Lecture Notes in Computer Science 11703

More information about this series at http://www.springer.com/series/7409

Khalid Saeed · Rituparna Chaki ·
Valentina Janev (Eds.)

Computer Information Systems and Industrial Management

18th International Conference, CISIM 2019
Belgrade, Serbia, September 19–21, 2019
Proceedings

 Springer

Editors
Khalid Saeed (ORCID)
Bialystok University of Technology
Bialystok, Poland

Rituparna Chaki (ORCID)
University of Calcutta
Calcutta, India

Valentina Janev (ORCID)
Mihajlo Pupin Institute
Belgrade, Serbia

ISSN 0302-9743   ISSN 1611-3349   (electronic)
Lecture Notes in Computer Science
ISBN 978-3-030-28956-0   ISBN 978-3-030-28957-7   (eBook)
https://doi.org/10.1007/978-3-030-28957-7

LNCS Sublibrary: SL3 – Information Systems and Applications, incl. Internet/Web, and HCI

This Springer imprint is published by the registered company Springer Nature Switzerland AG
The registered company address is: Gewerbestrasse 11, 6330 Cham, Switzerland

Preface

CISIM 2019 was the 18th of a series of conferences dedicated to computer information systems and industrial management applications. The conference was held during September 19–21, 2019, in Belgrade, Serbia, at Metropolitan Belgrade University.

More than 70 papers were submitted to CISIM by researchers and scientists from a number of reputed universities around the world. These scientific and academic institutions belong to Brazil, Bulgaria, Colombia, Czech Republic, France, India, Italy, Pakistan, Peru, Poland, Serbia, South Korea, Tunisia, and Vietnam. Most of the papers were of high quality, but only 70 of them were sent for peer review. Each paper was assigned to at least two reviewers initially, and the decision of acceptance was made after receiving two positive reviews. In case of conflicting decisions, another expert's review was sought for the respective papers. In total, about 150 reviews and comments were collected from the referees for the submitted papers. In order to maintain the guidelines of Springer's *Lecture Notes in Computer Science* series, the number of accepted papers was limited. Furthermore, a number of electronic discussions were held within the Program Committee (PC) chairs to decide about papers with conflicting reviews and to reach a consensus. After the discussions, the PC chairs decided to accept for publication in the proceedings book the best 43 of the total submitted papers. The main topics covered by the chapters in this book are biometrics, security systems, multimedia, classification and clustering, and industrial management. Besides these, the reader will find interesting papers on computer information systems as applied to wireless networks, computer graphics, and intelligent systems.

We are grateful to the three esteemed speakers for their keynote addresses. The authors of the keynote talks were Profs. Miroslav Trajanović, University of Niš, Serbia; Young Im Cho, Gachon University, South Korea; and Václav Snášel, Technical University of Ostrava, Czech Republic.

We would like to thank all the members of the PC, and the external reviewers for their dedicated efforts in the paper selection process. Special thanks are extended to the members of the Organizing Committee, both the international and the local ones, and the Springer team for their great efforts to make the conference a success. We are also grateful to Andrei Voronkov, whose Easy-Chair system eased the submission and selection process and greatly supported the compilation of the proceedings. The proceedings editing was managed by Prof. Jiří Dvorský (Technical University of Ostrava, Czech Republic), to whom we are indeed very grateful.

We hope that the reader's expectations will be met and that the participants enjoyed their stay in the beautiful city of Belgrade.

September 2019

Khalid Saeed
Rituparna Chaki
Valentina Janev

Organization

Conference Patrons

Dragan Domazet   Belgrade Metropolitan University, Serbia
Lech Dzienis   Białystok University of Technology, Poland

General Chair

Khalid Saeed   Białystok University of Technology, Poland

Conference Co-chairs

Marek Krętowski   Białystok University of Technology, Poland
Miroslava Raspopovi Mili   Belgrade Metropolitan University, Serbia
Rituparna Chaki   University of Calcutta, India
Agostino Cortesi   Ca' Foscari University of Venice, Italy

Program Committee

Chairs

Khalid Saeed   Białystok University of Technology, Poland
Valentina Janev   Mihajlo Pupin Institute, Serbia

Members

Waleed Abdulla   University of Auckland, New Zealand
Raid Al-Tahir   The University of the West Indies, St. Augustine, Trinidad and Tobago
Adrian Atanasiu   Bucharest University, Romania
Aditya Bagchi   Indian Statistical Institute, India
Valentina Emilia Balas   University of Arad, Romania
Jerzy Balicki   Warsaw University of Technology, Poland
Anna Bartkowiak   Wrocław University, Poland
Rahma Boucetta   National Engineering School of Gabes, Tunisia
Nabendu Chaki   University of Calcutta, India
Rituparna Chaki   University of Calcutta, India
Agostino Cortesi   Ca' Foscari University of Venice, Italy
Dipankar Dasgupta   University of Memphis, USA
Pierpaolo Degano   University of Pisa, Italy
Riccardo Focardi   Ca' Foscari University of Venice, Italy
Marina Gavrilova   University of Calgary, Canada
Jan Devos   Ghent University, Belgium

Additional Reviewers

Marcin Adamski	Białystok University of Technology, Poland
Andrea Albarelli	Ca' Foscari University of Venice, Italy
Samiran Chattopadhyay	Jadavpur University, India
Ayan Das	University of Calcutta, India
Dorota Duda	Białystok University of Technology, Poland
Tomasz Grześ	Białystok University of Technology, Poland
Wiktor Jakowluk	Białystok University of Technology, Poland
Sunirmal Khatua	University of Calcutta, India
Adam Klimowicz	Białystok University of Technology, Poland
Subhashis Majumder	Heritage Institute of Technology, India
Joyati Mondal	University of Calcutta, India
Mirosław Omieljanowicz	Białystok University of Technology, Poland
Jarosław Pempera	Wrocław University of Technology, Poland
S. P. Raja	Vel Tech Institute of Science and Technology, India
Grzegorz Rubin	Lomza State University, Poland
Mariusz Rybnik	University of Białystok, Poland
Maciej Szymkowski	Białystok University of Technology, Poland
Marek Tabędzki	Białystok University of Technology, Poland
Sławomir Zieliński	Białystok University of Technology, Poland

Keynotes

Intelligent Knowledge Sharing Technologies for Cloud Service Robot in Complex AI Environment

Young Im Cho

Faculty of Computer Engineering, Gachon University, South Korea
yicho@gachon.ac.kr

Abstract. In this talk, intelligent knowledge sharing technologies for cloud service robot is presented. The cloud robot industry does not have a common interface or communication standard between robots, unlike other computing industries. Since the operating system uses various operating systems such as Windows, Linux, RTOS, and Android, technology development is slowing down.

Therefore, it is necessary to standardize not only the operating system but also the robot application, the common interface and the communication standard in order to promote the robot industrial technology and activate the robot software market. Currently, there are VWNS robot software frameworks such as OPRoS (Open Platform for Robotics Services) in Korea and ROS (Robot Operation System) in the USA. The interfaces of application programs are standard of RoIS (Robot Interaction Service) and RLS (Robot Localization Service). However, since it is still in the development stage, it is necessary to build a common infrastructure that is more widespread and to standardize and globalize it.

In this presentation, we will present how to build a DB collection, a standard DB conversion algorithm design, and a cloud server environment for cloud service robot. The main contents of the development are first to grasp the requirements of the intelligent service robot (consumer) and to collect the data elements necessary for the mobile intelligence, manipulation intelligence, and social intelligence robot standard DB design, to be classified according to type.

We developed an algorithm for designing a standard DB schema to convert various data types into standard DB form. In addition, we will develop a DB collection system to enable each robot to serve a standard DB in the form of an open shared DB. In order to implement this function, it is important to build a shared platform in the cloud server environment.

Deep Learning for Massive Data Analysis

Václav Snášel

Faculty of Electrical Engineering and Computer Science,
VŠB – Technical University of Ostrava, Czech Republic
vaclav.snasel@vsb.cz

Abstract. Recent research trends in the areas of computational intelligence, communications, data mining, and computational models aim to achieve a multi-disciplinary balance between research advances in the fields of collective intelligence, data science, human-centric computing, knowledge management, and network science. The purpose of the lecture is to give perspective, challenges, and opportunities of application deep learning approach. Deep learning discovers an intricate structure in large data sets by using complex or compressed attributes. These methods have dramatically improved the state-of-the-art in visual object recognition, object detection, network science, and many other domains such as drug discovery and genomics. This talk will discuss some unifying approach for text, image, and network data. Then, this talk will provide some real-life deep learning applications.

Design of Osteofixation Devices – Personalised Approach

Miroslav Trajanović

Faculty of Mechanical Engineering, University of Niš, Serbia
miroslav.trajanovic@masfak.ni.ac.rs

Abstract. Treatment of patients after major bone trauma, regardless of whether they are caused by fractures, osteoporosis, cancer or infections, require application of implants, fixators, scaffolds or other osteofixation devices. The speed and quality of bone regeneration depends to a large extent on degree of adaptability of implants or fixators to a specific patient and a specific trauma. The personalized approach to design makes it possible to create the devices most suited to the patient.

For the design of personalized osteofixation devices, a 3D geometric model of bone before trauma is needed. However, in case of major trauma, there is usually no longer a part of the bone, so it is not possible to create a 3D model of the entire bone. The paper presents original methods for reverse engineering of human bones even in cases where there is no medical picture of the complete bone. Also, it is shown how such a model is applied for the design of personalized osteofixation devices.

Contents

Industrial Management and Other Applications

Machine Learning and High Performance Computing

Modelling and Optimization

Various Aspects of Computer Security

Biometrics and Pattern Recognition Applications

Evaluating Performance and Accuracy Improvements for Attention-OCR

Adam Brzeski[1,2]([⊠]) [iD], Kamil Grinholc[1,3], Kamil Nowodworski[1,4], and Adam Przybyłek[1] [iD]

[1] Faculty of Electronics, Telecommunications and Informatics,
Gdańsk University of Technology, Gdańsk, Poland
adam.brzeski@pg.edu.pl
[2] CTA.ai, Gdańsk, Poland
[3] Spartez, Gdańsk, Poland
[4] IHS Markit, Gdańsk, Poland

Abstract. In this paper we evaluated a set of potential improvements to the successful Attention-OCR architecture, designed to predict multiline text from unconstrained scenes in real-world images. We investigated the impact of several optimizations on model's accuracy, including employing dynamic RNNs (Recurrent Neural Networks), scheduled sampling, BiLSTM (Bidirectional Long Short-Term Memory) and a modified attention model. BiLSTM was found to slightly increase the accuracy, while dynamic RNNs and a simpler attention model provided a significant training time reduction with only a slight decline in accuracy.

1 Introduction

Optical Character Recognition is an important area of computer vision with numerous applications in document processing [25], factory automation, quality control [13], assisting visually impaired people [30] and many other fields, including recently actively researched autonomous cars [1]. Basic OCR (optical character recognition) approaches involve reading text from preprocessed images containing single lines of text. More advanced techniques include detecting text in the scene and capability to read multiline texts, often referred to as text recognition in unconstrained scene, text recognition in the wild, photo OCR or text spotting. This class of problems involves challenges of handling a variety of scenes, fonts and different types of distortions, which are more diverse and complex in real-world photographs than in document scans.

The process of text recognition is often split into separate text localization steps and a consecutive actual text recognition step. Examples of text localization methods include MSER [16] based on intensity analysis or deep learning approach by Gupta et al. [7], employing fully convolutional network in multiscale fashion to predict both text location and orientation. However, recently a lot of recognition was gained by end-to-end models, which combine text localization

© Springer Nature Switzerland AG 2019
K. Saeed et al. (Eds.): CISIM 2019, LNCS 11703, pp. 3–11, 2019.
https://doi.org/10.1007/978-3-030-28957-7_1

and recognition in one model and training procedure. One of the successful approaches in that area is the Attention-OCR architecture proposed by Wojna et al. [29].

At the same time, the increasing computational complexity of OCR and image analysis systems in general motivates discussion about processing efficiency. For many applications, high computational overheads of the algorithms coupled with a need of utilization of powerful GPU units are barriers for successful deployment. Also, long training procedures can generate substantial financial costs [23]. For this purpose, reducing the complexity of algorithms and models is an active area of research [5,9,17,26], which can result in significant savings. Progress in this field is also desired for machine learning models for optical character recognition, including especially advanced end-to-end systems.

2 Related Work

In the field of deep end-to-end systems Bartz et al. [3] proposed PhotoOCR system based on ResNet [8] convolutional neural network and BiLSTM network for locating text regions. ResNet architecture is also applied for predicting character probabilities at each possible position. Similarly to a previous work by Shi et al. [19], text localization step employs spatial transform networks (STN) [11] for generating transformation matrices of each line of text (or word). A recurrent configuration with BiLSTM network is here used, however. Similar approach with GRU networks was previously proposed by Sønderby et al. [22]. STN is followed by grid generator module that produces final text bounding boxes as well as sampled regions for the final text recognition phase. At the end, consecutive text characters are predicted using ResNet network with softmax classifier, which is applied with a fixed set of offsets over the text region. Final prediction is evaluated using CTC function. The method shows potential for application in unconstrained OCR setups, it does however need several minor modifications to be successfully applied.

Li et al. [12] employed VGG-16 [20] network for feature extraction followed by a dedicated text proposal network (TPN), which is applied in multi-scale sliding window mode. TPN is responsible for generating lists of text regions with assigned translations and shifts with respect to predefined anchors, and was inspired by Faster-RCNN network [18]. Anchor parameters are optimized for aspect ratios and scales typical for text regions in images. Detected regions are then encoded using feature maps and a LSTM network, and then passed to text detection network (TDN) and text recognition network (TRN). TDN consists of two fully-connected layers and is responsible for generating "textness" classification scores and refining text bounding boxes. The actual text recognition is finally performed by TRN constructed as LSTM network with attention function. However, the disadvantage of this approach is the requirement for text bounding boxes in addition to text labels during training of the model.

Finally, one of the most successful models in the field is Attention-OCR approach proposed by Wojna et al. [29]. The network consists of three major modules: feature extraction, attention mechanism and text-prediction using LSTM.

Feature extraction is performed using inception-resnet-v2 [24] convolutional neural network. Extracted feature maps are then used by LSTM to predict consecutive characters of the text in the image. Feature vectors are however passed to LSTM module after transformation by the attention mechanism. At each time step, attention mechanism selects meaningful areas of the image, are then used for spatial weighting of the features maps. Also, in order to improve location awareness of the network, one-hot coordinate encoding is used to append location information to the feature map elements.

A significant advantage of the Attention-OCR model is the fact that it only uses text labels for training and does not require text bounding boxes. The architecture is also fairly simple, and despite this the model achieved state-of-the art result on FSNS dataset [21]. The application of the method, however, is aggravated by large computational complexity resulting in long training times. Hence in this work we propose and evaluate potential improvements for Attention-OCR architecture.

3 Methodology

In the presented work we evaluate a set of optimizations for Attention-OCR architecture which can affect performance and accuracy of the model, which can possibly lead to higher training and processing efficiency. The evaluated optimizations are:

(a) dynamic RNNs - utilization of dynamic RNNs enables handling variable size sequences by adapting the number of time steps; in contrast, static RNNs automatically unrolls the graphs to a fixed number of time steps, which requires padding for shorter sequences and prevents processing of sequences longer than the defined length;
(b) BiLSTM - bidirectional LSTMs perform processing of time steps in both forward and backward directions, hence extending the context information at each step; BiLSTM layer is appended as additional encoder layer for convolutional features before the LSTM decoding layer;
(c) scheduled sampling - technique enabling using varying probability of passing ground truth tokens instead of outputs predicted by the network between timesteps over the training process; this enables using real labels at the beginning of the training and slowly moving to network predicted labels as training progresses; Bengio et al. [4] presented 3 types of sampling probability decay, including exponential, inverse sigmoid and linear decay;
(d) Luong attention - Bahdanau's attention model [2], which is employed by Attention-OCR implementation, can be replaced with simpler model proposed by Luong et al. [14]; Luong's model is considered more general and can possibly lead to higher accuracy rates.

Also, all of the evaluated model configurations employ coordinate encoding technique that extends feature vectors with one-hot encoded pixel coordinates, which potentially increases location awareness of the network. During the experiments, a set of model configurations were evaluated including various combinations of optimizations presented above, as well as the original Attention-OCR model, referred to as static RNN with Bahdanau.

Avenue des Sapins

Fig. 1. Sample image from FSNS datasets presenting four views of a street sign.

3.1 Dataset

Experiments were conducted on FSNS dataset [21] including over one million annotated images of french street signs acquired from Google Street View labeled with character sequences with maximum length of 37. Images in the dataset are composed of four views presenting a single street sign from different viewing angles (see Fig. 1). The dataset is split into train subset composed of around one million images, validation set of 16 000 images and test subset with 20 000 images.

3.2 Model Training and Evaluation

Models were trained on Nvidia DGX Station workstation using a single Tesla V100 GPU unit. For each model configuration 7 consecutive trainings were performed in order to analyse the reproducibility of the results. Each training involved 400 000 training steps using batch size of 32. SGD optimizer was used with 0.004 base learning rate and momentum of 0.9, which are the default values for Attention-OCR model[1].

We evaluated model configuration using sequence accuracy metric, calculated as a ratio of entirely correctly predicted sequences. Since we aim for capturing overall accuracy of model configurations, we decided to perform extensive model evaluation during training using merged validation and test sets, which enabled to improve the representativeness of the evaluation set, and consequently increased the confidence of the results. This was also justified by a fair ability of the Attention-OCR model to prevent overfitting, which can be observed in Fig. 3. Evaluation was performed every 10 000 steps.

---

[1] https://github.com/tensorflow/models/tree/master/research/attention_ocr.

Table 1. Sequence accuracies acquired on test set results for network configurations. Top results are in bold.

RNN	Attention	Other	Mean	Median	Max	Min	Std dev
Static	Bahdanau	-	0.825	0.825	0.830	0.818	0.005
Static	Bahdanau	Bi	**0.833**	**0.832**	**0.835**	**0.824**	0.004
Dynamic	Bahdanau	-	0.818	0.818	0.821	0.816	0.002
Dynamic	Bahdanau	Bi	0.822	0.822	0.825	0.818	0.003
Dynamic	Bahdanau	SS	0.787	0.777	0.816	0.770	0.020
Dynamic	Luong	-	0.808	0.807	0.812	0.805	0.003
Dynamic	Luong	Bi	0.816	0.816	0.819	0.813	0.002
Dynamic	Luong	SS	0.724	0.722	0.739	0.710	0.010

4 Results

4.1 Prediction Accuracy Evaluation

Sequence accuracy results presented in Table 1 show that evaluated modifications revealed marginal impact on model's accuracy. Transition from static to dynamic LSTM resulted in a slight degradation of average accuracy by 0.7 p.p. for the original Attention-OCR model (employing Bahdanau attention model) and by 1.0 p.p. for model extended to BiLSTM. Application of the Luong attention model resulted in a small accuracy drop and on average was lower by 0.8 p.p. in relation to the Bahdanau attention model, comparing three different configurations employing dynamic LSTMs. The improvement introduced by BiLSTM encoding is also not meaningful, however, along with Bahdanau attention and static graph, it contributes to the highest sequence accuracy achieved in the experiments.

Interestingly, application of scheduled sampling significantly degraded the accuracy, which resulted in 3.1 to 8.5 points lower accuracy than for the regular training. In addition, statistic analysis of accuracy results acquired during sevenfold trainings, presented in Fig. 2, show that scheduled sampling strongly decreased stability of accuracy results of the models. Also, the stability appears higher for dynamic than for static networks. Evaluation results collected during training processes for representative training executions of network configurations are presented in Fig. 3.

4.2 Performance Evaluation

Evaluation was performed by measurements of training time for each configuration during training conducted for 160 000 steps using batch sizes of 16 and 32. For each configuration three training processes were performed and results were averaged. Tests on batch size 16 were performed on Nvidia GeForce Ti 1080 GPU, while tests on batch size 32 were executed on DGX Station V100 GPU.

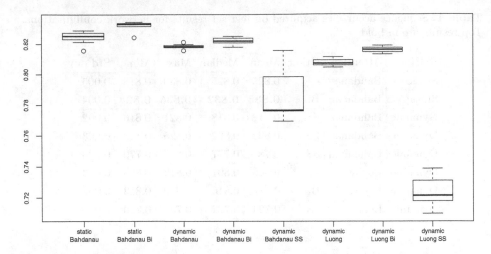

Fig. 2. Box plot of accuracy for each model configuration.

Results show that transition to dynamic networks provides an over 27% process-ing speed increase. Also, employing Luong attention with dynamic increased the performance gain to 51%. Scheduled sampling showed marginal impact on train-ing performance. In turn, BiLSTM had a strongly negative impact on training time by introducing 80% slowdown. Detailed results of performance evaluation are presented in Table 2.

Table 2. Performance evaluation results (averaged over 5 training runs). Top results are in bold.

RNN	Attention	Other	Batch size	Steps per second	Speedup
Static	Bahdanau	-	32	1.58	*baseline*
Static	Bahdanau	Bi	32	0.27	0.17
Static	Bahdanau	-	16	2.84	*baseline*
Dynamic	Bahdanau	-	16	3.63	1.28
Dynamic	Bahdanau	Bi	16	0.69	0.24
Dynamic	Bahdanau	SS	16	3.62	1.27
Dynamic	Luong	-	16	**4,31**	**1.51**
Dynamic	Luong	Bi	16	0.59	0.21
Dynamic	Luong	SS	16	4.27	1.50

5 Discussion

The experiments revealed several relationships between model's accuracy and performance in different configurations. First of all, switching to dynamic RNNs and Luong attention enabled significant reduction of training time at the cost of a slight accuracy drop. This might indicate higher versatility and overall computational efficiency of dynamic RNNs versus static and higher efficiency of simpler Luong attention model. On the other hand, static RNNs achieve higher accuracy and converge faster (see Fig. 3). Still, dynamic RNNs keep advantages of higher performance for short sequences and possibility to processes sequences of variable length.

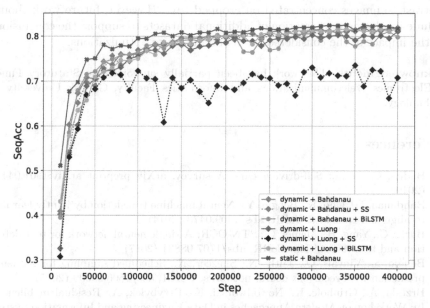

Fig. 3. Sequence accuracy evaluation results acquired during training for network configurations.

Conversely, extending the architecture to bidirectional model resulted in significant performance overhead with a slight accuracy improvement. Bidirectional model on top of static RNNs achieved highest sequence accuracy among all tested configurations. Despite the large performance overhead, bidirectional models can be still considered optimal for accuracy-critical applications.

Finally, quite surprisingly scheduled sampling clearly worsened the accuracy of the models. Intuitively, scheduled sampling should represent the idea of curriculum learning method and therefore have positive effect on the results. Such conclusions were confirmed by recent literature, e.g. by Goyal et al. [6] and Wang et al. [28]. However, other authors also report negative effect of scheduled sampling, including Wang et al. [27], Mathews et al. [15] and Huszar [10]. This might indicate that the effect of scheduled sampling strongly depends on the application or is highly sensitive to the shape of sampling probability function over training time.

6 Conclusions

In this study we evaluated a set of accuracy and performance related optimizations to Attention-OCR model [29]. We indicated dynamic RNNs and Luong attention model as potential performance improvements and bidirectional LSTMs as accuracy optimization. We conducted multiple trainings of each configuration in order to increase confidence of the results. The source code enabling reproduction of the results was made publicly available at GitHub[2].

The main limitation of this study is involvement of only a single dataset (FSNS) for accuracy and performance evaluation. It is still difficult to access large-size datasets that would include full-scene pictures with multiline text, in contrast to images concentrated on cropped text. However, future work should include involvement or creation of additional datasets to support the conclusions on the impact of the considered model architecture optimizations.

Acknowledgments. This work has been partially supported by Statutory Funds of Electronics, Telecommunications and Informatics Faculty, Gdansk University of Technology.

References

1. Badue, C., et al.: Self-driving cars: A survey. arXiv preprint arXiv:1901.04407 (2019)
2. Bahdanau, D., Cho, K., Bengio, Y.: Neural machine translation by jointly learning to align and translate. CoRR, abs/1409.0473 (2014)
3. Bartz, C., Yang, H., Meinel, C.: STN-OCR: A single neural network for text detection and text recognition. CoRR, abs/1707.08831 (2017)
4. Bengio, S., Vinyals, O., Jaitly, N., Shazeer, N.: Scheduled sampling for sequence prediction with recurrent neural networks. CoRR, abs/1506.03099 (2015)
5. Brzeski, A., Grinholc, K., Nowodworski, K., Przybyłek, A.: Residual mobilenets. In: Workshop on Modern Approaches in Data Engineering and Information System Design at ADBIS 2019 (2019)
6. Goyal, K., Dyer, C., Berg-Kirkpatrick, T.: Differentiable scheduled sampling for credit assignment. CoRR, abs/1704.06970 (2017)
7. Gupta, A., Vedaldi, A., Zisserman, A.: Synthetic data for text localisation in natural images. CoRR, abs/1604.06646 (2016)
8. He, K., Zhang, X., Ren, S., Sun, J.: Deep residual learning for image recognition. CoRR, abs/1512.03385 (2015)
9. Howard, A.G., et al.: Mobilenets: Efficient convolutional neural networks for mobile vision applications. arXiv preprint arXiv:1704.04861 (2017)
10. Huszár, F.: How (not) to train your generative model: Scheduled sampling, likelihood, adversary? arXiv e-prints, November 2015
11. Jaderberg, M., Simonyan, K., Zisserman, A., Kavukcuoglu, K.: Spatial transformer networks. In: Cortes, C., Lawrence, N.D., Lee, D.D., Sugiyama, M., Garnett, R., (eds) Advances in Neural Information Processing Systems, vol. 28, pp. 2017–2025. Curran Associates Inc (2015)

---

[2] https://github.com/Avenire/models.

12. Li, H., Wang, P., Shen, C.: Towards end-to-end text spotting with convolutional recurrent neural networks. CoRR, abs/1707.03985 (2017)
13. Liukkonen, M., Tsai, T.-N.: Toward decentralized intelligence in manufacturing: recent trends in automatic identification of things. Int. J. Adv. Manufact. Technol. **87**(9–12), 2509–2531 (2016)
14. Luong, M.-T., Pham, H., Manning, C.D.: Effective approaches to attention-based neural machine translation. CoRR, abs/1508.04025 (2015)
15. Mathews, A.P., Xie, L., He, X.: Semstyle: Learning to generate stylised image captions using unaligned text. CoRR, abs/1805.07030 (2018)
16. Nistér, D., Stewénius, H.: Linear time maximally stable extremal regions. In: Forsyth, D., Torr, P., Zisserman, A. (eds.) ECCV 2008. LNCS, vol. 5303, pp. 183–196. Springer, Heidelberg (2008). https://doi.org/10.1007/978-3-540-88688-4_14
17. Przybyłek, K., Shkroba, I.: Crowd counting á la bourdieu. In: Workshop on Modern Approaches in Data Engineering and Information System Design at ADBIS 2019 (2019)
18. Ren, S., He, K., Girshick, R.B., Sun, J.: Faster R-CNN: towards real-time object detection with region proposal networks. CoRR, abs/1506.01497 (2015)
19. Shi, B., Wang, X., Lv, P., Yao, C., Bai, X.: Robust scene text recognition with automatic rectification. CoRR, abs/1603.03915 (2016)
20. Simonyan, K., Zisserman, A.: Very deep convolutional networks for large-scale image recognition. arXiv preprint arXiv:1409.1556 (2014)
21. Smith, R., et al.: End-to-end interpretation of the French street name signs dataset. CoRR, abs/1702.03970 (2017)
22. Sønderby, S.K., Sønderby, C.K., Maaløe, L., Winther, O.: Recurrent spatial transformer networks. CoRR, abs/1509.05329 (2015)
23. Strubell, E., Ganesh, A., McCallum, A.: Energy and policy considerations for deep learning in NLP. arXiv preprint arXiv:1906.02243 (2019)
24. Szegedy, C., Ioffe, S., Vanhoucke, V., Alemi, A.A.: Inception-v4, inception-resnet and the impact of residual connections on learning. In: Thirty-First AAAI Conference on Artificial Intelligence (2017)
25. Tafti, A.P., Baghaie, A., Assefi, M., Arabnia, H.R., Yu, Z., Peissig, P.: OCR as a service: an experimental evaluation of Google Docs OCR, Tesseract, ABBYY FineReader, and Transym. In: Bebis, G., et al. (eds.) ISVC 2016. LNCS, vol. 10072, pp. 735–746. Springer, Cham (2016). https://doi.org/10.1007/978-3-319-50835-1_66
26. Tan, M., Chen, B., Pang, R., Vasudevan, V., Le, Q.V.: MnasNet: Platform-aware neural architecture search for mobile. arXiv preprint arXiv:1807.11626 (2018)
27. Wang, X., Takaki, S., Yamagishi, J.: An RNN-based quantized f0 model with multi-tier feedback links for text-to-speech synthesis. In: INTERSPEECH (2017)
28. Wang, Y., Gao, Z., Long, M., Wang, J., Yu, P.S.: PredRNN++: Towards A resolution of the deep-in-time dilemma in spatiotemporal predictive learning. CoRR, abs/1804.06300 (2018)
29. Wojna, Z., et al.: Attention-based extraction of structured information from street view imagery. CoRR, abs/1704.03549 (2017)
30. Yi, C., Tian, Y.: Assistive text reading from natural scene for blind persons. In: Hua, G., Hua, X.-S. (eds.) Mobile Cloud Visual Media Computing, pp. 219–241. Springer, Cham (2015). https://doi.org/10.1007/978-3-319-24702-1_9

Multi-muscle MRI Texture Analysis for Therapy Evaluation in Duchenne Muscular Dystrophy

Dorota Duda[✉][ORCID]

Faculty of Computer Science, Bialystok University of Technology, Bialystok, Poland
d.duda@pb.edu.pl

Abstract. The study presents a strategy for indicating the textural features that are the most appropriate for therapy evaluation in Duchenne Muscular Dystrophy (DMD). The strategy is based on "multi-muscle" texture analysis (simultaneously processing several distinct muscles) and involves applying statistical tests to pre-eliminate features that may possibly evolve along with the individual's growth. The remaining features, considered as age-independent, are ranked using the *Monte Carlo* selection procedure, from the most to the least useful in identifying dystrophy phase. In total 124 features obtained with six texture analysis methods are investigated. Various subsets of the top-ranked age-independent features are assessed by six classifiers. Three binary differentiation problems are posed: the first vs. the second, the second vs. the third, and the first vs. the third dystrophy phase. The best vectors of age-independent features provide a classification accuracy of 100.0%, 86.9%, and 100.0%, respectively, and comprise 16, 12, and 9 features, respectively.

Keywords: Duchenne Muscular Dystrophy · Therapy testing ·
Golden Retriever Muscular Dystrophy · GRMD ·
Magnetic Resonance Imaging · Texture analysis ·
Monte Carlo feature selection · Classification

1 Introduction

Duchenne muscular dystrophy (DMD) is a severe inherited disorder, found principally in males [1]. It is caused by mutations in the gene responsible for synthesizing dystrophin – a protein that maintains muscle integrity and function. The lack of dystrophin entails a progressive degenerating all the striated muscles. Affected individuals suffer from a broad spectrum of complications, including: the loss of motor ability, deformities, cardiomyopathy, and respiratory difficulties. Due to this reason, an extensive research on potential therapies for DMD is continually ongoing [2]. Unfortunately, no effective cure is available at present, and therapeutic practices can only improve the sufferers' quality of life. The patient's death usually occurs in his (or her) twenties [3].

© Springer Nature Switzerland AG 2019
K. Saeed et al. (Eds.): CISIM 2019, LNCS 11703, pp. 12–24, 2019.
https://doi.org/10.1007/978-3-030-28957-7_2

The research on any therapy requires establishing procedures for the objective assessment of treatment effects. So far, several measurement protocols have been proposed for classifying stages of patients with DMD [4]. They are based mainly on the evaluation of muscle strength and joint mobility (quantifying various functional activities, like: walking, going up and down the stairs, sitting and standing from a chair) or monitoring cardiac and respiratory muscle function. However, some protocols are reliable only when applied by the same professional (results can be biased by a subjective observer's assessment) or by experienced members of a well-trained group of specialists. In this context, the elaboration of other non-invasive biomarkers for application in DMD clinical trials becomes increasingly important. A growing interest is shown here in Magnetic Resonance Imaging (MRI), which offers a considerable range of possibilities for the characterization of muscle structure and function [5]. Proper interpretation of the image content is, however, a complicated task and requires applying advanced computer-aided approaches. The research has shown that potentially powerful MRI-based biomarkers can be provided by texture analysis (TA) [6].

Several studies have already investigated the potential of MRI-based TA in characterizing muscular disorders (the most recent of them are outlined in the next section). They have shown that using textural features as tissue descriptors can lead to a relatively high distinction between dystrophic and healthy muscles at different patient's ages [7–10], or among several phases of dystrophy development in affected individuals [11–13]. They have also proven that textural features can outperform other MRI biomarkers, not based on texture [7,11].

The common property of the above works is that they considered only the cases of untreated dystrophy, progressing incessantly with the growth of an individual. It was not assessed whether the "usefulness" of a given feature in distinguishing stages of dystrophy effectively resulted from the feature's evolution under the influence of the disease development. The fact that features can also change with the individual's growth, with which the dystrophy progresses, was not taken into account (with only one exception in [7]). Our preliminary study on MRI textures of healthy muscles at different individuals' ages has shown that many of generally robust textural features can be, in fact, age-dependent [14]. If texture analysis was to be used to test the therapy's effects in DMD, particular attention should be paid to such features, since their misuse may result in a wrong assessment of dystrophy response to treatment.

Another common property of mentioned works is that they performed texture analysis based on only one type of muscles at a time (e.g. [7,12,13]), or even ignoring the potential texture differences between distinct muscles [8]. Our previous research showed that a "multi-muscle" texture analysis of dystrophic muscles (simultaneously processing textural properties of several muscles) can lead to better classification results than those obtained when each muscle is considered separately [15].

In this study, MRI-based multi-muscle texture analysis is applied in characterization of dystrophic muscles. For the first time, "multi-muscle" feature vectors are constructed with the exclusion of age-dependent textural features.

The strategy proposed to indicate the most robust combination of features (and the most appropriate in terms of the therapy testing process) comprises several steps, including: indication and elimination of age-dependent features, construction of multi-muscle feature vectors, and selection of the best age-independent features. The final sets of features are evaluated by six different classifiers.

The study uses the *Golden Retriever Muscular Dystrophy* (GRMD) model, genetically homologous to human DMD one [16]. Three phases of canine growth and/or the disease development are distinguished in this model, in reference to histological changes in muscle structure: 0–4 months of age (the first phase), 5–6 months (the second phase), and 7 months and more (the third phase).

2 Related Works

Most of the studies on MRI-texture-based characterization of dystrophic muscles have appeared over the last five years. For example, Martins-Bach et al. [11] investigated the potential of MRI texture analysis in characterizing muscles in four mouse models of muscular dystrophy: the severely affected $Large^{myd}$ mouse, the worst double mutant $mdx/Large^{myd}$ mouse, the mildly affected mdx mouse, and normal mice. In their work, texture descriptors, derived from T2-weighted images, were calculated with the use of six TA methods (involving image histogram, image gradient, run-length matrices, co-occurrence matrices, autoregressive model, and wavelet transform). They were compared to non-texture-based MRI measures (e.g. transverse relaxation times of MRI contrast). The group of 40 textural features from co-occurrence matrices (contrast- and entropy-based) allowed to correctly identify all considered mouse strains, outperforming non-texture-based muscle T2 values.

Zhang et al. [10] carried out MRI texture analysis (separately for T1- and T2-weighted images) to differentiate between healthy and dystrophic patients with DMD. Their textural features (12 – in total) were based on the 2D discrete wavelet transform and were processed using principal component analysis (PCA). The classification system, applying non-linear Support Vector Machines (SVM) [17], correctly recognized as many as 97.1% cases.

In turn, Eresen et al. [13] tried to assess the disease severity (low or high) from *ex vivo* images acquired on GRMD dogs. They considered a total of 41 textural features (based on: the image histogram, co-occurrence matrices, run-length matrices, local binary pattern, and wavelet transform) calculated from pectineus muscle samples. Features were derived from six types of images: weighted MRI (T1- and T2-weighted), T1 and T2 MRI Maps, and Dixon MRI Maps (water fraction and fat fraction images). Classification was performed with the SVM method. The best system accuracies amounted to 88.9% if only one textural feature was used (e.g. wavelet transform- or histogram-based, from T1-weighted images), and – up to 100.0% for several different combinations of two features.

An important piece of research on possible strategies for muscle imaging texture analysis was conducted within the European COST Action, BM1304, MYO-MRI [6,18]. Some of our studies in this field [9,12,15] were also a part of that project. They all used the same database, composed of T2-weighted images from healthy and dystrophic dogs (GRMD model), acquired at three phases of canine growth and/or disease progression. Four different hind-limb muscles were considered: the *Extensor Digitorum Longus* (EDL), the *Gastrocnemius Lateralis* (GasLat), the *Gastrocnemius Medialis* (GasMed), and the *Tibial Cranialis* (TC).

In our preliminary work [9] we differentiated between affected and healthy dogs. Experiments were carried out separately for each of three phases. Each of the four muscles was considered independently. 39 textural features were calculated with eight TA methods, based on: the histogram, autocorrelation, gradient matrices, co-occurrence matrices, run length matrices, gray level difference matrices, fractional model, and Laws' filters. The best classification results, provided by the SVM classifier, amounted to 95.8%, 97.2%, and 91.4% of correctly recognized cases, for the first, the second and the third phase, respectively.

As an extension of the previous research [12], we measured the usefulness of each feature as tissue descriptor, based on its frequency of selections in a modified *Monte Carlo* (MC) procedure. The most useful features (mainly co-occurrence- and run length-based) were used in differentiation between GRMD and healthy dogs at each phase of canine growth, yielding high classification accuracies (first phase: 99.9%, second phase: 98.1%, third phase: 90.8%). However, even with the feature selection, differentiation among three phases of dystrophy in GRMD dogs turned out to be a difficult task (accuracy: 71.3%). Finally, that research suggested that sets of the best features could be quite different for each muscle.

In the next study [15] we proposed to simultaneously analyze features derived from the four different muscles. The multi-muscle texture analysis, followed by a modified *Monte Carlo* feature selection, was applied in recognition of four phases of dystrophy progression, including the "zero phase" – the absence of the disease. The simultaneous consideration of several muscles increased the classification accuracy by maximum 12.5% in comparison to the best corresponding result achieved with a single-muscle TA. A set of 17 most useful textural features ensured 82.1% of correctly recognized cases with the AdaBoost [19] classifier.

Finally, we used statistical analysis to indicate textural features with significantly different values for two adjacent phases of life in healthy dogs: (i) the first and the second phase, and (ii) the second and the third phase [14]. Depending on the pair of phases and the muscle type (each considered separately), from 16.2% to 64.9% of features demonstrated their age-dependency, among them – many features previously considered as "useful in recognizing the phase of dystrophy".

To our best knowledge, only one other work highlighted to possible age influence on MRI-derived muscle textures [7]. Similar studies were recently carried out on ultrasonic images of skeletal muscles [20], also confirming that quite a few of generally robust textural features can depend on age (in cited work – 15.9% of 283 tested features). It is highly probable that discarding many features can considerably reduce the ability of texture-based system to recognize a dystrophy phase. A solution can be performing here a multi-muscle texture analysis (which assures better tissue characterization than a single-muscle one) combined with the *Monte Carlo* selection procedure. The proposed approach can possibly prevent from a significant deterioration in the system's classification abilities.

This work examines which classification quality can be achieved by using multi-muscle TA combined with the MC selection from age-independent features. Obtained results are compared to those provided by the whole set of features, including the age-dependent ones, both in single-muscle and multi-muscle TA.

3   Indicating the Most Appropriate Combination of Age-Independent Textural Features

The proposed strategy for finding the best combination of textural features (the most suitable for therapy testing and guarantying the best possible differentiation of dystrophy phases) comprises several steps. They are depicted in Fig. 1. First, the assessment of the "feature dependency on age" is performed separately for each feature and for each muscle. Features showing significant differences in their values for distinct phases of growth in healthy individuals are indicated by means of statistical analysis. Since these features are recognized as possibly evolving with the individual's growth, they are eliminated from further investigation. Next, the remaining features (considered as "independent of age") are used for characterization of dystrophic muscles and they are combined in multi-muscle feature vectors. In this study, multi-muscle vectors are composed of features derived sequentially from the following muscles: EDL, GasLat, GasMed, and TC. Each vector is created based on muscles belonging to the same limb and segmented in the same image. The order of features corresponding to each muscle is strict and the same for each vector. Thus created multi-muscle vectors are labeled with a phase of dystrophy progression. In the next step, the usefulness of each feature in identifying phases of dystrophy in GRMD dogs is assessed. This step involves applying the modified *Monte Carlo* selection procedure, as described in [12]. Features are then ranked from the most to the least frequently selected (and therefore – from the most useful to the least useful one). The final step is determining how many of the top-ranked features is sufficient to guarantee the most satisfying differentiation of dystrophy phases.

Seeing that the differentiation among more than two dystrophy phases is rather a difficult task [12,15], this work focuses on only two-phase differentiation problems, taking into account all the three possible combinations of two phases: the first and the second phase (task abbreviated "1vs2"), the second and the third phase ("2vs3"), and – the first and the third phase ("1vs3").

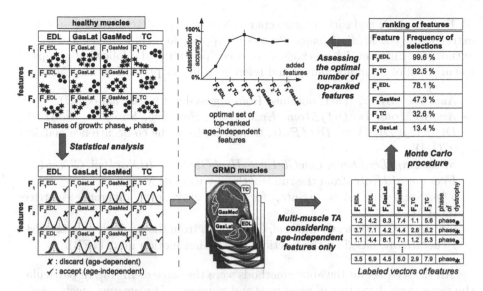

Fig. 1. Indicating the best possible multi-muscle vectors of age-independent features.

4   Experimental Setup

The experiments were performed on T2-weighted MRI images provided by the Nuclear Magnetic Resonance (NMR) Laboratory of the Institute of Myology in Paris, France. Images were derived from 5 GRMD dogs and 5 healthy controls, each examined several times (from 3 to 5) over a maximum of 14 months. Examinations were carried out in conformity with the *Guide for the Care and Use of Laboratory Animals* [21] and respected the European legislation on laboratory animals and animal studies. A detailed description of examination protocols can be found in [22]. Images were acquired on a 3T Siemens Magnetom Trio TIM scanner with a standard, circularly polarized extremity coil. The in-plane resolution was 0.56 mm × 0.56 mm, the slice thickness was 3 mm, and the inter-slice gap was 7.5 mm. The slice orientation was axial with respect to the long axis of the muscle. The repetition time was 3,000 ms, the first and the second echo time were 6.3 ms and 50 ms, respectively. All images had a size of 240 × 320 pixels.

In total, 38 examinations were taken into account. For the needs of this study, each examination was assigned to one of the three predefined phases of canine growth and/or dystrophy development. The assignment was based on the dog's age at the time of examination. In total, the first, the second and the third phase were represented by 7, 5, and 6 examinations, respectively, in GRMD dogs, and – by 7, 4, and 9 examinations, respectively, in healthy ones. For each examination, one series of 12 to 14 images was studied. Four types of muscles were considered: EDL, GasLat, GasMed, and TC. For each muscle, up to two *Regions of Interest* (ROIs) were manually segmented on each image – one for each limb, left and right. Only ROIs having at least 100 pixels were subjected to investigation.

For each ROI and each muscle separately, a total of 31 textural features were extracted by the *Medical Image Processing* application [23] implemented by the author. Six different TA methods were used, providing the following groups of features (all of them are named and referenced in our previous work [15]):

- *Avg*, *Var*, *Skew*, *Kurt*, obtained from a gray-level histogram (GLH),
- *AngSecMom*, *InvDiffMom*, *Entr*, *Corr*, *SumAvg*, *SumVar*, *SumEntr*, *DiffAvg*, *DiffVar*, *DiffEntr*, *Contrast*, from the co-occurrence matrices (COM),
- *ShortEmp*, *LongEmp*, *LowGlrEmp*, *HighGlrEmp*, *RlNonUni*, *GlNonUni*, *Fraction*, *RlEntr*, from the run length matrices (RLM),
- *gAngSecMom*, *gAvg*, *gEntr*, form the gray level difference matrices (GLDM),
- *GradAvg*, *GradVar*, *GradSkew*, *GradKurt*, from the gradient matrix (GM),
- *FractalDim*, based on the fractional Brownian motion model (FB).

All the settings for the above methods were the same as in [15]. In particular, the same were: directions of pixel runs and numbers of image gray levels considered for the COM, RLM, and GLDM methods, as well as distances between pixels in pairs for the COM, GLDM, and FB methods. In contrast, the GLDM-based *gAngInvDiffMom* and *gContrast* features were now not considered, as they are strongly correlated to the COM-based *AngInvDiffMom* and *Contrast*, respectively. Furthermore, the previously used *GradNonZero* feature was now omitted, since it produced the same values for a great majority of ROIs.

Features possibly evolving along with the individual's growth were indicated by means of statistical analysis performed separately for each binary differentiation task, for each muscle, and for each feature. Due to the specific properties of the available database, it was not possible to conduct analyzes adapted to dependent variables (in fact, the values of textual features obtained over the time from the same dog can be related one to another). The choice of tests adapted for independent samples was justified in our recent study [14]. Following that, the Shapiro-Wilk test was used to determine whether each of the two compared samples of feature values had the normal distribution. If both samples met this condition, the T-test was applied to check if the mean values of two samples were statistically different from each other at a significance level of 0.05. Otherwise, the Mann-Whitney U-test was used to check the above condition. The statistical analyses were performed by *Statistica* software [24].

At this step, some of the results presented in [14] were used. They included the list of features demonstrating their age-dependency for the following differentiation problems (concerning only the healthy individuals): (i) the first phase vs. the second phase, and (ii) the second phase vs. the third phase of canine growth. Additionally, the same statistical analyses were repeated for the third problem: the first phase vs. the third phase. The percentages of features considered as age-dependent and, therefore, eliminated from further investigation, are given in Table 1, separately for each differentiation task and for each muscle. The numbers of ROIs used for statistical analyses are presented in Table 2.

Table 1. Percentages of age-dependent features for each muscle and each binary differentiation task.

	EDL	GasLat	GasMed	TC
"1vs2"	21.6	16.2	64.9	64.9
"2vs3"	54.1	32.4	56.8	18.9
"1vs3"	48.4	19.4	32.3	35.5

Table 2. Numbers of ROIs used for statistical analysis for each muscle and each phase of canine growth.

	EDL	GasLat	GasMed	TC
First	97	73	124	126
Second	104	58	80	151
Third	209	116	173	238

Table 3. Multi-muscle TA: considered tuples of muscles, their abbreviations, and numbers of corresponding feature vectors for each binary differentiation task.

Tuple of muscles	Abbreviation	"1vs2"	"2vs3"	"1vs3"
(EDL, GasLat, GasMed, TC)	ELMT	23	35	24
(EDL, GasLat, GasMed)	ELM	24	37	27
(EDL, GasLat, TC)	ELT	24	38	26
(EDL, GasMed, TC)	EMT	34	56	42
(GasLat, GasMed, TC)	LMT	43	56	43

The multi-muscle texture analysis, performed in the next step, involved only the age-independent features. Multi-muscle feature vectors were based on the quadruple of muscles – (EDL, GasLat, GasMed, TC). As there were relatively few images on which all four muscles could be seen, this part of experiments was repeated for all possible triples of muscles. The considered combinations (tuples) of muscles and numbers of corresponding feature vectors are listed in Table 3.

Ranking of age-independent features, according to their importance in identifying phases of dystrophy in GRMD dogs, was created based on the modified *Monte Carlo* procedure run with the following settings. The single selection experiment, executed on a "truncated" data set, was repeated 250,000 times using *Weka* software [25] and was based on the best-first strategy with the forward search algorithm. During this process, a wrapper method [26] combined with *C4.5* tree [27] and 10-fold cross-validation were applied for evaluating each candidate subset of features. Truncated data sets were always created by a random choice of 2/3 of initial observations described by 1/3 of the initially used features.

Finally, different sets of top-ranked features were assessed with six classifiers (validated using 10-times 10-fold cross-validation), available in *Weka* tool:

- DT: *C4.5* Decision Tree,
- AB: Ensemble of Classifiers with the AdaBoost voting scheme, using the *C4.5* classifier as the underlying algorithm and trained for 100 iterations,
- RF: Random Forest [28], comprising a set of 100 *C4.5* trees,
- LR: Logistic Regression [29],

– NN: back-propagation Neural Network [30] using a sigmoid activation function and having one hidden layer,
– SVM: Support Vector Machines using a second-degree polynomial kernel.

5   Results and Discussion

The highest percentages of correctly identified dystrophy phases, obtained with the proposed strategy, are presented in Table 4, separately for each of the three considered classification tasks: the first vs. the second phase ("1vs2"), the second vs. the third phase ("2vs3"), and the first vs. the third phase ("1vs3"). Each result is followed by the name of classifier by which it was received and the number of age-independent top-ranked features in the best multi-muscle feature vector. Moreover, accuracies related to the use of all tested features (also including the age-dependent ones) in single-muscle TA and in multi-muscle TA combined with the MC selection procedure are also shown, for reference.

Table 4. The highest possible percentages (with standard deviation) of correctly identified phases of dystrophy, achieved with different approaches to texture analysis: "multi TA/MC age-indep" (proposed) – multi-muscle TA combined with MC-based selection from age-independent features only, "multi TA/MC all" – multi-muscle TA combined with MC-based selection from all possible features, and "single TA all" – single-muscle TA (separately processing each muscle from a given tuple of muscles) considering all possible features. For the first approach, results are followed by the classifier providing the result and the number of features in the best multi-muscle vector.

Task	Tuple	multi TA/MC age-indep			multi TA/MC all	single TA all
		Percentage	Classifier	Number	Percentage	Percentage
"1vs2"	ELMT	95.2 (4.0)	SVM	54	98.3 (3.2)	86.8 (6.5)
	ELM	97.7 (2.8)	LR	3	99.5 (1.5)	86.5 (6.7)
	ELT	88.3 (6.1)	RF	10	90.1 (5.2)	84.8 (7.5)
	EMT	100.0 (0.0)	SVM	16	100.0 (0.0)	86.3 (6.4)
	LMT	94.7 (2.9)	NN	47	96.0 (2.9)	92.4 (4.1)
"2vs3"	ELMT	86.9 (4.9)	SVM	12	88.7 (5.8)	80.8 (7.3)
	ELM	81.0 (5.9)	RF	15	89.1 (4.9)	75.5 (6.5)
	ELT	86.6 (4.6)	NN	6	91.2 (4.3)	83.9 (5.0)
	EMT	84.5 (4.3)	RF	11	86.6 (4.5)	78.3 (5.0)
	LMT	84.9 (4.9)	NN	4	86.8 (4.4)	75.1 (5.8)
"1vs3"	ELMT	100.0 (0.0)	NN	9	100.0 (0.0)	96.5 (3.7)
	ELM	93.5 (4.7)	LR	37	100.0 (0.0)	93.2 (6.9)
	ELT	99.0 (2.2)	NN	13	100.0 (0.0)	97.0 (2.9)
	EMT	91.3 (3.9)	SVM	8	97.0 (2.6)	89.3 (5.1)
	LMT	81.9 (5.8)	NN	3	96.0 (2.9)	81.0 (5.8)

Table 5. The best set of age-independent textural features for each binary classification task. Each feature is followed by the muscle from which the feature was derived.

"1vs2"		"2vs3"		"1vs3"	
Feature	Muscle	Feature	Muscle	Feature	Muscle
$RlEntr$	GasMed	$AngSecMom$	TC	$Entr$	EDL
$RlNonUni$	TC	$InvDiffMom$	TC	$Corr$	TC
$RlNonUni$	EDL	Avg	EDL	$GradAvg$	TC
$LowGlrEmp$	GasMed	$Entr$	GasMed	$AngSecMom$	EDL
$SumEntr$	EDL	$GlNonUni$	EDL	Var	GasLat
$Entr$	EDL	$Corr$	TC	$gAngSecMom$	GasMed
$Fraction$	EDL	$SumAvg$	EDL	$LongEmp$	EDL
$GlNonUni$	EDL	$LowGlrEmp$	EDL	$GradKurt$	TC
$LongEmp$	EDL	$LongEmp$	TC	$GradKurt$	GasMed
$GradKurt$	EDL	$GradVar$	GasMed		
$AngSecMom$	EDL	$SumEntr$	EDL		
$Entr$	TC	$SumEntr$	TC		
$GradSkew$	EDL				
Avg	GasMed				
$ShortEmp$	EDL				
$GradAvg$	EDL				

Comparing the results obtained for the same classification task and for the same tuple of muscles, it can be seen, that the multi-muscle TA combined with MC-based feature selection (even if performed on age-independent features only) always ensures better differentiation of dystrophy phases than that ensured by the single-muscle TA. The observed improvement in classification results ranges from 3.0% to 15.0%. However, as far as the multi-muscle TA is concerned, the elimination of the age-dependent features generally leads to a deterioration of results ("1vs2": up to 3.1%, "2vs3": up to 8.1%, "1vs3": up to 14.1%). Such a deterioration is different for each tuple, which should not come as a surprise since the number and combination of rejected features is different for each muscle. Despite this, for two classification tasks, "1vs2" and "1vs3", exists at least one tuple of muscles for which the 100.0% accuracy can be achieved. Only when differentiating between the second and the third dystrophy phase, the best possible result for age-independent features (86.9% of recognized cases) was by 4.3% inferior to the best observed when all the possible features were considered.

Table 5 lists the top-ranked features (starting from the most useful ones) that were included in the best multi-muscle vectors for each binary classification task, distinguishing between dystrophy phases. As can be noticed, such features constitute a small part of 124 originally calculated ones (31 for each of 4 muscles). When the first two phases of dystrophy are distinguished, the most important texture characteristics can be provided by the EDL muscle. In fact, not many EDL-derived features were rejected as age-dependent at this task, and the set of remaining features, to select from, was quite large. The transition from the second to the third phase possibly results in larger changes in the EDL muscle in healthy individuals (54.1% of its textural features were found to be significantly different between these two phases in healthy individuals – see Table 1), nevertheless the remaining set seems to contain many robust features. Relatively good texture characteristics are also provided by the TC muscle, which proves to be useful in distinguishing the third dystrophy phase from the two remaining ones. Finally, the least effective features turn out to be those derived from the GasLat muscle. Even if many of them do not evolve with age, they were selected neither in the first ("1vs2") nor in the second ("2vs3") differentiation problem.

6   Conclusion and Future Work

The study presented a strategy for indicating the textural features that are the most appropriate for therapy evaluation in Duchenne Muscular Dystrophy. This strategy was based on multi-muscle texture analysis (simultaneously considering several types of muscles) and involved applying statistical analysis to eliminate features that may possibly evolve under the influence of the individual's growth. The remaining features, considered as age-independent, were ranked basing on the *Monte Carlo* procedure, according to their usefulness in identifying dystrophy phases. Different sets of top-ranked age-independent features were assessed by six classifiers. The best vectors of features ensured a classification accuracy of 100.0% (problem "1vs2"), 86.9% (problem "2vs3"), and 100.0% (problem "1vs3") cases, and were composed of 16, 12, and 9 features, respectively.

The main limitation of the study is that, it was based on a relatively small database. The numbers of ROIs used for statistical analysis (Table 2) and the numbers of feature vectors obtained by multi-muscle TA (Table 3) were not large, what did not allow to obtain the highly reliable results. In the future, experiments should undoubtedly be repeated using more subjects. Also, because many considered features showed their age-dependency (see Table 1), which makes them inappropriate for therapy evaluation, other groups of features could be tested, e.g. – those based on local binary pattern or wavelet transform. Additional image series can be introduced as well; at least the T1-weighted and the Dixon ones. Finally, a model characterizing differences in texture evolution under dystrophy progression and under the individual's growth is worth to be elaborated.

Acknowledgments. I would like to thank Noura Azzabou from the Institute of Myology, NMR Laboratory, Paris, France for providing the database of images and ROIs on which the experiments were performed in this study. I also thank the participants of the COST Action BM1304, MYO-MRI for valuable discussions.

This work was supported by grant S/WI/2/18 (from the Bialystok University of Technology), founded by the Polish Ministry of Science and Higher Education.

References

1. Jasmin, L.: Duchenne Muscular Dystrophy: MedlinePlus Medical Encyclopedia. Medline Plus. U.S. National Library of Medicine (2017). http://www.medlineplus.gov/ency/article/000705.htm. Accessed 28 Feb 2019
2. Crone, M., Mah, J.K.: Current and emerging therapies for Duchenne muscular dystrophy. Curr. Treat. Options Neurol. **20**(8), 1–17 (2018)
3. Andrews, J.G., Wahl, R.A.: Duchenne and Becker muscular dystrophy in adolescents: current perspectives. Adolesc. Health Med. Ther. **9**, 53–63 (2018)
4. Escorcio, R., Voos, M.C., Martini, J., Albuquerque, P.S., Caromano, F.A.: Functional evaluation for Duchenne muscular dystrophy. In: Escorcio, R. (ed.) Muscular Dystrophy, Avid Science, pp. 1–28 (2019, in press)
5. Finanger, E.L., Russman, B., Forbes, S.C., Rooney, W.D., Walter, G.A., et al.: Use of skeletal muscle MRI in diagnosis and monitoring disease progression in Duchenne muscular dystrophy. Phys. Med. Rehabil. Clin. N. Am. **23**(1), 1–10 (2012)
6. De Certaines, J.D., Larcher, T., Duda, D., Azzabou, N., Eliat, P.A., et al.: Application of texture analysis to muscle MRI: 1-what kind of information should be expected from texture analysis? EPJ Nonlinear Biomed. Phys. **3**(3), 1–14 (2015)
7. Fan, Z., Wang, J., Ahn, M., Shiloh-Malawsky, Y., Chahin, N., et al.: Characteristics of magnetic resonance imaging biomarkers in a natural history study of golden retriever muscular dystrophy. Neuromuscul. Disord. **24**(2), 178–191 (2014)
8. Yang, G., Lalande, V., Chen, L., Azzabou, N., Larcher, T., et al.: MRI texture analysis of GRMD dogs using orthogonal moments: a preliminary study. IRBM **36**(4), 213–219 (2015)
9. Duda, D., Kretowski, M., Azzabou, N., de Certaines, J.D.: MRI texture analysis for differentiation between healthy and golden retriever muscular dystrophy dogs at different phases of disease evolution. In: Saeed, K., Homenda, W. (eds.) CISIM 2015. LNCS, vol. 9339, pp. 255–266. Springer, Cham (2015). https://doi.org/10.1007/978-3-319-24369-6_21
10. Zhang, M.H., Ma, J.S., Shen, Y., Chen, Y.: Optimal classification for the diagnosis of Duchenne muscular dystrophy images using support vector machines. Int. J. Comput. Assist. Radiol. Surg. **11**(9), 1755–1763 (2016)
11. Martins-Bach, A.B., Malheiros, J., Matot, B., Martins, P.C.M., Almeida, C., et al.: Quantitative T2 combined with texture analysis of nuclear magnetic resonance images identify different degrees of muscle involvement in three mouse models of muscle dystrophy: mdx, Largemyd and mdx/Largemyd. PLOS ONE **10**(2), e0117835, 1–16 (2015)
12. Duda, D., Kretowski, M., Azzabou, N., de Certaines, J.D.: MRI texture-based classification of dystrophic muscles. A search for the most discriminative tissue descriptors. In: Saeed, K., Homenda, W. (eds.) CISIM 2016. LNCS, vol. 9842, pp. 116–128. Springer, Cham (2016). https://doi.org/10.1007/978-3-319-45378-1_11
13. Eresen, A., Alic, L., Birch, S.M., Friedeck, W., Griffin, J.F., et al.: Texture as an imaging biomarker for disease severity in golden retriever muscular dystrophy. Muscle Nerve **59**(3), 380–386 (2019)
14. Duda, D.: MRI texture-based recognition of dystrophy phase in golden retriever muscular dystrophy dogs. Elimination of features that evolve along with the individual's growth. Stud. Log. Gramm. Rhetor. **56**(1), 121–142 (2018)
15. Duda, D., Azzabou, N., de Certaines, J.D.: Multi-muscle texture analysis for dystrophy development identification in golden retriever muscular dystrophy dogs. In: Saeed, K., Homenda, W. (eds.) CISIM 2018. LNCS, vol. 11127, pp. 3–15. Springer, Cham (2018). https://doi.org/10.1007/978-3-319-99954-8_1

16. Kornegay, J.N.: The golden retriever model of Duchenne muscular dystrophy. Skelet. Muscle **7**(9), 1–21 (2017)
17. Vapnik, V.N.: The Nature of Statistical Learning Theory, 2nd edn. Springer, New York (2000). https://doi.org/10.1007/978-1-4757-3264-1
18. Lerski, R.A., de Certaines, J.D., Duda, D., Klonowski, W., Yang, G., et al.: Application of texture analysis to muscle MRI: 2 - technical recommendations. EPJ Nonlinear Biomed. Phys. **3**(2), 1–20 (2015)
19. Freund, Y., Shapire, R.: A decision-theoretic generalization of online learning and an application to boosting. J. Comput. Syst. Sci. **55**(1), 119–139 (1997)
20. Nodera, H., Sogawa, K., Takamatsu, N., Mori, A., Yamazaki, H., et al.: Age-dependent texture features in skeletal muscle ultrasonography. J. Med. Invest. **65**(3.4), 274–279 (2018)
21. National Research Council: Guide for the Care and Use of Laboratory Animals. The National Academies Press, Washington, DC, USA (2011)
22. Thibaud, J.L., Azzabou, N., Barthelemy, I., Fleury, S., Cabrol, L., et al.: Comprehensive longitudinal characterization of canine muscular dystrophy by serial NMR imaging of GRMD dogs. Neuromuscul. Disord. **22**(Suppl. 2), S85–S99 (2012)
23. Duda, D.: Medical image classification based on texture analysis. Ph.D. Thesis, University of Rennes 1, Rennes, France (2009)
24. StatSoft Inc: Statistica, ver. 13.1 (2016). www.statsoft.com. Accessed 28 Feb 2019
25. Hall, M., Frank, E., Holmes, G., Pfahringer, B., Reutemann, P., Witten, I.H.: The WEKA data mining software: an update. SIGKDD Explor. **11**(1), 10–18 (2009)
26. Kohavi, R., John, G.H.: Wrappers for Feature Subset Selection. Artif. Intell. **97**(1–2), 273–324 (1997)
27. Quinlan, J.: C4.5: Programs for Machine Learning. Morgan Kaufmann, San Francisco (1993)
28. Breiman, L.: Random forests. Mach. Learn. **45**(1), 5–32 (2001)
29. Hosmer, D.W.J., Lemeshow, S., Sturdivant, R.X.: Applied Logistic Regression, 3rd edn. Wiley, Hoboken (2013)
30. Bishop, C.M.: Neural Networks for Pattern Recognition. Clarendon Press, Oxford (1995)

An Online Pattern Based Activity Discovery: In Context of Geriatric Care

Moumita Ghosh(✉)(iD), Sayan Chatterjee(iD), Shubham Basak(iD),
and Sankhayan Choudhury(iD)

Department of Computer Science and Engineering, University of Calcutta,
Kolkata, India
ghoshmoumita06@gmail.com, scsayan96@gmail.com, shubhambsk@gmail.com,
sankhayan@gmail.com

Abstract. The behavioral analysis of an elderly person living independently is one of the major components of geriatric care. The day-long
activity monitoring is a pre-requisite of the said analysis. Activity monitoring could be done remotely through the analysis of the sensory data
where the sensors are placed in strategic locations within the residence.
Most of the existing works use supervised learning. But it becomes infeasible to prepare the training dataset through repeated execution of a set
of activities for a geriatric person. Moreover, the geriatric people are
annoyed to use wearable sensors. Thus it becomes a challenge to discover the activities based on only ambient sensors using unsupervised
learning. Pattern-based activity discovery is a well-known technique in
this domain. Most of the existing pattern based methods are offline as the
entire data set needs to be mined to find out the existing patterns. Each
identified pattern could be an activity. There are a few online alternatives but those are highly dependent on prior domain knowledge. In this
paper, the intention is to offer an online pattern based activity discovery
that performs satisfactorily without any prior domain knowledge. The
exhaustive experiment has been done on benchmark data sets ARUBA,
KYOTO, TULUM and the performance metrics ensure the strength of
the proposed technique.

Keywords: Geriatric care · Unsupervised learning · Activity detection

1 Introduction

Nowadays, population aging and care for population aging are common phenomena [1]. It seeks out attention from the people of various domains such
as media-persons, policymakers, physicians, and adult-care social workers. The
major concern is their well-being that can be assessed through their daily activities. There are several types of basic activities such as eating, bathing, getting
dressed, etc. and these are called "Activities of Daily Living" (ADL) [13, 14].
Moreover, based on the existing socio-economic status it can be apprehended

© Springer Nature Switzerland AG 2019
K. Saeed et al. (Eds.): CISIM 2019, LNCS 11703, pp. 25–38, 2019.
https://doi.org/10.1007/978-3-030-28957-7_3

that within a couple of decades the elderly people need to reside independently. Certainly, there is a strong association between "Independent Living" and being able to perform daily activities. The smooth execution of ADLs play a crucial role to determine whether a person needs assistance; especially the degree of assistance from caregivers to survive alone in his/her residence.

There are many ways to assess the performance of daily activities. A person is monitored for a long time for the necessary behavioral analysis. The first step towards measuring performance is to get information about the activities. There are primarily two approaches to track the activities. These are either vision based or sensor based [2]. In vision based, a video camera is used to track the activities. But, the prominent form of activity tracking is sensor based as a camera-based tracking system violates some sort of privacy of the users. The sensor-based tracking system uses two types of sensors. Ambient sensors are placed in some strategic locations to sense the human movement. As opposed to this, wearable sensors are tied in some specific body position to track the activities. It may create some extent of annoyance to the geriatric people.

The activity recognition addresses the challenge of identifying the activity through the necessary analysis of sensory data. The said technique mostly relies on supervised learning [3,7]. The common practice of supervised learning is to perform some predefined activities in a scripted setting for the generation of training data. The generation of training data is a difficult job, especially in the target domain. Most of the time the geriatric persons are not willing to perform the same task repeatedly. As a result, using a scripted setting, the generation of training data is almost infeasible. The only alternative could be recognizing the activities in an unsupervised way and this is termed as "Activity Discovery" [11] in literature.

The approach of activity discovery is broadly categorized in two ways. Most of the activity discovery method relies on finding motifs/patterns to identify activities. It identifies the frequent and repeatable sequences over the entire data set. These repetitive sequences are called motifs [12]. This approach can detect only those activities for which motifs are found [5,10–12]. Thus, it fails to detect activities with lower frequency compared to the activities with higher frequencies. Another widely used approach is feature based activity discovery. In this approach, the similar data points are included in a cluster. The widely used approaches are k-Means, DBScan, Agglomerative, etc. [9]. The similarity among data points is measured using the different features [8] and similar data points form a cluster. Some of the features used to measure the similarity are mean, median, standard deviation, energy, integral, skewness, kurtosis, and root mean square, etc. [8].

In reality, geriatric people are annoyed to use wearable sensors. In the case of wearable sensors, finding the similarity among sensor events is not a challenging issue as distinct values trigger for different activities. But, in an ambient sensor especially in the case of binary motion sensors, finding the similarity among motion sensors is a challenging task. Location and time act as major features in most of the existing works. The domain knowledge is to be incorporated for measuring the correlation among motion sensors. It puts an extra burden to acquire the domain knowledge [15]. From the above discussion, it can be apprehended that to work with ambient motion sensors, pattern-based activity discovery could be a better solution for activity monitoring in a geriatric care environment.

In general, pattern means frequent occurrences of event sequences. The patterns that occur more than given predefined support are treated as activities [12]. Most of the pattern based approaches are offline [5] as the entire dataset needs to be present beforehand for necessary mining. In contrast, the existing online approaches depend on prior knowledge [10]. The above discussion demands the need for proposing an online discovery technique that uses only ambient sensors for a geriatric care application without using domain knowledge.

The paper is structured as follows. Section 2 describes the problem with an illustrative example. In Sect. 3, the solution of the problem, i.e. the proposed method of activity discovery is discussed in detail. Section 4 describes the experiment for the necessary validation. Section 5 concludes the discussion highlighting the specific contributions of the work.

2 Scope of the Problem

It is assumed that there is an elderly person in the house alone. She is capable of doing all her daily activities. Our concern is to identify some basic activities like Sleeping, Bed-to-toilet, Eating, Meal preparation, etc. The frequency of the activities in respective days may be different. The person is monitored through the generated spontaneous signals from the ambient (motion) sensors as placed in the strategic locations within the house. Also, we assume that the activities are performed sequentially. The challenge is to discover the activities online. Here the term "online" implies that within a finite amount of time (not real-time), the proposed solution will be able to discover the activities.

The ARUBA [4] baseline data, as created by Washington State University, is considered here for experimentation of the proposed discovery algorithm. Let us, consider the floor plan as given in ARUBA [4] and is depicted in Fig. 1. It can be seen from the diagram that several sensors are placed in some strategic locations. The sensors are only triggered whenever a person is within the range of a sensor as well as he is moving position. The scope includes an online activity discovery technique proposal and subsequent experimentation on the benchmark data set for ensuring the effectiveness of the proposed approach. however, we have used the raw dataset assuming that there is no noise. Moreover, the activity recognition, based on the output of the proposed discovery algorithm is also within the scope. The experimentation on existing benchmark data sets is also one of the targets to assess the effectiveness of the algorithm irrespective of the nature of a specific data set. As a result, the datasets TULUM and KYOTO [6] are also identified beside ARUBA [4] for necessary experimentation.

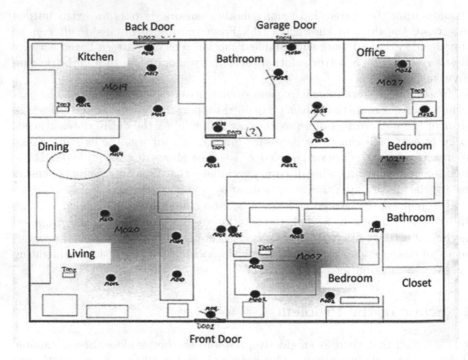

Fig. 1. Floor plan as mentioned in ARUBA.

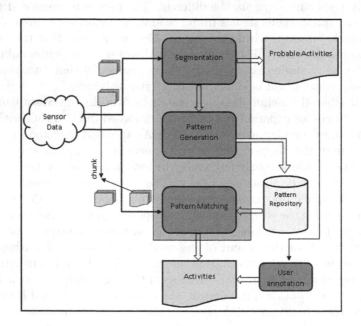

Fig. 2. Block diagram of activity discovery.

Table 1. Raw data as triggered in ARUBA data set

Date	Time	SensorId	Value	Annotation
04-11-2010	08:11:10 AM	M018	ON	Meal_Preparation begin
04-11-2010	08:11:15 AM	M019	ON	
04-11-2010	08:11:16 AM	M015	ON	
04-11-2010	08:11:17 AM	M018	OFF	
04-11-2010	08:11:19 AM	M019	OFF	
04-11-2010	08:11:21 AM	M015	OFF	
04-11-2010	08:11:23 AM	M019	ON	
04-11-2010	08:11:37 AM	M019	OFF	
04-11-2010	08:11:37 AM	M019	ON	
04-11-2010	08:11:39 AM	M019	OFF	

3   Proposed Approach

In general, activity discovery is conceptualized as in the block diagram depicted in Fig. 2. The sensors trigger as and when an activity takes place. The continuous execution of activities generates a stream of sensor data. Our approach is a two-fold approach. In the first form, it aims to segment the stream of sensor data activity wise and the subsequent pattern generation is carried out to detect the further occurrences of an activity. It is assumed that after activity-based segmentation, the discovered segment is labeled manually. The detailed discussion on each phase in the discovery process is given below.

3.1   Preliminaries: Proposed Solution

The following preliminaries are illustrated for substantiating the proposed discovery mechanism.

Data Representation: In this present article, we use the data set collected from the sensor based smart home like ARUBA [4], TULUM and KYOTO [6]. The data set consists of several tuples or rows. Each row represents one single event. The field of the tuples is Date, Time, sensor identifier and sensor value. A snapshot of related events is shown below in Table 1. This is the typical example of an activity called Meal Preparation.

Artifacts: The artifacts are described in the following section.
Event: Each tuple of a data set is called an event. From the above table, each of the rows is treated as an event. For example, the first row of the above Table 1 signifies that motion sensor M019 triggers on dated 2010-11-04 at 08:12:23.
Sequence: Several consecutive events are called sequence.

Chunk: A sequence of sensor data is called a chunk. This may or may not pertain to a particular activity. A chunk can be fixed length or variable length. The length of the chunk depends on the chunk selection strategy. If the chunk is selected event wise then a chunk must include a fixed number of events. The number of entries in all the subsequent chunks is equal. On the other hand, in the time-based chunk selection strategy, the number of entries differs from one chunk to another. Here, time is fixed. In the above table, a Chunk of length 10 (Chunk_SIZE) has been shown.

Buffer: One or more chunks containing sensor events pertaining to only a particular activity is defined as a buffer. It is supposed to be a chunk of a sensor event sequence that occurs from the starting of an instance of an activity to its end.

Segment: A buffer is cleared from memory after waiting for a predefined time, with the assumption that the activity instance has been completed. This buffer, after being mature, is termed as a segment.

Unique_sensor: The set of distinct sensors that appear in chunk or Buffer.

Dominant_sensor: The dominant sensors are those whose frequency of occurrence in a chunk or buffer is higher than a predefined threshold T.

Pattern: The descending order of top n most trigger events of a chunk. So, from the above example, pattern P is defined as $< M019, M015 >$. In the next subsection, the segmentation procedure is discussed in depth.

3.2   Segmentation

The activity discovery is executed by several distinct modules as depicted in Fig. 2. The stream of sensor data is the input to the activity discovery block. The details of each module are given below.

Before processing, the stream data is divided into chunks(collection of events). The chunk is either taken event wise or time wise. A fixed number of events are recorded in event-based strategy whereas, in time-based segmentation, the number of events in a segment may vary. In the target domain, the stream data may generate in discretely as the concerned sensors are only ambients. As a result, our choice could be time-based. In an online environment, event-based segmentation, one needs to wait a long time to fill the chunks in terms of event number such as twenty events. The most challenging part is to choose the interval of time as sometimes no data event may come or sometimes data appears at a higher rate. But, the problem persists irrespective of the fact of using time-based chunk selection or event-based technique as we deal with stream data. One solution is to select the chunk activity wise and that could be the fittest solution for our target domain. We have used the time-based segmentation for creating the initial chunks and the generated chunks are merged to form an activity through the proposed activity based segmentation. For the sake of completion in the experimentation phase, the time based as well as event-based segmentation are used for chunk creation to asses the performance variation between the said techniques.

The activity-based segmentation, i.e. the merging of the existing chunks, as generated through time-based/event-based technique, is done without any prior

---

Algorithm 1: Online Pattern based Segmentation Technique ($OPST$).

Input : $Wait\_time$, Stream of sensor events (S), $Chunk\_Size$, $Buffer\_list$
Output: Pool of Activity Patterns

1   $Chunk\_size$ = c_size
2   $Buffer\_list$ = b_list
3   $start = 0$
4   **while** *start in range of data stream* **do**
5   Cur_Chunk=content $[start:start+Chunk\_size]$
6   **if** $Buffer\_list == \{\}$ **then**
7 | $Cur\_Buffer = Cur\_Chunk$
8   **end**
9   **else**
10       $set\_diff = Unique\_Sensor.Cur\_Chunk \setminus Unique\_Sensor.Cur\_Buffer$
       // perform the set difference between the unique sensors of Current
       Chunk and Current Buffer and UniqueSensors is a function that
       calculates unique sensors of Current Chunk.
11   **if** $set\_diff == \{\}$ **then**
       // all the unique elements of current chunk is common to current
       buffer.
12        $Cur\_Buffer = Cur\_Buffer + Cur\_Chunk$ // Immediately current
       chunk is appended to current buffer.
13   **end**
14   **if** $set\_diff == \{all\ unique\ elements\ of\ Cur\_Chunk\}$ **then**
       // When all the unique elements of current chunk are uncommon to
       current buffer
15        $Cur\_Buffer = Cur\_Buffer + 1$ // the current chunk is not
       appended to current buffer;it will search for another new buffer
       to append the current chunk
16   Cur_Buffer=Cur_Chunk
17   **end**
18   **if** $set\_diff == \{Cur\_Chunk \setminus (Cur\_Chunk \cap Cur\_Buffer)\}$ **then**
       // When,some common elements are present is the current chunk,We
       have to wait for next chunk. $temp\_index = start + Chunk\_size + 1$
19        $temp\_Chunk$ = content $[temp\_index :temp\_index+Chunk\_size]$
       // Bringing the next Chunk in the temporary Chunk.
20        $set\_differ = Unique\_Sensor.Cur\_Chunk \setminus Unique\_Sensor.temp\_Chunk$
21   **if** $set\_differ == \{\}$ **then**
22 | $Cur\_Buffer = Cur\_Chunk$
23   **end**
24   **if** $set\_differ == \{Cur\_Chunk \setminus (Cur\_Chunk \cap temp\_Chunk)\}$ **then**
25          $output\_common = Cur\_Chunk \cap temp\_Chunk$
26          $Cur\_Buffer = alloutput\_common from Cur\_Chunk$
27   **end**
28   **end**
29   **end**
30   **foreach** *buf in Buffer_list* **do**
31       $Eva\_Buffer = Buffer\_list[buf]$
32   **if** $time.Cur\_Buffer[last\_ele] + Wait\_time <= time.Cur\_Chunk[first\_ele]$
      then
33 | Output Buffer as probbale activity segment
34   **end**
35   **end**
36 **end**

Algorithm 2: Pattern Generation.

Input   : Pool of Committed Activities(Com_Act)
Output: Pool of Activity Patterns

1 **foreach** *Activity in Pool of Activity Patterns* **do**
2 | *Sensor_List = getFrequency(Com_Act)//* `getFrequency is a function` `that calculates frequency of each distinct sensor in a segment of` `committed activity.`
3 | *Dom_Sensor_List = getDominant(Sensor_List)//* `It prunes top n` `number of sensors from the sensor list.`
4 | *Pattern = nonDecreasing(Dom_Sensor_List)//* `Arrage the dominating` `sensors in non decreasing order.`
5 | *Pattern_reposotory = Pattern//* `Store each pattern in pattern` `repository.`
6 **end**

---

domain knowledge. The rationale behind the concept is that if a set of events occurs in several consecutive chunks, then it could be a part of the same activity. As a result, the chunks must be merged in a single segment. This process will be continued until a new set of sensors is generated and that creates the initiation of a new chunk i.e. a new activity segment. Every new segment is given a predefined threshold time for its maturity. The activity is clear from the memory after the threshold time, and it is given to the experts for annotation. The maturity time selection strategy is described later. The detailed of the segmentation procedure is given in Algorithm 1.

Threshold Time: The selection of threshold time is dynamic. It has been decided for event-based and time-based respectively. The threshold time for maturity in event-based is fixed and can be derived through the experiment. In the case of time-based segmentation, the difference in times between the last event of the active segment and the first event of the next chunk is treated as threshold time. It adapts the varying property of different activities in terms of time duration.

Pattern Generation: The pattern is generated from a probable activity segment. The frequency of the dominating sensors is noted. Then sensors are arranged in nondecreasing order. The non-decreasing order of the sensors is called a pattern. The patterns generation process is described in the Algorithm 2.

Pattern Matching: The evolving patterns are is kept in a repository. Later, when another chunk will arrive, at first, the chunk is compared with predefined patterns to infer the same pattern can be derived from the chunk or not. If the pattern is found from the previously discovered set of patterns, we simply mark the chunk as an instance of a predefined activity and wait for its maturity. The basic principle of matching is depicted in the Algorithm 3.

Algorithm 3: Pattern Matching.

Input   : Cur_Chunk, Pool of Activity Patterns
Output: Committed Activity Segments

1 **foreach** *Activity in Pool of Activity Patterns* **do**
2     $Dom\_Cur\_Chunk = getDominant(Cur\_Chunk)$// It prunes top n number of sensors of Current Chunk.
3     $Pattern\_Chunk = nonDecreasing(Dom\_Cur\_Chunk)$// Arrage the dominating sensors in non decreasing order.
4     $Result = doMatch(Pattern\_Chunk, Cur\_Act\_Pat)$// Matching in between current chunk pattern and all available patterns.
5   **if** *Result is True* **then**
6        $Activity\_segment = Cur\_Chunk$ // Assigned current chunk as activity segment.
7   **end**
8   **else**
9        $OPST(Cur\_Chunk)$ // Create new activity segment.
10   **end**
11 **end**

---

4   Experimental Findings

We have identified three benchmark data sets ARUBA [4], KYOTO, TULUM [6] for the necessary experimentation. The objective is to measure the performance of the proposed discovery technique in terms of activity detection ratio. Aruba dataset [4] contains sensor data that was collected from the home of a volunteer adult. Aruba dataset collected from a house that consists of a bedroom, a kitchen, a bathroom, a dining room, and an office. The home Aruba included 31 sensors to collect environmental information. All activities are collected from a single inhabitant within the period of 2010-11-04 to 2011-06-11.

Kyoto dataset represents sensor events collected in the WSU smart apartment testbed during the summer of 2009. The apartment housed two residents R1, R2 and they performed their normal daily activities. Herein, 51 motion sensors, five temperature sensors, fifteen door sensors, a burner sensor, hot and cold-water sensors, and an electric sensor were used for the necessary data recording. In our problem, we consider only motion sensors as per the problem definition. WSU Tulum Smart Apartment 2009 is a two Resident test-bed. This dataset represents sensor events collected in the WSU smart apartment test-bed from April to July of 2009. The sensors consist of 18 motion sensors (M001 through M018) and two temperature sensors (T001 and T002). Ten activities are annotated by denoting the begin and end of each activity occurrence. The data set TULUM and KYOTO consider two residents. But, in this work, our intention is to detect the activities irrespective of the association of activity to its corresponding residence.

Table 2. Detection ratio in ARUBA.

Activity name	No. of activity instances occuring			Detection ratio in	
	In ground truth data ARUBA	In event based chunk selection	In time based chunk selection	In event based chunk selection	In time based chunk selection
Sleeping	2	1	2	0.5	1.00
Bed to toilet	1	1	1	1	1.00
Eating	4	3	4	0.75	1.00
House keeping	2	8	-	4.00	-
Meal preparation	9	12	9	1.33	1.00
Relax	5	7	4	1.40	0.80
Wash dishes	2	3	2	1.50	1.00
Work	2	2	2	1.00	1.00

Table 3. Detection ratio in TULUM.

Activity name	No. of activity instances occuring			Detection ratio in	
	In ground truth data ARUBA	In event based chunk selection	In time based chunk selection	In event based chunk selection	In time based chunk selection
R1_cook_breakfast	1	1	1	1.00	1.00
R1_eat_breakfast	2	1	2	0.50	1.00
R1_cook_lunch	1	1	1	1.00	1.00
Leave_home	1	1	1	1.00	1.00
R1_snack	14	11	9	0.78	0.64
Watch_tv	16	13	10	0.81	0.63

We have executed the said discovery on these three data sets. The time-based segmentation is used for creating initial chunks. To assess the variation between time-based and event-based, the second approach is also used in the experimentation phase. We present the result as obtained using both the techniques. We have done the experimentation with different chunk sizes for the event based chunk creation. We found that the chunk sizes of 10, 5, 5 respectively to perform the test for the dataset ARUBA, TULUM and KYOTO. All the cases, we assume the fixed wait time and is set as five minutes. As an outcome of the experimentation phase, the number of activity segments is 127, 109, 68 respectively in three data sets. In time-based chunk creation, the number of activity segments is found 133, 107, 68 respectively in three data set.

Table 4. Detection ratio in KYOTO.

Activity name	No. of activity instances occuring			Detection ratio in	
	In ground truth data ARUBA	In event based chunk selection	In time based chunk selection	In event based chunk selection	In time based chunk selection
R1 sleep	1	1	1	1	1
R1 wakeup	1	1	1	1	1
R1 grooming	1	1	1	1	1
R1 shower	1	2	1	2	1
R1 work	12	14	7	1.17	0.58

Table 5. Accuracy measured in ARUBA.

Activity name	Precision		Recall		F1-Measure	
	Event based	Time based	Event based	Time based	Event based	Time based
Sleeping	0.90	0.88	0.86	0.59	0.87	0.69
Bed to toilet	0.72	0.73	0.58	0.76	0.59	0.72
Eating	0.77	0.81	0.76	0.79	0.74	0.80
House keeping	0.89	0.99	0.28	0.09	0.37	0.17
Meal preparation	0.88	0.81	0.71	0.61	0.75	0.66
Relax	0.84	0.80	0.78	0.77	0.78	0.76
Wash dishes	0.65	1.00	0.66	0.65	0.63	0.77
Work	0.79	0.82	0.76	0.77	0.74	0.77

Table 6. Accuracy measured in TULUM.

Activity name	Precision		Recall		F1-Measure	
	Event based	Time based	Event based	Time based	Event based	Time based
R1_cook_breakfast	1.00	1.00	0.64	0.86	0.78	0.93
R1_eat_breakfast	0.19	0.74	0.41	0.77	0.26	0.75
R1_cook_lunch	0.69	1.00	0.73	0.86	0.71	0.93
Leave_home	0.89	0.94	0.56	0.89	0.69	0.92
R1_snack	0.75	0.85	0.30	0.51	0.36	0.58
Watch_tv	0.85	0.82	0.50	0.50	0.39	0.60

The following tables show the performance of the proposed discovery technique in terms of well-known parameters called Precision, Recall and F1 measure. are shown in Tables 5, 6 and 7. The activity detection ratio is also depicted in

Table 7. Accuracy measured in KYOTO.

Activity name	Precision		Recall		F1-Measure	
	Event based	Time based	Event based	Time based	Event based	Time based
R1 sleep	0.96	0.99	1.00	0.82	0.98	0.90
R1 wakeup	0.06	1.00	1.00	0.67	0.11	0.80
R1 grooming	0.70	0.71	1.00	1.00	0.82	0.83
R1 shower	0.24	0.29	0.77	0.90	0.37	0.43
R1 work	0.38	0.87	0.69	0.58	0.41	0.67

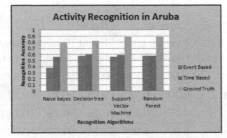

(a) Activity Recognition in ARUBA.

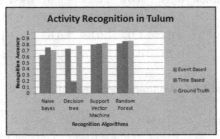

(b) Activity Recognition in TULUM.

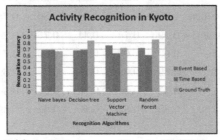

(c) Activity Recognition in KYOTO.

Fig. 3. Evaluation of activity recognition algorithms in different data sets.

the Tables 2, 3 and 4. The overall performance is satisfactory except few cases. It ensures the effectiveness of the proposed discovery algorithm. Moreover, activity recognition is done using five days of annotated data. We train the model using five days annotated data as per the detection is done by the proposed discovery on the five days data in the original data set. Based on the said training, recognition is performed using well-known approaches like Naive Bayes, Decision Tree, Support Vector Machine, and Conditional Random Field. The accuracies of the recognized activities are depicted in Fig. 3.

5   Conclusion

The scope of the paper is to deliver an online activity discovery in an ambient sensor based home care environment without any prior domain knowledge. The requirements are set keeping the geriatric care application in mind. The proposed solution will be suitable for use in the geriatric care domain where the online monitoring of an old aged person is highly needed. The solution does not require any training as well as any prior domain knowledge as it becomes an almost infeasible task in the above-said domain. The proposed pattern-based discovery uses time-based segmentation on the stream data for the creation of initial chunks. These created chunks are merged based on the said pattern matching and generate a segment that could be a probable activity. Thus the overall approach can be treated as an activity-based segmentation. The overall performance is satisfactory except few cases e.g. activity recognition result in ARUBA is not good enough whereas it shows much better for KYOTO and TULUM data set. The proposed online segmentation cum discovery approach is memory efficient. The algorithm works with the growing segment in memory and outputs the matured one. Moreover, further activities like annotation can be going on parallel while the discovery process is running for the other activities. Several issues remain for further investigation. The discovery needs to be modified for detecting scattered activity. The transitions between the activities have to be identified for better accuracy.

References

1. Elderly   in   india.   http://mospi.nic.in/sites/default/files/publication_reports/ ElderlyinIndia_2016.pdf
2. Benmansour, A., Bouchachia, A., Feham, M.: Multioccupant activity recognition in pervasive smart home environments. ACM Comput. Surv. (CSUR) 48(3), 34 (2016)
3. Brdiczka, O., Crowley, J.L., Reignier, P.: Learning situation models in a smart home. IEEE Trans. Syst. Man Cybern. B Cybern. 39(1), 56–63 (2008)
4. Cook, D.J.: Learning setting-generalized activity models for smart spaces. IEEE Intell. Syst. 2010(99), 1 (2010)
5. Cook, D.J., Krishnan, N.C., Rashidi, P.: Activity discovery and activity recognition: a new partnership. IEEE Trans. Cybern. 43(3), 820–828 (2013)

6. Cook, D.J., Schmitter-Edgecombe, M.: Assessing the quality of activities in a smart environment. Methods Inf. Med. **48**(05), 480–485 (2009)
7. Fleury, A., Noury, N., Vacher, M.: Supervised classification of activities of daily living in health smart homes using SVM. In: 2009 Annual International Conference of the IEEE Engineering in Medicine and Biology Society, pp. 6099–6102. IEEE (2009)
8. Gjoreski, H., Roggen, D.: Unsupervised online activity discovery using temporal behaviour assumption. In: Proceedings of the 2017 ACM International Symposium on Wearable Computers, pp. 42–49. ACM (2017)
9. Kisilevich, S., Mansmann, F., Nanni, M., Rinzivillo, S.: Spatio-temporal clustering. In: Maimon, O., Rokach, L. (eds.) Data Mining and Knowledge Discovery Handbook, pp. 855–874. Springer, Boston (2009). https://doi.org/10.1007/978-0-387-09823-4_44
10. Rashidi, P., Cook, D.J.: Mining sensor streams for discovering human activity patterns over time. In: 2010 IEEE International Conference on Data Mining, pp. 431–440. IEEE (2010)
11. Rashidi, P., Cook, D.J., Holder, L.B., Schmitter-Edgecombe, M.: Discovering activities to recognize and track in a smart environment. IEEE Trans. Knowl. Data Eng. **23**(4), 527–539 (2011)
12. Saives, J., Pianon, C., Faraut, G.: Activity discovery and detection of behavioral deviations of an inhabitant from binary sensors. IEEE Trans. Knowl. Data Eng. **12**(4), 1211–1224 (2015)
13. Thapliyal, H., Nath, R.K., Mohanty, S.P.: Smart home environment for mild cognitive impairment population: solutions to improve care and quality of life. IEEE Consum. Electron. Mag. **7**(1), 68–76 (2018)
14. Urwyler, P., Stucki, R., Rampa, L., Müri, R., Mosimann, U.P., Nef, T.: Cognitive impairment categorized in community-dwelling older adults with and without dementia using in-home sensors that recognise activities of daily living. Sci. Rep. **7**, 42084 (2017)
15. Ye, J., Stevenson, G.: Semantics-driven multi-user concurrent activity recognition. In: Augusto, J.C., Wichert, R., Collier, R., Keyson, D., Salah, A.A., Tan, A.-H. (eds.) AmI 2013. LNCS, vol. 8309, pp. 204–219. Springer, Cham (2013). https://doi.org/10.1007/978-3-319-03647-2_15

Ships Detection on Inland Waters Using Video Surveillance System

Tomasz Hyla[1]([✉]) [iD] and Natalia Wawrzyniak[2] [iD]

[1] West Pomeranian University of Technology, Szczecin, Poland
thyla@zut.edu.pl
[2] Marine Technology Ltd., Szczecin, Poland
n.wawrzyniak@marinetechnology.pl

Abstract. The video surveillance is used to monitor ships in order to ensure safety on waterways. The ships detection is a first step in a ship automatic identification process based on video streams. The paper presents a new algorithm for ships detection on inland waterways. The algorithm must detect moving ships of all kinds, including leisure craft, that are visible on a video stream and is designed to work for stationary cameras. Furthermore, it only requires an access to video streams from existing monitoring systems without any additional hardware or special configuration of cameras. The algorithm works in variable lightning conditions and with slight changes of background. In the paper, the test application implementing the algorithm is presented together with a series of experimental results showing the algorithm quality depending on different parameters' sets. The main purpose of the tests was to find the optimal set of twelve parameters that will become the default setting. All moving ships, including small boats and kayaks, must be detected, which is the main difference from existing solutions that mostly focus on detection of only one vessel type. In the proposed algorithm, all objects that are moving on water are detected and then non-ships are eliminated by usage of some logic rules and excluding additional image processing methods.

Keywords: Video surveillance · Ship detection · Inland waterway ·
Dynamic background · Real-time detection

1 Introduction

The ships traffic is monitored in order to ensure safety on waterways. Usually, the traffic is monitored using radar networks, Automatic Ship Identification (AIS) receivers, and video surveillance systems. These three systems complement each other. The video surveillance is mostly used to monitor non-conventional (according to International Convention for the Safety of Life at Sea (SOLAS)) ships and to confirm results of detection and recognition obtained from other systems. It is mostly used in restricted or special areas of heavy or complicated traffic. Currently, an operator must visually monitor ships that are passing in front of the cameras. Especially, when it is required to detect and identify a wide array of ships starting from large cargo vessels and ending at kayaks.

© Springer Nature Switzerland AG 2019
K. Saeed et al. (Eds.): CISIM 2019, LNCS 11703, pp. 39–49, 2019.
https://doi.org/10.1007/978-3-030-28957-7_4

The problems related to ship detection on inland waters were discussed by Wawrzyniak and Hyla [1]. The ship in a video stream can be detected using two basic approaches. The first one is to use a pixel-based detection method that allows detecting any moving object on constant or slightly changing background. The second approach is to use an object-based detection using a classifier. The second approach is better when it is possible to find a distinctive property of a class of objects, e.g., a mast of a sailing vessel, because it usually provides better detection result.

1.1   Related Works

One of the possible solutions to the ship detection problem was presented by Ferreira et al. [2]. The authors use two cameras: one camera with low resolution that detects movement and another camera with high resolution that is used to take a photo when the first camera detects movement. Their solution is designed to detect fishing vessels. They achieved the best results when using object-based detection based on Histogram of Oriented Gradients (HOG) classifier [3]. In contrast, Hu et al. [4] used pixel-based detection in their visual surveillance scheme for cage aquaculture that automatically detects and tracks ships. They used the median scheme to create a background image from previous N frames with some additional improvements that allowed to reduce the influence of sea waves. The problem of ship detection in the presence of waves was also addressed by Szpak and Tapamo [5]. They present techniques that solve a problem of moving vessels' tracking in the presence of a moving dynamic background (the ocean). Other works related to the problem of ship detection include [6, 7] and a survey [8].

Moving objects can be detected using a background subtraction algorithm or, to be more precise, using a background/foreground segmentation algorithm. The background subtraction algorithms were evaluated by [9] and compared by [10]. Several background subtraction algorithms are implemented in the OpenCV library [11]. To begin with, Gaussian Mixture-based Background- Foreground Segmentation (MOG) algorithm (that uses a mixture of K, $K = 3$ to 5) gaussian distributions to model each background picture. The probable values of background pixels are the ones that are more static and present in most of the previous frames [12]. Next, Gaussian Mixture-based Background- Foreground Segmentation Algorithm version 2 (MOG2) [13] is available which is an improved version of MOG.

The algorithm Godbehere-Matsukawa-Goldberg (GMG) [14] uses by default 120 frames for background modelling and per-pixel Bayesian segmentation. Another algorithm, *CouNT* (CNT) was designed by Sagi Zeevi [15] to reflect the human vision. It is designed for variable outdoor lighting conditions and it works well on IoT hardware. Other algorithms include k Nearest Neighbours (KNN) that implements K-nearest neighbours background subtraction from [16], the algorithm created during Google Summer of Code (GSOC) [11], and Background Subtraction using Local SVD Binary Pattern (LSBP) [17].

1.2   Motivation and Contribution

This paper is a part of an ongoing research in Ship Recognition (SHREC) [18] project, which concerns automatic recognition and identification of non-conventional (according to International Convention for the Safety of Life at Sea) ships in areas covered by River Information System and Vessel Traffic Service systems. The ships detection is a first step in a ship identification process based on video streams processing [19].

The main contribution is a new algorithm for ships' detection on inland waterways. The algorithm is designed to detect all kinds of moving ships and to work efficiently, so it can be used to process data from multiple cameras (20 or more) with usage of economically acceptable amount of server resources. Moreover, the test application implementing the algorithm is presented together with a series of experimental results showing the algorithm quality depending on different parameters' sets.

1.3   Paper Organisation

The rest of this paper is organised as follows. Section 2 introduces the novel detection algorithm. Section 3 contains description of test environment (test application, experimental data sets) and shows the results of several tests concerning detection quality depending on six different sets of parameters. The final section discusses results and concludes the paper.

2   Detection Algorithm

2.1·   Requirements and Problems

The ships' detection algorithm must detect moving ships that are present on a video stream. The algorithm is designed to work for stationary cameras and detect all kinds of ships, including leisure crafts. The algorithm should use only video streams from an existing monitoring system without any additional hardware or special configuration of cameras. The output of the algorithm are ships pictures cut out of frames in which ships were detected.

The task of selecting foreground objects in a scene is easy in indoor environment, but in outdoor environment it is much more difficult due to many factors that must be considered. It becomes easier when background and lightning are constant at the scene. This is the opposite situation for the one in which the developed detection algorithm should work.

The main problems related to detection of moving ships are [1]: the camera usually is not directed strictly at the water, several other moving objects are present in the frame (e.g., trees that moves in windy conditions), moving animals (e.g., birds) and people, different water state (waves), different camera angles or waterway crossroads, obstacles blocking the view, and different lightning conditions.

2.2   Algorithm Description

The algorithm uses the pixel-based approach. Mostly since it is designed to detect a wide range of ships and it is difficult to find the distinguishing features of each type of ship. The algorithm takes as an input 12 different parameters. A pseudocode for the algorithm is presented below. Several phases in processing a video frame can be distinguished. At first, a frame is pre-processed (lines 6–8), i.e., is resized, blurred and converted to grey scale (using all RGB channels or only using red channel). Next, the algorithm check weather to update the background model. Many background subtraction algorithms can be used. The model is not updated every frame, because in such case some slow-moving ships merge with the background.

Afterwards, the algorithm is looking for the contours on the mask and calculates bounding boxes for each contour. The filtering of objects that are not a ship is performed in two stages. In the first stage (lines 23–28), objects which lie entirely within negative regions are removed (the negative regions are pre-configured for each camera and mark the areas, i.e. land, a bridge, or sky). In the second stage (lines 29–33), the objects that are too small or have inadequate proportions are removed. Finally, the algorithm merges overlapping objects and cuts them out from the original frame. Then returns the resulting images.

```
Algorithm 1: Detect-Ships
Input: video_stream, detection_parameters = {alg_ext,
     res, blur_size, flag_red, n_init, n_learn,
     neg_regions, n_detect, min_width, min_height,
     max_ratio, min_area}
Output: array<bmp>
1   array<bmp> ships = init_empty_array();
2   frame_counter = 0;
3   fgbg = initiate_background_substractor(alg_ext);
4   foreach frame ff in video_stream do
5       frame_counter++;
6       f = resize_to(ff, res);
7       f = covert_to_gray(f, flag_red);
8       f = blur_frame(f, blur_size);
9       if ((frame_counter < n_init) or
10          (frame_counter mod n_learn != 0))
11      then
12          continue;
13      else
14          fgbg.update(f);
15      end
16      if (frame_counter mod n_detect != 0) then
17          mask = fgbg.get_mask();
18          contours = find_contours(mask);
19          array<br> tmp_ships = init_empty_array();
```

```
20        foreach contour c in contours do
21            br = get_bounding_rectangle(c);
22            flag = false;
23            foreach region r ∈ neg_regions do
24                if (br ⊆ r) then
25                    flag = true;
26                    break;
27                end
28            end
29            if ((flag == false) and
30                (br.width  > min_width) and
31                (br.height > min_height) and
32                (br.ratio  < max_ratio) and
33                (br.area   > min_area))
34            then
35            tmp_ships.add(br);
36            end
37        end
38        tmp_ships = merge_overlapping_br(tmp_ships);
39        foreach bounding_rectangle br in tmp_ships do
40            ship_bmp = get_frame_fragment(ff,res,br);
41            ships.add(ship_bmp);
42        end
43    end
44 end
```

Notation:
```
res            - resolution {1920x1080,720x540,960x540)
alg_ext        - a foreground extraction algorithm {FF, MOG,
                 MOG2, GMG, CNT, KNN, GSOC, LSBP}
flag_red       - convert to gray using only Red channel
                 {true/false}
n_init         - number of initialisation frames
n_learn        - alearning interval for alg_ext (number of
                 frames)
n_detect       - a detecting interval (number of frames)
neg_regions    - a set of polygons that describe frame area
                 not designeated for detection
max_ratio      - maxium height to width (or width to height)
                 ratio
```

3   Experimental Evaluation

The main purpose of the test was to find the optimal set of twelve parameters that will become default setting. Firstly, the performance of algorithms was tested [1] and, based on an expert opinion, values for nine parameters were set. Next, for the remaining three parameters two values have been selected, each with the greatest influence on the detection quality.

3.1   Test Environment

In order to test the algorithm, the test application was written in C# and is using Emgu CV version 3.4.3 (C# wrapper for OpenCV). The application (see Fig. 1) allows user to select different parameters and to see how they affect the detection quality. It is possible to watch detection performed by two methods simultaneously to allow for better comparison. Additionally, it is possible to store detection results into the files.

Fig. 1. A screenshot from the test application

The data set that contain more than 200 video samples was recorded on the waterways near Szczecin during the summer 2018. The 15 different video samples (Full High Definition 1920 × 1080, 30 fps, bitrate: 20 Mb/s, AVC Baseline@L4, duration: between 30 s and 120 s) that show different type of ships from different angles, recorded in different places, were selected for the test. The Fig. 2 shows screenshots of a few samples. The following parameters was set to the constant values: *blur_size = {21}, flag_red = {false}, n_init, = {250}, neg_regions = {loaded}, n_detect = {30}, min_width = {30}, min_height = {30}, max_ratio = {9}, min_area = {1000}.* The processing resolution and a background model update rate were tested with the following six sets of parameters:

Fig. 2. Examples of video samples

1. *res = {960 × 540}; n_learn = {1};*
2. *res = {960 × 540}; n_learn = {5};*
3. *res = {960 × 540}; n_learn = {10};*
4. *res = {1280 × 720}; n_learn = {1};*
5. *res = {1280 × 720}; n_learn = {5};*
6. *res = {1280 × 720}; n_learn = {10}.*

A test computer (Core i7-8700 K, 32 GB RAM, SSD 1TB, NVIDIA Quadro P4000) was used in the tests. The tests were run using 6 sets of parameters described above for each vide sample. Each test outputted a set of image files.

3.2 Results

The output images for each test were divided into the following categories:

1. correctly detected ships;
2. partially detected ships (an image contains a part of the ship);
3. artefacts (not ships) – anything else detected except water;
4. artefacts (not ships) – only water detected as object.

Additionally, the number of correctly detected different ships in each video sample was counted (i.e., ships that are present on at least one image). The samples from each category are presented on the Fig. 3.

The algorithm is designed to output possible ships' images that will be used further by a ships' classification algorithm. Therefore, the most important parameter is FNR (False Negative Rate) that shows how many ships were not detected at least once per passage in front of the camera. The FNR (see Fig. 4) is significantly lower when the background model is updated every 10 frames (three times per second). The FNR for

GSOC-10-720 is only 2% and for *GSOC-10-540* is 6%. The FNR for *GSOC-1-540* is 29% and for *GSOC-1-720* is 19%. Generally, higher resolution provides better detection results.

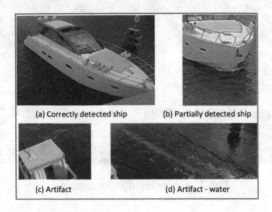

Fig. 3. Examples of different categories of output images

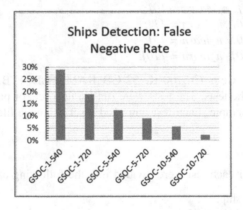

Fig. 4. Ships detection: False Negative Rate

In the following test, each video sample was tested using each set of parameters, which resulted in 90 tests. The results of each test were categorised into one of four categories mentioned above. Then, number of elements in each category was counted. The element was considered as the partial correct detection' result when it contains some distinguishable visible property showing that the element is indeed a ship. The ratios of each category broken down by different parameters' set are presented on the Fig. 5.

The best ratio of correctly detected ships to all detection results was achieved using *GSOC-5-540* (52%), *GSOC-5-540* (51%), and *GSOC-5-540* (51%). Further, counting together correct detection and partial detection the best results was achieved by *GSOC-*

5-540 (87%). The artefacts constitute 21% for *GSOC-10-720* (the worst case) and 13% for GSOC-5-540 (the best case). However, in the test results around 2/3 of artefacts contain water only. Mainly, some waves caused by passing ships and sudden wind gusts. The percentage of artefacts (incorrect detection results excluding water) varies from 3% *GSOC-5-540* to 6% (*GSOC-1-540, GSOC-1-720,* and *GSOC-10-720*).

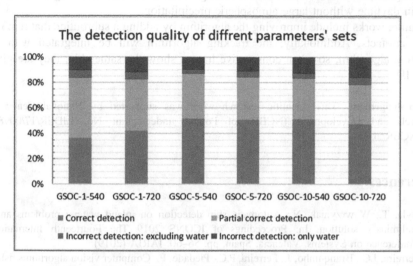

Fig. 5. The detection quality of different parameters' sets

4   Conclusion

The background model is updated not every frame, because in a such situation slow moving, long ships, for example barges, merge with a background. From the other hand, when the update rate is higher the background model has problems with capturing waves and merging them into the background. Therefore, the update rate around three times per second in our type of video streams is optimal. The higher resolution, i.e. HD 1280 × 720, provides better FNR. This probably results from the fact that small or slow-moving ships, after downsizing the frame, are more easily merged with the background model. The FHD resolution (1920 × 1080) might provide better FNR, but calculations take too long to use it practice.

It is worth to mention that some partial detection results are inevitable from the fact that a ship is moving outside the camera view. The highest number of water artefacts result from less frequent updates of the background model. Possibly, the ratio of erroneous artefacts could be increased by finetuning the filtering using negative regions. To sum up, the best set of parameters is *GSOC-10-720* as it will be easier to further minimize the number of artefacts than improve the FNR.

Our algorithm differs from solutions mentioned in the first section with a different design philosophy, use of GSOC background subtraction algorithm, and using all RGB channels to create grayscale image instead of using only red channel. In our approach, we try to detect all objects that are moving on water and then eliminate non-ships by usage of some logic but not image processing. Additionally, the algorithm must detect all moving ships, including small boats and kayaks, which is the main difference from existing solutions that mostly focus on only one vessel type.

The main limitation of the study is that the algorithm is designed to work with stationary FHD streams with good quality. It should work with 4 K and 720 p streams equally good, but it will require further testing. Other limitation is that algorithm works only in daytime without large atmospheric precipitation.

Future works include improving the algorithm by adding a subroutine that removes water artefacts. Additionally, the tracking algorithm will be integrated with the detection algorithm, so when consecutive frames show the same ship, they are given some ID.

Acknowledgement. This scientific research work was supported by National Centre for Research and Development (NCBR) of Poland under grant No. LIDER/17/0098/L-8/16/NCBR/2017.

References

1. Hyla, T., Wawrzyniak, N.: Automatic ship detection on inland waters: problems and a preliminary solution. In: Proceedings of ICONS 2019 The Fourteenth International Conference on Systems, Valencia, Spain, pp. 56–60. IARIA (2019)
2. Ferreira, J.C., Branquinho, J., Ferreira, P.C., Piedade, F.: Computer vision algorithms fishing vessel monitoring—identification of vessel plate number. In: De Paz, J.F., Julián, V., Villarrubia, G., Marreiros, G., Novais, P. (eds.) ISAmI 2017. AISC, vol. 615, pp. 9–17. Springer, Cham (2017). https://doi.org/10.1007/978-3-319-61118-1_2
3. McConnell, R.K.: Method of and apparatus for pattern recognition. US Patent 4,567,610 (1986)
4. Hu, W.-C., Yang, C.-Y., Huang, D.-Y.: Robust real-time ship detection and tracking for visual surveillance of cage aquaculture. J. Vis. Commun. Image Represent. **22**(6), 543–556 (2011)
5. Szpak, Z.L., Tapamo, J.R.: Maritime surveillance: tracking ships inside a dynamic background using a fast level-set. Expert Syst. Appl. **38**(6), 6669–6680 (2011)
6. Kaido, N., Yamamoto, S., Hashimoto, T.: Examination of automatic detection and tracking of ships on camera image in marine environment. In: 2016 Techno-Ocean, pp. 58–63 (2016)
7. Kim, Y.J., Chung, Y.K., Lee, B.G.: Vessel tracking vision system using a combination of Kaiman filter, Bayesian classification, and adaptive tracking algorithm. In: 16th International Conference on Advanced Communication Technology, pp. 196–201 (2014)
8. da Silva Moreira, R., Ebecken, N.F.F., Alves, A.S., Livernet, F., Campillo-Navetti, A.: A survey on video detection and tracking of maritime vessels. Int. J. Res. Rev. Appl. Sci. **20**(1), 37–50 (2014)
9. Brutzer, S., Höferlin, B., Heidemann, G.: Evaluation of background subtraction techniques for video surveillance. In: CVPR 2011, Colorado Springs, CO, USA, pp. 1937–1944 (2011)
10. Benezeth, Y., Jodoin, P.-M., Emile, B., Laurent, H., Rosenberger, C.: Comparative study of background subtraction algorithms. J. Electron. Imaging **19**(3), 1–30 (2010)
11. Emgu CV Library Documentation version 3.4.3. http://www.emgu.com/wiki/files/3.4.3/document/index.html. Accessed 15 Apr 2019

12. KaewTraKulPong, P., Bowden, R.: An improved adaptive background mixture model for real-time tracking with shadow detection. In: Remagnino, P., Jones, G.A., Paragios, N., Regazzoni, C.S. (eds.) Video-Based Surveillance Systems. Springer, Boston (2002). https://doi.org/10.1007/978-1-4615-0913-4_11

13. Zivkovic, Z.: Improved adaptive gaussian mixture model for background subtraction. In: Proceedings of the 17th International Conference on Pattern Recognition (ICPR 2004), vol. 2, pp. 28–31. IEEE Computer Society, Washington (2004)

14. Godbehere, A.B., Matsukawa, A., Goldberg, K.: Visual tracking of human visitors under variable-lighting conditions for a responsive audio art installation. In: 2012 American Control Conference (ACC), pp. 4305–4312 (2012)

15. Zeevi, S.: BackgroundSubtractorCNT Project. https://github.com/sagi-z/Background-SubtractorCNT. Accessed 15 Apr 2019

16. Zivkovic, Z., van der Heijden, F.: Efficient adaptive density estimation per image pixel for the task of background subtraction. Pattern Recogn. Lett. 27(7), 773–780 (2006)

17. Guo, L., Xu, D., Qiang, Z.: Background subtraction using local SVD binary pattern. In: 2016 IEEE Conference on Computer Vision and Pattern Recognition Workshops, Las Vegas, NV, pp. 1159–1167 (2016)

18. Wawrzyniak, N., Stateczny, A.: Automatic watercraft recognition and identification on water areas covered by video monitoring as extension for sea and river traffic supervision systems. Pol. Marit. Res. 25(s1), 5–13 (2018)

19. Wawrzyniak, N., Hyla, T.: Automatic ship identification approach for video surveillance systems. In: Proceedings of ICONS 2019 The Fourteenth International Conference on Systems, Valencia, Spain, pp. 65–68. IARIA (2019)

Signature Image Improvement with Gradient Adaptive Morphology

Kacper Sarnacki[1], Marcin Adamski[2(✉)], and Khalid Saeed[2]

[1] Warsaw University of Technology, Warsaw, Poland
k.sarnacki@mini.pw.edu.pl
[2] Bialystok University of Technology, Bialystok, Poland
{m.adamski,k.saeed}@pb.edu.pl

Abstract. The paper presents a method for improving signature images, by using a directional field guided morphology. The method adapts a circular or linear structural element and its orientation. There is presented the comparison of the algorithm with the results of binarization process and with the existing post-processing algorithms, such as the morphological opening, closing and median filtering. The experiments show that the authors' method significantly improves the quality of images by removing unwanted artifacts.

Keywords: Signature quality improvement ·
Gradient adaptive morphology · Directional field

1 Introduction

Studies on the automatic processing of images with handwritten documents have a long history. There are many approaches proposed in scientific literature and commercial solutions. Signatures are a special case of handwriting, where the main task is verifying signature authenticity or identifying the signer [1]. Systems that process handwritten documents are usually composed of several stages, such as preprocessing, feature extraction and classification.

This paper presents a new method of the post-processing of binarized images. As a result the image is characterized by a smaller number of errors. The idea of the algorithm is based on using a directional field for a local selection of the structural element used in morphological operations. Thanks to the selection of the shape and the orientation of the element, it is possible to reduce the number of errors, such as incorrect joining or filling the loops. The method also uses the coherence measure to limit the impact of errors during determining the directional field.

Whilst there are many studies on various approaches for the signature feature extraction and classification, there is not a lot of work in the literature devoted to the preprocessing of signature images [1, 2]. To reduce artefacts in a binary image,

© Springer Nature Switzerland AG 2019
K. Saeed et al. (Eds.): CISIM 2019, LNCS 11703, pp. 50–58, 2019.
https://doi.org/10.1007/978-3-030-28957-7_5

most of the works used a median filter [3, 4], an average filter [5] or basic morphology operations: dilation, erosion and their superposition, such as opening and closing [5, 6].

Our aim is to create an universal algorithm for improving the binarization process. One might find similar approach to image filtering, as proposed in this study, in work [7] where the spatially-variant structural elements were applied to grayscale and binary images. However, the authors of [7] used different technique for directional field estimation and selection of structural element. The direction field was estimated by using average gradient followed by regularization with vector flow.

The results of the authors' algorithm were tested on two databases: CEDAR [8] and DIBCO [9].

2   Outline of the Proposed Method

As an input of the algorithm we accept a grayscale image of a handwriting signature. The first step is to execute the binarization process. The proposed method does not assume any specific approach - one can choose any available solution for this purpose.

In parallel to the binarization process, a directional field (DF) is calculated based on a grayscale image. A precise, noise-resistant algorithm was proposed in [10]. It is a gradient based approach that was natively applied to fingerprint images. In addition, reliability of each value from a directional field is assessed by using the coherence measure given in [11].

The next step is the post-processing of a binary image using morphological operations. The dilation with locally adapted structural elements (SE) is applied. For each position in the binary image, the shape of structural element is selected based on the DF. The decision takes also into account the coherence measure. If the value of the coherence exceeds the selected threshold, a linear structural element is used with an orientation based on a value of the directional field. On the other hand, if the coherence measure is lower, it is assumed that a direction value is not reliable and a diamond shaped SE is used instead.

As the final step, additional filtering is performed using 4-neighbourhood test. The process fills small artefacts that were left after the morphological processing.

Figure 1 illustrates the flow of the image processing in the proposed algorithm.

3   Description of Used Techniques

3.1   Binarization

The image binarization is a technique of a segmentation widely used in many areas of the image processing. Typically, an input of the binarization algorithm is a grayscale image. The output is a binary map, where one of the values represents the background and the other is used for the segmented object (the foreground). In this paper we assume that the object (the signature line) is represented by a

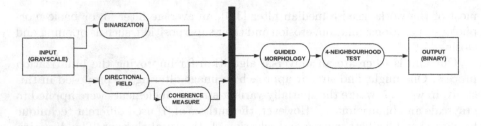

Fig. 1. The outline of the proposed method

value of zero (shown as black) and the background pixels have the value of one (shown as white). In general, the binarization can be described as an operation that assigns a value one or zero to each input pixel by comparing it to the threshold value, as shown in Eq. (1).

$$I_0 = \begin{cases} 1, \text{ if } I(x,y) > T \\ 0, \text{ otherwise} \end{cases} \tag{1}$$

where $I(x,y)$ is a pixel value in an image I at location x, y and T is a threshold value.

Many approaches to the binarization have been proposed in the image processing literature. The comprehensive review describes over 40 methods that can be found in [12], and more recent advances are presented in [13]. In this work we used Otsu binarization - an approach that have been applied to many systems using images with a text or other types of graphical objects.

Otsu Method [14]. Otsu method is one of the most widely used binarization techniques. The threshold value is computed globally for the whole input image based on the optimization procedure that maximizes intra-class variance between two classes of pixels defined by the threshold criterion (1). The intra-class variance σ_B^2, for a particular threshold value t, is computed using the Eq. (2).

$$\sigma_B^2(t) = P_0(t)P_1(t)(\mu_0(t) - \mu_1(t))^2 \tag{2}$$

where t is selected threshold, μ_i is the mean of input pixel values that are classified as a foreground ($i = 0$) and as a background ($i = 1$), and P_i is the sum of the normalized histogram values for the levels that belong to a particular class.

The value of the optimal global threshold (T_{opt}) is given by (3).

$$T_{opt} = \arg \max_{0 < t < L-1} \sigma_B^2(t) \tag{3}$$

where L is a number of pixels intensity levels.

3.2 Morphology

The mathematical morphology is a widely used tool in an image analysis for filtering and object detection [15]. It treats the image as a set of points and defines image operations based on the mathematical set theory. In this paper, morphological operations are applied to binary images obtained from the binarization algorithm. Such a binary image can be defined as a set of tuples in two dimensional integer space $\mathbb{Z}^2$, where each tuple $z = (x, y)$ represents object's pixel (black) at a given location (x, y).

Morphological operations usually take two operands: a set that represents an input image and a set representing so- called structural element. The structural element represents a subimage that contains an object of a basic shape such as a line or a disk. One of the elements in the SE set is selected as an origin. Usually the origin represents the center of the gravity of object corresponding to the structural element. Figure 2 shows examples of structural elements and their origins.

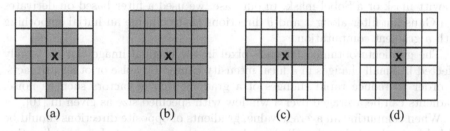

(a)   (b)   (c)   (d)

Fig. 2. Structural elements of size 5 represented as images: (a) diamond, (b) square, (c) horizontal line, (d) vertical line. Gray cells represent elements of the SE set. The position of the SE origin is marked by x.

Basic morphological operations include dilation (4) and erosion (5).

$$A \oplus B = \{z : (\hat{B})_z \cap A \subseteq A\} \tag{4}$$

$$A \ominus B = \{z : (B)_z \subseteq A\} \tag{5}$$

$$(B)_Z = \{c : c = b + z, b \in B\} \tag{6}$$

where A represents the input image, B is the structural element, (B) is the translation of B elements by z and $\hat{B}$ is reflection of B around its origin.

According to these equations, the result of dilation is formed by a set of positions z, for which the SE set translated by z is completely contained in A. The result of erosion is a set of z's for which the SE set translated by z has at least one common element with A.

When applied to an input image, erosion has an effect of shrinking or thinning objects. The operation can be also used for filtering - objects smaller than a structural element are completely removed. The erosion also deletes thin lines. As a result it removes small and thin structures that can be interpreted as noise.

Dilation thickens objects in an input image. As a consequence it may fill holes and merge nearby structures. This operation can be used to filter noise that is located inside object's perimeter. It can also be used to connect structures that where incorrectly separated. The best results are achieved by using the square SE of a size smaller than a size used during dilation.

3.3 Directional Field

The directional field is used to determine orientation of the line at the given area. For each position (x, y) in the image the value of the directional field $\theta(x, y)$ is computed. The example can be seen in Fig. 3.

The directional field can be computed using various methods, though, one of the most common and accurate approaches is using gradient operators [16]. Given a grayscale image I, the gradients G_x along x and G_y along y coordinates can be defined by (7).

$$\begin{bmatrix} G_x(x, y) \\ G_y(x, y) \end{bmatrix} = \begin{bmatrix} \frac{\partial I(x,y)}{\partial x} \\ \frac{\partial I(x,y)}{\partial y} \end{bmatrix} \tag{7}$$

The gradient values can be computed by convolving an input image with a Prewitt mask or a Sobel mask. In our case, we used a filter based on derivates of a Gaussian filter along x and y directions that combine an initial smoothing with a gradient computation.

The gradients obtained for each pixel in the original image can be largely affected by small changes in a local intensity caused by noise or other artefacts. In order to reduce rapid changes of a gradient due to factors such as noise, gradients can be averaged over a window with specified size as given in [10].

When computing an average value, gradients of opposite directions should be added instead of being cancelled out because they represent the same direction of a line. It is also beneficial to reduce the influence of gradients with a low magnitude. These values usually represent regions with no evident edges.

One way to compute the average value is by treating the gradient vector as a complex number, and then computing the sum of the squared gradients G_W for each position (x, y) in the input image, with the window W centered at (x, y) (8).

$$G_W(x, y) = \sum_{(x', y') \in W} (G_x(x', y') + jG_y(x', y'))^2 \tag{8}$$

In order to smooth the change in a gradient direction, an additional low-pass filtering can be applied. This step is achieved by normalizing vectors G_W to unit length, and then by applying the Gaussian filter $K(x, y)$ as shown in (9).

$$G_S(x, y) = \frac{G_W(x, y)}{|G_W(x, y)|} \otimes K(x, y) \tag{9}$$

The final orientation of a line at a point (x, y) is obtained as an argument of G_S as given in (10). Due to the initial squaring, the angle must be divided by 2 and shifted by $\frac{\pi}{2}$ (the gradient is perpendicular to line boundary).

$$\theta(x, y) = \frac{1}{2} \arg(G_S(x, y)) + \frac{\pi}{2} \tag{10}$$

The proposed method uses $\theta(x, y)$ to locally align the orientation of a linear structural element.

3.4   Coherence Measure

The reliability of directional field is not equal for every area. For instance lines intersection or dot like shapes make the information about gradients misleading. For this purpose a coherence measure was used. It aims to detect such areas. The coherence of directions in the neighbourhood of the given position is shown in (11).

$$r(x,y) = \frac{|\sum_{(x,y)\in W} G_s(x,y)|}{\sum_{(x,y)\in W} |G_s(x,y)|} \tag{11}$$

The value of the measure is in range $[0,1]$, where 1 is perfect coherence, 0 is lack of coherence. Figure 3 shows results of this threshold. The red colour represents areas with low value of the coherence measure.

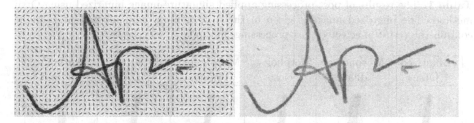

Fig. 3. On the left: Directional field values; On the right: Coherence measure for grayscale image. The more red color, the lower value of the measure. (Color figure online)

3.5   4-Neighbour Test

The aim of applying a 4-neighbourhood test is to eliminate some minor artefacts. Most of such artefacts after a guided morphology are one pixel size and the test can successfully detect them.

For each pixel, its four neighbours are analysed: if the colour of all neighbouring pixels is a background colour, the colour of the pixel is also changed to background colour.

4   Expermients

The experiments were conducted on images from two databases: CEDAR [8] and DIBCO [9]. The CEDAR database was used to perform initial visual evaluation. The results of the method were compared to the output of median filtering and standard morphology techniques: dilation, closing and opening.

Table 1 presents the output of the author's method compared to standard morphological operations and median filtering. The first column contains binarized section of the signature from CEDAR database. The whole signature image is given in Table 2. As one may notice in first column of Table 1, the binarized version obtained using Otsu method contains artifacts along signature line.

The aim is to filter the image to improve it without introducing new errors. However, as illustrated in second and third columns of Table 1, the dilate and closing morphological operations tend to close internal loop. On the other hand, the morphological opening breaks the line continuity. The result of the median filter is given in forth column. It preserved line continuity, but the line width was be severely thinned in places where the binarization artifacts were present. The author's method is presented in the last column of Table 1. It allowed to remove binarization defects with least amount of distortions compared to standard morphological and median filtering.

Table 2 shows a complete signature example in unprocessed, grayscale form, its binarized version by Otsu method and post-processed using author's approach.

Table 1. The results of post-processing applied signature image binarized using Otsu method. The binarized image is given in the first column. The subsequent columns contain the result of selected post-processing methods

Binarized (Otsu)	Morphology dilate	Morphology close	Morphology open	Median	Author's method

The DIBCO database contains handwritting images that have similar characteristics to signatures. This database also incorporates binary ground truth images that may be used to assess the effect of binarization and post-processing by comparing the method's output to ideal solution given by the ground truth image. Table 3 shows the results of such comparison obtained on a subset of 20 images from DIBCO database, each containing several words of handwritten text. The presented values are computed as the percent of pixels that were the same in the reference (ground truth) and method's output image - the accuracy measure. As can be seen the best result was obtained for author's method.

Table 2. Signature image from CEDAR database binarized by Otsu algorithm and post-processed using author's method

Grayscale singature image	Binarized (Otsu)	Post-processed (author's method)

Table 3. The accuracy measure for images selected from DIBCO database and binarized using Otsu method

Binarized (Otsu)	Morphology dilate	Morphology close	Morphology open	Median	Author's method
82,2%	88,1%	91,5%	91,3%	91,6%	91,9%

5 Conclusions

The method presented in this paper allows to reduce the number of artefacts arising during binarization for digitalized images of handwriting signatures. Its main contribution is the application of morphological operations guided by directional field to signature images and novel adaptive structural element selection. As it can be seen from the presented examples, in comparison with standard morphological and median filtering, the proposed approach results in smaller amount of the artefacts. The method can be applied to the output of any binarization technique as long as the initial grayscale image allows to compute directional field. Currently, the authors are working on the application of the proposed method in signature verification system.

Acknowledgements. This work was partially supported by grant S/WI/2/2018 from Białystok University of Technology and funded with resources for research by the Ministry of Science and Higher Education in Poland.

References

1. Impedovo, D., Pirlo, G.: Automatic signature verification: the state of the art. IEEE Trans. Syst. Man Cybern. Cybern. C Appl. Rev. **38**(5), 609–635 (2008)
2. Diaz-Cabrera, M., Morales, A., Ferrer, M.A.: Emerging issues for static handwritten signature biometrics. In: Pirlo, G., Impedovo, D., Fairhurst, M. (eds.) Advances in Digital Handwritten Signature Processing, pp. 111–122. World Scientific (2014)

3. Bajaj, R., Chaudhury, S.: Signature verification using multiple neural classifiers. Pattern Recogn. **30**(1), 1–7 (1997)
4. Kennard, D.J., Barrett, W.A., Sederberg, T.W.: Offline signature verification and forgery detection using a 2-D geometric warping approach. In: 21st International Conference on Pattern Recognition (ICPR), Tsukuba, Japan. pp. 3733–3736 (2012)
5. Huang, K., Yan, H.: Off-line signature verification based on geometric feature extraction and neural network classification. Pattern Recogn. **30**(1), 9–17 (1997)
6. Fierrez-Aguilar, J., Alonso-Hermira, N., Moreno-Marquez, G., Ortega-Garcia, J.: An off-line signature verification system based on fusion of local and global information. In: Maltoni, D., Jain, A.K. (eds.) BioAW 2004. LNCS, vol. 3087, pp. 295–306. Springer, Heidelberg (2004). https://doi.org/10.1007/978-3-540-25976-3_27
7. Verd-Monedero, R., Angulo, J., Serra, J.: Anisotropic morphological filters with spatially-variant structuring elements based on image-dependent gradient fields. IEEE Trans. Image Process. **20**(1), 200–212 (2011)
8. CEDAR database. www.cedar.buffalo.edu/NIJ/data/signatures.rar. Accessed 27 May 2019
9. DIBCO database. https://vc.ee.duth.gr/dibco2017/. Accessed 27 May 2019
10. Hong, L., Wan, Y., Jain, A.: Fingerprint image enhancement: algorithm and performance evaluation. IEEE Trans. Pattern Anal. Mach. Intell. **20**(8), 777–789 (1998)
11. Bazen, A.M., Gerez, S.H.: Systematic methods for the computation of the directional fields and singular points of fingerprints. IEEE Trans. Pattern Anal. Mach. Intell. **24**(7), 905–919 (2002)
12. Sezgin, M., Sankur, B.: Survey over image thresholding techniques and quantitative performance evaluation. J. Electron. Imaging **13**(1), 146–168 (2004)
13. Chaki, N., Shaikh, S.H., Saeed, K.: Exploring Image Binarization Techniques. Springer, New Delhi (2014). https://doi.org/10.1007/978-81-322-1907-1
14. Otsu, N.: A threshold selection method from gray-level histograms. IEEE Trans. Syst. Man Cybern. B Cybern. **9**(1), 62–66 (1979)
15. Gonzalez, R.C., Woods, R.E.: Digital Image Processing, 3rd edn. Pearson Prentice Hall, Upper Saddle River (2007)
16. Maltoni, D., Maio, D., Jain, A., Prabhakar, S.: Handbook of Fingerprint Recognition. Springer, London (2009). https://doi.org/10.1007/978-1-84882-254-2

An Algorithm for Detecting the Expressive Musical Gestures of Violinists Based on IMU Signals

Aleksander Sawicki$^{(\boxtimes)}$ (ID) and Sławomir K. Zieliński (ID)

Faculty of Computer Science,
Bialystok University of Technology, Bialystok, Poland
{a.sawicki,s.zielinski}@pb.edu.pl

Abstract. The article presents an algorithm for classifying the style of expression of violin playing based on IMU sensor, located on the violinists forearm. In the initial phase of research, the original set of measured signals was extended by transferring them to new coordinate systems. Additional motion dynamics signals, including estimated linear velocity, have been obtained using transformations typical for inertial navigation systems (INS). In the next part of the work, universal features as well as indicators typical for IMU signals were extracted. The final experiment concerned the comparative effectiveness of data classification, using features selected by mutual information and random forest algorithms. The evaluation of the performance of the proposed algorithm has been carried out using a publicly available database. The obtained level of classification accuracy exceeded 90%.

Keywords: IMU · Feature extraction · Feature selection · Classification · Musical expression

1 Introduction

Human communication involves transmitting verbal messages ("what has been said") combined with non-verbal cues ("how it was said") [1]. Similarly, in live performance of music it is possible to distinguish between "transmitting" music messages ("what has been played") and performing expressive gestures ("how it has been played") [2]. For the purpose of this study, expressive musical gestures are defined as the musicians' body movements, resulting in variations in musical articulation, dynamics or tempo [3, 4]. For example, in [5] the détaché expression was described as "alternating bow direction with a smooth, connected stroke and evenness of tone", while the group of a staccato style was described as "series of two or more stopped bow strokes in a single bow direction with resultant space between". According to the musicologists, expressive gestures play an important role in "communicating" music from musicians to audience [6]. While in the recent years, machine-learning algorithms has been successfully applied to music analysis and composition [7] little work has been done towards building music robots [8] capable of not only playing music but also mimicking body movements commonly seen in live performance of music. In order to build

© Springer Nature Switzerland AG 2019
K. Saeed et al. (Eds.): CISIM 2019, LNCS 11703, pp. 59–71, 2019.
https://doi.org/10.1007/978-3-030-28957-7_6

plausible models of musicians, a deeper understanding of the body movements would have to be acquired, e.g. by analyzing visual recordings or the signals derived from the sensors attached to a body of a musician. The contribution of this paper could be considered as an initial step towards the above long-term goal as it presents a method for the automatic classification of five expressive gestures, typically performed by violinists during live concerts, based on the signals captured by the inertial sensors attached to a violinist's forearm.

During the literature review, information was sought in all the above mentioned fields. A popular solution used by their authors was based on the extraction of parameters from raw signals measured by an accelerometer and a gyroscope. Scientific publications present a variety of features, including "universal" features, as well as those used only for inertial measurement unit (IMU) signals. An inspiration for the work was an approach presenting the possibilities of using procedures typical for inertial navigation system (INS) in data processing. In this study many advanced operations were used, such as a transformation of measurement signals to an additional coordinate system, estimation of gravitational acceleration, velocity and displacement components It should be noted that in the proposed approach the final displacement was chosen as the most important indicator. The possibility of using additional information about motion dynamics using velocity values seems to be promising.

The present research aimed at the following objectives: development of a violin expression style detection system based on IMU signals with an accuracy reaching minimum 90%; verification whether the set of selected features contains parameters determined from the estimated values of gravitational acceleration and linear velocity; verification whether the set of the most important features contains parameters of signals transformed in additionally created coordinate systems; and comparison of the accuracy of classification using features selected by the mutual information and random forest algorithms.

The original contribution of the work is two-fold. First, it provides a method for the automatic classification of the expressive music gestures commonly performed by violinists, based on the signals derived from the inertial sensors. Second, it identifies the most prominent features affecting the classification accuracy. In terms of its possible applications, the proposed method could potentially be used by musicologists in order to automatically analyze the gestures performed by violinists (as an aid for musicological research). It could also be used as a tool aiding violinists during rehearsals, e.g. assisting students while learning how to play a violin. Moreover, the proposed algorithms could be of interest by a community of researchers developing machine learning algorithms employing the signals from IMU sensors.

The paper is organized as follows: Sect. 2 provides a literature review on the topic of the processing of IMU signals and the extraction of their features. Sections 3 and 4 introduce the procedures of signal processing and features extraction used in the study while Sect. 5 shows the experiment results. Finally, the conclusions and the plans for future works are presented in Sect. 6.

2 Literature Review

Sarasúa et al. [3] developed and made publicly available [4] two datasets of gestures recorded during the musical performance. The first one concerned violinists performing standard pedagogical repertoire with variation in expressive musical gestures. The second one included the signals obtained from the pianists performing a repertoire piece with variations in time of performance and expression. It should be noted that the data set used in their publication contained recordings collected from 9 research participants, while the publicly available corpus only 8. This was an additional obstacle in the development of the method presented in this paper. The authors' aim was to develop a set of data dedicated to benchmarking algorithms developed by other scientists.

Many interesting solutions concerning the extraction of features from inertial motion sensors can be found in publications in the field of activities of daily living (ADL) [9, 10], human computer-interaction [11], or healthcare [12]. According to the literature, research is commonly carried out with the use of universal as well as specific for IMU sensors groups of features. Most of the approaches use raw, directly measured signals [9–11], although there are individual cases employing additional transformations, such as measurement signals transformed into additional coordinate systems or estimated displacement of the sensor in three-dimensional space [12]. A promising example was proposed by Li et al. [9], who used such sensors as triaxial accelerometer and a micro-Doppler radar for ADL classification. The following features were extracted among other from the motion signals: minimum value, mean, variance, RMS. The support vector machine (SVM) method was used for classification. Similarly to the above work, Zhang and Sawchuk [10] also investigated the utility of the motion sensors to undertake the task of the automatic ADL classification. They proposed to use a set of features specific to IMU signals. The examples of the metrics exploited by Zhang and Sawchuk include: movement intensity, eigenvalues of dominant direction, and averaged acceleration energy. The authors used a variant of the bag of words algorithm. In their work regarding the recognition of hand finger gestures, Georgi et al. [11] used the signals acquired from accelerometer, gyroscope and a set of EMG sensors. They exploited the technique of a sliding window from which such statistics as mean and standard deviation were extracted. Hidden Markov Model (HMM) algorithm was used as the classifier.

In order to determine the position of the upper limb, Comotti et al. [12] exploited the algorithms typical for inertial navigation. Their paper presents a number of advanced mathematical operations such as transformation vector between coordinate system, estimation of gravitational acceleration components, calculation of the linear velocity and location of the sensor.

From the above literature background, it can be concluded that the approaches to capturing information regarding body movements, feature extraction, and machine-learning algorithms are domain specific, and therefore the they should be "tailored" towards a given application. At the outset of this study, there were no direct pointers in the literature as to which methods should be taken to classify musical expression gestures, with the exception of the paper by Sarasúa et al. [3], who suggested that the IMU and EMG signals fed to the input of the classifier based on HMM. However, they did not provide any detailed information regarding pre-processing of the signals or feature extraction required to reduce the dimensionality of the data. Therefore, the methodology presented in this paper could be regarded as original, potentially directing other researchers in the area of the automatic recognition of musical expression gestures.

3   Dataset Processing

Original Dataset

The authors used a data set collated by Sarasúa et al. [4]. The repository contained the recordings of 8 musicians playing an excerpt from Kreutzer Etude No. 2 in C major. Each of the musicians played the above piece of music 10 times using 5 techniques (expressions): détaché, legato, spiccato, staccato, and martelé. Provided audio data were recorded with the use of microphones, while body movement was acquired with the use of the commercially available armband ("MYO") equipped with the motion sensors. The sensor of agreement with the axes in the North-East-Up convention [13] was placed on the forearm (in which the bow was held) with the X axis directed towards the wrist. Detailed photographs of device assembly are available in the publication [3]. According to that paper, the musicians did not report any problems hindering their performance, resulting from attaching the sensors to their forearms.

The armband device allowed the researchers to record both electromyogram (EMG) and inertial measurement unit (IMU) signals. The authors used only the inertial sensor data in their work, thus omitting the EMG signals. The data set represents a total of 13 channels of signals recorded at a sample rate of 50 Hz [4] as specified in Table 1. To the best of the authors' knowledge, the device manufacturer does not provide any detailed information regarding its technical specifications such as the sensors' sensitivity or the calibration details. The calibration procedure is proprietary. Considering the commercial use of the device and its intended functionality, the authors believe that the sensitivity of the band was adequate to record the movements of the musicians.

Table 1. Original dataset [4]

Name of signal	# of channel	Description
accel	3	linear acceleration acquired by accelerometer
gyroscope	3	angular velocity acquired by gyroscope
Euler_angles	3	sensor orientation in Euler angels form
quaternion	4	sensor orientation in quaternion form

It is easy to imagine a situation when the violinist, starting each recording session, is at a different angle in relation to the north. Even in the case of a perfectly repeated motion, the orientation data in quaternion form will have different number values. It was, therefore, necessary to carry out an additional 'calibration' process.

In their original work, Comotti et al. [12] tried to solve the above mentioned problem using an additional calibration quaternion related to the orientation of the place where the gestures were made. In the case of the available database [4], it was not possible to implement this method since information regarding the reference quaternion has not been included in the data corpus. The authors did not mention whether the participants were directed in the same direction during the repetitions.

In this article attempts have been made to eliminate the potential direction miss-alignment problem through the additional use of two coordinate systems. The former one was called "Calibration 1", whereas the latter one was referred to as "Calibration 2".

Calibration 1 Coordinate Systems

The first of the additional coordinate systems was used to determine the orientation relative to the initial one. In order to define it, an associative property of quaternion multiplication [13] described by Eq. (1) was used:

$$
{}_{t}^{W}q = {}_{t0}^{W}q \otimes {}_{t}^{t0}q,
\tag{1}
$$

where:

${}_{t}^{W}q$ – quaternion representing the rotation from world coordinates to object space at time t;

${}_{t0}^{W}q$ – quaternion representing the rotation from world coordinates to object space at initial time $t0$;

${}_{t}^{t0}q$ – quaternion representing the rotation from space at initial $t0$ to space at time t;

Equation (1) has been transformed to form (2)

$$
{}_{t}^{t0}q = {}_{t0}^{W}q^{*} \otimes {}_{t}^{W}q,
\tag{2}
$$

where:

${}_{t0}^{W}q^{*}$ – quaternion conjugated to the quaternion ${}_{t0}^{W}q$.

Based on the current orientation indicated by the sensor (i.e. ${}_{t}^{W}q$) and initial orientation at time $t0$ (i.e. ${}_{t0}^{W}q$), the quaternion representing the relative change of orientation was calculated (i.e. ${}_{t}^{t0}q$). The impact of the initial orientation value in relation to the North (*Yaw* angle) has been completely eliminated, however the initial values of the *Pitch* and *Roll* angles information has been lost.

Calibration 2 Coordinate System

The second of the additional coordinate systems is described as "Calibration 2". In this system, the initial value of the *Yaw* angle has been reset to zero. This process can also be understood as an "artificial" pointing of the object to the North.

This procedure was conducted in the following steps:

1. Storing information regarding orientation ${}_{t0}^{W}q$
2. Conversion of quaternion into three Euler angles (*Yaw, Pitch, Roll*)
3. Calculation of the conjugate quaternion ${}_{Yaw}^{W}q^{*}$
4. Multiplication of the quaternary ${}_{Yaw}^{W}q^{*}$ and quaternion ${}_{t}^{W}q$

where:

$_{Yaw}^{W}q^{*}$ quaternion representing rotation at an angle of −Yaw.

The method described above allowed to eliminate the influence of *Yaw* angle on the values of orientation readings It should be noted that the original values of *Pitch* and *Roll* angles are kept in this system.

Additional Motion Dynamic Signals

In order to obtain additional information about motion dynamics of the musical expression gestures, a velocity estimation algorithm typical for inertial navigation has been implemented. The schematic diagram divided into two sections "Gravity Elimination" and "Velocity Estimation" is shown in Fig. 1.

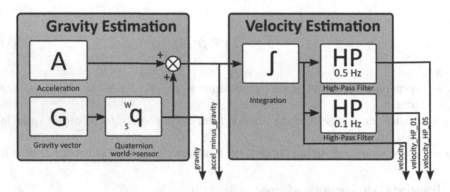

Fig. 1. Velocity estimation schematic

It can be assumed that the values measured by the accelerometer are the sum of absolute acceleration resulting from the motion of the object and the components of gravitational acceleration [12, 14–16]. Note that the gravitational acceleration depends on the sensor orientation. The process of isolating the above two components was carried out through transforming the known "global" gravitational vector to the coordinate system of the sensor using the following equation:

$$g^{s} = {}_{t}^{W}q^{*} \otimes [0, g] \otimes {}_{t}^{W}q, \qquad (3)$$

where:

g^{s} − gravity vector component in sensor coordinate system;

g − gravitational acceleration in world coordinate system ($[0 \quad 0 \quad -1]^{T}$).

In the first block, termed as "Gravity Estimation" in Fig. 1, individual values of gravitational acceleration in sensor coordinate system were estimated. In order to determine the absolute acceleration values, they were summed up with the accelerometer's measured values. The signals processed in this way were sent to the "Velocity Estimation" block, in which, as a result of numerical integration of the signal, linear velocity values were determined. The processed signal was subject to high-pass filtration. The cut-off frequency was set to 0.1 Hz and 0.5 Hz, respectively.

It should be emphasized that the estimated signals were represented in a coordinate system associated with the sensor. These vectors could be transformed into coordinate systems "Calibration 1" and "Calibration 2", which was also accomplished in this study. A list of all signals used in the further stages of the experiment is given in Table 2.

Table 2. Processed dataset

Signal name	# of channel	Description
Initial coordinate system/Data in sensor coordinate system		
accel	3	accelerometer raw data
gyroscope	3	gyroscope raw data
gravity	3	gravity acceleration components in acceleration measured data
accel_minus_grav	3	accel signal reduced by gravity components
velocity	3	accel_minus_gravity integration result
velocity_HP_01	3	velocity signal processed by a high pass filter with a 0.1 Hz cut-off frequency
velocity_HP_05	3	velocity signal processed by a high pass filter with a 0.5 Hz cut-off frequency
Callibration_1 coordinate system/Orientation relative to initial one		
quaternion_cal1	4	Orientation in quaternion form
Euler_cal1	3	Orientation in Euler angles
accel_cal1	3	accelerometer raw data transformed to Cal1 coordinate system
accel_cal1_minus_grav	3	accel_cal1 signal reduced by gravity components
velocity_cal1	3	accel_cal1_minus_gravity integration result
velocity_cal1 _HP_05	3	velocity_cal1 signal processed by a high pass filter with a 0.1 Hz cut-off frequency
velocity_cal1 _HP_01	3	Velocity_cal1 signal processed by a high pass filter with a 0.5 Hz cut-off frequency
Calibration_2 coordinate system/Initial *Yaw* rotation zeroed		
quaternion_cal2	4	Orientation in quaternion form
Euler_cal2	3	Orientation in Euler angles form
accel_cal2	3	accelerometer raw data transformed to Cal2 coordinate system
accel_cal2_minus_grav	3	accel_cal2 signal reduced by gravity components
velocity_cal2	3	accel_cal2_minus_gravity integration result
velocity_cal2 _HP_05	3	velocity_cal2 signal processed by a high pass filter with a 0.1 Hz cut-off frequency
velocity_cal2 _HP_01	3	Velocity_cal2 signal processed by a high pass filter with a 0.5 Hz cut-off frequency
Total:	65	

4 Feature Extraction

Further part of the proposed algorithm consisted in the extraction of features from a processed data set. According to the literature [9–11], the following statistics were extracted: minimum, maximum, mean, range, median, standard deviation, variation, median absolute deviation, root mean square, waveform length. Feature extraction was performed on all types of signals, including those not having strictly physical meaning, e.g. time series of quaternion w component. Each groups of features have been determined for all of the 65 signals available in the processed data set. The extraction of a group of features specific to IMU signals was performed.

Following the approach taken by Zhang and Sawchuk [10], the parameters related to energy or the direction of motion were also determined. The definitions of the physical features are listed below.

- **Mean of Movement Intensity (MMI):** MMI is defined as

$$MMI = \frac{1}{T}\sum_{t=1}^{T}\left(\sqrt{a_x(t)^2 + a_y(t)^2 + a_z(t)^2}\right). \qquad (4)$$

It is the mean of Euclidean norm of the acceleration vector after removing the gravitational components (accel_cal2_minus_grav). Components $a_x(t), a_y(t), a_z(t)$ are the acceleration values measured by along the x, y and z at time t.
- **Variance of Movement Intensity (VMI):** VMI is defined as

$$VMI = \frac{1}{T}\sum_{t=1}^{T}\left(\sqrt{a_x(t)^2 + a_y(t)^2 + a_z(t)^2} - MMI\right)^2. \qquad (5)$$

It is the variance of Euclidean norm of the total acceleration vector after removing the gravitational components.
- **Normalized Acceleration Magnitude Area (AMA):** AMA is using the following equation:

$$AMA = \frac{1}{T}\left(\sum_{t=1}^{T}|a_x(t)| + \sum_{t=1}^{T}|a_y(t)| + \sum_{t=1}^{T}|a_z(t)|\right). \qquad (6)$$

It represents the mean of sums of absolute acceleration vector after removing the gravitational acceleration values.
- **Averaged Acceleration Energy (AAE):** AAE is defined as the mean value of energy of acceleration vector after removing gravity. Energy is sum of the squared FFT component magnitudes.
- **Averaged Rotation Energy (AAE):** AAE is defined as the mean value of energy over all gyroscope axes.
- **Eigenvalues of Dominant Direction (EVA):** EVA is defined as the eigenvectors of the covariance matrix, created from the acceleration vector after removing the gravitational component (accel_cal2_minus_grav). Vectors represent most varying data direction (direction along which intensive motion occurs). The indicator is in the form of three-dimensional vectors.

As a result of feature extraction process, 664 parameters divided into 10 groups, such as minimum (1÷65), maximum (66÷130), mean (131÷195), range (196÷260), median(261÷325), standard deviation (326÷325), variation (391÷455), median absolute deviation (456÷520), root mean square, (521÷585), waveform length (586÷650), and physical (651÷650) were estimated. The described groups were used to extract traits of all available music performances (400 samples). The data in this form was then normalized to unity and contributed to the data selection algorithms.

5 Experiments and Results

Both the test and training set contained data from all participants of the study (musicians). The training set consisted of 60% (240 runs) and the test comprised 40% (160 runs) of available data. The accuracy of the classification was evaluated using random sub-sampling validation repeated ten times.

In the first stage of the experiment, with the help of two classifiers available in the scikit-learn package of the Python language: ExtraTrees and MutualInformation, the importance of all of the 664 features was automatically assessed. As a result, groups of 15, 20 and 25 of the most metrics were then selected. In the next stage of the study default ExtraTrees Classifier was used to train the model, and then predict the test set. The parameters of a random forest were as follows: the number of trees in the forest-5000; number required to split a node-2;a number of samples required to be at a leaf node-1. The obtained percentage accuracy of classification for 15, 20 and 25 features is presented in Fig. 2.

It can be noted that for all the analyzed variants, the classification of class d (détaché) was carried out with the least effectiveness. In the case of a classifier exploiting a set of 15 metrics this accuracy was equal to 84.69% and 82.81%, respectively (see Fig. 2(a) and (b)). For the sp (spiccato) classification, the effectiveness was relatively high, amounting to 95.00% and 95.94%, respectively.

In the case of the number of features amounting to 20, the random forest algorithm (c) has an advantage over mutual information (d) in most of the studied classes. For four of the five classes studied (détaché, l - legato, staccato, martelé) the accuracy obtained using the random forests was superior compared to the one achieved with the mutual information method. Selection of metrics based on the determination of the 25 most important features with the use of the random forest algorithm allowed to achieve the best quality of classification among all the examined possibilities. For all the studied classes, the classification accuracy exceeded 90%. This outcome was significant at $p < 0.05$ level, according to Bernoulli statistical trial.

Table 3 contains a list of features selected by the random forest method used in the configuration comprising 25 features. A number of occurrences means how many times in 10 trial runs a given feature was selected by the algorithm. The number of 10 describes that features were in each of the learning sets.

According to Table 3, a group of fourteen features was selected in each of the 10 iterations carried out. The selected metrics include indicators related to angles of rotation, values measured by accelerometer and gyroscope, as well as those related to the estimated value of gravity and velocity. A group of frequently selected features

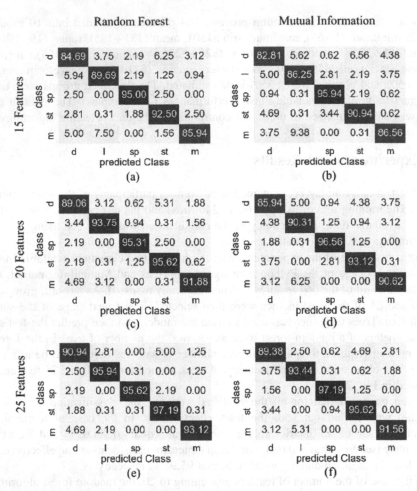

Fig. 2. Percentage classification result depending on feature selection algorithm: random forest (a), (c), (e) mutual information (b), (d), (f). d – détaché, l – legato, sp – spiccato, st – staccato, m – martelé

(9 and 8) contain parameters related to quaternion components in two additional coordinate systems (mad_quat_cal1_z, mad_quat_cal2_w). The indicators related to values measured by sensors as well as estimated speed values were selected less frequently (7, 6, 5). The presence of features associated with filtered velocity values in the rare group (1, 2, 3, 4) should be emphasized. It should be noted that even if the given characteristics were not often in the ranking, they were selected as one of the 25 most important out of 664 possible parameters.

It should be emphasized that the presented data sets do not include features associated with velocity signal processed by 0.1 Hz frequency high-pass filter. Additionally, in the automatic selection of features none of the indicators belonging to the so-called physical feature groups has been selected. Therefore, from the list of processed

Table 3. Feature use frequency

Feature name	Number of uses (maximum 10)
mean_euler_cal2_pitch, median_euler_cal2_pitch mean_accel_x, median_accel_x max_gyro_y, std_gyro_y, wl_gyro_x, mean_gravity_x, median_gravity_x, min_gravity_x mean_velocity_x, min_velocity_x, rms_velocity_x, std_velocity_x	10
mad_quat_cal1_z, rms_gyro_y, range_velocity_x	9
mad_quat_cal2_w	8
range_gyro_y	7
min_accel_x, std_gyro_z, var_velocity_x	6
mad_euler_cal2_yaw	5
min_accel_minus_gravity_y, rms_gyro_z, median_velocity_x	4
max_accel_x, wl_accel_y, max_gyro_z, wl_gravity_x	3
wl_quat_cal2_x, mad_velocity_x wl_accel_cal1_minus_gravity_y, wl_accel_cal1_pitch wl_accel_minus_gravity_y mad_gravity_z, median_gravity_z wl_gravity_z rms_velocity_cal2_HP_05_z, std_velocity_cal2_HP_05_z	2
max_velocity_cal2_x	1

signals (Table 3), 3 channels concerning the velocity time series processed by 0.1 Hz frequency high-pass filter can be eliminated. These signals may be considered insignificant for the classification process. The time-consuming process of implementing methods for determining the features of physical groups can also be omitted.

6 Conclusions and Future Work

The authors developed a comprehensive algorithm for classification of the expressive musical gestures performed by the violinists, based on the IMU signals. The method was tested on the publicly available repository of the signal recordings of forearm movements while playing Kreutzer Etude No. 2 in C major using 5 techniques.

According to the results, it is possible to identity some correlates between the expression gestures and the extracted features. Depending on the style of play, the musician move the bow with different dynamics. For example, in the détaché case the movement is slow and fluent, whereas in the case of staccato it is more intense and separated by periods of low activity [5]. In these cases, the groups of signal features accounting for motion dynamics proved to be significant. Angular velocity and the estimated value of velocity could be considered as the key exemplars of the signals representing the dynamics of the musicians' body movements. Consequently, the features created from these signals played an important role in the classification process.

The study proposed the creation of two additional coordinate systems. The features obtained from signals transformed into both of them ranked high. It should be noted that in addition to the features resulting from the *Pitch* angle in the "Calibration 2" system (which is equal to the originally determined Pitch angle) very often other features such as mad_quat_cal1_z or mad_quat_cal2_w were selected. It is therefore recommended to use both coordinate systems.

The dataset consisted of 664 column vectors, representing the extracted features, and comprised 400 rows, signifying the music performances. Therefore, methods such as random forest and mutual information were used to determine the most significant parameters. A solution that allows to achieve over 90% accuracy was developed with the use of 25 features selected by random forest algorithms. A direct use of the developed set of features for detecting the expressive musical gestures of pianist would result in low classification accuracy. This would be due to different directions of movement in relation to the orientation of the sensors. Methods presented in the article allowing to obtain additional information about the direction and velocity of movement could potentially improve the standard quality of classification.

Research work on the extraction of features from the available electromyogram (EMG) signals is planned for the future. The aim of the study will be to further improve the quality of classification by using additional data describing the musicians' muscles activities. Furthermore, it is planned to create an original database of recordings. The developed corpus will be made available to the public, and together with the previously used database [4] it will provide an opportunity to carry out more extensive research.

Acknowledgment. This work was supported by S/WI/3/2018 and WI/WI/11/2019 grants from Białystok University of Technology and funded with resources for research by the Ministry of Science and Higher Education in Poland.

References

1. Pelachaud, C.: Studies on gesture expressivity for a virtual agent. Speech Commun. **51** (7), 630–639 (2009). 107
2. Palmer, C.: Music performance. Ann. Rev. Psychol. **48**(1), 115–138 (1997)
3. Sarasúa, Á., Caramiaux, B., Tanaka, A., Ortiz, M.: Datasets for the analysis of expressive musical gestures. In: Proceeding MOCO 2017 Proceedings of the 4th International Conference on Movement Computing, Article No. 131 (2017)
4. Datasets for the Analysis of Expressive Musical Gestures repositorum. https://gitlab.doc. gold.ac.uk. Accessed 21 Jan 2019
5. Rabin, M., Smith, P.:Guide to orchestral bowings through musical styles. Univeristy of Wisconsin-Madisnon, Really Good Music, LLC
6. Peters, D., Eckel, G., Dorschel, A.: Bodily Expression in Electronic Music: Perspectives on Reclaiming Performativity. Routledge, New York (2012)
7. Williams, D., et al.: Affective calibration of musical feature sets in an emotionally intelligent music composition system. ACM Trans. Appl. Percept. (TAP) **14**(3), 17 (2017)
8. Zappi, V., Pistillo, A., Calinon, S., Brogni, A., Caldwell, D.: Music expression with a robot manipulator used as a bidirectional tangible interface. EURASIP J. Audio, Speech Music Process. **1**, 2 (2012)

9. Li, H., et al.: Multisensor data fusion for human activities classification and fall detection. In: 2017 IEEE SENSORS (2017)
10. Zhang, M., Sawchuk, A.A.: Motion primitive-based human activity recognition using a bag-of-features approach. In: Proceedings of IHI 2012 of the 2nd ACM SIGHIT International Health Informatics Symposium, pp. 631–640 (2012)
11. Georgi, M., Amma, C., Schultz, T.: Recognizing hand and finger gestures with IMU based motion and EMG based muscle activity sensing. In: Proceedings of BIOSTEC 2015 Proceedings of the International Joint Conference on Biomedical Engineering Systems and Technologies, vol. 4, pp. 99–108 (2015)
12. Comotti, D., Caldara, M., Galizzi, M., Locatelli, P., Re, V.: Inertial based hand position tracking for future applications in rehabilitation environments. In: Proceedings of 6th IEEE International Workshop Advances in Sensors and Interfaces (IWASI), pp. 222–227 (2015)
13. Dunn, F., Parberry, I.: 3D Math Primer for Graphics and Game Development. Wordware Publishing (2002)
14. Kang, W., Han, Y.: SmartPDR: smartphone-based pedestrian deadreckoning for indoor localization. IEEE Sens. J. **15**(5), 557 (2015)
15. Zhang, R., Höflinger, F., Reindl, L.: Inertial sensor based indoor localization and monitoring system for emergency responders. IEEE Sens. J. **13**(2), 838–848 (2013)
16. Sawicki, A., Walendziuk, W., Idźkowski, A.: The gravitational acceleration components elimination from the accelerometer measurement data. In: Photonics Applications in Astronomy, Communications, Industry, and High-Energy Physics Experiments 2016, Proceedings of SPIE, vol. 10031 (2016)

An Algorithm for Exact Retinal Vein Extraction

Maciej Szymkowski$^{(\boxtimes)}$ (iD), Dawid Najda, and Khalid Saeed (iD)

Faculty of Computer Science, Białystok University of Technology,
Białystok, Poland
{m.szymkowski, k.saeed}@pb.edu.pl,
dawid.najda97@gmail.com

Abstract. Recently more interest in retina-based human recognition is observable. It is connected with the fact that this biometrics trait can guarantee absolute certainty in the case of human identity. In the literature, one can easily observe that most of the algorithms are based on veins system and its pattern. A method to extract recently mentioned structure is presented in this paper. The proposed approach consists of three main parts: preprocessing, segmentation and unnecessary artifacts removal. During the research, the authors used different image processing methods for veins system extraction, especially diversified binarization algorithms and edge detection approaches were tested. In the time of the experiments the authors took into consideration not only accuracy but also proposed solution efficiency. Performed tests have shown that it is clearly possible to extract veins system with satisfactory precision and efficiency.

Keywords: Biometrics · Retina color images · Segmentation · Retinal veins · Image processing

1 Introduction

Nowadays, biometrics methods are one of the most important ways in which we can defend our data before hackers. The main reason why we use them is huge uniqueness of biometrics measurable traits and simplicity of their usage.

One of the most important is human retina. It is a representative of physiological biometrics. It was confirmed [1] that it is impossible to spoof this trait as well as we know there is no possibility to have two samples that are exactly the same. In the different sources [2] we can read that German Chancellor's retina was crafted and biometrics system accepted it as a real sample. It has to be claimed, there are no scientific evidences for this experiment was successful. Moreover, the author did not provide any information about biometrics system on which he carried out his experiment and how this system was implemented. We do not know how images were processed and how feature vector was constructed. Without this information we cannot be totally sure whether his results are real and if it is a possibility to spoof retina.

When we consider this biometrics trait for our safety system, we should also have in mind how to process its images and which features are the most informative. In this case, the most important part for human identification is veins system. It makes algorithm

© Springer Nature Switzerland AG 2019
K. Saeed et al. (Eds.): CISIM 2019, LNCS 11703, pp. 72–83, 2019.
https://doi.org/10.1007/978-3-030-28957-7_7

authors to consider how to highlight retinal veins. Sometimes also it is impossible to retrieve retinal veins images due to pathological changes within the veins. In the literature there are many different approaches to process retina images although some of them returns satisfactory results but in inefficient way. On the other hand, there are also algorithms that return results really fast, but they are not precise enough.

In this paper the segmentation algorithm for retinal veins is described. At the beginning the authors deals with preprocessing stage, during which image quality is improved and being prepared for further processing steps. The second stage is the main point of our approach. During it we carried out the segmentation process. As the last part, we implemented methods and algorithms for small artifacts (visible after second step) removal. One of this research main aims is to check whether it is possible to effectively extract retinal veins from retina color image with high accuracy.

This work is organized as follows: in the first section the authors describes different approaches and algorithms to retinal veins segmentation. In the second one the novel solution is presented. In this section it's all stages (preprocessing, segmentation and artifacts removal) are presented. Third chapter contains information about performed experiments, especially about different binarization methods and edge detection algorithms that were tested. Finally, the conclusions and future work are given.

2 How Others See the Problem

In the literature one can easily find multiple, different approaches to retinal veins segmentation. Most of the works are based on simple image processing algorithms. Novelty of the algorithm presented in this paper lies in the use of the latest image processing algorithms for retinal veins extraction.

An interesting approach to identify a man on the basis of his retina was presented in [3]. In the case of this algorithm the authors proposed an approach using color histogram as the trait of retina biometrics. In this paper, it was pointed out that interference of lighting and deformation of viewpoint during retina color image acquisition can have a huge impact on human recognition. The authors claimed that in color histogram deformation can be easily observed and its impact on identification can be easily reduced. This approach is really interesting although it can return unsatisfactory result in the case of retina color images with different brightness.

In [4] the Authors presented an algorithm for assessing the severity level of retinal arteriovenous nicking. The most important part, from our point of view, is a method for vessel segmentation. This procedure consists of a few steps: region of interest (ROI) as bounding rectangle extraction and method based on the fact that changing the length of a basic line detector can result in detection of all retinal veins. Another step in this algorithm is isolation the main vessel segments from unnecessary structures such as small artifacts. This algorithm returns satisfactory results, but its efficiency is too low.

Another thought-provoking method was presented in [5]. The Authors proposed an algorithm for blood vessels segmentation with morphological operations in images with diabetic retinopathy. The proposed approach consists of two main parts: the first one responsible for valley detection and the second for peak segmentation. After these two stages, image is constructed on the basis of their results. The main advantage of this approach is satisfactory efficiency although its disadvantage is time consuming method.

In [6] an approach to retinal blood vessel extraction based on Curvelet Transform and Fuzzy C-Means was described. The Authors claimed that at the beginning noise from retina color image is removed, then curvelet transform is used for retinal vasculature enhancement. Another stage of this algorithm is matched filtering for blood vessels intensification. The last step is fuzzy c-means method for vessels silhouette extraction from the background. On the basis of images presented in the paper we can claim that the proposed method returns satisfactory results although it processes image in a really huge time.

An algorithm for supervised pixel classification into arteries and veins was described in [7]. The Authors claimed that their approach can be easily used for diabetic retinopathy changes detection. Their algorithm consists of six basic steps: illumination correction, extraction of centerline pixel, feature extraction, training of neural network classifier, testing the data and final pixel classification. Their approach was tested on DRIVE database and returned around 85% of correct classification. We can assume that this method can assure quite good accuracy level although it is time consuming due to usage of neural network as pixel classifier.

In the literature, we can easily find another interesting approach connected with retinal veins segmentation. An interesting algorithm based on Laplace operator was presented in [8] whilst an algorithm based on direction and score information for person verification was described in [9]. Another algorithm for person identification on the basis of his retina was introduced in [10].

A thought-provoking approach was described in [11]. In it, the authors presented fully-automized algorithm for human identity recognition on the basis of their retina. They proposed a method composed of a few steps: feature extraction, phase correlation and feature matching for recognition. In the first step they used Harris corner detector for characteristic attributes extraction. Then, rotation angle of eye movement was estimated and finally feature vector was compared with all samples from the database with new similarity function proposed by the authors. The algorithm is really interesting although it is hard to rate how it will work in the case of retina color images with pathological changes.

3   Proposed Methodology

The authors have recently published articles in the field of retina image processing [12, 13]. Most of our current works were connected with pathological changes detection especially hard exudates visible in diabetic retinopathy. During the experiments, multiple image databases were used: authors own retina color images set, STARE [14] and DRIVE [15]. Usage of different databases allowed us to compare our results with diversified, recently published algorithms.

In this chapter, we present the worked-out algorithm. It was implemented on the basis of experiences gained during previous research. Moreover, it will be further used in our incoming experiments connected with improvement of automatic algorithm for pathological changes detection in retina color images. Proposed procedure consists of ten steps that we can group into three main stages: image preprocessing, segmentation and unnecessary artifacts removal. The first of them starts with Gaussian blur and is finished when image histogram is equalized. The second stage begins with mask applying in image and its last step is binarization. Artifacts removal and K3M thinning are algorithms that were included in the third stage which we called "Unnecessary elements removal". The whole algorithm was implemented with C# Programming Language, .NET Framework and Visual Studio 2019 development environment.

In Fig. 1 activity diagram of our algorithm was presented whilst Fig. 2. presents original sample of retina color image (a) and after Gaussian blur (b).

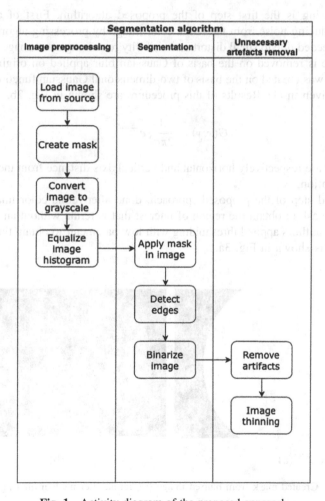

Fig. 1. Activity diagram of the proposed approach

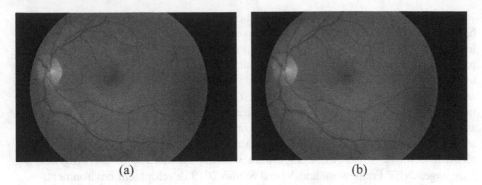

(a)   (b)

Fig. 2. Original retina image sample (a) and after Gaussian blur (b).

Pre-processing is the first step of the proposed algorithm. First of all, authors focused on reducing noise from the retina color image by processing algorithms. This operation is needed due to small distortions visibility remaining after image acquisition process. Noise is removed on the basis of Gaussian blur applied on original sample. The blur filter was created on the basis of two-dimensional Gaussian function. Formula used in it is given in (1). Results of this procedure are shown in Fig. 2b.

$$G(x,y) = \frac{1}{2\pi\sigma^2} e^{\frac{-x^2+y^2}{2\sigma^2}} \tag{1}$$

where x and y are respectively horizontal and vertical axis distance from the origin and σ means deviation.

The second step of the proposed approach, done after retina color image blur, is creation of a mask to obtain the region of interest that is retina without any additional elements. The authors applied thresholding with low parameter to obtain this structure. Sample mask is shown in Fig. 3a.

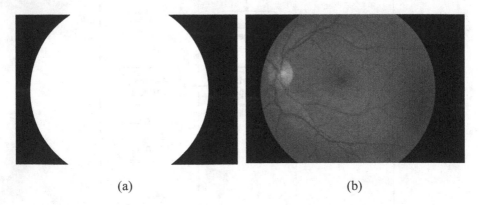

(a)   (b)

Fig. 3. Created mask from blurred image (a), retina after median filtering (b).

The next stage in pre-processing procedure is continuation of reducing noise from analyzed sample. In this case, the authors applied median filter with 3 × 3 mask. The result obtained after median filtering is presented in Fig. 3b.

Image enhancement is the next part of the algorithm. The authors focused on retina veins visibility enhancement and to prepare image for segmentation step.

In the case of samples used in this research, each retina color image is presented in RGB color scale. Due to the fact that the most important data is connected with retinal veins structure, the next step is conversion to grayscale. Information about color from each RGB channel is not necessary for segmentation stage. In the literature, we can observe that conversion to grayscale with green channel is a kind of a standard [16–18] in retina color image processing and its feature extraction. We selected green channel for image conversion to grayscale. Our experiments have shown that it gives the best visibility for retinal veins. Results of this operation are presented in Fig. 4a.

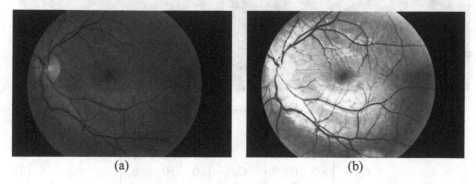

(a)   (b)

Fig. 4. Sample after conversion to grayscale with green channel (a) and after histogram equalization and applying mask in image (b).

After conversion to grayscale, image histogram is equalized. It is done for better retinal veins enhancement. This procedure allowed for better view of retinal veins due to contrast adjustment (it is accomplished by effectively spreading out the most frequent intensity values). Another step in the proposed approach is applying mask in image. We did this operation because by this we extracted region of interest that is real retina without any additional elements. In this algorithm we used mask presented in Fig. 3a. Retinal veins are clearly visible due to previous steps done in image enhancement. Results obtained after applying two recently mentioned methods are shown in Fig. 4b.

Edge detection is the third part of the algorithm. The authors applied Sobel edge detector in enhanced retina image. Sobel operator was created to detect edges in two dimensions (horizontal and vertical). The authors used two 3 × 3 kernels given in (2) to get information about the edges. Each pixel of image presented in Fig. 5 is calculated as an approximate absolute gradient magnitude for corresponding pixel of retina enhanced sample. The proper equation for this step is presented in (3).

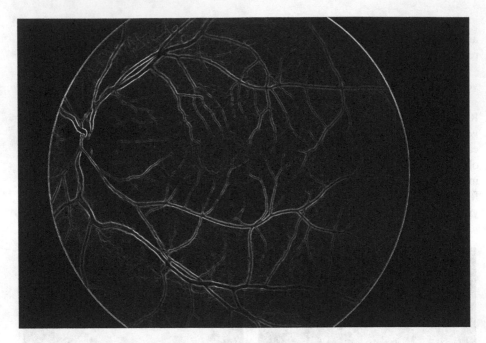

Fig. 5. Image after applying Sobel edge detection algorithm.

$$G_h = \begin{bmatrix} -1 & 0 & 1 \\ -2 & 0 & 2 \\ -1 & 0 & 1 \end{bmatrix} \quad G_v = \begin{bmatrix} 1 & 2 & 1 \\ 0 & 0 & 0 \\ -1 & -2 & -1 \end{bmatrix} \tag{2}$$

$$|G| = |G_h| + |G_v| \tag{3}$$

After edge detection the image is binarized. It means that we convert our sample from grayscale to a space consisting of two values: black and white. By this operation all edges belonging to retinal veins were visible and the image was ready to the next procedure, that is false elements removal. The results in this stage were obtained with low computational complexity Otsu algorithm [19] and are shown in Fig. 6a. However, after binarization process additional, unnecessary artifacts are observable and the shape of retinal veins is not clearly visible. Before thinning operation by which retinal veins structure is finally obtained, the authors cleared the retina image from unnecessary elements by using the artifact removal algorithm. Used procedure is based on calculation of vein length. If it is too short (on the basis of threshold value) then it is removed from the image (we assume that it does not represent veins). The results of this approach are presented in Fig. 6b.

The last part of the algorithm is thinning. K3M [20] thinning algorithm was used to obtain veins structure in form of one-pixel width lines. In Fig. 7 final form of the proposed approach is presented.

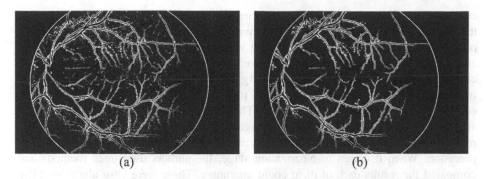

(a)   (b)

Fig. 6. Retina color image after Otsu binarization method (a) and after artifact removal (b).

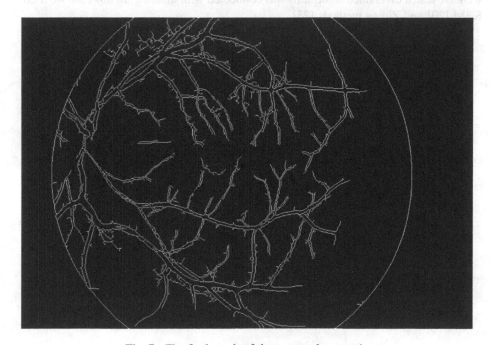

Fig. 7. The final result of the proposed approach.

4   Experiments

The significant part of the work is connected with performed experiments. The authors have to claim that they do not measure segmentation accuracy of the proposed algorithm with any automated method. Each result was consulted with experienced ophthalmologist. His comments allowed us to significantly improve our approach, more precise methods were used to segment retinal veins from retina color images. The algorithm proposed in this paper was tested on STARE, DRIVE and authors' own databases, a total of 150 retina color images. The experiments main point was connected with the created software implementation of the proposed algorithm. During the research we have used multiple different algorithms. In the first stage, we tested possibilities to convert image to grayscale with diversified channels: red, green, blue and average. Although, as mentioned above, the best results were obtained with green channel – the veins were clearly visible. By this we confirmed the statement from the literature [16–18]. In the next step we used multiple methods (with different masks) for edge detection – Sobel, Laplace, Canny. The result obtained with the last-mentioned algorithm is presented in Fig. 8. Once again, we decided to use the most precise method that was Sobel algorithm by which retinal veins were extracted with the highest precision. When it comes to binarization stage, the authors used three methods and compared the results each of them could guarantee. These were Otsu algorithm [19], Niblack method [21] and Bernsen binarization procedure [22]. The last stage in which we have tested diversified algorithms was connected with thinning. In this case we tried K3M [20] and Zhang methods [23].

Fig. 8. Result of Canny edge detection algorithm.

We have to claim that in the final version of the approach described in this paper we used solutions that returned the most precise results. By this statement, we understand that in each step the veins were clearly visible and selected methods gave us possibility to gain the most information about them.

The authors also tested time needed for obtaining retina veins image. The amount of time was measured in a programmatical way with C# Programming Language and object of StopWatch class. This experiment was done on Intel Core i9, 32 GB RAM, 512 SSD ROM computer. The time measured is 30 s. We would like to claim that this is significantly less than in the case of diversified algorithms we tested. The comparison results connected with this experiment are presented in Table 1.

Table 1. Comparison between different segmentation algorithms in terms of time needed for obtaining final image.

Algorithm	Measured time
Wan Mustafa et al. [5]	1 min 10 s
Kar and Maity [6]	1 min 45 s
Proposed approach	30 s

5 Conclusions and Future Work

In the last few years, it is easily observable that retina become one of the most popular biometrics trait. Its huge popularity is connected with its vast uniqueness and impossibility to spoof.

The approach presented in this paper was implemented in a real development environment with C# and .NET Framework. The algorithm was also tested on 150 samples. The authors used not only online available databases but also their own got from Medical University of Białystok, Faculty of Medicine, Department of Ophthalmology. In the future it will be considered to share this data collection online. The final result of the proposed solution is an image consists only of retinal vein. Our approach can also be used in the process of human identification. The feature vector can be easily obtained from information presented in the final image that is a result of our solution. Moreover, the final result of the algorithm can also be used in the process of pathological changes detection in retina color images. This conclusion is connected with the fact that one of the very beginning steps in this kind of algorithms is retinal veins extraction and removal. It is caused by the fact that changes cannot be observed in veins in the course of diversified illnesses (for example in diabetic retinopathy).

In the work, the authors do not use any automated accuracy measure method. It will be really hard to specify image parameters that could evaluate the accuracy of the proposed approach. Instead of this, each result was consulted with experienced ophthalmologist. His remarks helped us to significantly improve our approach.

The authors current work is to improve segmentation step of the proposed approach for better final image and to apply it in pathological changes detection algorithm, like hard exudates in diabetes.

Acknowledgment. The authors are thankful to Medical University of Białystok, Faculty of Medicine, Department of Ophthalmology, especially to Dr Emil Saeed, for their support and providing a sample database.

This work was supported partially by grant S/WI/3/2018 and by grant WI/WI/2/2019 from Białystok University of Technology and funded with resources for research by the Ministry of Science and Higher Education in Poland.

References

1. Vacca, J.R.: Biometric Technologies and Verification Systems. Butterworth-Heineman, pp. 85–87 (2007). ISBN 978-0750679671

2. https://www.scmagazineuk.com/starbugs-eyes-german-hacker-spoofs-iris-recognition/article/1479198. Accessed 15 Feb 2019

3. Hao, H., Kumar, D.K., Aliahmad, B., Che Azemin, M.Z., Kawasaki, R.: Using color histogram as the trait of retina biometric. In: 2013 IEEE ISSNIP Biosignals and Biorobotics Conference: Biosignals and Robotics for Better and Safer Living (BRC), Rio de Janerio, Brazil, 18–20 February, Proceedings (2013)

4. Nguyen, U.T.V., et al.: Automated quantification of retinal arteriovenous nicking from colour fundus images. In: 2013 IEEE 35th Annual International Conference of the IEEE EMBS, Osaka, Japan, 3–7 July, Proceedings, pp. 5865–5868 (2013)

5. Wan Mustafa, W.A.B., Yazid, H., Bin Yaacob, S., Bin Basah, S.N.: Blood vessel extraction using morphological operation for diabetic retinopathy. In: 2014 IEEE Region 10 Symposium, Kuala Lumpur, Malaysia, 14–16 April, Proceedings (2014)

6. Kar, S.S., Maity, S.P.: Extraction of retinal blood vessel using curvelet transform and fuzzy C-Means. In: 2014 IEEE 22nd International Conference on Pattern Recognition, Stockholm, Sweden, 24–28 August, Proceedings, pp. 3392–3397 (2014)

7. Chlabra, S., Bhusan, B.: Supervised pixel classification into arteries and veins of retinal images. In: 2014 IEEE International Conference on Innovative Applications of Computational Intelligence on Power, Energy and Controls with their Impact on Humanity, CIPECH 2014, Ghaziabad, India, 28–29 November, Proceedings, pp. 59–62 (2014)

8. Minar, J., Pinkava, M., Riha, K., Dutta, M.K., Sengar, N.: Automatic extraction of blood vessels and veins using laplace operator in fundus image. In: 2015 IEEE International Conference on Green Computing and Internet of Things (ICGCIoT), Noida, India, 8–10 October, Proceedings (2015)

9. Frucci, M., Riccio, D., Sanniti di Baja, G., Serino, L.: Using direction and score information for retina based person verification. Expert Syst. Appl. **94**, 1–10 (2018)

10. Choraś, R.: Retina recognition for Biometrics. In: 7th International Conference on Digital Information Management (ICDIM), Macau, China, 22–24 August, Proceedings (2012)

11. Dhghani, A., Ghassabi, Z.R., Abrishami Moghaddam, H., Moin, M.-S.: Human recognition based on retinal images and using new similarity function. EURASIP J. Image Video Process. **58**(1) (2013). https://doi.org/10.1186/1687-5281-2013-58

12. Szymkowski, M., Saeed, E., Saeed, K.: Retina tomography and optical coherence tomography in eye diagnostic system. In: Chaki, R., Cortesi, A., Saeed, K., Chaki, N. (eds.) Advanced Computing and Systems for Security. AISC, vol. 666, pp. 31–42. Springer, Singapore (2018). https://doi.org/10.1007/978-981-10-8180-4_3

13. Saeed, E., Szymkowski, M., Saeed, K., Mariak, Z.: An approach to automatic hard exudate detection in retina color images by telemedicine system based on d-Eye sensor and image processing algorithms. MDPI Sens. **19**(3) (2019). https://doi.org/10.3390/s19030695

14. http://cecas.clemson.edu/~ahoover/stare/. Accessed 30 Dec 2018

15. https://www.isi.uu.nl/Research/Databases/DRIVE/. Accessed 30 Dec 2018

16. Xu, L., Luo, S.: A novel method for blood vessels detection from retinal images. BioMed. Eng. Online **9**, 14 (2010)

17. Raja Sundhara Siva, D., Vasuki, S.: Automatic detection of blood vessels in retinal images for diabetic retinopathy diagnosis. Comput. Math. Methods Med. **2015**, 12 (2015)

18. Zhang, J., Cui, Y., Jiang, W., Wang, L.: Blood vessels segmentation of retinal images based on neural network. In: 8th International Conference on Image and Graphics, 2015 ICIG, Tianjin, China, Proceedings, pp. 11–17 (2015)

19. Otsu, N.: A threshold selection method from gray-level histograms. IEEE Trans. Syst. Man Cybern. **9**(1), 62–66 (1979)

20. Tabędzki, M., Saeed, K., Szczepański, A.: A modified K3M thinning algorithm. Int. J. Appl. Math. Comput. Sci. **26**(2), 439–450 (2016)

21. Saxena, L.P.: Niblack's binarization method and its modifications to real-time applications: a review. Artif. Intell. Rev. **51**(4), 673–705 (2019)
22. Eyupoglu, C.: Implementation of Bernsen's locally adaptive binarization method for gray scale images. In: 2016, Proceedings of 7th International Science and Technology Conference (ISTEC), pp. 621–625 (2016)
23. Zhang, T.Y., Suen, C.Y.: A fast parallel algorithm for thinning digital patterns. Commun. ACM **27**(3), 236–239 (1984)

Diagnosing Parkinson's Disease with the Use of a Reduced Set of Patients' Voice Features Samples

Krzysztof Wrobel[✉]

Institute of Computer Science, University of Silesia,
ul. Bedzinska 39, 41-200 Sosnowiec, Poland
krzysztof.wrobel@us.edu.pl
http://zsk.tech.us.edu.pl

Abstract. The paper proposes a method for diagnosing Parkinson's disease using a reduced set of patients' voice features samples. The Sequential Forward Selection and Sequential Backward Selection methods were used to reduce features. The data reduced were classified separately with the use of over a dozen popular classifiers. The effectiveness of diagnosing Parkinson's disease on a reduced set of data was determined for each classifier. Then it was compared with the results obtained for the data without any reduction of features.

The experiments carried out showed that, depending on the classifier used, the reduction of the set even to few features allowed increasing the effectiveness of classification. The research also allowed indicating the classifiers and features, with the use of which the best results of classification were obtained. The experiments were carried out on a publicly available database containing voice samples of patients with Parkinson's disease and of healthy patients.

Keywords: Parkinson's disease · Medical diagnosis ·
Data classification · Feature selection

1 Introduction

Parkinson's disease (PD) is a slowly progressing disease of the central nervous system. The basic symptoms of PD are slowed movements, difficulties in moving and speaking, and a lack of balance [1,2]. In general, the first symptoms of PD can occur already in people over the age of 50, although the average age of patients is 59 [3]. Therefore, an important task is to diagnose Parkinson's disease as early as possible in order to immediately start a therapy that will stop or slow down the disease process.

Currently, there are many methods for diagnosing PD [1–5]. One of them is an analysis of recorded voice samples of the patients [6–10]. The advantage of this method is its non-invasive character. Voice samples can be recorded and analyzed at any time, without the use of specialized and often expensive medical

© Springer Nature Switzerland AG 2019
K. Saeed et al. (Eds.): CISIM 2019, LNCS 11703, pp. 84–95, 2019.
https://doi.org/10.1007/978-3-030-28957-7_8

equipment. An additional advantage is the fact that the registration of samples does not have to take place in specialized hospital wards, but can be done at home, while samples can be sent for testing, e.g. by e-mail. The process of registration of samples and diagnosing can also be performed online via the Internet [7,11,12].

It is possible to extract appropriate voice features from the recorded sample and subject them to the process of classification. As a result, there is possibility to determine whether the analyzed sample comes from a sick or healthy person.

Studies on diagnosing Parkinson's disease with the use of voice samples were presented by many researchers [13,14]. For the purpose of classification of samples, there were used primarily Artificial Intelligence (AI) tools, such as Neural Networks [15], Support Vector Machines (SVM) algorithm [16] and the k-Nearest Neighbors (k-NN) method [17,18]. The tests were carried out on various databases and the results indicated that the effectiveness of classification often exceeded 90%. In many publications, e.g. [8,9], all features of patients' voice samples were analysed. However, in practice it may turn out that some of the features do not affect the effectiveness of classification and even make it worse. Therefore, the main motivation of this work is a will to determine only those features, which allow to achieve the best possible classification accuracy.

In this study, there was extracted a reduced set of features [19–21], with the use of which the highest effectiveness of classification was obtained. Feature reduction methods, such as Sequential Forward Selection and Sequential Backward Selection, were used for this purpose. There were also conducted studies aimed at determining how many test samples of the patient's voice are needed to determine the medical condition. The minimum number of samples was indicated.

2   Proposed Method

Let there be given a set of m patients $P = \{P_1, P_2, ..., P_m\}$. For each patient P_i, where $i = 1, ..., m$, there is given a set of n samples of the patient's voice $P_i = \{S_1, S_2, ..., S_n\}$. Each of the samples S_j is described by the set of features $S_j = \{f_1, f_2, ..., f_r\}$, for $j = 1, ..., n$. Based on the analysis of samples of the patient's voice P_i and features of these samples, the task is to diagnose whether the patient P_i is healthy or has Parkinson's disease.

Let's introduce the class $C = \{0, 1\}$, to which the patient P_i belongs. Class 0 means that the patient is healthy, while class 1 means that Parkinson's disease was diagnosed. Additionally, let $c_{ij} \in C$ means the class of a single sample j of the patient i.

Let us designate the decision about the membership of the sample S_{ij} in the class $c_{ij} \in C$ as:

$$d_{ij} = \Psi(S_{ij}), \tag{1}$$

where Ψ indicates the model of the classifier used, while S_{ij} designates the j-th sample coming from the i patient.

As n samples of the patient P_i were analyzed and each sample was classified separately, the final decision $d_i^{final} \in C$ on whether the patient P_i has Parkinson's disease or is healthy was made on the basis of majority voting:

$$d_i^{final} = \begin{cases} 0, & \text{if} \quad d_{ij}^0 \geq d_{ij}^1 \\ 1, & \text{if} \quad d_{ij}^0 < d_{ij}^1 \end{cases} \tag{2}$$

where:
$d_{ij}^1 = \sum_{j=1}^{n} d_{ij}$ - is the decision indicating that the sample comes from a patient with Parkinson's disease,
$d_{ij}^0 = n - d_{ij}^1$ - is the decision indicating that the sample comes from a healthy patient.

The voice samples from the tested database were subjected to the operation of algorithms for selection (reduction) of features. The test samples obtained from patient P_i were also subjected to the operation of feature reduction. For this purpose, the Sequential Forward Selection and Sequential Backward Selection methods were used separately.

Sequential Backward Selection (SBS) and Sequential Forward Selection (SFS) algorithms belong to a family of greedy algorithms for searching feature space. They are used to reduce the initial k_1-dimensional feature space X to the k_2-dimensional feature subspace X_r, where $k_2 < k_1$. The input parameter of both methods is a given number of features contained in the new subspace. The mechanism of SBS and SFS algorithms operation differs in the way of eliminating features. In the SBS algorithm, the X_r subspace is at the beginning initiated with the full space of features X ($X_r = X$). Then, in each iteration step, a feature whose removal has the least effect on the classification efficiency is eliminated. The end of the algorithm takes place when the set number of features is reached. In the case of the SFS algorithm, the X_r space is at the beginning initialized with an empty set ($X_r = \emptyset$). Then, in each iteration step, the feature for which the maximum classification efficiency is achieved is added to this set. Similar to SBS algorithm, the termination of the SFS algorithm takes place when the set number of features is reached. Both algorithms are described in detail in [23,24].

In the training stage, the given classifier Ψ was trained on a set of voice samples from the tested database. In the testing stage, the classifier Ψ was tested on a set of voice samples obtained from the patient P_i. As the Ψ classifier, the classifiers listed in Table 1 were substituted and tested separately. Classification results for tested classifiers are presented in Table 3.

In the last stage, the final decision on whether the diagnosed patient was healthy or had Parkinson's disease was made using a majority voting of a chosen Ψ classifier results on a set of samples.

Diagram presenting the operation of the method is shown in Fig. 1. In case of data classification without reduction of features the diagram is the same, but has no "Feature reduction" block.

The final decision calculated from formula (2) is assigned to the patient P_i as the predicted medical diagnosis concerning Parkinson's disease. This information is compared with the actual medical diagnosis, which makes it possible to calculate the error of classification. This error is given by the following formula:

$$err_i = |d_i^{final} - d_i^{real}|, \tag{3}$$

where:
d_i^{final} - predicted medical condition of the patient P_i,
d_i^{real} - actual medical condition of the patient P_i.

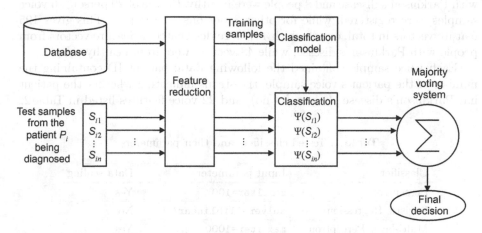

Fig. 1. Diagram presenting the operation of the research method.

3 Experiments and Results

During the experiments, there were used popular classifiers, data selection methods as well as a publicly available database of patient voice samples. Description of the tools used can be found in further sections of the study.

3.1 Classifiers Tested and Data Selection Methods

All experiments were carried out with the use of software written in Python language, using the scikit-learn library. This library contains implementations of popular and frequently used classifiers [22]. In the case of certain classifiers, a data pre-scaling method contributed to an increase in the effectiveness of classification. Scaling was performed using a method of the StandardScaler class of the scikit-learn library, which was described in detail in [22].

Table 1 shows the classifiers tested, their parameters, as well as the information whether the tested data were scaled or not.

For reducing the data, there were used the SBS and SFS methods along with the implementation available at this website: https://rasbt.github.io/mlxtend/user_guide/feature_selection/SequentialFeatureSelector/.

3.2 Database

The tested database was prepared and described in [25] and is publicly available in the UCI archive at the following address: https://archive.ics.uci.edu/ml/index.php. It contains voice samples from 32 people, out of whom 24 were people with Parkinson's disease and 8 people were healthy. In case of 29 persons, 6 voice samples were registered, while for other 3 persons - 7 samples. This gives 195 feature vectors in total, out of which 147 were designated as feature vectors from people with Parkinson's disease, while 48 vectors were from healthy people.

Each voice sample contained the following data: patient ID containing the number of the patient's voice sample, the status indicating whether the patient has Parkinson's disease (1 - yes, 0 - no), and 22 voice features listed in Table 2.

Table 1. Tested classifiers and their parameters.

Classifier	Input parameters	Data scaling
Perceptron	max_iter=100	Yes
Logistic Regression	solver='liblinear'	No
Multi-layer Perceptron	max_iter=1000	Yes
SVM (linear kernel)	kernel='linear'	No
SVM (non-linear kernel)	kernel='rbf', gamma='auto'	Yes
SVM (polynomial kernel)	kernel='poly', gamma='auto', degree=1	No
Decision Tree	criterion='entropy', max_depth=5	Yes
k-NN	n_neighbors=10, metric='euclidean', weights='distance'	Yes
Naive Bayes	default	No
Stochastic Gradient	max_iter=1000	Yes
Gaussian Process	default	Yes
Random Forest	default	No
Ada Boost	default	No
Gradient Boosting	default	No
Extra Trees	default	No
Bagging	DecisionTreeClassifier	No
Linear Discriminant	default	No
Quadratic Discriminant	default	Yes

3.3 Obtained Results

The purpose of the first experiment was to determine the effectiveness of classification on a reduced set of features and compare the results with the results obtained for the data without reduction of features. During the studies, the quantity and numbers of features (presented in Table 2), with the use of which a given result had been obtained, were also indicated. The detailed results of the tests are presented in Table 3, in which the highest effectiveness for a given classifier was marked in grey (if a given result was the same for the cases examined, the results were not marked).

When analyzing Table 3, it can be seen practically for every classifier tested that a higher effectiveness of classification was obtained for a reduced set of features. In addition, in the case of some classifiers, an analysis of even one feature increased the effectiveness of classification. The exceptions are SVM classifiers with a linear kernel, SVM with a polynomial kernel and Multi-layer Perceptron.

Table 2. Analyzed features of voice samples.

No.	Feature	Description
1.	MDVP:Fo(Hz)	Average vocal fundamental frequency
2.	MDVP:Fhi(Hz)	Maximum vocal fundamental frequency
3.	MDVP:Flo(Hz)	Minimum vocal fundamental frequency
4.	MDVP:Jitter(%)	Several measures of variation in fundamental frequency
5.	MDVP:Jitter(Abs)	
6.	MDVP:RAP	
7.	MDVP:PPQ	
8.	Jitter:DDP	
9.	MDVP:Shimmer	Several measures of variation in amplitude
10.	MDVP:Shimmer(dB)	
11.	Shimmer:APQ3	
12.	Shimmer:APQ5	
13.	MDVP:APQ	
14.	Shimmer:DDA	
15.	NHR	Two measures of ratio of noise to tonal components in the voice
16.	HNR	
17.	RPDE	Two nonlinear dynamical complexity measures
18.	D2	
19.	DFA	Signal fractal scaling exponent
20.	spread1	Three nonlinear measures of fundamental frequency variation
21.	spread2	
22.	PPE	

Table 3. The effectiveness of classification obtained for the reduced set of features and the whole set of features.

Classifier	SBS algorithm			SFS algorithm			All features
	Accuracy	Number of features	Feature no.	Accuracy	Number of features	Feature no.	
Perceptron	0.906	8	4,8,12, 13,17,18, 20,22	0.875	6	1,4,7, 11,21,22	0.781
Logistic Regression	0.844	5	2, 3, 18, 19, 21	0.875	3	1, 3, 21	0.812
Multi-layer Perceptron	0.906	22	All	0.906	22	All	0.906
SVM (linear)	0.844	1	19	0.844	1	19	0.844
SVM (non-linear)	0.875	2	2,20	0.844	1	22	0.844
SVM (polynomial)	0.875	2	1,21	0.875	11	1,2,4,5, 6,7,8,9, 17,19,21	0.875
Decision Tree	0.844	20	All \ {18,20}	0.875	1	22	0.844
k-NN	0.844	2	3,19	0.875	1	22	0.812
Naive Bayes	0.875	1	19	0.875	1	19	0.688
Stochastic Gradient	0.844	1	22	0.875	9	1,3,5,6, 9,11,13, 17,22	0.812
Gaussian Process	0.875	3	2,18,22	0.875	3	2,18,22	0.844
Random Forest	0.875	1	22	0.875	1	22	0.844
Ada Boost	0.875	1	22	0.875	1	22	0.812
Gradient Boosting	0.875	2	1,20	0.875	1	22	0.844
Extra Trees	0.906	2	16,19	0.875	1	22	0.812
Bagging	0.875	1	19	0.875	1	22	0.812
Linear Discriminant	0.906	6	3,4,6,17, 20,22	0.844	1	19	0.812
Quadratic Discriminant	0.844	6	5,9,11, 16,18,20	0.875	1	19	0.812

The same effectiveness of classification was obtained for SVM classifiers, but for a smaller set of features. In turn, in the case of the Multi-layer Perceptron classifier, the results for the whole and reduced set of features did not change.

In seven cases, better classification results were obtained for the Sequential Forward Selection method (if the effectiveness was the same, the smaller number of features decided about the superiority). For four cases, better results were obtained using the Sequential Backward Selection method. In the remaining seven cases, the result was the same.

The experiment allowed indicating the classifiers, with the use of which the best results were obtained. These were the following classifiers: Perceptron, Multi-Layer Perceptron, Extra Trees classifier and Linear Discriminant. The effectiveness of classification obtained with these classifiers was 0.906.

This experiment also allowed indicating the numbers of features, with the use of which the best classification results were obtained for individual classifiers. For the SBS method, there can be distinguished three features which occurred most often in the best results of classification. These are the features designated with numbers 19, 20, 22. These features appeared in the best results successively 8, 6 and 8 times. In turn, for the SFS method, the three most commonly occurring features were as follows: feature No. 22 (12 times), feature No. 19 (6 times) and feature No. 1 (5 times). The histogram showing the dependency between the number of occurrences of a given feature in the best result for individual classifiers (see: Table 3, column "Feature no.") is presented in Fig. 2.

Taking into account the results obtained for the SBS and SFS methods, it can be noticed that the features No. 19 and No. 22 are particularly important in diagnosing Parkinson's disease with the use of voice samples.

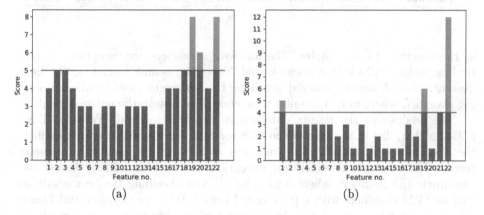

Fig. 2. The number of occurrences of features in the best result for the methods: (a) SBS, (b) SFS.

The second experiment examined the effectiveness of classification depending on how many test samples were taken from one patient. The tested database contained 6 or 7 test samples taken from a single patient. If there were 6 test samples available for the tested person, the test was limited to this number of samples. The tests were conducted separately for the SBS and SFS methods, and their results are summarized in Tables 4 and 5.

The analysis of the results presented in Table 4 shows that for the majority of classifiers the effectiveness of classification increases along with an increase

Table 4. The effectiveness of classification for different number of test samples in the SBS method.

Classifier	Number of test samples						
	$n = 1$	$n = 2$	$n = 3$	$n = 4$	$n = 5$	$n = 6$	$n = 7$
Perceptron	0.816	0.851	0.858	0.899	0.897	0.906	0.906
Logistic Reggression	0.799	0.803	0.829	0.810	0.850	0.844	0.844
Multi-layer Perceptron	0.858	0.879	0.881	0.906	0.906	0.906	0.906
SVM (linear)	0.843	0.844	0.859	0.850	0.862	0.844	0.844
SVM (non-linear)	0.859	0.845	0.871	0.869	0.875	0.875	0.875
SVM (polynomial)	0.852	0.838	0.863	0.858	0.875	0.875	0.875
Decision Tree	0.777	0.830	0.823	0.840	0.827	0.844	0.844
k-NN	0.813	0.828	0.814	0.828	0.818	0.844	0.844
Naive Bayes	0.826	0.847	0.873	0.858	0.893	0.875	0.875
Stochastic Gradient	0.831	0.839	0.854	0.847	0.859	0.844	0.844
Gaussian Process	0.841	0.851	0.865	0.866	0.875	0.875	0.875
Random Forest	0.728	0.813	0.795	0.861	0.836	0.875	0.875
Ada Boost	0.806	0.842	0.863	0.871	0.858	0.875	0.875
Gradient Boosting	0.852	0.862	0.880	0.866	0.876	0.875	0.875
Extra Trees	0.833	0.868	0.874	0.906	0.906	0.906	0.906
Bagging	0.808	0.836	0.854	0.869	0.853	0.875	0.875
Linear Discriminant	0.810	0.840	0.859	0.866	0.906	0.906	0.906
Quadratic Discriminant	0.781	0.815	0.784	0.791	0.777	0.844	0.844

in the number of test samples. The following classifiers are exceptions: Logistic Regression, SVM with a linear kernel, Naive Bayes and Stochastic Gradient descent, where 5 samples allowed obtaining the best result, and Gradient Boosting classifier, where only 3 samples were enough to obtain the optimal result.

The analysis of the results obtained in the SFS method (Table 5) allows noticing that, like in the case of the SBS method, for the majority of classifiers the effectiveness of classification increases along with the number of samples tested. The following classifiers are exceptions: SVM with a linear kernel and Quadratic Discriminant, where 5 samples allowed obtaining the best result, as well as SVM classifiers with a polynomial kernel, Bagging classifier and Linear Discriminant, where only 3 samples were enough to obtain an optimal result. In the case of the SVM (non-linear) classifier, the best result was obtained for one sample.

In respect of both feature reduction methods, it is also worth noting that although 7 test samples were available for some patients, there was no difference in the effectiveness of classification for six ($n = 6$) and seven ($n = 7$) test samples.

Table 5. The effectiveness of classification for different number of test samples in the SFS method.

Classifier	Number of test samples						
	$n = 1$	$n = 2$	$n = 3$	$n = 4$	$n = 5$	$n = 6$	$n = 7$
Perceptron	0.817	0.835	0.845	0.853	0.865	0.875	0.875
Logistic Reggression	0.836	0.833	0.85	0.849	0.859	0.875	0.875
Multi-layer Perceptron	0.858	0.879	0.881	0.906	0.906	0.906	0.906
SVM (linear)	0.843	0.844	0.859	0.85	0.862	0.844	0.844
SVM (non-linear)	0.848	0.837	0.848	0.844	0.844	0.844	0.844
SVM (polynomial)	0.878	0.871	0.883	0.875	0.875	0.875	0.875
Decision Tree	0.783	0.833	0.841	0.871	0.858	0.875	0.875
k-NN	0.779	0.84	0.838	0.871	0.858	0.875	0.875
Naive Bayes	0.826	0.847	0.873	0.858	0.893	0.875	0.875
Stochastic Gradient	0.835	0.834	0.86	0.852	0.875	0.875	0.875
Gaussian Process	0.841	0.851	0.865	0.866	0.875	0.875	0.875
Random Forest	0.728	0.813	0.795	0.861	0.836	0.875	0.875
Ada Boost	0.806	0.842	0.863	0.871	0.858	0.875	0.875
Gradient Boosting	0.757	0.818	0.807	0.861	0.836	0.875	0.875
Extra Trees	0.742	0.826	0.795	0.861	0.836	0.875	0.875
Bagging	0.851	0.848	0.88	0.877	0.877	0.875	0.875
Linear Discriminant	0.84	0.84	0.851	0.844	0.844	0.844	0.844
Quadratic Discriminant	0.838	0.847	0.873	0.858	0.893	0.875	0.875

4   Conclusions

The experiments carried out have shown that a reduction of features of voice samples increases the effectiveness of classification. For all the classifiers tested, the effectiveness of classification was greater than in the case of data classifications, in which the features were not reduced.

The experiments allowed indicating classifiers, for which the highest effectiveness of classification can be obtained. The best result of classification accuracy equal to 0.906 has been obtained ex aequo by 4 different classifiers: **Perceptron**, **Multi-Layer Perceptron**, **Extra Trees** and **Linear Discriminant**.

The experiments also allowed indicating the voice features that are particularly important in diagnosing Parkinson's disease. These were the following features: **DFA** - signal fractal scaling exponent, **PPE** - one of the three nonlinear measures of fundamental frequency variation.

In the course of the studies, there was also analyzed the influence of the quantity of test samples on the final result. For most classifiers, the rule was that the more test samples, the higher the effectiveness of classification. In several cases, the highest effectiveness of classification was obtained for the quantity of voice samples other than the maximum one.

In next stages of the studies, it is planned to create an ensemble of classifiers to increase the effectiveness of classification further. The competences of classifiers for the analysis of individual features of voice samples will also be examined.

Other databases of voice samples of healthy patients and those with Parkinson's disease, containing a larger number of records, will also be used.

References

1. Golbe, L.I., Mark, M.H., Sage, J.I.: Parkinson's Disease Handbook. The American Parkinson Disease Association Inc., New York (2010)
2. Parkinson, J.: An essay on the shaking palsy. London (1817)
3. Grosset, D., Fernandez, H., Grosset, K., Okun, M.: Parkinson's Disease Clinician's Desk Reference. CRC Press, Boca Raton (2009)
4. Lee, S.-H., Lim, J.S.: Parkinson's disease classification using gait characteristics and wavelet-based feature extraction. Expert Syst. Appl. **39**(8), 7338–7344 (2012)
5. Hariharan, M., Polat, K., Sindhu, R.: A new hybrid intelligent system for accurate detection of Parkinson's disease. Comput. Methods Programs Biomed. **113**(3), 904–913 (2014)
6. Tsanas, A., Little, M.A., McSharry, P.E., Ramig, L.O.: Nonlinear speech analysis algorithms mapped to a standard metric achieve clinically useful quantification of average Parkinson's disease symptom severity. J. R. Soc. Interface **8**(59), 842–55 (2011)
7. Sakar, B.E., Kursun, O.: Telemonitoring of changes of unified Parkinson's disease rating scale using severity of voice symptoms. In: Proceedings of the 2nd International Conference on E-Health and TeleMedicine, Istanbul, pp. 114–119 (2014)
8. Froelich, W., Wrobel, K., Porwik, P.: Diagnosing Parkinson's disease using the classification of speech signals. J. Med. Inform. Technol. **23**, 187–193 (2014)
9. Froelich, W., Wrobel, K., Porwik, P.: Diagnosis of Parkinson's disease using speech samples and threshold-based classification. J. Med. Imaging Health Inf. **5**(6), 1358–1363 (2015)
10. Rouzbahani, H.K., Daliri, M.R.: Diagnosis of Parkinson's disease in human using voice signals. Basic Clin. Neurosci. **2**(3), 12–20 (2011)
11. Tsanas, A., Little, M.A., McSharry, P.E., Ramig, L.O.: Accurate telemonitoring of Parkinson's disease progression by noninvasive speech tests. IEEE Trans. Biomed. Eng. **57**(4), 884–93 (2010)
12. Goetz, C.G., et al.: Testing objective measures of motor impairment in early Parkinson's disease: feasibility study of an at-home testing device. Mov. Disord. **24**(4), 551–556 (2009)
13. Morales, D.A., et al.: Predicting dementia development in Parkinson's disease using Bayesian network classifiers. Psychiatry Res. NeuroImaging **213**(2), 92–8 (2013)
14. Peker, M., Sen, B., Delen, D.: Computer-aided diagnosis of Parkinson's disease using complex-valued neural networks and mRMR feature selection algorithm. J. Healthc. Eng. **6**(3), 281–302 (2015)
15. Ene, M.: Neural network-based approach to discriminate healthy people from those with Parkinson's disease. Ann. Univ. Craiova **35**, 112–116 (2008)
16. Peker, M.: A decision support system to improve medical diagnosis using a combination of k-medoids clustering based attribute weighting and SVM. J. Med. Syst. **40**(5), 1–6 (2016)
17. Chen, H.-L., et al.: An efficient diagnosis system for detection of Parkinson's disease using fuzzy *k*-nearest neighbor approach. Expert Syst. Appl. **40**(1), 263–271 (2013)
18. Guruler, H.: A novel diagnosis system for Parkinson's disease using complex-valued artificial neural network with k-means clustering feature weighting method. Neural Comput. Appl. **28**(7), 1657–1666 (2017)

19. Wrobel, K., Doroz, R., Palys, M.: A method of lip print recognition based on sections comparison. In: IEEE International Conference on Biometrics and Kansei Engineering (ICBAKE), pp. 47–52 (2013)
20. Palys, M., Doroz, R., Porwik, P.: On-line signature recognition based on an analysis of dynamic feature. In: IEEE International Conference on Biometrics and Kansei Engineering (ICBAKE), pp. 103–107 (2013)
21. Porwik, P., Doroz, R.: Self-adaptive biometric classifier working on the reduced dataset. In: Polycarpou, M., de Carvalho, A.C.P.L.F., Pan, J.-S., Woźniak, M., Quintian, H., Corchado, E. (eds.) HAIS 2014. LNCS (LNAI), vol. 8480, pp. 377–388. Springer, Cham (2014). https://doi.org/10.1007/978-3-319-07617-1_34
22. Pedregosa, F., et al.: Scikit-learn: machine learning in python. J. Mach. Learn. Res. **12**, 2825–2830 (2011)
23. Ferri, F.J., Pudil, P., Hatef, M., Kittler, J.: Comparative study of techniques for large-scale feature selection. Mach. Intell. Pattern Recogn. **16**, 403–413 (1994)
24. Pudil, P., Novovicova, J., Kittler, J.: Floating search methods in feature selection. Pattern Recogn. Lett. **15**(11), 1119–1125 (1994)
25. Little, M.A., McSharry, P.E., Roberts, S.J., Costello, D.A., Moroz, I.M.: Exploiting nonlinear recurrence and fractal scaling properties for voice disorder detection. Biomed. Eng. Online **6**(1), 23 (2007)

Computer Information Systems

Big Data and the Internet of Things in Edge Computing for Smart City

Jerzy Balicki[1]([⊠])[iD], Honorata Balicka[2], Piotr Dryja[3][iD],
and Maciej Tyszka[3]

[1] Faculty of Mathematics and Information Science,
Warsaw University of Technology, Koszykowa St. 75, 00-662 Warsaw, Poland
j.balicki@mini.pw.edu.pl
[2] Faculty of Management and Commodity, Maritime University of Gdynia,
ul. Morska 81-87, 81-225 Gdynia, Poland
honoratabalicka@gmail.com
[3] Faculty of Telecommunications, Electronics and Informatics,
Gdańsk University of Technology, Narutowicza St. 11/12,
80-233 Gdańsk, Poland
piodryja@pg.gda.pl, tyszka.maciej@gmail.com

Abstract. Requests expressing collective human expectations and outcomes
from city service tasks can be partially satisfied by processing Big Data provided
to a city cloud via the Internet of Things. To improve the efficiency of the city
clouds an edge computing has been introduced regarding Big Data mining. This
intelligent and efficient distributed system can be developed for citizens that are
supposed to be informed and educated by the smart agents. Besides, we suggest
that these intelligent agents can be moved to the edge of the cloud and reduce
the latency of the big data receiving. Finally, some numerical experiments with
edge computing have been submitted to support this approach with optimization
of two criteria. The first one is the CPU workload of the bottleneck computer
and the second one is the communication workload of the bottleneck server.

Keywords: Big data · Internet of Things · Edge computing · Smart city

1 Introduction

Big data (BD) is very useful to achieve high-value information related to decision
support, business intelligence or forecasting in a city. Citizens of large cities should live
in the smart environment that can be effectively supported by smart clouds used the
Internet of Things (IoT). In consequence, a huge number of almost unlimited data
sources may provide Big Data about different features of human behaviors and human
environments. In results, it is possible to understand some aspects of human behaviors
that are important to prevent some crisis situations or to prepare an efficient annual
expenditure budget to satisfy a community expectation. Moreover, some disadvantages
of the city infrastructure can be identified and then improved [13].

Citizens are supposed to be informed and educated by the smart city agents.
Besides, we suggest that some agents can be moved to the edge of the cloud and reduce

K. Saeed et al. (Eds.): CISIM 2019, LNCS 11703, pp. 99–109, 2019.
https://doi.org/10.1007/978-3-030-28957-7_9

the latency of the big data receiving. Some limited data sources, such as logs from email servers or web browsers can be supported by many intensive sources like cameras, microphones and social networks. Furthermore, the Internet of Things increases the data capacity about the behavior of the citizens from the real-life sensors. Specifically, this data is coming with an extended system such as *SmartSantander* [29].

SmartSantander is a city-scale experimental research with several applications and services dedicated for smart cities. This system is strongly developed to be sufficiently large, open and flexible. Its goal is to enable horizontal and vertical federation with other experimental city facilities. Besides, it stimulates development of some mobile applications. Over 20,000 sensors are developed in cities: *Belgrade, Guildford, Lübeck,* and *Santander* [29].

Another example is the United Kingdom's nationwide fault-reporting website called *FixMyStreet* [25]. Thousands of people use it to report broken streetlights, car accidents, not cleared of snow streets, road potholes, or other inconvenience in the local area. System recognizes and redirects citizen complaints and remarks to the right page of the council website. Citizens do not need to know who is responsible for getting things fixed regarding automated monitoring [25].

A quality of Big Data depends on services provided by some public edge computing platforms and places of sensors' locations. Furthermore, there are important types of information from the IoT. BD services provided by some public cloud computing platforms can offer real-time insights about large-scale multimedia data for smart city systems. In addition, a query to BD database can be performed for multi-terabyte datasets in 1–2 s. The current technology causes that this service can be used due to its scalability [3].

The Internet of Things connects a wide variety of devices such as cars with built-in sensors, heart monitoring implants, biochip transponders on animals, or field operation devices that assist fire-fighters. These devices collect useful data and then autonomously flow data between other devices. Besides, we can consider smart thermostat systems and washer/dryers with Wi-Fi for remote monitoring. Radio-frequency identification (RFID) can support all objects and citizens in daily life. Furthermore, the tagging of things may be achieved through such additional technologies as barcodes, QR codes, or digital watermarking [12].

Our research results give solutions how the edge computing, Internet of Things and Big Data can improve the cloud effectiveness of smart city. A description of collective citizens' behavior modelling with support of the IoT and BD is submitted in Section 2. Then, the Internet of Things is characterized in Section 3. Next, Section 4 presents some studies under Big Data. Design principles of edge computing infrastructures for smart city are analyzed in Section 5. Finally, some conclusions are drawn in Section 6.

2 Related Work

Approaches for cloud computing are presented in many works [4, 10, 22]. Although, some new technologies are still developed in cities, the need for smarter cities is greater than till now. The concept of a smart city can be recognized as representing a crucible for invention. Besides, the smart city is an area for developing global integration. It is also a pattern answer for addressing the existing global issues related to environmental, societal, governance and economic areas [14]. There is a reasonable expectation that developing information and communication technologies such as cloud computing can be applied for integration smart city facilities and innovations. Cloud computing has been developed for many strategic e-government initiatives as some global government clouds. The edge of the cloud can improve some criteria of city system by moving processing of data for the sources of it.

Smart cities have to cope with some open important issues like growing population or traffic congestion [15]. These factors cause that home and public spaces are used in the more efficient way. Even currently, there is a huge issue with a deficiency of city resources like water and energy. So, an efficient management of resources is strongly required by automatic way. What is more, global warming and carbon emissions are some critical factors for future conditions in cities. Besides, the city infrastructure should be rapidly adjusted to the new ecosystems. In consequence, tighter city budgets should be prepared and controlled in more sophisticated way [31].

Some stats show that more than 50% of the world's population lives in cities [16]. It is predicted that 400 million people in China will move to cities in the nearest 15 years [18]. Population progress in cities is expected to increase about 90% [26]. Furthermore, global CO_2 emissions will grow of 80% as well as energy usage will increase of 75% [21]. A vision of smarter cities is related to better protection of natural environment and more efficient use of it [19]. Sustainable homes and buildings can be planned and efficient use of city resources can be developed. Citizens expect an efficient and sustainable transportation in livable city and also better urban planning [1].

To solve these open dilemmas some project are considered. Masdar City is a highly planned and specialized research project that is based on the high technology that incorporates a living environment [3]. A smart vision of Masdar City is based on environmental sustainability and efficiency. Additionally, an efficient use of resources is required. To avoid strong congestion an efficient and sustainable transportation can be developed. A road infrastructure is designed to be very friendly to pedestrians and cyclists.

Better urban planning is necessary to achieve a livable city. An important role plays sustainable buildings. For instance, the temperature in the streets can be controlled by building constructions. In Masdar, it is largely cooler than the nearby desert because of some wind towers. They can suck air from the high area, and then they can push a cool breeze through area on streets. An air is raised overhead the near land to create a minor cooling effect. In a design of buildings it is assumed they are clustered adjacent together to create protection from the sun for walkways. The main ideas behind the smart cities are widely described in [5, 17, 20]. Moreover, information about specific environments and applications are given in [23, 27, 28].

Some additional experiments with smart city that were carried out in Tsukuba Science City, Japan, permits to focus on some the most important fields of a smarter city: citizens, living, education, research, environment, governance, economy, healthcare, employment opportunities to a wide section of its residents, mobility, energy, building, infrastructure, and technology. Above key areas can be supported by smart human capital, social capital, and ICT infrastructure. The concept is dynamic like a process of becoming city more live able, resilient, and able to adjust quicker to current challenges.

3 Internet of Things

Next Generation Internet (NGI) and the Internet of Things are patterned on some technological trends that will reshape the internet over the next 10 years. Researchers should drive this technology revolution while contributing to making the future internet more human-centric. Increasingly these technological trends influence each other.

These technologies will allow users to access, process and deliver information in more natural, efficient and less intrusive ways, providing enhanced and personalized experiences. Advances in artificial intelligence are critical to turn information into knowledge and to embed autonomy and intelligence into a smart city and the connected devices.

Internet of Things and applications alter the way users, services and applications interact with the real world environment in a trusted way. The social networks, media and platforms transform the way we produce, consume and interact with content, services and objects, within and across users' groups and become the way our societies operate for communication, exchange, business, creation and knowledge acquisition. NGI will be multilingual and inclusive. Advances in language technologies help eliminate language barriers. NGI technologies also help to provide a new quality in digital learning as smart, open, and personalized learning solutions that are tailored to each individual's needs, competences and abilities.

Internet of Things consists of smart devices that are commonly used in daily life with using protocol IPv6. Technology G5 supports increasing the mobile communication rate up to 10 Gb/s. Things like smartphones, tablets, smartwatches, TV sets, monitoring sensors, medical devices, access control systems, and cars can be supported by quick access to the large databases. The 128-bit IP addressing system distinguishes about 3×10^{38} devices. A multicast addressing provides optimization for the distribution of city services [7].

Low Power Wireless Personal Area Networks (6LoWPAN) with the 2.4 GHz frequency is the IPv6 version that can be applied even to the smallest devices. In results, some low-power devices with limited processing capabilities are able to participate in the IoT. Low-power radio communication need wireless web connectivity at lower data rates 250 kbps for devices such as home automation, entertainment applications, office and factory environments. They use wireless sensors networks or the cellular networks. Currently, these devices are used to separate purposes and part of them can be developed to the common goals related to the smarter city. Besides, the protocol Routing Over Low power and Lossy networks (ROLL or RPL) determines routes for the networks with low power consuming and minimization energy losses. Also, the nano Internet Protocol (NanoIP) implements the efficient versions of the wireless TCP/IP algorithms with minimal latency and the memory capacity for addressing.

Security and privacy are supported by the protocol Datagram Transport Layer Security (DTLS) that inhibits message forgery for client/server communication. Spying and data restrictions in IoT are constrained. Because packets can be misplaced or reordered the DTLS introduces the transport layer security procedures on datagram transport.

Important roles play low cost air-interfaces, and systematic reduction of costs and sizes for the electronic chipsets. Some smart embedded things (devices or sensors) have capabilities to communicate and interact with the environment and other smart objects. They are smart, because they can act intelligently with an autonomous behavior. Smart things support an extended range of solutions based on cellular infrastructure and wireless sensor networks.

Figure 1 shows how the Internet of Things can support smart city applications. As far as we concern, education of citizens is the most crucial to achieve higher level of collective intelligence in a city. Well-educated society is able to adjust to new challenges quicker and it can be make decisions for much more difficult problems than dilemmas solved by ordinary people. Data are gathered from sensors connected via Internet of Things (Fig. 1). Big Data mining is required to use data for smart city applications. There are some levels of integration of sensors, data and applications. In consequence, we can expect new models of healthcare, social protection, transport, energy delivery, recycling, water management, and monitoring. To some extent, this process of change is similar to transformation in internet banking or e-commerce.

4 MapReduce for Smart City Infrastructures

MapReduce, first introduced by *Dean* and *Ghemawat*, can be described as a distributed and scalable solution for parallel processing and large data sets on clusters [12]. It has been gaining in popularity in the recent years as a one of the key concepts related to Big Data. There are many reasons *MapReduce* outstands other models and approaches. First of all, MapReduce was designed to be efficient in batch processing by using cheap, affordable commodity hardware instead of costly, high-end solutions. Such approach is financially rewarding and its usage can be considered not only by big market players. As in a large scale, hardware errors are something rather typical than exceptional, MapReduce is upfront designed to be fault-tolerant. Other significant advantage is its universality. MapReduce model does not assume anything about any problem domain, making it possible to use in variety of situations. Nowadays there are many implementations of MapReduce model in the market, some of them commercial with guaranteed support. One of the most popular is the open-source one offered by the Apache Hadoop project [2].

MapReduce requires two custom functions to be implemented by its user. These functions are map and reduce and are usually specific to a particular domain. The first one, map takes a key, value pair as an input, and performs computation to produce set of different intermediate key, value pairs. The intermediate keys are not expected to be unique. The second function, reduce is executed after the map function as it takes map output as its input. The reduce function is usually responsible for merging of input values to a smaller set. It is therefore possible to define the Map and Reduce as:

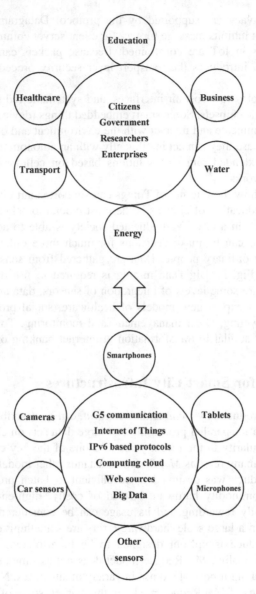

Fig. 1. Internet of Things for supporting some smart city applications.

$$\text{map}\,(k1, v1) \rightarrow \text{list}(k2, v2)$$
$$\text{reduce}\,(k2, \text{list}(v2)) \rightarrow \text{list}(v2)$$

There are four major execution phases in the MapReduce model. Let the text with random words be considered. The goal of an algorithm is to count the number of occurrences for every word. In the first phase, the input is split, and in the second phase each of the data splits is processed by the Map function in parallel (Fig. 2). The particular word e.g. *Cat* has the key and the '1' is the arbitrarily chosen value. In the third phase, all intermediate pairs produced in the second phase, are sorted and grouped by the key. In the reducing phase, the reduce function receives the key and the corresponding values as an input. In this case, the target of the reduce function is to sum the values and return the number of word occurrences to the output [24].

Because of the new technology needs, it is highly probable that IoT and Smart City markets will constantly grow and become one of the main producers of data. It is believed that there will have been 50 billion devices connected to the Internet by the year 2020 [6, 8]. Many of them could belong the Smart Cities infrastructure producing huge amount of valuable data, which would need to be processed in a fast and efficient manner. MapReduce is especially useful in processing massive historical data but may not be the optimal solution for real-time processing. In the context of Smart City, it may be used to answer variety of questions. For example, car monitoring by RFID tags are the smart way to detect traffic issues. Besides, it can support planning the road infrastructure accordingly. Other examples might be monitoring energy consumption in houses or people density in the means of public transportation.

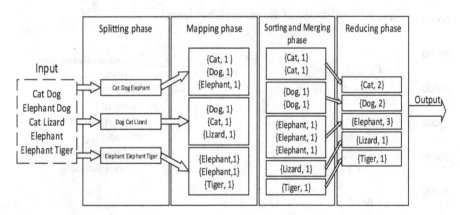

Fig. 2. MapReduce execution flow illustrated with the case of counting the number of occurrences of each word.

An interesting example of such Big Data analytics was the project made by IBM in the city of Da Nang in Vietnam [12]. The goal was to introduce a traffic management system as a response to a fast growing population of the city. With the data collected from many sources including buses and roads, this system helped to reduce traffic congestion by optimizing traffic lights synchronization. A similar project took place in Dublin, Ireland [12]. The data collected form Bus System (e.g. GPS data), CCTV monitoring system, weather monitoring system and others helped to improve public bus transportation services and reduce traffic congestions. All of these were achieved without any modification in city's historic infrastructure.

5 Design Principles of Edge Computing for Smart City

Intelligent agents based on genetic programming (*AGPs*) can optimize an edge resource management for big data queries [4]. Especially, they have been dedicated to global optimization of edge software agents in the city cloud. *AGP* uses the principle of selection, crossover and mutation to obtain a population of programs applied as a scheduler for efficient using Big Data by the edge. This scheduler optimizes some criteria related to load balancing and send a compromise solution to agents based on harmony search (*AHSs*) [5, 30].

AHS allocated to the platform *Windows 10/Intel i7* can find the compromise configuration of the computing cloud for at most 15 nodes, 50 middle-layer cloud agents and 15 virtual machines. Figure 3 shows an evaluation of the compromise configuration for the laboratory smart cloud that was found by *AHS1* [9, 11]. In this instance, workload is characterized by two criteria [5]. The first one is the CPU workload of the bottleneck computer (denoted as $\hat{Z}_{max}$), and the second one is the communication workload of the bottleneck server $(\tilde{Z}_{max})$.

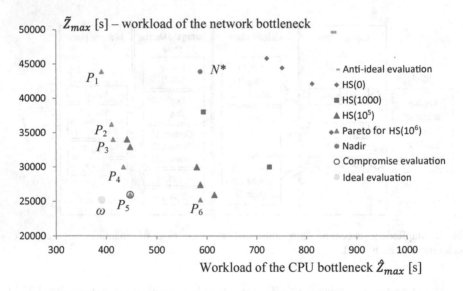

Fig. 3. The evaluation P_5 of compromise configuration found by *AHS1*.

The compromise configuration found by *AHS1* is specified in Table 1. The data distribution *W*-agent with number 5 as well as two edge *S*-agents (No. 6 and 27) should be moved to the node No. 1, where the third alternative of the virtual platform *VP* (*BizServer* E5-2660 v2) is assigned. Agent *AHS1* publishes this specification in the common global repository of cloud and the other agents can read it to make decision related to moving to some recommended nodes. However, reconfiguration of resource requires a bit of time. So, the edge agent reads the state of resources in the given cloud node, and then it makes decision whether to go to that node or not.

Table 1. A specification of a compromise configuration from AHS1.

Node i	1	2	3	14	5	6	7	8	9	10	11	12	13	14
VP j	3	8	3	9	8	9	8	3	9	3	3	3	3	3
No. W	5		11	4	9		2, 13	10		1, 8	6, 15	3, 7	14	12
No. S	6, 27	13, 23, 24, 30	7, 26	14, 21, 28	3, 15, 25	4, 5, 11, 22	19	2	1, 16, 18, 20	9	10	29	12, 17	8

On the other hand, the *AGP* cooperates with several *AHSs*. It takes into account their recommendation for resource using by middleware agents. Moreover, the *AGP* optimizes the resource usage for the whole grid starting from the configuration obtained by set of *AHSs* and trying to improve it by multi-criteria differential evolution.

6 Concluding Remarks and Future Work

Some intelligent agents in the edge computing can significantly support the efficiency of the proposed approach for smart city clouds. Multi-objective differential evolution multi-criteria genetic programming as relatively new paradigms of artificial intelligence can be used for finding Pareto-optimal configuration of the edge computing, too. These smart agents can cooperate with harmony search agents to solve NP-hard optimization problem of edge resources.

The major contributions of this paper are:

- An introduction a concept of transmission Big Data from sensors by the Internet of Things to the edge of the cloud;
- A development edge computing for smart city cloud;
- A presentation some outcomes from laboratory cloud simulations.

Our future works will focus on testing the other metaheuristics to find the compromise configurations for new criteria. Besides, quantum-inspired algorithms can be considered to support big data, too [3].

References

1. Altameem, T., Amoon, M.: An agent-based approach for dynamic adjustment of scheduled jobs in computational grids. J. Comput. Syst. Sci. Int. **49**(5), 765–772 (2010)
2. Apache Hadoop. http://hadoop.apache.org/. Accessed 17 April 2019
3. Ayed, B., Halima, A.B., Alimi, A.M.: Big data analytics for logistics and transportation. In: 4th International Conference on Advanced Logistics and Transport (ICALT), pp. 311–316. IEEE (2015)
4. Balicki, J.: Negative selection with ranking procedure in tabu-based multi-criterion evolutionary algorithm for task assignment. In: Alexandrov, V.N., van Albada, G.D., Sloot, P.M.A., Dongarra, J. (eds.) ICCS 2006. LNCS, vol. 3993, pp. 863–870. Springer, Heidelberg (2006). https://doi.org/10.1007/11758532_112

5. Balicki, J.: An adaptive quantum–based multiobjective evolutionary algorithm for efficient task assignment in distributed systems. In: Mastorakis, N., et al. (eds.) Recent Advances in Computer Engineering 2009, 13th International Conference on Computers, Rhodes, Greece, pp. 417–422. WSEAS, Athens (2009)
6. Balicki, J., Kitowski, Z.: Multicriteria evolutionary algorithm with tabu search for task assignment. In: Zitzler, E., Thiele, L., Deb, K., Coello Coello, C.A., Corne, D. (eds.) EMO 2001. LNCS, vol. 1993, pp. 373–384. Springer, Heidelberg (2001). https://doi.org/10.1007/3-540-44719-9_26
7. Balicki, J., Korłub, W., Szymanski, J., Zakidalski, M.: Big data paradigm developed in volunteer grid system with genetic programming scheduler. In: Rutkowski, L., Korytkowski, M., Scherer, R., Tadeusiewicz, R., Zadeh, L.A., Zurada, J.M. (eds.) ICAISC 2014. LNCS (LNAI), vol. 8467, pp. 771–782. Springer, Cham (2014). https://doi.org/10.1007/978-3-319-07173-2_66
8. Balicki, J., Korlub, W., Krawczyk, H., et al.: Genetic programming with negative selection for volunteer computing system optimization. In: Paja, W.A., Wilamowski, B.M. (eds.) Human System Interactions 2013, Gdańsk, Poland, pp. 271–278 (2013)
9. BOINC. http://boinc.berkeley.edu/. Accessed 17 April 2019
10. Cao, L., Gorodetsky, V., Mitkas, P.A.: Agent mining: the synergy of agents and data mining. IEEE Intell. Syst. **24**(3), 64–72 (2009)
11. Comcute grid. http://comcute.eti.pg.gda.pl/. Accessed 17 April 2019
12. Dean, J., Ghemawat, S.: MapReduce: simplified data processing on large clusters. Commun. ACM **51**(1), 1–13 (2008)
13. Galligan, S.D., O'Keeffe, J.: Big Data Helps City of Dublin Improves its Public Bus Transportation Network and Reduce Congestion. IBM Press (2013)
14. Guojun, L., Ming, Z., Fei, Y.: Large–scale social network analysis based on MapReduce. In: International Proceedings on Computational Aspects of Social Networks, pp. 487–490 (2010)
15. Kang, J., Sim, K.M.: A multiagent brokering protocol for supporting Grid resource discovery. Appl. Intell. **37**(4), 527–542 (2012)
16. Li, H.X., Chosler, R.: Application of multilayered multi–agent data mining architecture to bank domain. In: International Proceedings on Wireless Communications and Mobile Computing, pp. 6721–6724 (2007)
17. Mardani, S., Akbari, M.K., Sharifian, S.: Fraud detection in process aware information systems using MapReduce. In: International Proceedings on Information and Knowledge Technology, pp. 88–91 (2014)
18. Marz, N., Warren, J.: Big Data – Principles and Best Practices of Scalable Realtime Data Systems. Manning, Shelter Island (2014)
19. O'Leary, D.E.: Artificial intelligence and big data. IEEE Intell. Syst. **28**(2), 96–99 (2013)
20. Ostrowski, D.A.: MapReduce design patterns for social networking analysis. In: International Proceedings on Semantic Computing, pp. 316–319 (2014)
21. Qiu, X., et al.: Using MapReduce technologies in bioinformatics and medical informatics. In: International Proceedings on High Performance Computing, Networking, Storage and Analysis, Portland (2009)
22. Reed, D.A., Gannon, D.B., Larus, J.R.: Imagining the future: thoughts on computing. IEEE Comput. **45**(1), 25–30 (2012)
23. Shibata, T., Choi, S., Taura, K.: File–access patterns of data-intensive workflow applications. In: International Proceedings on Cluster, Cloud and Grid Computing, pp. 522–525. IEEE/ACM (2010)
24. Shvachko, K., et al.: The Hadoop distributed file system. In: MSST, pp. 1–10 (2010)

25. Snijders, C., Matzat, U., Reips, U.-D.: 'Big Data': big gaps of knowledge in the field of internet. Int. J. Internet Sci. 7(1), 1–5 (2012)
26. Twardowski, B., Ryzko, D.: Multi-agent architecture for real–time big data processing. In: International Proceedings on Web Intelligence and Intelligent Agent Technologies, vol. 3, pp. 333–337 (2014)
27. Vavilapalli, V.K.: Apache Hadoop YARN: yet another resource negotiator. In: International Proceedings on Cloud Computing, New York, USA, pp. 5:1–5:16 (2013)
28. Verbrugge, T., Dunin-Kęplicz, B.: Teamwork in Multi–agent Systems. A Formal Approach. Wiley, New York (2010)
29. Viegas, J.: Big data and transport. International Transport Forum (2013)
30. Węglarz, J., Błażewicz, J., Kovalyov, M.: Preemptable malleable task scheduling problem. IEEE Trans. Comput. 55(4), 486–490 (2006)
31. Zhou, D., et al.: Multi–agent distributed data mining model based on algorithm analysis and task prediction. In: International Proceedings on Information Engineering and Computer Science, pp. 1–4 (2010)

Some Artificial Intelligence Driven Algorithms For Mobile Edge Computing in Smart City

Jerzy Balicki[1]([✉]) [iD], Piotr Dryja[2] [iD], and Marcin Zakidalski[2]

[1] Faculty of Mathematics and Information Science,
Warsaw University of Technology, Koszykowa St. 75, 00-662 Warsaw, Poland
j.balicki@mini.pw.edu.pl
[2] Faculty of Telecommunications, Electronics and Informatics,
Gdańsk University of Technology, Narutowicza St. 11/12,
80-233 Gdańsk, Poland
piodryja@pg.gda.pl, mzakidalski@gmail.com

Abstract. Smart mobile devices can share computing workload with the computer cloud that is important when artificial intelligence tools support computer systems in a smart city. This concept brings computing on the edge of the cloud, closer to citizens and it can shorten latency. Edge computing removes a crucial drawback of the smart city computing because city services are usually far away from citizens, physically. Besides, we introduced a neuro-evolution approach for supporting smart infrastructures. Solutions related to using Tweeter's blogs by smart city apps are presented, too. Finally, the design principles of differential evolution for smart city are analyzed.

Keywords: Artificial intelligence · Edge computing · Smart city

1 Introduction

Artificial Intelligence (AI) is still fascinating; its provides some very efficient algorithms like metaheuristics or deep learning algorithms that produce the high quality solutions for NP-hard optimization problems or for classifications based on Big Data (BD) streams. Besides, the mobile devices can perform the selected AI algorithms combining an aggregation of data from sensors in real time and using low-energy consuming processors to achieve results without the extensive interactions with the cloud. This feature seems to be extremely useful for smart city systems.

In smart city, nanny applications and Big Data files are downloaded by several mobile phones to support city services. But, it would be too much burden to them because of limited processing power and memory. So, we propose to use edge servers that are physically local to citizens. Videoconferences or augmented reality can be hosted at the edge of the network connected a city cloud with the sensors and mobile devices. Moreover, the large application can be split on some modules performed both at the device and at the cloud. In the nearest future, the high transmission capacity offered by the communication 5G can support a lot of distributed systems including edge computing at the smart city clouds.

K. Saeed et al. (Eds.): CISIM 2019, LNCS 11703, pp. 110–119, 2019.
https://doi.org/10.1007/978-3-030-28957-7_10

The Internet of Things (IoT) was first offered for a development of a modern strategic industry by Auto-ID Center in 1999 [29]. IoT and some AI-driven algorithms permit on knowledge mining about some phenomena and features of city dynamics. In results, it is possible to better understanding some aspects of human behaviors, prevent some crisis situations or prepare an efficient annual expenditure budget to satisfy a community expectation. Besides, some disadvantages of the city infrastructure can be identified and then fixed [13]. Also, an urban plan can be optimized and the states of building can be better monitored.

Experiments with smart city systems like *SmartSantander* [29], *FixMyStreet* [25], and *Tsukuba Science City* [13] confirmed that we can focus on some the most important fields related to citizens, living, and education. Besides research, environment, and governance are some important aspects of the smart city model. Some authors indicate economy, healthcare, and employment opportunities as areas for development by new technologies. Mobility, energy management, infrastructure, and technology play crucial roles in the dynamic and smart city. Above key areas can be supported by smart human capital and social capital.

To order many important issues in this paper, the artificial neural networks for edge computing at smart city are described in Sect. 2. Then, a neuro-evolution approach is characterized in Sect. 3. Next, Sect. 4 presents some studies under Tweeter's blogs for smart city apps. The design principles of a differential evolution for the smart city are analyzed in Sect. 5. Finally, some findings are presented in Sect. 6.

2 Artificial Neural Networks for Smart City Applications

A rapid development of an artificial intelligence paradigm has been observed because of a discovery of deep learning from last decade. Deep learning belongs to the most exciting and efficient approaches for designing artificial neural networks (ANNs). Achievements and approaches related to development artificial neural networks for supporting mobile devices regarding edge computing are presented in [4, 10, 22]. Besides, ANNs and the Internet of Things open some new challenges for data analysis. One of such challenge is the need and the necessity for analyzing real-time and massive amount of data. At smart city, areas which could be improved by machine learning approaches are traffic issues, waste management, energy supply and demand governance. For instance, smart bins can use sensors indicating when to pick them up. ANNs are applied for the improvement of a waste segregation at the home sources. Regarding the traffic solutions, such tasks like the smart parking management, a time control of road lights, and the alternative road recommendations are reinforced by ANNs.

Traffic solutions could be also improved by leveraging available data. Some applications were done in field of estimating road congestion using the data about mobile phone network's load. In this domain, pre-trained ANN models, could be used as the fast and reliable way to notice the unusual situations like traffic jams. The other example is the analysis of RFID tags'. This smart technology is commonly used to mark objects in stores and warehouses. The trend in current technology development might result in such tags being placed to any everyday object.

Artificial neural networks can be adapted to analyze RFID tags [24]. The target of this application is to create the network that can serve as a helper during navigation in warehouse and looking for the selected RFID tag. This application might be enhanced and applied in the other domain like car navigation in a parking, or looking for parts in the mechanical store.

Some researchers also deliberate about possible architecture of IoT. Machine learning algorithms might be used into ubiquitous IoT as specific unit of it. It might as well serve as an output system and, simultaneously as a data source for other systems [32]. In [44] an approach to create such autonomous systems is presented. It might become the component of IoT setting.

Besides, artificial neural networks are developed as the classification and prediction applications for detecting the flood attack by computer viruses. The robust intruder detection systems are applied for multi-hop wireless mesh networks. Those networks are integrated with other networks via the special gateways that provide a common interface to the system. These gateways are resistant against malicious attacks. One of the attack is the distributed denial of service attack (DDOS), known also as a distributed flood attack. The efficient ANN-driven application should use the gateways. It is a feed forward network that is trained by the back propagation algorithm. The aim of this network is to recognize the pattern of the network traffic, which might be caused by the ongoing flood attack.

An ubiquity of smart devices brings another challenge – it is expected that all devices like fridges, watches, and cars would have their own IP addresses. Because of enormous amount of data produced by the machines, building some data analytical solutions by a standard approach are not efficient or even possible. Machine learning algorithms, including ANNs, are efficient in many applications. There are various directions in research related to ANNs and the Internet of Things what force the intensive progress in the Industry 4.0.

3 Agents and Neuro-Evolution Approach for Smart City

By definition [32], smart city is considered as an "environment which involves many technologies and multiple agents collecting data from sensors scattered around the whole city". Unfortunately, the linear increase in the number of sensors and agents imposes square growth in potential relations between those entities. Undoubtedly, much of this communication overhead might be addressed by the traditional measures such as choosing the centralized communication switch or performing any other form of centralized synchronization. When additionally the variety of potential local disturbances of the system is considered, the centralized approach to the idea of smart city seems to be reaching its maximal capacity.

Another approach to the idea of smart city would transfer more autonomy to agents. To retain some degree of responsiveness to the changing environmental conditions, agents would be equipped with a learning capability. The unwritten assumption of this approach is that the degree of freedom transferred to agents would not impose any kind of threat to the citizens of smart city (Fig. 1).

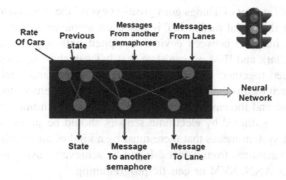

Fig. 1. The sensor – actuator – forward communication for the experiment with the JAnEAT framework

A solution JAnEAT for the decentralized traffic control was presented in [32]. Although this solution did not reach far beyond preliminary laboratory tests, this idea seems to be an extreme importance. The JADE framework is combined with the NEAT neuro-evolutionary learning algorithm. While the first component supplies the system with the necessary messaging infrastructure, the second one is responsible for determining the behavior of agents controlling the traffic lights. The first experiment included completely decentralized traffic control. The second one focused on wider usage of sensors (crossings, lanes, streets) and it included limited communication between adjacent agents.

The idea of the neuro-evolutionary traffic control is under further development in [33]. In this case, agents are no longer homogeneous. They are divided into classes (adaptive agents, observer agents). Main agents are responsible for information routing in the IoT network (including device detection). Adaptive agents performs neuro-evolutionary computations – effectively meaning preparing new versions of observer agents. Observer agents are responsible for changing lights in particular road intersections. Their effectiveness is evaluated against the specified fitness function.

This approach is effective even in different problem domains. A solution to the problem of decaying fruits is proposed in [34]. The set of sensors retrieves information concerning the conditions in which fruits are stored. The other sensors are calibrated to spot out symptoms of early decay of fruits. Those pieces of information combined conclude an input to a neuro-evolutionary algorithm which adjusts not only the size of fruit deliveries but also warns users of a pre-decay situation in particular fruit storage facilities.

4   Tweeter's Blogs for Smart City Apps

Twitter has already proved its application in the support of daily human interaction. To share information with greater audience we can use Twitter as a strong and easy tool. Range of Twitter together with the number of about 300 million users almost guarantees that our message can reach addressees [13].

But the idea of Internet of Things goes greatly beyond the information acquired and broadcasted using the social media. IoT is based on autonomous interaction not only between humans, but also between devices equipped with appropriate sensors. Following Stanford-Clark and IBM we can state that IoT can show up its power when the 3 'I's are combined together: Instrumented, Interconnected, and Intelligent [28]. An instrumented system means that devices should have special sensors to collect the data based on their state and the environment surrounding them. An interconnected system means that the data gathered by electronic sensors should be joined together. At the end, an intelligent system means that there must be a kind of an intelligent analysis on the top of the data acquired from devices. It can be achievable using machine learning techniques such as ANN, SVM or genetic programming.

Twitter is a great tool to support 'Interconnected' feature of Internet of Things idea because it becomes more widely used as a platform to exchange information, not only between humans but also between devices. According to [13], the first attempts to use Twitter as mean to post data generated by devices, are dated back to 2006. In that year, the user account was created for the plant sensors allowing posting a tweet when water is needed. Besides, a drone controlled in a city exclusively by tweets was proposed in 2014 [8].

But the usage of Twitter in the area of IoT is not limited to the examples presented above. It was proved, that Twitter can be used also in the systems which support general safety of society. As a response for the water flood which took place in the UK in 2013, the authorities decided to build a reliable system of early warning. As a part of that system, about 3000 sensors installed in the rivers send the river's level information via Twitter accounts. Thanks to that, people can track the river level in their nearest area [39].

Social media can protect against crisis situations in smart city. Department of Communications in Roanoke, Virginia, U.S. launched a social media, when a havy snowstorm hit in the winter of 2014. Citizens used the city's page to get information about snow removal. Besides, photos were viewed by more than 400,000 citizens. Social media pages can be connected to all city departments via an integration icon, now. News streams from Facebook and Twitter are visible by citizens as well as some view posts from a selected agency. It is permit to browse and see the city's videos and news releases via some social media platforms, such as Instagram and Flickr. Getting and sharing information from all the city's departments is much easier. Social Media Center works in more effective way than a phone hotline 311 regarding some criteria related to query, complain or ask for help. Another advantage is to give an economic boost in the form of increased tourism traffic. Publicity generated by photos and Facebook advertising attract tourists that give on average 450 additional "likes" every month [3].

To deal with some new tasks caused by social media, a city has announced a set of policies, which contain obeying the law and nonparticipation in creation some contentious remarks. An administrator of social media in a city department can cooperate with a consultant to improve many web pages, point out the pros and cons of them, and propose references for upcoming posts. Furthermore, some regular classes are carried out to review the effectiveness of pages, to deliver more training, and to discover more examples of new choices and tools. These conferences can also play a role of some brainstorming sessions. The main drawback of the social media approach is the high amount of a required effort with the constant entering of data. High-profile departments, such as communications, recreation, parks or police, usually post on a daily, and the others post less repeatedly.

From Roanoke case study, we can observe that social media can support a smart city as a model of metropolis, which integrates a number the information systems with the use of the Internet of Things to efficient management of urban resources. Smart city stems from the fact that several modern cities, especially the largest ones require overcoming crises in various areas, which mainly interfere.

5 Differential Evolution in Smart Cities

Metaheuristics are important part of artificial intelligence because one algorithm can be used for solving many different problems. Ken Price in 1996 invented the *differential evolution* (DA) to solve the *Chebychev Polynomial* fitting problem. From this days to now, the new metaheuristic was applied wildly. The advantages of *DA* are: doughty stabilization for non-convex optimization problem, multi-modal and non-linear functions, rapid convergence speed, good multi-variable solving function, easy programming and simple operations [30]. This algorithm is similar to the overall structure of the genetic algorithm. *DA* in mutation uses a perturbation of two members as the vector. A new vector is obtained by adding to third member previous vector. At the crossover operation, the algorithm with certain rules mixes the new vector with the pre-defined parameters to produce test vectors. At the next step, the test vector of function is compared to the target function. If the test vector is less than target function, the test vector instead of the target is in the next generation. The same number of competitors in next generation is produce by final choice of the operation on all members of the population [30].

In smart city, communication using radio signal play important role. Reducing the received power and increase received data error rate is the main problem when designing wireless communication systems in environment with tall structure like buildings. In the design process, it is necessary to achieve good directivity by varying different structures of the antenna arrays. *SBR/Image* method can be used to calculate path loss and apply *DA* to find the optimal excitation voltages by minimization the path loss. It is investigated three different shapes of antenna the L shape, the Y shape and the circular shape. The test simulation was preform on Yinzhuan road in New Taipei city [12].

Figure 2 shows positions of the buildings in a city area. The height of each in alphabetical order are 45, 50, 30, 35, 20 and 30 m, the thickness of the wall in each building is 30 cm. The transmitting investigated antennas array are put on the top building E. In the first case receiver Rx1 is chosen at (−55, 85) [m] and in second case they set receiver Rx2 at (−95, 85) [m]. Tables 1 and 2 compare three cases: the first case is an outcome without algorithm, the second case presents the solution obtained by *GA* algorithm and the third alternatives is related to *DE* algorithm. The results show that *DE* algorithm gives the best minimization of cost function of all approach [31].

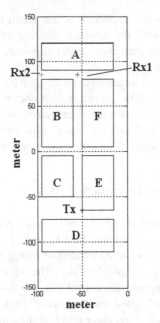

Fig. 2. The simplified layout geometry for simulation

Table 1. Comparison of path loss with and without algorithm in dB (the first case) [12]

Algorithm	Antenna arrays		
	L shape	Y shape	Circular shape
Without algorithm	80.0	77.7	83.3
GA	77.8	69.5	81.3
DE	76.2	68.6	79.8

Table 2. Comparison of path loss with and without algorithm in dB (the second case) [12]

Algorithm	Antenna arrays		
	L shape	Y shape	Circular shape
Without algorithm	104.8	109.9	108.2
GA	97.8	103.9	105.1
DE	97.0	102.9	105.0

6   Concluding Remarks and Future Work

Smart devices can share computing workload with the computer cloud that permits development artificial intelligence in a smart city. Some artificial neural networks and neuro-evolution algorithms can be applied for supporting some smart city tasks. Moreover, data from Tweeter's blogs can be processed by smart city apps. Differential evolution can be used for an efficient communication in smart city. These concepts bring computing on the edge of the cloud, closer to citizens, what can shorten latency and decreases communication rate.

Our future works will focus on testing the different artificial intelligence algorithms for smart city infrastructures.

References

1. Ayed, B., Halima, A.B., Alimi, A.M.: Big data analytics for logistics and transportation. In: 4th International Conference on Advanced Logistics and Transport (ICALT), pp. 311–316. IEEE (2015)
2. Balicki, J.: Negative selection with ranking procedure in tabu-based multi-criterion evolutionary algorithm for task assignment. In: Alexandrov, V.N., van Albada, G.D., Sloot, P.M.A., Dongarra, J. (eds.) ICCS 2006. LNCS, vol. 3993, pp. 863–870. Springer, Heidelberg (2006). https://doi.org/10.1007/11758532_112
3. Balicki, J.: An adaptive quantum-based multiobjective evolutionary algorithm for efficient task assignment in distributed systems. In: Mastorakis, N., et al. (eds.) Recent Advances in Computer Engineering 2009, pp. 417–422. WSEAS, Athens (2009). 13th International Conference on Computers
4. Balicki, J., Kitowski, Z.: Multicriteria evolutionary algorithm with tabu search for task assignment. In: Zitzler, E., Thiele, L., Deb, K., Coello Coello, C.A., Corne, D. (eds.) EMO 2001. LNCS, vol. 1993, pp. 373–384. Springer, Heidelberg (2001). https://doi.org/10.1007/3-540-44719-9_26
5. Balicki, J., Korłub, W., Szymanski, J., Zakidalski, M.: Big data paradigm developed in volunteer grid system with genetic programming scheduler. In: Rutkowski, L., Korytkowski, M., Scherer, R., Tadeusiewicz, R., Zadeh, L.A., Zurada, J.M. (eds.) ICAISC 2014. LNCS (LNAI), vol. 8467, pp. 771–782. Springer, Cham (2014). https://doi.org/10.1007/978-3-319-07173-2_66
6. Balicki, J., Korlub, W., Krawczyk, H., et al.: Genetic programming with negative selection for volunteer computing system optimization. In: Paja, W.A., Wilamowski, B.M.: Human System Interactions 2013, Gdańsk, Poland, pp. 271–278 (2013)
7. Banerjee, S., Agarwal, N.: Analyzing collective behavior from blogs using swarm intelligence. Knowl. Inf. Syst. 33(3), 523–547 (2012)
8. Batty, M., et al.: Smart cities of the future. Eur. Phys. J. 214(1), 481–518 (2012)
9. Bollen, J., Mao, H., Zeng, X.: Twitter mood predicts the stock market. J. Comput. Sci. 2(1), 1–8 (2011)
10. Cao, L., Gorodetsky, V., Mitkas, P.A.: Agent mining: the synergy of agents and data mining. IEEE Intell. Syst. 24(3), 64–72 (2009)
11. Caragliu, A., Del Bo, C., Nijkamp P.: Smart cities in Europe. Series Research Memoranda 0048. VU University Amsterdam, Faculty of Economics, Business Administration and Econometrics (2009)
12. Clohessy, T., Acton, T., Morgan L.: Smart City as a Service (SCaaS): a future roadmap for e–government smart city cloud computing initiatives. In: 7th International Proceedings on Utility and Cloud Computing, pp. 836 – 841. IEEE/ACM (2014)
13. Comcute grid. http://comcute.eti.pg.gda.pl/. Accessed 17 Apr 2019
14. Curtis, S.: How Twitter will power the Internet of Things. http://www.telegraph.co.uk/technology/twitter/11181609/How-Twitter-will-power-the-Internet-of-Things.html. Accessed 17 Apr 2019

15. Dean, J., Ghemawat, S.: MapReduce: simplified data processing on large clusters. Commun. ACM **51**(1), 1–13 (2008)
16. FixMyStreet Project. https://www.mysociety.org/projects/. Accessed 17 Apr 2019
17. Galligan, S.D., O'Keeffe, J.: Big data helps city of dublin improves its public bus transportation network and reduce congestion. IBM Press (2013)
18. Li, G.-Y., Liu, M.-G.: The Summary of differential evolution algorithm and its improvements. In: 3rd International Proceedings on Advanced Computer Theory and Engineering (iCACTE), pp 153–156 (2010)
19. Gea, T., Paradells, J., Lamarca, M., Roldan, D.: Smart cities as an application of internet of things: experiences and lessons learnt in Barcelona. In: 7th International Proceedings on Innovative Mobile and Internet Services in Ubiquitous Computing, pp. 552–557 (2013)
20. Liu, G., Zhang, M., Yan, F.: Large-scale social network analysis based on MapReduce. In: International Proceedings on Computational Aspects of Social Networks, pp. 487–490 (2010)
21. Kanter, R., Litow, S.: Informed and interconnected: a manifesto for smarter cities. Harvard Business School, Working Knowledge (2009). https://hbswk.hbs.edu/item/informed-and-interconnected-a-manifesto-for-smarter-cities. Accessed 17 Apr 2019
22. Komninos, N., Pallot, M., Schaffers, H.: Special issue on smart cities and the future internet in Europe. J. Knowl. Econ. **4**, 1–134 (2013)
23. Leppänen, T., Riekki, J., Liu, M., Harjula, E., Ojala, T.: Mobile agents-based smart objects for the internet of things. In: Fortino, G., Trunfio, P. (eds.) Internet of Things Based on Smart Objects. IT, pp. 29–48. Springer, Cham (2014). https://doi.org/10.1007/978-3-319-00491-4_2
24. Li, H.X., Chosler, R.: Application of multilayered multi-agent data mining architecture to bank domain. In: International Proceedings on Wireless Communications and Mobile Computing, pp. 6721–6724 (2007)
25. Macmanus, R.: The Tweeting House: Twitter + Internet of Things. http://readwrite.com/2009/07/20/the_tweeting_house_twitter_internet_of_things. Accessed 17 Apr 2019
26. Marz, N., Warren, J.: Big Data – Principles and Best Practices of Scalable Realtime Data Systems. Manning, Shelter Island (2014)
27. Nam, T., Pardo, T.A.: Conceptualizing smart city with dimensions of technology, people, and institutions. In: 12th International Proceedings on Digital Government Innovation in Challenging Times, pp. 282–291 (2011)
28. Naphade, M., Banavar, G., Harrison, C., Paraszczak, J., Morris, R.: Smarter cities and their innovation challenges. Computer **44**(6), 32–39 (2011)
29. Ning, H., Wang, Z.: Future internet of things architecture: like mankind neural system or social organization framework. IEEE Commun. Lett. **15**(4), 461–463 (2011)
30. O'Leary, D.E.: Artificial intelligence and big data. IEEE Intell. Syst. **28**(2), 96–99 (2013)
31. Ostrowski, D.A.: MapReduce design patterns for social networking analysis. In: International Proceedings on Semantic Computing, pp. 316–319 (2014)
32. Qiu, X., et al.: Using MapReduce technologies in bioinformatics and medical informatics. In: International Proceedings on High Performance Computing, Networking, Storage and Analysis, Portland (2009)
33. Reed, D.A., Gannon, D.B., Larus, J.R.: Imagining the future: thoughts on computing. IEEE Comput. **45**(1), 25–30 (2012)
34. Schaffers, H., Komninos, N., Pallot, M.: Smart cities as innovation ecosystems sustained by the future internet. Fireball White Paper (2012)
35. Smartsantander. Future Internet Research & Experimentation. http://www.smartsantander.eu/. Accessed 17 Apr 2019
36. Snijders, C., Matzat, U., Reips, U.-D.: 'Big Data': big gaps of knowledge in the field of internet. Int. J. Internet Sci. **7**(1), 1–5 (2012)

37. Twardowski, B., Ryzko, D.: Multi–agent architecture for real–time big data processing. In: International Proceedings on Web Intelligence and Intelligent Agent Technologies, vol. 3, pp. 333–337 (2014)
38. Twitter. https://about.twitter.com/company. Accessed 17 Apr 2019
39. Viegas, J.: Big data and transport. International Transport Forum (2013)
40. Węglarz, J., Błażewicz, J., Kovalyov, M.: Preemptable malleable task scheduling problem. IEEE Trans. Comput. **55**(4), 486–490 (2006)

Geographic Location Based Dynamic and Opportunistic RPL for Distributed Networks

Manali Chakraborty[✉], Alvise Spano, and Agostino Cortesi

Università Ca' Foscari, Via Torino, 153, 30172 Venezia, VE, Italy
{manali.chakraborty,alvise.spano,cortesi}@unive.it

Abstract. RPL or Routing Protocol for Low power and Lossy Networks (LLNs) is considered the most suited routing technology for IPV6. However, with the rapid advancements in networking and the paradigm shift towards IoT, RPL is facing some performance issues due to scalability, resource constraints and mobility. We propose a Geographic location-based Dynamic Opportunistic routing protocol (GDO-RPL) for point-to-point communication, whose algorithm has been extensively simulated within the Contiki Cooja environment. As a testbed for the proposed solution, we evaluated the scenario of an innovative 3D printing system that uses IIoT (Industrial Internet of Things) technologies, such as sensors installed within artifacts collecting data during the lifetime of the object in the environmental context for which it is intended.

Keywords: IoT · RPL · Additive manufacturing ·
Opportunistic routing · Distributed networks

1 Introduction

Along with the rapid advancement of Internet of Things (IoT), IPv6 becomes an obvious choice for implementing distributed networks. We consider in particular for underlying routing protocol, RPL, which is a distance-vector routing protocol and based on IPv6 for Low-power and Lossy Networks (LLNs). It was designed considering the requirements specified in RFC 5826 [2], RFC 5673 [3], RFC 5548 [4] and RFC 5867 [5].

This LLNs have the following specific characteristics [1]:

- it consists of a group of constrained nodes, which have limited processing and storage capabilities;
- nodes are connected via lossy links, typically supporting only low data rates, that are usually unstable with relatively low packet delivery rates;
- the traffic patterns are not simply point-to-point, but in many cases point-to-multipoint or multipoint-to-point;
- furthermore, such networks may potentially comprise up to thousands of nodes.

© Springer Nature Switzerland AG 2019
K. Saeed et al. (Eds.): CISIM 2019, LNCS 11703, pp. 120–131, 2019.
https://doi.org/10.1007/978-3-030-28957-7_11

1.1   Motivation

As outlined by some recent works on RPL discussed in Sect. 2, even though RPL is still recognised as the most suitable routing protocol for IoT and IPv6 at the moment, it still has some flaws, among which:

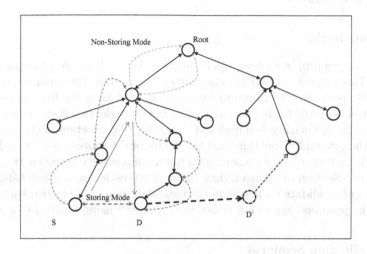

Fig. 1. Overhead in RPL route selection process.

1. In P2P communication, storing mode, a data packet travel upwards until a common ancestor and then return downwards to the destination, and in non-storing mode, it goes directly to the root and then travel downwards. This strategy creates congestion close to the root and greatly increases overhead and latency. In Fig. 1, we can see the overhead for both storing and non storing mode for P2P communication between S and D.
2. Another major concern for RPL is mobility. A mobile node can join any existing DODAG, at any point. However, in point-to-multipoint communication, as the mobile node moves from a parent to another, information disseminated via DAOs may rapidly become obsolete.

   Suppose, node D in Fig. 1 moves to D', then the present common ancestor cannot find a path to D' and there will be packet drop.
3. Scalability is another issue in RPL. In non-storing mode, the limiting factor is the size of the packet header containing the source routing information; this can include up to 8 IPv6 addresses (64 with a compressed header), but the longer the header the higher the overhead and the route repair latency. In storing mode, instead, the limiting factor is the memory available to store neighbor and routing tables. The nodes close to the root must store routing state for almost the entire DODAG, which can be challenging for resource-constrained devices.

Now, RPL is the tailor made solution keeping in mind the requirements of IPv6 based networks. However, these requirements were published 7 years ago [1], a relatively long time in the fast-paced world of networked computing in general and IoT in particular. Hence, with the rapid advancement in networking domain and the paradigm shift towards the IoT, it is high time to address these above mentioned issues.

1.2   Contribution

In this paper, we propose a geographic location based, dynamic and opportunistic RPL. This extension of RPL, generally aims to reduce the memory overhead and mobility issues in P2P communication. Instead of using the Root of the DAG or a common ancestor for both sender and receiver node, two nodes can communicate directly, or via some leaf nodes of the DAG. The selection of the routes are based on the geographic location, and the degree of the routes are chosen dynamically, such that they always ensure minimum connectivity between two nodes. Besides, the selection of routes follow the opportunistic routing mechanism [6], where a set of candidate node selects the most deserving node to transmit a data packet. The proposed algorithm is extensively tested using Contiki-Cooja.

1.3   Application Scenario

Additive Manufacturing (AM) or 3D printing is slowly gaining popularity as one of the most interesting and innovative domain for research purposes. Generally AM is used to develop 3D models, though the associated cyber physical system (CPS) can be used for several applications [7]. In this paper we have considered a scenario where IoT based network is used to collect information using sensors, placed on 3D artifacts designed by the 3D printers. These sensors can communicate between themselves and with a base station. The goal is to improve the production process by analyzing such data in order to make the overall communication system more efficient, robust and scalable.

1.4   Structure of the Paper

The rest of the paper is structured as follows: Sect. 2 discusses some relevant works in this domain, while the detailed methodology of our algorithm is described in Sect. 3. Section 4 presents the results and finally, Sect. 5 concludes the paper.

2   State of the Art

In RPL, three types of communication are supported;

- P2M or point to multipoint, from root node to lower level nodes in the DODAg. This communication goes downwards.

- M2P or multipoint to point, from nodes to root.
- P2P or point to point, between two distinct nodes in a network.

In order to achieve this three types of communication, RPL has two different modes of operation;

- Storing mode: In this mode, each node keeps a routing table containing mappings between all destinations reachable via its sub-DODAG and their respective next-hop nodes, learned while receiving DAOs.
- Non-storing mode: In this mode, the root is the only network node maintaining routing information.

Authors of [12], try to improve the performance of RPL under storing mode by improving the memory consumption of each node. They restrict the number of routing table entries for every storing node, by a predefined number N. If a storing node reaches the value N, it then create a new storing node among its children, and the process continues, until all the storing node are exhausted, and the mechanism turns into typical storing mode. This method tries to lower the burden of storing nodes, specially those are closer to roots, however, with increasing scalability and mobility, the routing tables at every storing node fail to capture the exact topology of surroundings.

In storing mode, if a node send a DAO and its parent can't store its information for memory issues, then the parent sends a DAO-NACK, to notify the node. The authors of [15], propose a multicast mechanism, where a node or a set of nodes, which can't store the information of their sub DODAG in the routing table anymore, joins a multicast group and declares themselves as junction node. When the root wants to communicate with a leaf node, for which it has no path, the root then multicasts the message to the multicast group. The members of that group then look for the destination in their routing tables and forward the packet accordingly. This method improves the performance of RPL in storing mode by changing the root's behaviour.

However, it still suffers from scalability and mobility issues [12]. Besides, as the size of the network grows, more messages are sent as broadcast message to every junction node, and inturn the junction nodes have to look up their routing table for the destination. Hence the cost of packet delivery increases.

Another modification over RPL has been proposed in [10]. This paper tries to improve the shortcomings of [12] and [15] by using a hybrid mode of operation for downward routing, i.e., for P2M and P2P routing. They distributes the routing information over root node and routing nodes. The root node stores the information of all the destination nodes, whereas, the router nodes store a routing table containing information about other routeing nodes. The P2P communication is performed using non-storing mode, (leaf-root-leaf), whereas the router to router communication is performed using storing mode. Authors claim that this method overcomes the disadvantages of both storing and non storing modes by showing lesser routing table entries than storing mode and decreasing the end-to-end delay than non-storing mode. However, the proposed method experiences performance degradation with mobility in the network.

In [16], an extension of RPL is proposed, that improves the performance of non-storing mode. It proposes that, when a node wants to send a packet to another node, then instead of sending it upwards to the root, it broadcasts a Route Request message (like AODV) and tries to build a DODAG originated at itself. In this way using a reactive path discovery method, the proposed work improves the traffic density near the root and ensures a better PDR by decreasing delay and hop count.

RPL is no doubt the best suitable choice for routing in IPv6 based networks with constraied nodes. However, with the advancement in IoT, RPL is facing some performance issues, due to scalability, resource constraint of nodes and scalability. The works discussed above try to propose extensions based on RPL, to overcome this problems. However, handling mobility in RPL is still an open problem.

2.1 Aim of the Paper

The primary objective in this paper is to design an extension of RPL which can perform efficiently in a scalable and mobile network. Now, RPL is a topology based routing or table based routing, where various nodes in the network (storing mode) or only the root (non-storing mode) stores the topology of the network and use this information to maintain a stable communication system in the network. Now this topology based routing methods stores the topology of the network, which is not very helpful for rapidly changing networks. On the other hand, geographic location based routing protocols are proved to be an improvement for this types of networks, as only the location information is needed for routing.

Location-based routing based methods are depending on the fact that every node knows its location, as well as the destination node's location. It has low communication overhead because advertisements of routing tables, like in traditional routing protocols, are not needed. Therefore, Location-based routing conserves both energy and bandwidth since route request and state propagation are not required after one-hop distance. Location-based routing uses the location information for nodes to provide higher efficiency and scalability. However, the location information always have some degree of inaccuracy in it. Specially, if the network supports mobility, then its very difficult to keep track with the nodes' locations. Another major drawback of geographic location based routing is fault tolerance, which results in poor throughput and PDR.

Hence we tried to merge this two types of routing in such a way that each of them can make another one stronger and results in a better routing for IPv6.

3   Proposed Solution

In this paper, we propose a geographic location based, dynamic routing protocol for point to point communication.

We assume that, every node in this system stores the information of its one hop neighbours as depicted in Fig. 2. However, broadcasting the message to this entire neighbour list can still incur a great overhead on both computation and memory. Besides, its completely absurd to involve a node in the routing process if its on the exactly opposite direction of the destination node. Thus, we proposed a geographic location based routing, where the nodes will communicate with their one hop neighbours which are on the way to the destination node.

3.1 Information Stored at Each Node

Every node N should store the following informations:

1. Its own geographic address. Let (x_i, y_i) denotes the address of node N_i.
2. Address of its one hop neighbor nodes.
3. Address of the destination node.

Let us consider a node S. If we consider the one hop neighbors of S as,

$$S_N = \{S'_1, S'_2, \ldots, S'_M\}$$

where, M is the total number of one hop neighbours of S.

Given α, S_N^α is the set of neighbouring nodes of S, which falls under the angle α. In Fig. 2 the neighbour nodes of S for 360°, 180° and 90° have been shown.

Every node will select the degree of angel based on the total number of neighbouring nodes. Our main purpose of this work is to maintain a equilibrium between performance and resources. Hence, we provide dynamic node selection for next hop transmission, considering a certain level of performance assurance. If we have selected 180° as an angel, then the probability of a single node in the neighbourhood of being on that 180° angle is 1/2. Similarly, the probability of a single node to remain in 90° angle is 1/4.

Hence, in order to assure atleast one path towards the destination, the collective probability should be greater than 1.

Thus,

$$\mid S_N^\alpha \mid \leq \frac{2\pi}{\alpha}$$

3.2 Neighbour Discovery

Every node, when it wants to join a network, broadcasts DIO message to find its DODAG instance and preferred parent. Each DIO message contains the predefined routing metric of the network, such as path reliability, hop count, bandwidth, latency, etc. and an objective function which determines the preferred parent towards the root for every node. Since a node broadcasts this DIO message, nodes in its one-hop distance can listen to this message, and update its neighbour tables accordingly.

Now, this DIO messages are rebroadcasted by each node according to an adaptive technique, the Trickle algorithm [6], which strikes a tradeoff between reactivity to topology changes and energy efficiency. Trickle ensures that DIOs are advertised aggressively when the network is unstable, and instead rebroadcast at an increasingly slow pace while the network is stable. This ensures that every node remains updated with its surrounding topology.

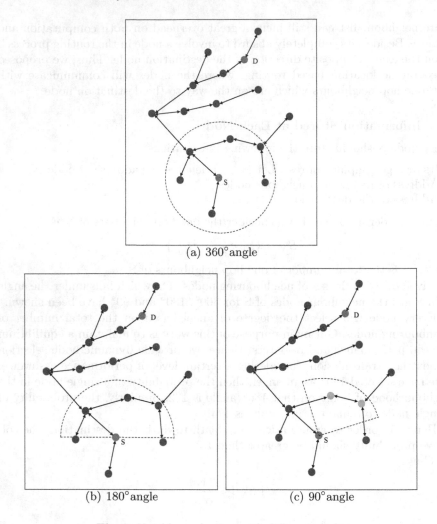

(a) 360° angle

(b) 180° angle   (c) 90° angle

Fig. 2. Neighbor selection with different angles

3.3   Route Establishment

Suppose a node S_0 wants to send a packet to a destination node D: the Algorithm 1 runs on each node of the network, implementing a routing mechanism: nodes are dormant and awake when a unicast message is received, triggering the execution of the algorithm; the only exception is the starting node S_0 initiating the whole iteration. It is capable of routing a message M coming from a neighbor source node S to a target node among its neighbors in a recursive way; base case is when the destination node D directly belongs to the neighborhood. Please note that the information of the initial node S_0 is not forwarded to subsequent nodes, and $S \equiv S_0$ only for the second iteration.

Moreover, the algorithm assumes a discovery process has already taken place: every node must know its own address, as well as its one-hop neighbour addresses and their geographical coordinates. In the pseudo-code some function calls appear, whose semantics are straightforward:

GetMyNeighbors returns the neighbors of the self node, which have previously been discovered.

Unicast unicast the message argument to the given node.

InitAngle calculates the starting, ending, increment and direction angles in function of the source and self nodes. Parameters α_1, α_2 and δ could be constants such as $10°$, $180°$ and $10°$ respectively, or even be the result of a finer computation. ϕ is calculated as the direction from which source node S originates with respect to the self node: assume (S_x, S_y) and $(\texttt{self}_x, \texttt{self}_y)$ are the coordinates of S and self respectively, then:

$$\phi = \arctan 2(\texttt{self}_y - S_y, \texttt{self}_x - S_x)$$

RestrictNeighbors calculates the subset of nodes laying within the angular range given as pair of arguments.

Length calculates the length of a list of nodes.

Farthest calculates the farthest node among those passed as argument, comparing each one's distance from self (Fig. 3).

Algorithm 1: RouteMessage(M, S, D)

   input: the message M
   input: source node S
   input: destination node D
1 *let self be the current node*;
2 nodes ← GetMyNeighbors();
3 **if** $D \in$ nodes **then**
4 | Unicast(M, D);
5 **else**
6 | $(\alpha_1, \alpha_2, \delta, \phi)$ ← InitAngle(self, S);
7 | **for** $\alpha = \alpha_1$ **to** α_2 **step** δ **do**
8 | restricted ← RestrictNeighbors(nodes, $\phi - \frac{\alpha}{2}, \phi + \frac{\alpha}{2}$);
9 | **if** Length(restricted) $\geq \frac{2\pi}{\alpha}$ **then**
10 | nodes ← restricted;
11 | break;
12 | **end**
13 | **end**
14 | target ← Farthest(nodes);
15 | Unicast(M, target);
16 **end**

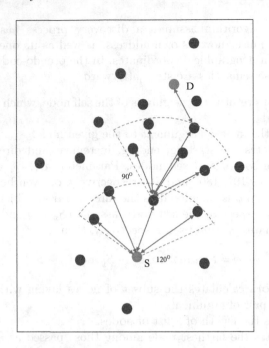

Fig. 3. Route selection process.

4   Results

We simulate our proposed algorithm using Contiki-Cooja [13,14]. The simulation settings are described in Table 1. Figure 4 shows the variation of total time needed to transmit a packet successfully for various node density in the network.

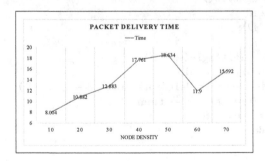

Fig. 4. Packet delivery time vs Node density.

Table 1. Simulation settings

Network simulator	COOJA under Contiki O.S (2.7)
Simulation time	1 h
Radio environment	UDGM (Unit Disk Graph Medium)
Area of deployment	600 * 600 m2
Emulated nodes	Sky motes
Transmission range	40 m

4.1   Application Domain

As we already mentioned earlier, we have considered the IIoT (Industrial Internet of Things) technology based Additive manufacturing system as our application domain. Now, the primary objective of this project is to secure the transmission between new generation sensors inside of manufactured products that, in particular, will further allow us to analyse the circumstantial data and plan predictive maintenance and process improvement strategies.

In order to achieve this goal the most important requirement is a reliable, robust and secure communication system. Considering the scalability of both the network and generated data, inconsistent and vulnerable nature of sensors and the distributed and heterogeneous network structure, inspired us to think of RPL as the most appropriate solution.

The proposed extension of RPL has several advantages over the existing RPL, such as,

- Every node in the network stores the neighborhood information, which confirms with the distributed nature of the network. This also helps to remove the bottleneck near the root node of every DODAG, especially with a scalable network.
- The degree of routes are dynamically chosen during runtime, ensuring the reliability of the system. Every node selects a set of candidate nodes for forward transmission in such a way, that there always a path towards destination.
- However, if a node selects multiple nodes for next hop transmission and those nodes further repeat the same process, then the control message overhead of the network will increase cumulatively with a chance of duplicate path problem. Hence, our proposed method uses opportunistic route selection paradigm, where the set of candidate nodes will select only one forwarding node, based on the objective functions of the network.
- Since our solution does not involve the root node or common ancestral parent in P2P communication, the time required to transmit a data packet does not depend on the position of the node in the hierarchical structure.

Hence, we can claim that our proposed solution will perform better in this application scenario.

5   Conclusions

The proposed extension over RPL in this paper is responsible for handling the existing issues, such as scalability and mobility in RPL. The proposed routing algorithm is used to identify neighbours of a node that guarantees a reliable transmission towards the destination. The degree of routes is depended directly on the reliability of the process. Thus, the algorithm makes sure that there exist at least one path towards the destination by hopping through nodes: each one finds the best-candidate among its strict neighborhood by guessing the preferred direction. We have used Contiki-Cooja to verify our proposed work. The results clearly show that our method performs better than RPL. The algorithm is parametric over the increment and the width of the rotating angle seeking for such candidate: in our tests we used 10° increments within a 180° maximum span. Future work may focus on making the probability constraint in the condition of the major if statement aware of number and density of neighbors.

Acknowledgments. Work partially supported by the project "ADditive Manufacturing & Industry 4.0 as innovation Driver (ADMIN 4D)", for providing the support required for carrying out the research work.

References

1. Winter, T., et al.: RPL: IPv6 routing protocol for low-power and lossy networks. Internet Engineering Task Force (IETF), 6550 Category, ISSN: 2070–1721, March 2012
2. Brandt, A., Buron, J., Porcu, G.: Home automation routing requirements in low-power and lossy networks. IETF RFC 5826
3. Pister, K., Thubert, P., Dwars, S., Phinney, T.: Industrial routing requirements in low-power and lossy networks. IETF RFC 5673
4. Dohler, M., Watteyne, T., Winter, T., Barthel, D.: Routing requirements for urban low-power and lossy networks. IETF RFC 5548
5. Martocci, J., Mil, P.D., Riou, N., Vermeylen, W.: Building automation routing requirements in low-power and lossy networks. IETF RFC 5867
6. Chakraborty, M., Deb, N., Chaki, N.: POMSec: pseudo-opportunistic, multipath secured routing protocol for communications in smart grid. In: Saeed, K., Homenda, W., Chaki, R. (eds.) CISIM 2017. LNCS, vol. 10244, pp. 264–276. Springer, Cham (2017). https://doi.org/10.1007/978-3-319-59105-6_23
7. Yampolskiy, M., King, W.E., Gatlin, J., Belikovetsky, S., Brown, A., Skjellum, A.: Security of additive manufacturing: attack taxonomy and survey. Addit. Manuf. **21**, 431–457 (2018)
8. Chakraborty, M., Chaki, N., Cortesi, A.: A new intrusion prevention system for protecting smart grid from ICMPv6 vulnerabilities. In: IEEE Xplore Digital Library Proceedings of the 3rd International Workshop on Smart Energy Networks & Multi-Agent Systems (SEN-MAS 2014), The Federated Conference on Computer Science and Information Systems (FedCSIS), Warsaw, Poland (2014)

9. Chakraborty, M.: Advanced monitoring based intrusion detection system for distributed and intelligent energy theft: DIET attack in advanced metering infrastructure. In: Gavrilova, M.L., Tan, C.J.K., Chaki, N., Saeed, K. (eds.) Transactions on Computational Science XXXI. LNCS, vol. 10730, pp. 77–97. Springer, Heidelberg (2018). https://doi.org/10.1007/978-3-662-56499-8_5
10. Oh, S., Hwang, D., Kim, K., Kim, K.-H.: A hybrid mode to enhance the downward route performance in routing protocol for low power and lossy networks. Int. J. Distrib. Sens. Netw. **14**(4) (2018). https://doi.org/10.1177/1550147718772533
11. Brown, W.: Distributed network architecture: scalability and load balancing in a secured environment. White Paper by Tyco Security Products (2018)
12. Gan, W., Shi, Z., Zhang, C., et al.: MERPL: a more memory efficient storing mode in RP. In: 19th IEEE International Conference on Networks (ICON), Singapore, 11–13 December 2013, pp. 1–5. IEEE, New York (2013)
13. Contiki: The Open Source Operating System for the Internet of Things (2017). http://www.contiki-os.org/
14. VMware Virtualization for Desktop & Server, Application, Public & Hybrid Clouds (2018). http://www.vmware.com/uk
15. Kiraly, C., Istomin, T., Iova, O., et al.: D-RPL: overcoming memory limitations in RPL point-to-multipoint routing. In: IEEE 40th Conference on Local Computer Networks (LCN), Clearwater Beach, FL, 26–29 October 2015, pp. 157–160. IEEE, New York (2015)
16. Baccelli, E., Philipp, M.: The P2P-RPL routing protocol for IPv6 sensor networks: tested experiments. In: Software, Telecommunications and Computer Networks, September 2011

Dynamic Scheduling of Traffic Signal (DSTS) Management in Urban Area Network

Abantika Choudhury[1]([⊠]), Uma Bhattacharya[2], and Rituparna Chaki[3]

[1] RCC Institute of Information Technology, Kolkata 700015, India
abantikachoudhury@gmail.com
[2] Indian Institute of Engineering Science and Technology,
Shibpur, Howrah 711103, India
uma_bh2000@yahoo.co.in
[3] Calcutta University, Kolkata 700106, India
rituchaki@gmail.com

Abstract. Nowadays vehicular ad hoc network (VANET) is a promising area of research. One of the aspects of this area is traffic congestion control. Due to the limited capacity of road networks, road traffic congestions are becoming a vital problem in most of the metropolitan cities or large cities throughout the world. That creates the chances of casualties and other types of losses related to time, fuel, finance etc. Congestion also causes a considerable amount of pollution. In this paper, we concentrate on traffic light scheduling in the intersection or junction point of road network for congestion control. We propose an approach to optimize the timing of traffic light dynamically by using scheduling algorithm to reduce the congestion in various junction points in urban area network. The proposed mechanism is used for connected intersection system where every objects and traffic lights will be connected with each other and can share information. We use V2I connectivity system via road side unit (RSU) for our methodology. The Traffic Management controller (TMC) is able to collect the traffic related information of an intersection from RSU. Several researchers worked on this problem. But the performance of the proposed method is simulated and the results show that the proposed method performing better in terms of queue length and the waiting time of vehicle in intersection area with respect to other methodologies.

Keywords: VANET · RSU · TMC · V2I · Traffic Congestion ·
Traffic light scheduling

1 Introduction

Nowadays, traffic congestion becomes a big problem. Therefore wastage of time and fuel are increasing for the travelling vehicles due to the increase of traffic intensity. Traffic efficiency is one of the main applications that have been developed over road networks using VANETs. Not only is this but a huge amount of pollution is also occurred. To preserve the time and fuel and control the pollution, the congestion control of the traffic in roadways can take a major role. There are several ways to reduce the congestion. One of the schemes is traffic light scheduling. Especially in the

© Springer Nature Switzerland AG 2019
K. Saeed et al. (Eds.): CISIM 2019, LNCS 11703, pp. 132–143, 2019.
https://doi.org/10.1007/978-3-030-28957-7_12

city, the junction of the road networks is crowded with vehicles. Because, the vehicles need to wait to cross the roads in the junction points. But in the peak hours the number of vehicles becomes very high. They need to wait for long time to cross the road. Traffic lights control the traffic flows at each road intersection. They provide safe scheduling that allows all conflicting traffic flows to share the road intersection. Several research works is going on in this area. Optimization of dynamic traffic light scheduling scheme is made in such a way so that the traffics, waiting in the junction should not wait for unnecessarily long time. The scheme increases the traffic flow in the roadways and minimizes the waiting time for the traffic. The queuing delay at each signalized road intersection decreases traffic fluency, which decreases traffic efficiency throughout the road network. To enhance the performance of traffic efficiency, several researchers have developed intelligent and efficient algorithms to schedule the increase the flow of traffic at each signalized road intersection. The efficient schedule for each traffic light should reduce the waiting delay time of traveling vehicles at each road intersection and increase the throughput of road intersections.

In this paper, an intelligent traffic light controlling algorithm is introduced considering a real-time traffic characteristics of all traffic flows that will cross the road intersection. The introduced algorithm is intended to schedule the traffic flows at each road intersection, while reducing the expected queuing length and waiting time of vehicle and increasing the throughput of the road intersection. A virtual ready area has been considered around each road intersection. Vehicles inside the boundaries of this area are ready to cross the intersection. However, the vehicles receive a red signal from the traffic light begin to decrease their speed and prepare to stop at the closest empty space to the road intersection. Similarly, the vehicles receive green signal from traffic light, start the engine, accelerate the speed and exit the road area. The flows of traffic are density is scheduled to pass first. Moreover, the assigned time of each phase of the timing cycle is set based on the real-time traffic distribution inside the ready area.

2 Related Work

In this section we briefly discuss about the related research work in this field. Intelligent Traffic Light Controlling (ITLC) [1] algorithm is proposed considering the real-time traffic characteristics of each traffic flow are going to cross the road junction. The methodology proposed here for scheduling the time phases of each traffic light. A new approach [2] for smart traffic light control at intersection is proposed. A connected intersection system where every object like vehicles, sensors, and traffic lights all are connected and sharing information to one another. The controller is able to collect effectively and mobility traffic flow at intersection in real-time. In the work [2] authors also propose the optimization algorithms for traffic lights by applying algorithmic game theory. Two game models (Cournot Model and Stackelberg Model) are used to deal with difference scenarios of traffic flow. In this regard, based on the density of vehicles, controller will make real-time decisions for the time durations of traffic lights to optimize traffic flow. In [3], an algorithm is proposed for system to control the traffic by measuring the realtime vehicle density using canny edge detection with digital image processing. The procedure offers traffic control system. Besides that, the complete technique from image acquisition to edge detection and green signal allotment using sample images of different traffic conditions is depicted. A study, inspired by recent advanced vehicle technologies [4], considering for improvement of traffic flow in real-time problem. The algorithm depicts a new approach to manage traffic flow at the intersection by scheduling of traffic light signal. The method is based on process synchronization and connected vehicle technology. The traffic deadlock is also considered for huge number of traffic. The simulation shows the potential results comparing with the existing traffic management system. A new approach [5] is proposed for traffic flow management at intersection. By IoT, based on connected object, A model is designed which communicating among objects to improve traffic flow at intersection with real time problem. In this scheme, traffic congestion is also considered in case of high traffic volume. Traffic Congestion Investigating System by Image Processing [6] from CCTV Camera is proposed to check a traffic condition from a traffic image on road. The system brings a traffic image from a CCTV camera to process in the system as an input. Then, the system finds for traffic congestion and gets the results in three traffic conditions as Flow, Heavy, and Jammed. Finally, a user can use the system for a transportation planning or an intersection traffic control. In this paper [7], a new traffic system recommendation based on support real-time flows in highly unpredictable sensor network environments is proposed. The proposed algorithm includes two phases. First phase is proposed to deal with the real-time problem and second phase, the algorithm is based on Depth First Search (DFS) algorithm to recommend the paths which meet demands of drivers based their context. A unique Intelligent Road Traffic Monitoring And Management System [8] is proposed to improve traffic flow and safety of road users. An Intelligent Road Traffic Monitoring and Management System (IRTMMS) [8] based on the VANET is proposed in this paper. A new scheme [9] proposes that reduces the traffic congestion problems and improves the performance decreasing the vehicle waiting time and their pollutant emissions at intersections. Combination of vehicle-to-vehicle (V2V) and vehicle-to-infrastructure (V2I) communications is used to fulfill the goal. The main traffic input for applying traffic assessment in this approach is the queue length of vehicle clusters at the intersections. A new approach is proposed [10] where road-side facilities communicate the traffic light cycle information to the approaching vehicles. Based on this information, the vehicles determine their optimal speeds and other appropriate actions to take to cross road intersections with minimum delays. The survey [11] of adaptive signal control strategies to optimize traffic signal is done where authors divided the procedure in three categories depending on level of traffic involvement. Two secure intelligent traffic light control schemes [14] are done using fog computing whose security are based on the hardness of the computational Diffie–Hellman puzzle and the hash collision puzzlerespectively. Designing of a dynamic and efficient traffic light scheduling algorithm [15] that adjusts the best green phase time of each traffic flow, based on the real-time traffic distribution around the signalized road intersection. This proposed algorithm has also considered the presence of emergency vehicles, allowing them to pass through the signalized intersection as soon as possible. The phases of each traffic light are set to allow any emergency vehicle approaching the signalized intersection to pass smoothly. In case of multiple emergency vehicles approach the signalized intersection have been investigated to select the most efficient and suitable schedule. A survey [16] of different traffic density estimation methodologies is described, where one can get the vivid idea about the trends of research work in this aspect. A multi-agent traffic signal control system based on vehicular ad hoc network (VANET) is proposed [17] where real-time and accurate vehicle information obtained by vehicular ad hoc network is used. By constructing a distributed architecture using multi-agent technology, and realizing vehicle road communication using communication module of intersection agent, a more intelligent signal timing strategy is constructed by discrete fuzzy controller. A novel preemptive algorithm for optimization of traffic signals in VANETs [18] proposes to reduce large queuing at crossroads by allowing smooth movement of traffic on the roads without much waiting. The proposed algorithm selects green light timings according to real time vehicular density and can select any phase out of predefined order depending on the traffic density on that phase to reduce the congestion. A new scheme for dynamic traffic regulation method is proposed based on virtual traffic light (VTL) [19] for Vehicle Ad Hoc Network (VANET). In our framework, each vehicle can express its "will"—the desire of moving forward—and share among one another its "will"-value and related traffic information at a traffic light controlled intersection. A decentralized model based on multi-agent systems (MAS) and complex event processing (CEP) [20] is proposed. The new control scheme improves green light time to reduce the average waiting time of vehicles. This improvement is provided by the observation of the intersection through Cyber Physical Systems (CPS). The paper [21] proposes an auto-adaptive model for smart regulation traffic lights. The research work provides an intelligent traffic light control system to avoid the traffic congestion and to give a free way to emergency vehicles to reach their respective places without any delay. This system uses IR sensors to detect the vehicles density before signal. This will help the Arduino to change the signal timing based on the number of vehicles. For traffic clearance, the radio frequency transmitter and receiver are used. To detect the emergency vehicles and will change the signal color from red to green. Thus, this intelligent traffic light control system will help us to avoid traffic congestion and provide traffic clearance for emergency vehicles to reach their destination.

3 Proposed Methodology

Phase: A phase is a set of routes of vehicles. The vehicles of all the routes in the same phase can cross the junction simultaneously without colliding each other (Figs. 1, 2, 3 and 4).

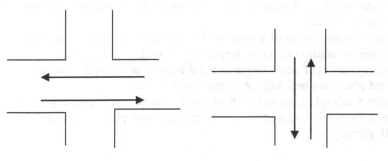

Fig. 1. Phase 1   **Fig. 2.** Phase 2

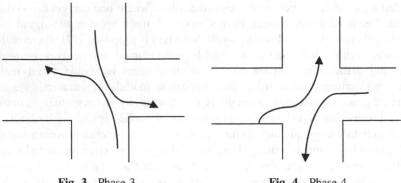

Fig. 3. Phase 3   **Fig. 4.** Phase 4

Row of Vehicles: A row of vehicles is defined as the number of vehicles standing beside each other (perpendicularly to the road) during the red signal.

Queue length of a route = number of vehicles in a route.

Queue length of a phase = summation of number of vehicles in all the routes of a phase.

Queue length of a lane = number of vehicles in all the routes of a lane (Fig. 5).

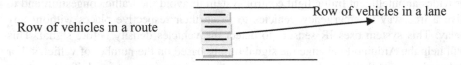

Row of vehicles in a route   Row of vehicles in a lane

Fig. 5. Row of vehicles for route and lane

Assumption: A lane has three routes to follow. The routes are right turn route, straight route and left turn route. The right turn route is always open. So, in present work, only straight route and left turn route are considered for traffic light scheduling.

3.1   Tasks of RSUs

- Receives message from each vehicle of all the routes.
- Calculates number of vehicles for each route of all phases from the received message of vehicles.
- Calculates queue length of a route as the number of vehicles of the route.
- Calculates summation of queue length of two routes of each phase.
- Calculates sub set of queue length as the difference between the queue length of the selected phase and next highest queue length phase.
- Calculates sub set of queue length of highest queue length phase as the difference between the queue length of the highest queue length phase and next highest queue length phase.

- Calculates row of vehicles for highest queue length phase as the number of vehicles standing beside each other (perpendicularly of a road).
- Counts number of rows of vehicles for selected subset of highest queue length phase as the ratio of number of vehicles of the subset of queue length and number of vehicles of each row.
- If total number of vehicles of the routes in a phase is $p_j\_tot\_sub\_veh_i$, (where j denotes the phase number and i denotes the route number) and the number of vehicle of a row is $row\_veh_{i,j}$ where i and j denotes the route and phase respectively. For a particular phase p_j
- Number of rows = $(\sum_{i=1}^{n} p_j\_tot\_sub\_veh_i)/row\_veh_{i,j}$
- Calculates duration of green signal for highest queue length phase as the time required for a sub set of queue length of highest phase to cross the junction.
- Calculates the duration of red signal for other phases as equal like the duration of green signal.
- Sends duration of green signal for highest queue length phase and red signal for other phases to Traffic Management Controller (TMC).
- Calculates congestion of each incoming lane having red signal as the distance of the last row of vehicle from the junction. The distance is calculated as the summation of all the inter row distance of the lane and distance of first row from the junction.
- Compare congestion of incoming lane with a predefined threshold of that lane and sends a message to TMC in case the congestion of lane crosses the threshold.
- The threshold value is calculated as-
- Congestion threshold = length of the lane/2.
- Repeats the same steps of operations.

3.2   Tasks of TMC or VANET Authority

- Receives green signal duration of one phase and red signal duration of other phases from RSUs.
- Assigns green signal for one phase and red signal to other phases as per the information of RSUs.
- Receives congestion message of congested lane from RSUs (if congestion occurred).
- Increases the waiting time of the routes of connecting junction coming towards the congested lane (if congestion occurred).
- Calculates the increment of waiting time as (duration of green signal of the congested lane)/2 (Table 1).

Table 1. Different notations used in the algorithm 1

Notation	Description
Q_len	Queue-length
T_g	Time duration of green signal
T_s	Start-up time
T_a	Acceleration time
T_r	Time duration for red signal
D_{L-I}	Distance of the last vehicle location from the intersection
S	Speed of vehicle
New_Q_len	Queue length after arrival of new vehicles
new_T_g	Time duration of green signal for New_Q_len
del_T_g	Difference of new T_g and T_g
T_{wth}	Waiting time threshold
T_{wt}	Waiting time
T_{max}	Maximum time duration for green signal for the highest queue-length phase
q-len$_{max}$	value of highest queue-length
T_{wt_p}	Waiting time of phase p
p_T_{wth}	Phase suffering from T_{wth}
p_T_{wt}	Phase suffering from T_{wt}
P_T_g	Phase enjoying T_g
P_T_{wt}_Q_len	Queue length of phase suffering from T_{wt}

3.3 Proposed Algorithm

(See Algoritm 1)

Algorithm 1: Traffic light scheduling

Input: phases.
Output: T_g, P_T_g, Q_len, T_{wt}
if (phase)
    If beacon signal (D_{L-I}, direction to move)
        Q_len <- $Q\_len + 1$
        Return Q_len
   End
        Sort Q_len from highest to lowest
End
while Q_len is highest
       Calculate $T_g = T_s + T_a + D_{L-I} /S$
       Calculate V_{new} in time T_g
       New_Q_len <- $Q\_len + V_{new}$
       Calculate new_$T_g = T_g + del\_T_g$
       Allot new_T_g for selected phase
End
Calculate $T_{wth} = T_{max}$ x (q-len$_{max}$/ q-len)
 if ($T_{wt\_p} = T_{wth}$) then
  if p_T_{wt} < 2 then
    allot T_g for P_T_{wt} and $T_r = T_{wth}$ for P_T_g
  else if   p_T_{wt}_Q_len1 > p_T_{wt}_Q_len2
        allot T_g for P_T_{wt}_Q_len1 and T_r for P_T_g
         else allot T_g for P_T_{wt}_Q_len2 and T_r for P_T_g
  End
End

3.4   Flow Chart

(See Fig. 6)

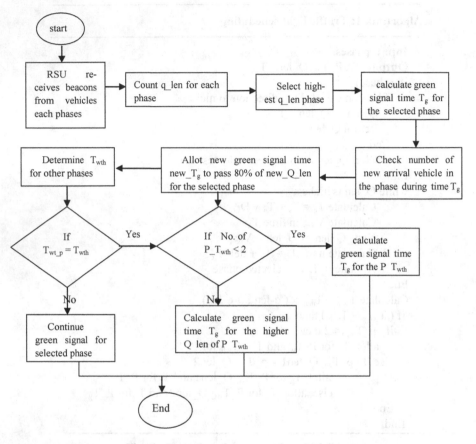

Fig. 6. Flow chart for proposed methodology

3.5   Performance Analysis

To evaluate the algorithm, a network of six intersections (4 point intersection) is taken for consideration. Different number of vehicles is taken as input of the network for various times. For simulation, SUMO 0.25.0 is used for creating the network and the vehicle movement. The communication with RSU is done by omnetpp 4.9. The parameters taken for comparison are average queuing length of vehicles in a particular intersection and the average waiting time of the vehicles at the end of the simulation. The comparison graphs are given below. It is assumed that average speed of the vehicles is 60 km/hr, acceleration speed is 6 km/hr² and start time is 20 s, inter vehicular distance is 2 m. Figs. 7 and 8 depicts the comparison graph with the proposed method and other two methods (one is Xiao et al. (2017) and Punam et al. (2015)). The proposed method gives better result than that of other two methodologies Xiao et al. (2017) and Punam et al. (2015).

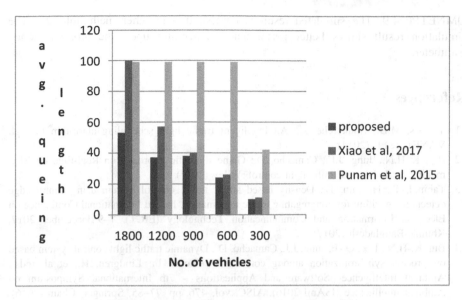

Fig. 7. No. of vehicles vs. average queuing length

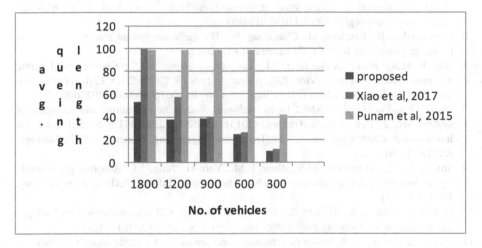

Fig. 8. No. of vehicles vs. average waiting time

4 Conclusion

The research work done in this paper is concentrating on traffic light scheduling in urban area road network. A methodology in order to optimize the traffic light scheduling is proposed to control the road traffic congestion in urban road network. The proposed methodology is established by the implementation of a new scheduling algorithm. The proposed method targets to reduce the queuing length of road traffic and their average waiting time. The algorithm is simulated on SUMO 0.25.0 and

OMNETPP 4.9. The simulated result is compared with other methodologies. The simulation result shows better performance depending upon the aforementioned parameter.

References

1. Younes, M.B., Boukerche, A.: An Intelligent traffic light scheduling algorithm through VANET. IEEE (2014)
2. Bui, K.-H.N., Jung, J.E., Camacho, D.: Game theoretic approach on Real-time decision making for IoT-based traffic light control. Wiley (2017)
3. Tahmid, T., Hossain, E.: Density based smart traffic control system using canny edge detection algorithm for congregating traffic information. In: 3rd International Conference on Electrical Information and Communication Technology (EICT). 7–9 December 2017, Khulna, Bangladesh (2017)
4. Bui, K.-H.N., Lee, O.-J., Jung, J.J., Camacho, D.: Dynamic traffic light control system based on process synchronization among connected vehicles. In: Lindgren, H., et al. (eds.) Ambient Intelligence- Software and Applications – 7th International Symposium on Ambient Intelligence (ISAmI 2016). AISC, vol. 476, pp. 77–85. Springer, Cham (2016). https://doi.org/10.1007/978-3-319-40114-0_9
5. Bui, K.-H.N., Camacho, D., Jung, J.E.: Real-time traffic flow management based on inter-object communication: a case study at intersection. Mob. Netw. Appl. **22**(4), 613–624 (2017). https://doi.org/10.1007/s11036-016-0800-y
6. Eamthanakul, B., Ketcham, M., Chumuang, N.: The traffic congestion investigating system by image processing from CCTV camera. IEEE (2017)
7. Bui, K.-H.N., Pham, X.H., Jung, J.J., Lee, O.-J., Hong, M.-S.: Context-based traffic recommendation system. In: Vinh, P.C., Alagar, V. (eds.) ICCASA 2015. LNICST, vol. 165, pp. 122–131. Springer, Cham (2016). https://doi.org/10.1007/978-3-319-29236-6_13
8. Ghode, P.S., Pochhi, R.: VANET based intelligent road traffic monitoring and management system. Int. J. Res. Advent Technol. (2015). (E-ISSN: 2321-9637) Special Issue 1st International Conference on Advent Trends in Engineering, Science and Technology, ICATEST 2015
9. Shaghaghi, E., Jabbarpour, M.R., Noor, R.M., Yeo, H., Jung, J.J.: Adaptive green traffic signal controlling using vehicular communication. Front. Inform. Technol. Electron. Eng. **18**, 373 (2017)
10. Djahel, S., Jabeur, N., Barrett, R., Murphy, J.: Toward V2I communication technology-based solution for reducing road traffic congestion in smart cities. IEEE (2015)
11. Florin, R., Olariu, S.: A Survey of vehicular communications for traffic signal optimization. Veh. Commun. **2**, 70–79 (2015)
12. Younes, M.B., Boukerche, A.: Intelligent traffic light controlling algorithms using vehicular networks. IEEE Trans. Veh. Technol. **65**, 5887–5899 (2015)
13. Younes, M.B., Boukerche, A.: An intelligent traffic light scheduling algorithm through VANETs. In: International Workshop on Performance and Management of Wireless and Mobile Network. IEEE (2014)
14. Liu, J., et al.: Secure intelligent traffic light control using fog computing. Future Gener. Comput. Syst. (2017)
15. Younes, M.B., Boukerche, A.: An efficient dynamic traffic light scheduling algorithm considering emergency vehicles for intelligent transportation systems. Wirel. Netw. (2017) https://doi.org/10.1007/s11276-017-1482-5

16. Darwish, T., Bakar, K.A.: Traffic density estimation in vehicular ad-hoc networks: a review. Ad Hoc Netw. **24**, 337–351 (2014)
17. Huang, X., Zhang, Q., Wang, Y.: Research on multi - agent traffic signal control system based on VANET information. In: 20th International Conference on Intelligent Transportation Systems (ITSC). IEEE (2017)
18. Bedi, P., Jindal, V., Garg, R., Dhankani, H.: A preemptive approach to reduce average queue length in VANETs. IEEE (2015)
19. Shi, J., Peng, C., Zhu, Q., Duan, P., Bao, Y., Xie, M.: There is a will, there is a way – a new mechanism for traffic control based on VTL and VANET. In: 16th International Symposium on High Assurance Systems Engineering. IEEE (2015)
20. Elchamaa, R., Dafflon, B., Ouzrout, Y., Gechter, F.: Agent based monitoring for smart cities: application TO traffic lights. In: 10th International Conference on Software, Knowledge, Information Management and Applications (SKIMA). IEEE (2016)
21. Karthiga, R.S., Vanmathi, J., Dharani, D., Janaranjani, S., Sudarsan, P.: Intelligent traffic light control system using arduino. Int. J. Sci. Eng. Res. **9**(3) (2018)

Evaluation of the Existing Tools for Fake News Detection

Agata Giełczyk$^{(\boxtimes)}$ ⓘ, Rafał Wawrzyniak, and Michał Choraś

UTP University of Science and Technology Bydgoszcz, Bydgoszcz, Poland
agata.gielczyk@utp.edu.pl

Abstract. The extreme growth and adoption of Social Media and User Generated Content (UGC) websites, in combination with their poor governance and the lack of quality control over the digital content being published and shared, has led information veracity to a continuous deterioration. Therefore, there is a growing need for reliable information assurance, called by both private and public users and authorities. Due to the popularity of the social media and Internet availability all over the world, anyone can provide a piece of information on the web. This may create a ready channel for spreading false, not verified or confusing information, which may be called 'fake news'. In order to protect the user from online disinformation, some tools have already been proposed. In this article we have described the available online tools and evaluated them using the same dataset, which was created for this study. We have provided the results proving that fake news detection is an increasingly more pressing, yet a difficult research problem.

Keywords: Online disinformation · Fake news detection · Online tools

1 Introduction and Context

Nowadays, information plays a key role in the society. Access to the information and news is incredibly easy using a connection to the Internet and social media. The simplicity of providing new pieces of information leads to the phenomenon called 'fake news'. Using the ENISA definition [6], it can be explained as 'false, inaccurate, or misleading online information designed, presented and promoted with malicious intent or for profit'. Said profit may be financial (e.g. clickbait advertisement), economical or even political. A more detailed definition of this emerging problem was presented in paper [3], where some possible approaches to automatic detection of fake news were delineated as follows:

- journalist analysis – in this kind of approach the journalist former articles are analyzed, if there were any fake information before, the websites of trusted news agencies are less likely to produce fake online information in comparison to the newly created websites of private blogs;
- text analysis – the news text may be compared to the news released on approximate time;

© Springer Nature Switzerland AG 2019
K. Saeed et al. (Eds.): CISIM 2019, LNCS 11703, pp. 144–151, 2019.
https://doi.org/10.1007/978-3-030-28957-7_13

- metadata analysis – if the author provided the metadata or tag, those may be also used in order to classify the specific piece of information as true or fake;
- image analysis – images used for online disinformation often are modified instances of existing images or have simply been used before in different context, e.g. in older news.

Due to the fact that online disinformation has become an increasingly more pressing issue recently, there is already some work published in this domain. Authors in [13] enumerated some linguistic features that are used in order to proceed the text analysis: language features (number of syllabs, number of words in categories like noun, verb etc.), lexical features (amount of unique words and their frequency in the text), psycholinguistic features (comming from dictionary-based text mining), semantic features (for example the toxicity score obtained from Googles API available at https://www.perspectiveapi.com/#/) and subjectivity (e.g. subjectivity and sentiment scores of a text using the TextBlobs API - http://text-blob.readthedocs.io/en/dev/). They emphasize that labeling data for the reseach In [12] authors presented a promising approach to fake news detection using geometric deep learning, Currently they are working on a tool called FABULA AI, that is said to be released as a commercial APIs for the world's social networks and publishers by the end of 2019. In [14] the CSI model is presented. Authors claim that such a complex problem as fake news detection needs a complex solution. Thus, they combine information obtained from text, response and source and present encouraging results. In [1,2] a harmonic algorithm using the graph theory for fake news detection is implemented. A possible solution for fake news detection and understanding was proposed in [15] and is called FakeNewsTracker. It uses auto-encoding networks and linguistic features (eg. news content) for detection. In [3] authors presented an overall framework and an image-based solution.

The research in fake news detection is also a major subject of several European Union research projects, such as e.g. SocialTruth funded within H2020 Programme.

Moreover, some broader initiatives such as SOMA (Social Observatory for Disinformation and Social Media Analysis) active at disinfobservatory.org have been initiated.

The article is structured as follows: in Sect. 2 the currently available online tools are characterised. In Sect. 3 the dataset created for this study is presented. In Sects. 4 and 5 we provide the obtained results, conclusions and plans for future work, respectively.

2   Overview of the Evaluated Tools

Due to the increase in the significance of the fake news problem, several solutions have already been proposed and released. In this article we focus on free online tools. They are mostly created as extensions to the browsers. They use different approaches for fake news detection, namely: image, author and textual analysis.

Therefore in this section we provide a short overview of the online tools selected and used in this research.

2.1 SurfSafe

The SurfSafe tool is a free browser extension released by RoBhat labs in August 2018 available online [17]. The main idea of this tool is to compare the images from news to a database of images. The images stored in the database are culled from both trusted and fact-checking sites. If the image was modified or used in fake context, the whole news piece is considered to be fake. Moreover, the text analysis is performed - the text from the news is compared to the text found within the image on another site. The SurfSafe user may adjust the set of trusted websites.

2.2 Fake News Detector AI

The Fake News Detector AI is a tool available online [7]. Unfortunately, there is no information about the algorithms involved in the detection procedure, other than the short message 'use a neural network'. The online interface provides the information 'true', 'false' or 'unknown error' for each link that the user wants to verify.

2.3 TrustedNews

The next tool involved in the research is called TrustedNews and may be found online [18]. It was released by the MetaCert organization in 2017. This tool can provide a wider set of results - trustworthy, untrustworthy, satire, biased, malicious, clickbait, generated and unknown. Trusted News is powered by the MetaCert Protocol, and it is claimed to use 'independent, politically objective data sources to measure the truthfulness of news content'.

2.4 Fake News Detector

The Fake New Detector is available online [8]. It involves the feedback provided by the other users of the tool. It can give one of the following answers: legitimate (real), fake news, clickbait or biased. What is very important, this is an open source project and its repositories are available on the Github platform.

2.5 Fake News Guard

This tool is a passive one working as a browser extension [9]. It verifies any page visited by the user and any link displayed in Facebook. However, it is difficult to evaluate the way this tool works. Authors only claim that it combines the linguistic approach, network analysis and artificial intelligence. Apart of that, each user can report the source, if it is suspected of being fake.

2.6   Decodex

Decodex is an online tool released in France [5]. It labels the pieces of information as 'info', 'satire' and 'no information', which may alert the user about potential fake news. Apart from the tool, the detailed user guide is available on the website. The authors encourage users to verify the information before sharing it, to verify the source of the news (and use only the trustworthy sources) and to verify the image used in the specific context.

3   Dataset Creation

For the research purposes we have gathered a set of 20 websites providing news. Most of them (12) contain text written in the Polish language, while the rest of the news is provided in English.

All the elements were manually classified and labelled as real, fake, fake clickbait or satire. The details of the dataset are presented in Table 1. We did not use any dataset that has been published already because of two reasons: no information about URL address or providing only the URL of the publisher (Kaggle [10]) or some of provided URLs in the databases are not valid - the news have been already removed from the servers (FakeNewsNet [16]).

Table 1. Details of the dataset used in the research - link, language and classification (real, fake, fake clickbait or satire)

No.	Website	Lang.	Classification
1	https://wyborcza24.pl/koniec-prezesa-nbp-jest-seks-tasma-z-pania-dyrektor/	Polish	fake
2	https://wiadomosci.wp.pl/piotr-d-zatrzymany-za-szpiegostwo-dla-chin-brejza-kariera-przyspieszyla-za-rzadow-pis-6337360732755585a	Polish	real
3	http://szczepienie.blogspot.com/2018/06/poszczepienne-polio-w-wenezueli_14.html	Polish	fake
4	https://gazetalubuska.pl/synoptycy-alarmuja-czeka-nas-zima-stulecia/ar/12503592	Polish	fake
5	https://www.visittheusa.com/trip/pacific-coast-highway-road-trip	English	real
6	https://www.theonion.com/	English	satire
7	https://superekspress.pl/fundacja-tvn-kulczyk-holding-sprowadzi-polski-5-tys-uchodzcow-wybudujemy-meczety/	Polish	fake
8	https://martabrzoza.pl/nowotwory/szwajcaria-zabronila-wykrywanie-raka-mammogramem/	Polish	fake
9	https://wpolityce.pl/polityka/385517-ujawniamy-ujawniamy-sad-najwyzszy-uniewinnil-prokuratora-ktory-prowadzil-samochod-po-po-pijanemu-uzasadnienie-nie-wiedzial-ze-mial-alkohol-we-krwi	Polish	fake clickbait
10	https://www.naturalnews.com/2019-01-11-vaccine-shot-killed-famed-cancer-doctor-in-mere-minutes-total-organ-failure.html?fbclid=IwAR0ZmLqauVPTyfEUpjpbGLpouv11lDRpcoXDJ8-FM6YMlRKeuXfFpjZstxI	English	fake clickbait

Table 1. (*continued*)

No.	Website	Lang.	Classification
11	https://gazetawroclawska.pl/wypadek-na-klimasa-ukrainiec-wjechal-w-drzewo/ar/12969637	Polish	fake clickbait
12	https://www.clickhole.com/	English	satire
13	https://zmianynaziemi.pl/wiadomosc/w-wodach-atlantyku-plywa-ponad-500-letni-rekin-polarny	Polish	fake clickbait
14	https://innpoland.pl/139543,naukowcy-wcale-nie-znalezli-512-letniego-rekina-okazuje-sie-ze-ma-zaledwie-390-lat	Polish	real
15	https://edition.cnn.com/2016/08/11/health/greenland-sharks-long-lives/index.html	English	real
16	https://www.polityka.pl/tygodnikpolityka/kraj/1692966,1,polska-nie-chce-przyjac-10-sierot-z-aleppo-powody-sa-absurdalne.read	Polish	fake clickbait
17	https://www.rp.pl/Banki/312089996-Wielka-fuzja-dwoch-liderow-PKO-BP-i-Pekao.html&cid=44&template=restricted	Polish	fake
18	https://babylonbee.com/	English	satire
19	https://awazetribune.com/	English	satire
20	http://dailybonnet.com/	Eglish	fake clickbait

4   Experiments and Results

All the online tools introduced in Sect. 2 were used during the research. We have installed them as browser extensions or have used the dedicated online interface. While using the extensions, it was necessary to visit the investigated websites. The web-based interfaces on the other hand allowed for simply pasting the web address before coming up with the evaluation. The classification performed by each tool is presented in Table 2, where the listing number of the website, manual classification and the tools' classification are given.

Table 2. News classification performed manually (Classification) and by various tools: 1 - SurfSafe, 2 - Fake News Detector AI, 3 - Trusted News, 4 - Fake News Detector, 5 - Fake News Guard, 6 - Decodex

No.	Classification	1	2	3	4	5	6
1	fake	–	fake	–	–	–	–
2	real	–	real	–	–	–	–
3	fake	fake	fake	–	–	–	–
4	fake	–	fake	–	fake	–	–
5	real	real	real	–	real	–	–
6	satire	–	real	satire	satire	satire	satire
7	fake	fake	fake	–	fake	–	–
8	fake	–	fake	–	–	–	–

Table 2. (*continued*)

No.	Classification	1	2	3	4	5	6
9	clickbait	fake	fake	–	clickbait	–	–
10	clickbait	fake	fake	–	fake	clickbait	–
11	clickbait	fake	fake	–	clickbait	–	–
12	satire	–	real	satire	clickbait	satire	satire
13	clickbait	–	fake	–	clickbait	–	–
14	real	real	real	–	–	–	–
15	real	real	real	real	real	–	real
16	clickbait	–	real	–	clickbait	–	–
17	fake	–	–	–	fake	–	–
18	satire	–	real	satire	–	–	–
19	satire	–	fake	satire	–	satire	–
20	clickbait	–	fake	–	–	fake	–

Then the accuracy of the detection was estimated. It is expressed with Eq. 1, where WL - well classified samples and N - total number of samples (here $N = 20$). We assumed that 'clickbait' is well classified when is labeled as 'clickbait' or 'fake'. The 'satire' is well classified when is labeled as 'satire' of 'fake'. 'Fake' and 'real' pieces of information are classified well only when the result is 'fake' or 'real', respectively.

$$Acc = \frac{WL}{N} \cdot 100\% \qquad (1)$$

The detailed results of the accuracy are presented in Table 3.

The table illustrates that the highest accuracy was obtained using the Fake News Detector AI (75%), while the poorest using Decodex (15%).

The provided data demonstrates that the outperforming tool was very successful in detecting the real news (100%), promising results were achieved for fake news and clickbait, but far weaker for satire.

For detecting the satire the TrustedNews tool achieved the best results on our dataset - it has classified all satire samples correctly. However, for the other categories it was significantly less successful.

The average value and standard deviation are also presented in the table. All methods give the average accuracy close to 39%. Nevertheless, the standard deviation values are very high, because the obtained accuracy results are very different for each tool and each category.

Table 3. Accuracy for different tools: 1 - SurfSafe, 2 - Fake News Detector AI, 3 - Trusted News, 4 - Fake News Detector, 5 - Fake News Guard, 6 - Decodex for all samples and 4 separate categories: 'fake', 'real', 'satiric' and 'clickbait' with average and standard deviation

Category	1	2	3	4	5	6	AVG	STD DEV
All samples	40%	75%	25%	55%	25%	15%	39%	22%
'Fake'	33%	83%	0%	50%	0%	0%	28%	34%
'Real'	75%	100%	25%	50%	0%	25%	46%	37%
'Satire'	0%	25%	100%	25%	75%	50%	46%	37%
'Clickbait'	50%	83%	0%	83%	33%	0%	42%	39%

The dataset contains sources written in the Polish and English languages. In Table 4 the accuracy of the detection is presented once again. It illustrates the dependency between the language of the content and the obtained accuracy.

It is worth focusing on two tools: TrustedNews and Fake News Guard - they provide over 60% for English content but give 0% for Polish sources. Thus, it is possible that these two tools do not contain non-English samples in the training set or database.

Table 4. Accuracy for different tools: 1 - SurfSafe, 2 - Fake News Detector AI, 3 - Trusted News, 4 - Fake News Detector, 5 - Fake News Guard, 6 - Decodex for both languages and each language separately

Language	1	2	3	4	5	6
Both	40%	75%	25%	55%	25%	15%
Polish	42%	83%	0%	58%	0%	0%
English	38%	63%	63%	50%	63%	38%

5   Conclusions and Future Work

In this article we have provided the description, evaluation and comparison of the existing online tools for the fake news detection. We also present the results of classification performed by those six tools, namely: SurfSave, Fake News Detector AI, TrustedNews, Fake News Detector, Fake News Guard and Decodex.

What is remarkable is that many attempts of classification have failed - we have got either 'error' or 'no result' feedback from the utilities. It may indicate that the evaluation databases or training sets of the tools are not sufficiently large or relevant. However, existing online tools hardly ever provided a pair of contradictory results (e.g. 'false' and 'real'). Thus, it seems to be reasonable to use more than one tool at the same time in order to protect the users from online disinformation. We have also verified whether the language of news has an impact on fake news detection. And, in case of some tools, it seems that they provide better accuracy for English text and sources.

Our research clearly shows the need for more robust solutions (e.g. lifelong learning approach to machine learning, NLP, fact checkers, AI etc.) [4,11] such as those to be developed by the EU framework programme projects like H2020 SocialTruth among others.

Acknowledgement. This work is funded under SocialTruth project, which has received funding from the European Unions Horizon 2020 Research and Innovation Programme under Grant Agreement No. 825477.

References

1. Agrawal, R., et al.: Identifying fake news from twitter sharing data: a large-scale study. arXiv preprint arXiv:1902.07207 (2019)
2. de Alfaro, L., et al.: Reputation systems for news on twitter: a large-scale study. arXiv preprint arXiv:1802.08066 (2018)
3. Choraś, M., Giełczyk, A., Demestichas, K., Puchalski, D., Kozik, R.: Pattern recognition solutions for fake news detection. In: Saeed, K., Homenda, W. (eds.) CISIM 2018. LNCS, vol. 11127, pp. 130–139. Springer, Cham (2018). https://doi.org/10.1007/978-3-319-99954-8_12
4. Choraś, M., Kozik, R., Renk, R., Hołubowicz, W.: The concept of applying lifelong learning paradigm to cybersecurity. In: Huang, D.-S., Hussain, A., Han, K., Gromiha, M.M. (eds.) ICIC 2017. LNCS (LNAI), vol. 10363, pp. 663–671. Springer, Cham (2017). https://doi.org/10.1007/978-3-319-63315-2_58
5. https://www.lemonde.fr/verification/. Accessed 18 Apr 2019
6. ENISA: Strengthening network and information security and protecting against online disinformation ('fake news'). https://www.enisa.europa.eu/publications/enisa-position-papers-and-opinions/fake-news/. Accessed 18 Apr 2019
7. http://www.fakenewsai.com/. Accessed 18 Apr 2019
8. https://fakenewsdetector.org/en. Accessed 20 Apr 2019
9. http://fakenewsguard.com/index.html. Accessed 18 Apr 2019
10. https://www.kaggle.com/mrisdal/fake-news. Accessed 26 Apr 2019
11. Kozik, R., Choras, M., Keller, J.: Balanced efficient lifelong learning (B-ELLA) for cyber attack detection. J. UCS **25**(1), 2–15 (2019)
12. Monti, F., Frasca, F., Eynard, D., Mannion, D., Bronstein, M.M.: Fake news detection on social media using geometric deep learning. arXiv preprint arXiv:1902.06673 (2019)
13. Reis, J.C., Correia, A., Murai, F., Veloso, A., Benevenuto, F., Cambria, E.: Supervised learning for fake news detection. IEEE Intell. Syst. **34**(2), 76–81 (2019)
14. Ruchansky, N., Seo, S., Liu, Y.: CSI: a hybrid deep model for fake news detection. In: Proceedings of the 2017 ACM on Conference on Information and Knowledge Management, pp. 797–806. ACM (2017)
15. Shu, K., Mahudeswaran, D., Liu, H.: FakeNewsTracker: a tool for fake news collection, detection, and visualization. Comput. Math. Organ. Theory 1–12 (2018)
16. Shu, K., Mahudeswaran, D., Wang, S., Lee, D., Liu, H.: FakeNewsNet: a data repository with news content, social context and dynamic information for studying fake news on social media. arXiv preprint arXiv:1809.01286 (2018)
17. https://www.getsurfsafe.com/. Accessed 20 Apr 2019
18. https://trusted-news.com/. Accessed 20 Apr 2019

A Model-Driven Approach for Simplified Cluster Based Test Suite Optimization of Industrial Systems – An Introduction to UMLTSO

Ayesha Kiran[✉], Farooque Azam, Muhammad Waseem Anwar,
Iqra Qasim, and Hanny Tufail

Department of Computer and Software Engineering,
College of Electrical and Mechanical Engineering, National University
of Sciences and Technology (NUST), Islamabad, Pakistan
{akiran17, iqra.qasim16,
hanny.tufail16}@ce.ceme.edu.pk,
{farooq, waseemanwar}@ceme.nust.edu.pk

Abstract. Software testing is a significant but costly activity of software development life cycle, because it accounts for more than fifty-two percent (>52%) of entire development cost. Testing requires the execution of all possible test cases in order to find defects in software. However, the selection and implementation of right test cases is always challenging for large scale industrial systems. In this context, clustering is a renowned approach for achieving optimization. However, it is difficult to optimize test cases through clustering due to its implementation complexity and time-consuming nature. Hence, a model based simple mechanism is strongly needed for optimization of generated test cases while preserving the coverage criterion. In this paper, a Unified Modeling Language profile for Test Suite Optimization (UMLTSO) is presented that models the optimization process for test case generated from java source code. Particularly, UMLTSO is capable of modeling test case generation, coverage criteria application and optimization using clustering approaches. This offers the rationale for converting the UMLTSO source code into target test cases for optimization based on different coverage criteria e.g. code coverage. The applicability of UMLTSO is validated through two industrial case studies.

Keywords: Testing · Optimization · Model-based optimization · Test case · Clustering

1 Introduction

In Software Development Life Cycle (SDLC), testing plays a crucial role. It strengthens the product quality before delivering it to the client. Testing of software is a deal between time, budget and quality. In a typical software development project, more than 52% of the budget is spent on software testing in terms of time and cost. Hence, it is essential to control the cost of testing process as much as possible due to its monotonous and time-consuming nature. For controlling this cost, test data optimization can

© Springer Nature Switzerland AG 2019
K. Saeed et al. (Eds.): CISIM 2019, LNCS 11703, pp. 152–163, 2019.
https://doi.org/10.1007/978-3-030-28957-7_14

be done during testing [1]. However, the objective of software testing cannot be achieved by simply decreasing the test data. All the potential lapses existing in industrial product or software must be adequately uncovered by the test data. Amongst several available solutions, the procedure of finding the optimum solution is regarded as optimization. Fittest dataset can be filtered out with the help of optimization and then it can be utilized to test different software or product related properties. The process of test suite optimization consists of five main steps. In first step, test cases generated from software requirements specifications or source code of a software program are used as an input. In second step, for evaluating these test cases according to some given requirement, an analysis is performed. On account of analysis performed in second step, initial test suite is selected from the pool of generated test cases. Then, an adequate cluster based optimization algorithm, or technique (e.g. K-mean, K-mediod), selected as per given requirements e.g. specific coverage criteria, fault effectiveness etc., is applied on test suite. Finally, an optimized test suite is produced as output.

Test-suite optimization speeds up regression testing by identifying and removing redundant tests based on a given set of requirements. Until now, many research efforts have been devoted on test suite optimization. As a result, various algorithms/techniques for test suite optimization have been introduced intensively. But, it is evident that less attention has been given to model based test suite optimization, therefore this research area needs to be explored further. Model-based processes encompass few features that provide additional benefit as compared to code-based heuristics. Hence, the main objective of this research is the development of a Unified Modeling Language (UML) profile for improving the efficiency and effectiveness of test suites generated from source code. It focuses on three main activities: transformation of source code into test cases, adoption of coverage criteria for test cases and optimization of test cases based on clustering techniques.

Principally, in this paper a UML profile is introduced to model the optimization process based on clustering techniques. This profile reduces the implementation complexity as well as time cost of cluster-based optimization approach. Test cases are defined by a coverage criterion such as statement coverage and the optimized test suite has to satisfy all the requirements as the original test suite. UMLTSO consists of several stereotypes for modelling complex optimization requirements. This results in transformation of the source code into target optimized test cases. Furthermore, UMLTSO can be utilized to automate the exploration of our approach by using it on actual testing environment.

The organization of paper is as follows: review of literature and summary of the present research is given in Sect. 2. Section 3 presents the proposed approach for test suite optimization based on MDA. Validation of UMLTSO using two case studies is done in Sect. 4, the discussion and advantages of proposed UML profile are presented in Sect. 5 and finally conclusion is stated in Sect. 6.

2 Literature Review

In this section, a survey of different studies that relate to test suite optimization techniques, is performed. Garousi et al. [2] states that the important part of Software Development Life Cycle (SDLC) is testing phase. Moreover, major economic disasters can be lead due to inadequate testing of software. For instance, in 2017 a report named "Software fail watch" is published by Tricentis GmbH which reveals that, in 2017 alone, a financial loss of 1.7 trillion globally is caused due to failure of software. Esfandyari and Rafe [3] explains that exhaustive testing of software takes into consideration the interaction of components and system configuration, but due to limited strategies of sampling and computational restrictions it is impractical to conduct. Similarly, Qi et al. [4] discuss that exhaustive testing is infeasible for real situations. Such as, if we have ten parameters for a system and each of these parameter can have ten different values, then a total to one thousand and ten (1010) likely combinations are generated. If the execution time of each combination is one minute, then eventually the completion of whole test takes twenty thousand years.

Singh and Shree [5] describes that the coverage of given testing requirement cannot be checked by a single test case. Therefore, a pool of test cases or a test set is required to be generated. According to Khan et al. [6], the cost and time of manual testing can be reduced by automating the whole process. The idea of automatic test case generation for a given program is presented by automatic software testing. Kothari and Rajavat [7] analyzed that in software testing the key issue is preparation of test suite or a test set that is employed on a function and then get the outcomes. But, the software testing cost significantly increases because of its time consuming nature. Many research articles have suggested that test case much be optimized in order to reduce the cost and efforts of quality assessment or the software testing process. Lin et al. [8] propose that regression testing cost is reduced by an important approach known as test suite reduction. This technique works on the basis of relationship among test requirements of the system that is being tested and the test cases of regression test set. Yamuç [9] states that test suite reduction emphasizes on the recognition of test cases which are redundant. Once these redundant test cases are identified, they can be removed from the test suites. Coviello et al. [10] propose that similar entities can be grouped into a cluster with the help of clustering algorithms. In addition to that, authors propose a prototype tool named CUTER (ClUstering-based TEst suite Reduction) for inadequate reduction of test cases. For the underlying process, CUTER employ the hierarchical agglometric algorithm. This cluster-based tool is also implemented as an eclipse plug-in.

Wang et al. [11] describe that present studies have proposed several techniques for reducing the size of test cases. But, a common framework is always shared by these approaches. Firstly, some characters such as, high coverage, high-partition which can preserve the efficiency of new test suite with the original one. Then, on the basis of these characters a series of test requirements is generated. Subsequently, for getting an optimized test suite that satisfy all testing requirements, a heuristic algorithm is applied. Lastly, information about coverage and execution of optimized test suite is collected. Anwar et al. [12] explains that although many techniques have been introduced for the purpose of optimization until now, but a better solution is still required for improving this process. Test suite optimization is a multi-dimensional problem, however, most of the current researches have dealt with it as a single objective one. According to Gebizli et al. [13], test cases can be automatically generated from system models with the help of Model-based testing (MBT). The efficiency of generated test cases is influenced by the content of these models. Similarly, Dadkhah [14] discusses that automation of generated test cases is based on software system design and UML models formulated from requirement specification. In order to find out that the requirements which are defined by software users are correctly supported, testing based on the specified requirements can be done. For accomplishing this task, it is necessary to follow the relationship among test cases and user requirements. This work can easily be done with the help of model based Semantic-based testing.

In another work, Gebizli et al. [15] explains that MBT systematizes test case generation based on models that represent the desired behavior of the system under test (SUT). The effectiveness of the generated test cases relies on the correctness and completeness of these models. Critical faults can be left undetected if the associated scenarios are not reflected to the models. Granda [16] defines that a transformation strategy is used in Model-Driven Testing (MDT) paradigm for test model generation. There are several benefits of MDT, for example, it is platform independent, rules have to be specified only once and then it can be re-used for test case generation from several requirements models with the help of same derivation, the test cases can be generated in different target codes. Seo et al. [17] analyzed transformation process of models for test case generation with the help of sequence diagrams. In this work, authors have also given the transformation rules for model execution. M D Kumar et al. [18] propose a novel approach which consists of sequence diagram transformation into Sequence Diagram Graph (SDG) and then test cases are generated from SDG. The Relational Definition Language (RDL) is also used for providing the traceability among models. Granda et al. [19] states that even though some approaches for development of test cases from UML models have been introduced, it is required to rigorously assess the completeness of defined derivation rules. A plan and design of a controlled experiment that examines the strategy for test case generation, in order to evaluate its completeness from the viewpoint of those testers, is also proposed.

According to Kalaee and Rafe [20], from the behavioral models of system under test, the systematic derivation of executable test cases can also be done through MBT approach. In many systems, low-cost implementation of a system model as compared to the complete system execution makes it more realistic than the code-driven testing approach. But, the test case generation approach aided by model checking has a major disadvantage in terms of scalability. They cannot be transferred to industry due to the problem of state space explosion. Hence, it is evident from literature that even though some research work aimed at model-based heuristic for optimization, but broader research is still required for fulfilling the needs of several domains i.e. testing based on modeling, software product lines etc. through model-based clustering methods. Heuristics based on modeling encompasses few features e.g. complexity management through abstraction, automatic mechanism, which provide additional benefit as compared to code-based heuristics. So, there is a strongly needed to develop a generic framework based on MDA for automating the whole test suite optimization process.

3 Proposed Profile

Model Driven Architecture (MDA) is distinguished methodology for development of applications that considerably streamline the design as well as verification of system that is being developed [21]. For complex application development, MDA is mostly taken into consideration. In this approach, one kind of UML mechanism for extension is a Profile based on UML. There are several specialized language elements like symbols and icons. Following key elements are composed in UML profile: (1) Classes are depicted using meta-class in profile. (2) The meta-class operation illustrates the functioning of UMLTSO. (3) Stereotype tagged values are the elementary mechanisms of UML profile. (4) Association is a meta-class that links the classes. The characteristics related to behavior of a system can be shown by means of dynamic modeling whereas they can be defined through sequence and state machine diagram. The structural aspects of a system are incorporated in structural modeling and they can be termed with the help of class diagram which comprises of relationships and attributes. For the structural view, we have considered class diagram, stereotypes and tagged values in this paper. In Fig. 1, the proposed UMLTSO is shown.

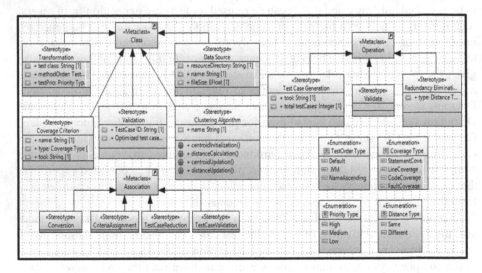

Fig. 1. Proposed unified modeling language profile for test suite optimization (UMLTSO)

3.1 UMLTSO Description

The stereotypes for UMLTSO have been presented in this section. A description of each stereotype along the base class and tagged value is given. There are twelve (12) stereotypes for managing test suite optimization process and their description is as follows:

Data Source Stereotype. This stereotype is used for retrieval of the code. It takes the path of an open source software, system etc. from where code is taken for optimization of generated test cases. Its base class is Class. Following are its three tagged values:

- Resource directory: EString [1] represents path of data source from where the code/dataset is taken as input
- Name: EString [1] represents name of data source
- File Size: EInt [1] represents size of code

Transformation Stereotype. This stereotype is used for the transformation of the source code into test cases. Its base class is Class. Following are its three tagged values:

- test class: EString [1]
- method Order: TestOrder Type [1] represents that test methods will be executed in the selected order type e.g. in order of names, sorted in ascending order
- testPrio: Priority Type [1] represents the priority of a test class

Coverage Criteria Stereotype. This stereotype provides the option to users for selection of coverage type as per their requirement. It represents the type of coverage criteria which should be undertaken throughout optimization process e.g. code coverage. Its base class is Class. Following are its three tagged values:

- Name: EString [1] represents name of coverage type
- Type: Coverage Type [1] represents type of coverage criteria for optimization
- tool: EString [1] represents the tool from which the selected coverage type is applied

Clustering Algorithm Stereotype. This stereotype allows the users to apply the clustering algorithm for optimization of generated test cases. Its base class is Class. It incorporates one tagged value and four operations which are given below:

- Name: EString [1] represents name of applied clustering algorithm
- CentroidInitialization which randomly select test cases as the center of the initial cluster
- distanceCalculation calculate the distance between the test cases of the non-center point and the centers of the clusters
- centroidUpdation take re-utilization of the non-central point in the cluster to replace the center point,
- distanceUpdation update the distance value constantly

Validation Stereotype. This stereotype helps to validates that final optimized test cases fulfills the selected coverage criteria. Its base class is Class. Following are its two tagged values:

- test case id: EInt [1] represents the id of optimized test cases which are selected on the basis of selected coverage criteria and clustering algorithm.
- Optimized test cases: EInt [1] represents the total number of test cases after optimization.

Test Case Generation Stereotype. This stereotype allows to generate the test cases from the source code through a test case generation tool which is passed as a string. Its base class is Operation. It incorporates two tagged value which are given below:

- tool: EString [1] represents the tool from which the test cases are generated
- total testCases: EInt [1] represents the count of initially generated test cases from selected tool

Redundancy Elimination Stereotype. This stereotype is used to remove the sample points with similar distance. Its base class is Operation. It incorporates one tagged value which is given below:

- Type: Distance Type [1] represents whether the test cases have similar or different distance.

Validate Stereotype. This stereotype is utilized for providing the total count of reduced test cases after the application of clustering algorithm and it checks that coverage criterion is successfully satisfied. Its base class is operation.

Conversion Stereotype. It is used for conversion of source code into test cases. Its base Class is Association.

Criteria Assignment. This stereotype is utilized for assigning a coverage criterion. Its base Class is Association.

Test Case Reduction Stereotype. This stereotype is utilized for optimizing the test cases. Its base Class is Association.

Test Case Validation Stereotype. This stereotype is utilized for the validation of optimized test cases which are produced after the application of clustering algorithm. Its base Class is Association.

4   Validation

In this section, we demonstrate the application of our profile to define the optimization for evolving source code. To do this, motivation examples are used as case studies to evaluate the feasibility of UMLTSO profile application on selected source code. According to the requirements, code.org represents the data source. To accomplish its task, three different data structures namely the File size, Name and Resource Directory, are utilized. Transformation represents the conversion of source code into test cases, it also has data structures i.e. test class, methodType, and testPrio. Coverage type depicts the application of coverage criteria for optimization, it holds Coverage type, Tool and Name.

4.1   Case Study 1: K-Mean Algorithm

For the validation of proposed UMLTSO, an industrial case study of Automatic Teller Machine (ATM) is taken into consideration. User can perform transaction through

ATM. But only one bank account is associated with a user. User have the access to their account balance, withdraw cash (i.e., take money out of an account) and deposit funds (i.e., place money into an account). The model of K-mean algorithm through UMLTSO is depicted in Fig. 2.

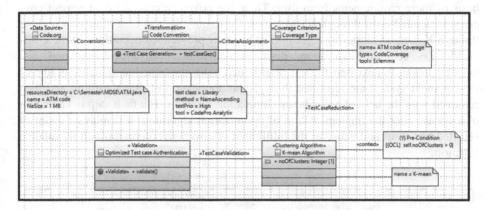

Fig. 2. The model of K-mean Algorithm through UMLTSO

On the left side of Fig. 2, a data source (code.org) is shown that retrieves the java source code of ATM through a string and then request its conversion into test cases. Initially, it requests the user to choose the test class, decide an order of method and then select the priority of test. For completing this request, the transformation (code conversion) starts the conversion process with the help of a tool (CodePro Analytix). After this transformation process, a request for the application of coverage criterion is sent. The Coverage Criterion (Coverage Type) then displays different options of coverage i.e. code coverage, statement coverage, line coverage and fault coverage. After the selection of coverage criteria, clustering algorithm (K-mean algorithm) is applied for optimization. It determines the number of the clusters as a pre-condition and then randomly selects centroid with the help of centroidInitialization function. The remaining data elements are assigned to the nearest cluster according to the distance values calculated through distanceCalculation function. Centroid of the cluster as well as distance value is updated continuously through centroidUpdation and distanceUpdation function according to the data elements in each cluster, until the criterion function converges and ends. The last step is validation of test cases (Optimized Test Case Authentication), it shows the total count of reduced test cases after the application of K-mean algorithm and checks that coverage criterion is successfully satisfied through validate function.

4.2 Case Study 2: K-Mediod Algorithm

For the second case study, we have considered the Enterprise Resource Planning (ERP) system as shown in Fig. 3. It's a business process management software that manages and integrates a company's financials, supply chain, operations, reporting, manufacturing, and human resource activities. As company's needs change and they expand, this ERP system keeps up with them. So, in the first step ERP source code is retrieved through data source. In this case study, the test class is selected as ERP, test method is name ascending and test priority is high.

The source code is transformed into different test cases through JUnit tool on the basis of these requirements from user. Then, the coverage criteria i.e. statement coverage is applied on it through EMMA tool. Consequently, test case reduction is done through K-mediod clustering algorithm. It has four pre-defined operations in the UML profile i.e. centroidInitialization, distanceCalculation, centroidUpdation and distanceUpdation. In next step, the test cases which holds the same functionality of library management system are identified through the application of this algorithm and then removed with the help of redundancy elimination function. The final step is validation of test case after the implementation of optimization algorithm. It displays a count of selected test cases and validates the fulfillment of coverage criteria through its validate function.

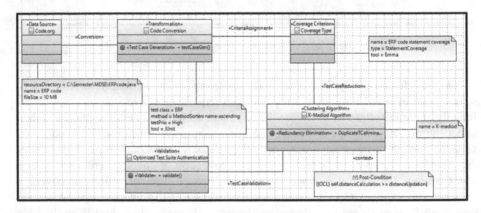

Fig. 3. The model of k-mediod algorithm through UMLTSO

5 Discussion

Software testing is done to assure the quality of software before delivering it to the clients. The quality of product, and the estimation of its reliability along verification and validation is done through the process of testing. However, the effort involved in testing is tedious and it costs more than fifty-two (>52%) of the total development cost [22]. In software testing, optimization of test data is done to control this cost. The software testing depends mainly on three main phases: test case generation, test execution and test evaluation. The later two parts are easy to implement. However, knowledge up to a certain level is required for first part. In recent years, Model Driven Architecture (MDA) has emerged as a major area for dealing with problems of software testing. The key benefit of one of its sub-area i.e. MBT (Model Based Testing), is automation of test case generation. Several MBT tools are also developed for meeting increased software testing requirements through advanced testing solutions. Several model-based heuristics have been proposed until now for generation of test suite in order to perform software testing. However, in literature, focus is mostly given on UML model based automatic generation of test cases, rather than optimization of test cases.

Researchers and practitioners have worked on various optimization approaches from decades. However, test suite optimization is still an open area of research as each of these approach has its own advantages and limitations. For example, Ant Colony Optimization (ACO), which is a meta-heuristic technique tries to identify the smallest path from all the test cases, but it does not cover all the required test cases. Similar to greedy algorithm, its convergence rate is slow to some extent and also gets trapped in local optimum [23, 24]. Greedy based approaches have good capability in cost reduction but the time taken by these approaches for performing reduction task constantly increases as soon as the test suite complexity increases and also its ability of fault detection gets worse in general [8]. From this analysis, it is evident that there is no single technique that is superior to all problems of test suite optimization. Hence, there is a need to introduce a generic framework for optimization of automated test cases.

In this regard, we have proposed a profile named UMLTSO which offers higher level of abstraction for test suite optimization. Subsequently, the complexity of optimization process is considerably reduced by applying UMLTSO. Moreover, it facilitates the automation of target test case generation process as well as their optimization from the java source code. Before the generation of test cases, the static analysis of source code is also performed using different tools like Mockito, JTest etc. By using the proposed profile, improvement can be made in quality along the elimination of friction as well as improved decision through rapid prototyping. It also helps the testers to measure accuracy as well as effectiveness before actually developing the system. UMLTSO also enhances the development time and reduces the cost. Although we intend to make a UML profile for automating test suite optimization process, there are few things that still need to be addressed. UMLTSO is based on clustering approach e.g. K-Mean and K-Mediod, for performing optimization task. In case of K-Mean algorithm, it is difficult to predict K-value, so it needs to be defined at run time. On the other hand, K-mediod algorithm performs better than K-mean but it has higher time complexity. A complete UML profile for automating test suite optimization process is defined, but we are still working for the validation of well-formedness of proposed UMLTSO profile as well as evaluation of its performance. The working on transformation engine is also under progress for automatic generation of optimized test cases with the help of UMLTSO source models for early verification of software.

6   Conclusion

This paper describes a Unified Modeling Language profile for Test Suite Optimization (UMLTSO) of test cases generated from source code by using the characteristics of clustering techniques. In the proposed approach, twelve stereotypes are utilized for characterizing the optimization requirements in software test cases by means of models.

This specifies the foundation to convert the UMLTSO source code into test cases for timely verification of testing requirements. Subsequently, UMLTSO considerably reduces the complexity for implementation of test case optimization strategy in testing of industrial systems. The validation of UMLTSO applicability is done with the help of ATM and ERP case studies on two clustering algorithms i.e. K-mean and K-mediod. However, this work is yet under development and we are working on the transformation engine for automatic generation of target optimized test cases from UMLTSO source code using clustering approach for timely verification of industrial system.

References

1. Mall, R.: Fundamentals of software engineering. PHI Learning Pvt. Ltd (2014)
2. Garousi, V., Özkan, R., Betin-Can, A.: Multi-objective regression test selection in practice: an empirical study in the defense software industry. Inf. Softw. Technol. **103**, 40–54 (2018)
3. Esfandyari, S., Rafe, V.: A tuned version of genetic algorithm for efficient test suite generation in interactive t-way testing strategy. Inf. Softw. Technol. **94**, 165–185 (2018)
4. Qi, R.Z., Wang, Z.J., Li, S.Y.: A parallel genetic algorithm based on spark for pairwise test suite generation. J. Comput. Sci. Technol. **31**(2), 417–427 (2016)
5. Singh, S., Shree, R.: A combined approach to optimize the test suite size in regression testing. CSI Trans. ICT **4**(2–4), 73–78 (2016)
6. Khan, R., Amjad, M., Srivastava, A.K.: Optimization of automatic generated test cases for path testing using genetic algorithm. In: 2016 Second International Conference on Computational Intelligence & Communication Technology (CICT), pp. 32–36. IEEE (2016)
7. Kothari, S., Rajavat, A.: Minimizing the size of test suite using genetic algorithm for object-oriented program. In: International Conference on ICT in Business Industry & Government (ICTBIG), pp. 1–5. IEEE (2016)
8. Lin, C.T., Tang, K.W., Wang, J.S., Kapfhammer, G.M.: Empirically evaluating greedy-based test suite reduction methods at different levels of test suite complexity. Sci. Comput. Program. **150**, 1–25 (2017)
9. Yamuç, A., Cingiz, M.Ö., Biricik, G., Kalıpsız, O.: Solving test suite reduction problem using greedy and genetic algorithms. In: 2017 9th International Conference on Electronics, Computers and Artificial Intelligence (ECAI), pp. 1–5. IEEE (2017)
10. Coviello, C., Romano, S., Scanniello, G.: Poster: CUTER: ClUstering-based TEst Suite Reduction. In: IEEE/ACM 40th International Conference on Software Engineering: Companion (ICSE-Companion), Gothenburg, pp. 306–307 (2018)
11. Wang, X., Jiang, S., Gao, P., Ju, X., Wang, R., Zhang, Y.: Cost-effective testing-based fault localization with distance-based test-suite reduction. Sci. China Inf. Sci. **60**(9), 092112 (2017)
12. Anwar, Z., et al.: A hybrid-adaptive neuro-fuzzy inference system for multi-objective regression test suites optimization, pp. 1–15 (2018)
13. Gebizli, C.Ş., Metin, D., Sözer, H.: Combining model-based and risk-based testing for effective test case generation. In: 2015 IEEE Eighth International Conference on Software Testing, Verification and Validation Workshops (ICSTW), Graz, pp. 1–4 (2015)
14. Dadkhah, M.: Semantic-based test case generation. In: 2016 IEEE International Conference on Software Testing, Verification and Validation (ICST), Chicago, IL, pp. 377–378 (2016)
15. Gebizli, C.S., Sözer, H.: Improving models for model-based testing based on exploratory testing. In: 2014 IEEE 38th International Computer Software and Applications Conference Workshops, Vasteras, pp. 656–661 (2014)

16. Granda, M.F., Condori-Fernández, N., Vos, T.E.J., Pastor, O.: Towards the automated generation of abstract test cases from requirements models. In: 2014 IEEE 1st International Workshop on Requirements Engineering and Testing (RET), Karlskrona, pp. 39–46 (2014)
17. Coviello, C., Romano, S., Scanniello, G., Marchetto, A., Antoniol, G., Corazza, A.: Clustering support for inadequate test suite reduction. In: 2018 IEEE 25th International Conference on Software Analysis, Evolution and Reengineering (SANER), pp. 95–105. IEEE (2018)
18. Dhineshkumar, M., Galeebathullah: An approach to generate test cases from sequence diagram. In: 2014 International Conference on Intelligent Computing Applications, Coimbatore, pp. 345–349 (2014)
19. Granda, M.F.: An experiment design for validating a test case generation strategy from requirements models. In: 2014 IEEE Fourth International Workshop on Empirical Requirements Engineering (EmpiRE). IEEE (2014)
20. Kalaee, A., Rafe, V.: Model-based test suite generation for graph transformation system using model simulation and search-based techniques. Inf. Softw. Technol. **108**, 1–29 (2018)
21. Anwar, M.W., Rashid, M., Azam, F., Kashif, M.: Model-based design verification for embedded systems through SVOCL: an OCL extension for system verilog. J. Des. Autom. Embed. Syst. **21**(1), 1–36 (2017)
22. Zhang, X., Shan, H., Qian, J.: Resource-aware test suite optimization. In: 9th International Conference on Quality Software QSIC 2009, pp. 341–346. IEEE (2009)
23. Zhang, Y.-N., Yang, H., Lin, Z.-K., Dai, Q., Li, Y.-F.: A test suite reduction method based on novel quantum ant colony algorithm. In: 2017 4th International Conference on Information Science and Control Engineering (ICISCE), pp. 825–829. IEEE (2017)
24. Kumar, S., Ranjan, P., Rajesh, R.: Modified ACO to maintain diversity in regression test optimization. In: 2016 3rd International Conference on Recent Advances in Information Technology (RAIT), pp. 619–625. IEEE (2016)

Linking Open Drug Data: Lessons Learned

Guma Lakshen[1], Valentina Janev[2](✉) [iD], and Sanja Vraneš[2]

[1] School of Electrical Engineering, University of Belgrade, Belgrade, Serbia
jlackshen65@yahoo.com
[2] Mihajlo Pupin Institute, University of Belgrade, Belgrade, Serbia
{valentina.janev, sanja.vranes}@institutepupin.com

Abstract. Linked Open Data illustrates the concept that provides an optimum solution for information and dissemination of data, through the representation of the data in an open machine-readable format and to interlink it from diverse repositories to enable diverse usage scenarios for both humans and machines. The pharmaceutical/drug industry was among the first that validated the applicability of the approach for interlinking and publishing open linked data. This paper examines in detail the process of building Linked Data application taking into consideration the possibility of reusing recently published datasets and tools. Main conclusions derived from this study are that making drug datasets accessible and publish it in an open manner in linkable format adds great value by integration to other notable datasets. Yet, open issues arose clearly when trying to apply the approach to datasets coded in languages other than English, for instance, in Arabic languages.

Keywords: Linked data · Drugs application: Arabic datasets · Quality · Lessons learned

1 Introduction

The World Wide Web has emerged in 1989 with an objective to tackle the widely spread difficulties to exchange information between different systems that arose in the 1980s, such as incompatible networks, disk/data formats, as well as character-encoding schemes [1]. The power the web possesses today lies in the amount of information it holds that represents a goldmine for data-driven applications and services. Its weakness, however, is caused by a potential design flaw: it was envisioned as a virtual documentation system. Storing the documents in unstructured form makes extracting information a manual and often tedious task. To obtain information, perform detailed analysis, create new products or additional documents, an efficient approach is needed to code the data and describe the data sources. More precisely, we need a standard, machine-readable format that allows for large-scale integration of, and reasoning on, data on the Web.

1.1 About Linked Data Approach

In 2001, Sir Tim Berners-Lee, the Director of the Wide Web Consortium outlined his vision for the Semantic Web as an extension of the conventional Web and as a world-wide

K. Saeed et al. (Eds.): CISIM 2019, LNCS 11703, pp. 164–175, 2019.
https://doi.org/10.1007/978-3-030-28957-7_15

distributed architecture where data and services easily interoperate [2]. Additionally, in 2006, Berners-Lee proposed the basic principles for interlinking linking datasets on the Web through references to common concepts known as Linked Data principles [3].

Thus Linked Open Data (LOD) movement was initiated for organizations to make their existing data available in a machine-readable format. In the last decade, the Linked Data approach has been adopted by an increasing number of data providers leading to the creation of a global data space that contains many billions of assertions—the LOD cloud, http://lod-cloud.net/. The cloud has increased from 12 datasets in 2007 to 1,229 with 16,113 links (as of April 2019, https://www.lod-cloud.net/).

1.2   Motivation

Due to the standardization and development of semantic web technologies, data being published on the web as linked data added tremendous value to institutions, research centers, and enterprises. In the drug industry, the rapidly increasing amount of data on the web opens new opportunities for integrating and enhancing drug knowledge on a global scale. The pharmaceutical/drug industry was leading others in expressing interest in validating uuthe approach for publishing and integrating open data. Linked Open Drug Data LODD endpoint was created in 2011, https://www.w3.org/wiki/HCLSIG/LODD [4], which is a set of linked datasets related to Drug Discovery. It includes data from several datasets including DrugBank (https://www.drugbank.ca/), DailyMed, LinkedCT, SIDER, ClinicalTrials.gov, RxNorm, and NCBI Entrez Gene, a detailed comparison of the LODD datasets can be accessed at https://www.w3.org/wiki/HCLSIG/LODD/Data, notably this page was last updated on 28th December 2012. Later, in 2014, the 3rd release of Bio2RDF (http://bio2rdf.org/ or https://github.com/bio2rdf/) was published as the largest network of Linked Data for the Life Sciences (35 datasets).

This motivates the authors to examine the use of available Linked Data tools for interlinking local drug datasets (from one or more countries) with datasets integrated in the LOD cloud. In this paper the authors proposes improvements in the Linked Data lifecycle in tasks related to quality assessment in the process of consuming the open data. The framework enhances the existing methodology of integrating (transforming/interlinking) open data and proposes integration of quality assessment services for improving the overall performance of the Linked Drug Data application.

The paper is structured as follows. Section II introduces the business objectives, gives a review on Linked Data methodologies and proposes an approach for building a Linked Data application. Section III presents in detail the process of transforming the Arabic drug datasets as a linked data and discusses the results and benefits for end-users. Section IV points to lessons learned in relation to the flexibility of using the created graph and challenges with quality assessment issues. Section V concludes the paper with hints for future work.

2 Building Linked Data Apps

2.1 Pharmaceutical/Drug Industry: Business Objectives

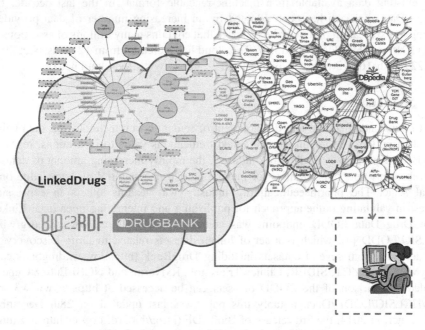

Fig. 1. Integrating public and private datasets.

The goal of the target application is to enable end-users to answer inquiries about drug availability in the open datasets (e.g. DrugBank, DBpedia, see Table 1) and enrichment of local data with information from the Web. The end-user will benefit from the interlinking of private datasets with public data and enrichment of local data with information from the Web (Fig. 1).

Examples of key business queries are:

1. For a particular drug, retrieve relative information in the Arabic language (if it exists) from other identified datasets, such as DrugBank and DBpedia.
2. For a particular drug, retrieve equivalent drugs, and compare their active ingredients, contradictions, and prices.
3. For a particular drug, retrieve valuable information about equivalent drugs with different commercial names, manufacturers, strengths, forms, prices, etc.
4. For a particular drug, retrieve its reference information to highlight possible contradiction, e.g., in combination with other drugs, allergies, or special cases (e.g., pregnancy).
5. For a particular active ingredient, retrieve advanced clinical information, i.e., pharmacological action, pharmacokinetics, etc.
6. For a particular drug, retrieve its cost, manufacturer, and country.

Table 1. Linked datasets - examples

DataSet	Description
DrugBank	DrugBank is a web-enabled database containing comprehensive molecular information about drugs, their mechanisms, their interactions, and their targets. First described in 2006, DrugBank has continued to evolve over the past 12 years in response to marked improvements to web standards and changing needs for drug research and development. See https://www.drugbank.ca/
DBpedia	DBpedia is an ongoing project designed to extract structured data from Wikipedia. It contains RDF data about 2.49 million things out of which is 218 million triples describing 2300 drugs. DBpedia is updated every three months. See https://www.DBpedia.org

2.2 Survey of Linked Data Methodologies

In literature, not many papers dealt with Linked Data methodologies i.e. the process of generating, linking, publishing and using Linked Data, to name a few: *Best Practices for Publishing Linked Data* (W3C-Government Linked Data Working Group 2014) [5], *A Cookbook for Publishing Linked Government Data on the Web* (Hyland et al. 2011) [6], *Linked Data Life Cycles* (Hausenblas et al. 2016) [7], *Guidelines for Publishing Government Linked Data* (Villazón-Terrazas et al. 2011) [8], *Managing the Life-Cycle of Linked Data with the LOD2 Stack* (Auer et al. 2012) [9], and *Methodological guidelines for consolidating drug data* (Jovanović and Trajanov 2017) [10], see Table 2 below for a brief comparison. One of the first Linked Data methodologies was developed in the European research project LOD2 (2010–2014) [9] that was mainly dedicated to the publishing process, i.e. opening the data in a machine-readable format and establishing the prerequisite tools and technologies for interlinking and integration of heterogeneous data sources in general. Jovanović and Trajanov [10] proposed a new Linked Data methodology with a focus on reuse which provides guidelines to data publishers on defining reusable components in the form of tools and schemas/services for the given domain (i.e. drug management).

Table 2. Survey on linked data methodologies

Authors	Title/Steps	
W3C Government Linked Data Working Group [5]	***Best Practices for Publishing Linked Data*:**	
	(1) Prepare stakeholders, (2) Select a dataset, (3) Model the data, (4) Specify an appropriate license, (5) Good URIs for linked data, (6) Use standard vocabularies,	*Initialization*
	(7) Convert data, (8) Provide machine access to data,	*Innovation*
	(9) Announce new data sets, (10) Recognize the social contract	*Validation & Maintenance*

(continued)

Table 2. (*continued*)

Authors	Title/Steps	
Hyland et al. [6]	*A Cookbook for Publishing Linked Government Data on the Web*:	
	(1) Identify, (2) Model, (3) Name, (4) Describe,	*Initialization*
	(5) Convert, (6) Publish,	*Innovation*
	(7) Maintain	*Validation & Maintenance*
Hausenblas et al. [7]	*Linked Data Life Cycles*:	
	(1) Data awareness, (2) Modeling,	*Initialization*
	(3) Publishing, (4) Discovery, (5) Integration,	*Innovation*
	(6) Use-cases	*Validation & Maintenance*
Villazón-Terrazas et al. [8]	*Guidelines for Publishing Government Linked Data*:	
	(1) Specify, (2) Model,	*Initialization*
	(3) Generate, (4) Publish,	*Innovation*
	(5) Exploit	*Validation & Maintenance*
Auer et al. [9]	*Managing the Life-Cycle of Linked Data with the LOD2 Stack*:	
	(1) Extraction,	*Initialization*
	(2) Storage, (3) Authoring, (4) Interlinking, (5) Classification,	*Innovation*
	(6) Quality, (7) Evolution/Repair, (8) Search/Browsing/Exploration	*Validation & Maintenance*
Jovanovik and Trajanov [10]	*Methodological guidelines for consolidating drug data*:	
	(1) Domain and Data Knowledge, (2) Data Modeling and Alignment,	*Initialization*
	(3) Transformation into 5-star Linked Data, (4) Publishing the Linked Data Dataset on the Web,	*Innovation*
	(5) Use-cases, Applications and Services	*Validation & Maintenance*

2.3   Proposal for a Piloting Methodology

Taking into consideration that end-use organization might be interested to implement innovations in existing drug data management, the authors propose to split the implementation of the Linked Data application development into three phases as follows [11]:

Phase I: INITIALIZATION

Business objectives and requirements: Requirement specification, technical characterization, and setting up of the demo site; establishing acceptance (success) criteria for pilot applications validation based on performance characteristics, usability, as well as EU and national regulations (e.g., related to data access and security measures);

Data categorization and description: Analysis of the datasets to be published in linked data format and selection of vocabularies and development other specifications for metadata description.

Phase II: INNOVATION

Integrating datasets in the form of a knowledge graph: Data access, transformation, and enrichment.

Generic component selection and tool customization for the pilot applications: Customization of linked data components for use in the targeted domain.

Specific tools development: Integration of security measures to deal with possible communication threats.

Phase III: VALIDATION

Continuous validation of the open-source tools that have been reused, providing feedback for improving the solution components, and testing for imperfect data.

3   Testing the Piloting Methodology in the Drug Domain

The authors tested the proposed methodology for development of the Linked Drug Data Application with datasets from the pharmaceutical/drug industry from the Arabic region. The Arab world also known as the Arab nation currently consists of the 22 Arab countries of the Arab League and has a combined population of around 422 million inhabitants. The Arabic language content in the World Wide Web is less than 3%; the situation is even worse regarding Arabic open data, Arabic linked data, and Arabic drug open linked data. As far as medical data available in the Arab region, there are only a handful of Arabic drug applications such as Webteb [12], Altibbi [13], and 123esaaf [14], which provide their services in Arabic and English, but unfortunately, the data is not open and most are not free. Arabic language content on the web is less than 3%. The situation is even worse regarding Arabic open data, linked data, and open linked data on drugs. This limitation of Arabic content encourages the researcher to enrich the Arabic user experience by utilizing semantic web technologies to interlink their data with other languages, including English.

3.1   Phase I - Data Categorization and Description

As a use case scenario, the authors selected four drug data files from four different Arabic countries, Iraq, Saudi Arabia, Syria, and Lebanon as shown in Table 3. Most of the open published files in the Arab region are either in PDF or XLS format. The reasons for choosing XLS format were data fidelity, ability to source from a wider range of public sector domains, and to have increased value that comes from many information linkages. The authors believe that for many years to come, more drug data will be published in XLS format in the Arab countries.

The selected datasets are open data published by health ministries or equivalent bodies in the respected governments. They are regularly updated, usually after a two-year period. As it can be noticed from the difference in the number of columns, the structure of the datasets is not unified, which makes the unification and mapping of data necessary.

The data quality of the selected files is too low; most of XLS documents do not represent the generic name or their ATC code which makes the data almost unusable for further transformation.

Table 3. Selected Arabic open drug datasets

Country	No. of tuples	No. of columns
Iraq	9090	9
Lebanon	5822	15
Saudi Arabia	6386	10
Syria	9375	7

3.2   Phase II - Integrating Datasets in a Form of a Knowledge Graph

In what follows we will describe the steps required in the process of transforming, and linking the Arabic drug data in a form of a knowledge graph.

Data Cleaning
OpenRefine (http://openrefine.orgVersion 2.6-rc1) was used to clean the selected data in order to make it coherent and ready for further operations according to the methodology. A well-organized cleaning operation minimizes inconsistencies and ensures data standardization among a verity of data sources.

Ontology Definition and Data Mapping Schema
Some of the ontologies and vocabularies which a data publisher needs to have in mind biomedical ontologies. The schema comprises classes and properties are Schema.org (https://schema.org/), DBpedia Ontology UMBEL (http://umbel.org/), DICOM (https://www.dicomstandard.org/), and the DrugBank Ontology used, as well as other from the Schema.org vocabulary: the *schema:Drug* class (https://health-lifesci.schema.org/Drug), along with a large set of properties which instances of the class can have, such as generic *drug name, code, active substances, non-proprietary Name, strength value, cost per unit, manufacturer, related drug, description, URL, license, etc.* Additionally, in order to align the drug data with generic drugs from DrugBank, properties *brandName, genericName, atcCode and dosageForm* from the DrugBank Ontology were used. The relation rdfs:seeAlso can be used to annotate the links which the drug product entities will have to generic drug entities from the LOD Cloud dataset. The nodes are linked according to the relations these classes, tables or groups have between them. There exist a few tools for ontology and vocabulary discovery which should be

used in this operation such as Linked Open Vocabularies (LOV, http://lov.okfn.org/) and DERI Vocabularies (http://datahub.io).

Data Conversion

Create RDF dataset: The previously mapped schema can produce an RDF graph by using RDF-extension of LODRefine tool. This step transforms raw data into RDF dataset based on a serialization format. Transformation process can be executed in many different ways, and with various software tools, e.g. OpenRefine (which the authors used), RDF Mapping Language (http://rml.io/spec.html), and XLWrap (http://xlwrap.sourceforge.net/), among others.

Interlinking

LODRefine was used for reconciliation in interlinking the data. In this case, columns atcCode, genericName1, activeSubstance1, activeSubstance2 and activeSubstance3 reconciled with DBpedia. This operation enables interoperability between organization data and the Web through establishing semantic links between the source dataset (organization data) with related datasets on the Web. Link discovery can be performed in manual, semi-automated, or fully-automated modes to help discover links between the source and target datasets. Since the manual mode is tedious, error-prone, and time-consuming, and the fully-automated mode is currently unavailable, the semi-automated mode is preferred and reliable. Link generation yields links in RDF format using *rdfs: seeAlso* or *owl:sameAs* predicates. The activities of link discovery and link generation are performed sequentially for each data source. The last activity within the interlinking stage is the generation of overall link statistics which showcase the total number of links generated between the source and target data sources.

Storage/SPARQL Endpoints

OpenLink virtuoso server (version 06.01.3127, https://virtuoso.openlinksw.com/) on Linux (x86_64-pc-Linux-gnu), Single Server Edition was used to run the *SPARQL endpoint*.

Publication

RDF graph can be accessed on the following link: http://aldda.b1.finki.ukim.mk/. For publishing linked data on the web, a linked data API is needed, which makes a connection with the database to answer specific queries. The HTTP endpoint is a webpage that forms the interface. A REST API is used to make a web application. It makes it possible to give the linked data back to the user in various formats, depending on the user's requirements. The linked data can be made visible in HTML on a website as HTTP links or as RDF data in a browser or a graphic visualization in a web application, which would be the most user-friendly.

3.3   Phase II - Specific Tools Development

The authors have made experiments and tested the quality of the public datasets that are used for enrichment, in particular the DBpedia. The DBpedia knowledge base contains information on many different domains that is automatically extracted from Wikipedia, based on infoboxes. The automatic extraction has obvious advantages in terms of speed and quantity of data (ensures wide coverage), but it also poses some quality issues.

When it comes to quality assessment of the DBpedia Arabic Chapter, there are problems specific to the Arabic language that result in:

1. Presentation of characters as symbols via web browsers due to errors during the extraction process.
2. Wrong values in numerical data, due to the use of Hindu numerals in some Arabic sources.
3. Occurrence of different names for the same attribute, for instance, the birth date attribute appears in various infoboxes by different names: one time as "الميــلاد تــاريخ" [birth date], another time as "الــولادة تــاريخ" [delivery date], the third time as "الميــلاد" [birth].
4. Inconsistency of names between the infobox and its template; for instance, there is a template called "مدينــة" [city] while the infobox name is called "مدينــة معلومــات" [city information].
5. Geo-names templates formatting problems when placed in the infobox.
6. Errors in *owl:sameAs* relations and problems in identifying the *owl:sameAs* relations due to heterogeneity in different data sources.

However, some of the problems present in other DBpedia chapters are also identified in the Arabic chapter, specifically:

7. Wrong Wikipedia Infobox information; for example, the height of minaret of the grand mosque in Mecca (the most valuable mosque for all Muslims) is given as 1.89 m, where the correct height is 89 m.
8. Mapping problems from Wikipedia, such as unavailability of infoboxes for many Arabic articles; for example, "Man-made river in Libya يالصــناع النهــر," which is considered as the biggest water pipeline project in the world, or not containing all the desired information.
9. Object values incompletely or incorrectly extracted.
10. Data type incorrectly extracted.
11. Some templates may be more abstract, thus cannot map to a specific class.
12. Some templates are unused or missing inside the articles.

Hence, what is needed when working with open data is tools for quality assessment of datasets prior to interlinking with the private datasets.

3.4   Phase III – Validation of Scenarios for Querying Pharmaceutical/Drug Datasets

Visualization and Querying

After publishing the data in Linked Data format it becomes available to other web applications for retrieving and visualization. The use of standard vocabularies for modeling the data allows the end-users to use different visualization opportunities e.g. freely available libraries can be used that offer diverse types of visualization such as a table or in a diagram formatted in different ways. Custom visualization applications can be used to enable a user to interact with data (Fig. 2).

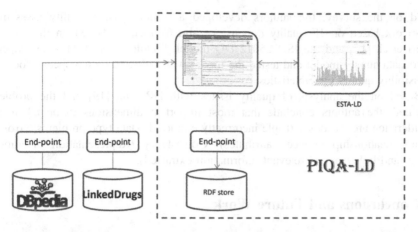

Fig. 2. Knowledge Graph Visualization and Querying.

4 Lessons Learned

4.1 About the Linked Data Format and the Knowledge Graph

The linked data approach, based on principles defined back in 2006 and on best practices for publishing and connecting structured data on the web (as elaborated by ICT experts), can play an important role in the domain of semantic interoperability. Web data, including drug data, is published most often in a two-star format data, i.e., PDF or XLS format (see Berners-Lee's categorization of open data). However, the authors decided to use the RDF, because it is recommended by W3C, and it has advantages, such as an extensible schema, self-describing data, de-referenceable URIs. Further, since RDF links are typed, it enables good structure, interoperability, and safely linking different datasets.

Before converting XLS data to RDF, the authors selected a target ontology to describe the drugs contained in the drug availability dataset. Authors selected the LinkedDrugs ontology [10], Schema.org vocabulary, and DBpedia, as they have the needed properties and provide easier interlinking possibilities for further transformation. The Web Ontology Language allows complex logical reasoning and consistency checking for RDF and OWL resources. These reasoning capabilities helped the authors to harmonize the heterogeneous data structures found in the input datasets.

4.2 About the Quality of Open Data

Many authors have pointed out issues such as the completeness, conciseness, and consistency of open data. In 2014, Kontostas et al. [15] provided several automatic quality tests on LOD datasets based on patterns modeling various error cases, and they detected 63 million errors among 817 million triples. At the same time, Zaveri et al. [16], conducted a user-driven quality evaluation which stated that DBpedia indeed has quality problems (e.g., around 12% of the evaluated triples had issues). They can be summarized as incorrect or missing values, incorrect data types, and incorrect links.

Based on the survey, the authors developed a comprehensive quality assessment framework based on 18 quality dimensions and 69 metrics. Based on the work of Zaveri et al. [17] and the ISO 25012 DQ model, Radulović et al. [18] developed a linked data quality model and tested the model with DBpedia with a special focus on accessibility quality characteristics.

Based on the analysis of quality issues with DBpedia [19] and the problems identified, the authors conclude that most important dimensions to be taken into consideration are Accuracy (triple incorrectly extracted; Data type problems; errors in implicit relationship between attributes); Consistency (Representation of number values) and Relevancy (Irrelevant information extracted).

5   Conclusions and Future Work

Most of the available drug datasets nowadays are still provided in 2-star format and in English language due to the fact that the English language is widespread among physicians and pharmacists and also a predominant language in communications between physicians and pharmacists. In order to showcase the possibilities for large-scale integration of drug data, the authors proposed a piloting methodology and tested the approach with datasets from Arabic countries. The authors presented the transformation process of 2-star drug data into a 5-star Linked Open Data with DrugBank and DBpedia. The OpenLink virtuoso server (version 06.01.3127) on Linux (x86_64-pc-linux-gnu), Single Server Edition is used to run our SPARQL endpoint (see http://aldda.b1.finki.ukim.mk/sparql).

The paper showcases the benefits from the Linked Data approach and for the first time discusses the issues with drug data from Arabic countries (authors selected four drug data files from four different Arabic countries, Iraq, Syria, Saudi Arabia, and Lebanon).

Taking into consideration the issues identified with quality of the open data (in particular, the issues with drug data from Arabic countries), the future work will include implementation of a stable and open-source web applications that will allow the end-user to fully explore and assess the quality of the consolidated dataset, and if possible, to repair the errors observed in the Arabic Linked Drug dataset.

Acknowledgments. The research presented in this paper is partly financed by the Ministry of Science and Technological Development of the Republic of Serbia (SOFIA project, Pr. No: TR-32010) and partly by the EU project LAMBDA (GA No. 809965).

References

1. Halpin, H.: Social Semantics: The Search for Meaning on the Web. Semantic Web and Beyond, vol. 13. Springer, New York (2013). https://doi.org/10.1007/978-1-4614-1885-6
2. Berners-Lee, T., Hendler, J., Lassila, O.: The Semantic Web. Sci. Am. (2001)
3. Berners-Lee, T.: Design issues: Linked Data. http://www.w3.org/DesignIssues/LinkedData.html. Accessed 1 May 2019

4. Jentzsch A., et al.: Linking open drug data. In: Triplification Challenge of the International Conference on Semantic Systems (2009)
5. W3C, Best Practices for Publishing Linked Data (2016). http://www.w3.org/TR/ld-bp/. Accessed 1 May 2019
6. Hyland, B., Wood, D.: The joy of data: a cookbook for publishing linked government data on the web. In: Wood, D. (ed.) Linking Government Data, pp. 3–26. Springer, New York (2011). https://doi.org/10.1007/978-1-4614-1767-5_1
7. Hausenblas, M.: Linked Data Life Cycles (2016). http://www.slideshare.net/mediasemanticweb/linked-data-life-cycles
8. Villazón-Terrazas, B., Vilches-Blázquez, L.M., Corcho, O., Gómez-Pérez, A.: Methodological guidelines for publishing government linked data. In: Wood, D. (ed.) Linking Government Data. Springer, New York, NY (2011). https://doi.org/10.1007/978-1-4614-1767-5_2
9. Auer, S., et al.: Managing the life-cycle of linked data with the LOD2 stack. In: Cudré-Mauroux, P., et al. (eds.) ISWC 2012. LNCS, vol. 7650, pp. 1–16. Springer, Heidelberg (2012). https://doi.org/10.1007/978-3-642-35173-0_1
10. Jovanovik, M., Trajanov, D.: Consolidating drug data on a global scale using linked data. J. Biomed. Semant. 8(1), 3 (2017)
11. Janev, V., Mijović, V., Milosević, U., Vraneš, S.: Linked data apps: lessons learned. In: Trajanov, D., Bakeva, V. (eds.) ICT Innovations 2017 Web Proceedings, Communications in Computer and Information Science book series (CCIS, volume 778) (2017). ISSN 1865-0937
12. WebTeb. https://www.webteb.com/aboutusen
13. Altibbi. https://www.altibbi.com/
14. esaaf. https://www.123esaaf.com/
15. Kontokostas, D., Westphal, P., Auer, S., Hellmann, S., Lehmann, J., Cornelissen, R.: Test driven evaluation of linked data quality. In: Proceeding of the 23rd International Conference on World Wide Web, New York, NY, USA, pp. 747–758 (2014). http://dx.doi.org/10.1145/2566486.2568002
16. Zaveri, A., et al.: User-driven quality evaluation of DBpedia. In: Proceedings of the 9th International Conference on Semantic Systems, New York, NY, USA, pp. 97–104 (2013)
17. Zaveri, A., Rula, A., Maurino, A., Pietrobon, R., Lehmann, J., Auer, S.: Quality assessment for linked data: a survey. Semant. Web Interoperability Usability Appl. 7(1), 63–93 (2016). https://doi.org/10.3233/SW-150175
18. Radulović, F., Mihindukulasooriya, N., García-Castro, R., Gómez-Pérez, A.: A comprehensive quality model for linked data. Semant. Web Interoperability Usability Appl. 9(1), 3–24 (2018). https://doi.org/10.3233/SW-170267. Special issue on Quality Management of Semantic Web Assets (Data, Services and Systems)
19. Lackshen, G., Janev, V., Vraneš, S.: Quality assessment of Arabic DBpedia. In: Proceedings of 8th International Conference on Web Intelligence, Mining and Semantics, 25–27 June 2018, Novi Sad, Serbia. ACM, New York (2018). https://doi.org/10.1145/3227609.3227675

Cluster Based Framework for Alleviating Buffer Based Congestion for Wireless Sensor Network

Soumyabrata Saha[1](✉) and Rituparna Chaki[2]

[1] JIS College of Engineering, Kalyani, West Bengal, India
som.brata@gmail.com
[2] University of Calcutta, Kolkata, West Bengal, India
rituchaki@gmail.com

Abstract. In wireless sensor networks, event based applications prone to traffic congestion and unforeseen event detection produce an unremitting generation of traffic throughout the network. The congestion control procedure is used to monitor the process of adapting the total amount of data and concerns to control the network traffic levels to an acceptable value. The performance control mechanism can be conceded through robust congestion control techniques to uphold the operational networks under different conditions. Congestion in sensor networks has to be controlled to achieve high energy efficiency, to prolong the life of the system, improve equity, the quality of service in terms of throughput, packet loss and delay. The information gleaned from an extensive review is shared to reinforce the knowledge base to design a scalable distributed cluster based framework for alleviating buffer based congestion in WSNs and evenly dispense the energy usage among all nodes within the networks. The results show that the proposed technique is simple, efficient and capable of successful dealing with congestion in WSN while preserving the performance characteristics of the network.

Keywords: Wireless sensor networks · Cluster · Buffer · Congestion · Throughput

1 Introduction

Advancement in wireless sensor networks have been growing interest in perceptive and optimizing network routing and the impending use in real life applications like military, environmental, health, space exploration, vehicular movement, disaster management, combat field reconnaissance etc. Immense and random placement of sensor nodes on a monitored field renders node communication an intricate task to be achieved and interference, congestion, and routing related issues may affect the network communication at any point of time. Due to the circumscribed communication range, packet forwarding in sensor networks is usually performed through multi-hop fashion. Routing challenges in wireless sensor networks stem from the unique characteristics of these networks, such as limited energy supply, computing power, bandwidth on the wireless links, and congestion, which impose severe restrictions on the design of

© Springer Nature Switzerland AG 2019
K. Saeed et al. (Eds.): CISIM 2019, LNCS 11703, pp. 176–190, 2019.
https://doi.org/10.1007/978-3-030-28957-7_16

efficient routing protocols of WSNs. Routing protocol must reassure uniform energy dissipation across the network, quickly converge irrespective of the network node density, and be flexible in terms of the routing framework and the route computation metric.

A node in a sensor network is a small embedded computing device that interfaces with sensors and communicates using short-range wireless transmitters. Sensor nodes act autonomously but courteously to form a logical network where data packets are routed through hop-by-hop fashion towards management nodes those are acknowledged as sinks or base stations.

Depending on the numerous applications, the generation of large, sudden, and correlated impulses of data would be delivered to the sinks without disrupting the performance of the sensing application. This high generation rate of data packets is intermittently unrestrained and often leads to congestion. Congestion control is an exceedingly imperative area within wireless sensor networks, where as traffic becomes greater than the aggregated or individual capacity of the underlying channels. Special considerations are obligatory to develop more classy techniques to avoid, detect, and resolve congestion. The main sources of congestion include buffer overflow, channel contention, interference, packet collision and many-to-one nature. Buffer overflow occurs when the numbers of incoming packets are greater than the available buffer space. Contention occurs between different flows and different packets of a flow. Interference is caused by instantaneous transmissions along multiple paths within physical immediacy of each other. Packet collisions indicate lower level congestion and leads to packet drops.

Usually two types of congestion may occur in WSNs; Node Level Congestion where within a particular node if the buffer is used to keep the packets to be transmitted overflows that causes packet loss, the queuing delay increase and leads to retransmission that consumes additional energy. Link Level Congestion where multiple active sensor nodes within range of one another attempt to access transmission medium simultaneously, the packets coming out of the buffer may not reach next hop due to the collision between the sensor nodes. Network congestion causes the eminence of the channel to degrade, increases the rate of packet loss and leads to drops in buffers, increased delays and affects the event detection trust worthiness at the sink and requires retransmissions. Congestion has unswerving impact on energy efficiency and decreases the network throughput, lifetime and creates fidelity.

Congestion in WSNs is more convoluted in comparison to conformist networks as it may emerge in different types and different places. Pertaining to the reason of congestion incidence, network issues that can be categorized in different types. In Type H1 congestion within a particular location many nodes attempt to transmit concurrently, resulting in losses due to interference and thereby dropping the throughput of all nodes in the area. In Type H2 congestion within a particular node, the buffer used to hold packets that are transmitted through flows employing conformist dentition congestion. Type W1 congestion is identified as source congestion, where densely deployed sensors generating data events during a calamity state would craft persistent hotspots very close to the sources. Type W2 congestion is recognized by sink congestion where even meagerly deployed sensors generate low data rates which could potentially create ephemeral hotspots wherever in the sensor field. Type W3 congestion is recognized as forwarder congestion, where a sensor network would have more than one flows which would intersect with one another.

The rest of the paper is organized as follows. Different congestion techniques have been presented in the Sect. 2. In Sect. 3, we have presented a cluster based framework for alleviating buffer based congestion for WSNs. The main aim of hierarchical clustering routing is to efficiently maintain the energy consumption of sensor nodes by involving them in multi-hop communication within a particular region. Result analysis has been presented in Sect. 4. In Sect. 5, this paper concludes and identifies some of the future directions with open research issues.

2   Related Works

In this section, we have presented the study on diverse congestion control approaches based on the following ways such as; congestion detection, congestion is mitigated, congestion notification is performed, and congestion can be avoided. In [6], algorithms that deal with congestion in WSNs can be initially classified in three major categories as; Congestion control, Congestion avoidance, and Reliable data transport. Congestion control algorithms that take reactive actions when congestion arises in the network and their target is to control it. Congestion avoidance algorithms that take actions in order to prevent congestion from happening and involved in MAC and network layer operations. Reliable data transport algorithms are used to control congestion in a network, and attempt to recover all or part of the lost information. In accordance with the control schemes can be used to resolve congestion, such as; traffic control that controls the load, resource control that increase resources, and employ MAC layer enhancements that could help more in the direction of interference-based congestion. Congestion mitigation algorithms can be classified in the way they perceive congestion, how they notify other nodes of this incident and how they face congestion. There are four different ways that algorithms use to detect congestion are identified as; Buffer occupancy, Wireless channel load, Buffer occupancy-wireless channel load, and Packet transmission time metrics. Congestion is mitigated either by rate reduction that is identified as traffic control or by the creation of alternative paths from the source to the sink which is known as resource control.

Based on the deployment strategy congestion control schemes are classified into centralized and distributed approaches. Centralized congestion control schemes where all related actions to avoid or control congestion are carried out by the sink node that sporadically collects data from the sensor node, detects the possibility of congestion and accordingly takes action to overcome congestion. In distributed congestion control, the congestion schemes and spans those are distributed in nature and this scheme contains buffer based and cross layer congestion control techniques.

HTAP [7] is a scalable and distributed framework for minimizing congestion and ensures reliable data transmissions in event based networks. CODA [8] is used to detect the congestion in the network area that attempts to face congestion by implementing congestion detection, open-loop hop-by hop backpressure notification, and closed-loop multi-source AIMD-like traffic control to mitigate congestion. CCF [9] is a distributed and scalable mechanism that provides congestion detection on the basis of packets service time and congestion mitigation through traffic control. In [10], Hull et al. proposed Fusion algorithm that detects congestion by monitoring the queue size of each node and performing channel sampling at fixed intervals. COMUT [11] is a cluster based congestion control mechanism for supporting multiple classes of traffic in WSNs where each cluster node detects congestion through traffic intensity estimation and this estimation is broadcast to the cluster head that evaluates the congestion level. In [12], Popa et al. proposed BGR protocol that detects congestion based on buffer occupancy and wireless usage, exponentially averaged to eliminate noise. PCCP [13] refutes the congestion control that argue in favor of providing equal fairness to each sensor node in a multi-hop WSNs by attaching a weighted fairness to each sensor node. TARA [14] focuses on the adaptation of the network's extra recourses in case of congestion, alleviating intersection hot spots and measured not only the buffer occupancy but also the channel loading in order to detect congestion. CONSISE [15] contributes to sink-to-sensor congestion and can be the reverse path contention and broadcast storms, due to packets that broadcast from sinks to sensors. DAlPaS [16] is a dynamic and distributed hop-by-hop congestion control technique that employs a resource control method for congestion mitigation and attempts to choose an alternate path where congestion occurs. FACC [17] focuses on the fairness issue along with the congestion control techniques where intermediate nodes are categorized into 'near-sink nodes' and 'near-source nodes'. In CADA [18] the congestion level of a node is measured by an aggregation of buffer occupancy and channel utilization. UHCC [19] is designed based on a cross layer design that tries to reduce packet losses while guaranteeing priority-based fairness with lower control overhead and this mechanism consists of two components: congestion detection and rate adjustment.

Siphon [20] uses a combination of hop-by-hop and end-to-end congestion control depending on the location of the congestion that aims to maintain application fidelity, detection and avoidance of congestion by introducing several virtual sinks with a multiple range radio within the sensor network. BRCBA [21] consists of three schemes as, upstream source count, buffer occupancy based rate control, and the snoop based MAC level ACK and this technique can reduce collision drop rate, increase delivery ratio and improve the network's energy efficiency in comparison to other existing approaches. TADR [22] is used to route packets around congestion areas and disperse excessive packets along multiple paths consisting of idle and low loaded nodes. ANAR [23] is used to alleviate network congestion that is based on cross-layer information and employs existing information from the Request-to-Send and Clear-to-Send packets within the MAC scheme. TALONet [24] implements three schemes: different levels of transmit power to alleviate congestion in the data link layer, buffer management for avoiding buffer level congestion and multi-path detouring technique to increase resources for congested traffic flows. Flock-CC protocol [25] focuses on designing a robust and self-adaptable congestion control protocol that works on Swarm Intelligence paradigm.

TADR [26] protocol defines a hybrid scalar potential field comprising of depth and queue length field while the former provides the backbone for routing the packets to the sink along the shortest available paths, and the latter makes the TADR traffic aware. I2MR [27] is aided with the congestion control mechanism that reserves multiple alternative paths for routing data to eliminate congestion. In [28] Mehm et al. proposed congestion detection, considering the buffer occupancy and the buffer role is twofold: (a) contains the detected data and (b) accommodates the relay packages. ADCC [29] is a congestion control scheme that based on home automation and is equally useful for general sensor network based on the duty cycle adjustment of the sensor devices. In [30] Li et al. introduced a cross layer congestion control system where the multiple trajectories of the source to sink are first established and followed by the cross-layers information is shared in the form of a status frame. In [31] Meera S. et al. proposed congestion control in wireless sensor networks using prioritized interface queue that introduced the dual queue to control congestion using cross layer approach and the intelligent routing selects the best node having low traffic to forward the packets.

WSNs applications can be classified into three data delivery models: event-based, continuous-based, and query-based. In WSNs most event-driven applications are interactive, delay intolerant and mission critical i.e., the data generated from sensor nodes must be delivered within short span of time through a sink node to a processing center for further actions. In application based on continuity, the applications controlled by queries in the WSNs are similar to the applications controlled by events, except that the data is extracted by the receiving node while in the applications controlled by events, the data sent from the originating nodes to the receiver. In a WSN that involves an event-driven or a query-driven application, where a transient congestion situation is expected to arise, congestion mitigation or avoidance mechanisms should be adopted as a method of controlling counter-trafficking traffic. Through the extensive literature review it is observed that the congestion may greatly affect the performance of the whole network and in the next section we would present a cluster based framework for alleviating buffer based congestion for wireless sensor network is based on the self-organization of the network into clusters, each of which autonomously and proactively monitors congestion within its localized scope.

3 Proposed Framework

The preceding section leads to the observation of diverse routing to control congestion of WSNs in which numerous sensors collected data to the aggregation node could not cross routes that are largely coupled to hindrance and experience high packet loss and arbitrary packet delays due to the congestion. Here packet drops are one of the prime attribute to queue over flows and media access strife as the queue overflow is even more critical due to the limited queue size.

The assumptions made for this framework are as follows: all sensor nodes in the network are immobile and homogeneous; sensor nodes are generally energy constrained; each sensor node has a unique identifier and uniformly deployed over the target area to continuously monitor the environment; every sensor node can directly communicate with its immediate neighbor; the transmission range of each node is same on one condition; the data collections have been done based on the locality and the collection rate of each sensor node is different and unknown to each other.

The contributions of our work are to estimate buffer based congestion and the apposite action would be taken on a node based on a self-organized clustering network, each monitor independently and cumbersome way congestion. The projected framework has interrelated constituent distinctiveness that is exceedingly effectual in dealing with multiple interfering flows and achieving high delivery ratios, low delays, higher throughput, along with substantial energy savings in terms of considerable reduction in packet lost through effective regulation of the network load.

In this scheme, we have considered the technique [2–4] for weight based cluster head selection mechanism. The proposed scheme is divided in three modules. Section 3.1 is used for Cluster Formation and Hierarchical Tree Creation, Threshold Based Buffer Occupancy module has been described in Sect. 3.2. Alternative Path Creation technique is presented in Sect. 3.3 (Table 1).

Table 1. Data Dictionary

Variable	Description	Variable	Description
Ch_i	Cluster Head	W_{Ch_i}	Weight Factor of Cluster Head
Cm_{in}	Cluster Member	Ch_Es	Residual Energy of Cluster Head
Msg_Id	Message Id	Hp_Cnt	Hop Count
Sn_i	Node Id	$q_i(t)$	Data Packet
E_{S_i}	Residual Energy of Node S_i	NACK	Negative Acknowledgement
ΔTh_{Chs}	Threshold Value	$BFMS_i$	Maximum Buffer Size of Node S_i
Val_i^n	Data in bucket	D_{pi}	Data Packet Identifier
Cnt_i	Number of data in the bucket	W_{bq}	Weighted Buffer Queue Length
B_{thp}	Buffer Threshold for Priority Data	B_{thr}	Buffer Threshold for Regular Data

3.1 Cluster Formation and Hierarchical Tree Creation

The objective of clustering is to accomplish effective congestion inference where the nodes use network monitoring at the cluster level to reflect the traffic load within a local spatial region.

The objective of this phase is to construct clusters of almost same sizes. After cluster head selection process [2–4] has been completed, cluster head broadcast a CH_ADV_MSG {Ch_i, Msg_Id, W_{Ch_i}, Ch_Es, Hp_Cnt, TTL} for the network nodes. Accordingly, nodes send a reply CM_RPLY_MSG {Ch_i, Sn_i, Nd_lc, W_{Ch_i} Msg_Id, E_{S_i}, Hp_Cnt, TTL} to join as the cluster member of that cluster. Depends upon the equation $\sum_{i=1}^{n} W_{S_i} \leq (W_{Ch_i})$, each cluster head would add maximum number of sensor nodes to its cluster and sends CHM_FRM_MSG {Ch_i, Cm_{in}, W_{Ch_i}, Ch_Es, E_{S_i}, Hp_Cnt, TTL} to the cluster members of the corresponding cluster head and cluster formation has been executed. Sink node act as root of the tree with its own level to 0. Cluster head belong to transmission range of sink node add himself as the child of sink node and assign its own level incremented by one. The above process is applicable for all the remaining clusters in the network and tree formation has been executed. It is possible for sensor node to be the last one that receives the CH_ADV_MSG when there are no other nodes to forward the packet and responds by NACK through broadcasting to indicate that any packet cannot be routed from this node and all the recipient nodes are aware of this situation and final level of the tree is recorded.

Algorithm 1: Cluster Formation and Hierarchical Tree Creation

Ch_i broadcast a CH_ADV_MSG for the rest of the nodes

For each node in the network:

If any node is already another cluster head or cluster member

    Then discards the previous message

Else

    Check the $Max(W_{S_i}, P_{S_i}, E_{S_i})$ and $Min(dist(Sn_j, d_{Ch_i})$ and it sends a reply CM_RPLY_MSG to appropriate Ch_i

    If $\sum_{i=1}^{n} W_{S_i} \leq (W_{Ch_i})$ is TRUE

        Then Ch_i sends CHM_FRM_MSG and corresponding node add as Cm_{in} of corresponding Ch_i

    Else

        Then it discards the previous message

    Ch_i maintains the location information of each member and used for establishing the route to each cluster member

Set the level of sink node to 0

Sink node sends RT_MSG for its neighbor cluster heads.

If $\{dist (Sn_j, d_{Ch_i}) < Th_{dist}\}$ is TRUE

    Then Ch_i copies all the information to its corresponding MSG_HS_TBL and performs operation

        Increase its own level by one.

        Reply with SNC_MSG and becomes the child of the sender node.

        Forward RT_MSG for its next hop neighbor nodes.

If any Ch_i receives the RT_MSG from more than one sender

    Then it will join as a child with $Max(W_{Ch_i})$ and $Min(dist(Sn_j, d_{Ch_i})$

Else

    If any Ch_i receives RT_MSG more than one sender with same level

    Then ignore RT_MSG

    Else Continue

If there are no unexplored nodes are present in the network,

    Then Ch_i broadcast the NACK for the network nodes and the final level of the tree is recorded by the network nodes.

Else

    Ch_i forward RT_MSG for the next hop neighbor nodes.

END

By using the above procedure sensor node can join as a cluster member to the cluster head and cluster head add itself as the child node of the sink node and hierarchical tree creation has been executed.

3.2 Threshold Based Buffer Occupancy

The level of congestion in each sensor node is detected using the buffer occupancy and the adaptive threshold value on the buffer capacity of that node. The buffer occupancy of node S_i at time $t + 1$ is given by:

$$[p_i(t+1) = p_i(t) + u_i(t) - v_i(t)], \tag{i}$$

Where $u_i(t)$ and $v_i(t)$ are the incoming and outgoing packet traffic rates of node S_i at time t. The threshold value of node i is calculated as:

$$\left[\infty_i(t+1) = \frac{v_i(t)}{u_i(t)} \left(BFMS_i - p_i(t) \right) \right]$$ (ii)

Where, $u_i(t) > 0, v_i(t) > 0, u_i(t) > v_i(t)$ and where $BFMS_i$ is the maximum buffer size of node S_i and $\infty_i(t+1)$ is the threshold value of buffer for the given flow rate considering the remaining capacity of node S_i. $\infty_i(t+1)$ is inversely proportional to the incoming traffic and directly proportional to the outgoing traffic and remaining buffer capacity. The threshold value decreases as the incoming traffic increases, $\infty_i(t+1)$ specifies the desired queue level at $(t+1)$ based on the current traffic. Equation (ii) can be applied under the condition that there is data flow in the node or that the incoming traffic is larger than the outgoing traffic. The threshold $\infty_i(t+1)$ is set to ∞_{MAX}, when outgoing traffic exceeds incoming traffic or $u_i(t) = 0$, the threshold allows nodes in the system to tolerate bursting data flows. The buffer occupancy of a node is compared with its threshold value to detect congestion.

- There would not be any congestion if $p_i(t) < \infty_i(t)$
- If $p_i(t) = BFMS_i$ and $u_i(t) > v_i(t)$, then the packets received by node S_i will be dropped. This results in buffer overflows and congestion.
- The proposed method detects congestion, when $\infty_i(t) < p_i(t) < BFMS_i$, the buffer occupancy exceeds the threshold value, the level of congestion increases, as the number of packets increases to more than the threshold value, the occurrence of congestion also increases.

In this proposed framework, the buffer occupancy level of the concern node would be clued-up to the neighbor nodes for their further execution which helps the nearby neighbors to take pronouncement whether they would send the data to the particular upstream neighbor or use any alternative path for data transmission. After receiving the message neighbors would take decision accordingly and no outmoded data would be transferred which helps to minimize superfluous energy depletion and consequently congestion would be minimized to afford better throughput.

Data from far away nodes traverse through multi-hop path, involving more number of nodes in data forwarding; the corresponding energy depletion also increase. Due to congestion, this data might be dropped. Thus redundant transmission is required for successful data delivery. However, this involves more energy depletion for same data in comparison to the data transfer from nearby neighbors. The resulting throughput would be decreased. The threshold level has been identified using Eq. (ii) and corresponding data storage would depend on the specified threshold value. The data packet identifier is recorded as   .

$$\left[D_{pi} = \frac{\lambda * hopcnt}{\beta * Ne_i} \right]$$ (iii)

We have considered the benchmark value as 5, and data packet identifier greater than benchmark value would refer to data from far away nodes and are 'priority' data, whereas data from nearby nodes known as 'regular' data. Weighted buffer queue length is defined as

$$[W_{bq} = \sum_{i=1}^{n} D_{pi}] \tag{iv}$$

where 'n' is the total number of data packets are present in the buffer. Separate locations are identified in the corresponding buffer for priority and regular data, so that priority data may not be dropped due to lack of buffer space.

We have introduced the buffer threshold 'B_{thp}' for priority and 'B_{thr}' for regular data. After updation of data, corresponding buffer threshold value would be recorded and this updated value would be informed to neighbors through 'PACK'. Out of total buffer space, 50% is reserved for priority data and 40% are allotted for regular data. 50% spaces are prearranged for the priority data and 40% spaces are allotted for regular data. The remaining spaces are allotted as reserved that might be used in any of the two categories depending on the data flow. If a node's buffer occupancy exceeds the threshold and its data has higher priority among neighborhood, the corresponding congestion level bit in the outgoing packet header is set. When congestion occurs, other nodes should reduce their data forwarding rate to mitigate congestion. After the cluster formation, the level of congestion within each cluster would be determined and this information would be informed accordingly as the sources of the data flows can aptly control their sending rates. Congestion level of the WSNs can be measured through the estimation of the traffic intensity both within and across multiple clusters.

Algorithm 2: Threshold Based Buffer Occupancy

For each node of the network,

Calculates the buffer threshold value using $\infty_i(t+1) = \frac{v_i(t)}{u_i(t)}(BFMx_i - p_i(t))$

By using the data packet identifier $D_{pi} = \frac{\lambda * \square opcnt}{\beta * Ne_i}$ and based on the benchmark vale the data categorization has been made as priority and regular data.

Design the buffer space for storing the priority data, regular data along with reserve space.

At each time interval (t_i) sensor node (S_i) checks the buffer occupancy level

   If buffer occupancy level of sensor node is greater than buffer threshold

      Then sensor node forwards the PACK message to the neighbors to notify the current buffer occupancy level.

      After receiving the PACK message corresponding neighbors would not forward any data for the required destination and wait for the next updated messages.

   Else

      Continue the data transfer process to deliver the data packet for the required destination.

END

Using this above approaches, threshold based buffer occupancy technique has applied to minimize the congestion.

3.3 Alternative Path Creation

As sensor nodes receive more number of data packets from the neighbor sensors compared to the forwarding data packets to the other neighbors, the buffer occupancy level of the corresponding node reaches maximum limits, and packet drop would be started. $\sum_{i=1}^{k} Rx_i \geq Tx_{max}$ By using this equation, the congestion detection method is able to calculate the total receiving rate $\sum_{i=1}^{k} Rx_i$ and compare it with its maximum transmission rate Tx_{max}. In order to avoid this situation, when the buffer occupancy of a node reaches a specific threshold limit, node changes its Flag to False and communicates this fact through a ACK_{BF} message to its neighbor nodes. After receiving the ACK_{BF} message, neighbor nodes stop transmitting data packets to this particular node and find for the alternative path. When the congested node recovers from the overload situation it reverts its Flag to True and informs the neighboring nodes through ACK_{BNF} about this fact. The sensor nodes can change their indicator to False when the energy level is below the threshold value as it becomes exhausted.

As the algorithm is dynamic in nature, the number of hops to the sink may change when the state of nodes changes at a level closer to the sink. The choice of the next node to forward data, after avoiding the congested node, depends on the following parameters as; Flag checking, the number of hops to the sink, the remaining energy, and the buffer occupancy. Using this approach in an easy and simple way each node can find the next node with the minimum calculation.

Algorithm 3: Alternative Path Creation

Sensor nodes check the buffer occupancy level along with the congestion detection method is able to calculate the total receiving rate which is compare with the maximum transmission rate, i.e. $\sum_{i=1}^{k} Rx_i \geq Tx_{max}$

If the buffer occupancy of a node reaches a specific threshold limit || If the energy level of the node is below the threshold value

    Then $\{f(S_i(Flag) = False\}$ and broadcast the ACK_{BF} message to the neighbors and transfer the data through alternative path which may identified during the Hierarchical Tree creation, where member node may receive request message from more than one cluster head and may join in only one cluster at a time but additional received message details are also maintained for alternative path selection process.

Else

    Continue receive the data packet from neighbor nodes and forward to the next hop neighbors.

END

By using the above process the required data would be transferred via alternative path as the actual path is not able to carry the data due to congestion.

4   Result Analysis

The simulation model consists of a network model that has a number of wireless nodes, which represents the entire network to be simulated. We have implemented different sets of simulations using the well-known tool MATLAB to evaluate the performance of our proposed framework and compare with existing algorithms [1–5].

In this section the performance metrics namely, network lifetime, number of dead nodes in each round, throughput, average energy consumptions have been considered. In Fig. 1, we have depicted a relation between numbers of nodes involved in cluster formations vs. required energy. It has been observed that the proposed scheme requires less energy consumption compared with other existing algorithms [1–5].

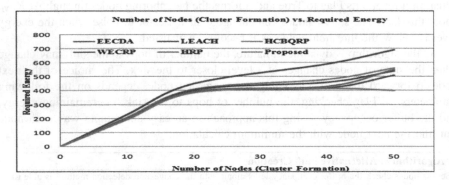

Fig. 1.   Number of nodes (Cluster Formation) vs. required energy

Throughput is defined as the total number of message send or received in per time unit. In this proposed scheme, throughput is measured in terms of data delivery in per time unit by varying the number of sensor node. From Fig. 2, we have observed that the new scheme achieves better throughput comparative with [1–5].

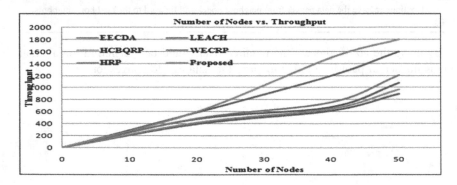

Fig. 2.   Node number vs. throughput

In the proposed framework, cluster formation along with hierarchical tree creation, threshold based buffer occupancy design, communication among network nodes, minimize the redundant data transmission have executed warily that very less numbers of sensor nodes are affected due to lack of energy. According to Fig. 3, as less numbers of dead nodes are present here and it has identified that less energy has been dissipated in comparisons with the existing approaches [1–5].

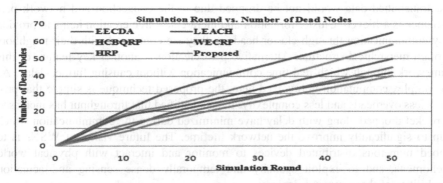

Fig. 3. No of dead node vs. simulation round

Network lifetime is defined as the time until when all sensor nodes would die out of their energy and it depends upon the average energy spent in the network. From the Fig. 4, it has identified that the proposed provides better the network lifetime than the existing approaches [1–5].

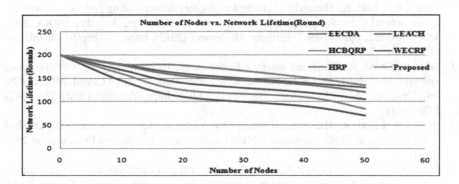

Fig. 4. Node number vs. network life time (Round)

Here we have considered distributed cluster based framework for alleviating buffer based congestion for wireless sensor networks where number of packet transmission from source to sink has been decreased which helps to minimize the average energy consumption comparing with the existing approaches as LEACH [1], HCBQRP [2], WECRP [3], HRP [4], EECDA [5].

5   Conclusions

The authors have presented a detail survey of different congestion control mechanisms for WSNs and presented a cluster based framework for alleviating buffer based congestion for WSNs. This proposed approach concern with the threshold based buffer occupancy and reserve the space for the regular and priority data. The buffer occupancy level would be conversant to all concern neighbor nodes prior to the data delivery, so that transmitted data would not be dropped due to the congestion and network performance is achieved. Cluster formation and hierarchical tree creation helps to provide easy communication through cluster heads as they are connected with their neighbors through hierarchical structure. Alternative path creation is another key feature of this framework through which real time communication without causing further delay. As no complex computation is involved here, the proposed technique is simple that provides less overheads and less complexity. It has identified that throughput has increased as packet dropped along with delay have minimized during the communication which help to significantly improve the network lifetime. The future vision of WSNs is to embed numerous distributed devices to monitor and interact with physical world phenomena, and to exploit spatially and temporally dense sensing and actuation capabilities of those sensing devices.

References

1. Heinzelman, W.R., Chandrakasan, A., Balakrishnan, H.: Energy efficient communication protocol for wireless micro-sensor networks. Published in the Proceedings of the 34th Hawaii International Conference System in 2000 (2000)
2. Saha, S.B., Chaki, R.: Hierarchical cluster based query driven routing protocol for wireless sensor networks. In: Satapathy, S.C., Avadhani, P.S., Abraham, A. (eds.) INDIA 2012. ASIC, vol. 132, pp. 657–667. Springer, Heidelberg (2012). https://doi.org/10.1007/978-3-642-27443-5_76
3. Saha, S., Chaki, R.: Weighted energy efficient cluster based routing for wireless sensor networks. In: Cortesi, A., Chaki, N., Saeed, K., Wierzchoń, S. (eds.) CISIM 2012. LNCS, vol. 7564, pp. 361–373. Springer, Heidelberg (2012). https://doi.org/10.1007/978-3-642-33260-9_31
4. Saha, S.B., Chaki, R.: Hierarchical routing protocol for wireless sensor network. Published in the Proceedings of 8th International Multi Conference on Information Processing in 2014 (2014)
5. Kumar D., Aseri T.C., Patel R.B., EECDA: energy efficient clustering and data aggregation protocol for heterogeneous wireless sensor networks. Int. J. Comput. Commun. Control. VI(1), 113–124 (2011)
6. Sergiou, C., Vassiliou, V., Paphitis, A.: A comprehensive survey of congestion control protocols in wireless sensor networks. IEEE Commun. Surv. Tutorials 16(4), 1369–1390 (2014). Fourth Quarter
7. Sergiou, C., Vassiliou, V., Paphitis, A.: Hierarchical Tree Alternative Path algorithm for congestion control in wireless sensor networks. Int. J. Ad Hoc Netw. 11, 257–272 (2013)

8. Wan, C.Y., Eisenman, S.B., Campbell, A.T.: CODA: congestion detection and avoidance in sensor networks. In: Proceedings of the 1st International Conference Network Sensor System, pp. 266–279 (2003)

9. Ee, C.T., Bajcsy, R.: Congestion control and fairness for many to one routing in sensor networks. In: Proceedings of the 2nd International Conference Embedded Network Sensor System, pp. 148–161 (2004)

10. Hull, B., Jamieson, K., Balakrishnan, H.: Mitigating congestion in wireless sensor networks. In: Proceedings of the 2nd International Conference Embedded Network Sensor System, pp. 134–147 (2004)

11. Karenos, K., Kalogeraki, V., Krishnamurthy, S.V.: Cluster based congestion control for supporting multiple classes of traffic in sensor networks. In: Proceedings of the 2nd IEEE Workshop EmNets, pp. 107–114 (2005)

12. Popa, L., Raiciu, C., Stoica, I., Rosenblum, D.S.: Reducing congestion effects in wireless networks by multipath routing. In: Proceedings of the IEEE ICNP, pp. 96–105 (2006)

13. Wang, C., Sohraby, K., Lawrence, V., Li, B., Hu, Y.: Priority-based congestion control in wireless sensor networks. In: Proceedings of the International Conference on Sensor Networks, Ubiquitous, and Trustworthy Computing, vol. 1, pp. 22–31 (2006)

14. Kang, J., Zhang, Y., Nath, B.: TARA: topology-aware resource adaptation to alleviate congestion in sensor networks. IEEE Trans. Parallel Distrib. Syst. 18(7), 919–931 (2007)

15. Vedantham, R., Sivakumar, R., Park, S.-J.: Sink-to-sensors congestion control. Ad Hoc Netw. 5(4), 462–485 (2007)

16. Sergiou, C., Vassiliou, V.: DAlPaS: a performance aware congestion control algorithm in wireless sensor networks. In: Proceedings of the 18th ICT, pp. 167–173, May 2011

17. Yin, X., Zhou, X., Huang, R., Fang, Y., Li, S.: A fairness-aware congestion control scheme in wireless sensor networks. IEEE Trans. Veh. Technol. 58(9), 5225–5234 (2009)

18. Fang, W.-W., Chen, J.-M., Shu, L., Chu, T.-S., Qian, D.-P.: Congestion avoidance, detection and alleviation in wireless sensor networks. J. Zhejiang Univ. Sci. C 11(1), 63–73 (2010)

19. Wang, C., Li, B., Sohraby, K., Daneshmand, M., Hu, Y.: Upstream congestion control in wireless sensor networks through cross-layer optimization. IEEE J. Sel. Areas Commun. 25 (4), 786–795 (2007)

20. Wan, C.Y., Eisenman, S.B., Campbell, A.T., Crowcroft, J.: Siphon: overload traffic management using multi-radio virtual sinks in sensor networks. In: Proceedings of the 3rd International Conference on Embedded Network SenSys, pp. 116–129 (2005)

21. Alam, M.M., Hong, C.S.: Buffer and rate control based congestion avoidance in wireless sensor networks. In: Proceedings of the KIPS, pp. 1291–1293, May 2007

22. He, T., Ren, F., Lin, C., Das, S.: Alleviating congestion using traffic aware dynamic routing in wireless sensor networks. In: Proceedings of the IEEE SECON, pp. 233–241 (2008)

23. Hsu, Y.P., Feng, K.-T.: Cross-layer routing for congestion control in wireless sensor networks. In: Proceedings of the IEEE Radio Wireless Symposium, pp. 783–786 (2008)

24. Huang, J.M., Li, C.Y., Chen, K.H.: TALONet: a power efficient grid-based congestion avoidance scheme using multi-detouring technique in wireless sensor networks. In: Proceedings of the Wireless Telecommunication Symposium, pp. 1–6 (2009)

25. Antoniou, P., Pitsillides, A., Blackwell, T., Engelbrecht, A., Michael, L.: Congestion control in wireless sensor networks based on bird flocking behavior. Comput. Netw. J. 57(5), 1167–1191 (2013)

26. Ren, F., He, T., Das, S.K., Lin, C.: Traffic aware dynamic routing to alleviate congestion in WSN. IEEE Trans. Parallel Distrib. Syst. 22(9), 1585–1599 (2011)

27. Teo, J.Y., Ha, Y., Tham, C.-K.: Interference minimized multipath routing with congestion control in WSN for high rate streaming. IEEE Trans. Mob. Comput. 7(9), 1124–1137 (2008)

28. Vuran, M.C., Akyildiz, I.F.: XLP: a cross layer protocol for efficient communication in wireless sensor networks. IEEE Trans. Mob. Comput. **9**(11), 1578–1591 (2010)
29. Lee, D., Chung, K.: Adaptive duty-cycle based congestion control for home automation networks. IEEE Trans. Consumption Electron. **56**(1), 42–47 (2010)
30. Li, Z., Zou, W., Qi, T.: A cross-layer congestion control strategy in wireless sensor network. In: Proceedings of IEEE IC-BNMT (2011)
31. Meera, S., Jayakumari, R.B., Senthilkumar, V.J.: Congestion control in wireless sensor networks using prioritized interface queue. In: International Conference on Recent Trends in Computational Methods, Communication and Controls (2012)

Type-Driven Cross-Programming for Android and LEGO Mindstorms Interoperability

Alvise Spanò[✉], Agostino Cortesi, and Giulio Zausa

Università Ca' Foscari, Via Torino, 153, 30172 Venice, VE, Italy
{alvise.spano,cortesi}@unive.it, mail.zausa.giulio@gmail.com

Abstract. We present Legodroid, a Java library for Android that allows cross-programming LEGO Mindstorms through an Android device to exploit its extra computational capabilities in a seamless way. From a programmer's perspective, the paradigm it suggests for programming the EV3 is straightforward and resembles a standard *main* function in the likes of `leJOS`, which natively runs on the EV3 side though. Moreover, the library imposes type-driven coding patterns for interacting with motors and sensors, which guide developers in writing correct code with less runtime errors thanks to a rigid discipline over types. This is particularly effective in Android, whose component-based pattern complicates coding of traditional long-running algorithms for robots. Compared to `leJOS`, Legodroid users reported shorter bugfixing times and a more accessible paradigm for programming the robot, which had a positive impact on how much resources could be put in writing smarter algorithms and sophisticate interactions.

Keywords: Android · Java · LEGO Mindstorms · EV3 · Type-driven development · Type soundness · Design patterns

1 Introduction

LEGO Mindstorms is an educational platform including an SDK for programming the main control unit - namely the EV3 brick - by using RoboLab, a visual language meant to learn coding and problem solving [38]. Alternative ways of programming the brick in a more traditional way exist as well:

(a) Using `leJOS`: a Java-based SDK ported from the LEGO NXT Kit [35] offering classes and methods for accessing EV3 motors and sensor in an object-oriented fashion; programs run directly on the EV3 device.

(b) Sending *commands* from a remote device: the EV3 brick runs an interpreter of instructions, constantly listening to incoming wifi[1] or bluetooth connections

---

[1] At the time of writing, Legodroid does not support wifi connections, as the bluetooth counterpart is preferable in most cases. A `WifiConnection` class is expected by design though and will be added in a future update.

© Springer Nature Switzerland AG 2019
K. Saeed et al. (Eds.): CISIM 2019, LNCS 11703, pp. 191–209, 2019.
https://doi.org/10.1007/978-3-030-28957-7_17

and processing requests; requests are structured streams of bytes, formatted according to the *EV3 Communication Developer Kit* specification [36].

(c) Flashing the brick ROM with a new custom firmware is an option for those willing to take over the system and reprogram it from scratch.

While option (a) produces programs running on the EV3 brick, with its limited performance[2], option (b) unleashes the computational power of external connected devices hosting and running the program. Legodroid facilitates the latter approach: it consists in a Java library for Android with a strongly-typed API for programming the EV3 brick from a remote device in a type-driven disciplined way. Application business logic can be implemented on the Android side: interaction with the brick is seamless, allowing the programmer to design complex algorithms that apparently run on the robot but actually don't. Benefits of this Android-based approach include:

– computing power: Android devices, from mobile phones to tablets, have a much more powerful CPU than the EV3;
– development environment: Android Studio [19] is an advanced IDE, offering debugger, code analyzers and other powerful tools for developing apps in a comfortable way;
– third party technologies: the whole Android SDK is at your fingertips, including a powerful UI, background services and components; plus, many third party libraries are available for Android.

Legodroid introduces a new way for programming LEGO Mindstorms compared to other APIs, by making the application Android-centric but not only: it imposes a sound style, where error-prone coding habits are discouraged by a disciplined use of types. Additionally, it offers a straightforward paradigm for programming the robot: regular Java code packed into one callback representing the robot *main* function; within its scope users are allowed to access to the sensors and motors connected to the brick.

The library is mainly addressed to two kinds of audience:

(1) juniors willing to learn coding: we argue that type-driven programming, despite being a methodology mostly explored by a niche of advanced programmers, effectively aids in teaching coding and problem solving even at the basic level, thanks to the educational power of a strict discipline over types;
(2) experienced developers willing to explore new ways of programming Android and improve their programming skills through a sophisticate use of types in Java.

We put the library to the test by developing 17 different apps controlling LEGO Mindstorms robots for different purposes. In Sect. 4 of this paper we show the outcome of this experiment, confirming that type-driven programming

---

[2] The EV3 CPU is a 300 MHz TI Sitara AM1808 (ARM926EJ-S Core) with 64 MB of RAM.

reduces bug fixing time and favours quick deployment of stable applications, allowing programmers to focus on the business logic of the application and on the algorithms.

1.1 Type-Driven Development

Type-driven programming wants to bring the type-sound coding discipline coming from the world of functional languages to the world of mainstream application development, where traditionally less care is put on types and static safety. Literature on the matter is scarce and mostly of industry origin, type-driven programming being more of a programming methodology than an actual scientific achievement; still, we believe its teachings and benefits are particularly meaningful in an era where dynamic languages have become mainstream and widely used for writing small as well as big software, training generations of coders against a disciplined use of types.

Also known as *typeful programming*, its principles have been foreseen decades ago by a handful of knowledgeable computer scientists [7], albeit it has quite never broken through despite the advancements of technology, arguably because of its difficulty [29]. Type-driven development relies on a accurate type design and compile-time validation of code, as opposed to writing down unthoughtful algorithms dealing with untyped or barely typed data. The basic idea behind it is that "a strong type system can not only prevent errors, but also guide you and provide feedback in your design process" [31], which admittedly requires a deep understanding of types and how to exploit the compiler as a tool for validating code.

Recently, interest in type-driven development has increased: the Haskell and F# communities have been promoting the benefits of *designing with types* for years [41], showing how writing programs with the Hindley-Milner type system [10] shifts the emphasis towards type design and improves the programmer's understanding of the static properties of software [32]. Even more advanced languages based on dependent type systems such as Idris [5] brought type-driven development to new heights [6], by conducting the programmer to the correct implementation in a quasi-mechanical way, putting the basis for a form of *assisted* programming guided by rich type information.

Although not all programmers can realistically learn dependent types [43], we believe that any programmer could be trained in respecting the basic type-driven programming principles to some extent, even without dependent types or complex In this paper we claim that the fundamental principles of type-driven programming can be ported to mainstream languages like Java, and any programmer, at any level of skill, can benefit of it at the cost of learning the core concepts of functional programming.

1.2 Core Principles

The type-driven approach is particularly recommended when writing libraries. Libraries impose styles, patterns [13] and discipline to programmers designing applications and are often responsible for the quality of the outcome in terms of code maintainability, scalability and safety. A modern library should carefully find a balance between two opposite characteristics:

Flexibility. Exported functions must be generic and cover a wide range of scenarios, exploiting forms of polymorphism;

Type Safety. Operations must be constrained to certain data types, guiding the programmer in writing correct code.

We synthesize a handful of type-driven qualitative principles that have been put on test in designing and implementing Legodroid.

I Make code more general via higher-order functions [14]. Custom behaviours can be formulated via callbacks instead of overriding methods in sub-classes, which leads to a greater use of parametric polymorphism in place of subtyping. The higher-order function approach, obviously originating from the functional world, has been incrementally adopted by mainstream languages in recent years and is nowadays not unaccepted from the object-oriented programming community as it used to be in the past [23]. It fits better the immutable programming style, reducing *statefulness* in code and thus errors due to state invalidity [42].

II Never allow the programmer declare uninitialised variables, but rather emulate the functional let-binding by constructing objects in a valid state. Nullness checking is crucial: adding Java annotations @NotNull and @Nullable, combined with an aggressive use of the `final` qualifier, raises code quality in a measurable way [8]. This has an impact on how classes and constructors are designed: avoiding no-argument constructors discourages the "create empty and populate with setters"-sort of approach, which in turn discourages unneeded mutable data [9].

III Reduce side effects to the minimum [20]. Arguably, most mutable data structures in imperative programs are involuntary so, since mutability is the default condition for variables and fields in most mainstream languages. Overuse of assignments is a common source of runtime bugs in presence of concurrent code, for instance, and in general contributes to the proliferation of runtime errors, whereas programming with immutable data tends to lift errors up to the type level.

Manipulating immutable data types, moreover, does not make code slower: this is a common misconception that happens to be true less often than not, since most OO languages implement call-by-reference parameter passing and data is never copied unless explicitly cloned [2]. Quite the opposite, this is another point in favour of immutability, as modifying function parameters is another error-prone practice that compilers today discourage.

IV Use strong types even for intermediate result. A wise use of types and generics [4] can literally drive the programmer to the correct solution, by rendering unwanted chains of function calls impossible due to type mismatches. Control flow reflects data flow; and data is ultimately validated by types [46].

Despite these may seem in contradiction with classic OOP practices and advises, it has been observed that object-orientation *adds* abstractions, in the form of heavyweight type names that represent operations, whereas the functional approach *subtracts* abstractions thanks to anonymous functions, i.e. lambda expressions [22]. Abstractions are useful and powerful in many cases, but overly complicated class hierarchies are hard to understand: for example, reducing the number of heavyweight types representing callbacks relieves the programmer of memorizing dozens of type names that represent functions somehow, and could therefore be anonymized. This has another advantage in terms of design: it reduces the number of classes and interfaces to those cases modelling actual data types, which aids in separating data from behaviour [2].

2 Library Breakdown

In this section we describe the architecture of Legodroid in terms of types, API design and patterns. We motivate aspects of the type-driven design in particular. Before delving into it, a few words on the notation we are using in this paper.

Notation 21 (Subtyping). *We write* $T \preceq S$, *where* T *and* S *are types, for indicating that* T *is a subtype of* S; *its symmetric counterpart* $S \succeq T$ *holds as well.*

Notation 22 (Qualified Names). *Method names are suffixed by brackets, e.g.* *run() is a bare method name, whereas the notation* **EV3.run()** *specifies the class it belongs to.*

Legodroid is designed with 3 layers of API. Each layer strictly wraps the underlying one and supports extensions.

Low level API. It deals with serialization and byte-level manipulation of commands for communicating with the EV3 brick according to the *EV3 Communication Developer Kit* specification [36]. The **comm** sub-package, detailed in Sect. 2.2, contains the **Bytecode** class, aimed at building commands by appending op-codes and manipulating parameters at the byte level in a straightforward way. Users willing to extend the library with new commands can limit use of such low-level primitives to small self-contained methods.

Mid level API. Class **Api**[3] provides the core primitives for interacting with EV3, such as reading SI or PCT values from a sensor. The *EV3 Firmware Development Kit* defines these as half-baked data types translating, respectively, into **float** and **short** in Java. Extending the library at this level means to add new methods implementing EV3 instructions that are currently unsupported by Legodroid, manipulating arrays of floats or short according to the specification in Sect. 4 of [37].

High level API. The **Api** class offers a family of *getter* methods constructing strong-typed handles to sensors and motors defined in the **plugs** package. Such handles exhibit methods performing high-level operations over sensors

---

[3] We refer to the **EV3.Api** nested static class as **Api** for brevity.

and motors and are distinct classes within the `plugs` sub-package. Extending the library at this level means to extend the `Api` class with new methods constructing new handles, which provide the methods implementing new commands for the brick in the same way as classes in `plugs` do.

The reason why the `Api` class includes two layers of API is subtle: from a user perspective the high-level methods and handles dealing with sensors and motors should be enough for most situations. Mid-level methods like `getSiValue()`, `getPercentValue()` and `execAsync()` are not enough, in number, to justify the architectural overhead of an additional class. Users willing to implement new high-level methods have all they need at their fingertips.

We now delve into the details of each package of Legodroid. This is not a replacement for the documentation of the library but rather the explanation of how its major feature impact programming in a *typeful* way.

2.1 `legodroid.lib.util`

Package `legodroid.lib.comm` contains general utilities such as the definition of functional interfaces [27] for supporting older versions of Android preceding Java 8; and a `Prelude` class containing miscellaneous utility functions.

Interfaces `Function` and `Consumer` reproduce `java.util.Function` and `java.util.Consumer` as defined in the JDK 8+, providing compatible functional interfaces working with Android API 21, which does not include Java 8 features. A more formal way for describing such functional interfaces would be using arrow types, assuming that $\varnothing$ represents the `unit` type.

$$\texttt{Function<A, B>} \equiv A \to B$$
$$\texttt{Consumer<T>} \equiv T \to \varnothing$$
$$\texttt{Runnable} \equiv \varnothing \to \varnothing$$

`ThrowingConsumer<T, E>` extends the functional interface `Consumer<T>` adding an extra type parameter $E \preceq \texttt{Throwable}$ that statically tracks the exception possibly thrown by the `Consumer` callback through a constrained generic. The Java `throws` declaration in method signatures can be modelled by a special arrow type where the exception is annotated:

$$\texttt{ThrowingFunction<A, B, E} \preceq \texttt{Throwable>} \equiv A \to B \triangle E$$
$$\texttt{ThrowingConsumer<T, E} \preceq \texttt{Throwable>} \equiv T \to \varnothing \triangle E$$
$$\texttt{ThrowingRunnable<E} \preceq \texttt{Throwable>} \equiv \varnothing \to \varnothing \triangle E$$

In order to make these interfaces compatible with their inherited parent functional interfaces, an additional `callThrows()` method is defined which adds the `throws E` declaration, whereas the original `call()` method is overridden and traps any exception raised by `callThrows()` by converting it to a non-checked `RuntimeException`. This allows for the best of both worlds: either executing the callback knowingly expecting an exception or totally trapping it, type-wise.

Finally, class `Prelude` is just a container for utility functions, among which `trap()` is arguably the most useful: `trap()` picks a function and executes it within a try-catch block trapping any exception possibly raising from it. Overloaded versions for different functional interfaces exist as well, the behaviour emerging clearly from the following functional type signatures:

$$\texttt{trapFunction} : \forall \alpha\ \beta\ (\gamma \preceq \texttt{Throwable}).\ (\alpha \to \beta \bigtriangleup \gamma) \to \alpha \to \beta \bigtriangleup \varnothing$$
$$\texttt{trapConsumer} : \forall \alpha\ (\beta \preceq \texttt{Throwable}).\ (\alpha \to \varnothing \bigtriangleup \beta) \to \alpha \to \varnothing \bigtriangleup \varnothing$$
$$\texttt{trapRunnable} : \forall \alpha \preceq \texttt{Throwable}.\ (\varnothing \to \varnothing \bigtriangleup \alpha) \to \varnothing \to \varnothing \bigtriangleup \varnothing$$

Mind that these arrow-based type representations are not meant to be accurate, but rather to display how functional manipulation occurs in a more readable way. Java does not provide arrow types in its type system [33]; there is no `unit` type, being `void` only a keyword for expressing methods with no return statement and not a type constructor [26]; also, currying is technically possible but not as straightforward as in functional languages, where the application syntax models the lambda-calculus term for application [1]. These are complications that ultimately make the actual implementation different from the clean type signature.

2.2   `legodroid.lib.comm`

Package `legodroid.lib.comm` in Fig. 1 shows the architecture of types related to the communication facilities provided by the library. Channels represent the basic abstractions offering communication primitives: a `Channel` can send a `Command` and receive a `Reply`, both of which are subclasses of `Packet`. Low-level communication with EV3 is based on exchanging data as untyped byte arrays formatted according to the official specification defined by LEGO in the *EV3 Communication Development Kit* [36]: *direct commands* sent by the client and consequent replies coming from EV3 require a byte-per-byte encoding, which includes a header followed by a an extra sequence of bytes carrying the custom content of each request; the header consists of fixed byte fields such as the length of the packet, the sequence number, the command type, the attached data etc. Class `Const` binds all C-style preprocessor symbols defined in the official header files as static numeric constant fields in Java, mostly used by the `Bytecode` class for serializing commands.

The `Connection<C>` interface represents the contract for constructing channels of type `C`, where `C` $\preceq$ `Channel`, essentially implementing a *typed factory* pattern tracking the type information associated to the result type, as opposed to the old-fashioned, classic factory pattern which is often considered an obsolete unsound way of constructing objects [12]. Interestingly, `Connection` is equivalent to the `java.util.Supplier` interface defined by JDK 8+, making it a functional interface *de facto*, albeit with type `C` being upper-bounded to type `Channel`. We can, in other words, write the following type equation:

$$\texttt{Connection<C} \preceq \texttt{Channel>} \equiv \texttt{Supplier<C>} \equiv \varnothing \to \texttt{C} \bigtriangleup \varnothing$$

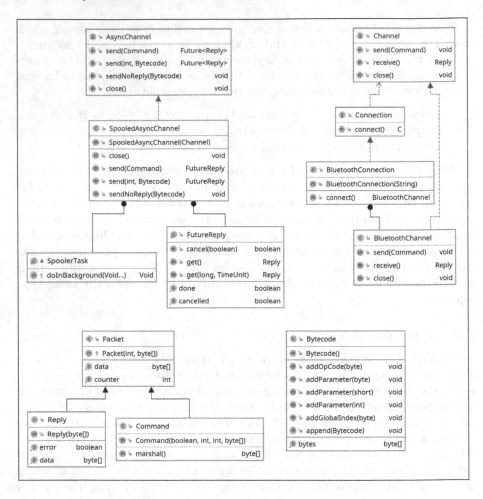

Fig. 1. UML Class Diagram of package `legodroid.lib.comm`

2.3 `legodroid.lib`

The root package of the library contains the main classes for programming with
Legodroid, as shown in Fig. 2. Class `EV3` stands at its core and exhibits most of
the type-driven practices. An instance of type `EV3` represents a physical instance
of the EV3 brick and can basically do one thing: executing a callback as if it was
the *main* function for that brick, running on the Android device as a standalone
thread which constantly communicates with the brick in a transparent way.

The `run()` method takes a function `Api → ∅` (or a `Consumer<Api>` function
object) as argument and executes it within an Android `AsyncTask` that traps
and logs any unexpected exception. It also behaves like a singleton, granting only
one callback is running at any given time on the brick. Perhaps surprisingly, the

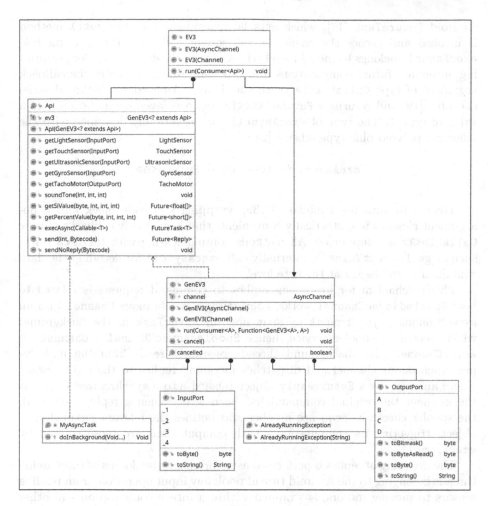

Fig. 2. UML Class Diagram of package `legodroid.lib`

EV3 class does not provide any method for interacting with sensors and motors: the `Api` class does; and objects of type `Api` cannot be freely constructed - this is a crucial design point of the whole library. An object of type `Api` is passed to the `Consumer<Api>` callback being passed to the `EV3.run()` method by the programmer as the robot *main* function: no other legal way of obtaining an object of type `Api` exists, which is a strong type-driven principle that discourages error-prone programming approaches. Pattern 32 in Sect. 3 shows its details.

2.4   Concurrency in the Safe Way

In Legodroid concurrent computations occur often and are wrapped by *future* computations [40], also known as *promises* [21]. The implementations extends

Android `FutureTask` [17], which gets lazily evaluated as the `get()` method is invoked and caches the result for subsequent calls. In class `Api`, method `execAsync()` belongs to the mid level API and is the basic primitive for performing automatic future computations in a type-safe way. It executes the callback argument of type `Callable<T>`[4] with the default Android single-thread serial executor [16] and returns a `FutureTask<T>`, i.e. a delayed computation over a value of type `T`. The type of `execAsync()` can be formally described with the following polymorphic type scheme [24]:

$$\texttt{exeAsync} : \forall \alpha.\ (\varnothing \rightarrow \alpha) \rightarrow \texttt{Future<}\alpha\texttt{>}$$

Thanks to Java 8+ lambdas [34,39] wrapping any code block into a no-argument closures is syntactically convenient, that is why only callbacks of type `Callable<T>` are supported. All methods communicating with the EV3 brick, such as `getPercentValue()`, internally call `execAsync()` for decoding the data contained in the `Reply` at the byte level.

This mechanism for processing replies to command requests is related to how `SpooledAsyncChannel` works, converting a synchronous `Channel` into an asynchronous `AsyncChannel` by spawning an `AsyncTask` in the background which acts as a spooler service, hence `SpooledAsyncChannel : Channel →` `AsyncChannel`. The background thread constantly reads from the underlying synchronous channel and dispatches incoming replies to the right *owner*; where an owner is a `FutureReply` object pushed into a synchronized queue at the moment the original command has been sent. When a reply is received, the spooler checks its sequence number and notifies the relevant `FutureReply` object, triggering its computation - such computations are those created by `execAsync()`.

The decoding of replies is performed asynchronously by dozens of short-living threads belonging to the Android thread pool: any input operation, from reading sensors to moving motors, is wrapped within a future computation - in other words, the whole high level API returns objects of type `Future<`τ`>`, for some type τ. From the user's perspective, blocking calls to `Future.get()` are required to retrieve any result; subsequent calls do not trigger the computation again, enabling a form of lazy evaluation [25]. Virtually, by postponing `Future.get()` calls to the very point where the result is needed may lead to minor performance gains due to massive concurrency, depending on the level of support from the Dalvik virtual machine [11] for fine-grained future computations [44,45].

Admittedly, other systems in literature use a more sophisticate approach to programming with futures, for instance by generating transparent proxies for delayed computations [30], whereas Legodroid proposes a lighter-weight library based solution. Our point is: how realistically useful is a solution relying on external tools, analyzers and code generators that time makes obsolete and

---

[4] The functional interface `Callable<T>` represents functions with no arguments and a result of type `T`, in the same way as `Supplier<T>` does, whose functional type can be written as $\varnothing \rightarrow$ `T`.

incompatible with the ever-changing technology underlying Java and its world? A pure library surely cannot yield the same results, but we believe it is a good compromise of usability and safety that arguably has a better chance to survive the test of time.

2.5 Generalized EV3

Class EV3 is actually a subclass of the more general GenEV3<A> parametric class, where A $\preceq$ Api. This mixes generics with subtyping, object-orientation with generic programming, in order to achieve extensibility and type safety at the same time [3]. Nested static types InputPort, OutputPort and Api are defined within EV3 rather than GenEV3 for simplicity and name brevity, hiding the super-class to casual users. EV3 instantiates the type parameter A with the Api concrete type, which is enough for most applications; programmers willing to extend the Api class with additional custom methods are allowed do so by applying the subclass as type argument to GenEV3<A>. The sample below shows how:

```
public class MainActivity {
    static class MyApi extends EV3.Api {
        MyApi(GenEV3<? extends EV3.Api> ev3) {
            super(ev3);
        }
        public void myAdditionalCommand() {
            // implementation
        }
    }

    protected void onCreate(Bundle b) {
        BluetoothConnection conn =
            new BluetoothConnection("MyEV3Brick");
        BluetoothChannel ch = conn.connect();
        GenEV3<MyApi> ev3 = new GenEV3<>(ch);
        ev3.run(this::legoMain, MyApi::new)));
    }

    private void legoMain(MyApi api) {
        api.myAdditionalCommand();
    }
}
```

Since the legoMain() function passed to GenEV3.run() picks a parameter of type MyApi, calls to additional methods are allowed without any cast or undisciplined pattern.

This generalization comes at the cost of providing one extra argument to GenEV3.run(): a function of type GenEV3<A> $\rightarrow$ A, required for constructing the object of type A to be passed to the *lego main*. Such second argument could be omitted if the Java type system supported *constructor constraints*: type parameter A could have been constrained to be *constructible* from an object of type GenEV3<A>. Alternatively, lambdas can replace this missing feature at the cost of explicitly passing a constructor reference, like MyApi::new in the example [28]. This is also a preferable solution than a factory, which would otherwise require additional classes and verbosity [12].

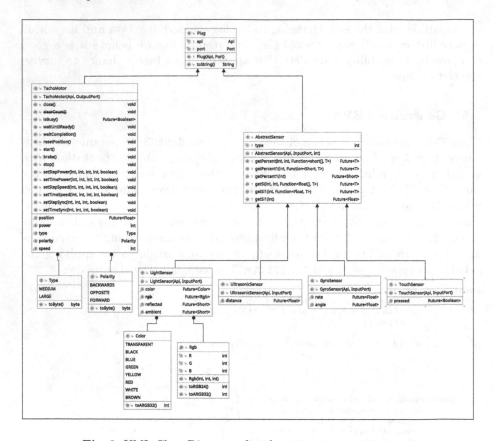

Fig. 3. UML Class Diagram of package `legodroid.lib.plugs`

2.6 `legodroid.lib.plugs`

Figure 3 shows the classes representing sensors and motors. Each one exposes methods for reading sensors (`GyroSensor`, `LightSensor`, `TouchSensor`) or moving motors (`TachoMotor`) in a typed way:

1. ports are distinct enum types (`EV3.OutputPort`, `EV3.InputPort`);
2. minor flags representing motor polarity and type[5] are enum types as well;
3. all sensor and motor classes inherit from a common superclass `Plug<P>` where P represents the port type: this makes subclasses instantiate the generic P with some concrete type at inheritance time;
4. sensors inherit from a common abstract class `AbstractSensor`: protected methods `getPercent()`, `getPercent1()`, `getSi()` and `getSi1()` are commodities for quickly implementing actual sensor subclasses.

---

[5] Refer to the documentation of EV3 firmware instructions (op-codes `opOutput_Polarity` and `opOutput_Set_Type`) in section 4.9 of [37].

The classes included in this package behave as *handles* for accessing LEGO accessories, such as sensors and motors, connected to the I/O ports. As explained in Sect. 2, extending the library for supporting new accessories requires extending the `Plug` abstract class (or even `AbstractSensor`) and implementing the relevant communication primitives in function of the mid-level methods mentioned above.

3   Type-Driven Patterns

This section describes in detail the most interesting type-driven programming patterns used in Legodroid. These are the result of combining design patterns existing in literature and in the industry with the formal and sound approach of the functional language scientific community.

3.1   Objects as Evidences

Using objects as *evidences* for constructing other objects is a type-driven practice any strongly typed language can benefit of.

Pattern 31 (Objects as Evidences). *In order to ensure that a given set of operations O becomes available only after some state S_k has been reached within a sequence of increasingly mutating states $S_1 .. S_n$ such that $1 \leq k \leq n$ and $n > 0$, the following pattern can be followed:*

- *operations O can be translated into methods of a stateless object of type O;*
- *each state S_i can be translated into an object of type S_i for $i \in [1, n]$:*
  - *each object S_i holds the information for the state S_i;*
  - *an object of type S_i, for $i > 1$, can only be constructed by providing an argument of type S_{i-1}, i.e. the previous state;*
  - *the initial state S_0, implemented by an object of type S_0, can be constructed explicitly from scratch;*
- *objects of type O can only be constructed given an argument of type S_k.*

Each object constructor formally behaves like a function $S_i : S_{i-1} \rightarrow S_i$, where only S_0 is initially given and no alternative way of instantiation exists for the remaining states.

In Legodroid this type-driven practice emerges from the type architecture:

- in order to access EV3 motors and sensors, the programmer needs an object of type `Api`;
- an object of type `Api` can only be obtained as argument passed to the callback of type `Consumer<Api>` the programmer passes to the `EV3.run()` method;
- an object of type `EV3`, which represents a physical EV3 brick connected to the Android device, requires an object of type `AsyncChannel`, which provides the I/O primitives for asynchronous communication between Android and the brick itself;

- AsyncChannel's can be created given a synchronous Channel by using the SpooledAsyncChannel class, which can be seen as a function of type Channel $\rightarrow$ AsyncChannel;
- a Channel can be created by calling Connection.connect(): class BluetoothConnection implementing Connection<BluetoothChannel> behaves like a *factory* for producing objects of type BluetoothChannel, which are synchronous channels;
- a Connection requires the target peer in order to be constructed, e.g. BluetoothConnection requires the name the EV3 brick physically uses for pairing with Bluetooth, whereas WifiConnection requires the IP address of the brick.

Each step in this chain represents a state S_i in our generalized Pattern 31: the initial state S_0 here is a string constant and subsequent states $S_1..S_3$ are represented by each object in the flow:

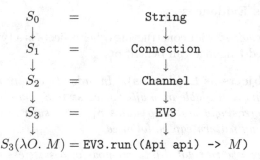

$$
\begin{array}{ccc}
S_0 & = & \texttt{String} \\
\downarrow & & \downarrow \\
S_1 & = & \texttt{Connection} \\
\downarrow & & \downarrow \\
S_2 & = & \texttt{Channel} \\
\downarrow & & \downarrow \\
S_3 & = & \texttt{EV3} \\
\downarrow & & \downarrow \\
S_3(\lambda O.\ M) & = & \texttt{EV3.run((Api api) -> } M\texttt{)}
\end{array}
$$

The final step is different: we do not consider it as a further state S_4, but rather as a dictionary of operations O that requires state S_3 and is eventually passed to the *lego main* block M. In Java the chain above is implemented by the following code:

```
String name = "MyEV3BrickName";
Connection conn = new BluetoothConnection(name);
Channel ch = conn.connect();
AsyncChannel ach = new SpooledAsyncChannel(ch);
EV3 ev3 = new EV3(ach);
ev3.run((Api api) -> /* lambda body M */);
```

The last line introduces the next pattern.

3.2 Limiting Access to a Resource

Let us assume a general scenario where a given resource R has to be accessible in a restricted environment, a mere binding does not meet the robust discipline we are looking for, as once an object has been bound to a variable name there is no mechanism for unbinding it from the environment. Callbacks and lambdas are an effective tool for controlling the scope of a resource R, since the application of the argument R is performed and controlled by its owner.

Pattern 32 (Lambdas for Scoped Access). *Users willing to access a resource R must provide a callback f by either defining a lambda, an anonymous class or a functional object[6] parametric over the resource R. The owner applies R to f and can control what happens before and after the function application.*

The following example shows a minimal implementation of this general pattern (not an excerpt of Legodroid):

```
public class FunProxy<R> {
    private R resource;
    public FunProxy(R resource) {
        this.resource = resource;
    }
    public <T> T perform(Function<R, T> f) {
        // do something before
        T result = f.apply(resource);
        // do something after
        return result;
    }
}
```

Admittedly, this pattern does not prevent the user from saving the pointer to the protected resource for later use outside of its controlled scope. The Java compiler detects the simplest scenario and forbids assignments to plain variables captured by a closure:

```
String copy;        // target pointer in closure
FunProxy<String> p = new FunProxy<>("MyString");
p.perform((res) -> { copy = res; })  // illegal!
```

However, a well-known workaround exists: putting the copy inside the cell 0 of a `final` array of size 1 [15]. We believe such a syntactic overhead discourages most programmers though.

This pattern has a number of applications, ranging from synchronizing access to a resource by locking and unlocking a mutex, to trapping exceptions by surrounding the application with a try-catch block (`Prelude.trap()` in package `legodroid.lib.util` is an example). Even without performing any operation, the callback alone is useful: assume the dictionary of operations O described in pattern 31 is our resource R, then we can merge the two patterns for restricting the use of `Api` objects to the scope of a callback.

4   Experimental Results

Legodroid is open source and available on GitHub at the following URL:
https://github.com/alvisespano/Legodroid

The repository includes an Android Studio project with two modules: the library and a demo app showing the main patterns and features.

We extensively tested the library with undergraduate students of the Software Engineering course[7] Over 100 students divided into small teams of 3–5 people

---

[6] In Java 8+ all the mentioned language constructs are equivalent type-wise.
[7] Bachelor degree in Computer Science, year 2018-19, at DAIS, Università Ca' Foscari Venezia.

produced 17 Android apps performing complex interactions with LEGO Mind-storms devices. The LEGO physical devices created by each team ranged from wheeled machines capable of processing the environment via sensors and avoiding obstacles, to printers capable of moving a pen up and down on a scrolling paper, rendering an input image with dots, to automatic equation solvers printing each reduction step on a paper.

Teams using Legodroid were 7 out of 17; the remaining teams either used leJOS (8 teams) or flashed the brick with a custom firmware (2 teams).

Anyhow all teams had to interact with the EV3 from an Android device in a non-trivial way. Apps were supposed to exploit the additional computational power of Android, though depending on how teams designed their system this requirement has been more or less fulfilled. A few teams wrote entire algorithms with leJOS, reducing the Android contribution to a remote UI; others exploited the Android mobile, moving robot logic to the Android code to varying degrees.

We observed that teams using Legodroid reported a smoother development experience compared to those working with leJOS. The type-driven patterns offered by the library were positively received by all teams. Advanced coding practices have not been entirely understood by the majority, which is reasonable for a junior developer, though this did not prevent them to take full advantage of those patterns. This is a strong point in favour of type-driven programming: types impose such a strict, yet clear, discipline that any possible misuse of the API is rejected by the compiler, putting the development process on a rail that forcefully led teams to the correct implementation. This sense of guidance and safety has been particularly appreciated by our teams and arguably counterbalances the lower understanding due to type complexity.

The comfortable programming style allowed teams to put more effort into smarter algorithms and advanced interaction. The same did not apply to leJOS users, who had a harder time implementing their applications, even though leJOS wraps low level operations as much as Legodroid does, offering comparable levels of abstraction. Android makes the difference here: its programming pattern requires extra care when managing object references due to complications arisen from activity life-cycle [18]. This impacted those apps interacting with leJOS: despite the longer development time, teams using leJOS could not finalize their code, presenting runtime bugs and weird behaviours at different levels.

Teams reported their appreciation for how Legodroid immutable data types can be constructed and reconstructed safely, in a stateless fashion that fits how Android transitions through different construction/destruction phases. Positive feedback was given to the *lego main* control flow, which is straight, in the likes of leJOS native code and unlike the respective Android side, which consisted in fragmented code spread throughout many callbacks. The event-driven style was often used, which is less than ideal for encoding long algorithms and introduce bugs that could arguably be avoided by a type-driven discipline.

5 Conclusions

We presented Legodroid, an Android library for interacting with LEGO Mindstorms devices through type-driven programming patterns that guide the user into writing robust code. This cross-programming practice has been put on test by a number of junior teams designing and implementing several original LEGO systems exploiting the Android platform capabilities in a non-trivial way. Teams using Legodroid reported a smoother coding experience compared to teams using alternate solutions such as leJOS, as our library imposes a type-driven style that enhances the development process in various ways, making sophisticate interaction between the mobile device and the robot seamless and sound.

References

1. Barendregt, H.P.: Functional programming and lambda calculus. In: Formal Models and Semantics, pp. 321–363. Elsevier (1990)
2. Bloch, J.: Effective Java. Pearson Education India (2016)
3. Bracha, G.: Generics in the Java Programming Language (2004)
4. Bracha, G., Odersky, M., Stoutamire, D., Wadler, P.: Making the future safe for the past: adding genericity to the Java programming language. ACM SIGPLAN Not. **33**(10), 183–200 (1998)
5. Brady, E.: Programming and reasoning with algebraic effects and dependent types. ACM SIGPLAN Not. **48**, 133–144 (2013)
6. Brady, E.: Type-Driven Development with Idris. Manning (2016)
7. Cardelli, L.: Typeful programming. In: Formal Description of Programming Concepts, pp. 431–507 (1991)
8. Chalin, P., James, P.R.: Non-null references by default in Java: alleviating the nullity annotation burden. In: Ernst, E. (ed.) ECOOP 2007. LNCS, vol. 4609, pp. 227–247. Springer, Heidelberg (2007). https://doi.org/10.1007/978-3-540-73589-2_12
9. Chalin, P., James, P.R., Rioux, F.: Reducing the use of nullable types through non-null by default and monotonic non-null. IET Softw. **2**(6), 515–531 (2008)
10. Damas, L., Milner, R.: Principal type-schemes for functional programs. POPL **82**, 207–212 (1982)
11. Ehringer, D.: The Dalvik virtual machine architecture. Tech. Rep. **4**(8) (2010)
12. Ellis, B., Stylos, J., Myers, B.: The factory pattern in API design: a usability evaluation. In: Proceedings of the 29th International Conference on Software Engineering, pp. 302–312. IEEE Computer Society (2007)
13. Gamma, E., Helm, R., Johnson, R., Vlissides, J.: Design patterns: abstraction and reuse of object-oriented design. In: Nierstrasz, O.M. (ed.) ECOOP 1993. LNCS, vol. 707, pp. 406–431. Springer, Heidelberg (1993). https://doi.org/10.1007/3-540-47910-4_21
14. Gibbons, J.: Design patterns as higher-order datatype-generic programs. In: Proceedings of the 2006 ACM SIGPLAN Workshop on Generic Programming, pp. 1–12. ACM (2006)
15. Goetz, B.: State of the Lambda, 4th edn. (2011). http://cr.openjdk.java.net/~briangoetz/lambda/lambda-state-4.html
16. Google Inc.: Android Executor Interface Documentation (2012). https://developer.android.com/reference/java/util/concurrent/Executor

17. Google Inc.: Android FutureTask Class Documentation (2012). https://developer.android.com/reference/java/util/concurrent/FutureTask
18. Google Inc.: Understand the Activity Lifecycle (Android documentation) (2014). https://developer.android.com/guide/components/activities/activity-lifecycle
19. Google Inc.: Android Studio download page (2019). https://developer.android.com/studio/
20. Haack, C., Poll, E.: Type-based object immutability with flexible initialization. In: Drossopoulou, S. (ed.) ECOOP 2009. LNCS, vol. 5653, pp. 520–545. Springer, Heidelberg (2009). https://doi.org/10.1007/978-3-642-03013-0_24
21. Haller, P., Prokopec, A., Miller, H., Klang, V., Kuhn, R., Jovanovic, V.: Futures and promises (2012). http://docs.scala-lang.org/overviews/core/futures.html
22. Kestelyn, J.: How Apache Spark, Scala, and Functional Programming Made Hard Problems Easy at Barclays (2015). https://blog.cloudera.com/blog/2015/08/
23. McClean, J.: Lambdas are not functional programming (2018). https://medium.com/@johnmcclean/lambdas-are-not-functional-programming-63533ce2eb74
24. Mycroft, A.: Polymorphic type schemes and recursive definitions. In: Paul, M., Robinet, B. (eds.) Programming 1984. LNCS, vol. 167, pp. 217–228. Springer, Heidelberg (1984). https://doi.org/10.1007/3-540-12925-1_41
25. Nguyen, D., Wong, S.B.: Design patterns for lazy evaluation. ACM SIGCSE Bull. **32**, 21–25 (2000)
26. Odersky, M., Wadler, P.: Pizza into Java: translating theory into practice. In: POPL (1997)
27. Oracle Corp: JDK 8 Documentation: Package java.util.function (2010). https://docs.oracle.com/javase/8/docs/api/java/util/function/package-summary.html
28. Oracle Corp: Method References (Java Documentation) (2017). https://docs.oracle.com/javase/tutorial/java/javaOO/methodreferences.html
29. Petricek, T.: Type-First Development (2015). http://tomasp.net/blog/type-first-development.aspx/
30. Pratikakis, P., Spacco, J., Hicks, M.: Transparent proxies for java futures. In: Proceedings of the 19th Annual ACM SIGPLAN Conference on Object-Oriented Programming, Systems, Languages, and Applications, OOPSLA 2004, pp. 206–223. ACM, New York (2004)
31. Seemann, M.: Type Driven Development (2015). https://blog.ploeh.dk/2015/08/10/type-driven-development/
32. Seemann, M.: Type Driven Development (2015). https://blog.ploeh.dk/2016/02/10/types-properties-software/
33. Setzer, A.: Java as a functional programming language. In: Geuvers, H., Wiedijk, F. (eds.) TYPES 2002. LNCS, vol. 2646, pp. 279–298. Springer, Heidelberg (2003). https://doi.org/10.1007/3-540-39185-1_16
34. Subramaniam, V.: Functional programming in Java: harnessing the power of Java 8 Lambda expressions. In: Pragmatic Bookshelf (2014)
35. The Lego Group: LEGO Mindstorms NXT Education Kit (2011). https://www.generationrobots.com/media/Lego-Mindstorms-NXT-Education-Kit.pdf
36. The Lego Group: EV3 Communication Developer Kit (2013). https://le-www-live-s.legocdn.com/sc/media/files/ev3-developer-kit/lego
37. The Lego Group: EV3 Firmware Developer Kit (2013). https://le-www-live-s.legocdn.com/sc/media/files/ev3-developer-kit/lego
38. The Lego Group: ROBOLAB Reference Guide (2013). http://www.legoengineering.com/robolab-programming-references/
39. Warburton, R.: Java 8 Lambdas: Pragmatic Functional Programming. O'Reilly Media Inc., Sebastopol (2014)

40. Welc, A., Jagannathan, S., Hosking, A.: Safe futures for Java. In: Proceedings of the 20th Annual ACM SIGPLAN Conference on Object-Oriented Programming, Systems, Languages, and Applications, OOPSLA 2005, pp. 439–453. ACM, New York (2005)
41. Wlaschin, S.: Designing with Types (2013). https://fsharpforfunandprofit.com/series/designing-with-types.html
42. Wlaschin, S.: Designing with Types: Making illegal states unrepresentable (2013). https://fsharpforfunandprofit.com/posts/designing-with-types-making-illegal-states-unrepresentable
43. Xi, H., Pfenning, F.: Dependent types in practical programming. In: Proceedings of the 26th ACM SIGPLAN-SIGACT Symposium on Principles of Programming Languages, pp. 214–227. ACM (1999)
44. Zhang, L., Krintz, C., Nagpurkar, P.: Language and virtual machine support for efficient fine-grained futures in Java. In: Proceedings of the 16th International Conference on Parallel Architecture and Compilation Techniques, PACT 2007, pp. 130–139. IEEE Computer Society, Washington, DC (2007)
45. Zhang, L., Krintz, C., Soman, S.: Efficient support of fine-grained futures in Java. In: International Conference on Parallel and Distributed Computing Systems (PDCS). Citeseer (2006)
46. Zibin, Y., Potanin, A., Ali, M., Artzi, S., et al.: Object and reference immutability using java generics. In: Proceedings of the 6th Joint Meeting of the European Software Engineering Conference and the ACM SIGSOFT Symposium on the Foundations of Software Engineering, pp. 75–84. ACM (2007)

Industrial Management and Other Applications

Implementation of the Single Minute Exchange of Die (SMED) Principles for the Improvement of the Productivity in a Steel Company in Colombia

Lina María Altamar Guerra[1] , Xiomara Noriega Fontalvo[1] ,
Juan Carlos Cabarcas[1] , Dionicio Neira[2] ,
and Javier Velasquez[2(✉)]

[1] Universidad del Atlántico, Barranquilla, Colombia
linamari_1220@hotmail.com,
xiomynoriega_12@hotmail.com,
juancabarcas@mail.uniatlantico.edu.co
[2] Universidad de la Costa, Barranquilla, Colombia
{dneiral,jvelasqu3}@cuc.edu.co

Abstract. This study aims to analyze the process conditions for the reference changeover in a pipe forming mill in a metalworking company in Colombia, focusing on the high set-up times of this machine. High set up times in this machine causes, excessive idle time, low productivity, and complains due to tardy orders. Based on the principles of SMED, each of the set-up activities was analyzed. The methodology allowed the reclassification of some activities as external, as well as the identification of deficiencies in personnel formation, housekeeping, lack of tools, and other factors affecting the set-up time. Different actions were implemented with the commitment of directives, operators, production management, and other areas. The discipline showed for all the involved areas allowed to achieve exceptional results.

Keywords: SMED · 5S method · Set-up time · Productivity ·
Metalworking company

1 Introduction

Due to the globalized economy companies all around the world has been forced to find ways to continuously improve their processes to remain competitive [1]. In production processes there are factors that become critical constraints causing high lead times, inefficiencies and an increase of costs. Currently in the analyzed company (AC), the manufacturing process of structural tubular profiles presents delays in its production time, due to high set up time. The set-up time is particularly high when producing the structural tubular profile in the tube-forming, therefore the design of SMED based strategies that help in the reduction of time losses in the production process was necessary. The SMED technique is one of the most successful approaches in the reduction of equipment set up time, increasing process productivity. This increase in

K. Saeed et al. (Eds.): CISIM 2019, LNCS 11703, pp. 213–231, 2019.
https://doi.org/10.1007/978-3-030-28957-7_18

the productivity gives to the organization an improvement in its competitiveness, considering that better productivity allows companies to reduce costs, and to increase flexibility (ability to rapidly adapt to changes in demand) [2, 3]. So, the implementation of this technique in the process will be of great help to solve the current problem of high set up times and low productivity.

This paper is organized as follows, in Sect. 2 a literature review of SMED, 5S, cycle time and change of reference is performed. Section 3 describes the SMED implementation process. Section 4 drive some conclusions considering the SMED implementation process and its outcomes.

2 Literature Review

2.1 Single Minute Exchange of Die (SMED)

The SMED has been defined as the theory and techniques designed to perform die changes in less than 10 min. According to SMED principles a reduction in set up times allows the organization to work with smaller batches, that is, shorter process times, which results in a substantial improvement of delivery times and in a reduction in work in process and finished good inventory [4].

2.1.1 SMED Steps

Step 1: Study of the changeover operation. The basis of this step is the well-known principle "What is not known cannot be improved". The purpose of this step is to understand the changeover procedure, what the operators do, and ask them why to do they do things the way they are doing them. In this stage a detailed analysis of the set-up process is carried out with the following activities:

- Record changeover times: It is necessary to perform a statistical analysis of all the activities made in the changeover operation to determine its mean and standard deviation. It is also important to identify causes of high activities execution times and causes for variability in activity times.
- Study the current conditions of change: It is recommended to record the set-up operation on video. It is also important to take pictures of the operation. Then these pictures and video can be projected to the operators in order they analyze their work and realize what they are doing wrong and can be improved. This process is important to get the operators involved and committed with the SMED project.

Step 2: Separate internal and external activities. In this phase it will be necessary to make a list of the sequential activities carried out during the setup, to identify which are internal (necessary to be performed in with a stopped machine) and external (can be performed with the machine in normal operation). This step allows to detect basic problems that have become part of the work routine.

Step 3: Convert internal activities into external ones. One of the basic principles of SMED and Lean Manufacturing is that machine should be adding value to product (on operation) all the planned time. Any stop during the planned time is considered a waste, no matter if this stop is expected (set ups) or unexpected (breakdowns). Keeping on mind that any stop is considered a waste (*muda*) it is necessary to eliminate them or reduce them as much as possible. At this stage it is necessary to make a thorough review of the internal activities, to make the conversion to external ones, in as much activities as possible. Another important aspect to consider is the elimination of adjustments, since it is considered that adjustment operations usually represent 50 to 70% of the internal preparation time. Therefore, it is very important to reduce this adjustment time to shorten the total set up time.

- Improve internal and external activities: The objective of this stage is to perfect every elementary activity (both external and internal). This stage implies in many cases reductions in activities improved in the previous stages. This work is of a high level of detail and, and it also requires a lot of imagination and the design of novel devices and tools.
- In this step, the minimum internal activities that remain can be diminished and the others, although external, can also be improve [5].

2.2   Methodology of the 5S

The 5S are the initials of five Japanese words that name each of the five phases that make up the methodology:

- *SEIRI - ORGANIZATION*: It consists in identifying and separating the necessary materials from the unnecessary ones.
- *SEITON - ORDER*: It consists of establishing the way in which the necessary materials must be located and identified, so that it is easy to find them.
- *SEISO - CLEANING*: It consists of identifying and eliminating the sources of dirt, ensuring that all media are always in perfect state.
- *SEIKETSU- STANDARDIZATION*: Simple and visible rules for all
- *SHITSUKE- DISCIPLINE AND HABIT*: It consists of working permanently in accordance with established norms [6].

2.3   Change of Reference (Changeover, or Set Up)

It is the process that must be followed when going from making a certain reference to a different one, which involves adjusting the parts of the different steps (assemblies) of the pipe forming mill, considering the specifications of each reference, incurring preparation and enlistment times [7].

3   Study Case

3.1   Step 1: Study of the Changeover Operation

Structure of the Structural Pipe Forming Mill
The pipe forming mill is the machine used to manufacture and shape the structural tubular profiles of TCR (Round Reference), TSR (Square Reference) and TRR (Rectangular Reference). This machine consists of a forming zone and a finishing zone where the tube is given its final measurement before being cut. These zones are made

up of 15 steps that must be adjusted depending on the reference that is required for production purposes. The structural tube forming mill has the following structure:

- Formation stages: A stage can be defined as a motorized structure formed by different parts and supports. There are 15 stages in the mill. The stages have the following elements (Table 1)

Table 1. Elements from Stage 1 to Stage 15.

Elements stages		
Stage	Items	Components
Stage 1 and Stage 2	Upper shaft: support	These contain the formation dice for the different structural tubular profiles references
	Upper shaft dice	Piece of steel, used to transform the sheet into a pipe
Stage 3	Upper shaft	Solid shaft forming the tube, within its elements can be found separators, the calibration system and dice
	Lower shaft	Solid tube forming shaft, inside its elements can be found separators and dice
Stages 4–15	Upper shaft	Solid shaft forming the tube, within its elements are separators, calibration system and dice
	Intermediate shaft	Tube forming shaft is formed by two structures that contain vertical dice located in the middle of the passage
	Lower shaft	Solid tube forming shaft, within its elements are separators and dice

- Formation shafts: The shafts located in the different steps have the following structure (Tables 2 and 3):

Table 2. Shafts elements

Shafts elements	Components
Upper shaft elements	Solid shaft, Calibration system, Cardan, Separators, Formation dice, Synchronization axis
Intermediate shaft elements	Covers, Axis, Formation dice, Hose
Elements Welding roller	Covers, Axis, Formation dice, Support

Table 3. Standard times of possible changes

Change scenarios	Standard time
Change square/rectangular to round and vice versa	5 days
Round to round change	3 days
Change square/rect to square/rect	2 days

Types of Changes Between the Different References

- Square/rectangular to round change and vice versa: It is necessary to dismantle all the formation steps and change all the formation dice, as well as change of the Welding rollers, change in the chocks of the cutter on the fly, change of the formation dice from stage 1 and 2 and calibration.
- Round to round change: They have 14 common rollers (shafts) so it is not necessary to disassemble the stages (8, 9, 10) only changes are made in the spacers, as well as change in the rollers of the Welding roller, change in the shims of the cutter on the fly, change of the training dice of stage 1 and 2 and calibration.
- Change square/rectangular (rect) to square/rect: The complexity of this change depends on the reference to produce, the most critical case is the disassembly of 8 rollers and 4 formation steps, as well as change in the rollers of the Welding roller, change in the shims of the cutter on the fly, change of the formation dice of step 1 and 2 and calibration, the less critical case is the change of reference between thicknesses $150 \times 150 \times 6$ and $\times 150 \times 4$.

Likewise, for each setting scenario, changes must be made for each of the elements of the mill.

Study of Preparation Set Up Times in the Pipe Forming Mill

This stage was recorded on video. Taking of times for possible scenarios of change:

- Times Square-Rectangular change: Change of square pipe $5 \times 135 \times 135$ to rectangular pipe $6 \times 300 \times 100$. This change took 35 h.
- Round-Round change times: Reference change Round-Round $114 \times 8 - 152 \times 6$. This change took 48 h.
- Round-Square change times: Round reference change - Square $152 \times 6 - 200 \times 200$. This change is the most extensive change that the tube-forming mill has. It took 83 h.

Considering that the elements to change are the same and what varies is the amount of the changed elements, filming was made in the process of changing each of the elements. So, a specific timestamp for each of the changes in the Mill components could be determined.

3.2 Step II: Classification of Activities and Identification of Opportunities for Improvement of the Set-up Activities

- Classification of Upper shaft dice activities

The total duration time of this change should be 2 h and 1 min but currently it takes 2 h and 17 min.

Improvement Opportunities

Activity 2: This activity implies high waiting times because existing cranes are not enough, and it consumes a lot of time while this resource is available for the assembly and disassembly of the pieces.

Activities 3 and 8: The slings used are long, and entangled, making it difficult the lifting and the dismantling of the parts. Time is also lost wrapping them, disarming them and placing them in a correct position to reduce the rolling of the pieces.

Activity 4: Can be converted as an external activity. The donkeys, used to support the shaft during dismantling, even when this activity is external, these are located at the same moment that the activity is carried out, instead of doing it before the set up.

Activity 6: Nuts and screws are removed with non-automatic tools such as manual screwdrivers, this can be optimized with more advanced tools to speed up the work.

Activity 9: Many times, the die gets stuck and rudimentary tools such as a chisel and keys are used. This can be optimized by looking for more effective and automated methods to remove large parts such as dice.

- Classification of activities Upper shaft Separators

The total duration of this group of activities should be 35 min and they currently take 01 h and 11 min.

Improvement Opportunities

Activity 2: Excessive revisions can be avoided, through strategies that allow the easy and effective review of the procedure to be followed, with all the characteristics of the components and the parts to be changed.

Activity 3: Can be converted in an external activity. Currently, due to the lack of many tools necessary for the assembly and disassembly of certain components in the line of pipe 2102, the operators must lend the hammers and other resources in the line of pipe 2103.

Activity 4: Can be converted in an external activity. Interruptions that currently occur to search for separators are not justified, this must always be done externally (Tables 4 and 5).

Table 4. Classification of upper shaft activities given

Components	No	Activities	External	Internal
Upper shaft dice	1	The safety pin and wedges are removed		√
	2	Wait crane	√	
	3	Location of slings to remove the upper shaft		√
	4	Preparation of donkeys	√	
	5	Location of the upper shaft on the donkeys or supports available		√
	6	The calibration system nut is removed		√
	7	The fixing bar is disassembled		√
	8	The slings are located and the calibration system is undocked		√
	9	Separators are removed and then the dice too.		√
	10	The dice is disarmed		√
	11	The dice is selected according to the reference to be mounted		√
	12	The dice is loaded and suspended to add the conical cover and is located next to the shaft.		√

(*continued*)

Table 4. (*continued*)

Components	No	Activities	External	Internal
	13	Separators that are not necessary are removed		√
	14	The sling is placed to lift the shaft in order to move spacers that are not necessary		√
	15	The dice are located on the shaft		√
	16	The dice are pushed into position with the wooden trunk		√
	17	The required separators are searched	√	
	18	The shaft is suspended when required to locate spacers		√
	19	The separators are located on the shaft and subsequently measured		√
	20	The grease is applied to the bearings and these are located		√
	21	The calibration system is mounted to the shaft and then screwed		√
	22	The axis is moved to its respective formation step and wedges are added		√

Table 5. Classification of activities upper axis separators

Components	No	Activities	External	Internal
Horizontal formation shafts, separators	1	The operators look for the specification drawings for the identify the settings depending on the reference to be mounted	√	
	2	The operators check the drawings and discuss for the adequate separators they should use	√	
	3	They proceed to look for the necessary tools (hammer) to correctly change the separators	√	
	4	Interruptions to find the necessary separators	√	
	5	Disarm of separators that are not necessary		√
	6	Assembly of spacers that are required		√

- Classification of roller activities Squeeze roller (SR)

Similar analysis was performed in the case of the squeeze roller. It was determined that the total duration time of this activity should be 1 h, and 46 min and it takes 1 h and 58 min now, concluding that this activity is consuming 10% more than the time it should. The activities related with the squeeze roller are 19 from which 16 were classified as internal and three as external. The main improvement opportunities were related with the need to make a better planning prior the execution of the activities.

- Classification of change activities for welding roller

The total duration time of this activities should be 1 h, and 31 min and they take 1 h and 43 min now, this activity is consuming 12% more than the time it should. The activities related with the welding roller are 11 from which 3 were classified as external and 8 as internal. The main improvement opportunities were related to the reduction of the clutter in the work area, which makes it difficult to locate tools, and there is also lack of certain tools. There are problems related to the immediate availability of the cranes. There is significant loss of time before assembly and disassembly operations, therefore, evaluate the amount of material that is purchased to reduce waiting times.

- Classification of set up activities Step 1 and Step 2

The total duration time of this activity should be 1 h, and 51 min and it takes 2 h and 40 min now, this activity is consuming 31% more than the time it should.

Improvement Opportunities
Activities 1 and 23: The methods to remove screws are slow and uncomfortable for operators. This activity can be optimized by acquiring more effective resources.

Activity 2: The stage is dismantled on the floor to then re-locate the slings and make the stage assembly on some spacers. There are other alternatives that could optimize the execution of this activity no need to dismantle the step.

Activity 9: This activity can be improved through the acquisition of more effective automatic tools for the disassembly of robust parts such as the formation dice.

Activity 19: In many occasions' operators look for the grease containers at the same moment that the operators are going to apply it (Table 6).

Table 6. Classification of set up activities Step 1 and 2

Components	No	Activities	External	Internal
Step 1 and 2 change	1	Remove main shaft screws (both sides)		√
	2	Location of slings		√
	3	Disassembly in crane		√
	4	Location of supports		√
	5	Mounting the passage in the supports		√
	6	Location eyebolts on the rides of the die		√
	7	Location of slings in the lateral eyebolts		√
	8	Remove clamping caps from the die		√
	9	Remove die and locate vertically on wooden supports		√
	10	Location of eyebolts on die surface		√
	11	Location of slings		√
	12	Horizontal mounting given		√
	13	The disassembly and assembly for the other die is repeated		√
	14	Elevation of the die to remove the shaft		√

(continued)

Table 6. (*continued*)

Components	No	Activities	External	Internal
	15	Drive shaft with wooden support		√
	16	Clean the die		√
	17	Remove shaft and bearing		√
	18	Add bearing and cap to the new shaft		√
	19	Add grease		√
	20	Add ring to the die		√
	21	External measurements	√	
	22	Fitting the die		√
	23	Screwed		√
	24	Repeat the same disassembly and assembly activities for the other		√

• Classification of activities changes cutter on the fly (Table 7)

Adding times of internal activities, the total duration time of this activity should be 2 h and 43 min and it takes 3 h and 39 min now.

Table 7. Classification of activities cutter on the fly

Components	No	Activities	External	Internal
Clan 4	1	Remove the clan's outer screws		√
	2	The operator checks the plan to determine which shims should be located	√	
	3	Search for tools	√	
	4	Search for shims and put them in the workplace	√	
	5	Remove screws (4) from the shims located on the plates (2)		√
	6	Location of the shims according to the reference as indicated		√
	7	Add the screws (2) of clan 4		√
	8	Dialogue with the supervisor about required shims in the plane	√	
	9	Test the clan by activating the controllers.		√
Clan 1	10	Approach of the operator to the clan by turning the valve		√
	11	Remove the clan's outer screws		√
	12	Remove plates (2)		√
	13	Plane query	√	
	14	Search for shims	√	
	15	Remove screws (4) from the plates		√

(*continued*)

Table 7. (*continued*)

Components	No	Activities	External	Internal
	16	Add required slums		√
	17	Add clan outer screws		√
Clan 2	18	Check the plan in order to rectify the necessary shims		√
	19	Remove shoes		√
	20	Search for shims	√	
	21	Location of the shims in order to place the roller at the required height		√
Clan 1	22	Open or close the side rollers of the press entrance		√
	23	Raise or lower the upper roller according to the reference		√

Opportunities for Improvement

Activity 2: Can be converted into an external activity. The specification drawings must be checked before proceeding to stop the machine for set up activities. This activity is currently made now when the shims are going to be mounted, which delays the activities.

Activity 3: Can be converted into an external activity. Frequent machine stops to search for tools, and the clutter in the work area makes it difficult to locate them. Some tools are missing.

Activity 5: Can be improved by replacing rudimentary tools with automatic tools.

Activity 8: Can be converted into an external activity. Getting informed of the shims that must be in Clan 4 is a task that must be external, this means, that the operator should be informed of the shims that will be needed with their respective characteristics before beginning with the set up as it constitutes a planning activity.

Activity 18: There are many interruptions due to technical drawing revision. The revision of the drawings can be optimized to facilitate the understanding of the process by the operators and make faster and more practical the development of this task.

3.3   Step III: Design of Strategies Based on Lean Manufacturing Techniques

- Hoisting Ears: The ears are previously designed mechanical structures which have two lifting points at each end of the upper part of it and serve as lifting tools, serving as an intermediary between the load and the crane. For the realization of the changes of horizontal shafts, it is necessary the accommodation of slings to perform the lifting of the calibration system of the upper shaft and then its location in the correct position.
- Hoisting headgear: The headgear is a structure that has an opening in the form of eyelet, which allows to the operator to raise and handle the load in different positions, with the help of a crane, together with the hoisting ear this proposal will help the replacement of slings for assembly and roller (shaft) removal.

- Automation of tools

Electric drills: The use of non-automatic tools tends to influence the times of high reference change, operators are up to 10 min in the screws of the plates of subjection of the SR, with the use of tools such as ratchet and its respective sockets. The proposal consists of changing these tools for more agile ones that facilitate the activity, such as three electric drills and their respective dice.

Bearing extractor: This procedure is tedious and sometimes it is also high time consuming in the dismantling of the dice, as well as there are occasions that the bearing and covers come out easily even when using hammer and chisel, there are also times where these parts get stuck and are difficult to remove, making it difficult to change dice.

During the project a survey for more advanced tools was made in order to find tools or devices that would allow greater efficiency in the disassembly of formation dice, in this way it was found that the suitable tool for this task is the bearing extractor, which is an advanced mechanical tool that allows the removal of heavy parts when these do not come out easily. The bearing extractor allows to remove the bearing and the covers of the dice in less time and simplifies the work to the operators.

Installation of console cranes: It was concluded that the crane utilization percentage was very high and waiting times for cranes also, since there were not the necessary number of cranes available or sometimes these were not used correctly. The percentage of use of crane in the change Welding roller is equivalent to 56%, in the horizontal roller's changes SR is 43% and in the changes step 1 and 2 is 43%. These high crane utilization rates are due to the size and weight of the parts to be changed. In addition to interruptions to locate the crane in a different part of the plant where is required to move some component. This means that it is rare to find a crane unoccupied and ready to be used in the place that is needed. It is proposed to evaluate the possibility of acquiring at least one additional crane.

- Planning proposals

Tools: Operators often interrupt the operation since they do not have immediate availability of the tools because they are not present in the workplace while the activities are carried out, therefore it is necessary to suspend to go to search the tools that are needed to continue the operation. The search for tools is a planning activity that if not carried out correctly can generate unnecessary interruptions during the internal tasks of changes.

In the production line there is a lack of many tools that could simplify the operations performed by the operators and the place where they are located is not organized. Considering the 5S SEITON-ORDER technique, it is proposed to organize each one considering its usefulness and its size, thus reducing the time it takes for the operator to find the tool he needs by reducing clutter in the work area.

It is proposed the identification and separation of the necessary materials from the unnecessary ones (SEIRI-ORGANIZATION), taking into account that there are many tools that are needed for the efficient realization of the activities, it will be necessary to carry out an inventory of tools identifying the tools that operators do not use or are unnecessary and those that needed and they do not currently have.

Separators: The separators are not organized, which makes it difficult for operators to have immediate disposition of these and, they are slow to locate in the middle of the mess the separator they need according to the reference that is going to change. Continuing with the principles of order posed by the 5S to solve the lack of organization of the separators and reduce the time in the search for them, it was proposed the creation of supports where they could be located according to the measures, in addition make an inventory of separators, where they detect missing or those that are in poor condition and thus acquire the necessary.

Checklist: It is important that before proceeding to start the activities of reference changes the personnel have clarity of the necessary tools, this is part of the correct planning of the process to avoid losses of time due to interruptions to look for tools. This strategy consists on making a checklist in which the necessary tools to carry out the activity are indicated. The checklists will be made for each respective change since the same tools are not used for each part of the mill to be changed.

Rapid change software: The lack of organization, makes the operators delay looking for separators, to comply with the assigned measure. Separators that are sometimes not available in inventory or that the measure assigned in the plan is already located in the outgoing reference. The proposal consists of using the inventory of separators and a software that will indicate the separators that you need and that they have, all this with the purpose of omitting the mental calculations or calculations made with the cell phone calculator. The inclusion of this software will also help the operators to identify which separators are armed in the mill. The software contains the option to enter the incoming reference and the outgoing reference and the stage that you want to verify allowing the personnel to easily verify what is already mounted in the machine and what is needed to be mounted.

- Station of rapid change: When performing the process time taking it become evident that the element that consumes more time to be changed is the horizontal formation shaft. It is proposed to have a rapid change station that would be dedicated to carry out the tooling transfer of horizontal formation shaft and these would later be placed on supports, i.e. the axes at the time of stopping the machine would already be armed with the reference to produce, just waiting for the assembly. Approximately 28 solid spare axles and 28 empty tubes in which the assemblies of the references contained in supports will be located, in the exchange station the axle will be placed with the incoming reference and the solid shaft. This shaft will have a power system, that will be responsible for transferring all the tooling with movements in the jaw cylinders.

3.4 Step IV: Simulation of the Process of Production of Structural Tubular Profiles Implementing the Proposals of Improvement of Station of Rapid Change for Horizontal Axes of Formation

With the initial time collection, a classification was made of how much time each element of the machine took depending on the amount that each of these elements has shown in Table 8 below:

Table 8. Times of duration of each element in the machine.

Element of the mill to change	Time C/u	Min	No. element	(Min * number of elements)	Total time (*HRS*)
Horizontal training axis	2:17	137	30	4110	68,5
SR rollers	1:58	118	13	1534	25,566
Welding roller	1:43	103	1	103	17,166
Turkish head	3:21	201	1	201	3,35
Cutting machine on the fly	3:39	219	1	219	3,65
TOTAL TIME SQUARE-ROUND CHANGE					57

It can be observed that the element of the mill that consumes the most time in the change of reference is the horizontal formation axis and the change that takes more time is when it is required to change the reference from round to square and vice versa.

To reduce these times, it is necessary to implement the rapid change station (prototype that will facilitate this process), as well as the purchase of spare axles to externalize this activity and locate more groups of operators in the change of the rollers of the SR, the use of spare axles. This time was not possible to calculate through practice; therefore, the software FLEXSIM ® was used to simulate the use of this prototype.

By entering the collected times and the approximate operating times of the proto-type, it was possible to obtain an estimate of the time and a reduction of approximately 80% of the time observed (Table 9).

Table 9. Comparison between current time and simulation time

Activity	Horizontal reference axis changes round reference		
Current time of operation	2:43:00	Approximate time with rapid change station	00:32 min

After the implementation of the proposals to reduce set up times in the pipeline forming mill, the time associated with the different reference changes was again taken to determine the percentage of reduction of the set-up time. The results for each scenario are shown

• New duration time reference change Square/Rectangular: 8 h, 54 min
• New duration time Reference change Round/Round: 18 h, 20 min
• New duration time reference change Square/Round: 20 h.

Comparative times general changes initial conditions vs new conditions (Table 10):

Table 10. Comparison of times before vs. current times

Reference change	Duration before (hr)	New duration time (hr)	% decrease
Square-Rectangular	35:00:00	8:54:00	75%
Round-Round	48:00:00	18:20:00	62%
Square-Round	83:00:00	20:00:00	76%

Considerable reductions have been obtained in the time it takes to perform the three possible types of reference change. The net set up time is equal to the sum of the activities that are carried out when the machine is stopped, that is, internal activities, because with the proposals based on SMED currently all activity that can be performed when the machine is producing a reference different, it will be done effectively externally, to use the time of stop of the mill only in activities of replacements and adjustments, assemblies and disassembles. In accordance with this and considering that the internal activities were reduced and optimized, the total set up time is much smaller, including the change that consumed the most time, that is (Round-Square) could be done in approximately 20 h, when previously making this change took even 5 days, which is equivalent to a reduction of approximately 75.90% of the required time.

It is important to point out that the duration of the reference changes is currently determined by the sum of the duration times of the internal activities, since these are the activities forcing the machine to stop.

Likewise, the times associated to the changes in the different components of the Mill were taken and the following results were obtained.

- New change times Step 1 and 2 (Table 11)

Table 11. New change times optimized Step 1 and 2

Activity	Time (h/mm)	Strategy implemented
Remove main shaft screws(both sides)	0:04	Optimized with automatic tool (drill)
The coupling of the lifting headband and the ears is made	0:01	Hooks and lifting ears
Remove die and locate vertically pm wooden supports	0:03	Optimizing with automatic tools (bearing extractor)
The disassembly and assembly for the other die is repeated	0:10	Optimizing with automatic tools (bearing extractor)

- New change times for Cutter on the fly (Table 12)

Table 12. New shifting times for cutter on the fly

Parts	Activity	Time (h/mm)	Strategy implemented
Clan 4	Remove the clan's outer screws	0:02	Optimized with automatic tools (drill)
	Remove screws (4) from the shims located on the plates (2)	0:10	Optimized with automatic tools (drill)
	Add the s crews (2) of clan 4	0:02	Optimized with automatic tools (drill)
Clan 1	Remove the clan's outer screws	0:02	Optimized with automatic tools (drill)
	Remove screws (4) from the plates	0:13	Optimized with automatic tools (drill)
	Add clan outer screws	0:02	Optimized with automatic tools (drill)
Clan 2	Check the plan in order to rectify the necessary shims	0:03	Optimized by quick change software

- New change times for horizontal axis (shaft) separators (Table 13)

Table 13. New change times for horizontal axis separators

Activity	Time (h/mm)	Strategy implemented
Disarm separators that are not necessary	0:15	
Assembly of spacers that are required	0:15	Optimized with the creation of new separators of lighter material that facilitates its assembly and disassembly

- New change times for welding roller (Table 14)

Table 14. New change times for Welding Roller

Activity	Time (h/mm)	Strategy implemented
The superior dice are removed	0:13	Optimized with automatic tools (bearing extractor)
The lower dice are removed	0:10	Optimized with automatic tools (bearing extractor)

(continued)

Table 14. (*continued*)

Activity	Time (h/mm)	Strategy implemented
The vertical axis and the bearings of the lower die are removed	0:02	Optimized with automatic tools (bearing extractor)
Arm and disarm the upper die	0:07	Optimized with automatic tools (bearing extractor) and by immediate availability of crane console eliminating movements and waiting times

- New change times for Horizontal Squeeze Roller (Table 15)

Table 15. New change times for horizontal Squeeze Roller

Activity	Time (h/mm)	Strategy implemented
The fixing screws are removed	0:03	Optimized with automatic tools (drill)
The screws are removed, the prisoner is uncoupled and the separator plate is	0:03	Optimized with automatic tools (drill)
The die is removed	0:04	Optimized with automatic tools (bearing extractor)
Shaft assembly	0:10	Optimized with the acquisition of new cranes that minimize times and movements. Due to the almost immediate availability of these in most cases

- Comparative Mill components change times: initial conditions vs. new conditions:

Previously, the change that took the longest time was the one associated with the flight cutter, it took approximately 3 h and 39 min to carry out all the disassembly and assembly in this element, to move from one reference to another, so that a 41% reduction in this time is important to reduce the total time of change. On the other hand, it can be observed that the upper horizontal formation shaft and its associated changes spend a total time of 2 h and 17 min. When compared with the cutter on fly the time spent in this change in much smaller. Nevertheless, the importance of its reduction and the implementation of the rapid change station lies on the fact that that each set up implies changing many of these rollers. On the other hand, there is only one cutter on the fly in the mill. In a reference change the total time spent in these shafts was 619 min and with inclusion of the rapid change station it only took 30 min.

Compliance with Programmed Production with Implemented Strategies
After the implementation of the strategies proposed in this project, an increase in the productivity of the pipe line 2102 of approximately 25.60% was obtained. This achievement was possible after 6 months of implementation of the action plans. The above assumes a growth of tons/month of 225.86% in the period between January and July (Tables 16 and 17).

Table 16. Comparison of times initial vs new times in the components of the Mill

Changes	Time before (h/mm)	Current time (h/mm)	% of reduction
Changes step 1 and 2	2:40	121	49,38%
Changes horizontal axis separators	1:11	0:30	57,75%
Roller changes Welder	1:43	1:24	18,45%
Cutter changes on the fly	3:39	2:09	41,10%
Changing horizontal rollers in Squeeze Roller	1:58	1:09	41,53%

Table 17. Increase in production after strategies

Month	Tons	Strategy implemented	Percentage fulfilled of tire expected production
January	143	——————	34%
February	142	——————	33%
March	160	Request for necessity tools for the pipe 02	34%
		Implementing the tool checklist	
April	275	Installation of lifting bands by welding	61%
		Installation of lifting lugs by welding	
May	222	Installing brackets for separators	46%
June	389	Installation of console cranes	86%
July	452	Use of fast change software	140%

4   Conclusions and Analysis of Results

The reduction of the downtimes and idle times allows the companies the minimization in the size of the batches, making it possible the reduction of the inventories in process and finished goods [8]. In the case of AC with the implementation of SMED, the pipe mill capacity better exploited, increasing its productivity being able now to meet the demand and look for additional markets. The company had large amounts of inventory but there were frequent shortages of some items causing disconformities among the customers. The proposed strategies not only based on SMED but in the 5S technique also, allowed to achieve reductions in times never thought. For example, the square-round change that previously took 5 days, then of the implementation of 86% of the proposals, times were obtained for this change of only 20 h, this was the time that was most reduced.

The most critical change is the one that takes place in the horizontal axis of formation, because these structures are present in all steps of the pipe mill 2102 (28 upper axes in total) that is, there are more of these than of any other part, therefore any time that could be reduced in these was fundamental at the time of obtaining significant decreases in the changes of references, after the implementation of the strategies a saving was obtained in times in the changes of the upper axes of training given of 32 min, which implies a significant saving in dead time, the implementation of the ears and the headbands, allowed to reduce the dismantling time of the axes higher than 10 min when previously it took 27 min, i.e., the mere implementation of 61% of the proposals allowed to reduce this time by more than 50%, which strongly supports the importance of this project, however with the proposed rapid change station, it is expected that the total replacement time of these axes will be only 30 min, which implies a reduction of approximately 78% compared to the previous duration, which was approximately 2 h 17 min.

It is not enough just with the application of the 4 stages of SMED to obtain considerable reductions of the set-up times, the adequate planning and organization during the execution of the activities is fundamental because it allows the saving of movements and human errors which result in losses of time even when the activities are carried out externally or are assigned in parallel. The proposal of the checklists for example, is a strategy aimed at improving the planning of activities, its implementation solved the problem of interrupting the work to search for tools and the useless movements associated with it, causing time gains, for example the interruption time was zeroed to look for separators that previously supposed the loss of 15 min.

By converting a preparation activity into an external one, not only production downtime is being reduced, but also the risk of unforeseen events occurring with the machine stopped so that any corrective action can be carried out without delaying the process.

The favorable results obtained with the implementation of 84% of the proposals are attributed largely to the fact of having actively involved the personnel that is directly related to the execution of the activities necessary for the reference changes.

This application evidences the impact that an adequate SMED implementation process may have in the productivity of a company. In this sense it is important to point out that this implementation includes commitment of personnel and companies' directors.

References

1. Landinez-Lamadrid, D.C., Ramirez-Ríos, D.G., Neira Rodado, D., Parra Negrete, K., Combita Niño, J.P.: Shapley value: its algorithms and application to supply chains. INGE CUC 13(1), 61–69 (2017)

2. Mo, J.P.T.: The role of lean in the application of information technology to manufacturing. Comput. Ind. **60**(4), 266–276 (2009)
3. McIntosh, R.I., Culley, S.J., Mileham, A.R., Owen, G.W.: Changeover improvement: a maintenance perspective. Int. J. Prod. Econ. **73**(2), 153–163 (2001)
4. Ulutas, B.: An application of SMED methodology. Int. J. Mech. Aerospace Ind. Mechatron. Manuf. Eng. **5**(7), 2017
5. Thun, J.-H., Drüke, M., Grübner, A.: Empowering Kanban through TPS-principles – an empirical analysis of the Toyota Production System. Int. J. Prod. Res. **48**(23), 7089–7106 (2010)
6. Michalska, J., Szewieczek, D.: The 5S methodology as a tool for improving the organisation. J. Achievements Mater. Manuf. Eng. **24**(2), 211–214 (2007)
7. Anzanello, M.J., Fogliatto, F.S.: Learning curve modelling of work assignment in mass customized assembly lines. Int. J. Prod. Res. **45**(13), 2919–2938 (2007)
8. Benjamin, S.J., Uthiyakumar Murugaiah, M., Marathamuthu, S.: The use of SMED to eliminate small stops in a manufacturing firm. J. Manuf. Technol. Manage. **24**(5), 792–807 (2013)

Teleagro: IOT Applications for the Georeferencing and Detection of Zeal in Cattle

Paola Ariza-Colpas[1]([⊠]), Roberto Morales-Ortega[1],
Marlon Alberto Piñeres-Melo[2], Farid Melendez-Pertuz[1],
Guillermo Serrano-Torné[3], Guillermo Hernandez-Sanchez[3],
and Hugo Martínez-Osorio[3]

[1] Universidad de la Costa, CUC, Barranquilla, Colombia
{parizal, rmoralesl, fmelendel}@cuc.edu.co
[2] Universidad del Norte, Barranquilla, Colombia
pineresm@uninorte.edu.co
[3] Extreme Technologies, Barranquilla, Colombia
{gserrano, ghernandez, hmartinez}@extreme.com.co

Abstract. The loss of reproductive efficiency of animals and cattle rustling have become one of the main concerns of farmers. The decrease in reproductive efficiency is mainly due to the low percentage in heat detection. Reproductive efficiency is commonly measured by the interval between births, which affects the daily milk production of the cow during its productive life and the income associated with the sale of milk from its production, conditioning the profitability of the farmers. The zeal for its part consists of the theft of bovine cattle that usually is used for its commercialization, bringing considerable losses. According to figures from the Observatory of Human Rights and International Humanitarian Law of the Fundacion Colombia Ganadera, Fundagán, only during 2014 there were 164 cases of cattle rustling, resulting in the loss of 3,798 cattle throughout the country, which represents a loss for the producers of 15 billion of Colombian money. This project proposes the development of a technological platform that combines hardware, software and communications systems of the latest technology and with open standards to provide an economic and reliable solution to the Colombian and Latin American livestock industry. In Colombia, there is a history of products and prototypes that have been developed to alleviate this problem, no platforms of similar benefits have been found that are accessible to farmers in the country. In this article, the different stages developed to obtain a validated prototype with the beneficiary entity and their respective results are socialized.

Keywords: Technological system · Georreferenced detection ·
Zeal of bovine cattle

K. Saeed et al. (Eds.): CISIM 2019, LNCS 11703, pp. 232–239, 2019.
https://doi.org/10.1007/978-3-030-28957-7_19

1 Introduction

Livestock has a key importance for Latin America and the Caribbean, and is a source of basic food for the food security of its population, according to FAO studies, more than 1 billion people worldwide depend on the livestock sector, and 70% of the 880 million rural poor living on less than USD 1.00 per day depend at least partially on livestock for subsistence. Traditional livestock produces very little employment and economic value compared to agriculture and generates a negative impact on the environment [1, 2]. The poverty, social exclusion and violence that Colombia faces are the expressions of a problem that arose from a traditional agrarian structure, outdated, not very innovative and that has deep roots in the excessive concentration of land.

The livestock sector has traditionally been less tradable, although some subsectors of it are in the perspective of becoming tradable to the extent that beef is eventually exported, currently its trade is restricted to border areas; the production, in a high proportion, is dedicated to the internal demands of the producing countries. In Colombia, meat exports historically do not represent 1% of production. One of the limitations that bovine entrepreneurs have to enter the world market is that the incorporation of technologies into the processes of animal nutrition and nutrition, genetics and animal reproduction, mitigation and adaptation to climate change, which reduce costs, improve The efficiency of the use of food depends on the importation of technology and capital investment.

There is in the Department of Cesar in Colombia, a low productivity in the livestock sector caused among other factors by the non-incorporation of technological tools that improve the efficiency of the production process such as the timely detection of bovine zeal and the prevention of theft of cattle due to their high costs, considering that 80.7% of the producers of the Department are medium and small producers, with existing solutions in the market higher than the profit margins of the producer. The prolongation of the production cycle is associated with deficient technological parameters such as birth, weight gain, age of sacrifice among others; In turn, this condition gives the business a low liquidity, subjecting it to a high degree of speculation, while deepening the livestock cycles that undermine the profitability of the activity.

The article is organized in the next section. First, the brief of literature about the technologies for cattle are shown. Second, we explain the structure of the proposed solution. Third, each of the components of the hardware architecture is detailed. Fourth, the conclusions of the experimentation are shown and future works. Finally, the researchers thank all those who supported the development of this project.

2 Brief Review of Literature

In Colombia, projects have been developed in recent years aimed at solving both the problem of detection of heat of cattle and cattle rustling. There is a product in the Colombian market called Celotor (http://www.celotor.com/) which detects the zeal of cattle by placing an RFID chip on the back of the cows to detect when the bull is riding them. Once the mount of the bull is detected, the farmer is informed immediately through a text message (SMS) and the information is stored on a website. While this may be a good solution, it has the disadvantage that it depends on the presence of a riding bull and that the means of communication used is the GSM network which may have low coverage rates in some rural areas [3]. The cost of acquisition of the bulls (the price of a bull is equivalent to 4 heifers) as well as their care are an important expense for small farmers, in addition the mere presence of the bull does not guarantee that all cows in heat will be assembled. affects the accuracy of the method. The Celotor product is the technification of the visual observation method traditionally used by breeders to detect heat [4].

The Mariana University (Pasto, Nariño, Colombia), carried out in 2014 a prototype of surveillance system for livestock farms as prevention of cattle rustling. The prototype monitors biological variables (animal temperature) and its georeferencing and transmits the information to a central computer. The prototype uses Xbee transmission technology. From our point of view, the choice of Xbee technology is not appropriate for this type of project due to its cost, transmission capacity and relatively high energy consumption. The prototype has not yet developed into a commercial product and does not solve the problem of estrus detection in cattle [5].

As background of the project we can mention that Extreme Technologies is a Colombian company with ten (10) years of experience dedicated to the design, development and implementation of advanced technology solutions for the corporate market, especially for companies in the commercial, industrial, logistics and home public services [6]. Extreme Technologies provides IT services based on advanced technological systems that integrate the most modern information and communication technologies. Its business lines include remote data transmission, location-based services, mobile asset tracking and web and mobile computing software solutions. Serves clients from various sectors of the economy in Latin America, providing global quality services and adding value to its customers by optimizing their business processes [7].

3   Architecture of the Hardware Solution

3.1   General Operation of the Solution

The devices will send daily information on their temperature variables and steps of the animal autonomously, also if there is a variation of the established thresholds that show a possible estrus state or in case of having changed georeferenced zone by triangulation. This information will be sent to the Gateway, which will redirect it to the server to be registered and, if necessary, send a message to each of the parties, such as the breeder, the breeders' federation and the nearest points that have a bull. reproduction. If it is a case of unauthorized transfer of the animal, it would not be notified to the point that they have breeding bulls but to the nearest authorities to act. See Fig. 1.

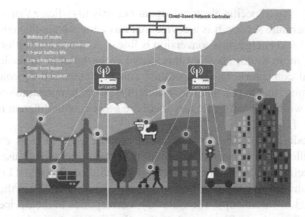

Fig. 1. General operation of the solutions

3.2 Local Operation of the Solution

Each animal will have an intrauterine device that will monitor the temperature of the cow and wirelessly transmit the data periodically and/or event, it must have an energy autonomy of the same duration of the main device located on the neck of the animal, from which it will be sent to the server along with the other parameters or variables. See Fig. 2.

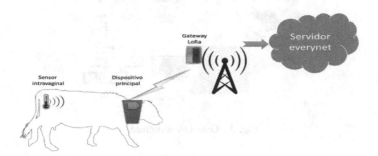

Fig. 2. Local operation of the solutions

Next, each of the components of the solution is specified. The intravaginal sensor, is an autonomous internal sensor, responsible for monitoring the temperature and transmitting it locally to the main device. The main device: It is the autonomous device, responsible for centralizing the information received from peripherals such as the temperature sensor, GPS, accelerometer, etc [8, 9]. This information is processed together with the parameters established in the thresholds to generate the periodic reports or by event, to transmit them to the server. The pedometer or step sensor, It is a device that has a transducer that converts the kinetic energy into an electrical signal allowing the detection of inclination and vibration, variables by means of which it is capable of delivering a specific electrical signal per axis to indicate that a step has been taken. The temperature sensor: It is a device that has a transducer that converts thermal energy into electrical energy, this conversion is linear, so the amplification of the output signal is very simple to do, allowing this signal to be brought to readable levels by analog to digital converters. The temperature can be transferred by conduction, convection or radiation; due to this there are different types of temperature sensors for each category, while within the same category there are sensors with different resolutions for each application [10, 11].

The RF Module, The RF communication module is a wireless communication device, which allows the transfer of information without the need to use conventional means such as cell phone networks, products such as Sigfox, Xbee and Lora, have been taken into account due to its scope, low consumption and reliability in the transmission of data. (RN2903 of Microchip). The Gateway, corresponds to the device that receives the information from the LoRa network and redirects the information to the everynet server. It is responsible for centralizing the information delivered by the RF modules and allowing them access to the Internet and georeferencing by triangulation of each device [12, 13] (Fig. 3).

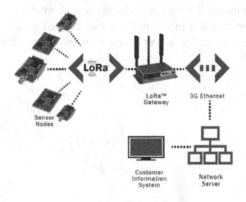

Fig. 3. Gateway structure.

The Server, corresponds to the platform on which the data will be hosted, for viewing or downloading through its API [14]. The diagram of the devices of the solution is shown below in Fig. 4.

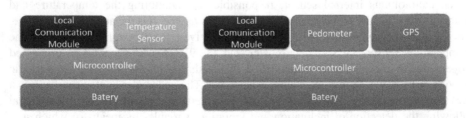

Fig. 4. Intravaginal and principal dispositive.

4   Results

The Table 1, also shows the approximate current consumption of the devices, both in Sleep mode and in active mode. It also shows what would be the consumption of current minute by minute, the first 30 min of operation:

Table 1. Operations result

Peripheral	Active (mA)	Sleep Mode (mA)
GPS	14	0.135
Temp	1	0.001
LoRa	122	0.0014
Micro	9	0.0025

Activity frecuence GPS	GPS	Temp	LoRa	Micro
1	14	1	122	9
2	0.135	0.001	0.0014	0.0025
5	14	1	0.0014	9
6	14	1	0.0014	9
7	0.135	0.0001	0.0014	0.0025
10	14	1	0.0014	9
11	14	1	0.0014	9
12	0.135	0.001	0.0014	0.0025
15	14	1	122	9
16	14	1	0.0014	9
17	0.135	0.001	0.0014	0.0025
20	14	1	0.0014	9
21	14	1	0.0014	9
22	0.135	0.001	0.0014	9
25	14	1	0.0014	9
26	14	1	0.0014	9
27	0.135	0.001	0.0014	9
30	14	1	122	9

The above is represented graphically in the figure shown below (Fig. 5).

Note that every 15 min there is a peak consumption when the LoRa module transmits data. Every 5 min only the microcontroller and the GPS module wake up to be able to evaluate if there is any alarm, and immediately go back to sleep.

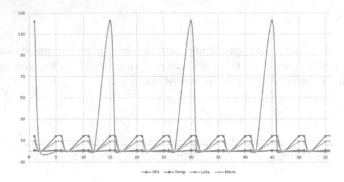

Fig. 5. Approximate current consumption of the devices

5 Conclusions

This research proposed a development of hardware to be incorporated in cattle for the identification of estrus and its respective georeferencing. For this, each of the stages of the project "Technological system of georeferencing and detection of cattle" financed by Colciencias was developed.

The methodological design of the project has taken as a reference the prototyping model as a method of system development. The methodology begins with the identification and validation of the basic requirements. In this stage the project team will integrate the specialists of FEGACESAR in order to limit the minimum structure and the required scalability of the equipment and systems for the detection of heat and georeferencing of animals. In this stage all the behavioral, physical and biological conditions that identify the zeal and georeferencing of the animals and the implementation of electronic sensors for their detection will be investigated and evaluated. The specialists of the accompanying research group will also be integrated to validate the different data transmission alternatives and the requirements in terms of coverage, costs and energy consumption. The final validation of the minimum structure will be carried out using the validation methodology by expert judgment. The second stage of the methodology includes an iterative process of design and implementation. Initially, the architecture of the hardware, software and wireless communications systems for the detection of heat and georeferencing. Consistent with this methodology, it will begin with a Description/Prescription layer, which concludes with the requirements and prescriptions, which links with a conceptual layer that concludes with the specifications of the system and which links with an implementation layer which concludes with the information system and the presentation system.

Once the system architecture is defined, the web and mobile data management and access systems was designed with the following elements: data management, data access and storage, and data security. Since the interaction with the hardware equipment that interacts with the animals are fundamental for this stage, the following configuration has been defined as the minimum elements with which the minimum viable hardware prototype will be made.

Acknowledgment. To the company extreme technologies for the development of the information platform and to the company Fegacesar, for allowing the piloting of this solution.

References

1. Chanvallon, A., et al.: Comparison of three devices for the automated detection of estrus in dairy cows. Theriongenology **82**(5), 734–741 (2014). https://doi.org/10.1016/j.theriogenology.2014.06.010
2. Duponte, M.W.: The Basis of Heat (Estrus) Detection in Catle. University of Hawaii at Manoa, 8–10 April 2007
3. Pérez, L.A.Q., Romero, J.A., Rojas, R.L.: Evaluación de dos protocolos de inseminación artificial a término fijo (IATF) con dos inductores de ovulación (benzoato de estradiol y cipionato de estradiol) en vacas raza criollo caqueteño en el departamento del Caquetá. REDVET. Revista Electrónica de Veterinaria **16**(9), 1–11 (2015)
4. Gaignard, L., Charon, A.: Gestion de crise et traumatisme: les effets collatéraux de la vache folle. De l'angoisse singulière à l'embarras collectif. Travailler **2**, 57–71 (2005)
5. de la Rosa, C.A.: An inexpensive and open-source method to study large terrestrial animal diet and behaviour using time-lapse video and GPS. Methods Ecol. Evol. **10**(5), 615–625 (2019)
6. Desiato, R., et al.: Data on milk dioxin contamination linked with the location of fodder croplands allow to hypothesize the origin of the pollution source in an Italian valley. Sci. Total Environ. **499**, 248–256 (2014)
7. Iwashita, H., et al.: Push by a net, pull by a cow: can zooprophylaxis enhance the impact of insecticide treated bed nets on malaria control? Parasites Vectors **7**(1), 52 (2014)
8. Bhattarai, N.R., et al.: Domestic animals and epidemiology of visceral leishmaniasis, Nepal. Emerg. Infect. Dis. **16**(2), 231 (2010)
9. Doherr, M.G., Zurbriggen, A., Hett, A.R., Rüfenacht, J., Heim, D.: Geographical clustering of cases of bovine spongiform encephalopathy (BSE) born in Switzerland after the feed ban. Vet. Rec. **151**(16), 467–472 (2002)
10. Palechor, M., Enrique, F., De La Hoz Manotas, A.K., De La Hoz Franco, E., Ariza Colpas, P.P.: Feature selection, learning metrics and dimension reduction in training and classification processes in intrusion detection systems. J. Theor. Appl. Inf. Technol. **82**(2), 291–298 (2015)
11. De-La-Hoz-Franco, E., Ariza-Colpas, P., Quero, J.M., Espinilla, M.: Sensor-based datasets for human activity recognition–a systematic review of literature. IEEE Access **6**, 59192–59210 (2018)
12. Palechor, F.M., De la Hoz Manotas, A., Colpas, P.A., Ojeda, J.S., Ortega, R.M., Melo, M.P.: Cardiovascular disease analysis using supervised and unsupervised data mining techniques. JSW **12**(2), 81–90 (2017)
13. Mendoza-Palechor, F.E., Ariza-Colpas, P.P., Sepulveda-Ojeda, J.A., De-la-Hoz-Manotas, A., Piñeres Melo, M.: Fertility analysis method based on supervised and unsupervised data mining techniques. Int. J. Appl. Eng. Res. **11**(21), 10374–10379 (2016)
14. Calabria-Sarmiento, J.C., et al.: Software applications to health sector: a systematic review of literature. J. Eng. Appl. Sci. **13**(11), 3922–3926 (2018)

The Role of Innovation in Cloud–Based ERP Adoption

Thanh D. Nguyen[1,2]([⊠]) [iD], Tu T. Huynh[1], Uyen H. Van[1],
and Tien M. Pham[1]

[1] Banking University of Ho Chi Minh City, Ho Chi Minh City, Vietnam
thanhnd@buh.edu.vn, tuht.mis@gmail.com,
uyenvh.mis@gmail.com, tienpm.mis@gmail.com
[2] Bach Khoa University, Ho Chi Minh City, Vietnam

Abstract. Enterprise resource planning based on cloud computing provides modern software solutions for the organizations. Furthermore, although there are several different studies for each topic of information systems, such as the illustrious theories of technology adoption (TAM, UTAUT), the related theories of innovation (DOI, TOE), there are not many works, which integrate with the various theories of information systems. This study investigates the role of innovation in the adoption of enterprise resource planning based on cloud computing. A total of 232 cloud–based ERP participants have been surveyed and analyzed by structural equation modeling. The findings demonstrate the components of technology–organization–environment (TOE) and the concept of innovation in the structural relationships with technology adoption. Interestingly, innovation has a positive effect on the cloud–based ERP adoption.

Keywords: Cloud–based ERP · Innovation · Technology adoption · TOE

1 Introduction

Information Technology (IT) is changing the relationship among the stakeholders of organizations, and contributing to the important role in supporting GDP growth in the countries [2]. Enterprise resource planning based on cloud computing (cloud–based ERP) supports that organizations can achieve the benefits of ERP solutions with disregard in IT infrastructure [20]. Moreover, the cloud–based ERP solutions help reduce the pressure on the IT department in organizations [22], just a specific cost for using enterprise resource planning system, the organizations can select a standard software package from suppliers or a customized software package to resolve the organization's business needs. Notwithstanding, cloud–based ERP solutions depend heavily on the suppliers, which is extremely important in choosing the right supplier [30]. In Vietnam, there are only 1.1% of organizations applying ERP solutions [49], in which, most of the ERP projects do not meet with the desired objectives [33]. Although cloud–based ERP solutions are being considered by numerous organizations, technology adoption depends on several different factors [20].

The theory of Diffusion of Innovation (DOI) is proposed by Rogers [41] to consider the adoption and widespread diffusion of new technology, DOI also related to the

© Springer Nature Switzerland AG 2019
K. Saeed et al. (Eds.): CISIM 2019, LNCS 11703, pp. 240–252, 2019.
https://doi.org/10.1007/978-3-030-28957-7_20

framework of Technology–Organization–Environment (TOE). One of the authors proposed the first theoretical framework of TOE that is Tornatzky et al. [46], the TOE framework is identified in three contexts: technology, organization, and environment. In the related works, many authors studied in–depth about innovation, a component of the DOI, for example, Oturakci & Yuregir [36]; Stanko [44]; Zahra et al. [54]. Besides, The theories of DOI and TOE can also integrate with the other theories of information systems. Some scholars propounded the illustrious theories of technology adoption, for instance, Davis [13] proposed TAM; Venkatesh et al. [51] proposed UTAUT, which consider the acceptance and use of information systems. In particular, there are many works on each topic of these theories, such as the theories of technology adoption, the theory of DOI, the framework of TOE. However, there are not many works, which integrate with the related theories of information systems, e.g., technology adoption (e.g., TAM, UTAUT), related theories of innovation (e.g., DOI, TOE). Indeed, for an information system to be accepted and valued, which requires many different components, for example, technical, organizational, and environmental components, three main components of the TOE framework. Distinctly, innovation is considered a critical factor in technology adoption [10, 15, 38]. In addition, there are many studies related to each context of information systems, for instance, the adoption of ERP (e.g., Liu & Wang [28]), cloud (e.g., Gangwar et al. [18]), cloud–based ERP (e.g., Albar & Hoque [3]). Therefore, the well–known theories of TAM, UTAUT, the theory of DOI, and the theoretical framework of TOE are considered as the foundational theories for the study of technology adoption, with the specific context of "cloud–based ERP".

2 Theoretical Basis and Research Model

2.1 Enterprise Resource Planning Based on Cloud Computing

Cloud computing (Cloud) is an interesting concept in the world and one of the new development trends of modern technology [34]. However, cloud computing is not an entirely new technology, it is a combination among elements of available IT services [20]. Some scholars argued that cloud computing is the future representation of IT use in organizations. Specifically, Velte & et al. [50] believed that the power of cloud computing has a profound impact on the IT industry, the organizations will not need to install software on their systems and not need to buy hardware or software, simply, they can hire these IT services from the providers.

Enterprise resource planning (ERP) is a new trend of the world, this is an information system to help organizations managing resources and operational management, ERP integrates different modules into one system to support the core functions of the organization [27]. The ERP combines single activities into a whole, integrates most of the relevant activities of the organization into a system [40]. ERP offers many benefits, such as improving business performance by keeping business processes running smoothly, supporting management in providing decision–making information, making organizational operations more flexible [42].

Cloud–based ERP is the enterprise resource planning placed into the environment of the cloud computing [31]. The Enterprise resource planning based on cloud computing can provide flexibility, cost efficiency, scalability, compatibility, availability, and data configured for any organization or business [48]. In addition, cloud–based ERP is also gaining rapid growth in the global [3].

2.2 Literature Review

Technology Adoption is demonstrated in many studies about IT and information systems. Specifically, The Theory of Reasoned Action (TRA) based on the perspective of social psychology to identify behavioral trends, which is proposed by Fishbein & Ajzen [16]. The Theory of Planned Behavior (TPB) is developed by Ajzen [1], based on the foundational theory of TRA and added a new dimension of perceived behavioral control. The Technology Acceptance Model (TAM) is proposed by Davis [13], based on the theories of TRA and TPB to explain the behavior of technology users. The Unified Theory of Acceptance and Use of Technology (UTAUT) is the first built by Venkatesh et al. [51] to explain the behavioral intention and use behavior information systems. UTAUT is based on many foundational theories (TRA, TPB, TAM, C–TPB–TAM, DOI, MM, MPCU, and SCT). In which TRA, TPB, and TAM have the most influence on UTAUT. The theory of UTAUT is built with these factors of performance expectancy, effort expectancy, social influence, and facilitating conditions. Venkatesh et al. [52] continue to develop a new theory based on the UTAUT, that integrates more dimensions of hedonic motivation, price value, and habit, called UTAUT2.

Diffusion of Innovation (DOI) is proposed by Rogers [41] to appreciate and consider how new technology is adopted and widely disseminated. According to Rogers [41], the factors influence on new technology adoption are relative advantage, compatibility, complexity, trialability, and observability. Rogers [41] also divides the new technology adoption with these categories, including innovators, early adopters, early majority, late majority, and laggards. Moore & Benbasat [32] also advances the elements for DOI, such as relative advantage, compatibility, ease of use, result demonstrability, image visibility, trialability, and voluntariness. The theory of DOI is studied in many areas (e.g., information and communication, sociology, marketing research, research and development, knowledge management...) as in Bharati & Chaudhury [7]; Chen et al. [10]; Zahra et al. [54]. On the other hand, DOI is also a premise for the development of many theoretical information systems, including the theoretical framework of Technology–Organization–Environment (TOE). The framework of TOE is defined by Tornatzky et al. [47] in three contexts: technology, organization, and environment. Especially, TOE is widely integrated with the other theories of information systems (e.g., TPB, TAM, UTAUT...), and routinely used in many studies of IT and information systems. For example, e–commerce (e.g., Awa et al. [6]), ERP (e.g., Liu & Wang [28]), cloud (e.g., Gangwar et al. [18]), cloud–based ERP (e.g., Albar & Hoque [3]; Gupta et al. [20]).

The theory of DOI and the theoretical framework of TOE are considered as the appropriate foundational theories to research cloud–based ERP [3]. Although cloud–based ERP is a potential enterprise system, there are not many related works in Vietnam (except, e.g., Nguyen & et al. [34]). Hence, in–depth research on cloud–based ERP is extremely essential and meaningful research both in theory and practice.

2.3 Research Model

From the practical issues of cloud–based ERP, the theoretical basis of the illustrious theories of technology adoption, the related theories of innovation, and the related works, a theoretical model that emphasizes the role of innovation in the technology adoption, which is proposed as in Fig. 1. Accordingly, the components of the model are based on the theoretical basis of the theories of diffusion of innovation (DOI) of Moore & Benbasat [32]; Rogers [41], the theoretical framework of Technology–Organization–Environment (TOE) of Tornatzky et al. [46], the well–known theories of technology adoption, including TAM of Davis [13]; UTAUT of Venkatesh et al. [51, 53]. The conceptual components of the research model are interpreted as follows.

Cloud–based ERP adoption (CEA) harmonizes with the theoretical basis of behavioral intention, which is considered in the illustrious theories of technology adoption as in TAM of Davis [13]; UTAUT of Venkatesh et al. [51], as a basis for the relationships of behavioral intention. For the innovation, technology adoption is the process of synthesizing, developing and adapting to new ideas within the organizations [22], the prediction to be able to control or react with changes that effect to the organizations [12]. Hence, cloud–based ERP adoption is that users intent to accept cloud–based ERP system in the business of the organization [3].

TOE components in the research, the model include three components as in the theoretical framework of TOE of Tornatzky et al. [46]: Technology–Organization–Environment. In particular, the components of the technology (T) in this study are proposed with two dimensions: IT infrastructure and performance expectancy.

- *IT infrastructure (ITI)* is viewed as a base system to meet the IT needs perfectly, to serve the operation system [43], shared in the whole organization as a service, and coordinated focus [53]. IT infrastructure includes hardware, software, network, and data [37]. It is a fundamental element in any information system [20], which is a factor of great interest in implementing cloud–based ERP in organizations [8].
- *Performance expectancy (PEE)* is the degree to which an individual believes that use an information system supporting them achieve efficiency in their work, and will accept and use new technology if they know that this technology fetches more benefits [51]. This concept is similar to the concept of perceived usefulness in TAM of Davis [13]. Performance expectancy is a very critical factor in the theory of acceptance and use of technology [51, 52].

The components of technological context have the positive relationships with the technology adoption from the foundational theory of DOI of Rogers [41], the theoretical framework of TOE of Tornatzky et al. [46], and which is confirmed in related works as in the theory of UTAUT of Venkatesh et al. [51, 52]. Hence, for cloud–based ERP, these hypotheses are proposed:

- *H1: IT infrastructure has a positive impact on cloud–based ERP adoption.*
- *H2: Performance expectancy has a positive impact on cloud–based ERP adoption.*

The components of the organization (O) in the framework of TOE in this study are proposed with two dimensions: top management support and organizational culture.

– *Organizational culture (ORC)* is a collection of belief values and assumptions that often occur in organizations that affect the perception and behavior of individuals [24]. Organizational culture is also considered a collection of the common understanding of organizational activities [14]. This concept is one of the critical factors that creates a conducive environment for innovation in core competencies [11], the organizational culture has a positive impact on technology adoption [3].
– *Top management support (TMS)* is the support activities of senior management or head of the organization in creating ideas for the system objective, analysis and design, system development, and system deployment [39]. The concept of top management support has a significant impact on the intention to use or the adoption technology of cloud–based ERP [3]. This relationship is also confirmed in these empirical studies as in Ali & Soar [4]; Awa et al. [6]; Gupta et al. [20].

The components of organizational context have the positive relationships with the technology adoption from the foundational theory of DOI of Rogers [41], the theoretical framework of TOE of Tornatzky et al. [46], and which is reconfirmed in empirical studies as in Awa et al. [6]; Jesus & et al. [25] with top management support, in Albar & Hoque [3]; Gonzalez & DeMelo [19] with organizational culture. Thus, for cloud–based ERP, these hypotheses are proposed:

– *H3: Organizational culture has a positive impact on cloud–based ERP adoption.*
– *H4: Top management support has a positive impact on cloud–based ERP adoption.*

The components of the environment (E) in the framework of TOE in this study are proposed with two dimensions: competitive pressure and external support.

– *Competitive pressure (COP)* is the level of pressure that organizations have to dangle from direct competitors in the industry [35], this pressure creates an effort for organizations applying new technologies [29]. Other side, information systems encourage competition in the industry [9], related to information capacity, flexibility, and innovation process [5]. The concept of competitive pressure is one of the most influential factors in the adoption of cloud–based ERP [21].
– *External support (EXS)* is related to the activities of IT service providers [17], support from suppliers or consultants [45]. This concept is also related to the innovation process, from the IT capacity of the organization, which obtains from the experiential learning of suppliers to applying into organizations [5]. External support has a direct impact on the adoption of cloud–based ERP [6].

The components of environmental context have the positive relationships with the technology adoption from the foundational theory of DOI of Rogers [41], the theoretical framework of TOE of Tornatzky et al. [46], and which is reconfirmed in empirical studies as in Albar & Hoque [3]; Jesus & et al. [25] with competitive pressure, in Awa et al. [6]; Kim & et al. [26] with external support. Therefore, for cloud–based ERP, these hypotheses are proposed:

– *H5: Competitive pressure has a positive impact on cloud–based ERP adoption.*
– *H6: External support has a positive impact on cloud–based ERP adoption.*

Innovation (INN) is the level that users accept to apply innovation earlier than others in the social context [41]. In the organizational context, innovation involves individual characteristics or management attitudes, and their response to with technological innovation [41], the internal features of the organization, such as complexity, organizational structure, organizational size [46], and the external features of the organization, such as system openness [41], competitive pressure [5].

The relationship between the innovation and the technology adoption is based on the foundational theory of DOI of Rogers [41], the theoretical framework of TOE of Tornatzky et al. [46], and that is reconfirmed in empirical works as in Jesus et al. [25]; Kim et al. [26]; Zahra et al. [54]. Thence, a hypothesis is proposed:

– *H7: Innovation has a positive impact on cloud–based ERP adoption.*

3 Research Method

3.1 Research Process

Two phases of the research process: (1) the first phase of this study that uses preliminary research with the qualitative method, and (2) the second phase of this study that uses formal analysis with the quantitative method.

In the first phase, from the theoretical basis of the related theories of innovation (DOI, TOE), the well–known theories of technology adoption (TAM, UTAUT), and other related works, it constructs a draft scale. Then, the senior experts on cloud–based ERP system are philosophized for strengthening the content accuracy of the draft scale.

In the second phase, the formal research handles the adjusted scale as a formal scale, this work employs a 5–point Likert questionnaire, there are five levels: strongly disagree – disagree – unclear – agree – strongly agree, which measures the assessment levels of manifest variables. In the formal scale, there are four observable quantities of IT infrastructure; four observable quantities of performance expectancy; four observable quantities of organizational culture; three observable quantities of top management support; four observable quantities of competitive pressure; three observable quantities of external support; four observable quantities of innovation; and three observable quantities of cloud–based ERP adoption. The method of convenience sampling is chosen for surveying and collecting data. In the interview, the questionnaires are sent to participants who have used or intended to use the cloud–based ERP by an online link (Google Docs). There are 232 valid samples of 28 manifest variables in the formal scale are collected for this research. Next, after collecting data, the method of structural equation modeling is applied for analyzing data by softwares of SPSS and AMOS.

3.2 Data Description

(1) Gender: it has a small difference with 43.97% participants of the male, 55.17% participants of the female, and 0.86% participants of the other. *(2) Age:* the 20–30 groups and the 31–40 groups are the majority with 62.07%, and 25.86%, respectively, followed by the 41–50 up to 10.34% percent, and over 50 is the lowest about 1.72%.

(3) Education: 81.04% participants of the university degree, postgraduate and intermediate/college amount to 12.93% and 6.03% participants, respectively. *(4) Job Position:* the percent of the staff is the highest with 53.79%, there are 20.69% participants who are team leaders, and managers, others and directors amount to 7.76%, 6.03% and 1.72%, respectively. *(5) Experience:* the most percent is under 5 years with 55.60%, followed by 6 – 10 years and 11–20 years account for 31.02% and 11.21%, respectively, and over 20 years is the lowest about 2.16%. *(6) Cloud–based ERP:* most of the participants use Ecount ERP with 43.97%, Bitrix cloud ERP amounts to 27.59%, Infor cloud suite accounts for 15.95%, and similarities exist between Teamcrop cloud ERP and other kinds of cloud–based ERP are roundly 6% participants.

4 Research Results

4.1 Exploratory and Confirmatory Factor Analysis

The first Exploratory Factor Analysis (EFA) dropped one observable quantity of the dimension of competitive pressure (COP_3) and one observable quantity of the dimension of organizational culture (ORC_1), because of the EFA factor loading < 0.50. Then, in the second EFA, eight factors are extracted from 26 observable quantities and grouped into eight factors in the rotated component matrix, which conform with the theoretical model, these grouped factors: IT infrastructure, performance expectancy, organizational culture, top management support, competitive pressure, external support, innovation, cloud–based ERP adoption. The EFA factor loading of manifest variables ranges between 0.612 and 0.882. Furthermore, the index of Kaiser–Meyer–Olkin (KMO) measure of sampling adequacy = 0.796, sphericity Bartlett's test with approximate Chi–square/dF = 8.672 (p–value = 0.000), so the manifest variables are appropriate. Thus, the measurement scale is valuable. Moreover, the Total Variance Extracted (TVA) = 71.331%, which explains the data difference roundly 71.331%.

The first Confirmatory Factor Analysis (CFA) continues to rescind one observable quantity of the dimension of performance expectancy (PEE_4), because of the CFA factor loading < 0.50. Next, the second CFA with 25 observable quantities: the measurement scale indexes as CMIN/dF = 1.158; GFI = 0.929; NFI = 0.907; TLI = 0.981; CFI = 0.986; RMSEA = 0.026 (p–value = 0.004), so the manifest variables in the measurement model are assorted with the data. The CFA loading of observable quantities ranges between 0.601 and 0.865. Besides, the Composite Reliability (C.R.) of dimensions, including IT infrastructure, performance expectancy, organizational culture, top management support, competitive pressure, external support, innovation, cloud–based ERP adoption values from 0.723 to 0.884 (Table 1). In addition, the value of Average Variance Extracted (AVE) ranges from 0.505 to 0.718. Hence, the measurement scales obtain the convergence value. Besides, the value of AVE for each element is larger than the square correlation coefficient (r^2), respectively (Table 1). Therefore, the measurement scales are also the discriminant value.

Table 1. Data, composite reliability, and square correlation coefficient

	Mean	CR	ITI	PEE	ORC	TMS	COP	EXS	INN	CEA
ITI	3.651	0.805	0.583*							
PEE	3.875	0.824	0.004	0.614*						
ORC	3.832	0.822	0.077	0.001	0.708*					
TMS	3.427	0.723	0.204	0.053	0.072	0.505*				
COP	3.853	0.794	0.002	0.030	0.008	0.001	0.672*			
EXS	3.491	0.884	0.168	0.078	0.093	0.141	0.001	0.718*		
INN	3.351	0.810	0.113	0.002	0.001	0.181	0.003	0.135	0.595*	
CEA	3.683	0.775	0.198	0.008	0.088	0.201	0.009	0.377	0.248	0.518*

CR: Composite Reliability; * *AVE: Average Variance Extracted*

4.2 Structural Equation Modeling

The results of Structural Equation Modeling (SEM) with the estimation of Maximum Likelihood (ML): theoretical model scale indexes as CMIN/dF = 1.162; GFI = 0.923; NFI = 0.901; TLI = 0.981; CFI = 0.985; RMSEA = 0.028 (p–value = 0.002). Thus, the theoretical model is adequate to fit with the research data.

The estimation of SEM is manifested as in Table 2, including the structural modeling and the testing results of all hypotheses. Under the cloud–based ERP, paths from components of the technology (IT infrastructure and performance expectancy) to technology adoption element, the path from the IT infrastructure to the cloud–based ERP adoption is statistical significance with the γ coefficient = 0.160 with p–value < 0.05, thus, the hypothesis H1 is supported. Contrarily, the data does not support the relationship between performance expectancy and technology adoption, because of the p–value > 0.05, hence, the hypothesis H2 is not supported. Paths from components of the organization (organizational culture and top management support) to technology adoption factor, although the path from the organizational culture to the cloud–based ERP adoption is statistical significance with the γ coefficient = 0.175 (p–value < 0.05), thus, hypothesis H3 is supported, the data do not support the path from the top management support to the technology adoption (p–value > 0.05), hence, the hypothesis H4 is not supported. Paths from components of the environment (competitive pressure and external support) to technology adoption dimension, the data do not support the relationship between the competitive pressure and the technology adoption (p–value > 0.05), so the hypothesis H5 is not supported, Inconsistently, the path from the external support to the cloud–based ERP adoption is statistical significance with the γ coefficient = 0.361 (p–value < 0.001), thus, the hypothesis H6 is supported.

Interestingly, the role of innovation in technology adoption with the positive impact of the innovation on the cloud–based ERP adoption, which is statistical significance, with the γ coefficients = 0.288 (p–value < 0.005), thus, the hypothesis H7 is supported.

Table 2. Structural equation modeling and testing results of hypotheses

H	Path	Estimate	SE	CR	p–value	Result
H1	CEA ← ITI	0.160	0.055	2.056	0.037	Supported
H2	CEA ← PEE	0.051	0.073	0.742	0.458	Not supported
H3	CEA ← ORC	0.175	0.054	2.248	0.025	Supported
H4	CEA ← TMS	0.096	0.092	0.871	0.384	Not supported
H5	CEA ← COP	0.095	0.043	1.383	0.167	Not supported
H6	CEA ← EXS	0.361	0.056	4.407	0,000	Supported
H7	CEA ← INN	0.288	0.057	3.067	0.002	Supported

SE: Standard Error; CR: Critical Ratio

4.3   Result Discussion

The research results externalized that one out of two dimensions of each component in the framework of Technology–Organization–Environment (TOE) is statistical significance with technology adoption dimension, including IT infrastructure in technology component, organizational culture in organization component, and external support in environment component which influence on the cloud–based ERP adoption, that confirmed the foundational theory of DOI of Moore & Benbasat [32]; Rogers [41], the theoretical framework of TOE of Tornatzky et al. [46], the well–known theories of TAM of Davis [13]; UTAUT of Venkatesh et al. [51, 52]. Besides, the research results also reconfirmed the empirical works about the impact of the IT infrastructure [8, 20, 53], organizational culture [3, 14, 19], and external support [5, 6, 26] on the technology adoption dimension. Distinctly, the external support has a significant impact on the cloud–based ERP adoption with the largest influence ($\gamma = 0.361$). Concomitantly, the data does not support the paths from the performance expectancy, top management support, and competitive pressure to the cloud–based ERP adoption.

Interestingly, the role of innovation in the cloud–based ERP adoption is significant with a large coefficient ($\gamma = 0.288$), this result confirmed the foundational theory of DOI of Moore & Benbasat [32]; Rogers [41], the theoretical framework of TOE of Tornatzky et al. [46], and reconfirmed several empirical works, such as Jesus et al. [25]; Kim et al. [26]; Zahra et al. [54]. Hence, along with three components of the TOE (IT infrastructure, organizational culture, and external support), the innovation has an important role in the cloud–based ERP adoption, details as in Fig. 1.

The structural equation modeling indicated that the components of the TOE and the innovation may be totally explained roundly 58.4% ($R^2 = 0.584$) in technology adoption with the context of cloud–based ERP. Originally, this research result can be compared with the theoretical results of TAM of Davis [13] amounted to 40%, and UTAUT of Venkatesh et al. [51] accounted for 56% in the technology adoption. Moreover, this explanation can be also collated with the empirical results of Gupta et al. [20] and Kim et al. [26] amounted to 57% and 41% in the cloud–based ERP adoption, respectively. Wonderfully, the exemplification of this study is better than when compared with the well–known theories of technology adoption (TAM, UTAUT), the empirical studies. Furthermore, this study investigated the important role

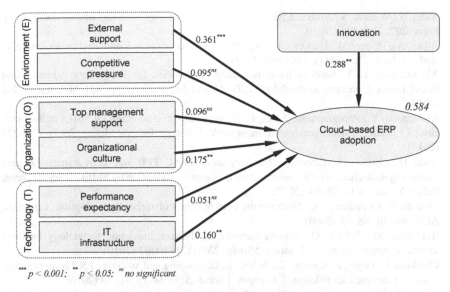

*** $p < 0.001$; ** $p < 0.05$; ns no significant

Fig. 1. Cloud–based ERP adoption model and testing results

of innovation in a structural model of cloud–based ERP adoption, which is not only contributing to the theories of DOI and TOE, but also furnishing to the theories of technology adoption.

5 Conclusion

This study investigated the role of innovation in the technology adoption in the specific context of cloud–based ER, which is one of the first works to integrate the various theoretical topics of information systems. Specifically, the theory of Diffusion of Innovation (DOI), the theoretical framework of Technology–Organization–Environment (TOE), the illustrious theories of technology adoption (TAM, UTAUT). While the theoretical framework of TOE mainly considers three components of technology, organization, and environment; the theory of DOI, the well–known model of TAM and the theory of UTAUT typically dissect the intention to use and use behavior of information systems or new technology adoption. Hence, the theoretical basis is considered as the foundational theories for this study have been appropriate. Interestingly, the research results not only integrate the related theories of information systems, but also accentuate the important role of innovation in the adoption of cloud–based ERP, which are significant academic contributions.

References

1. Ajzen, I.: From intentions to actions: a theory of planned behavior. In: Kuhl, J., Beckmann, J. (eds.) Action Control, pp. 11–39. Springer, Heidelberg (1985)

2. Akter, S., Wamba, S., Ambra, J.: Enabling service systems by modeling quality. Int. J. Prod. Econ. **207**, 210–226 (2019)
3. Albar, A., Hoque, M.: Factors affecting cloud ERP adoption in Saudi Arabia: an empirical study. Inform. Dev. **35**(1), 150–164 (2019)
4. Ali, O., Soar, J.: Technology innovation adoption theories. In: Technology Adoption and Social Issues: Concepts, Methodologies, Tools, and Applications, pp. 821–860. IGI Global (2018)
5. Alshamaila, Y., Papagiannidis, S., Li, F.: Cloud computing adoption by SMEs in the north east of England: a multi–perspective framework. J. Enterp. Inform. Manag. **26**(3), 250–275 (2013)
6. Awa, H., Ojiabo, O., Emecheta, B.: Integrating TAM, TPB and TOE frameworks and expanding their characteristic constructs for e–commerce adoption by SMEs. J. Sci. Technol. Policy Manag. **6**(1), 76–94 (2015)
7. Bharati, P., Chaudhury, A.: Studying the current status of technology adoption. Commun. ACM **49**(10), 88–93 (2006)
8. Binsawad, M., Sohaib, O., Hawryszkiewycz, I.: Factors impacting technology business incubator performance. Int. J. Innov. Manag. **23**(01), 1950007 (2019)
9. Charland, P., Leger, P., Cronan, T., Robert, J.: Developing and assessing ERP competencies: basic and complex knowledge. J. Comput. Inform. Syst. **56**(1), 31–39 (2016)
10. Chen, M., Lin, Y., Huang, W.: The study on firm acceptance of cloud service introduction from the innovation diffusion theory. Int. J. Appl. Syst. Stud. **7**(3), 117–137 (2017)
11. Corfield, A., Paton, R.: Investigating knowledge management: can KM really change organisational culture? J. Knowl. Manag. **20**(1), 88–103 (2016)
12. Damanpour, F.: Organizational complexity and innovation: developing and testing multiple contingency models. Manag. Sci. **42**(5), 693–716 (1996)
13. Davis, F.: Perceived usefulness, perceived ease of use, and user acceptance of information technology. MIS Q. **13**(3), 319–340 (1989)
14. Deshpande, R., Webster, F.: Organizational culture and marketing: defining the research agenda. J. Mark. **53**(1), 3–15 (1989)
15. DeZubielqui, G., Lindsay, N., Lindsay, W., Jones, J.: Knowledge quality, innovation and firm performance: a study of knowledge transfer in SMEs. Small Bus. Econ. **53**(1), 145–164 (2019)
16. Fishbein, M., Ajzen, I.: Belief Attitude Intention and Behavior An Introduction to Theory and Research. Addison–Wesley, Reading (1975)
17. Frambach, R., Barkema, H., Nooteboom, B., Wedel, M.: Adoption of a service innovation in the business market: an empirical test of supply–side variables. J. Bus. Res. **41**(2), 161–174 (1998)
18. Gangwar, H., Date, H., Ramaswamy, R.: Understanding determinants of cloud computing adoption using an integrated TAM–TOE model. J. Enterp. Inform. Manag. **28**(1), 107–130 (2015)
19. Gonzalez, R., DeMelo, T.: The effects of organization context on knowledge exploration and exploitation. J. Bus. Res. **90**, 215–225 (2018)
20. Gupta, S., Kumar, S., Singh, S., Foropon, C., Chandra, C.: Role of cloud ERP on the performance of an organization: contingent resource based view perspective. Int. J. Logistics Manag. **29**(2), 659–675 (2018)
21. Gutierrez, A., Boukrami, E., Lumsden, R.: Technological, organisational and environmental factors influencing managers' decision to adopt cloud computing in the UK. J. Enterp. Inform. Manag. **28**(6), 788–807 (2015)
22. Hashem, I., Yaqoob, I., Anuar, N., Mokhtar, S., Gani, A., Khan, S.: The rise of "big data" on cloud computing: review and open research issues. Inform. Syst. **47**, 98–115 (2015)

23. Higgins, J.: Innovation: the core competence. Plann. Rev. **23**(6), 32–36 (1995)
24. Hofstede, G.: Organizations and Cultures: Software of the Mind. McGrawHill, London (1991)
25. Cruz-Jesus, F., Oliveira, T., Naranjo, M.: Understanding the adoption of business analytics and intelligence. In: Rocha, Á., Adeli, H., Reis, L.P., Costanzo, S. (eds.) WorldCIST 2018 2018. AISC, vol. 745, pp. 1094–1103. Springer, Cham (2018). https://doi.org/10.1007/978-3-319-77703-0_106
26. Kim, D., Hebeler, J., Yoon, V., Davis, F.: Exploring determinants of semantic web technology adoption from IT professionals' perspective: Industry competition, organization innovativeness, and data management capability. Comput. Hum. Behav. **86**, 18–33 (2018)
27. Klaus, H., Rosemann, M., Gable, G.: What is ERP? Inform. Syst. Front. **2**(2), 141–162 (2000)
28. Liu, H., Wang, X.: Strategy research of enterprise information planning based on TOE–TAM model: case study for ERP implementation of a discrete manufacturing. In: DBTA Proceedings (2010)
29. Majumdar, S., Venkataraman, S.: New technology adoption in US telecommunications: the role of competitive pressures and firm–level inducements. Res. Policy **22**, 521–536 (1993)
30. Marston, S., Li, Z., Bandyopadhyay, S., Zhang, J., Ghalsasi, A.: Cloud computing–the business perspective. Decis. Supp. Syst. **51**(1), 176–189 (2011)
31. Mell, P., Grance, T.: The NIST definition of cloud computing. In: NIST Special Publication 800–145. NIST (2011)
32. Moore, G., Benbasat, I.: Integrating diffusion of innovations and theory of reasoned action models to predict utilization of information technology by end–users. In: Kautz, K., Pries-Heje, J. (eds.) Diffusion and Adoption of Information Technology, pp. 132–146. Springer, Boston (1996)
33. Nguyen, T.D.: A structural model for the success of information systems projects. Sci. Technol. Dev. J. **18**(2), 109–120 (2015)
34. Nguyen, T.D., Nguyen, T.T., Misra, S.: Cloud-based ERP solution for modern education in Vietnam. In: Dang, T.K., Wagner, R., Neuhold, E., Takizawa, M., Küng, J., Thoai, N. (eds.) FDSE 2014. LNCS, vol. 8860, pp. 234–247. Springer, Cham (2014). https://doi.org/10.1007/978-3-319-12778-1_18
35. Oliveira, T., Martins, M.: Understanding e–business adoption across industries in European countries. Industr. Manag. Data Syst. **110**(9), 1337–1354 (2010)
36. Oturakci, M., Yuregir, O.: New approach to Rogers' innovation characteristics and comparative implementation study. J. Eng. Technol. Manag. **47**, 53–67 (2018)
37. Pearlson, K., Saunders, C., Galletta, D.: Managing and Using Information Systems: A Strategic Approach, 7th edn. Wiley, New York (2016)
38. Pitt, L., Berthon, P., Robson, M., Prendegast, G.: Does corporate entrepreneurship influence innovation in service firms? In: WMC 1997 Proceedings, pp. 639–645 (2015)
39. Porter, M., Millar, V.: How information gives you competitive advantage. Harvard Bus. Rev. **63**(4), 149–160 (1985)
40. Rich, D., Dibbern, J.: A team–oriented investigation of ERP post–implementation integration projects: how cross–functional collaboration influences ERP benefits. In: Piazolo, F., Felderer, M. (eds.) Innovation and Future of Enterprise Information Systems, pp. 115–127. Springer, Heidelberg (2013)
41. Rogers, E.: Diffusion of Innovations: Simon & Schuster (1995)
42. Rouhani, S., Mehri, M.: Does ERP have benefits on the business intelligence readiness? an empirical study. Int. J. Inform. Syst. Change Manag. **8**(2), 81–105 (2016)
43. Silver, M., Markus, M., Beath, C.: The information technology interaction model: a foundation for the MBA core course. MIS Q. **19**(3), 361–390 (1995)

44. Stanko, M.: Toward a theory of remixing in online innovation communities. Inform. Syst. Res. **27**(4), 773–791 (2016)
45. Themistocleous, M.: Justifying the decisions for EAI implementations: a validated proposition of influential factors. J. Enterp. Inform. Manag. **17**(2), 85–104 (2004)
46. Tornatzky, L., Fleischer, M., Chakrabarti, A.: The processes of technological innovation. Lexington Books, Lexington (1990)
47. Tornatzky, L., Klein, K.: Innovation characteristics and innovation adoption–implementation: a meta–analysis of findings. IEEE Trans. Eng. Manag. **29**(1), 28–45 (1982)
48. Usman, U., Ahmad, M., Zakariya, N.: Factors influencing cloud enterprise resource planning adoption in SMEs. In: Information Science & Applications, pp. 235–245 (2016)
49. VCCI: Statistical report on ICT usage in enterprises, Vietnam Chamber of Commerce and Industry (2018)
50. Velte, A., Velte, T., Elsenpeter, R.: Cloud Computing: A Practical Approach. McGraw–Hill, New York (2010)
51. Venkatesh, V., Morris, M., Davis, G., Davis, F.: User acceptance of information technology: toward a unified view. MIS Q. **27**(3), 425–478 (2003)
52. Venkatesh, V., Thong, J., Xu, X.: Consumer acceptance and use of information technology: extending the unified theory of acceptance and use of technology. MIS Q. **36**(1), 157–178 (2012)
53. Weill, P., Broadbent, M.: Leveraging the New Infrastructure: How Market Leaders Capitalize on Information Technology. Harvard Business, Boston (1998)
54. Zahra, B., Egide, K., Diane, P.: Technology adoption and diffusion: a new application of the UTAUT model. Int. J. Innov. Technol. Manag. **15**(06), 1950004 (2018)

Application of Work Study to Process Improvement: Fruit Nectar Case

Mayra A. Macías-Jiménez[✉] ⓘ, Alfonso R. Romero-Conradoⓘ,
Luis C. Acosta-Fontalvoⓘ, and Jairo R. Coronado-Hernándezⓘ

Universidad de la Costa, Barranquilla 080001, Colombia
{mmacias3,aromero17,lacosta3,jcoronad18}@cuc.edu.co

Abstract. Work study is an extensively used technique for examining the methods to carry out activities in a company and proposing actions for productivity improvement. This paper presents a work-study application to a fruit nectar process inside a food company using 5W1H and ECRS techniques. A critical analysis was conducted in three previously selected activities, according to its improvement potential. Results allowed optimizing distances along the process and improving ergonomic conditions for workers. Savings included a total distance of 10.2 m, two transportation activities and two delays activities per production cycle. Also, the standard time was determined in one of the prioritized activities. Our results demonstrated that work study techniques are tools suitable to be implemented in most economic sectors for productivity improvements. However, the technique itself will not be effective without a commitment from top-level management for implementing the corrective actions proposed.

Keywords: Work study · Productivity improvement · Fruit nectar process · Food industry · 5W1H · ECRS

1 Introduction

Productivity is considered a key component for nations economic growth. It is defined as the relationship between the obtained results and the used resources for a specific purpose [1]. Efforts towards productivity enhancement in economic sectors have included Work Study (WS) approaches for optimizing resource utilization [2, 3]. WS allows proposing operational improvements based on a systematic analysis of productivity related factors [4].

WS implies the implementation of two techniques: Method study (MS) and Work Measurement (WM). MS is used to determine the specific way a task must be done by a worker, and WM allows establishing the required times to perform that task regarding allowances for fatigue and personal needs [2, 5].

WS applications can be found in a wide variety of industrial sectors., e.g. manufacturing, food industry, medicine, etc. However, in recent literature, there are no studies on WS application to fruit preserve industry. Therefore, this paper focus on the implementation of WS, 5W1H (5W: Why, What, Where, When, Who, 1H: How), and ECRS (Eliminate, Combine, Reorganize and Simplify) techniques, with the objective

© Springer Nature Switzerland AG 2019
K. Saeed et al. (Eds.): CISIM 2019, LNCS 11703, pp. 253–264, 2019.
https://doi.org/10.1007/978-3-030-28957-7_21

to improve the productivity of the production process of fruit pulp in a fruit preserve industry from Colombian Caribbean region.

The novel contribution of the paper is the implementation of work study techniques for fruit pulp products. The use of these tools allows reducing the traveled distance and the elimination of non-value-added operations in the studied process.

The rest of the paper is structured as follows. In the next section, a literature review about WS applications is discussed. Section 3 presents the research stages, Sect. 4 shows an application of the techniques mentioned above to the selected process. While Sect. 5 describes the conclusions of the research.

2 Literature Review

The effects of WS applications is a topic that has attracted attention in the literature. In recent years, articles on WS have been growing and new approaches have been emerging. Previously used WS techniques have included tools like line balancing (LB), 5W1H, and ECRS.

In a production line, workers can have musculoskeletal injuries due to the repeatability and inappropriate methods [6]. Therefore, recent research about line balancing tries to consider not only tasks duration and precedence but also physical demand or ergonomic factors.

This technique can be applied in a wide variety of sectors. In the agro-industry, WS and notions of line balancing with continuous improvements concepts were applied to improve productivity in a pasteurized milk manufacturer [7]. Also, similar approaches were used to perform a study in a large-sized frozen chicken producer with the aim of enhancing productivity. In this study, the analysis of the process under a work-study perspective was conducted, and an ECRS based line balancing was proposed [8].

As the literature suggests, it is common to find studies with a combination of these techniques. Such is the case of a work-study, 5W1H and, ECRS application, that was performed in a tomato cake production line [9]. In this research, non-value-added activities and hidden costs of waste were eliminated. Another application in the manufacturing sector was carried out to a line balancing for an electronics company [10]. In this contribution, WS, 5W1H, and ECRS principles were implemented to propose a new layout scheme, improving the productivity rate of two production lines by 22% and 15% respectively.

A similar implementation of these approaches was conducted in a hydraulic component company [11]. A line balancing scheme was proposed and included the reallocation of work content for the relative operation and other improvements. In this case, the productivity enhancement for the production line was 45.6%.

Another WS application in manufacturing to improve productivity was carried out in the shoemaking industry [12]. The improvements consisted of reducing the cycle time, workers' fatigue, and combining work stations in the production line.

The scope of WS sometimes includes only the identification of the current state and the proposal of improvement strategies, without any implementation results. This kind of pattern can be found in a study focused on WM carried out in a brewing company [13]. Basically, the technique was used to identify areas for productivity improvement in the brewing and packaging processes. The main results from the paper were the busy time and idle rate calculation, which allowed to present some suggestions for productivity enhancement.

Also, in India, a case study in a battery manufacturing plant was conducted [14]. The research included the application of WS techniques for proposing an improved layout, a flow process chart, and a technology upgrade plan. WS techniques have been successfully applied in a steel-pipe manufacturing company too [15]. The aim of this study was determining the process standard times.

Reviewing the available literature is possible to identify that previous research have applied WS techniques together with 5W1H, ECRS, and LB, for different fields including agro-industry. However, no previous studies have been carried out in the fruit preserve industry. It represents an important opportunity regarding the rise of production and consumption of fruit preserve products.

3   Methodology

The article shows a descriptive study for the application of WS techniques in a fruit preserve company. The methodological procedure followed was based on the guidelines of de ILO (International Labor Office) [16]. Figure 1. shows the research stages.

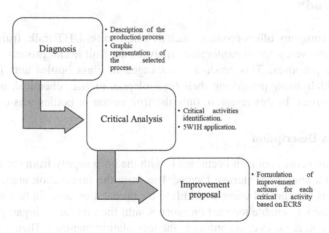

Fig. 1. Methodology steps

First, the research started with a diagnostic phase that includes the description of the process. For this purpose, primary information sources and direct observation were used, and a posterior critical analysis was conducted. In this stage, the operations with the biggest improvement potential were identified and prioritized. Once these operations were listed, they were analyzed using the 5W1H technique, which was applied to process leaders.

The improvement actions resulting from the first stage were adjusted based on the ECRS method, aiming to reduce the non-value operations, optimizing traveled distances, and improving the overall performance of the process. Finally, a WM study was conducted in the operation with the biggest improvement potential.

Table 1 describes the questions for the 5W1H application.

Table 1. Questions for the 5 W1H technique.

Purpose	5W/1H	Items
Eliminate unnecessary parts of the work (E)	What/Why	What is really done? Why do you have to do it?
Combine when it is possible (C) or Reorder the activities sequence (R)	Where/Why	Where is it done? Why is it done there?
	When/Why	When is made? Why is it done at that time?
	Who/Why	Who does it? Why does that person do it?
Simplify the operation (S)	How/Why	How is it done? Why is it done in that way?

4   Case Study

The selected company offers products such as whole milk, UHT milk, fruit nectar, and fruit juice. However, after an exploratory analysis, the fruit nectar process was selected for the study purposes. This product is packaged in glass bottles and Tetra Pak ® packages, which allow preserving their organoleptic, physic, chemical, and microbiological properties. In this research, only the fruit nectar in bottles was considered.

4.1   Process Description

The production process of fruit nectar starts with the pulp supply from the raw material warehouse to a temporary storage located 4 m from the preparation area.

The pulp is transported using a forklift to the preparation area. In this area, water is added to the tank to enable the suction process until the mix tank. Sugar, pepsin, citric and ascorbic acid are added, according to the formulation manuals. Then, the content in the tank is mixed for 15 min.

A sample from the mix is sent to lab analysis for determining levels of acidity, pH, °Bx (degrees Brix), and viscosity. After a positive result from the analysis, the mix is homogenized and pasteurized, to 3000–4000 psi and 98 °C–100 °C, respectively.

Simultaneously, in a secondary line, the bottles are transported from the warehouse to the preparation area and stay in a waiting zone while a conveyor belt provides the supply of bottles. Once the conveyor belt has enough space to locate the new bottles, the forklift moves again to this zone to locate the bottles in the dispenser machine. This machine moves the bottles to the washing area where bottles are cleaned and vaporized at a fixed temperature.

Once the nectar is pasteurized, it is packed at a temperature between 86 °C and 94 °C. The process starts with the filler machine and continues to an encapsulated machine. Once the bottle is filled, heated, and capped, it goes into a cooling tunnel for 20 min. Then, the product reaches a temperature below to 40 °C, acidity 0.3–0.2, pH 3.0–3.4, °Bx 10.5–12.8 and viscosity 20–13.

Finally, the product is labeled, and manual inspection is performed. The nectar is sent to the packing machine, where the product is organized in packages according to the desired format (24 or 30 units per box). Once this operation is finished, the packages are located on a cardboard tray and sent to an oven. After the seal and the code are inspected, the product is stowed and delivered to a finished products warehouse and are ready for distribution purposes.

Process Representation

Process Diagram. Figure 2 illustrates graphically how the process works.

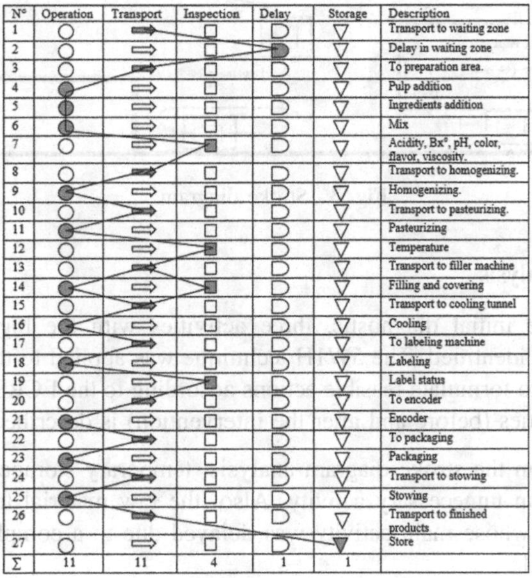

N°	Operation	Transport	Inspection	Delay	Storage	Description
1	○	⇒	□	D	▽	Transport to waiting zone
2	○	⇒	□	D	▽	Delay in waiting zone
3	○	⇒	□	D	▽	To preparation area.
4	●	⇒	□	D	▽	Pulp addition
5	●	⇒	□	D	▽	Ingredients addition
6	●	⇒	□	D	▽	Mix
7	○	⇒	■	D	▽	Acidity, Bx°, pH, color, flavor, viscosity.
8	○	⇒	□	D	▽	Transport to homogenizing.
9	●	⇒	□	D	▽	Homogenizing.
10	○	⇒	□	D	▽	Transport to pasteurizing.
11	●	⇒	□	D	▽	Pasteurizing
12	○	⇒	■	D	▽	Temperature
13	○	⇒	□	D	▽	Transport to filler machine
14	●	⇒	■	D	▽	Filling and covering
15	○	⇒	□	D	▽	Transport to cooling tunnel
16	●	⇒	□	D	▽	Cooling
17	○	⇒	□	D	▽	To labeling machine
18	●	⇒	□	D	▽	Labeling
19	○	⇒	■	D	▽	Label status
20	○	⇒	□	D	▽	To encoder
21	●	⇒	□	D	▽	Encoder
22	○	⇒	□	D	▽	To packaging
23	●	⇒	□	D	▽	Packaging
24	○	⇒	□	D	▽	Transport to stowing
25	●	⇒	□	D	▽	Stowing
26	○	⇒	□	D	▽	Transport to finished products
27	○	⇒	□	D	▽	Store
Σ	11	11	4	1	1	

Fig. 2. Fruit nectar process diagram

Stroke Diagram. Figure 3 presents a diagram of the workspace, where the activities done by the workers and the respective distances involved are included.

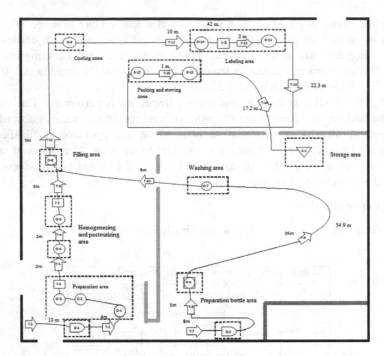

Fig. 3. Stroke diagram

4.2   Critical Analysis

As a result of the initial diagnostic, three activities with the biggest potential of improvement were identified. The 5W1H technique was applied to the process leader, with the objective to formulate feasible actions according to the ECRS approach. Then, the status of activities (before and after the intervention) is described.

Pulp Supply. From the stroke diagram analysis, temporary storage of the fruit tank was identified as an unnecessary activity. Also, the raw material transportation was done by a worker whose main activity was delayed due to a complimentary activity previously assigned.

The improvement proposal consisted of including a direct fruit pulp transportation activity to the preparation zone within the forklift truck schedule, avoiding the temporary storage zone. This small action allowed the elimination of one transportation and one delay activity, saving 4 m. in terms of traveled distance.

Waiting Zone in the Washing Area. In the case of the bottle treatment line, a delay activity was identified. It was due to the lack of available space in the conveyor belt when a new bottle batch had to be processed.

Before the intervention, the pallet of remaining bottles was removed by the forklift operator and stored in a temporal warehouse. Once the space needed in the belt was available, the operator came back to the warehouse and transport the bottles back to the belt.

After the 5W1H, the improvement proposal was rescheduling shifts for the forklift operator. One transportation and one delay activity were eliminated in the waiting area, which represented savings of 6.2 m of the traveled distance. Figures 4 and 5 illustrate the changes made in the process and the stroke diagram, respectively.

N°	Operation	Transport	Inspection	Delay	Storage	Description
1	○	⇒	□	D	▽	To preparation area.
2	●	⇒	□	D	▽	Pulp addition
3	◐	⇒	□	D	▽	Ingredients addition
4	◐	⇒	□	D	▽	Mix
5	○	⇒	■	D	▽	Acidity, Bx°, pH, color, flavor, viscosity.
6	○	⇒	□	D	▽	Transport to homogenizing.
7	●	⇒	□	D	▽	Homogenizing.
8	○	⇒	□	D	▽	Transport to pasteurizing.
9	●	⇒	□	D	▽	Pasteurizing
10	○	⇒	■	D	▽	Temperature
11	○	⇒	□	D	▽	Transport to filler machine
12	●	⇒	■	D	▽	Filling and covering
13	○	⇒	□	D	▽	Transport to cooling tunnel
14	●	⇒	□	D	▽	Cooling
15	○	⇒	□	D	▽	To labeling machine
16	●	⇒	□	D	▽	Labeling
17	○	⇒	■	D	▽	Label status
18	○	⇒	□	D	▽	To encoder
19	●	⇒	□	D	▽	Encoder
20	○	⇒	□	D	▽	To packaging
21	●	⇒	□	D	▽	Packaging
22	○	⇒	□	D	▽	Transport to stowing
23	●	⇒	□	D	▽	Stowing
24	○	⇒	□	D	▽	Transport to finished products
25	○	⇒	□	D	▼	Store
Σ	11	10	4	0	1	

Fig. 4. Improved fruit nectar process diagram

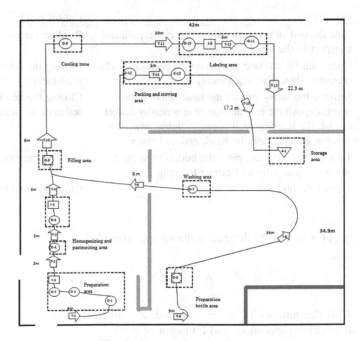

Fig. 5. Improved stroke diagram.

Addition of Fruit Pulp. In this operation, an activity with improvement potential was detected through direct observation: The loading operation of the pulp tank, which was carried out under inadequate ergonomic conditions. These conditions could generate musculoskeletal injuries in the mid-term. The use of a hoist was proposed, and this action was implemented by the top-level management.

In this operation, the worker carries the pulp tank to a weighing machine located to 1 m from the preparation zone. Once the worker has the tank's weight measure, he put on the PPE (Personal Protective Equipment) needed to handle raw material. This equipment consists of a mask, gloves and an apron.

The worker removes a security ring and the cover and put it on in a temporary storage space. After, the worker opens the tank, cut the internal protection, clean the material excess and with the help of a hose, adds water to the tank to enable the pulp extraction.

For this purpose, the worker introduces an extractor into the tank, turns on and continues adding water to avoid an obstruction into the pipe that transport pulp from the preparation tank to the mix tank. Once, 176 kg ± 15 kg of pulp was extracted, the worker proceeds to turn off the extractor and remove it from the tank. Now, the worker takes the PPE off and waits for one of the two available mix tanks was empty to repeat the steps previously described.

Work Measurement. To the WM purposes, this activity was split into five elements, whose description and cut-off points are shown in Table 2.

Table 2. Operation elements.

Element	Description	Cut-off point
A	Hold the tank of raw materials with a crane, pull, and transport to the weighing machine	Reading the weight
B	Open mini-locker, take and put on the necessary PPE (Personal Protective Equipment)	Closing the lid of the mini-locker
C	Remove the safety ring of the tank, remove the cover, deposit the ring and cover in a nearby basket, tear off the inner protective paper, throw away the material excess, clean by hand, and add water	Closing the key that activates the water hose
D	Turn on the extractor, press the button to insert it, add water gradually and extract the pulp	Turn off the extractor
E	Takes EPP off	Close the mini-locker

Then, Eq. (1) was used to determine the sample size [16].

$$N = \frac{Z^2 pq}{e^2} \tag{1}$$

Where, N is the number of cycles required, Z statistical value, p working proportion, q no working proportion, and e margin of error.

The confidence level selected was 95% (5% standard error), and 10 preliminary observations were made to determine the values of p and q, which correspond to 0.9 and 0.1, respectively (Table 3).

Table 3. Preliminary observations to determine p and q values.

Observations	p (working)	q (no working)
1	✓	
2	✓	
3	✓	
4	✓	
5		✓
6	✓	
7	✓	
8	✓	
9	✓	
10	✓	
$\sum$	9	1

To determine the margin of error, Eq. (2) was used.

$$Margin\ of\ Error\ =\ Z\ *\ \sigma p \qquad (2)$$

Where,

$$\sigma p\ =\ standard\ error\ in\ the\ proportion$$

$$Z\ =\ Value\ to\ the\ confidence\ level\ selected$$

Adopting the parameters selected above, the margin of error is 9.8%.

$$Margin\ of\ error\ =\ 1.96(5\%)$$

$$Margin\ of\ error\ =\ 9.8\%$$

After, the calculations were conducted, and it was obtained 36 cycles.

$$N = \frac{(1.96)^2(0.9)(0.1)}{(9.8\%)^2}$$

$$N = 36$$

The observed time is presented in a supplementary file [17]. Work measurement was conducted using a stopwatch time study, and a control chart [18] for assessing consistency is presented in Fig. 6. According to this chart, there are no points out of control, which means that the process is stable over time.

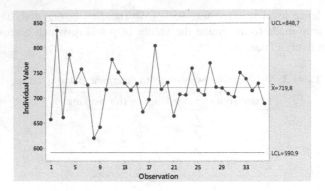

Fig. 6. Control chart for observed time.

After, the normal and standard time determination was conducted using the Eqs. (3) and (4)[1], respectively. To the normalization of observed time, performance rating was used. For standard time calculation, an allowance was added to normal time. The allowance refers to extra time added to compensate situations that force workers to stop the work, such as fatigue, delays, and other needs [19].

The results of normal time calculations are shown in Table 4. Finally, the standard time for each element and for the overall operation is presented in Table 5.

$$Normal\ time\ (T_n) = Observed\ time * performance\ rate = \bar{t} * \bar{V} \qquad (3)$$

$$Standard\ time = \sum_{A}^{E} T_n(1 + \%\ allowance) \qquad (4)$$

Therefore, the standard time for conducting the pulp addition operation is 813.27 standard seconds (13.55 standard min).

Table 4. Normal time determination

Cycles	Element				
	A	B	C	D	E
1–5 (s)	97.14	23.90	192.92	383.64	15.34
6–10 (s)	89.46	28.00	179.93	378.09	15.80
11–15 (s)	92.17	24.72	213.29	393.06	15.89
16–20 (s)	94.44	25.88	207.63	380.02	15.25
21–25 (s)	94.37	26.58	198.67	373.76	15.83
26–30 (s)	97.76	23.38	207.31	379.52	15.78

(continued)

---

[1] The allowances established are 13% (Personal: 6%, fatigue: 4%, and break: 3%).

Table 4. (*continued*)

Cycles	Element				
	A	B	C	D	E
31–35 (s)	91.30	25.55	200.30	392.15	16.18
36 (s)	96.54	22.56	178.56	375.46	15.01
Average time $\bar{t}$ (seconds)	94.15	25.07	197.33	381.96	15.64
Rating factor $\bar{V}$ (%)	95.50	97.25	104.41	100.63	96.00
Normal time t_n (normal seconds)	89.91	24.38	206.03	384.37	15.01

Table 5. Time study results

Element	Cycles	Average cycle time (sec.)	Rating factor (%)	Normal time (normal sec.)	Standard time (standard sec.)
A	36	94.15	95.50	89.91	101.60
B	36	25.07	97.25	24.38	27.55
C	36	197.33	104.41	206.03	232.82
D	36	381.96	100.63	384.37	434.33
E	36	15.64	96.00	15.01	16.97
$\sum$	–	714.15	493.79	719.70	813.27

5 Conclusions

This study examined a WS, 5W1H and ECRS application for enhancing the performance of a fruit nectar production process. The research showed that WS techniques were able to get an appropriate diagnosis and identifying improvement opportunities.

The implemented improvements in this case study had an impact on the work methods and represented a reduction in the number of delays and transportation activities. These actions affected the total traveled distance, with overall savings of 10.2 m per cycle.

Moreover, it was possible to determine the standard time in the pulp addition operation (13.55 standard min), a critical activity with big improvement potential. The standard time is the basis for quantifying the work content in a task through WM. For that purpose, previous methods standardization is required. Therefore, WM was carried out only in pulp addition operation, regarding it was the only one with standardized methods. Further studies include performing a comparative analysis for takt time reduction and the implementation of WM in other activities in the production line.

References

1. Duran, C., Cetindere, A., Aksu, Y.E.: Productivity improvement by work and time study technique for earth energy-glass manufacturing company. Proc. Econ. Financ. **26**, 109–113 (2015). https://doi.org/10.1016/S2212-5671(15)00887-4

2. Chisosa, D.F., Chipambwa, W.: An exploration of how work study techniques can optimize production in Zimbabwe's clothing industry. J. Text. Apparel Technol. Manag. **10**, 1–11 (2018)
3. Malashree, P., Kulkarni, V.N., Gaitonde, V.N., Sahebagowda, M.: An experimental study on productivity improvement using workstudy and ergonomics (2018)
4. Prokopenko, J.: Productivity Management: A Practical Handbook. International Labour Organization, Geneva (1987)
5. Roncancio Avila, M., Reina Moreno, D., Hualpa Zuñiga, A., Felizzola Jimenez, H., Arango Londoño, C.: Using learning curves and confidence intervals in a time study for the calculation of standard times. Inge Cuc. **13**, 18–27 (2017). https://doi.org/10.17981/ingecuc. 13.2.2017.02
6. Coronado-Hernandez, J.R., Ospina Mateus, H.: Incorporating ergonomic risks into U-shaped assembly line balancing problem. WPOM - Work. Pap. Oper. Manag. **4**, 29–43 (2013). https://doi.org/10.4995/wpom.v4i2.1164
7. Chueprasert, M., Ongkunaruk, P.: Productivity improvement based line balancing: a case study of pasteurized milk manufacturer. Int. Food Res. J. **22**, 2313–2317 (2015). https:// www.scopus.com/record/display.uri?eid=2-s2.0-84945325467&origin=inward&txGid=f3b2 71df3fda1d19864a135d28f7db5a
8. Ongkunaruk, P., Wongsatit, W.: An ECRS-based line balancing concept: a case study of a frozen chicken producer. Bus. Process Manag. J. **20**, 678–692 (2014). https://doi.org/10. 1108/BPMJ-05-2013-0063
9. Jia, S.: The research and application of program analysis in a production assembly line. In: 2017 4th International Conference on Industrial Engineering and Applications, ICIEA 2017, pp. 368–371 (2017). https://doi.org/10.1109/IEA.2017.7939240
10. Feng, J.Y.: The application and study of work study in electronic production packaging line balancing. Adv. Mater. Res. **933**, 538–542 (2014). https://doi.org/10.4028/www.scientific. net/AMR.933.538
11. Li, W.L., Song, C.L., Han, L.S.: Application of the work study to balancing hydraulic component assembly lines. Adv. Mater. Res. **452–453**, 206–210 (2012). https://doi.org/10. 4028/www.scientific.net/AMR.452-453.206
12. Mishra, R.: Productivity improvement in automobile industry by using method study. Int. J. Sci. Eng. Appl. Sci. **1**, 361–363 (2015). ISSN 2278-1684
13. Mwanza, B.G., Mbohwa, C.: Application of work study for productivity improvement : a case study of a brewing company, pp. 296–305. IEEE (2016)
14. Singh, M.P., Yadav, H.: Improvement in process industries by using work study methods : a case study. Int. J. Mech. Eng. Technol. **7**, 426–436 (2016). https://www.scopus.com/inward/ record.uri?eid=2-s2.0-85018504950&partnerID=40&md5=a5ebf0b930b759c8537d148eef 65c59f
15. Akansel, M., Yagmahan, B., Emel, E.: Determination of standard times for process improvement: a case study. Glob. J. Bus. Econ. Manag. Curr. Issues **7**, 62 (2017). https://doi. org/10.18844/gjbem.v7i1.1876
16. International Labour Office: Introduction to work study (1992)
17. Macías-Jiménez, M.A., Romero-Conrado, A.R. Acosta-Fontalvo, L.C. Coronado-Hernández, J.R.: Additional file: of application of work study to process improvement: fruit nectar case. Figshare. Dataset (2019). https://figshare.com/articles/Additional_file_of_Application_of_ Work_Study_to_process_improvement_Fruit_nectar_case_/8247425, https://doi.org/10.6084/ m9.figshare.8247425.v2
18. Minitab Inc.: Minitab 18.1 (2017)
19. Hartanti, L.: Work measurement approach to determine standard time in assembly line. In: Proceedings of 31st IASTEM International Conference, pp. 49–52 (2016)

UML Profiling for Software Systems in Medical Device Manufacturing

Muhammad Asim Minhas[(⊠)], Farooque Azam,
Muhammad Waseem Anwar, Iqra Qasim, and Hanny Tufail

National University of Sciences and Technology, Islamabad, Pakistan
{muhammad.minhas18, iqra.qasim16,
hanny.tufail16}@ce.ceme.edu.pk,
{farooq, waseemanwar}@ceme.nust.edu.pk

Abstract. Quality is a major concern in Medical Device Manufacturing (MDM). Conformance with prevailing regulatory standards is of profound importance in MDM. Due to critical nature and dependability of the domain, development of Workflow management information systems (WMIS) that truly depict the domain concepts along with the associated quality and regulatory parameters could be a challenging task. A Medical Device (MD) is not considered acceptable unless a documented conformance evidence is provided which supports the adequacy of the medical product to be used for its intended purpose. Therefore, WMIS for these manufacturing setups must provide an argumentative linkage between the development processes and corresponding regulatory requirements. In this paper, we have proposed a UML Profile Architecture for development of WMIS for medical device manufacturing setups. A case study from MD industry is included to discuss the benefit and applicability of the proposed methodology in detail.

Keywords: Medical Device Manufacturing (MDM) · UML Profile ·
Medical devices · Workflow management information system

1 Introduction

Medical devices, being safety critical in nature, require strict compliance with international standards. Each and every phase of product's lifecycle has stringent quality and safety requirements. Manufacturers of these medical devices have to provide strong evidences to prove conformance with these standards. There are various international standards like ISO, FDA etc. Each standard has its own implications and set of rules for each development phase of the MD. Medical device manufacturers experience increasing challenge of implementing a complex MD while ensuring high quality safety standards [4]. ISO 13485, Medical devices – Quality management systems – Requirements for regulatory purposes, is an internationally agreed standard that sets out the requirements for a quality management system (QMS) specific to the medical device industry.

Provision of workflow management information systems for such domains is also critical due to high risk factor involved in the manufacturing process. Software has to cover not only the core production workflows but also need to encompass the

© Springer Nature Switzerland AG 2019
K. Saeed et al. (Eds.): CISIM 2019, LNCS 11703, pp. 265–277, 2019.
https://doi.org/10.1007/978-3-030-28957-7_22

regulatory requirements of the applied standards. In other words, assurance of conformity and adherence to these standards lies at the heart of the medical device industry. A small human mistake could result into loss of human life. Formalism and automation with care and responsibility are recommended to minimize the chance of errors and mistakes at all stages. State of the art automated tools and equipment is used to achieve this goal. The developed software must be capable of handling manufacturing processes along with capturing all associated QMS parameters effectively to provide documented evidence to regulatory authorities for conformity assurance.

One effective solution is to use UML profile. i.e. A UML profile provides the facility to define domain concepts by extending the existing UML meta model. Through UML Profile, domain concepts can be defined with the help of stereotypes and UML meta model concepts can be extended. The main benefit is that the domain artifacts are already available in the tools and editors. The domain experts use the straightforward graphical user interface just to define their own business process models and as a result they get a fully functional automated software according to their needs and expectations.

A UML Profile Architecture (UPA) is proposed in this paper to define domain specific concepts as discussed earlier. First of all, as a reference to the regulatory standard, we selected ISO-13485. After analysis of this ISO Standard, we combined all requirements (Clause-8) in the form of a document and defined its relationships with the business process modeling. The objective of this research is to define generalized domain concepts in the form of a UML Profile to achieve benefits of generating Workflow management information systems (WMIS) with conformity of regulatory standard requirements across any medical device industry. The case study at the end of this paper shows that this approach results in to faster development of software with less cost and increased level of confidence on the adherence of the standards in practice.

This paper is organized as: Sect. 2 deals with the literature review whereas the proposed methodology is given in Sect. 3. Description of the case study is provided in Sect. 4 followed by discussion on the proposed methodology in Sect. 5. In Sect. 6, conclusion and future research work is discussed.

2 Literature Review

Various UML profiles have been proposed. [1] introduces the composition and function of workflow management system, and then discusses the advantages of using UML and Rose in modeling a workflow management system. It also provides the reason why system modeling is so useful to a software system at each phase of the development. It gives a general framework for workflow management systems by categorizing workflows in three dimensions, definition of business processes, control of the processes and finally running the interactive functions. In [2], the authors propose assurance case generation for safety regulatory requirements of medical devices. The authors provide with a concept of Goal Structure Notation (GSN) in order to combine software development process with assurance information in order to reduce the burden of medical device manufacturers. The concept of GSN is then applied on Rational Unified

Process (RUP) to develop Generic Insulin Infusion Pump (GIIP) case study. In order to fulfil the requirements of Food & Drug administration (FDA), which says that an assurance case is necessary before marketing of the GIIP, the authors provided a detailed guide map to automatically satisfy these requirements thereby getting two-fold advantage. i.e. medical device along with its software system, both get their conformance with FDA requirements using GSN and RUP in combination.

In paper [3], a UML profile approach is proposed for designing database applications using Sharp Architect RAD Studio. Paper [4] discusses the application of model-based system engineering (MBSE) approach within medical device domain to map regulatory requirements to components within the system that addresses those requirements. The paper used SysML as the reference architecture to design all interfaces and interactions of a specific device with the social-technical environment found in hospitals, clinics and user environment for devices that are integrated in the human system.

Various process modelling techniques involved in medical device development and their complexities have also been discussed briefly in paper [5]. The author provides key issues that are involved in medical device development domain and pointed out seven major factors that the designers must keep in their mind during development. Paper [6] describes a methodology for using OCL and UML profile for regulatory requirements in safety critical systems from safety requirements point of view. It also explains how system structure is identified, UML Profile is generated and OCL constraints are attached on M1 level models to capture the safety requirements.

In [7], a reference of ISO-13485 standard for medical device quality management system requirements is listed. Paper [8] is aimed to provide a documentation template for usability engineering process for medical devices. It connects the usability perspective of the medical device to the regulatory requirements of the domain and gives a more refined version of documentation of an already existing NBR 62366 (a digital thermometer) document structure. Paper [9] is a systematic literature review on how to extract regulatory and legal requirements to check for compliance or non-compliance of a system under consideration. It also suggests a methodology for prioritization of these requirements. An over-all goal-oriented approach is proposed to model the legal aspects and the support compliance as well as methods that provide templates for modeling compliant business processes.

Software development lifecycle is decomposed in to various categories with respect to the safety and risk levels in [10]. Medical devices are categorized in to thee classes: A, B and C. Each class is then assigned numerical values pertaining to the degree of contribution with the specific regulatory requirements. Regulation of networked mobile devices and mobile medical applications have also been discussed. Finally, in paper [13], a graphical as well as textual based technique is proposed for domain specific language engineering. The author(s) explained how tool-based support can be provided in both graphical and textual domains without loss of information and context in order to enable designers from both backgrounds accomplish their task concurrently. The transformation process is also explained in detail with the help of an industrial case study. In [14], the author has proposed a novel Model Based Software Engineering MBSE approach to automate the design verification of embedded systems by defining a new language SVOCL. Paper [15] provides a model driven approach for development of domain specific code generators and their application. In [16], the author has tried to prove that a combination of plan driven Software Development Lifecycles along with Agile Methodologies are the most effective choice for Medical Device Software Development. [17] provides a systematic approach for the development of code generators by categorizing software in to various types. A concept of High Confidence Medical Device Software has been introduced in [18]. The author argues that model driven software methodologies can lead to more reliable, dependable and safe software systems in the domain of implantable medical devices. In [19], a safety analysis of closed loop medical systems has been suggested. The author relates a simulation-based analysis of patient data model with timed automata to prove that the safety properties still remain conserved. In [20], an approach for analysis of the requirement documents have been discussed that can control and counter the malicious and security attacks on medical device software.

In the light of the above-mentioned literature review, it is evident that no research work has been performed which combines the four concepts of workflow management information system, medical device manufacturing, UML Profile and regulatory requirements assurance. In our research, we have combined these concepts in a logical way and applied UML profile that would enable the domain experts to not only automatically generate workflow information systems but these workflow systems will satisfy the regulatory requirements for the medical device domain.

3   Proposed Profile

In this paper, a UML Profile is proposed to define generalized domain concepts for development of Workflow Management Information Systems (WMIS). The first and foremost step of UML profile definition is to elicit all domain requirements. A preliminary analysis of the medical device domain manufacturing revealed following requirements. These requirements were common across a range of medical devices.

- Operator
- Product
- Lot
- Process
- Process Description
- Process Validation Criteria
- Post Process Verification
- Raw Material
- Process Dependencies
- Process Priority

The next step is to see what are the regulatory requirements against the above-mentioned domain concepts. In order to simplify this step, we take ISO-13485, which provides requirements of quality management system for medical devices. Due to scope limitation and simplicity, we take Clause-8 and see what specific requirements are needed to be fulfilled to get conformance with Clause 8 of ISO-13485 and how we can achieve a workflow management information system which intrinsically handles all of these requirements. CL-8 has two parts as described in Table 1.

Table 1. Measuring and monitoring requirements. ISO-13485 Clause-8

Clause #	Title	Compliance Policy	Document Ref
8.2.4.1	General Requirements	"The manufacturer must monitor and measure the characteristics of the product to verify that product requirements have been met. This is carried out at appropriate stages of the product realization process in accordance with the planned arrangements and documented procedures. Evidence of conformity with the acceptance criteria is maintained. Records indicate the person(s) authorizing release of product. Product release and service delivery do not proceed until the planned arrangements have been satisfactorily completed"	☐ Quality Plan ☐ Test Procedures ☐ Parameter Sheets
8.4.2.2	Particular Requirements for Active Implantable & Implantable Medical Devices	"Identification of personal performing any inspection is recorded on Process Travel Card/Inspection Record at Manufacturer's Production premises"	☐ Process Travel Card ☐ Inspection Record

After analyzing requirements as depicted in Table 1, it revealed that quality plan, test procedures and parameter sheets are the types of documents which have static nature. i.e. once defined they merely need to be updated. On the other hand, a very crucial record for the manufacturing process is 'Process Travel Card'. It has highly dynamic attributes.

In manual processing this document moves along with the production lot to all operators one by one and each one of them fill in the parameters as the production carries on. This process continues until we get a finished product. The criticality of PTC can be understood with the following facts.

1. PTC is used for the traceability of the whole production lot.
2. In case of a non-conformance, PTC is analyzed to find out the reasoning of non-conformance.
3. PTC provides a means to control sequence of the production flow of medical device manufacturing.
4. All process and product verification and validation related data is contained in PTC.

5. PTC is a documented evidence for the conformance of production lot to the pre-vailing international standard.
6. The criticality of the PTC can be understood by the fact that a production lot without corresponding PTC cannot be sold or marketed or in case of any error or mis-information, the whole production lot has to be discarded.
7. Even after sale of the medical product, PTC is a means for back tracking of the production lot.
8. PTC is retained during the whole product lifecycle of the product. For medical implants, it could range from 10–15 years.

In the light of the above-mentioned facts, we took PTC as our focus point. Every medical device manufacturing setup has to incorporate PTC in its domain to satisfy the above-mentioned requirements. We implement a UML Profile architecture to con-ceptualize PTC for the domain under consideration.

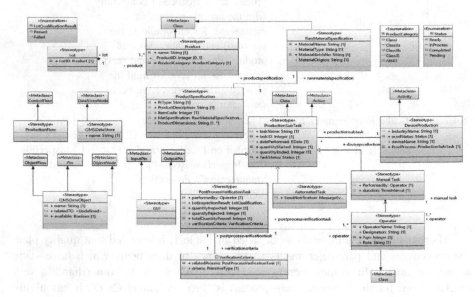

Fig. 1. UML profile for workflow management system in medical device

3.1 UML Profile

The proposed UML Profile is shown in Fig. 1. The UML Profile is developed using Papyrus Eclipse Tool. Two basic types of models are proposed i.e. Static and behav-ioral. Static models include class diagrams that will define the static structure of all the domain concepts and their relationships as well. Whereas behavioral model such as activity diagram shall be used to depict the dynamic nature of the production process. Apart from the production control, the important factor is to provide data storage facility after completion of each subsequent process. This is achieved through 'QMSDataObject'.

This object is responsible to store data related to each process and it is then available to the next process if it is required. Here we assume that achieving an adequate data storage of required information will enable us later on to manipulate this data according to our requirement. i.e. Any kind of graphical user interface or document will be generated later, when the data related to one complete production lot becomes available.

Stereotypes

The description of all stereotypes is briefly stated in Table 2. A stereotype is a profile class which defines how an existing meta class may be extended as part of a profile. It enables the use of a platform or domain specific terminology in place of, or in addition to, the ones used for the extended meta class.

Table 2. Stereotypes defined in UML profile

Stereo type	Description	Usage
≪Product≫	Refers to Medical Device of which the manufacturing setup is under consideration	For definition of structural concepts
≪Product Specification≫	Provides data related to the specific type of product	Structural Concepts/Process Flow Model
≪Raw Material Specification≫	Provides material and its associated data which the MD is made up of	Structural Model/Process Flow Model
≪Operator≫	Person responsible for execution of an action involved in an activity	Structural Model/Process Flow Model
≪ProductCategory≫	An enumeration that provides categorization of Medical Device	———do———
≪Process Verification≫	This domain concept deals with the post process verification of the medical device to make sure that all qualification parameters have been met and that the device is ready for the subsequent process	Behavior Model/Activity Diagram
≪ProcVerification Description≫	A specialization of the above mentioned domain concept	Behavior Model
≪ProductionFlow≫	Refer to control the sequential flow of the manufacturing	———do———
≪QMSDataStore≫	The domain concept which defines the store node for all kinds of data	Structural Model
≪ProductionSubTask≫	Denotes an atomic action performed in order to achieve an objective that has a meaningful contribution in the manufacturing process	Behavior Model/Activity Diagram

(continued)

Table 2. (*continued*)

Stereo type	Description	Usage
≪Automated Task≫	Represents an automated task performed via Automated Assembly/Device	Behavior Model
≪Manual Task≫	A task that will be executed by an actor	Behavior Model
≪LOT≫	Provides a concept of collection of the same kind of product that is adequate for batch processing	Structure Model
≪GUI≫	The domain concept primarily responsible for receiving input from the operator related to the QMS data of a production task	———do———
≪QMSDataObject≫	It holds data as well as behavior to achieve a specific kind of data representation which is one of the major concerns of the UML Profile	Both structure as well as behavior application
≪DeviceProduction≫	Represents the overall production activity for the whole process starting from the raw material to the finished product	Behavior Model/Activity Diagrams

4 Validation

In this section, we take example of Cardio Vascular Stent Manufacturing Company. Coronary Stents are human implantable medical devices used to clear blockage in the heart arteries. It is a class-III medical device with high level of risk involved in it. To apply the proposed profile, we repeat the same steps as discussed earlier. i.e. Firstly, we discovered all the requirement for stent manufacturing domain.

4.1 Case Study

Figure 2 shows process flow chart for Stent Manufacturing Setup (SMS). The information provided at each phase of the production is saved in PTC as evident from the figure. The UML is applied on the activity diagram representing the production workflow of the Cardio Vascular Stent Manufacturing. The class diagram of SMS is shown in Fig. 3 whereas the activity diagram model after profile application is shown in the Fig. 4.

The process flow diagram shows the lifecycle of the medical device called stent right from its start as a raw material to its finished form as a deliverable stent. The complete process can be divided in to the following steps.

1. To process the production, batch credentials are provided acting as guideline for the subsequent processes.
2. These parameters become available to the Raw Material Section which starts from issuance of the material for processing.

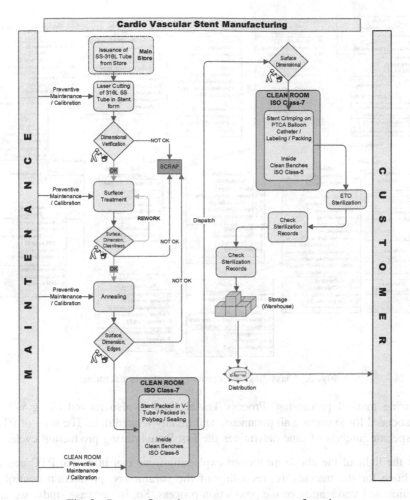

Fig. 2. Process flow chart- coronary stent manufacturing

3. After recording all information of raw material, it is then routed physically to the operator of Laser Cutting Process. In this process, stents are obtained by Laser Cutting of the tube. All process parameters along with the machine parameters are once again entered.
4. After completion of laser cutting process, a post process verification is performed to check the validity of laser cutting process.
5. During this phase, the stents are dimensionally verified to check whether each stent conforms to the design parameters. Here, the whole batch either gets passed or rejected completely in case of a non-conformance. The operator enters his remarks and verification results in PTC and route it for the subsequent process. This process gets continued till the last phase of the production as shown in Fig. 2.

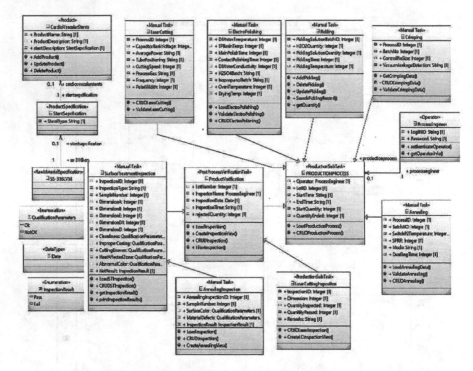

Fig. 3. Class diagram- coronary stent manufacturing

6. During manual processing, Process Travel Card is also moved along with the associated lot to capture all parametric and quality related data. The state of PTC at a specific interval of time determines the Lot Status during production cycle.

In the light of the above-mentioned explanation, we can infer that PTC acts as a back bone for the traceability, recording of the parameters, production control and validation and verification of the production process. So, in our case study, we apply the proposed UML Profile to conceptualize the concept of PTC and associated regulatory requirements.

5   Discussion

After application of the proposed profile and a detailed analysis of the case study, we have achieved the following benefits.

1. A domain specific language for process travel card implementation in medical device manufacturing industry.
2. An intrinsic conformance to the regulatory requirements for the MDM industry.
3. Provision of a leverage to domain experts by defining existing domain concepts thereby reducing the amount of work they might have to do.
4. Automated generation (GUI & related artifacts) of reliable and efficient WFMIS for production control and automation with appreciable fast development.

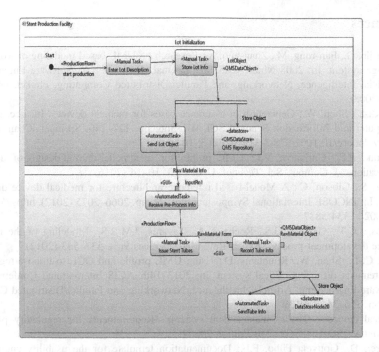

Fig. 4. Stent manufacturing. activity diagram

If proposed methodology is compared with the conventional software development approaches as the author presented in [21], it can be clearly stated that the proposed approach has substantial benefits as compared to code centric development approaches such as development effort, maintainability, bug probability, effort to learn, extendibility and most importantly model driven approach takes approx. only one fourth of the total time as compared to other approaches. Table-1 presented in [21] can be consulted for further elaboration of these advantages of model driven approach.

6 Conclusion

Model driven approaches such as UML Profile can be applied effectively to achieve specific business objectives in the systems generated in an automated fashion, having capability to seamlessly handle related regulatory requirements. Meeting the regulatory requirements involved in Medical device manufacturing industry could be challenging task but using the domain specific concepts in the form of a UML Profile makes this task easy and beneficial over to the conventional approaches. It is also evident that state of the art tools and techniques are a must to meet the growing quality demands for safety critical devices. In future, we would like to enhance the proposed UML profile to get full support of the complete QMS system by covering all clauses of the regulatory requirements.

References

1. Hong-jie, G., Fan-rong, M., Zhan-guo, X.: Research on UML-based modeling of work-flow manage system. In: 2008 Ninth ACIS International Conference on Software Engineering, Artificial Intelligence, Networking, and Parallel/Distributed Computing, Phuket, pp. 835–839 (2008)
2. Lin, C.-L., Shen, W.: Generation of assurance cases for medical devices. In: Lee, R. (ed.) Computer and Information Science. SCI, vol. 566, pp. 127–140. Springer, Cham (2015). https://doi.org/10.1007/978-3-319-10509-3_10
3. Oleynik, P.P., Gurianov, V.I.: UML profile for metamodel-driven design of database applications. J. Comput. Sci. Technol. Updates 3, 10–14 (2016)
4. Corns, S., Gibson, C.: A Model-based reference architecture for medical device development. In: INCOSE International Symposium, vol. 22, pp. 2066–2075 (2012). https://doi.org/10.1002/j.2334-5837
5. Santos, I.C.T., Gazelle, G.S., Rocha, L.A., Tavares, J.M.R.S.: Modeling of the medical device development process. Expert Rev. Med. Devices 9(5), 537–543 (2012)
6. Ling, C.-L., Shen, W., Kountanis, D.: Using UML profile and OCL to impose regulatory requirements on safety-critical system. In: 2013 14th ACIS International Conference on Software Engineering, Artificial Intelligence, Networking and Parallel/Distributed Computing, pp. 356–361 (2013)
7. Medical devices—Quality management systems—Requirements for regulatory purposes Committee ISO-13485/TC 210 Edition 2016-03
8. Scherer, D., Gouveia Filho, F.F.: Documentation template for the usability engineering process for medical devices. In: Lhotska, L., Sukupova, L., Lacković, I., Ibbott, Geoffrey S. (eds.) World Congress on Medical Physics and Biomedical Engineering 2018. IP, vol. 68/2, pp. 69–73. Springer, Singapore (2019). https://doi.org/10.1007/978-981-10-9038-7_13
9. Ghanavati, S., Amyot, D., Peyton, L.: A systematic review of goal-oriented requirements management frameworks for business process compliance. In: 2011 Fourth International Workshop on Requirements Engineering and Law, Trento, pp. 25–34 (2011)
10. Hrgarek, N.: Certification and regulatory challenges in medical device software development. In: Proceedings of the 4th International Workshop on Software Engineering in Health Care (SEHC 2012), pp. 40–43. IEEE Press, Piscataway (2012)
11. Object Management Group: UML 2.0 Superstructure. http://www.omg.org/cgibin/doc?ptc/2004-10-02
12. OMG: UML 2.0 OCL Specification. http://www.omg.org/docs/ptc/03-10-14.pdf
13. Maro, S., Steghöfer, J.-P., Anjorin, A., Tichy, M., Gelin, L.: On integrating graphical and textual editors for a UML profile based domain specific language: an industrial experience. In: ACM SIGPLAN International Conference on Software Language Engineering (2015). https://doi.org/10.1145/2814251.2814253
14. Anwar, M.W., Rashid, M., Azam, F., Kashif, M.: Model-based design verification for embedded systems through SVOCL: an OCL extension for system verilog. J. Des. Autom. Embedded Syst. 21(1), 1–36 (2017)
15. Roth, A., Rumpe, B.: Towards product lining model-driven development code generators. In: 2015 3rd International Conference on Model-Driven Engineering and Software Development (MODELSWARD), Angers, pp. 539–545 (2015)

16. Mc Hugh, M., Cawley, O., McCaffcry, F., Richardson, I., Wang, X.: An agile V-model for medical device software development to overcome the challenges with plan-driven software development lifecycles. In: 2013 5th International Workshop on Software Engineering in Health Care (SEHC), San Francisco, CA, pp. 12–19 (2013). https://doi.org/10.1109/SEHC.2013.6602471

17. Nazari, P.M.S., Rumpe, B.: Using software categories for the development of generative software. In: 2015 3rd International Conference on Model-Driven Engineering and Software Development (MODELSWARD), Angers, pp. 498–503 (2015)

18. Jiang, Z., Mangharam, R.: High-confidence medical device software development. In: High-Confidence Medical Device Software Development (2015). keywords: {Test; Verification; Risk Analysis; Program Verification; Software Model Checking}

19. Pajic, M., Mangharam, R., Sokolsky, O., Arney, D., Goldman, J., Lee, I.: Model-driven safety analysis of closed-loop medical systems. IEEE Trans. Ind. Inform. **10**(1), 3–16 (2014)

20. Lindvall, M., Diep, M., Klein, M., Jones, P., Zhang, Y., Vasserman, E.: Safety-focused security requirements elicitation for medical device software. In: 2017 IEEE 25th International Requirements Engineering Conference (RE), Lisbon, pp. 134–143 (2017)

21. Krogmann, K., Becker, S.: A case study on model-driven and conventional software development: the palladio editor. In: Software Engineering 2007 - Beiträge zu den Workshops, Fachtagung des GI-Fachbereichs Softwaretechnik in Hamburg, vol. 27, pp. 169–176, 30 March 2007

Economic Losses Reduction Through the Implementation of Statistical Process Control: Case Study in the Process of Medical Accounts in a Technology Company

Ginna Ospino Barraza⑩, Dionicio Neira Rodado⑩,
Luz Adriana Borrero López⑩, Javier Velásquez Rodríguez$^{(\boxtimes)}$⑩,
and Geraldin Royert⑩

Universidad de la Costa, Barranquilla, Colombia
ginnaospino1234@gmail.com, {dneira1,lborrero2,
jvelasqu3,groyert1}@cuc.edu.co

Abstract. Statistical process control (SPC) is one of the most important tools for process continuous improvement. Its usefulness lies on the fact that it helps in the identification of causes of variation in the process. This allows the decision maker to take the corresponding actions in such a way that the improvement of the associated indicators is achieved. In this particular case, the methodology of the SPC was used to intervene a process of verification and collection of medical accounts by a technology company. The errors in these accounts can cause that the health companies do not pay the correct amount to hospitals. This situation may affect the service to users or that the health companies have economic losses. The implementation of the statistical process control (SPC) had a big impact in the identification of problems, stabilization of the process, and improvement of satisfaction and reduction of quality costs.

Keywords: Statistical process control · Quality cost ·
Continuous improvement · Control charts

1 Introduction

Improvement in quality through statistical process control is a strategy that directly relates with the reduction of economic losses in organizations. The lack of quality is quickly detected by customers and causes customer losses and discomfort [1]. This is a very critical situation for any organization that wants to remain in the market, considering that is very difficult to attract again customer when they left the company due the poor quality in service or product supplied. The absence of quality strongly affects competitiveness in any organization [2, 3], therefore it is important to emphasize that any expense in quality improvement, should be considered as investment that in the future will bring benefits translated into profitability and greater customer satisfaction. This is the main reason for authors to apply statistical process control for various problems presented in the service sector [4–6].

K. Saeed et al. (Eds.): CISIM 2019, LNCS 11703, pp. 278–290, 2019.
https://doi.org/10.1007/978-3-030-28957-7_23

Spiess et al. [7] proposed the use of control charts in the molecular monitoring of minimal residual disease in chronic myeloid leukemia (CML), given that they are a common validation tool to maintain a high quality of the process through the continuous registration of the control parameters.

On the other hand, Eissa [8], shows the benefits of statistical control in the monitoring and control of pharmaceutical products to ensure the continuity and effectiveness of the products to final consumers, for which he used the graphics of control G. The tools provide an effective solution to monitor and control the withdrawal of products from the drug market by offering corrective and preventive visions for the problem of defective products through an effective bidirectional communication between the regulatory agencies and the drug manufacturing companies.

Eissa [9], used the control charts by attributes to mediate the trends found in the outbreaks of certain selected states of the United States. This author found that these trend graphs could be valuable not only in the evaluation and prediction of the process, but also to develop a simplified type of quantitative risk assessment based on the magnitude, frequency and threshold of the outbreak observed in each state.

The studies described above show that effective quality management is the main way to achieve the objective of improving quality in administrative processes and services, however there are still shortcomings in the application of quality techniques and methodologies to achieve relevant quality improvements. Among the causes commonly described are the lack of quality culture in the organizations, the low commitment of the teams, the resistance to change of methods, and not being aware of the economic impact of variations and mistakes in the process have [7–10].

In the case of this research, statistical process control and quality costs analysis is applied to improve the quality of the process of medical bills in a technology company in the city of Medellin. This type of analysis had not been carried out to improve operating costs of this type of company. The analysis carried out and the implementation of the corresponding corrective and preventive actions, allowed the company to improve the operating costs and the companies' service level. The process under study is responsible for the correct liquidation of bills. Errors in this process may cause economic losses both for the hospital and the health provider, and may also affect the patients, delaying treatments, surgeries and other procedures.

2 Methodology

In order to address the problem, a methodology based on seven steps was proposed. These steps and the expected results of each one of them can be observed on Fig. 1. The steps are described below:

- **Data collection:** Data was collected mainly by direct observation, through a survey's application. In each case, the type of error, administrative operator, amount of the transaction, among other aspects, are identified.
- **Characterization of the process:** Identification of the inputs, outputs, customers, and activities, as well as the percentage of defective bills. This phase includes the definition of the indicator to be monitored, and the identification of the baseline.

- **Control chart construction**: Once the process has been characterized and with the collected data, a *p*-control chart with variable limits will be constructed. The chart will have variable limits considering, that the amount of processed invoices varies every day.
- **Analysis of points:** Once the control chart is constructed, it will be determined which points are atypical to debug and analyze them in order to be able to identify special causes of variation and be able to take corresponding corrective actions. For this analysis, Pareto and Ishikawa diagrams will be used.
- **Improvements implementation:** Once the atypical points were analyzed and the improvement actions are determined, these actions will be implemented.
- **Improvements impact analysis:** Once the effectiveness of the improvement actions implemented and the stability of the improved process is verified, an economic valuation of the impact of the actions will be carried out. This valuation includes an analysis of the quality costs.

3   Study Case

As it was mentioned before, the process focus of this study is Medical Accounts. The importance of this process lies on the fact that the company processes around 220.000 bills monthly. This represents an income of 100.000 USD for the company in case that the percentage of defective bills remains below a threshold value (5% in this case). The main objective of the process Medical Accounts is to manage the documentation of Medical Accounts of a Healthcare provider. In case that the customer detects that the proportion of bills with mistakes exceeds the threshold value the company has to pay a penalty, affecting its profits. This process implies the reception of the documentation, its digitalization, loading the digitalized document in magnetic media, detailing and auditing of bills, until its delivery to the client, including its storage. In order to monitor the process, the company takes samples and put them in a graph but without any statistical analysis. The implementation of the seven steps described in the methodology is shown below:

Phase 1 Collection of Information
The quality diagnosis of the Medical Accounts process was made, through the errors reported by the client, for which three Pareto levels were developed with the aim of identifying causes and knowing exactly the problems of non-quality. The study is included among the errors generated in July and August, 503 cases of error were analyzed, which is constituted as 503 non-compliant invoices. An error is the same as a poorly operated invoice. Below, results obtained and analysis of cases reported by Pareto levels are presented. The total amount of bills inspected in those two months were 18910.

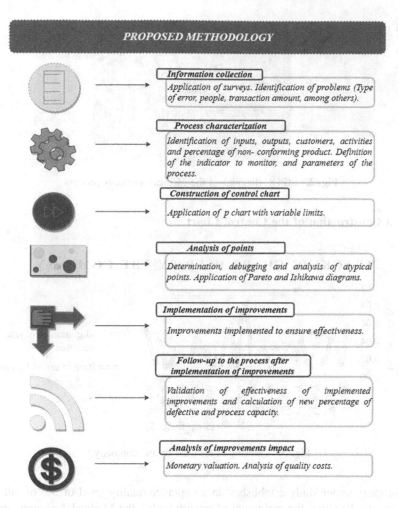

Fig. 1. Methodological scheme of the investigation.

Phase 2 Process Characterization

Once the information of the processed and defective invoices was collected, the SIPOC diagram (Fig. 2) was constructed and the current percentage of defective bills is determined by the division of the 503 defective bills out of the 18910 inspected bills, obtaining:

$$p = 0,0266$$

This percentage allows the calculation these two indicators to determine the quality of the process.

$$Z_{bench} = 1,94 \qquad C_p = 0,739$$

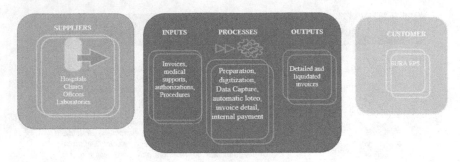

Fig. 2. SIPOC diagram of the medical accounts process

Phase 3 Construction of the Control Chart

TRACKING CHART USED BY THE COMPANY

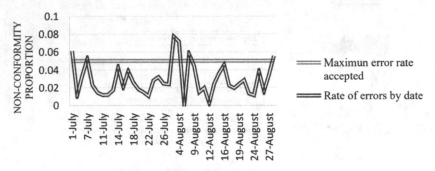

Fig. 3. Tracking chart used by the company.

The company under study establishes an acceptance quality level of 5% of bills with mistakes, this becomes the main goal of quality within the Medical Accounts process. The graph shown on Fig. 3 is the one currently used by the company to monitor the process. However, this graph is not useful to determine the stability of the process, i.e. if the value of p in the population varies or if the daily sample values do not allow to accept the hypothesis that the proportion of medical accounts with errors remains the same. The shortcoming of the method currently used by the company lies on the fact that the influence of the sample size is not considered and that the value that the company has as the upper limit of control is a specification limit.

The importance of controlling the proportion of defective invoices is that the customer (Health provider) penalizes the company in case the proportion of invoices with errors are greater than this percentage. Invoices with errors can involve delays in procedures and economic losses to the Health Provider. Taking into account this situation, it was proposed the implementation of a p control chart with variable upper and lower control limits that allows the company to monitor the process in relation to its stability. In other words, what is interesting is to be able to determine if at any moment there is enough statistical evidence to reject the hypothesis that the value of p remains the same. Through the use of this control chart the process can be monitored regardless of the size of the sample taken each day. Being sure that the proportion of defective bills remain equal, the ability of the process to meet the proposed goal of not exceeding 5% of defective bills, can be guaranteed.

The control chart initially obtained can be seen on Fig. 4. However, many samples exceeded the control limits, which forced the depuration of the corresponding observations, and the analysis of the root causes of the abnormal variation of these samples. Once the depuration process was finished, the chart shown in Fig. 5 was obtained. According to it, the value of $\bar{p}$ is 0.024 (2.4%), which was taken as the estimate for the population.

The new control chart allowed the organization to monitor the process and determine when the population changes its proportion of defective bills, either to a higher value or a lower value. Similarly, the impact of improvement actions on the performance of the process can be observed. And the most important thing is that regardless of the size of the analyzed sample, the value of the proportion of a particular day could be higher than the 5% established as an objective, without this implying that the proportion of the process has increased, thus avoiding false alarms. In the same way there will be points that although they are within the target value of 5%, they will be an indication that the process is not working with the value p = 0.024, when the sample size is large enough. Before fully implementation of the p chart, it is necessary to identify special causes of variation of the 19 points of the 41 that were debugged. This behavior indicates that the process is not stable. Once the causes of excess of variation were tackled, new samples were taken in order to have a reliable statistical control tool.

The values for the upper and lower control limit for the p-control chart were calculated as follows:

$$UCL_p = \bar{p} + Z_{\alpha/2} * \sigma_p \qquad LCL_p = \bar{p} + Z_{\alpha/2} * \sigma_p$$

$$\sigma_p = \sqrt{\frac{(\bar{p} * (1 - \bar{p}))}{n_i}} \qquad n_i \rightarrow \textit{number of elements in sample i}$$

The value used for α (Type I error) was 0,0027 obtaining a value of $Z_{\alpha/2} = 3$

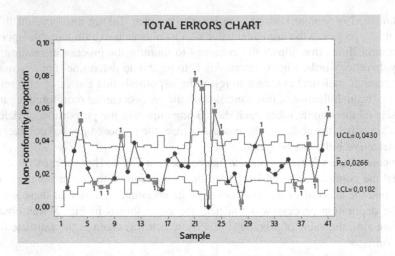

Fig. 4. Control charter P variable limits

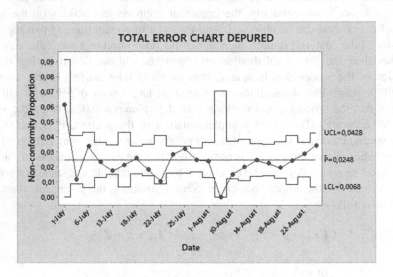

Fig. 5. p-control chart after depuration

Phase 4 Analysis of the Atypical Points

Once the atypical points were identified, an analysis of special causes was carried out in order to establish appropriate corrective and preventive actions. To carry out this analysis, Pareto and Ishikawa diagrams were used. First, a first level Pareto diagram was used to identify which is the most frequent error found among the bills (Fig. 6).

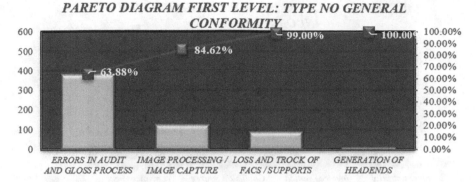

Fig. 6. First level Pareto diagram

From this first analysis it is evident that the main quality problems are given in the typology of audit error and bill processing with an absolute frequency of 65.61% indicating that it is the main problem. That's why this problem was further analyzed to identify its root causes. On the other hand, the generation of headers turned out to be the error of least frequency, however, it can be inferred that this can cause errors in audit, since an error in the header of the invoice, as it is a gross value, can generate a wrong liquidation of the account.

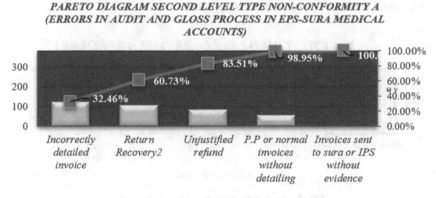

Fig. 7. Pareto diagram Second level

For this second Pareto (Fig. 7), the audit and bill processing process errors were analyzed and it could be determined that the first cause for those errors in the processing of bills is the problem of incorrectly detailed invoices with an absolute frequency of 115 of the total of 330 cases of error in bill processing, as well as the returns retrieves with absolute frequency of 86. Then a third level Pareto diagram was carried out in order to be able to identify the causes of incorrectly detailed invoices and propose more effective corrective and/or preventive actions.

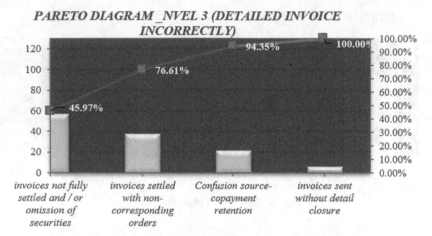

Fig. 8. Pareto diagram – Third level (Part 1)

For this first part of the Pareto study corresponding to the third level of incorrectly detailed invoices (Fig. 8), there are errors given by invoices that have not been settled in full and/or omission of values, which constitutes a high error recurrence, in addition to being of great impact on the customer. This has big impact in the company, considering that when an invoice is paid incorrectly, the payment of the total bill is being denied. This type of situation generates the loss of the company's profitability, as well as evidence of inefficient operational management.

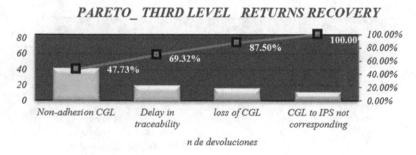

Fig. 9. Pareto diagram third level (Part 2)

On the other hand, on Fig. 9, the third level Pareto can be observed for the Recovery of returns. From which it can be observed that the most relevant problems are the non-printing of the CGI and the delays in the traceability of the bills.

Next, the scheme of the root cause diagram is presented for the problem of greater recurrence in the study of the three Pareto levels: errors in audit and glossing process. The root causes are mainly due to the lack of knowledge and competence of the operative team, it is necessary to develop training plans on critical issues for the audit and detail to minimize the error. As it is also important to tackle the indexing process, ensuring greater efficiency in the capture of the header of the invoice, this way no erroneous headers would be generated when downloading the information from the company web (Fig. 10).

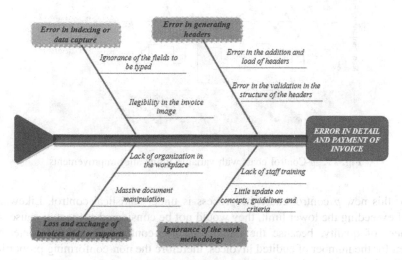

Fig. 10. Root cause diagram

Phase 5 Improvements Implementation

Taking into account the findings found through the analysis of causes, the company constructed an improvement plan that contained:

- Staff training plan to indicate the importance of each of the records and doubts about the process were resolved.
- A plan of awareness so that people will be empowered of the process.
- A plan to strengthen quality audits
- Regular biweekly meetings for monitoring and analysis of indicators

These actions were implemented at the same time. In this sense, in order to strengthen quality audits, the quality audit process was modified, specifying some particular control action to be carried out along the process.

Quality Audit Test

A pilot test was carried out during the following month, with the purpose of visualizing the behavior of the quality of the process for that period, a total of 72,492 invoices were inspected, with a capacity of 8 quality auditors within the process, responsible for the efficient management of this quality. The proposed methodology was carried out through the use of the information system where the non-compliant invoices are registered, together with the type of error, audit date, and operation auxiliary involved, finally the *p* type control chart is constructed (Fig. 11).

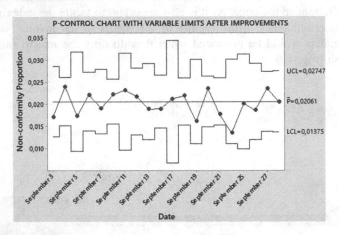

Fig. 11. p-Control chart with variable limits after improvements

For this new *p* control chart the process is under statistical control. Likewise, in case of exceeding the lower limit, they would not be considered suspect or cause of the detriment of quality, because the number of non-conforming invoices detected is reduced for the number of audited invoices, therefore the non-conforming proportion is low. In other words, within this month the value obtained from 0.02 of bills with problems is maintained, in addition to that there are no points outside the control limits in that period. The new values of Cp and Zbench are:

$$Z_{bench} = 2,05$$

$$C_p = 0,77$$

These values represent important savings for the company as evidenced in the phase of quality cost analysis. This implies also a reduction of 23.07% of the initial value, and the advantage of having a stable process.

Phase 7 Analysis of Quality Costs
To determine the amount of resources required in the quality audit of the Medical Accounts process, it was necessary to conduct a study of the costs of investing in quality improvement related to the number of auditors to be hired, as well as the cost of the absence of the quality generated by the multiple errors of the operation causing large reprocessing. In this sense, the cost of prevention, external failure, internal failure and measuring were determined, considering the impact to the health provider, the final user, the hospital and the company itself.

The graph of quality (measuring and prevention) and non-quality (external and internal failures) costs is constructed in order to find the point where the error can be minimized at a reasonable operating cost (Fig. 12).

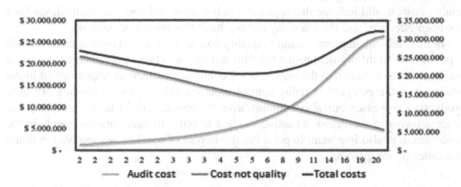

Fig. 12. Graph of quality and non-quality costs

The graph shows that as the number of auditors increases, the cost of quality increases given that the workforce destined to review bills is greater, therefore the volume of bills reviewed will be a significant amount, and the defective bills would decrease drastically, likewise the cost of non-quality is reduced since reprocessing and returns would be presented to a lesser extent.

Besides, it can be deduced that the quality and non-quality costs reach a significant approximation, while the cost of quality with a number of auditors of 8 is \$ 11,300,842, and the cost of non-quality is \$ 11,150,105, indicating that a little more is invested in quality but the percentage of non-conforming would be drastically reduced. Allowing to establish that the number of auditors required to perform the quality audit of the process of medical accounts, in this case would be 8 auditors, given that at that point the cost of quality and not quality can be minimized.

The auditors will be those operating assistants with a high level of competence and knowledge within this process.

4   Conclusions

The analysis of the P control chart applied within the company showed that the process is based on a quality goal, the 5% that is the non-conforming percentage allowed for the client, can generate erroneous conclusions about the stability and behavior of the process, finding points outside the control limits when in reality the process is under control, or vice versa. For example, on Fig. 5 it can be observed that the first day the sample yielded a value of 6%, but this did not become an alarm because the value was within the variable control limits of the chart. In this type of case, feedback, correction and improvement actions can be deployed unnecessarily or actions may be required and they are not deployed, since no problem is detected.

The study of costs of quality and not quality generated an important basis for the realization of the economic study of the implementation of quality in the Medical Accounts process, allowing to visualize the costs associated with the non-quality within the operation, becoming an important indicator of quality, because an increase in non-quality costs would indicate that reprocessing has increased and that the methods have not been effective, and the company did not have this economic analysis.

In this case, the implementation of quality cost analysis and statistical control made it possible to truthfully demonstrate the impact of the actions implemented in such a way that it was certain that the implemented controls presented an improvement in the total cost of the company. Quality control tools are suitable for monitoring not only production processes but also administrative processes, and in both cases help the process owner in the decision making process in order to make improvements in the processes. It is also important to point out the impact of training and motivation in the outcomes of any process.

References

1. Antosz, K., Stadnicka, D.: Lean philosophy implementation in SMEs – study results. Procedia Eng. **182**, 25–32 (2017)
2. Neira Rodado, D., Escobar, J.W., García-Cáceres, R.G., Niebles Atencio, F.A.: A mathematical model for the product mixing and lot-sizing problem by considering stochastic demand. Int. J. Ind. Eng. Comput. **8**(2), 237–250 (2016)
3. Rohani, J.M., Zahraee, S.M.: Production line analysis via value stream mapping: a lean manufacturing process of color industry. Procedia Manuf. **2**(2), 6–10 (2015)
4. Malik, A., Blumenfeld, S.: Six Sigma, quality management systems and the development of organisational learning capability. Int. J. Qual. Reliab. Manag. **29**(1), 71–91 (2012)
5. Cudney, E.A., Venuthurumilli, S.S.J., Materla, T., Antony, J.: Systematic review of Lean and Six Sigma approaches in higher education. Total Qual. Manag. Bus. Excell. 1–14 (2018)
6. Lee, C.K.M., Tan, C., Ru, Y., Yeung, C.L., Choy, K.L., Ip, W.H.: Analyze the healthcare service requirement using fuzzy QFD (2015)
7. Spiess, B., et al.: The benefit of quality control charts (QCC) for routine quantitative BCR-ABL1 monitoring in chronic myeloid leukemia. PLoS ONE **13**(4), 1–12 (2018)
8. Eissa, M.: Rare event control charts in drug recall monitoring and trend analysis of data record: a multidimensional study. Glob. J. Qual. Saf. Healthc. **2**(2), 34 (2019)
9. Eissa, M.: Attribute control charts for outbreaks trend of selected states in the USA: a case report of the insight into pattern. Int. Med. **1**(1), 11–14 (2019)
10. Cleophas, T.J., Zwinderman, A.H.: Machine Learning in Medicine - A Complete Overview. Springer, Cham (2015). https://doi.org/10.1007/978-3-319-15195-3

Machine Learning and High Performance Computing

Production Effectiveness Improvement with the Use of Tabu Search

Anna Burduk[✉] ⓘ, Kamil Musiał ⓘ, Dagmara Górnicka ⓘ,
and Joanna Kochańska ⓘ

Faculty of Mechanical Engineering,
Wrocław University of Technology, Wrocław, Poland
{anna.burduk, kamil.musial, dagmara.gornicka,
joanna.kochanska}@pwr.edu.pl

Abstract. The paper deals with the production downtime problem. Every production process may be affected by the risk of occurrence of the unplanned breaks. It can be caused by various factors, for example lack of components or machines failures. These result not only in the disturbance of production process flow, but also in the waste in the form of downtime. Machines failures can be caused by various factors, which may be difficult or even impossible to predict. Due to their random character, machine failure often results in operators idleness. The aim was to propose the solution of this problem. The proposed improvement was to develop the trainings schedule. These would take a part during the time of repairing the machine, so the waste would be reduced. The tool used to develop optimal training schedule was Tabu Search algorithm, a meta-heuristic method of supporting the decision-making process.

Keywords: Tabu Search · Training schedule · Machine failures ·
Waste in production process · Production process improvement

1 Introduction

Nowadays continuous improvement of production processes is kind of a condition that needs to be fulfilled by companies in order to stay competitive [1, 4, 5]. Thus, companies aim to reduce the waste sources, which can be caused by various factors. However, some of these factors are very difficult or even impossible to predict. An example of them are machines failures. Despite of taking preventive actions, they often have random character. The industry reality indicates that the occurrence of the machine failure often results in production stoppage. This causes the operators idleness and they usually take an additional break or they are even sent home, especially in the case of failures requiring a longer time to repair the machine. In order to solve this problem, the situation of failures was analysed. The analysis was based on quarter-a-year period of research, in automotive industry. It appeared that one of the tasks that can be done during downtime are operators trainings. Thus, the training schedule was proposed. This solution allows to use the downtime and replace the idleness by doing trainings, that would have to take place anyway.

© Springer Nature Switzerland AG 2019
K. Saeed et al. (Eds.): CISIM 2019, LNCS 11703, pp. 293–302, 2019.
https://doi.org/10.1007/978-3-030-28957-7_24

Because of the diversity of trainings, to develop the training schedule, Tabu Search was used. It is a kind of meta-heuristic algorithm, that is widely used in decision-making problems. Tabu Search allows to define and analyse the problem by using mathematical formulas [2]. It allows to find the solution that (in the local area) is close to the optimal one [3]. Tabu Search works through taboo lists that are being used to define the search prohibitions and changing the current solution to the new one.

2   Production Downtime – Case Study

The research has been performed in the automotive company that produce brakes used in trucks. The base of proposing the solution was an observation of production process through a quarter-of-year period. The most important task was monitoring all productions breaks, that was not planned. These are very important issues, because every stopping of production process generates important waste, not only in the financial area but also as delays of orders realisation. The observed downtimes were analysed for potential reasons. These are shown in Fig. 1 as a Ishikawa diagram, the *cause and effect* diagram that is being often used in production processes.

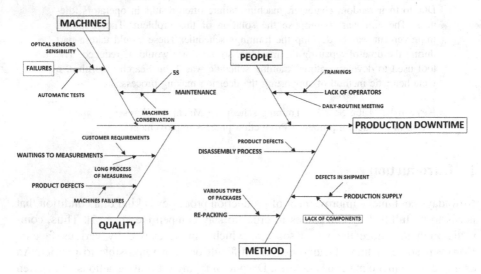

Fig. 1. Ishikawa diagram – production downtime reasons

The production process and Ishikawa diagram analysis allows to observe that the longest downtimes are caused by machines failures and lack of the components (marked in red at Fig. 1). The time of downtime caused by machine failures and lack of components were measured and listed in Table 1.

The conclusion of observation is, that downtimes in company are two types. The data was also shown in diagram (Fig. 2).

Table 1. Downtime caused by machine failures and lack of components

Week	Downtime [min]		
	Total [min]	Machine failures	Lack of components
W1	605	165	440
W2	1320	480	840
W3	1260	320	940
W4	1640	650	990
W5	820	235	585
W6	520	0	520
W7	375	25	350
W8	740	170	570
W9	605	90	515
W10	865	320	545
W11	285	100	185
W12	790	85	705
Total amount of downtime [min]:	9825	2640	7185
Average downtime in one week [min]:	818,75	220	598,75

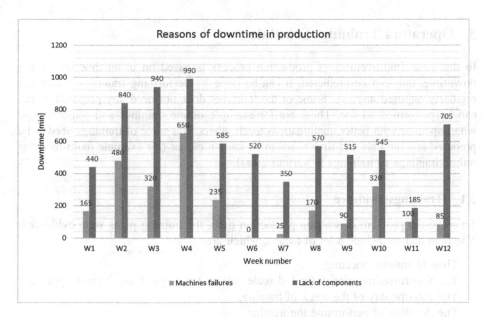

Fig. 2. Reasons of downtime in production – by weeks

One of the types of downtimes are caused by machines failures. These type of breaks are almost 27% of all downtimes. The second type of breaks are caused by lack of components which is over 73% of downtime (Fig. 3).

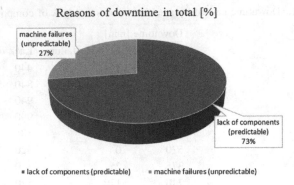

Fig. 3. Reasons of downtime of production in total

Machines failures are the type of downtime reasons, that cannot be predicted. They are 27% of the measured time. The second type are caused by lack of components that can be predicted with high level of certainty and are over 73% of downtimes measured. Thus, most of the measured time is possible to predict and it is the area where the improvement will be implemented.

3 Operators Trainings Schedule

In this case, improvement of production process is based on using time during the downtime, that can be predicted. It can be done by performing trainings, which are regularly required anyway. Some of the trainings does not need any preparation and can be performed ad-hoc. These are for example online trainings and self-trainings, when operator with better qualifications teach others. But some of trainings need to be prepared and the date and time needs to be known earlier (for example multi-modules online trainings or trainings in various areas).

3.1 Trainings Evidence

To solve the problem of wasting production time, the training plans were evidenced. The plan had to include a lot of factors, which are:

- Time of training/meeting,
- Trainings/meeting priority (in 1–3 scale, where 1 is highest and 3 lowest priority),
- The date/the day of the week of training,
- The deadline of performing the training.

The trainings were categorized as example of one-week trainings plan and listed in Table 2.

Every day of production has to include daily routine meeting and a break. The daily routine meeting can be performed at any time of the shift, but the break needs to be planned in the period of 2 h in the shifts half. The online training 1 needs to be performed till Thursday (4th day of the week), because it was planned earlier to be done

Table 2. An example of one-week training plan

Type	Priority	Time [h]	First available day	Last available day	Ad-hoc type (Yes/No)
Daily routine meeting	1	0,5	1	1	Yes
Daily routine meeting	1	0,5	2	2	Yes
Daily routine meeting	1	0,5	3	3	Yes
Daily routine meeting	1	0,5	4	4	Yes
Daily routine meeting	1	0,5	5	5	T (in 4 or 5 h of shift)
Break	1	0,33	1	1	T (in 4 or 5 h of shift)
Break	1	0,33	2	2	T (in 4 or 5 h of shift)
Break	1	0,33	3	3	T (in 4 or 5 h of shift)
Break	1	0,33	4	4	T (in 4 or 5 h of shift)
Break	1	0,33	5	5	T (in 4 or 5 h of shift)
Online training 1	1	1	1	4	Yes
Online training 2	2	4	1	5	Yes
Online training 3	3	2	1	5	Yes
Online training 4	3	1	3	5	Yes
Inner training 1	1	1	1	4	Yes
Inner training 2	2	2	3	5	No
Inner training 3	2	0,5	1	5	No
Inner training 4	3	0,5	1	5	Yes
Inner training 5	3	0,25	1	5	No
Inner training 6	3	4	1	5	No
Inner training 7	3	3	1	5	Yes
Outer training 1	2	8	1	5	No
Outer training 2	3	4	1	5	No
Failures and improvements discussion	1	0,5	4	5	Yes

till the end of the month (and, in this case, Thursday is the last day of the month). The failures and improvements discussion was being performed at Friday morning so far, but it can be done ad-hoc at Thursday or Friday as well. The priority 1 means, that the training or meeting needs to be done in the certain time. The priority 2 is recommended to perform training at this time. The priority 3 means, that the training can be delayed.

3.2 Tabu Search Implementation

Heuristic algorithms allow to find and implement various types of improvements, but they do not guarantee that found solution is the best one [6]. They are being more and more often used in manufacturing and production processes as computer aided methods [7–9, 12, 13]. One of the heuristic methods is Tabu Search, an algorithm that searches the space of all the solutions, doing sequence of movements [10, 11]. There are also forbidden moves that are named taboo. The way of algorithm working is that it achieves local optimum, by storing information about possible solutions. These are listed in the form of taboos (TL).

Algorithm **Tabu Search** (S_{start}, max_counter, max_iteration)

Set S = S_{start} and n_iteration = 0
Repeat
    counter = 0

    best_solution = 0

    n_iteration = n_iteration + 1

        Repeat

            counter = counter+1

            Execute **neighboring_solution_check** ($S,S_{counter}$)

            Execute **Tabu_list_check** (S,S_n)

                if ($f(S_{counter})$ > best_solution **then** (best_solution = $f(S_{counter})$ and (counter2= counter))

           until (counter = max_counter)

    Execute **Add_to_Tabu_list** ($S,S_{counter}$)

    S= $S_{counter2}$

    If best_solution > S **then** S = best_solution
Until niter = max_iter

Where:
Neighboring solution check:
The algorithm checks all neighboring solutions (differing in one bit):

$$
\begin{array}{ccccccc}
\mathbf{0} & 1 & 0 & 0 & 1 & 0 & 1 \\
1 & \mathbf{0} & 0 & 0 & 1 & 0 & 1 \\
1 & 1 & \mathbf{1} & 0 & 1 & 0 & 1 \\
1 & 1 & 0 & \mathbf{1} & 1 & 0 & 1 \\
1 & 1 & 0 & 0 & \mathbf{0} & 0 & 1 \\
1 & 1 & 0 & 0 & 1 & \mathbf{1} & 1 \\
1 & 1 & 0 & 0 & 1 & 0 & \mathbf{0} \\
\end{array}
$$

Check Tabu List:
Specific transition between data solutions in previous moves is checked. If so, such a solution is not taken under consideration and then the best solution, according to the specified criterion, is chosen:

$$1 \quad 1 \quad 1 \quad 0 \quad 1 \quad 0 \quad 1$$

Add to Tabu List:
Solution mentioned above is added to a list of prohibited movements (TL): If a found solution is the best found so far, the algorithm remembers it as the solution algorithm. The algorithm then repeats the operation with specified number of times.

Case study:
Analyzed issue can be presented as a binary sequence:

$$1 \quad 0 \quad 0 \quad 0 \quad 1 \quad 1 \quad 1 \quad 0 \quad 1 \ldots$$

Bits represent the tasks available to proceed in specific time – when free time slot appears. The value of "1" means that the task is pulled into schedule, the value of "0" – not taken into schedule. For instance, specific 4 of 7 tasks are taken into schedule:

$$1 \quad 1 \quad 0 \quad 0 \quad 1 \quad 0 \quad 1$$

For:

n events with priority $1 - e_{1,1}, e_{1,2}, \ldots e_{1,n}$
m events with priority $2 - e_{2,1}, e_{2,2}, \ldots e_{2,m}$
k events with priority $3 - e_{3,1}, e_{3,2}, \ldots e_{3,k}$

with fixed lasting event time:

$$t_{1,1}, t_{1,2}, \ldots t_{1,n},$$

$$t_{2,1}, t_{2,2}, \ldots t_{2,m}$$

$$t_{3,1}, t_{3,2}, \ldots t_{3,k}$$

and for the free time slot t_s because of failure or lack of production parts the algorithm allocates the events with priority 1 to fulfill the time slot.

$$0 \, t_{1,1} + 1 \, t_{1,2} + \ldots + 1 \, t_{1,n} \leq t_s$$

If the time gap is not completely managed, the algorithm repeats the action assigning events with priority 2 and finally with priority 3.

$$(0\,t_{1,1} + 1\,t_{1,2} + \ldots + 1\,t_{1,n}) + (0\,t_{2,1} + \ldots + 1\,t_{2,m}) + (1\,t_{3,1} + \ldots + 0\,t_{3,k}) \leq t_s$$

Triple execution of the procedure ensures correct management of priorities without taking them into account in the algorithm itself.

Finally, we receive a set of selected tasks from among all available ones, while maintaining their priorities. The total time of all selected tasks cannot exceed the length of the time gap, as mentioned in the above equation and should be as large as possible, as the function of the goal below says.

$$F(c) = (0\,t_{1,1} + 1\,t_{1,2} + \ldots + 1\,t_{1,n}) + (0\,t_{2,1} + \ldots + 1\,t_{2,m})$$
$$+ (1\,t_{3,1} + \ldots + 0\,t_{3,k}) \to MAX$$

The algorithm has been set to 50 iterations for each priority.

4 Results

The aim was reached by using Tabu Search, which allowed to increase the effectiveness of production process by using part of the time that was wasted before. The Tabu Search results are listed in Table 3.

Table 3. Downtime usage improvement by Tabu Search

Week	Downtime [min]		
	Total	Time that can be used for training	Time that cannot be used for training
W1	605	320	18
W2	1320	250	22
W3	1260	240	0
W4	1640	650	47
W5	820	400	0
W6	520	340	15
W7	375	260	112
W8	740	300	82
W9	605	180	18
W10	865	320	0
W11	285	100	0
W12	790	260	0
Total amount of downtime [min]:	9825	3620	314
Average downtime in one week [min]:	818,75	301,67	26,17

The average time of downtime, which was about 13 h, can be particularly used on operators trainings. According to Tabu Search results, the average time that can be spent on trainings, is more than 300 min, which means about 5 h. It is the 37% of total downtime. The data was shown in the diagram (Fig. 4).

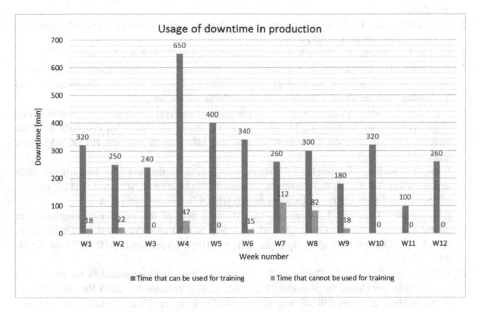

Fig. 4. Usage of downtime in production

There was a possibility to use whole downtime caused by lack of components in almost half of an analyzed period (W3, W5, W10, W11 and W12). In the rest of weeks, the time that was possible to use was higher than the time that cannot be used.

5 Summary

For the purpose of research, Tabu Search allowed to achieve the aim, which was improving production process effectiveness by using time, that was wasted earlier. This time was proved to be machines failures and lack of components. But the results of the research shows also, that it can be improved. In some cases, Tabu Search was not able to plan the training proper enough, because the downtime was much longer than the predicted one. Moreover, in 8 of 12 weeks Tabu Search planned longer trainings than the real downtime. It was caused by the fact, that the predicted time was longer than the actual one. This is not the same thing as waste, because the time would need to be spent on trainings anyways. Both imperfections of Tabu Search can be improved thanks to a better valuation of downtime of the company. The final result is, that Tabu Search allows to use average 37% of downtime, which is very desirable in described company. It also shows that Tabu Search has high potential of being used in this or similar kind of problems.

References

1. Musiał, K., Kotowska, J., Górnicka, D., Burduk, A.: Tabu search and greedy algorithm adaptation to logistic task. In: Saeed, K., Homenda, W., Chaki, R. (eds.) CISIM 2017. LNCS, vol. 10244, pp. 39–49. Springer, Cham (2017). https://doi.org/10.1007/978-3-319-59105-6_4
2. Hu, T., Chen, L.: Traffic signal optimization with greedy randomized tabu search algorithm. J. Transp. Eng. **1040**(8) (2012)
3. Glover, F., Laguna, M.: Tabu Search. Kluwer Academic Publishers, Norwell (1997)
4. Zwolinska, B., Grzybowska, K., Kubica, L.: Shaping production change variability in relation to the utilized technology. In: DEStech Transactions on Engineering and Technology Re-search (ICPR 2017). Destech Publications, Inc. (2017)
5. Sobaszek, Ł., Gola, A., Kozłowski, E.: Application of survival function in robust scheduling of production jobs. In: Ganzha, M., Maciaszek, M., Paprzycki, M. (eds.) Proceedings of the Federated Conference on Computer Science and Information Systems (FEDCSIS), New York (2017)
6. Jeleń, Ł., Kulus, M., Jurek, T.: Pattern recognition framework for histological slide segmentation. In: Saeed, K., Homenda, W. (eds.) CISIM 2018. LNCS, vol. 11127, pp. 37–45. Springer, Cham (2018). https://doi.org/10.1007/978-3-319-99954-8_4
7. Bożejko, W., Pempera, J., Wodecki, M.: Minimization of the number of employees in manufacturing cells. In: Graña, M., et al. (eds.) SOCO'18-CISIS'18-ICEUTE'18 2018. AISC, vol. 771, pp. 241–248. Springer, Cham (2019). https://doi.org/10.1007/978-3-319-94120-2_23
8. Zufferey, N., Respen, J., Thevenin, S.: All-terrain tabu search approaches for production management problems. In: Amodeo, L., Talbi, E.-G., Yalaoui, F. (eds.) Recent Developments in Metaheuristics. ORSIS, vol. 62, pp. 59–73. Springer, Cham (2018). https://doi.org/10.1007/978-3-319-58253-5_4
9. Delgoshaei, A., Mirzazadeh, A., Ali, A.: A hybrid ant colony system and tabu search algorithm for the production planning of dynamic cellular manufacturing systems while confronting uncertain costs. Braz. J. Oper. Prod. Manage. **15**(4), 499–516 (2018)
10. Cordeau, J.F., Gendreau, M., Laporte, G.: A tabu search heuristic for periodic and multi-depot vehicle routing problems. Networks **30**(2), 105–119 (1997)
11. Grabowski, J., Wodecki, M.: A very fast tabu search algorithm for the permutation flow shop problem with makespan criterion. Comput. Oper. Res. **31**(11), 1891–1909 (2004)
12. Rojek, I., Dostatni, E., Hamrol, A.: Automation and digitization of the material selection process for ecodesign. In: Burduk, A., Chlebus, E., Nowakowski, T., Tubis, A. (eds.) ISPEM 2018. AISC, vol. 835, pp. 523–532. Springer, Cham (2019). https://doi.org/10.1007/978-3-319-97490-3_50
13. Ociepka, P., Gwiazda, A.: Concept of hybrid system for computer aided of machines design process. Sel. Eng. Probl. (4) (2013)

Gentle AdaBoost Algorithm with Score Function Dependent on the Distance to Decision Boundary

Robert Burduk$^{(\boxtimes)}$ ⓘ and Wojciech Bozejko$^{(\boxtimes)}$ ⓘ

Faculty of Electronic, Wroclaw University of Science and Technology,
Wybrzeze Wyspianskiego 27, 50-370 Wroclaw, Poland
{robert.burduk,wojciech.bozejko}@pwr.wroc.pl

Abstract. This paper presents a new extension of Gentle AdaBoost algorithm based on the distance of the object to the decision boundary, which is defined by the weak classifier used in boosting. In the proposed approach this distance is transformed by Gaussian function and defines the value of a score function. The assumed form of transforming functions means that the objects closest or farthest located from the decision boundary of the basic classifier have the lowest value of the scoring function. The described algorithm was tested on four data sets from UCI repository and compared with Gentle AdaBoost algorithm.

Keywords: Gentle AdaBoost algorithm ·
Distance to the decision boundary · Score function

1 Introduction

Boosting is a machine learning effective method of producing a very accurate classification rule by combining a weak classifier [1]. The weak classifier is defined to be a classifier which is only slightly correlated with the true classification i.e. it can classify the object better than random classifiers. In boosting the weak classifier is learned on various training examples sampled from the original learning set. The sampling procedure is based on the weight of each example. In each iteration, the weights of examples are changing. The final decision of the boosting algorithm is determined on the ensemble of classifiers derived from each iteration of the algorithm. One of the fundamental problems of the development of different boosting algorithms is choosing the weights and defining rules for an ensemble of classifiers. In recent years, many authors presented various concepts based on the boosting idea [2–6].

In this paper we consider modification of the Gentle AdaBoost algorithm with linear basic classifiers. The proposed modification concerns the calculation of the scoring function. The value of the scoring function depends on the modified distance of the object from the decision boundary.

ⓒ Springer Nature Switzerland AG 2019
K. Saeed et al. (Eds.): CISIM 2019, LNCS 11703, pp. 303–310, 2019.
https://doi.org/10.1007/978-3-030-28957-7_25

This paper is organized as follows: Sect. 2 introduces the necessary terms of the boosting algorithm. In the next section there is our modification of Gentle AdaBoost algorithm. Section 3 presents the experiment results comparing Gentle AdaBoost with our algorithm. Finally, some conclusions are presented.

2   Boosting Algorithms

In the work [11] weak and strong learning algorithms were discussed. The weak algorithms can classify the object better than random classier, on the other hand, strong algorithms can classify the object accurately. Schapire formulated the first algorithm to "boost" a weak classifier. The main idea in boosting is to improve the prediction of weak learning algorithms by creating a set of weak classifiers which is a single strong classifier. The well-known and widely applied is AdaBoost algorithm. Its main steps are as follows [12]:

1. Let $w_{1,1} = ... = w_{1,n} = 1/n$
2. For $t = 1, 2, ...T$ do:
   a. Fit f_t using weights $w_{t,1}, ..., w_{t,n}$, and compute the error e_t
   b. Compute $c_t = \ln((1 - e_t)/e_t)$.
   c. Update the observations weights:

$$w_{t+1,i} = w_{t,i} \exp(c_t, I_{t,i}) / \sum_{j=1}^{n} (w_{t,i} \exp(c_t, I_{t,i})), \quad i = 1, ..n.$$

3. Output the final classifier:

$$\hat{y}_i = F(x_i) = sign(\sum_{t=1}^{T} c_t f_t(x_i)).$$

Table 1. Notation of the AdaBoost algorithm

i	Observation number, $i = 1, ..., n$.
t	Stage number, $t = 1, ..., T$.
x_i	A p-dimensional vector containing the quantitative variables of the ith observation.
y_i	A scalar quantity representing the class membership of the ith observation, $y_i = -1, 1$.
f_t	The weak classifier at the tth stage.
$f_t(x_i)$	The class estimate of the ith observation at the tth stage.
$w_{t,i}$	The weight of the ith observation at the tth stage, $\sum_i w_{t,i} = 1$.
$I_{t,i}$	Indicator function, $I(f_t(x_i) \neq y_i)$.
e_t	The classification error at the tth stage, $\sum_i w_{t,i} I_{t,i}$.
c_t	The weight of f_t.
$sign(x)$	$= 1$ if $x \geq 0$ and $= -1$ otherwise.

One of the main steps in the algorithm is to maintain a distribution of the training set using the weights. Initially, all weights of the training set observations are set equally. If an observation is incorrectly classified (at the current stage) the weight of this observation is increased. Similarly, the correctly classified observation receives less weight in the next step. In each step of AdaBoost algorithm the best weak classifier according to the current distribution of the observation weights is found. The goodness of a weak classifier is measured by its error. Based on the value of this error the ratio is calculated. The final prediction of AdaBoost algorithm is a weighted majority vote of all weak classifiers (Table 1).

Gentle AdaBoost calculates its weak hypothesis by optimizing the weighted least square error iteratively [7]. Experimental results show that the Gentle AdaBoost has a similar performance to other boosting algorithms like Real AdaBoost and Logit Boost, and in many cases outperforms these two types of boosting algorithms.

3   Distance Score Boost

In this section, we proposed Distance Score Boost algorithm that is a modification of Gentle AdaBoost algorithm. In particular, the method of calculating the weights of objects as well as the weights of the basic classifiers is not changed. However, base classifiers are not calculated by optimizing the weighted least square error iteratively. We propose that each base classifier had a scoring function, which depends on the distance to the decision boundary defined by this base classifier. In order to calculate the value of the scoring function, the distance of the object from the decision boundary is transformed by a function

$$SC(x_i) = \frac{1}{\sigma\sqrt{2\pi}} \exp\left(-\frac{(kd(x_i) - \mu)^2}{2\sigma^2}\right),$$

where $d(x_i)$ is the distance from the object x_i to the decision boundary. Our goal is not to provide a probabilistic interpretation of the score function, therefore, it

Table 2. Distance Score Boost algorithm

1.	Scale all features into the range $[0, 1]$
2.	Set the initial weights $w_{1,1} = ... = w_{1,n} = 1/N$
3.	For $t = 1, 2, ...T$ do:
a.	Train a base classifier f_t using weights $w_{t,1}, ..., w_{t,n}$
b.	Compute for each object x_i distance to the decision boundary defined by f_t - $d(x_i)_t$
c.	Transform the distance to score $SC(x_i)_t = \frac{1}{\sigma\sqrt{2\pi}} \exp\left(-\frac{(kd(x_i)_t - \mu)^2}{2\sigma^2}\right)$
d.	Update the observations weights: $w_{t+1,i} = \frac{w_{t,i}\exp(-y_t SC(x_i)_t)}{\sum w_{t,i}\exp(-y_t SC(x_i)_t)}$
3.	Output the final classifier: $\hat{y}(x_i) = sign\left(\sum_{t=1}^{T} SC(x_i)_t\right).$

is farther not transformed. Before the learning process feature scaling is used to bring all values into the range $[0, 1]$. The proposed algorithm is labeled DSBoost and it is as follows (Table 2):

The proposed transformation function is based on the normal distribution. We assume that the objects closest or farthest located from the decision boundary of the basic classifier have the lowest value of the scoring function. In addition, we assume that the base (weak) classifier forms a linear decision boundary. An example of such a weak classifier is recursive partitioning with one split (especially ID3 algorithm with one split).

4 Experiments

The main aim of the experiments was to compare the proposed Distance Score Boost algorithm with Gentle AdaBoost method. As the weak classifier ID3 algorithm with one split was used. In the experiments we use the implementation of Gentle AdaBoost algorithm described in [12]. The results are obtained via 10-fold-cross-validation method. In the experiments, the value of the parameter μ was tested. Other parameters have not changed and the following values have been adopted for them: $k = 20$, $\sigma = 5$.

In the experimental research we use 4 publicly available binary data sets from UCI machine learning repository. Table 3 presents the properties of the data sets which we used in experiments. For all data sets the feature selection process [8–10] was performed to indicate four most informative features.

Table 3. Properties of the data sets used in the experiments

Data sets	Features	Classes	Observations
Cancer	8	2	699
Parkinson	22	2	195
Pima	8	2	768
Sonar	60	2	208

Results for the fifty iterations of Gentle AdaBoost and Distance Score Boost algorithms are shown in Figs. 1, 2, 3, 4, 5, 6, 7 and 8. The results were presented for two measures of classification quality – classification error and kappa statistic. For Distance Score Boost algorithm the value of the parameter μ has been changed $\mu = 5, \mu = 10, \mu = 15$. Other parameters have not changed.

The obtained results indicate that the proposed algorithm can improve the quality of the classification in comparison to Gentle AdaBoost algorithm. The results depend on the data set and the quality of the classification is not always observed. In addition, the value of the parameter μ also affects the quality of the classification. For the examined data sets, the best value of this parameter is $\mu = 5$.

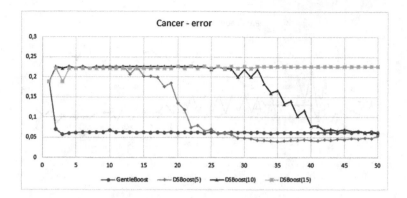

Fig. 1. The error for the Cancer data set

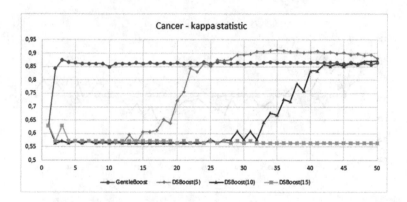

Fig. 2. The kappa statistic for the Cancer data set

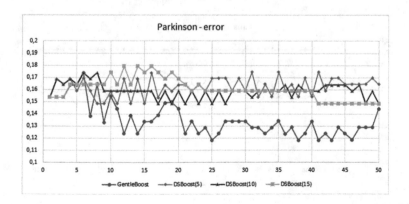

Fig. 3. The error for the Parkinson data set

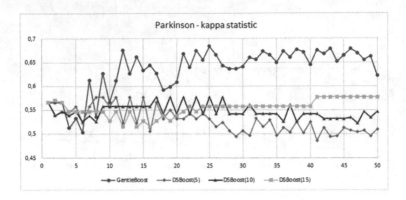

Fig. 4. The kappa statistic for the Parkinson data set

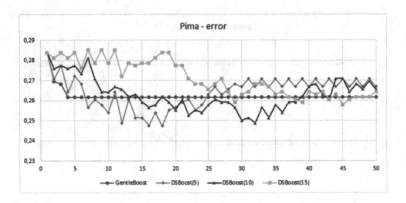

Fig. 5. The error for the Pima data set

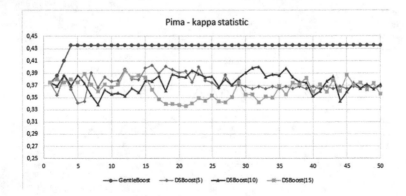

Fig. 6. The kappa statistic for the Pima data set

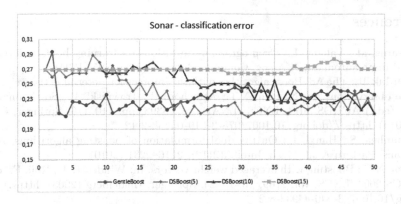

Fig. 7. The error for the Sonar data set

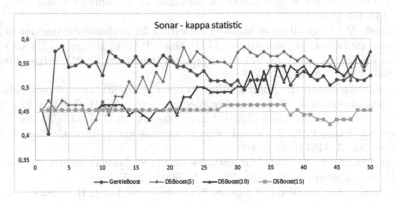

Fig. 8. The kappa statistic for the Sonar data set

5   Conclusions

In this paper we presented the new Distance Score Boost algorithm. It is a modification of Gentle AdaBoost algorithm where we use the score function, which depends on the distance from the decision boundary defined by each base (weak) classifier. The proposed function has no probabilistic interpretation. However, it determines the assurance of the object belonging to a class label that depends on the distance of the object from the decision boundary.

In this paper we focus on one parameter μ of the proposed method. In our future work, we want to extend our analyses to other parameters. In addition, we will adopt more kinds of boosting algorithms such as Real AdaBoost and Logit Boost.

Acknowledgments. This work was supported in part by the National Science Centre, Poland under the grant no. 2017/25/B/ST6/01750.

References

1. Kearns, M., Valiant, L.: Cryptographic limitations on learning boolean formulae and finite automata. J. Assoc. Comput. Mach. **41**(1), 67–95 (1994)
2. Burduk, R.: The AdaBoost algorithm with the imprecision determine the weights of the observations. In: Nguyen, N.T., Attachoo, B., Trawiński, B., Somboonviwat, K. (eds.) ACIIDS 2014. LNCS (LNAI), vol. 8398, pp. 110–116. Springer, Cham (2014). https://doi.org/10.1007/978-3-319-05458-2_12
3. Chunhua, S., Hanxi, L.: On the dual formulation of boosting algorithms. IEEE Trans. Pattern Anal. Mach. Intell. **32**(12), 2216–2231 (2010)
4. Oza, N.C.: Boosting with averaged weight vectors. In: Windeatt, T., Roli, F. (eds.) MCS 2003. LNCS, vol. 2709, pp. 15–24. Springer, Heidelberg (2003). https://doi.org/10.1007/3-540-44938-8_2
5. Freund, Y., Schapire, R.: Experiments with a new boosting algorithm. In: Proceedings of the Thirteenth International Conference on Machine Learning, Bari, Italy, pp. 148–156 (1996)
6. Wozniak, M.: Proposition of boosting algorithm for probabilistic decision support system. In: Bubak, M., van Albada, G.D., Sloot, P.M.A., Dongarra, J. (eds.) ICCS 2004. LNCS, vol. 3036, pp. 675–678. Springer, Heidelberg (2004). https://doi.org/10.1007/978-3-540-24685-5_117
7. Wu, S., Nagahashi, H.: Analysis of generalization ability for different AdaBoost variants based on classification and regression trees. J. Electr. Comput. Eng. **2015**, Article ID 835357, 17 pages (2015). https://doi.org/10.1155/2015/835357
8. Guyon, I., Elisseeff, A.: An introduction to variable and feature selection. J. Mach. Learn. Res. **3**, 1157–1182 (2003)
9. Rejer, I.: Genetic algorithms for feature selection for brain computer interface. Int. J. Pattern Recogn. Artif. Intell. **29**(5), 1559008 (2015)
10. Szenkovits, A., Meszlényi, R., Buza, K., Gaskó, N., Lung, R.I., Suciu, M.: Feature selection with a genetic algorithm for classification of brain imaging data. In: Stańczyk, U., Zielosko, B., Jain, L.C. (eds.) Advances in Feature Selection for Data and Pattern Recognition. ISRL, vol. 138, pp. 185–202. Springer, Cham (2018). https://doi.org/10.1007/978-3-319-67588-6_10
11. Freund, Y., Schapire, R.: A decision-theoretic generalization of on-line learning and an application to boosting. J. Comput. Syst. Sci. **55**(1), 119–139 (1997)
12. Dmitrienko, A., Chuang-Stein, C.: Pharmaceutical Statistics Using SAS: A Practical Guide. SAS Press, Cary (2007)

Software Development Metrics Prediction Using Time Series Methods

Michał Choraś[1,3], Rafał Kozik[1,3], Marek Pawlicki[1,3(✉)], Witold Hołubowicz[3], and Xavier Franch[2]

[1] ITTI Sp. z o.o., Poznań, Poland
mpawlicki@itti.com.pl
[2] GESSI, UPC, Barcelona, Spain
[3] UTP University of Science and Technology, Bydgoszcz, Poland

Abstract. The software development process is an intricate task, with the growing complexity of software solutions and inflating code-line count being part of the reason for the fall of software code coherence and readability thus being one of the causes for software faults and it's declining quality. Debugging software during development is significantly less expensive than attempting damage control after the software's release. An automated quality-related analysis of developed code, which includes code analysis and correlation of development data like an ideal solution. In this paper the ability to predict software faults and software quality is scrutinized. Hereby we investigate four models that can be used to analyze time-based data series for prediction of trends observed in the software development process are investigated. Those models are Exponential Smoothing, the Holt-Winters Model, Autoregressive Integrated Moving Average (ARIMA) and Recurrent Neural Networks (RNN). Time-series analysis methods prove a good fit for software related data prediction. Such methods and tools can lend a helping hand for Product Owners in their daily decision-making process as related to e.g. assignment of tasks, time predictions, bugs predictions, time to release etc. Results of the research are presented.

Keywords: Software engineering · Software development ·
Prediction · Metrics · Time series

1 Introduction and Context

Nowadays, increasing interdependences among software components can be observed in the IT domain. Every industry relying on software solutions is impacted by software development challenges, and with the domain being a growing one, it has a fair share of such issues. Some of them include optimization of the software code development process, minimization of the risk of software failures (quality assurance, code testing/debugging) and the software solutions security. Those aspects - to be addressed during the code development - are critical for businesses, service providers, end customers, and thus for society as a whole.

© Springer Nature Switzerland AG 2019
K. Saeed et al. (Eds.): CISIM 2019, LNCS 11703, pp. 311–323, 2019.
https://doi.org/10.1007/978-3-030-28957-7_26

A diverse range of interests by different stakeholders is involved in the issues related to code quality and code development optimization, making it a complex, intricate, multifaceted issue. Some of those facets include:

- Growing complexity of software solutions in terms of code lines volume - software solutions become increasingly more sophisticated, with the total number of code lines inflating several hundred percent with each subsequent release. Desktop applications, mobile OS or web-based solutions contain millions of lines of code, with e.g. all Google web services exceeding 2 billion lines [11]. The abovementioned trend of growing source code volume poses serious challenges in analysis, processing and reasoning from such data. It becomes a big data exploration problem, especially in the case of near real-time analysis and prediction.
- The emerging trend of including software components in IoT assets, microdevices, smart home systems, smart city systems, etc. adding to that the spike in popularity of cloud-based interconnection of assets.
- The software quality dictates the reputation, market position and competitiveness of the product vendors. The estimates state that a software bug can cause a fall in the product stock price by an average of 4% to 6% (for companies experiencing multiple software failures). This generates almost 3 billion dollars of market losses (QASymphony 2016, [23]). Moreover, substandard quality of code impacts the overall cost of the software development, deployment and maintenance [12]. According to QASymphony data, the process of debugging software during its design phase costs 4 to 5 times less than that of fixing bugs after its release.
- The growing cost of software testing and debugging - although the process of debugging software during its design phase costs significantly less than fixing bugs after its release, it is still non-trivial task that consumes a significant part of budgets and companies' effort. It might have less of an impact for bulky companies and software houses. However SMEs and small entities providing software solutions, often operating on constrained budgets and finite resources, are becoming increasingly more focused on techniques allowing automation and adequacy of the testing process, to be competitive in relation to big players on the market [9]. The costs of quality assurance and testing in IT are growing from each year. Currently, IT organizations spend approximately 1/3 of their budgets on quality assurance with the trend of inflating this value to approx. 40% in the next three years [5, 20].
- Raising concerns about the software (or solutions including software components) security - software flaws and bugs can impact not only the usability, functional value and user experience, but also the security of users. This is due to the fact that bugs in the design or implementation phase can be exploited by cyber-criminals. According to the article presented by [1], consequences of cyber attacks cost the British companies about 18 billion per year in terms of lost revenues.

Based on the above considerations, we state that there is a clear need for decision makers (project managers, product owners, development team leaders) in the software engineering process for an automated quality-related analysis of developed code. This should include code analysis and correlation of development data derived from available tools with management-related issues such as effort allocation, scheduling, workload accumulation and others.

Moreover, we believe that accurate prediction of such indicators can be beneficial in the software development process optimization and can raise the overall quality of software products and reduce further debugging and maintenance costs. In reality, one of the typical needs and challenges for product owners in their daily duties is to plan and predict time estimates for the current and future tasks in backlogs. Of course, those decisions depend on predicting other fundamental aspects like estimated foreseen number of bugs, failed tests as well as other software related and process metrics.

In the previous work of the H2020 Q-Rapids project consortium [10,14,15, 17,22], the concept of quality-aware decision making based on key strategic indicators is proposed. The overall goal of the project is to support strategic decision-making processes by providing strategic indicators in the context of quality requirements in agile and rapid software development. For the purposes of the project, a strategic indicator is defined as a specific aspect that a software development company has to consider as crucial for the decision making process during software development. Aspects such as e.g. time-to-market, maintenance cost, customer satisfaction, etc. can be considered as strategic indicators depending on the context. These strategic indicators are built on top of the measurements and factors calculated on the basis of the software development related data, stored in the management tools such as GitLab or SonarQube.

While in the previous work we focused on the data gathering and processing it towards quality metrics, indicators and requirements generation [7,21], we hereby target the prediction of the software related metrics.

The paper is structured as follows: in Sect. 2 an overview of time series methods and models is provided. In Sect. 3 the sample prediction results are presented. Conclusions are drawn thereafter.

2 Time Series Analysis

In this paper we investigate four models that can be used to analyze time-based data series for prediction of trends observed in the software development process, based on the information obtained from mentioned tools (e.g. GitLab). Those models are (1) Exponential Smoothing, (2) Holt-Winters Model, (3) Autoregressive Integrated Moving Average (ARIMA) and (4) Recurrent Neural Networks (RNN).

Time series analysis can be defined as the decomposition of a given X_t signal into a trend T_t, a seasonal component S_t and the residual component e_t (an example is shown in Fig. 1).

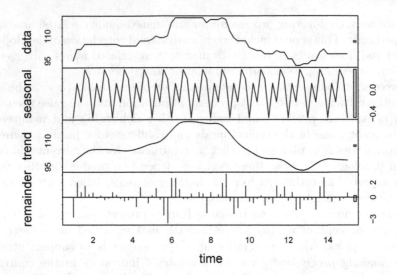

Fig. 1. Seasonal decompositioning of signal representing number of open issues in Git-Lab repository management system.

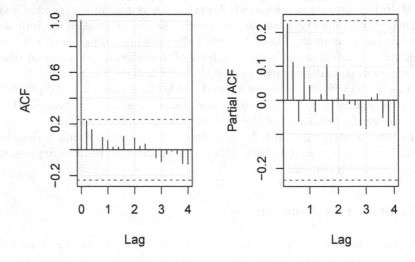

Fig. 2. ACF and PACF correlograms

The simplest way to obtain the trend of a signal is to use linear filter on the X_t:

$$T_t = \sum_{i=-\infty}^{\infty} \lambda_i X_{t+i} \tag{1}$$

An example of linear filter is a moving average with equal weights:

$$T_t = \frac{1}{2a+1} \sum_{i=-a}^{a} X_{t+i} \tag{2}$$

2.1 Exponential Smoothing

Exponential smoothing is a method for refining time series data using the exponential window function. In contrast to the simple moving average technique, the forecasting of data trends using exponential smoothing is characterized by exponentially decreasing weights of past observations, instead of equally weighted observations. This method is especially beneficial in forecasting time series characterized by a low variation of trend and seasonal changes. Numerous recent works show the viability of exponential smoothing for prediction purposes. In the project management area, [3] and [13] propose improvements to well-known Earned Value Management (EVM) project control methodology and Earned Duration Index (EDI) parameter by enhancing it with exponential smoothing to predict project progress and calculate project completion time and cost. In both cases, application of exponential smoothing was easy to incorporate to the traditional forecasting methodologies, raised their accuracy and reduced errors. For example, EVM enhanced by this technique led to the production of 14.8% more accurate time predictions and 25.1% more accurate cost predictions based on the data from 23 real-life projects examined by [3]. Exponential smoothing has been also applied to forecast financial/industrial indicators and variable physical quantities. [29] propose three methods using exponential smoothing to predict solar irradiance over time, based on historical data. Three variations of the method were examined: exponential smoothing with seasonal-trend decomposition, Global Horizontal Irradiance (GHI) time series decomposition (forecasted separately into a direct component and a diffuse component and then recombined) and the regression-based reconstruct of GHI through employing exponential smoothing for cloud coverage forecasting. [26] compared several methods based on exponential smoothing to forecast palm oil production in a given time. Those were: single ES, double ES (Holt Model), triple ES (Holt-Winters Model), triple ES additive and multiplicative. Due to the fact that historical data contain a seasonal component, authors recommend triple exponential smoothing additive as the suggested method for prediction, in this case, giving a smaller error value in the forecasted results.

Exponential smoothing predicts the next value of a given time series using geometric weighted sum of past data samples.

$$\hat{x}_{t=r}(1) = \alpha \cdot x_r + \alpha(1-\alpha) \cdot x_{r-1} + \alpha(1-\alpha)^2 \cdot x_{r-2} + \cdots \tag{3}$$

However, the exponential smoothing model should only be used with signals that have no systematic trend and seasonal components.

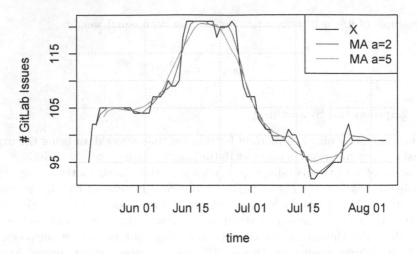

Fig. 3. Original signal X and moving averages $a = 2$ and $a = 5$

2.2 Holt-Winters Model

Triple exponential smoothing (called Holt-Winters Model) is an example of a method appropriate for forecasting data points in a series that are repetitive over a given period (are "seasonal"). One of the cases studied in literature and similar to our work, where the seasonal component can impact the overall prediction of a given phenomenon is in software reliability forecasting, addressed by [27]. Authors experimented with non-parametric method for prediction of the number of software bugs in a testing environment, employing the Holt-Winters model and comparing it to well-known parametric software reliability models. According to the study, parametric models developed for prediction of software reliability generally assume that bug detection process is a Markov process or a non-homogeneous Poisson process, that the fault intensity is proportional to the number of remaining faults and fault detection rate is constant. Authors have noticed an advantage of non-parametric methods (such as exponential smoothing) over parametric ones through a decreased volume of historical data and a reduced computational effort necessary to obtain accurate predictions. Specifically, using double or triple exponential smoothing (which addresses seasonal variations as well) reduces the impact of predicted abnormal data and eliminates the interference. The experimental results show that use of Holt-Winters model pays off not only in better forecasting than double exponential smoothing and than traditional, parametric models, but also that it results in extremely accurate predictions in terms of a precise number of software failures emerging in the future. Apart from software engineering, numerous publications address the problem of forecasting of seasonal variations with the use of the Holt-Winters method in domains other than software engineering. For example, [25] uses triple exponential smoothing to predict cloud resource provisioning to model cloud workload with multi-seasonal cycles, while some other sources examine Holt-Winters model in seasonal sales prediction and tourist attendance peaks forecasting.

As described above, the Holt-Winters model can be used in order to deal with the limitations of the exponential smoothing model. The Holt-Winters model has three smoothing parameters, namely α (for the constant level value), β (for the trend), and γ (for seasonal variations).

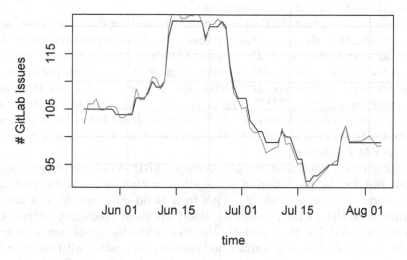

Fig. 4. Holt-Winters fitted model (red) for GitLab issues time series (black) (Color figure online)

2.3 ARIMA

ARIMA stands for Autoregressive Integrated Moving Average. ARIMA is composed of an autoregressive and a moving average model, where the autoregression

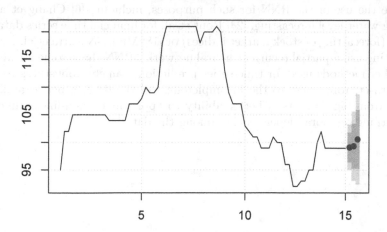

Fig. 5. Holt-Winters prediction for next 3 days. The gray bars indicate the confidence levels (95% dark gray and 80% light gray) (Color figure online)

model involves regressing the variables based on past values. The model is commonly denoted as ARIMA(p,d,q) where parameters p, d, and q are non-negative integers, which control three main components of the model: (i) the order (the number of time lags) of the autoregressive model, (ii) the degree of differencing, and (iii) the order of the moving-average.

It must be noted that ARIMA models are defined for stationary time series. In order to obtain it, the non-stationary time series has to be differenced until the non-stationarity is eliminated. The number of differencing iterations corresponds to the d parameter of the model. In order to chose the other two parameters (p and q) we must analyze the autocorrelation diagram (ACF) and the partial autocorrelation diagram (PACF). From the diagram shown in Fig. 2, we may conclude that p will be 0, because ACF function drops below the significance threshold (dashed line) after lag 0. Similarly, we can estimate the $q = 0$ value using the PACF diagram.

Autoregressive Integrated Moving Average (ARIMA) is a technique successfully applied for the prediction of non-stationary time series in different areas (e.g. finances or cybersecurity [2]). QoS in a cloud environment is a case for examination of the ARIMA model for cloud workload prediction purposes [4]. Authors concluded that their model is able to improve the prediction accuracy of up to 91%, contributing to a better cloud resources allocation with no impact on the cloud environment performance. ARIMA has also been studied for the purposes of prediction in software engineering. For example, a comparative analysis of ARIMA, neural networks and a hybrid technique for Debian bug number prediction can be found in [19], where a model including a combination of ARIMA an Artificial Neural Networks has been presented as a promising approach to improve prediction accuracy. On the other hand, [16] shows that hybrid model based on the Singular Spectrum Analysis (SSA) and ARIMA outperforms other models in prediction of software failures during the software testing process.

Furthermore, Recurrent Neural Networks (RNN) gain traction in the context of forecasting and prediction based on time series data. A number of publications describe the use of the RNN for such purposes, including [6] Chang et al. for flooding water level forecasting, [24] Rout et al. for financial time series data prediction (forecasting of stock market indices) or [18] Muller-Navarra et al. for sales forecasting using partial recurrent neural networks. RNNs have some advantages over other methods used for time series prediction, namely: robustness to noise in a dataset, robustness to the incompleteness of the data, a better ability to predict from big datasets, a better ability to approximate non-linear functions and learning temporal dependencies among the data [8].

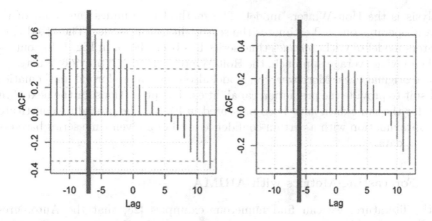

Fig. 6. Identified correlated facts: backlog size and the cognitive complexity (left), backlog size and the number of duplicated lines (right).

3 Prediction of Software Metrics Using Time Series Analysis

In our research we have used real data coming from SW development team working on commercial and research IT products (web applications) from several projects. The software team consists of up to 10 individuals, and they extensively use GitLab and SonarQube. According to the procedure described in the previous publications concerning Q-Rapids approach to data gathering and analysis, we have created connectors to those software management tools in order to calculate metrics, factors and strategic indicators. Hereby, our work facilitates adding the prediction aspect to help product owners in their daily decision making.

3.1 Predicting Metrics Trends

In our research we have attempted the application of numerous Time Series prediction methods with regard to software quality and fault prediction. The first of the discussed methods utilizes simple moving averages. The moving average is a useful tool that smooths out input signal. The algorithm calculates the average over a specific period of time. Among others, it helps to eliminate the noise from the input time series. In principle, a moving average with a short time frame will react faster to signal changes than a moving average with a longer time period. Two moving averages (for a time period a = 2 and a = 5), are shown in Fig. 3. In the presented example we have used a moving average to analyse a number of issues opened in a repository manager (in our case GitLab). The common use case of two moving averages is as follows. When the moving average with a shorter period crosses above the moving average with a longer one it may indicate that the trend of the observed signal will be rising. For example, we can see this for June 14 in Fig. 3. A more sophisticated approach for time series analysis is the Holt-Winters model. The method determines the trend of the data it operates on, and estimates the seasonality of the series. The fitted Holt-Winters model of GitLab issues time series has been shown in Fig. 4. In contrast to the moving average approach, the Holt-Winters algorithm provides a better fit for the original data. Moreover, the model also uses a more formal mathematical tool suit to provide the prediction capabilities. The predictions for the next three days for the same data have been presented in Fig. 5. The procedure constitutes an approximation with a certain confidence level of a given time series based on the raw data.

3.2   Forecasting Metrics with ARIMA

In the literature, we can find numerous examples [28] that the Autoregressive Integrated Moving Average often outperforms the Holt-Winters algorithm. Therefore, forecasting using the ARIMA model has also been attempted in this work.

In general, we have observed that ARIMA seasonal model allowed us to achieve a higher (than the Holt-Winters algorithm) fitting degree and lower forecasting error. For example, in Fig. 6 we have shown, that for a short time frame prediction, the ARIMA model allowed us to identify that the increasing trend of number of items in sprint backlog may cause deterioration of the code quality (increased cognitive complexity and number of duplicated lines). In that case we have used 3 ARIMA models: one to predict the backlog size, one to predict the cognitive complexity, and one to predict the number of duplicated lines. Statistically significant correlations have been spotted with auto correlation function (ACF).

4   Quantitative Evaluation of Prediction Models

In this section we have formally evaluated different prediction models used to forecast various projects and software quality metrics. We have used commonly adapted forecast accuracy metrics, such as RMSE (Root Squared Mean Error), MAE (Mean Absolute Error), MASE (Mean Absolute Scaled Error), and MAPE (Mean Absolute Percentage Error). For each metric we define error as forecast error, which is a deviation e_{T+h} of the forecast $\hat{y}_{T+h}$ from the observation y_{T+h} within a predefined time lag h:

$$e_{T+h} = y_{T+h} - \hat{y}_{T+h} \tag{4}$$

Moreover, here we assume that we split the time series y in to a training set $\{y_1, \cdots, y_T\}$ and testing set $\{y_T, y_{T+1} \cdots\}$. In our experiments we have evaluated the prediction effectiveness of following models, namely (described in previous section) ARIMA and Holt-Winters, and random walk forecast. The effectiveness results for different scenarios have been reported in Tables 1, 2 and 3.

Table 1. Effectiveness comparison of forecast models (sprint backlog size)

	RMSE	MAE	MASE	MAPE
ARIMA	0.448	0.281	9.258	16.830
Random Walk	0.496	0.335	11.267	19.492
Holt-Winters	0.570	0.409	14.669	24.526

In the first experiments we have used different forecasting models to predict amount of task in a sprint backlog. The results show that the ARIMA model achieves the lowest error rates. Surprisingly, we may notice that the highest errors are reported for Holt-Winters prediction model.

Table 2. Effectiveness comparison of forecast models (tasks in progress)

	RMSE	MAE	MASE	MAPE
ARIMA	0.268	0.160	11.339	12.561
Random Walk	0.286	0.215	14.773	17.995
Holt-Winters	0.308	0.235	16.836	19.124

We have identified the similar results also for other metrics, namely the number of task under development (tasks in progress) and the number of delayed tasks.

Table 3. Effectiveness comparison of forecast models (delayed tasks)

	RMSE	MAE	MASE	MAPE
ARIMA	0.369	0.161	223.958	7.208
Random Walk	0.487	0.251	171.567	13.963
Holt-Winters	0.671	0.461	55.947	24.017

5   Conclusions

In this paper we have addressed the problem of the analysis of the software development and quality data. Our thesis was that the time-series analysis methods are well suited to the challenge of software related data prediction. Such methods and tools (e.g. offered by H2020 Q-Rapids Project) can be helpful to Product Owners in their daily decisions related to e.g. assignment of tasks, time predictions, bugs predictions, time to release etc. We conducted our experiments on real case data in order to forecast various project-related characteristics. We have compared different forecasting tools such as ARIMA, Random Walk, and Holt-Winters. Our experiments have shown that ARIMA model performs well on our data. It achieved the lowest prediction errors among compared ones.

Acknowledgments. This work is funded under Q-Rapids project, which has received funding from the European Union's Horizon 2020 research and innovation programme under grant agreement No. 732253.

References

1. Tovey, A.: Cyber attacks cost British industry 34bn a year (2018). http://www.telegraph.co.uk/finance/newsbysector/industry/defence/11663761/Cyber-attacks-cost-British-industry-34bn-a-year.html
2. Andrysiak, T., Saganowski, Ł., Choraś, M., Kozik, R.: Network traffic prediction and anomaly detection based on ARFIMA model. In: de la Puerta, J.G., et al. (eds.) International Joint Conference SOCO'14-CISIS'14-ICEUTE'14. AISC, vol. 299, pp. 545–554. Springer, Cham (2014). https://doi.org/10.1007/978-3-319-07995-0_54
3. Batselier, J., Vanhoucke, M.: Improving project forecast accuracy by integrating earned value management with exponential smoothing and reference class forecasting. Int. J. Project Manage. **35**(1), 28–43 (2017)
4. Calheiros, R.N., Masoumi, E., Ranjan, R., Buyya, R.: Workload prediction using ARIMA model and its impact on cloud applications' QoS. IEEE Trans. Cloud Comput. **3**(4), 449–458 (2015)
5. Capgemini. Capgemini: World Quality Report 2016–17 (2017). https://www.capgemini.com/world-quality-report-2016-17/. Accessed 9 Oct 2017
6. Chang, F.-J., Chen, P.-A., Ying-Ray, L., Huang, E., Chang, K.-Y.: Real-time multi-step-ahead water level forecasting by recurrent neural networks for urban flood control. J. Hydrol. **517**, 836–846 (2014)
7. Choraś, M., Kozik, R., Puchalski, D., Renk, R.: Increasing product owners' cognition and decision-making capabilities by data analysis approach. Cogn. Technol. Work **21**(2), 191–200 (2019)
8. Dorffner, G.: Neural networks for time series processing. Neural Netw. World **6**, 447–468 (1996)
9. Felderer, M., Ramler, R.: Risk orientation in software testing processes of small and medium enterprises: an exploratory and comparative study. Softw. Qual. J. **24**, 519–548 (2015)
10. Franch, X., et al.: Data-driven requirements engineering in agile projects: the Q-rapids approach, pp. 411–414, September 2017
11. Desjardins, J.: QASymphony, how many millions of lines of code does it take? (2017). https://informationisbeautiful.net/visualizations/million-lines-of-code/
12. Jones, C., Bonsignour, O.: The Economics of Software Quality, 1st edn. Addison-Wesley Professional, Boston (2011)
13. Khamooshi, H., Abdi, A.: Project duration forecasting using earned duration management with exponential smoothing techniques. J. Manage. Eng. **33**, 04016032 (2016)
14. Kozik, R., Choraś, M., Puchalski, D., Renk, R.: Platform for software quality and dependability data analysis. In: Zamojski, W., Mazurkiewicz, J., Sugier, J., Walkowiak, T., Kacprzyk, J. (eds.) DepCoS-RELCOMEX 2018. AISC, vol. 761, pp. 306–315. Springer, Cham (2019). https://doi.org/10.1007/978-3-319-91446-6_29
15. Guzmán, L., Oriol, M., Rodríguez, P., Franch, X., Jedlitschka, A., Oivo, M.: How can quality awareness support rapid software development? – A research preview. In: Grünbacher, P., Perini, A. (eds.) REFSQ 2017. LNCS, vol. 10153, pp. 167–173. Springer, Cham (2017). https://doi.org/10.1007/978-3-319-54045-0_12

16. Liu, G., Zhang, D., Zhang, T.: Software reliability forecasting: singular spectrum analysis and ARIMA hybrid model, pp. 111–118, September 2015
17. López, L., et al.: Q-rapids tool prototype: supporting decision-makers in managing quality in rapid software development. In: Mendling, J., Mouratidis, H. (eds.) CAiSE 2018. LNBIP, vol. 317, pp. 200–208. Springer, Cham (2018). https://doi.org/10.1007/978-3-319-92901-9_17
18. Müller-Navarra, M., Lessmann, S., Voß, S.: Sales forecasting with partial recurrent neural networks: empirical insights and benchmarking results. In: 2015 48th Hawaii International Conference on System Sciences, pp. 1108–1116 (2015)
19. Pati, J., Shukla, K.K.: A comparison of ARIMA, neural network and a hybrid technique for Debian bug number prediction, pp. 47–53, September 2014
20. Jorgensen, P.C.: Software testing: a craftsman's approach (2016)
21. Kozik, R., Choraś, M., Puchalski, D., Renk, R.: Q-rapids framework for advanced data analysis to improve rapid software development. J. Ambient Intell. Hum. Comput. **10**, 1927–1936 (2019)
22. Q-Rapids: Q-rapids H2020 project (2018). http://www.q-rapids.eu/
23. QASymphony: QASymphony, The Cost of Poor Software Quality (2016). https://www.qasymphony.com/blog/cost-poor-software-quality/
24. Rout, A.K., Dash, P.K., Dash, R., Bisoi, R.: Forecasting financial time series using a low complexity recurrent neural network and evolutionary learning approach. J. King Saud Univ. - Comput. Inform. Sci. **29**(4), 536–552 (2017)
25. Shahin, A.A.: Using multiple seasonal holt-winters exponential smoothing to predict cloud resource provisioning. CoRR, abs/1701.03296 (2016)
26. Siregar, B., Butar-Butar, I.A., Rahmat, R.F., Andayani, U., Fahmi, F.: Comparison of exponential smoothing methods in forecasting palm oil real production. J. Phys.: Conf. Ser. **801**(1), 012004 (2017)
27. Wang, J., Wu, Z., Shu, Y., Zhang, Z., Xue, L.: A Study on software reliability prediction based on triple exponential smoothing method (WIP), pp. 61:1–61:9 (2014)
28. Wang, Z.-H., Lu, C.-Y., Pu, B., Li, G.-W., Guo, Z.-J.: Short-term forecast model of vehicles volume based on ARIMA seasonal model and holt-winters. In: ITM Web Conferrence, vol. 12, p. 04028 (2017)
29. Yang, D., Sharma, V., Ye, Z., Lim, L.I., Zhao, L., Aryaputera, A.W.: Forecasting of global horizontal irradiance by exponential smoothing, using decompositions. Energy **81**, 111–119 (2015)

Tag-Cloud Based Recommendation for Movies

Sambo Dutta[1], Soumita Das[1], Joydeep Das[2(✉)], and Subhashis Majumder[1]

[1] Department of Computer Science and Engineering, Heritage Institute of
Technology, Kolkata, WB, India
sambodutta@gmail.com, soumitamum210@gmail.com,
subhashis.majumder@heritageit.edu
[2] The Heritage Academy, Kolkata, WB, India
joydeep.das@heritageit.edu

Abstract. Most of the recommendation systems aim to make suggestions for individuals rather than a group of users. However, people are
sociable and most of the items to be recommended like movies, restau-
rants, tourist destinations, etc. are for group consumption. Making recommendations for a group is not a trivial task due to the diverse and
conflicting interests of the group members. In this paper, we present a
framework for recommending movies to a group of users. Existing recommendation systems for movies use users' ratings as a measure to suggest
individual recommendations or use them to generate the group profile
by using aggregation methods in case of group recommendations. In this
work, we focus on two things: exploiting the tags assigned to the movies
by the users and leveraging the semantic information present in them to
make recommendations. The assigned tags along with their weightages
are used to form tag clouds for individual group members as well as for
movies. Following this a *Group Score* is computed for each movie on the
basis of the content similarity of the tag cloud of the group and the tag
cloud of the movie. The movies having *top-N Group Score* are recommended to the group. To verify the effectiveness of this framework, experiments have been conducted on the MovieLens-10M and MovieLens-20M
datasets. Results obtained clearly demonstrate how the accuracy of the
recommendations increase with the increase in the homogeneity of preferences within the group members.

Keywords: Group recommendation · Movie tags · Tag cloud ·
Similarity measure

1 Introduction

The objective of any recommendation system is to predict the items that a user
may like or dislike among a list of items. Recommendation systems are of two categories namely collaborative filtering (CF) and content based filtering. CF based
systems rely on the past user interaction with the items in the database such
as user ratings, votes, etc. [16], while content based systems simple rely on the
analysis of the content associated with users or items [9]. In recent years group
recommendations are becoming popular [1,6]. Due to the diversity of interests
in a single group, it becomes a challenge to make recommendations of items for

© Springer Nature Switzerland AG 2019
K. Saeed et al. (Eds.): CISIM 2019, LNCS 11703, pp. 324–336, 2019.
https://doi.org/10.1007/978-3-030-28957-7_27

a group which will be in accordance with the preferences of most of the group members. In literature, there are two most common strategies to generate group recommendations. The first recommendation strategy is to generate personalized recommendations for each group member. Subsequently, these individual recommendation lists are merged based on different aggregation techniques to generate a single recommendation list that cater to the interests of the group as a whole [1]. The second strategy is to employ the aggregation techniques to generate a group profile by combining individual preferences [5]. This group profile is then treated as a pseudo user and recommendations are made using traditional recommendation algorithms. In this paper, we employ the second strategy.

Most of the group recommendation systems developed till now implement CF technique [1,13] to generate the group profile. However, the semantic information available in the tags or reviews of the group members have not been fully explored. In this work, we propose a framework that primarily relies on the tags assigned to the movies by the users and the frequency of their occurrences. These tags not only help in capturing the content of the movies but the frequency of occurrence also helps in estimating the correct weightage of the tags among the group members. The tags and their corresponding weightages are used to compute the individual tag clouds of the group members and also the tag clouds of the movies to be considered for recommendation. Following this, a group tag cloud is generated by combining the individual tag clouds based on aggregation techniques. This group tag cloud is then compared with the movie tag cloud to compute the similarity score between the two using the lexical database Word-Net [3,7]. We name this similarity score as *Group Score* and on the basis of this score *top-N* recommendations are generated for the group. In case of identical *Group Score*, movies having a higher *Popularity Score* are ranked higher. *Popularity Score* is the measure of the popularity of a movie in terms of the number of unique users who tagged it. Our recommendation framework with different modules is depicted in Fig. 1. We have verified our algorithm using Precision and Normalized Discounted Cumulative Gain ($nDCG$) metrics on MovieLens-10M and Movielens-20M datasets. Experimental results show that precision and $nDCG$ values improve when the similarity between group members is higher. Finally, we state that our proposed design is not only simple but can also be easily extended to make group recommendations on items other than movies.

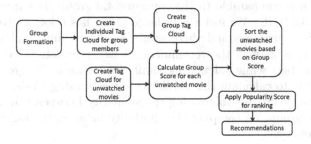

Fig. 1. Our framework

2   Related Work

In the domain of movies, Polylens is the first recommender system that provides recommendations for groups of users [11]. It is a CF based group recommender system, where a single neighborhood is formed for the group and then the individual recommendations are merged based on least misery technique. Research pertaining to aggregating individual recommendations produced by a CF method to generate group recommendations was addressed by Baltrunas et al. [1]. Recommendations for a group of users were built using 5 rank aggregation techniques and were tested for group having 2, 3, 4 and 8 members. Removal of natural noise (biasness) in ratings becomes a challenge for group recommender systems. Castro et al. [4] developed a fuzzy tool for noise removal from ratings in order to provide more accurate group recommendations by incorporating fuzzy profiling, global and local noise management. Seo et al. [14] added a deviation element to the aggregation method used for providing group recommendations. Items with low deviations are preferred over items with high deviations. GroupReM is a group recommender system that instead of using user ratings, leverages the semantic information from tags to generate recommendations [12]. Although it uses word-correlation factor to find movies based on group preferences, it ignores the weightage of each tag in the individual or the group profile. In our work, we have employed the tag cloud technique [15] to assign a correct weightage to each tag, which helps to depict the preferences of individuals or of the group as a whole accurately. We then go on to find the tag similarity to predict movies to groups based on the similarity between the group tag cloud and the movie tag cloud using an appropriate scoring system.

3   Our Framework

3.1   Group Formation

The first task of any group recommendation system is to form groups of optimal size. However, to the best of our knowledge none of the available datasets that are used to evaluate recommender systems provide built-in groups of users. Our primary focus is to form cohesive groups having optimal sizes from the users present in the MovieLens dataset. We have varied the group size between 3 to 8 members which is comparable to the experimental group sizes used in some of the earlier works [1,12]. We feel a very large group has a lot of diversity in the preferences of its members and there would hardly be any similarity between their choices, thus making the recommendations irrelevant. Since we are only considering the tags while calculating similarity between the group members, it is not possible to calculate this similarity directly using Cosine similarity or Euclidean distance. So, for calculating the similarity between two users (say u_1 and u_2) of the group, we compute the similarity between the tag clouds of the two users as follows.

$$Similarity\,(u_1, u_2) = \frac{1}{n} \sum_{i=1}^{n} \max_{1 \leq j \leq m} sim\,(tag_{i\_u_1}, tag_{j\_u_2}) \qquad (1)$$

where, n is the number of tags in the tag cloud of user u_1, m is the number of tags in the tag cloud of user u_2 and $sim()$ is a function that calculates the similarity between two tags using the lexical database WordNet [7]. Note that $similarity\,(u_1, u_2) \neq similarity\,(u_2, u_1)$. Equation 1 ensures that when one tag, say t_1 in the tag cloud of u_1 is exactly matched with a tag, say t_2 in the tag cloud of u_2, it is not penalized for the lower similarity measure between t_1 and any other tag in tag cloud of user u_2. Thus two users with exactly the same tag clouds will always have a similarity of 1. Note that the similarity value for an ordered pair of users will always lie in the range [0, 1]. Finally, for the Group Similarity, we take an average of all the user pair similarities. This ensures that the Group Similarity is also in the range [0, 1]. In our work, we randomly form groups of a predetermined number of users to verify our algorithm.

3.2 Individual Tag Cloud Formation

A tag cloud of an individual user consists of the tags and their corresponding frequencies used by that user. Once we find the tag that has been used most frequently, along with its frequency of occurrence, we use this frequency as the $max\_uTag\_frequency$ for that user. Subsequently, we calculate the weightage for each tag in the tag cloud of the user, $userNum$ using the following formula:

$$Weightage(userNum, usertag) = \frac{frequency_{usertag}}{max\_uTag\_frequency} \qquad (2)$$

where, $frequency_{usertag}$ is the frequency of the tag. By assigning this weightage we have a measure of the relevance of each tag to the user. Equation 2 gives us a tag weightage which lies in the range [0, 1]. Table 1 shows a sample user tag cloud. In the example given in Table 1, $classic$ is the most frequently used tag. Thus the $max\_uTag\_frequency$ will be 6. We calculate the weightage by dividing the individual frequency of each tag by 6. Using the above procedure we form individual tag clouds for all the group members.

Table 1. A sample user tag cloud

Tags	Frequency	Weightage
Classic	6	1
Cult	3	0.5
Sequel	5	0.83
Drama	1	0.16

3.3   Group Tag Cloud Formation

In this module, we merge all the individual tag clouds of the group members to form the group tag cloud. First we list the tag clouds belonging to a group and then add the weightages of each tag assigned by the group members. After this addition operation we divide this group weightage of each individual tag in the group tag cloud by the total number of members in the group to get the average weightage for the group as shown in Eq. 3. This ensures that all the weightages of the tags lie in the range $[0, 1]$.

$$Group\_Weightage(usertag) = \frac{\sum_{i=1}^{n} Weightage(i, usertag)}{n} \qquad (3)$$

where $usertag$ is a tag in the group tag cloud, n is the number of group members and $Weightage(i, usertag)$ maps the weightage of that particular tag in the tag cloud of user i using Eq. 2. If a tag is not present in the tag cloud of user i its weightage is considered to be 0. Figure 2 shows an example of a tag cloud. Here we have three user tag clouds $U1$, $U2$ and $U3$ and the corresponding group tag cloud G generated by merging the user tag clouds. The tag $classic$ occurs both in the tag cloud of $U1$ and $U3$ but not present in the tag cloud of $U2$. We calculate its weightage in the group tag cloud by adding the weightages of $classic$ for users $U1$ and $U3$, and then dividing the sum by the number of users in the group, which is 3. So the group weightage for $classic$ is $(1 + 0 + 0.16)/3 = 0.38$. In spite of being the most used tag in the user tag cloud $U1$, the weightage of $classic$ reduces in the group since it has a low weightage for $U3$ and is absent in the tag cloud of $U2$. Thus we obtain a normalized weightage measure for all the tags in the group tag cloud.

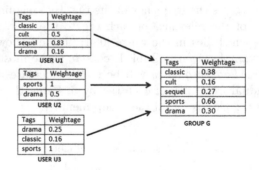

Fig. 2. A sample group tag cloud

3.4   Movie Tag Cloud Generation

We first list all the movies in the dataset which has not been watched by any of the group members. Next we develop a scoring system for all the unwatched movies and rank them. To calculate the *Group Score* for an unwatched movie we need to compare the similarity in content of the group tag cloud and the movie tag cloud. Hence we need to generate the movie tag cloud first. The procedure for forming the movie tag cloud is similar to the one used for forming individual user tag cloud. Here, all the tags ever used by any user to describe a particular movie are listed. Following this the frequency of each unique tag is calculated and we use the frequency of the tag, which is used most frequently in the tag cloud of the movie as the $max\_mTag\_frequency$ for that movie. The weightage for each tag in the tag cloud of the movie $movieNum$ is then calculated using the following formula:

$$Weightage(movieNum, movietag) = \frac{frequency_{movietag}}{max\_mTag\_frequency} \qquad (4)$$

where $frequency_{movietag}$ corresponds to the frequency associated with this tag. This weightage forms the basis for measuring the relevance of each tag assigned to the movie. Equation 4 gives us a weightage of all the tags in the range $[0, 1]$. An example of a movie tag cloud is shown in Table 2.

Table 2. A sample movie tag cloud

Tags	Frequency	Weightage
Classic	3	0.5
Cult	6	1
Animation	5	0.83
Action	1	0.16

3.5 Calculating Group Score

Once the movie tag clouds are formed we compare these tag clouds with our group tag cloud to assign the *Group Score* for the unwatched movies. We use WordNet [7] to compare the similarity between two tags. It groups English words into sets of synonyms called synsets, provides short definitions and usage examples, and records a number of relations among these synonym sets or their members. WordNet can thus be seen as a combination of dictionary and thesaurus. The similarity value returned by WordNet lies in the range $[0, 1]$ based on how closely related the two tags are. We get a value of 1 if the two tags are an exact match or if they are highly linked and a value of 0 if they are highly dissimilar. Now, with this similarity measure we multiply the weightage of the two corresponding tags to get a score. Since both the movie tag cloud and the group tag cloud may consist of a large number of tags, we will be comparing each tag from the group tag cloud with each of the tags in the movie tag cloud. From this list of scores the maximum score will be selected as the *Group Score* for that movie. The *Group Score* for a movie mov is calculated as follows.

$$GroupScore = \max_{1 \leq i \leq n, 1 \leq j \leq m} [sim(group\_tag_i, movie\_tag_j)$$
$$* Group\_Weightage(group\_tag_i) * weightage(mov, movie\_tag_j)] \qquad (5)$$

where n and m are the total number of tags in the group tag cloud and movie tag cloud respectively. $sim()$ calculates the similarity between two tags using Word-Net, $Group\_Weightage(group\_tag_i)$ and $weightage(mov, movie\_tag_j)$ functions map the weightage of the corresponding tags from the group and the movie tag cloud using Eqs. 3 and 4 respectively. Although two tags might be an exact match giving the result 1, but if the weightage of these two tags are low the *Group Score* will also be low. Thus Eq. 5 captures how similar a particular movie tag is to a group tag and their respective relevance to the movie tag cloud and group tag cloud. Note that, *Group Score* will again be in the range [0, 1].

3.6   Recommendation

We recommend a *top-N* movie list to the members of the group on the basis of the *Group Score*. However, there may arise a situation when more than one movie has the same *Group Score*. To overcome this issue, we find the *Popularity Score* of each movie in order to rank a more popular movie higher. The *Popularity Score* of a movie refers to the number of unique users who have tagged the movie. After calculating the popularity scores we normalize these values for all movies in the list L to keep it in the range [0, 1] using the formula below.

$$PopularityScore^l = \frac{I^l - L_{\min}}{L_{\max} - L_{\min}} \tag{6}$$

$PopularityScore^l$ is the normalized popularity score of a movie l in the list L while I^l is its un-normalized popularity score. $L_{\max}$ and $L_{\min}$ are the minimum and maximum popularity scores for the movies in L. Movies with the same *Group Score* will be recommended in the descending order of their popularity score.

4   Data Description

4.1   Dataset

We have conducted experiments on the MovieLens-10M and 20M datasets [8]. MovieLens-10M dataset contains 10000054 ratings and 95580 tags applied to 10681 movies by 71567 users while MovieLens-20M has 20000263 ratings and 465564 tags assigned by 138493 users to 27278 movies. In both the datasets only those users are included who have rated at least 20 movies. Since the datasets do not have any pre-defined groups, we use our own group formation procedure to form groups and subsequently provide recommendations to the groups.

4.2   Preprocessing

We observed two important features in the MovieLens dataset: (1) Instead of assigning tags, about 30% of the users had used complete sentences to describe a particular movie, and (2) There were some irrelevant tags like dialogues of the movie, or an expression used to describe the movie. To solve these problems, we used Natural Language Toolkit [2] to first remove the stop-words like the, is, which, etc. and then extract nouns and adjectives from the sentences. An example is shown below.

Original tag: This was based on a book.
Tags generated: book.
Original tag: I was scared by the horror
Tags generated: horror.

4.3   Evaluation Metrics

We evaluate the effectiveness of a ranked list using *Precision* and Normalized Discounted Cumulative Gain (*nDCG*) [10] metrics.

$$Precision = \frac{t_p}{t_p + f_p} \tag{7}$$

t_p or true positive implies the number of recommended items that were relevant to the group based on the training dataset while f_p or false positive denotes the number of irrelevant items that have been recommended. We have measured *precesion@10* to evaluate the effectiveness of *Top-10* recommended items.

$nDCG_N$ score imposes a penalty or discount on the relevant items that are ranked lower. This penalty is logarithmically proportional to the relative position of each relevant item in a ranked list (see Eq. 9). We have used $nDCG_{10}$ to evaluate the performance of *Top-10* recommended movies. A high $nDCG_{10}$ score implies that in the *Top-10* ranked list, the movies relevant to the preferences of the group members are ranked higher which makes the recommendations more effective. This metric is defined below.

$$nDCG_{10} = \frac{1}{P} \sum_{i=1}^{P} \frac{1}{Q_i} \sum_{k=1}^{Q_i} \frac{DCG_{10,k}}{IDCG_{10,k}} \tag{8}$$

where P is the number of groups with a pre-determined number of group members and Q_i denotes the number of users in the i-th group. $IDCG_{10,k}$ is the best possible $DCG_{10,k}$ value for the recommendations generated for the k-th group member. $IDCG_{10,k}$ is computed as $DCG_{10,k}$ (see Eq. 9) using an ideal ranking such that the 10 recommendations are arranged in descending order based on their relevant judgment scores in the ranked list.

$$DCG_{10,k} = \sum_{j=1}^{10} \frac{2^{relevance_j} - 1}{log_2(1 + j)} \tag{9}$$

where $relevance_j$ is the relevancy judgment factor of the recommended movie at the j-th ranked position. It takes a value of 1 if the movie is a relevant recommendation for k-th group member and is assigned a 0 if it is not.

5   Results and Discussions

We have generated groups of 3 to 8 members across MovieLens-10M and 20M datasets. Our experiments are performed by partitioning the datasets into five disjoint sets for 5-fold cross-validation. One set is used as the test set and the other four as training sets which results in five disjoint training/testing sets. Experiments are conducted on each set, and then the average results are reported. On the basis of the group formation strategy, we have conducted experiments over three types of groups: (1) highly similar groups (2) moderately similar groups and (3) dissimilar groups. The group classification is shown in Table 3.

Table 3. Classification of groups

Category of groups	Similarity measure
Highly similar	0.60 – 1.0
Moderately similar	0.30 – 0.59
Dissimilar	0.0 – 0.29

For determining the *precision* values, we have conducted experiments on 20 groups for each of the group categories (*highly similar, moderately similar* and *dissimilar*) across MovieLens 10M dataset. Similarly we have experimented with 30 groups for MovieLens 20M dataset. So for each fixed group size of 3 to 8, $60\,(20*3)$ groups are formed and since there are 6 different group sizes, we will have a total of $360\,(60*6)$ groups for MovieLens 10M dataset. On the other hand, for MovieLens 20M dataset, $90\,(30*3)$ groups are formed for a fixed group size and in total there will be $540\,(90*6)$ groups. The *precision* results for MovieLens-10M and 20M datasets are depicted in Fig. 3. The results show that when the group similarity measure increases between group members, the *precision* of recommendation also increases. As expected, highly similar group is likely to have greater *precision* for the recommendation list than the other two types of groups and likewise a moderately similar group achieves better *precision* than a dissimilar group. However, the remarkable fact that we noted is that even for a dissimilar group with similarity measure as low as 0.2, our framework achieves an average *precision* of 0.72 and 0.718 for the MovieLens 10M and 20M datasets respectively.

Similarly, for calculating $nDCG$ values, we have formed 50 groups for each of the group categories (*highly similar, moderately similar* and *dissimilar*). Thus for a fixed group size, $150\,(50*3)$ groups are formed, which further results in a total of $900\,(150*6)$ groups for the 6 different group sizes across each of the 10M and 20M datasets. We have reported the $nDCG$ values for MovieLens-10M and 20M datasets in Fig. 4. In most cases the $nDCG$ values turned out to be best for highly similar groups and here also the moderately similar groups always performed better than the dissimilar groups. The $nDCG$ value for a dissimilar group records a minimum of about 0.856 for 10M dataset and about 0.861 for 20M dataset whereas the $nDCG$ for a highly similar group achieves an average of 0.9185 and 0.935 for 10M and 20M datasets respectively.

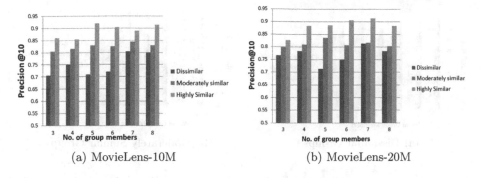

Fig. 3. Recommendation performance in terms of presicsion

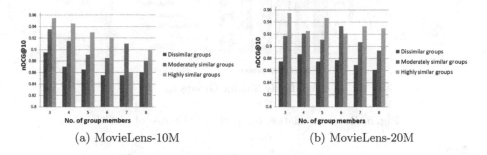

Fig. 4. Recommendation performance in terms of nDCG

In order to prove the accuracy and efficiency of our framework over other content-based and memory-based approaches we conduct further experiments. We compare our approach *TC+Popularity* with other approaches like *TC_Without Popularity, Equal_Weightage, Collaborative Filtering* and *Popularity*. For each approach, groups of members ranging from 3 to 8 have been formed. The comparison has been further classified into *dissimilar, moderately similar* and *highly similar* groups. For each comparison based on *Precision* and *nDCG*, we have formed 100 groups with a pre-defined degree of cohesiveness and group size. Thus in total $1800[100 * 3\ (group\ categories) * 6\ (different\ group\ sizes)]$ groups have been formed across the MovieLens 10M and MovieLens 20M datasets.

TC+Popularity consists of two core components. First one uses the tag cloud technique to form the group tag cloud representing the preferences of the group members, and the movie tag cloud to represent the content of a particular movie. The *Group Score* is assigned by comparing the group tag cloud and the movie tag cloud. The second component is the *Popularity Score* which is used to rank the popular movies higher in case of identical *Group Score*.

We compare the above technique with *TC_WithoutPopularity* which does not include the *Popularity Score* feature. A highly popular movie may find itself below a less popular movie in case of identical *Group Score* in the recommended list. In *Equal_Weightage* technique, tags are not assigned any weightage on

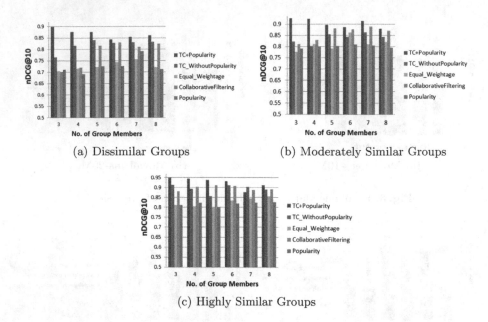

(a) Dissimilar Groups   (b) Moderately Similar Groups

(c) Highly Similar Groups

Fig. 5. Recommendation comparisons in terms of nDCG

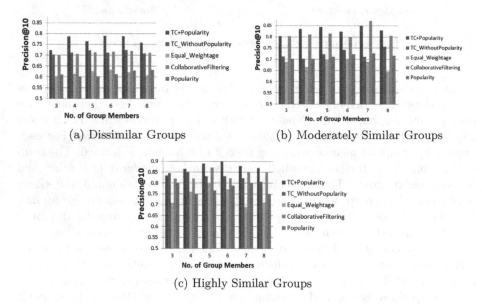

(a) Dissimilar Groups   (b) Moderately Similar Groups

(c) Highly Similar Groups

Fig. 6. Recommendation comparisons in terms of precision

the basis of their frequencies of usage and the *GroupScore* is calculated only using the similarity between the two tags. For comparing with a *Collaborative Filtering* method, we use the standard memory-based collaborative filtering algorithm while in *Popularity* based recommendation technique, we recommend items which are most popular among users on the basis of their consumption. Here, the popularity of a movie is calculated by counting the number of users who have tagged that particular movie. We report these comparison results in terms of *nDCG* and *precision* for *dissimilar, moderately similar* and *highly similar* groups in Figs. 5 and 6 respectively. We can notice that *TC + Popularity* outperforms the other comparative methods in almost all the cases.

The tag cloud technique proves to be a principal component in our framework as without the corresponding weightages of the tags it would be impossible to decipher how significant a particular tag is for the movie or for the group. In case of any noisy tags in the dataset the irrelevant tags will be given equal importance as any relevant tags. This causes error in prediction and thus we observe that *Equal Weightage* method records the lowest *precision* and *nDCG* values. The *Popularity Score* is another vital part of our framework. When a situation arises that multiple movies have equal *Group Score*, then we recommend them in order of their popularity. The results of *TC_WithoutPopularity* in terms of *precision* and *nDCG* verifies our intuition and proves that users are more likely to watch a popular movie than an unpopular one. Content based recommendations have always been a critical problem as there are no explicit ratings to signify the users' satisfaction with the items. The idea of tag cloud successfully captures users' preferences within a group and the content of the movie while *Popularity Score* serves as a basis for ranking the recommended items.

6   Conclusion and Future Work

In this paper, we have presented a group recommendation framework on the basis of the semantic information available in the tags assigned by users. We have exploited the weightage of each tag to form the group tag cloud, which is then used to recommend movies to the group by measuring its content similarity with the movies. The popular movies are ranked higher in the recommendation list. Empirical study conducted on the MovieLens dataset shows that our framework is effective and efficient in recommending movies to groups with both high and low degree of cohesiveness. In future, we plan to investigate the correctness of the assigned tags to the movies to remove noisy tags and also have an intent to incorporate a certain degree of fairness to every member of the group. Each member of the group must be satisfied with the recommendations up to a certain threshold. This threshold may be calculated using machine learning techniques.

References

1. Baltrunas, L., Makcinskas, T., Ricci, F.: Group recommendations with rank aggregation and collaborative filtering. In: Proceedings of the Fourth ACM Conference on Recommender Systems, RecSys 2010, pp. 119–126 (2010)
2. Bird, S., Loper, E.: NLTK: the natural language toolkit. In: Proceedings of the ACL-02 Workshop on Effective Tools and Methodologies for Teaching Natural Language Processing and Computational Linguistics, vol. 1, pp. 63–70 (2002)

3. Budanitsky, A., Hirst, G.: Semantic distance in wordnet: an experimental, application-oriented evaluation of five measures. In: Workshop on Wordnet and Other Lexical Resources, Second Meeting of the North American Chapter of the Association for Computational Linguistics (2001)
4. Castro, J., Yera, R., Martínez, L.: A fuzzy approach for natural noise management in group recommender systems. Experts Syst. Appl. **94**, 237–249 (2018)
5. Christensen, I., Schiaffino, S.: A hybrid approach for group profiling in recommender systems. J. Univers. Comput. Sci. **20**(4), 507–533 (2014)
6. De Pessemier, T., Dooms, S., Martens, L.: Design and evaluation of a group recommender system. In: Proceedings of the Sixth ACM Conference on Recommender Systems, RecSys 2012, pp. 225–228 (2012)
7. Fellbaum, C.: WordNet: An Electronic Lexical Database. MIT Press, Cambridge (1998)
8. Harper, F.M., Konstan, J.A.: The movielens datasets: history and context. ACM Trans. Interact. Intell. Syst. **5**(4), 1–19 (2016)
9. Lops, P., de Gemmis, M., Semeraro, G.: Content-based recommender systems: state of the art and trends. In: Ricci, F., Rokach, L., Shapira, B., Kantor, P. (eds.) Recommender Systems Handbook, pp. 73–105. Springer, Boston (2011)
10. Manning, C.D., Raghavan, P., Schutze, H.: Introduction to Information Retrieval. Cambridge University Press, Cambridge (2008)
11. O'Connor, M., Cosley, D., Konstan, J.A., Riedl, J.: PolyLens: a recommender system for groups of users. In: Proceedings of the Seventh Conference on European Conference on Computer Supported Cooperative Work, ECSCW 2001, pp. 199–218 (2001)
12. Pera, M.S., Ng, Y.K.: A group recommender for movies based on content similarity and popularity. Inf. Process. Manage. Int. J. **49**(3), 673–687 (2013)
13. Pujahari, A., Padmanabhan, V.: Group recommender systems: combining user-user and item-item collaborative filtering techniques. In: Proceedings of the 2015 14th International Conference on Information Technology, pp. 148–152. IEEE (2015)
14. Seo, Y.D., Kim, Y.G., Lee, E., Seol, K.S., Baik, D.K.: An enhanced aggregation method considering deviations for a group recommendation. Experts Syst. Appl. **93**, 299–312 (2018)
15. Sinclair, J., Cardew-Hall, M.: The folksonomy tag cloud: when is it useful? J. Inform. Sci. **34**, 15–29 (2008)
16. Su, X., Khoshgoftaar, T.: A survey of collaborative filtering techniques. Adv. Artif. Intell. **2009**, 1–19 (2009)

Real Time Key Frame Extraction Through Parallel Computation of Entropy Difference

Nandita Gautam[✉], Debdoot Das, Sunirmal Khatua,
and Banani Saha

Computer Science Department, University of Calcutta, Kolkata 700098, India
nanditagautam43@gmail.com, dasdebdoot@gmail.com,
enggnimu_ju@yahoo.com, bsaha_29@yahoo.com

Abstract. The advancement of image processing in the field of Artificial Intelligence has created various research prospects in the area of object detection, pattern recognition etc. Capturing real time video stream for multiple cameras within a region of interest has become a common phenomenon for an Intelligent Situation Awareness System. Video processing is an important application which is rapidly developing nowadays as an area of extensive research. Content retrieval as well as information collection from a video requires both syntactic and semantic analysis. For a large video data, some set of frames are used to represent the video content. These are identified as key frames. Several algorithms have been defined to extract key frames from a stored video file. The existing algorithms that have been defined for key frame extraction are based on sequential mode. This paper looks into the extraction of key frames for any real time video stream. The experimental results show that there is an effective reduction in the execution time to a huge extent in the case of distributed processing as compared to the sequential processing of frames. In this paper, we propose a distributed framework to regulate the speed of key frame generation for heterogeneous speed of incoming video.

Keywords: Real time streaming · Key frames · Parallel computing · Entropy

1 Introduction

With the development of software tools there has been an enormous development in the way data is processed nowadays. Digital image processing has been a vast area of research in the field of science and technology. Video processing is an important technique that helps in efficient content retrieval for a video stream. A video stream is understood to be a sequence of frames. The most informative frames which carry maximum information about the video content are known as representative frames or key frames [1]. The key frame generation provides a framework and abstraction for video browsing. The requirement is to get the frames which give the best possible information about the video stream. These key frames must give accurate information about the event. The information should be compact and the abstraction must be done efficiently. Here, efficiency refers to the fast retrieval of information that can be viewed quickly by the users. This means that the abstraction must be user friendly. Several

© Springer Nature Switzerland AG 2019
K. Saeed et al. (Eds.): CISIM 2019, LNCS 11703, pp. 337–346, 2019.
https://doi.org/10.1007/978-3-030-28957-7_28

existing algorithms based on video skimming and video summary have been adopted for video abstraction. These algorithms aim to identify key frames for an existing video stream by using techniques based on entropy difference calculation, shot detection, mosaic or content of the video. These techniques use static video input for the extraction of the key frames.

In this paper we have taken spatio-temporal real time video stream as our input data. In case of a high speed of input stream, the processing time of the frames as well as the rate of generation of the key frames poses another challenge for practical purposes. In our work, we propose a distributed architecture that has been used to regulate the speed of the key frames at the output with respect to the incoming frames.

In the first section, the importance of entropy difference calculation has been mentioned. Since entropy is a good way to determine the unpredictability of a set of data [2], this technique is a very effective way for identifying the key frames from a video being streamed in. Entropy is dependent on the context in which the measurement is taken. Higher entropy distributions better describe the regions that contain the crucial objects of a video sequence. Therefore, change in the object occurrence of these regions will affect the relevant information of the video sequence thus making it an efficient approach to extract the key frames.

In the next section, it is explained why there is a need for parallel processing and how it is beneficial when the video streaming is being done in real time. For a large size video data where the speed of key frame generation is expected to be faster than the input frames per second, there arises a need for task distribution. This task distribution [5] helps to speed up the computation as well as regulate the speed of generated key frames with respect to the speed of the video being streamed in. The major portion of this work focuses on deploying a distributed architecture so as to make the processing faster. In case of a spatio temporal real time video stream, the speed of the streaming is very high. Thus, in order to analyse a region of interest (ROI), the process of key frame extraction for generating a desired number of key frames must be substantially fast. In this context we deal with majorly three sections; the color quantization over the input frames, entropy calculation and parallel processing [11] of the incoming frames for desired key frame generation.

2 Related Work

Video skimming and video summary are two important techniques that are efficiently used for retrieval of video content for stored video data. Video skimming is based on retrieving frames that generate high contrast or the most interesting parts of the original video. On the other hand video summary is based on uniform generation of the representative frames that give the best abstraction of the overall video. This method is more user-friendly than the former one as this method as the information represented by this method is more meaningful.

Various categories of video summary technique are content based, shot based, mosaic based [2] and entropy based. In our proposed work, the concept of entropy difference has been adopted. Entropy is a very popular technique as it gives a statistical measure of randomness that can be used to characterize the texture of the input image.

It gives information about the degree of randomness of the data being observed and also lets us determine the unpredictability of a set of data in an effective way. Higher entropy distributions better describe the regions that contain the crucial objects of a video sequence. Therefore, change in the object occurrence of these regions will affect the relevant information of the video sequence thus making it an efficient approach to extract the key frames. The entropy difference technique has been discussed as follows:

2.1   Entropy Difference Technique

In this method the global entropy information of the frame is calculated by taking the sum total of the gray level entropies. The key frame is chosen by comparing the selected entropies of the current key frame and the consecutive frame entropy. The frame entropy difference is matched with a certain threshold value exceeding which the next key frame is chosen [4].

In order to eliminate as much as we can the possibility of the change of brightness during the key-frame comparison, we need to quantize our image to 256 colors. Let $h_f(k)$ be the histogram of the frame f and k the grey level such that $0 < k < 2^{b-1}$, where b is the number of bits in which the image quantization levels can be represented. The probability of appearance of this gray level in the frame will be:

$$p_f(k) = h_f(k)/(M.N)$$

The information quantity $Q_f(k)$ transmitted by an element is equal to the log (base 2) of the inverse probability of appearance $p_f(k)$

$$Q_f(k) = -log_2(p_f(k))$$

The above information quantity multiplied by its probability of appearance gives us the entropy E generated by the source for this quantization level.

$$E = \sum_{k=1}^{kmax} Qf(k).pf(k)$$

2.2   Distributed Computing Environment

Distributed computing is a model in which components of a software system are shared among multiple computers to improve efficiency and performance. In this paper, we use distributed computing for speeding up the process of key frame identification. We use the MapReduce architecture [3] for executing this work.

MapReduce is a framework using which we can write applications to process huge amounts of data, in parallel, on large clusters of commodity hardware in a reliable manner. Mapper task is the first phase of processing that processes each input record and generates an intermediate key-value pair. In our work mapper helps to perform the task distribution [6]. The job of the reducer is to process the data that comes from the mapper. We efficiently deploy this map reduce technique in our work.

3 Problem Statement

A video is a sequence of frames through which content is retrieved and information is extracted. For real time video analysis the frames per second (fps) of the video should match with the speed of the analysis. Thus, in order to avoid the overflow of frames in the analyser, there is a need for selecting some particular frames for the video analysis. These frames are identified as the key frames for that video file or video data. There are several existing algorithms that have been used for the identification of key frames for the video files stored on the cloud or a filesystem. In this paper, we consider the input from real time video sources such as drone camera (quadcopter camera), CCTV camera, Digital video camera or any other medium from where live video streaming can be retrieved.

The video sequence can be of heterogeneous formats such as .avi, .mp4, .flv etc. The speed (fps) of these sources are also heterogeneous in nature [8]. Our challenge is to convert these heterogeneous speed (fps) into speed required by the analyser (homogeneous). The number of processors required to speedup the execution is based upon the analysis of the required fps. When this task is performed sequentially over the entire sequence of frames the time taken is much larger as compared to distributed computation. In this paper, we propose an architecture for this distributed processing of the frames. We have used the concept of map-reduce programming for executing this task [9]. The mapper class is used for task distribution whereas the reducer task acts as the aggregator for combining the results obtained from the mapper class.

The next section broadly explains the framework for the execution of the mapper and the reducer tasks. We explain how this distributed architecture speeds up the overall process of generation of the key frames.

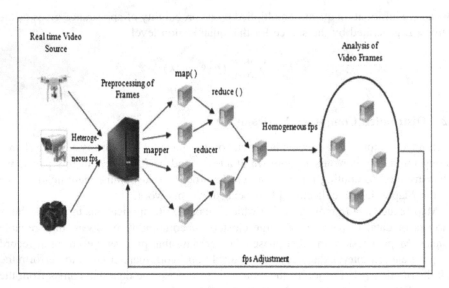

Fig. 1. Proposed architectural framework

4 Proposed Methodology

In this section, we propose an architecture in which the video can be streamed in through any real time sources such as drone camera, cctv camera, digital video camera etc. These videos can be of different formats as mentioned above. The frames per second generated by these video streams are heterogeneous in nature. These are brought to a processing environment (for example Matlab) for initial preprocessing. This preprocessing involves the color quantization of the image. This involves steps such as the conversion of the RGB image to a grayscale image (Fig. 1).

After this initial preprocessing, the task distribution is performed so as to segregate the incoming frames and allot them to separate processors for further computation. In our work, we have defined a mapper function [7] for executing this frame distribution among the processors. At each of the individual processors alloted by the map function, a set of key frames are generated by using the entropy difference technique. Next, the key frames generated by each of the processor are combined together to generate the final output set of key frames. The mapper and the reducer task has been explained as follows:

4.1 Mapper Task

In the mapper, the frames are distributed among certain number of processors. It is upto the mapper task how this distribution [9] of frames is done between the processors. At each of the processors, the map function performs certain computations so as to generate the set of key frames for that particular processor.

4.2 Reducer Task

The reducer method performs the task of aggregating the set of generated frames from each processor. This reduce function works as an aggregator [7] to arrange the generated set of key frames into a logical sequence.

After this aggregation a set of key frames are produced which are further analysed. Based on this analysis the number of processors used in the mapper task is selected. For a faster speedup (frames per second), the number of processors are increased. This fps adjustment is done based on the speed of the incoming frames. Speed of key frame generation has to be less than or equal to the processing speed of the network or else the frames would overflow. We should choose the maximum speed at which frames can be fed to the network to maximize amount of data to be processed, without overflowing. That is why the speed of output from key frame identification module should be at most the processing speed of the network.

In our program, the video input has been streamed in from CCTV camera. The video segmentation is done by initially generating the set of frames from the video sequence. A compression is applied on the generated set of frames by doing color quantization. The color quantization is done to convert the RGB scale to gray scale. This process of conversion of the RGB scale to gray scale is done sequentially for the generated set of frames. After this initial preprocessing of the frames these are distributed among the cores with the help of the mapper. In our analysis 12 cores have been taken [10]. At each of the core the map ( ) function is executed. In the map ( ) function we define the method of entropy difference calculation that has been used for the extraction of key frames. Here the entropy difference calculation among the consecutive frames involves major computations. The initial frame is selected as the key frame. If the frame entropy difference between the current frame and its consecutive frame is greater than T_H, then the consecutive frame is chosen as key frame. This is performed for all the frames allotted to that core by the mapper [12].

In order to perform syntactic and semantic analysis over a given region of interest, the threshold value has an essential role to play. The threshold limit is dependent on the number of key frames to be generated. This has been elaborated in the next subsection (Fig. 2):

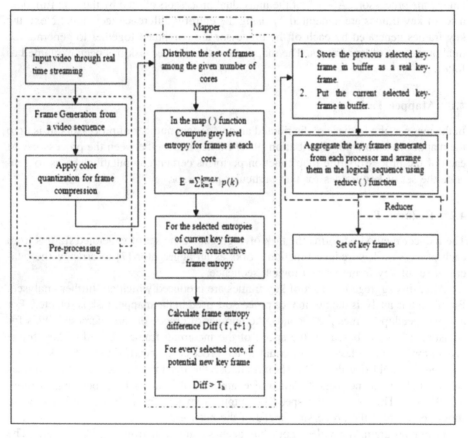

Fig. 2. Proposed workflow for the distributed processing

4.3   Threshold Estimation for Regulating the Key Frame Generation Speed

In order to get the desired number of key frames we estimate a threshold limit. The threshold value is set up to estimate the number of key frames generated for an input sequence of frames. Suppose the neural network can process x frames per second. Then it passes the parameter for number of key frames per second as x to the key frame identification module. The module then chooses a threshold value such that it can output x key frames per second. Then it outputs x frames per second to pipe to the speed of the neural network.

In our work, we first set the minimum and maximum limits for the threshold. Then, the number of frames required by the user is being accepted as the input. For the iterative calculation we set the condition that the threshold for the number of required key frames will be calculated with an accuracy of 0.00001. Next, we select a threshold between the two limits by applying the logic of simple binary search. After that, the key frames are generated as mentioned above. Lastly, it is checked that the number of generated key frames is equal to that required. If so, then it breaks out of the iterative condition and presents that list of identified key frames. If not then a simple technique of binary search is being applied, it checks if more key frames are needed or less key frames are needed. If more are needed, it reduces the threshold, by setting a lower max limit, and repeats. If less key frames are needed, it increases the threshold by increasing the min limit, and repeats. Figure 3 depicts the key frames identified in our experiment for CCTV surveillance of a university campus area. For a slight change in the degree of randomness, the frame is being detected as a key frame.

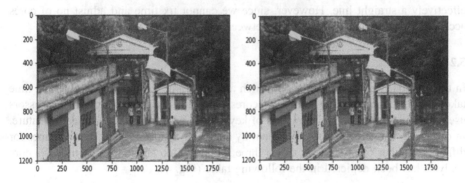

Fig. 3. Identified key frames in our work for CCTV surveillance of university campus area

After all the key frames have been generated by the processors these are sent to the reducer. The reducer aggregates these frames and using the reduce function the frames are arranged in a logical representation. For generating a less number of key frames, a small value of threshold is selected and vice-versa. Thus, we conclude that the threshold value (T_H) is to be set depending on the speed of the neural network using which the analysis is being performed.

5 Experiments

5.1 Experimental Setup

In this work, the spatio-temporal real time video stream is being input from a CCTV camera. In our experiment, we have used Basler network cameras with rapid frame rates of up to 120 frames per second and 1080p full HD resolution. The speed of the stream is recorded as 120 fps in our work. Our next task is to generate the array of pixel values for each frame of the video stream. There are in-built libraries embedded in this hardware device which give us the direct pixel values in array representation. This saves the overhead of encoding the frames to an array matrix for performing the experiment.

For implementation, we use the OpenCV platform in python program-ming. A pre-installed set of camera IPs are provided which are actually source of live feeds of streaming data of video content. Next, the OpenCV video processing library is used to convert video streams into image frames. Then, the key frames are selected based on the calculation of Entropy values. We use python built in libraries which are numpy, shared array and python multi-processing modules. The multi-processing module is used for the parallel computation that is for executing the core distribution between the frames. The logic for the distributed execution can be explained as follows.

Let us break up a video processing time into a few parts. Say it takes x seconds for the loading part(sequential), y seconds for the entropy calculation(concurrent) part, and z for the combining part(sequential). So, for a video of frame rate say A, it would take x + y + z seconds on a single core. We assume that for each new process, the fork/join and other housekeeping tasks take w seconds. So, for b cores, the time would be x + y/b + z + bw. For a video of frame rate say 3A, the time would be 3x + 3y/b + 3z + bw. This is effectively a straight line. However, since we cannot fix time and adjust no of cores accordingly, we cannot show a graph between frame rate and no of cores.

5.2 Results

In this section, we present two plots which are key frame v/s threshold value and time taken for execution v/s the number of cores. The plot between number of processors used and the time taken for extraction of key frames is asymptotically linear in nature. In our work, we perform our experiment by analysing the same set of input frames for different number of processors. For a three minute video streaming the time v/s core analysis has been depicted in the following table (Fig. 4):

Number of cores	Time taken
1	2:31
2	1:32
4	1:03
6	0:56
8	0:52
16	0:46
32	0:42

Fig. 4. Time and number of core analysis

Here the plot of threshold v/s key value and time v/s number of cores has been shown in Figs. 5 and 6 respectively. The threshold value is selected using a binary search logic as discussed in Sect. 5.2. A small value for threshold limit will generate lesser number of key frames as compared to a greater value. Also, as we keep increasing the number of cores for a large set of input frames, the time taken keeps on decreasing.

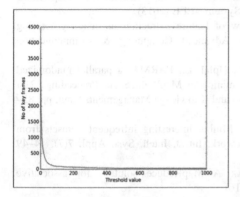

Fig. 5. Key frames v/s threshold value

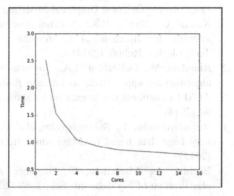

Fig. 6. Time v/s no. of cores

6 Conclusion

In this paper, .mp4 format has been used. However, the library we used utilized FFmpeg under the cover, which can decode almost all open/proprietary formats. The necessity of core distribution is to counter the speed mismatch between the incoming frames per second of the input stream and the key frame generated per second in real time scenarios. The parallel distribution using map-reduce provides an effective solution for key frame extraction by reducing the computation time. This has been established in this paper. The number of key frames generated in the output increases in parts of the video with a lot of action. The results obtained in the work are accurate. However, the value of the threshold is an area of further research.

Acknowledgements. This publication is an outcome of the Research and Development work undertaken project entitled 'Object Identification through Syntactic as well as Semantic Interpretation from given Spatio-Temporal Scenarios' under DRDO (ERIP/ER/1404742/M/01/1661) as well as the Visvesvaraya PhD Scheme of Ministry of Electronics & Information Technology, Government of India, being implemented by Digital India Corporation.

We would like to express our sincere gratitude to all the members for this opportunity.

References

1. Prabhdeep, S., Arora, A.: Analytical analysis of image filtering techniques. Int. J. Eng. Innov. Technol. (IJEIT) **3**(4), 234–237 (2013)
2. Nancy, E., Kaur, S.: Image enhancement techniques: a selected review. IOSR J. Comput. Eng. **9**(6), 84–88 (2013)
3. Du, W., Qian, D., Xie, M., Chen, W.: Research and Implementation of MapReduce Programming Oriented Graphical Modeling System, IEEE (2013)
4. Kumar, G., Bhatia, P.K.: A detailed review of feature extraction in image processing systema. In: International Conference on Advanced Computing & Communication Technologies, Rohtak (2014)
5. Riondato, M., DeBrabant, J.A., Fonseca, R., Upfal, E.: PARMA: a parallel randomized algorithm for approximate association rules mining in MapReduce. In: Proceedings 21st ACM International Conference on Information and Knowledge Management, Maui, pp. 85–94 (2014)
6. Ramakrishnudu, T., Subramanyam, R.B.V.: Mining interesting infrequent itemsets from very large data based on MapReduce framework. Int. J. Intell. Syst. Appl. **7**(7), 44–49 (2015)
7. Bechini, A., Marcelloni, F., Segatori, A.: A MapReduce solution for associative classification of big data. Inf. Sci., 1–69 (2016)
8. Phali, V., Goswani, S., Bhaiya, L.P.: An extensive survey on feature extraction techniques for facial image processing. In: Sixth International Conference on Computational Intelligence and Communication Networks, Bhopal (2014)
9. The NIST Definition of Cloud Computing (2014). http://csrc.nist.gov/publications/nistpubs/800-145/SP800-145.pdf
10. Image Recognition in the Cloud – EvoDevo (2014). http://www.nextcentury.com/our-technology-solutions/image-processing/image-recognition-in-the-cloud-evodevo
11. Amazon AWS (2014). http://aws.amazon.com/
12. Hadoop Image Processing Interface (2014). http://hipi.cs.virginia.edu/

Sequence Analysis for Relationship Pattern Extraction

Tomáš Martinovič[(✉)] [ID], Kateřina Janurová [ID], Jan Martinovič [ID],
Kateřina Slaninová [ID], and Václav Svatoň

IT4Innovations, VSB – Technical University of Ostrava, 17. listopadu 2172/15,
708 00 Ostrava-Poruba, Czech Republic
{tomas.martinovic,katerina.janurova,jan.martinovic,katerina.slaninova,
vaclav.svaton}@vsb.cz

Abstract. Analysis of the relationship between a large number of
sequences is a significant problem in many different applications such
as business processes, sport, voting, weblogs, etc. Generally, studying
relationship is based on clustering the sequences and creating a network
of relationships. Interpretation and validation of such results require
a domain expert knowledge. In this paper, we propose a methodology
which is able to provide an insight into the sequence dataset prior to
the analysis and independently of a domain expert. Such information
may be used to direct the analysis, identify sequences of interest and
expose special patterns in the sequences. This methodology leverages
tools such as transition matrix, Shannon entropy, complexity index, pairwise state occurrence, etc. Due to the low computational complexity of
these methods, this approach is possible to use on the large datasets and
help to identify the subsets of such datasets which should be inspected
closer with more sophisticated tools. Ability to extract relevant information using the aforementioned tools was validated on two datasets, one
from business processes simulation and the other from robot soccer game
simulation.

Keywords: Sequence analysis · Process modelling · Data mining ·
Shannon entropy · Complexity index

1 Introduction

The main motivation of the presented research is to provide the fundamental
feedback to creators of simulation application. There are many different simulation systems in various fields such as business processes [4,13] or robot simulators
[3,12]. Such simulators are used to predict the effects of changing the business
structure or to create the basis for the robot intelligence with the minimal costs.
However, any mistake in the simulator may lead to costly errors when the final
products are used in reality. Therefore it is of utmost importance to continuously review the outputs of the simulators and improve them. This can be

© Springer Nature Switzerland AG 2019
K. Saeed et al. (Eds.): CISIM 2019, LNCS 11703, pp. 347–358, 2019.
https://doi.org/10.1007/978-3-030-28957-7_29

done by analysing the sequences extracted from the output logs of these simulations. Such sequences contain information about the processes occurring in the simulations. To this end, there are various software tools that analyze output from the simulators. In business process the most prominent ones are ProM and Disco [1,2]. These software tools provide a range of different methods to the user that can help him understand the individual processes. The main problem for the newcomer to the field of sequence analysis is overwhelming amount of information to study in new datasets. It is difficult to know what is important when analyzing new data and also a senior maintainer of the simulator may easily miss some fundamental responses of the system. In this paper we provide a methodology to identify the states and sequences of interest by using the apriori analysis based on the simple measures such as state transition and entropy. We show that by visualizing this information it is possible to find central states or groups of sequences without any need for the more sophisticated analysis such as clustering and computing sequence distances.

1.1 Problem Definition

In our work, we generally deal with the analysis of processes that can be represented as a set of sequences of states consisting of discrete or categorical data with or without a timestamp. The final set of all possible states of a process is referred to as an alphabet A, with the size $a = |A|$. The state sequence s_k of length l_k is defined as ordered sequence $s_k = (s_{k,1}, s_{k,2}, ..., s_{k,l})$ where $s_{k,i} \in A$. The set of sequences is then referred to as $s = (s_1, s_2, ..., s_m)$, where m represents the number of all sequences.

2 Tools Overview

Since this study is focused on the information which can be extracted before the actual expert analysis of the data, the tools used are mainly the ones, which can be computed quickly without dependence on the character of the input sequences. Specifically, we use the descriptive statistics, such as counts of the states in the dataset and in the individual sequences, sequences length, and state transitions, Shannon entropy and sequence complexity. These tools can be used to extract the information about the dynamics of the sequences, find central states, give intuition about the sequences states distribution.

2.1 State Transitions

Examining the state transitions provides a number of useful information such as states with the most transitions to the other states, identifying constant subsequences, or identifying uncommon transitions. The state transition count, denoted as $ST_{i,j}$, is a sum of the number of transitions from the state $s_{k,i}$ to the consecutive state $s_{k,j}$ across all sequences s_k, for $k \in \{1, 2, \ldots, m\}$.

The state degree is then defined as the number of states to which the transition exists:

$$D(s_i) = |ST_{i,j} > 0|, j = 1, ..., a. \tag{1}$$

Most of the time it is more effective to store the transition in sparse format. In our case, we store the counts of traversal from the current state to the desired state. An example of the state transition is shown in Table 1.

Table 1. Transition counts example table.

From	To	Occurrences
1	2	2023
1	5	20
2	1	129
2	5	254
3	4	23
⋮	⋮	⋮

2.2 Shannon Entropy

In information theory, Claude Shannon introduced the concept of information entropy, also called Shannon entropy [9]. This measure is computed for each sequence separately. This entropy quantifies the expected amount of information in a message and it is defined as:

$$H(s_k) = -\sum_i^a p_{k,i} \log p_{k,i}, \tag{2}$$

where $p_{k,i}$ is the probability of a state i to occur in sequence s_k. Convention that $0 \log 0 = 0$ is accepted.

In this setting, entropy is zero if one state is bound to occur and it is highest if several states have the same probability to occur. Therefore, the maximal value of entropy for a different states is $-\log(1/a)$. Thus, if the number of states occurring in the message is known, it is possible to normalize the Shannon entropy to the interval of $[0, 1]$, where 0 means that one state is always occurring and 1 stands for the uniform states distribution in a sequence. In this paper, we used two types of Shannon entropy computed on the state sequences. The first one, called sequence Shannon entropy, was computed on the sequence with the probabilities of the state happening in the sequence. The second was computed with the probabilities of the state occurring in the whole dataset and is called global Shannon entropy. For the sequence Shannon entropy, 0 means that there is only one state in the sequence and 1 means that there is an equal probability of states occurring in the sequence. In the global Shannon entropy, 0 means that there is only one state in all the sequences and 1 means that there is an equal probability of states occurring in across all the sequences and there is uniform state distribution in the given sequence.

2.3   Complexity Index

The complexity index, introduced in [7], combines the number of transitions in the sequence and the longitudinal entropy in the form of geometric mean between the normalised entropy and the number of state changes in sequence normalised by the length of the sequence. It is defined as:

$$C(s_k) = \sqrt{\frac{(l_d(s_k) - 1)}{(l(s_k) - 1)} \frac{H(s_k)}{H_{max}}}, \tag{3}$$

where $H_{max} = log(a)$ represents the theoretical maximum value of the entropy given by the alphabet A, $(l_d(s_k)-1)$ number of distinct transitions and $(l(s_k)-1)$ number of transitions in sequence s_k.

3   Experiments

In the experiments, we show that even with the apriori analysis without the expert knowledge, we are able to identify states of interest, transition patterns and basic characteristics of the sequences. Providing such information to the domain expert speeds up the process of further analysis. For example, in our case providing this information to the creators of the simulation systems points out to the possibilities of improving the simulator. For the computation and visualization of the results we used R statistical software [8] and packages tidyverse [14], igraph [5] and TraMineR [6].

3.1   Datasets

To show that the methodology brings value in different settings, we use two datasets from separate environments. The first dataset is created as a simulation of the business processes analyzed in [11]. In this case, it is important to find out the relationships between the employees of a company and the customers in day to day business. Business processes contain over 500 different states in the 415 sequences. This is due to the fact, that every customer has its own set of states. In this case it is more difficult to find the relationships between the individual states, however, it is possible to identify some pattern in the business processes. Extracting the information from this dataset may help domain expert to identify repeating patterns, patterns leading to the repeating patterns, or the rare transitions. Closer inspection of such sequences or states may lead to a deeper understanding of the data.

The other dataset consists of the sequences from the simulation of the robot soccer game analyzed in [11]. Sequences are made up of the rules used by one of the robot teams to play the game. Each sequence is finished when the holding of the ball switch sides. The selection of the rules used to play the game is determined by the positions of the robots of both teams. There were only 11 rules used in simulation and therefore the alphabet is quite small in this case.

This dataset contains 62 sequences from one robot soccer game. There are different types of dynamics between the rules, which are determined by a strategy, a collection of relations between the rules. The main interest in this dataset is to determine, if there are some rules which should be broken down into more rules, or if there are some rules which are transient and therefore exploitable by the other team since the following rules are predictable.

3.2 Results

First, we will present results that can be extracted from the states transitions on the business processes data. In Fig. 1 is shown the state transitions as a directed network, we will see that there are too many states to get a good picture of the relations of individual states. However, even this visualization shows that there are two groups of states which are not related and that there seem to be some cycles in the bigger group of states on the left.

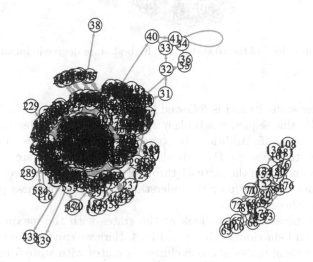

Fig. 1. Complete graph of state transitions of business processes dataset.

Additionally, it is possible to extract several types of networks based on the state degree and number of outgoing or incoming transitions. If we take the states with the top 10 state degree and visualize only direct connection to these state we will get Fig. 2. Here it is clear that the states 20, 5, 29, 69 and 68 are the states with the most connections. Other states from this group are hidden in between the states 20 and 5, where they share a connection to states 5 and 20 and some other states.

Another possible subsetting is to take the states which have the maximal number of outgoing transitions. Once again, when we will take the top 10 states in this category, we will get a graph extracting the states which are at the beginning of sent messages. In Fig. 3 it can be seen, that there is a cycle which

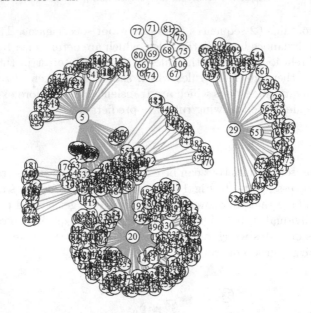

Fig. 2. State transitions of the 10 states with highest state degree in business processes dataset.

begins with the state 29 and is followed by the states 30 to 41. In between the state 32 and 41, this sequence is broken up into three other subsequences either 32 followed by 33 or 35. Additionally, sometimes state 40 jumps to the state 33 and sometimes to the state 41. This shows that when the states jump to the state 29 it will end up in the state 41 through three possible subsequences. Such information may help the user to understand the inner business processes by exploring what these states are.

Last shown possibility is to look at the states with the maximal incoming transitions. Such behaviour is shown in Fig. 4. Here we can see the same process as with the outgoing states and one cluster of states with state 5 in the center. This shows that besides the process shown already in the Fig. 3, there is a number of processes which are directed toward the state 5, what points to the need of deeper analysis of the sequences with the state 5. In this analysis, we used the top 10 states for every type of states subsetting, but this number could be a parameter chosen by the user before the start, so the process could work automatically.

Another analysis may be done using computation of the sequence Shannon entropy and global Shannon entropy. In Fig. 5 is shown a plot of sequence Shannon entropy to the global Shannon entropy, with the color of the points based on the sequence length and the size of the points based on the complexity index. Here it is clear, that the longer sequences of this dataset have higher global Shannon entropy. Actually, these are all the sequences which contain the business process which begins with state 29. This shows that these measures are able

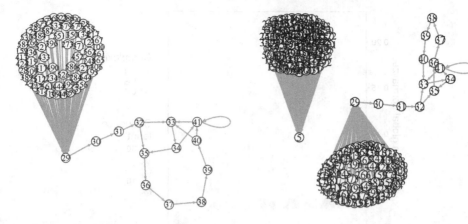

Fig. 3. State transitions of the 10 states with the most outgoing transitions in business processes dataset.

Fig. 4. State transition of the 10 states with the most incoming transitions in business processes dataset.

to discern groups of sequences with similar behaviour. The points are transparent so that we can see if there are several sequences with the same values of the sequence Shannon entropy and the global Shannon entropy. It is clear, that there is a large number of sequences with the sequence Shannon entropy equal to 1 since the points there are very dark, what means there are several points plotted on top of each other.

Another interesting information can be seen when we plot the complexity index to the Shannon entropy of the sequence, color points by the sequence length and set the point size by the global Shannon entropy. This is shown in Fig. 6. Despite showing the same information, this plot indicates several groups of interesting sequences. There are several groups of sequences where sequence Shannon entropy equals 1 and have different complexity index and global Shannon entropy. These groups are actually sequences of length 2 which contain state 20, sequences of length 3 which contain state 20 and sequences which have a length of 3 or 5 and contain states which occurred only once in the dataset. Like this, it would be possible to create clusters of sequences with similar behaviour. Another special sequence happens when there is high sequence Shannon entropy and high complexity index of 0.61 and very low global Shannon entropy of 0.004. This sequence is a sequence of length 12 with 11 distinct states which occurred only in this sequence. Such behaviour is indicated by the high sequence Shannon entropy and low global Shannon entropy. Similar case happens for the sequence which has complexity index lower than 0.4, but relatively high sequence Shannon entropy of 0.79. However, in this case, there is one state, specifically state 192, which repeats itself several times in the sequence. Thus the complexity and the sequence Shannon entropy are lower, while the global Shannon entropy is still very low with the value of 0.008.

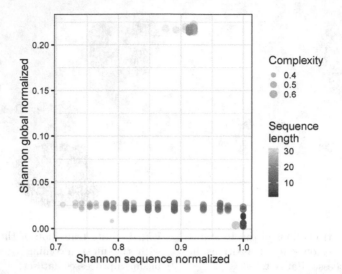

Fig. 5. Scatter plot of sequence Shannon entropy vs global Shannon entropy for the business processes dataset.

In the case of the robot soccer dataset, we start with the same approach. First, a graph of the state transition is shown in Fig. 7. This network is much more readable thanks to a low number of unique states in robot soccer dataset. Here it is possible to see, that most of the time states of the sequences will not change and will transfer to themselves. We added the number of transition from one state to another labeled by the red numbers. The two most central states are state 1 and 2, this shows that the rules 1 and 2 are preferred when deciding strategy. From the perspective of robot soccer, this means, that it would be a good idea to create several similar rules, so the rules will change more often. This is desirable because if there are rules which are used often, the opponent team will start using rules which respond to the given rules. Another information gained from Fig. 7 is that there are several cycles e.g. 9, 10, 11, 1, or short cycles like transitions between rules 2 and 3.

From Figs. 8 and 9 it is possible to see, that there are many sequences with 0 sequence Shannon entropy and different global Shannon entropy. This is due to the fact, that such sequences have only one state with a different amount in repetition in the dataset. We can see that the sequence Shannon entropy is scattered across the whole interval of [0, 1] with more sequences closer to 1. This means that there are more sequences which contain the states with approximately uniform distribution in the sequence. The sequences with low sequence Shannon entropy consist of one predominant rule which is repeated often and some minor rules. The low values of complexity index in Fig. 9 signify that the sequences in this dataset are made mostly of repetitive states, what could be seen already in Fig. 7.

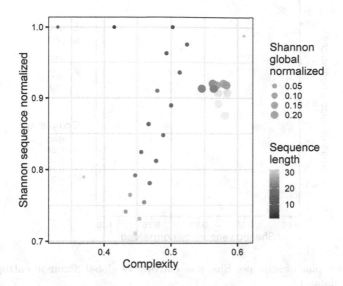

Fig. 6. Scatter plot of complexity index vs sequence Shannon entropy for the business processes dataset.

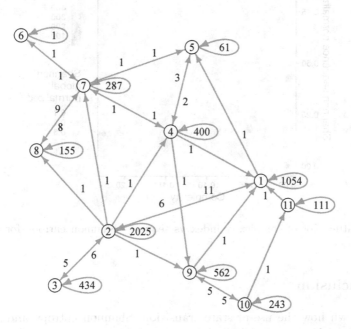

Fig. 7. Complete graph of state transitions in the robot soccer dataset.

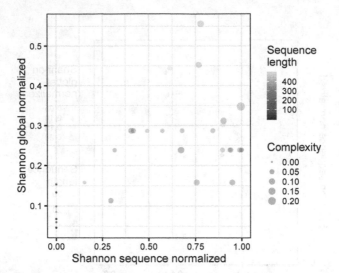

Fig. 8. Scatter plot of sequence Shannon entropy vs global Shannon entropy for the robot soccer dataset.

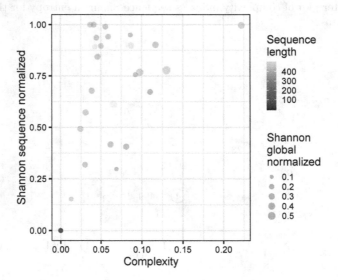

Fig. 9. Scatter plot of complexity index vs sequence Shannon entropy for the robot soccer dataset.

4   Conclusion

It was shown how the use of state transition, Shannon entropy and complexity index can lead to exploiting interesting information about the sequences which can be used as a feedback for the users responsible for simulation configuration. This was validated on two datasets which had a completely different structure of the sequences from two different usecases. The state transition and their visualization are very helpful, especially when visualizing the data with a smaller amount of states. In case of a dataset with many states, it was shown that subsetting the most central states helps to find the hidden dynamics of the sequences. Shannon entropy and complexity was very useful in the first dataset from the business process domain without the use of clustering approach [10], where it could identify the specific types of the sequences without the use of clustering algorithms. Additionally, these measures can give intuition about the characteristics of the sequences in the dataset, such as states distribution and the state frequencies in the dataset. Such information can then be used for further analysis of the highlighted states and sequences. Due to sparse computation of the state transitions and linear computational complexity of Shannon entropy and complexity index all of the characteristics are computed in matter of seconds for the given datasets.

For the future work, it would be interesting to find another measures and tools that could be used in an automated way for such apriori analysis and extend the pipeline of this analysis to provide as much relevant information as possible.

Acknowledgement. This work was supported by The Ministry of Education, Youth and Sports from the National Programme of Sustainability (NPS II) project "IT4Innovations excellence in science - LQ1602".

References

1. Disco. https://fluxicon.com/disco/. Accessed 20 Apr 2019
2. Prom tools. http://www.promtools.org/doku.php. Accessed 20 Apr 2019
3. Robocup. https://www.robocup.org/. Accessed 20 Apr 2019
4. Signavio gmbh. https://www.signavio.com/. Accessed 20 Apr 2019
5. Csardi, G., Nepusz, T.: The igraph software package for complex network research. InterJournal Complex Syst. 1695 (2006). http://igraph.org
6. Gabadinho, A., Ritschard, G., Müller, N.S., Studer, M.: Analyzing and visualizing state sequences in R with TraMineR. J. Stat. Softw. **40**(4), 1–37 (2011)
7. Gabadinho, A., Ritschard, G., Studer, M., Müller, N.S.: Indice de complexité pour le tri et la comparaison de séquences catégorielles. Revue des nouvelles technologies de l'information (RNTI) **E-19**, 61–66 (2010)
8. R Core Team: R: A Language and Environment for Statistical Computing (2018). https://www.r-project.org/
9. Shannon, C.E.: A mathematical theory of communication. Bell Syst. Tech. J. **27** (1948)
10. Slaninová, K., Martinovič, J., Šperka, R., Drázdilová, P.: Extraction of agent groups with similar behaviour based on agent profiles. In: Saeed, K., Chaki, R., Cortesi, A., Wierzchoń, S. (eds.) CISIM 2013. LNCS, vol. 8104, pp. 348–357. Springer, Heidelberg (2013). https://doi.org/10.1007/978-3-642-40925-7_32
11. Slaninová, K., Vymětal, D., Martinovič, J.: Analysis of event logs: behavioral graphsD. In: Benatallah, B., et al. (eds.) WISE 2014. LNCS, vol. 9051, pp. 42–56. Springer, Cham (2015). https://doi.org/10.1007/978-3-319-20370-6_4

12. Visser, A., Ito, N., Kleiner, A.: RoboCup rescue simulation innovation strategy. In: Bianchi, R.A.C., Akin, H.L., Ramamoorthy, S., Sugiura, K. (eds.) RoboCup 2014. LNCS (LNAI), vol. 8992, pp. 661–672. Springer, Cham (2015). https://doi.org/10.1007/978-3-319-18615-3_54
13. Vymetal, D., Sperka, R.: MAREA - from an agent simulation application to the social network analysis. In: 18th Annual International Conference on Knowledge-Based and Intelligent Information and Engineering Systems KES-2014. Procedia Computer Science. Gdynia Maritime University, Pomeranian Sci & Technol, Gdynia, Poland, vol. 35, pp. 1416–1425, 15–17 September 2014. https://doi.org/10.1016/j.procs.2014.08.198
14. Wickham, H.: tidyverse: easily install and load the 'Tidyverse' (2017). https://CRAN.R-project.org/package=tidyverse, r package version 1.2.1

Performance of User Data Collections Uploads to HPCaaS Infrastructure

Pavel Moravec[1,2](✉) (iD), Jan Kožusznik[1,2](✉) (iD), Michal Krumnikl[1,2] (iD),
and Jana Klímová[2] (iD)

[1] Department of Computer Science, FEECS VŠB – Technical University of Ostrava,
17. listopadu 15, 708 33 Ostrava-Poruba, Czech Republic
{pavel.moravec,jan.kozusznik,michal.krumnikl}@vsb.cz
[2] IT4Innovations, VŠB – Technical University of Ostrava,
17. listopadu 15, 708 33 Ostrava-Poruba, Czech Republic
jana.klimova@vsb.cz

Abstract. When offering the HPC as a Service middleware to remote
users wishing them to use a HPC infrastructure, we are facing a problem
of uploading large data collections for processing. On one hand, as users
perform calculations on local infrastructures as well, they typically make
use of the most common 1 Gb/s connectivity and the institution's connectivity to the Internet is not influencing transfer rates. On the other hand,
the institution offering the HPC as a Service middleware may be distant
both geographically and network-wise. Furthermore, the amount of data
to be transferred ranges from hundreds of gigabytes to several terabytes.
In this paper, we study the common protocols used for secure data transfers and evaluate results on IT4Innovations infrastructure. Changes to
the upload to HEAppE middleware developed in our institution are also
discussed.

Keywords: Big data · High-Performance Computing (HPC) ·
HPC as a Service · Collection · SCP · SFTP · Rsync · HEAppE

1 Introduction

Modern biomedical research generates vast collections of images or other data
that often have to be processed computationally before meaningful biological
insights may be gained. One of the main sources of such huge collections is
light sheet fluorescence microscopy [12]. As an example, one of the popular technique, called Selective Plane Illumination Microscopy (SPIM) [4] is extremely
demanding in terms of data storage and pre-processing, since it allows imaging
of cellular and developmental processes over longer time periods at high spatial
and temporal resolution and across relatively large samples.

However, such experiments can easily produce terabytes of multidimensional
image data, which often cannot be processed by researchers locally on their
computers [11]. As a result, the collections have to be processed remotely in

© Springer Nature Switzerland AG 2019
K. Saeed et al. (Eds.): CISIM 2019, LNCS 11703, pp. 359–369, 2019.
https://doi.org/10.1007/978-3-030-28957-7_30

cloud or HPC environment. The HPC as a Service (HPCaaS) concept provides a convenient solution if the user lacks access to a suitable local HPC infrastructure, enabling users to remotely access an HPC infrastructure without the need to purchase and manage physical servers.

One important task which has to be solved by the HPCaaS middleware is the upload of data collections to the remote HPC cluster [7]. The data may be part of the cutting-edge research and its confidentiality during the transfer may be required by the researcher submitting them for the calculation. Also, should the transfers of data collections take a long time, this may become a significant factor against doing the calculation remotely.

Presently, our HPCaaS middleware is using SSH File Transfer Protocol (SFTP) to upload the data collections to the server and provide calculated results.

In this paper, we will show some drawbacks of this solution, compare it with other secure ways of user data upload available on our cluster and suggest improvements, which would still ensure the confidentiality of transferred data but increase the overall performance whilst keeping in mind the cluster limitations and not requiring the user to significantly modify their workflows to submit the data for processing.

The rest of the paper is organized as follows: In the following section, we will discuss the communication protocols which may be used for secure transfer of data collections to an HPC cluster, whilst ensuring the data confidentiality. In the next section we will briefly discuss the HPCaaS middleware developed for our clusters – HEAppE. Consequently, we will discuss the experimental setup for both synthetic and real-life tests. The last section before conclusion deals with the results of our experiments and the conclusions we draw from them.

2   Data Transfers

To transfer data to the HPC infrastructure in the use cases we are developing, the users need to use either a simple web interface of some external utility, or upload data directly through our service. As the support for GridFTP on `globus.org` web site, which allowed background data transfers between servers [1] with a very high overall performance [5] was dropped this January, allowing only personal or paid endpoints, a suitable and reasonably fast replacement has to be selected.

In this section, we will discuss the possible secure (encrypted) data transfer options, which can be used to copy files to the HPC cluster storage.

2.1   SSH-Based Transfers

This group of transfers uses encrypted communication channel provided by an Secure Shell (SSH) protocol [6]. However, most client or server side implementations of this protocol have a limit of application-level channel window size about 1–2 MB (32 or 64 × 32 KB) [9], which is significantly less than the transport layer is able to provide.

As a transfer channel in SSH, we may use a shell executing `rsync` command, Secure copy protocol (SCP), or SSH File Transfer Protocol (SFTP), which are part of the SSH protocol definition. For the two latter cases, no special tools are to be installed on the server, but the support of them in the used SSH client/server must be implemented and enabled.

2.2 HTTPS-Based Data Transfers

Hypertext Transfer Protocol Secure (HTTPS, HTTP over TLS) [10], as an encrypted variant of the widespread HTTP communication protocol used for transferring information between computers in the World Wide Web, seems as a reasonable and common choice. However, its direct use for data collection upload may be limited by the firewalls, as neither the nodes with the collection to be transferred nor the computational nodes have ports which would allow HTTPS servers to be run on them.

We may use a dedicated node with a running HTTPS server, or an external storage for the data collection, where both the collection and results may be uploaded as they are created. However, this means that if such intermediary exists, the retrieval of the calculated results from the cluster may be delayed.

However, we need to limit our usage of HTTP 1.1, as HTTP/2 protocol [3], although it is primarily meant to use encryption, creates only a single TCP channel between the client and the server. This impacts the performance of embedded streams which are created on the fly and must be serialized into the single TCP connection.

2.3 iRODS

The integrated Rule-Oriented Data System (iRODS) [15] follows concepts of Storage Resource Broker (SRB) [2] and both systems were created by the Data Intensive Computing Environment (DICE). SRB is a middleware that provides uniform API to access heterogeneous storage resources. iRODS was rewritten from a scratch and it is offered as open source software. As name of iRODS suggests, one of the main features is a capability to create automatic workflows base on defined rules. Rule Engine is an important part of iRODS architecture.

Next crucial iRODS feature is a data virtualization. Storage space is shared by instances of iRODS server running on connected nodes. These nodes act as storage resources. Data are represented as data objects, data objects are grouped to collections and collections are organized into zones. Data objects appears to clients similarly as files and collections as directories and sub-directories. However, data objects in the same collection could be physically stored on different storage resources and there could even be more than one storing the same data object.

Other features are data discovery and secure collaboration. iRODS contains metadata about stored data objects that enables locating of relevant data in large data set. There are also defined system of permissions to access data objects by users. Data could be also shared among different users.

iRODS uses own transfer protocol offering support for parallel transfer. However, this was the main feature for us when we were deciding different strategies for a huge data transfer.

2.4 Other Options

Other options include use of UDP-based data transfers using BBCP[1], protocols using multiple streams such as Stream Control Transmission Protocol (STCP) [13], which however do not provide data encryption by themselves and are not evaluated in this paper.

BitTorent and other peer-to-peer networks may not provide encryption either, and although they mitigate the problems with firewalls, they might still require an external web site with tracker and are more suitable for transfers where multiple copies seeding the data collection exist, which is not our typical use case.

One of the remaining options is to reduce overall Round-Trip-Time by providing a direct link between the networks [16]. As the users of the supercomputer are potentially from all over the world, this solution is not feasible in our case.

3   HPC as a Service Middleware – HEAppE

HPC as a Service is a well-known term in the area of HPC [8], as it enables users to access a remote HPC infrastructure without them needing to buy and manage their own data center infrastructure or physical servers. This lowers the entry barrier for users who are interested in massive parallel computations but do not have the necessary level of expertise in this area.

To provide end users with simple and intuitive access to the supercomputing infrastructure, an application framework called High-End Application Execution Middleware (from now on referred to as HEAppE) was developed at the IT4Innovations national supercomputing center.

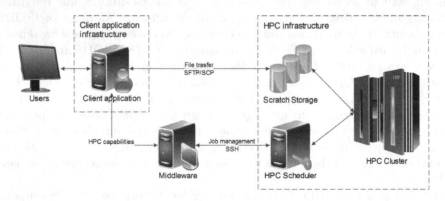

Fig. 1. Accessing an HPC environment via HPC as a Service middleware – HEAppE

---

[1] http://www.slac.stanford.edu/~abh/bbcp/.

HEAppE is software designed to be universal, which enables unified access to different HPC systems through a simple object-oriented client-server interface using standard web services.

It provides the necessary functionality for job submission, management, monitoring and reporting, user authentication and authorization, file transfer, encryption, and various notification mechanisms, the implementation is utilizing a mid-layer that manages and provides information about submitted and running jobs and their data between the client application and the HPC infrastructure (Fig. 1).

HEAppE has already been successfully used in several projects; for example, providing What-If analysis in the crisis decision support system Floreon+ [14], satellite image data analysis and in the area of molecular diagnostics and personalized medicine, the usual workflow with HEAppE consists of a one-time Command Template preparation through cooperation of HPC center specialist and the end-user. After that the computations can be routinely executed by the end-user.

However, in the previously used scenarios, the data collections have already been uploaded to the HPC environment by other means (often downloading fresh data as they are collected). But in our case, the user wants a specific, often publicly not available, collection to be processed.

4 Experiment Setup

For our experiment, we have decided to use nodes on both IT4Innovations clusters. The first tests were executed on the Salomon supercomputer consisting of 1 008 compute nodes, each equipped with 2 × 12-core Intel Xeon E5-2680v3 (2.5 GHz CPU) processors and 128 GB RAM, providing a total of 24 192 compute cores using x86-64 architecture and 129 TB RAM. The supercomputer uses a 7-dimensional Enhanced hypercube Infiniband network (56 Gb s^{-1}). This supercomputer will be the place where most calculations will be executed.

The second set of tests was executed on the older, smaller, cluster called Anselm. It consists of 180 compute nodes, each equipped with 2×8-core Intel Sandy Bridge E5-2665 (2.4 GHz CPU) with 64 GB of RAM and 23 GPU-accelerated compute nodes with 96 GB RAM, each equipped with 2×8-core Intel Sandy Bridge E5-2470 (2.3 GHz CPU) plus some special-purpose nodes. The cluster uses a high-bandwidth, low-latency InfiniBand QDR network (IB 4×QDR, 40 Gb s^{-1}) with fully non-blocking fat-tree topology.

Both of these clusters should provide a theoretical throughput of 2170 MB s^{-1} for a TCP connection over the InfiniBand network according to their documentation. However, the collections will be transferred to the login nodes through the shared connectivity of IT4Innovations, which is 4 × 10 Gb s^{-1} (unless the user uses a VPN connection, where the throughput is further reduced).

Finally, should the HEAppE middleware download data from a computational node, it will be limited to 1 Gb s^{-1} Gigabit Ethernet connectivity through utilizing network address translation. In this case, the data collection transfers would suffer significantly. As a result, the HEAppE middleware is run on a dedicated node making use of the full connectivity.

5   Results

For the first experiment, we have measured the data collection transfer performance from a typical user computer having Gigabit Ethernet connection using a variety of readily available tools. The second test was dealing with the possibility to make the transfers embedded in SCP parallel. The last test has been executed on dedicated nodes, where we were able to modify the operating system settings for the computational nodes and fine-tune the TCP protocol settings to achieve better overall performance.

5.1   Real-Life Experiment – Transfer from User Station with Arbitrary RTT

In this test we have used a representative of 10 GB subset of an existing data collection obtained from SPIM microscopy. The subset consists of 26 large files (387 MB each) and 5 smaller files (2 × 4 kB, 16 kB, 1.2 MB and 4.5 MB).

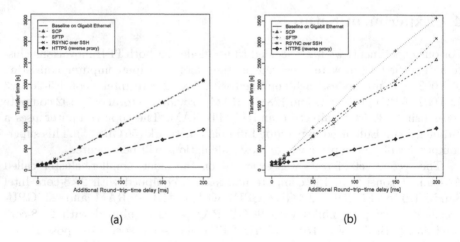

(a)   (b)

Fig. 2. Arbitrary RTT with (a) no jitter and (b) 100 μs jitter

We introduced arbitrary Round-Trip-Time (RTT) of 1 to 200 ms and a small jitter in the delay and measured the result. The test shows that even when we are using the same SSH connection, there are differences in using SCP, SFTP and rsync protocol over SSH, even when a small jitter is introduced. The delay plays a significant role for the data transfer performance, especially when using the SSH channel.

Whilst a user operating on the local network will reach the sub-ms delay and the jitter will be negligible, a user operating from the other institution in the Czech Republic will be experiencing a RTT of up to 10 ms and the 0.1 ms jitter and users from neighboring countries between 15 and 35 ms with similar jitter. Should the user uploading a data collection be from a different continent, the RTT can and will be over 100 ms, reaching 200 ms for Far East and exceeding 300 ms for Australia as our tests as well as data from RIPE RTT measurements indicate.

As one can see in Fig. 2, the performance is hindered significantly for the remote users, especially for SSH-based channels.

We have also tried to increase the number of parallel connections over 10, but in some cases (e.g. during the communication with CESNET data storage), this lead to blacklisting of the node executing tests by the data storage.

5.2   SSH-Based Connection on 10G+ Ethernet Networks

In this experiment, we tested data transfers between the Salomon supercomputer and a set of possible targets, which include the Anselm supercomputer located in the same computer room (but on another network), and nodes on CESNET data storage both in Ostrava (located in the same campus) and Pilsen. All of these transfers have been done on 10 Gigabit Ethernet or faster networks.

Table 1. Upload and download of data using a single SSH-based channel for SCP (in MiB s^{-1})

	Collection upload	Collection download
Pilsen CESNET data storage	30	88
Ostrava CESNET data storage	104.70	109.35
Different Salamon's SC node	107.50	102.90
Anselm cluster node	105.04	103.60

This covers the scenario where a user who wants to process their data collection is in the same country and the data is uploaded to a data storage hosted in the data center with a connectivity of 10 Gb s^{-1} or higher.

As we are able to see in Table 1, the transfers were influenced by other traffic on the login nodes, but mainly they were limited by the maximum SSH window size, which makes a single SSH connection not suitable on networks with transfer speeds above 1 Gb s^{-1}.

However, most collections consist of multiple files (or a single, large matrix may be split into several blocks transferred individually and merged on the recipient's side), so we should be able to create multiple channels in parallel.

To make the transfer easy to parallelize, we have created an artificial collection of 20 512 MB files, which were transferred using the arbitrary number of

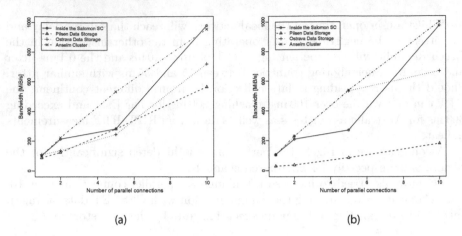

(a)   (b)

Fig. 3. Multiple SSH connections with parallel transfers (a) downloading and (b) uploading the collection

SSH connections. The results are summarized in Fig. 3. Repeatedly, there has been an unexpected performance drop when transmitting the artificial collection between two supercomputer nodes using 5 parallel streams.

5.3   Synthetic Transfers Between Anselm Nodes

In the last experiment, we have decided to test the data transfers between two dedicated Anselm cluster nodes in the same InfiniBand switch, thus removing any speed limitations on the network side.

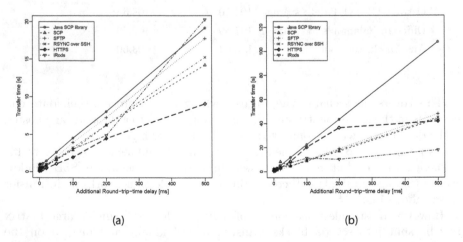

(a)   (b)

Fig. 4. Synthetic transfers of collections of with the size of (a) 10 MB and (b) 100 MB

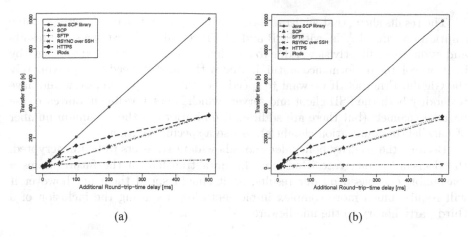

(a)   (b)

Fig. 5. Synthetic transfers of collections of with the size of (a) 1 GB and (b) 10 GB

The transfers were also done between allocated RAM disks to prevent the communication to be hindered by additional transfers to the data storage or the local SSD disk write speeds. In this scenario, we have tested both the previously evaluated methods, as well as the iRods data management software with a variety of simulated RTT delays and transferred data sizes.

We have set up a Nginx HTTPS server and iRods with default configurations and tested them together with previously used methods of data transfer from the first experiment. We have also used the JSch library[2] as the baseline for our tests, since it was used in the original implementation of the HEAppE collection upload library.

The results are summarized in Figs. 4 and 5, limited to the RTTs bellow 500 ms, which should be a reasonable upper bound for wired data transfers. As we can see from the results, the SSH-based transfers – SCP/SFTP/rsync over SSH behave almost the same with default implementations. The Nginx web server in default configuration behaves slightly worse for lower round-trip times, but the performance can be fine-tuned and improved. The JSch library, due to its native implementation in Java was performing the worst. The iRods has been a clear winner once the transfer was set up and running, being outperformed only for data collections smaller than 100 MB, where the overhead to set up its communication channels played a significant role for higher RTTs.

6   Conclusion

In this paper, we have evaluated the data collection transfer on both real collection sample and artificially generated data against several targets. The selection of proper transfer protocol is crucial for users transferring huge amount of data since it can significantly shorten the time needed for data transfers.

---

[2] www.jcraft.com/jsch/.

The results show, that whilst the usage of a single SSH channel is still a viable solution on wired LANs, with SCP and SFTP reaching almost the same results and rsync being slightly slower due to a higher number of exchanged messages by its protocol, the performance is still limited with transfer speed of approximately the Gigabit Ethernet. If we want to speed the transfers up more, we would have to modify both the SSH client and server, which is not possible in our case, use parallel channels (but there are additional limitations in the maximum number of parallel communication channels), or use a specific solution.

Because the security policy does not allow data transfers to be unencrypted, the decision to integrate iRods for the data transfers in the future seems a reasonable one based on our results, as it should speed them up, however it will require much more complex implementation, requiring the inclusion of a third-party library to the middleware.

Acknowledgement. This work was supported by the European Regional Development Fund in the IT4Innovations national supercomputing center – path to exascale project, project number CZ.02.1.01/0.0/0.0/16_013/0001791 within the Operational Programme Research, Development and Education.

References

1. Allcock, B., et al.: Data management and transfer in high-performance computational grid environments. Parallel Comput. **28**(5), 749–771 (2002). http://www.sciencedirect.com/science/article/pii/S0167819102000947
2. Baru, C., Moore, R., Rajasekar, A., Wan, M.: The SDSC storage resource broker. In: IBM Toronto Centre for Advanced Studies Conference (CASCON 1998), Toronto, Canada, November 1998
3. Belshe, M., Peon, R., Thomson, M.: Hypertext Transfer Protocol Version 2 (HTTP/2). RFC 7540, May 2015. https://rfc-editor.org/rfc/rfc7540.txt
4. Huisken, J., Swoger, J., Bene, F.D., Wittbrodt, J., Stelzer, E.H.K.: Optical sectioning deep inside live embryos by selective plane illumination microscopy. Science **305**(5686), 1007–1009 (2004)
5. Liu, Z., Balaprakash, P., Kettimuthu, R., Foster, I.: Explaining wide area data transfer performance. In: Proceedings of the 26th International Symposium on High-Performance Parallel and Distributed Computing, HPDC 2017, pp. 167–178. ACM, New York, (2017). https://doi.org/10.1145/3078597.3078605
6. Lonvick, C.M., Ylonen, T.: The Secure Shell (SSH) Protocol Architecture. RFC 4251, January 2006. https://rfc-editor.org/rfc/rfc4251.txt
7. Marx, V.: The big challenges of big data. Nature **498**, 255 EP (2013). https://doi.org/10.1038/498255a
8. Parashar, M., AbdelBaky, M., Rodero, I., Devarakonda, A.: Cloud paradigms and practices for computational and data-enabled science and engineering. Comput. Sci. Eng. **15**(4), 10–18 (2013)
9. Rapier, C., Bennett, B.: High speed bulk data transfer using the SSH protocol. In: Proceedings of the 15th ACM Mardi Gras Conference: From Lightweight Mash-Ups to Lambda Grids: Understanding the Spectrum of Distributed Computing Requirements, Applications, Tools, Infrastructures, Interoperability, and the Incremental Adoption of Key Capabilities, MG 2008, pp. 11:1–11:7. ACM, New York, (2008). https://doi.org/10.1145/1341811.1341824

10. Rescorla, E., Schiffman, A.M.: The Secure HyperText Transfer Protocol. RFC 2660, August 1999. https://rfc-editor.org/rfc/rfc2660.txt
11. Reynaud, E.G., Peychl, J., Huisken, J., Tomancak, P.: Guide to light-sheet microscopy for adventurous biologists. Nat. Methods **12**(1), 30–34 (2014)
12. Stelzer, E.H.K.: Light-sheet fluorescence microscopy for quantitative biology. Nat. Methods **12**, 23 (2014)
13. Stewart, R.R.: Stream Control Transmission Protocol. RFC 4960, September 2007. https://rfc-editor.org/rfc/rfc4960.txt
14. Svatoň, V., et al.: Floreon$^+$: a web-based platform for flood prediction, hydrologic modelling and dynamic data analysis. In: Ivan, I., Horák, J., Inspektor, T. (eds.) GIS OSTRAVA 2017. LNGC, pp. 409–422. Springer, Cham (2018). https://doi.org/10.1007/978-3-319-61297-3_30
15. Xu, H., et al.: iRODS primer 2: integrated rule-oriented data system. In: Synthesis Lectures on Information Concepts, Retrieval, and Services. Morgan & Claypool Publishers (2017). https://doi.org/10.2200/S00760ED1V01Y201702ICR057
16. Yamanaka, K., et al.: High-performance data transfer for full data replication between iter and the remote experimentation centre. Fusion Eng. Des. **138**, 202–209 (2019). http://www.sciencedirect.com/science/article/pii/S0920379618306926

Research of the Possibilities of Neural Network Predictive Modeling of Hydrodynamic Processes Based on Singularly Perturbed Problems

Assiya Zhumanazarova⑩ and Young Im Cho$^{(\boxtimes)}$⑩

Department of Computer Engineering, Gachon University,
Gyeonggi-do 461-701, Korea
assiya_mukhamaddin@mail.ru, yicho@gachon.ac.kr

Abstract. The use of artificial neural networks in predicting the dynamics of systems of natural phenomena, economic and technological processes, medical and environmental problems is a modern scientific approach to managing the development and safety of the environment and human society. Many physical processes and practical sciences in such systems are based on the laws of hydrodynamics, so the mathematical and predictive modeling of hydrodynamic processes have of theoretical and applied significance. Mathematical models of some hydrodynamic processes are described by differential equations with boundary and initial conditions. The purpose of this work is a theoretical study of the possibilities of neural networks for predictive modeling of hydrodynamic processes based on their mathematical models. The results of the work are the consideration of a singularly perturbed problem as a mathematical model and the definition of the theoretical basis of neural networks for predictive modeling of hydrodynamic processes.

Keywords: Neural networks · Singular perturbation · Asymptotic estimates · Hydrodynamics · Predictive modeling

1 Introduction

Artificial intelligence technologies are capable of solving computationally complex practical problems in a short time. For the application of such technologies have been developed various scientific and research methods that can significantly speed up the process and reduce production costs. Neural networks are one of the priority technologies in the field of artificial intelligence. The relevance of the research on artificial neural networks is related to the fact that the method of processing information by the human brain differs from the methods used by digital computers. Systems of neural networks achieve the best accurate results in the study of the functionality of various technological processes.

Neural networks can be used for prediction in the study of various physical processes of the real world. The formation of mathematical models of physical processes is an initial condition for the study of such processes. Differential equations with small

© Springer Nature Switzerland AG 2019
K. Saeed et al. (Eds.): CISIM 2019, LNCS 11703, pp. 370–382, 2019.
https://doi.org/10.1007/978-3-030-28957-7_31

parameters at higher derivatives have important applications as mathematical models of many physical processes. Asymptotic methods have been developed for their solution, which allow determining the behavior of solutions under given boundary and initial conditions. The study of the asymptotic behavior of solutions is necessary to determine the character of the process and make the correct decision when implementing mathematical models. The mathematical formulation of many problems in physics, mechanics, chemistry and engineering, for example, problems associated with the study of underground hydromechanics and hydrodynamic parameters of the reservoir, is directed towards such equations. In this paper, a linear integro-differential equation with a small parameter at the high derivatives under given initial conditions is considered on relation to the mathematical model. The main mathematical results of this work can be the basis for the further investigation of the possibilities of neural networks for construction predictive models of hydrodynamic processes.

In the following parts of this work, the basic concepts of modeling hydrodynamics problems and systems of their applications, the motivation and relevance of modeling such systems using mathematical methods and neural networks, also theoretical substantiations of given mathematical model are considered.

2 Modeling Hydrodynamic Processes

Mathematical models presented in the form of differential equations control many hydrodynamic processes. In such equations, the presence of small parameters at high derivatives plays an important role from the point of view of a more detailed and accurate description of the process being studied. However, in some extreme situations, when it is necessary to make a correct decision based on the prediction results, the use of mathematical models may be ineffective. Require models with the ability to determine the hidden unknown parameters for an accurate description of the prediction process and system management. The prediction problems are intended for research, identification of possible states of many physical, chemical processes and natural phenomena and their use in decision making. In this part, the possibilities of neural network technology to create a model for predicting hydrodynamic processes based on the proposed mathematical model are investigated on a theoretical level.

2.1 Mathematical Approach

In hydrodynamics problems, the mathematical description of the state of a moving fluid is carried out using functions that determine the distribution of the velocity of the fluid and any of its two thermodynamic quantities, pressure and density. Hydrodynamics have applied in various theoretical and applied directions, like the theory of nonlinear waves, plasma physics, nonlinear optics, electrodynamic problems, the mechanism of turbulence, and the mechanics of liquid crystals. Relativistic hydrodynamics is used in astrophysical issues, in the study of radiation objects and in the theory of multiple particle formation during collisions [1].

Mathematical modeling is the main method of various applied problems of hydrodynamics. For solving a number of such problems, differential equations of various types are used. Scientific studies of hydrodynamic processes for the construction of their mathematical models were conducted in different directions. A mathematical model of the hydrodynamic processes of the blood of the brain was developed in the work [2] using the theory of hydrodynamics to visualize blood flow in the brain vessels.

The focus of the work [3] is directed to the computation of water flows and hydrodynamics as these determine the transport of concentrations and other properties of water and form the basis for transport estimates and results. Mathematical modeling of physical phenomena with high accuracy in hydrodynamics is an important problem from the point of view of studying the influence of viscosity, density, compressibility of a liquid on wave processes to ensure safety in the construction of hydraulic structures, in the use of resources of large water objects. In solving such hydrodynamic problems, asymptotic methods have the applied significance, since it is quite possible to determine the dependencies between the exact and approximate models.

One of the most difficult and unsolved problems in hydrodynamics is the modeling of turbulence. Turbulence occurs when the velocity and size of a streamlined body are exceeded or viscosity decreases, also under nonuniform boundary and initial conditions at the boundary of the streamlined body. The problem of hydrodynamic turbulence is that it is not possible, based only on the hydrodynamic equations, to predict exactly when the turbulent mode should begin and what exactly should happen in it without experimental data [4].

2.2   A Neural Network Based Predictive Modeling

Potential applications of artificial neural networks are those where human intelligence is not effective, and traditional calculations are laborious, time consuming and do not match the requirements. Achievements of artificial neural networks are associated with the development of their theoretical foundations by effective mathematical methods for modeling the structures and architectures of neural networks, as well as with the optimal choice of various algorithms [5]. In complex dynamic systems, where there are difficult problems that require accurate results and correct decision-making based on these results, it is necessary to apply the technologies of neural networks in addition to traditional methods. Neural networks are a means of parallel execution of complex logical predicates. Neural networks can implement problems of information protection and prediction, optimization problems, security, and decision-making in control systems where it is impossible to apply any of mathematical calculation method [6].

For the application of neural networks to solve hydrodynamic problems for the purpose of prediction, many research works has been conducted in different directions. Artificial Neural Networks (ANNs) with different topologies have been evaluated to be used to predict hydrodynamic coefficients of permeable paneled breakwater in [7], ANNs were applied as a modeling tool and validation the accuracy of the model against actual flow in [8], and for prediction the effectiveness of hydraulic fracturing in [9].

There are various approaches to developing a model of hydrodynamic processes using neural networks, such as the combined use of neural networks and direct solutions of differential hydrodynamic equations, as well as the structure of a neural network to approximate the results of computational experiments obtained by the traditional methods. In this case, the general structure of the predictive model of hydrodynamic processes should be determined based on the first approach in order to apply integro-differential equations as the basis of a neural network under given initial conditions. According to the principle of operation of this type of modeling, process prediction is based on the results of observation the behavior of variables. The neural networks use the values obtained in the mathematical model for learning to predict and set parameters and unknown initial conditions of the process. In Fig. 1 was given the assumed structure of the model, obtained based on this principle [10].

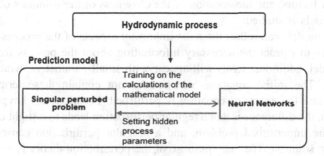

Fig. 1. Model structure

For model efficiency, various algorithms that use destructive and constructive computational strategies determine the optimal neural network architecture. In this case, constructive methods can be applied that suggest starting with simple networks and adding connections as the required accuracy of learning is achieved [11]. In accordance with the structure of the proposed mathematical model, it is assumed that the form of the equation, the influence of a small parameter and specified initial conditions, as well as the features of the simulated hydrodynamic process in determining the input and output parameters, as well as in setting up the neural network architecture will be considered. The presence of small parameters in these equations can increase the accuracy of prediction of the neural network model.

Based on theoretical studies, it can be concluded that neural networks have of practical importance as a means of modeling a unified system for predicting hydrodynamic processes. To create prediction models, problems are selected that must be solved by neural networks, and then the process of setting up the network architecture is performed using the appropriate optimal algorithm. A comparative analysis of the probability values of the expected result based on the estimation identifies possible problems of a particular process. Neural networks are able to find optimal solutions and improve the efficiency of prediction based on the results obtained.

The main components of prediction systems for hydrodynamic processes:

- Definition of variables of the mathematical model and parameters of the physical properties of hydrodynamic processes for training,
- Neural network architecture settings and algorithm selection,
- Comparative analysis of the output for prediction.

3 Mathematical Model Description

3.1 Singular Perturbed Problems

In mathematical modeling of real processes, it is inevitable to neglect some factors whose influence on the process seems insignificant. There are two types of models: simplified and extended. In the simplified models, small factors are not presented, and these models are simple enough to study. To determine the influence of these unaccounted factors on the process, an extended model will be constructed taking into account small factors, and the question of the closeness of the solutions obtained from these two models is studied.

Extended models can reflect the most important aspects of the process and provide an opportunity to extract the necessary information about the process from it. In the extended model, additional terms will appear with small parameters, which are called perturbations. The initial equation, which does not contain these terms, is called unperturbed, and the extended equation is perturbed. Perturbations have regular and singular types, the difference is that a regular perturbation leads to a slight change in the solution of the unperturbed problem, and a singular perturbation causes significant changes in the solution. The main purpose of the perturbation theory is to determine if the difference between the solutions of the simplified and extended models tends to zero when the small parameter tends to zero [12].

In the theory of singularly perturbed problems, asymptotic methods of a small parameter have been developed, which allow obtaining approximate analytical representations of solutions. Small parameter methods have applied in mechanics, physics, and in the development of methods of computer technology. Many problems of celestial mechanics, hydrodynamics, gas dynamics, and the theory of elasticity, the theory of oscillations and waves, and other problems of applied mathematics have features that do not allow for exact solutions. To study the solutions of such problems, their approximations obtained by approximate methods are used. The asymptotic expansions of these solutions are performed by a small parameter that naturally appears in the equations [13]. Singularly perturbed problems for linear and nonlinear differential and integro-differential equations with initial and boundary conditions were investigated in the works [14–16] and other numerous research papers, and various asymptotic methods were developed.

The practical value of asymptotic methods is the possibility of effectively finding the asymptotic approximations using simpler problems. This paper presents one of such methods for solving a singularly perturbed problem with initial conditions. The main question of this considering problem is whether the difference between the solutions of a singularly perturbed and unperturbed problem tends to zero when the small parameter tends to zero. The study of solutions using their asymptotic estimates is of theoretical importance for the development of the theory of singularly perturbed problems and the solution of specific applied problems.

Based on the above theoretical basis, it can be assumed that the study of singularly perturbed problems in relation to the theory of fluid mechanics and the theory of neural networks can be both theoretically and practically an important step.

3.2 Problem Solving Methodology

In this part, we aim to form of the general principles of methods for solving singularly perturbed problems. Therefore, the main results of applying one particular method to solve the Cauchy problem for linear integro-differential equations with a small parameter at the two high derivatives are presented [17]. In this problem, the roots of the characteristic equation of a homogeneous equation corresponding to a given perturbed equation were used to construct a fundamental system of solutions. The asymptotic representations of the Cauchy functions defined by the fundamental solution system were used for the analytical representation of the solution of the given problem. To study the asymptotic behavior of the solution, we considered the asymptotic estimates of the solution and the estimate of the difference of solutions of the singularly perturbed and unperturbed problems.

Problem Statement. Consider singularly perturbed Cauchy problem

$$L_\varepsilon y \equiv \varepsilon^2 y''' + \varepsilon A(t)y'' + B(t)y' + C(t)y$$

$$= F(t) + \int_0^1 [L_0(t,x)y(x,\varepsilon) + L_1(t,x)y'(x,\varepsilon)]dx \tag{1}$$

$$y(0,\varepsilon) = \alpha_0, \quad y'(0,\varepsilon) = \alpha_1, \quad y''(0,\varepsilon) = \alpha_2, \tag{2}$$

where $\varepsilon > 0$ is a small parameter, $\alpha_0, \alpha_1, \alpha_2$ are some known constants.

The main conditions

1. The functions $\mu_1(t), \mu_2(t)$ are roots of the equation

$$\mu^2 + A(t)\mu + B(t) = 0, \tag{3}$$

$$\mu_k(t) \le -\gamma \equiv const < 0, \quad \mu_1(t) \ne \mu_2(t), \quad 0 \le t \le 1.$$

2. The number 1 for sufficiently small ε is not eigenvalue of the kernel

$$J_\varepsilon(t,s) = \frac{1}{\varepsilon^2} \int_s^1 [L_0(t,x)K(x,s,\varepsilon) + L_1(t,x)K'(x,s,\varepsilon)]dx,$$

where $k(t,s,\varepsilon)$ is the solution of the homogeneous equation

$$L_\varepsilon y \equiv \varepsilon^2 y''' + \varepsilon A(t)y'' + B(t)y' + C(t)y = 0 \tag{4}$$

with initial conditions

$$K(s, s, \varepsilon) = 0, \quad K'_t(s, s, \varepsilon) = 0, \quad K''_t(s, s, \varepsilon) = 1.$$

The roots of the characteristic equation [18]

$$\varepsilon^2 \lambda^3 + \varepsilon A(t)\lambda^2 + B(t)\lambda + C(t) = 0 \tag{5}$$

have the following asymptotic representations:

$$\lambda_k(t, \varepsilon) = \frac{1}{\varepsilon}[\mu_k(t) + O(\varepsilon)], \quad k = 1, 2, \quad \lambda_3(t, \varepsilon) = \lambda(t) + O(\varepsilon). \tag{6}$$

The Fundamental System of Solutions. The fundamental system of solutions [19] of the homogeneous Eq. (4) has the following asymptotic formulas:

$$y_k(t, \varepsilon) = \exp\left(\frac{1}{\varepsilon}\int_0^t \mu_k(x)dx\right)[z_k(t) + O(\varepsilon)], k = 1, 2,$$

$$y_3(t, \varepsilon) = \exp\left(\int_0^t \lambda(x)dx\right)[1 + O(\varepsilon)]. \tag{7}$$

Cauchy Functions. The Cauchy functions [14] have the asymptotic representations:

$$K_1(t, s, \varepsilon) = \exp\left(\int_s^t \lambda(x)dx\right)[1 + O(\varepsilon)],$$

$$K_2(t, s, \varepsilon) = \frac{\varepsilon}{\mu_1(s)\mu_2(s)(\mu_2(s) - \mu_1(s))z_1(s)z_2(s)}$$

$$\cdot \left[\mu_1^2(s)z_1(s)\left(z_2(s)\exp\left(\int_s^t \lambda(x)dx\right) - z_2(t)\exp\left(\frac{1}{\varepsilon}\int_s^t \mu_2(x)dx\right)\right)\right.$$

$$\left. + \mu_2^2(s)z_2(s)\left(z_1(t)\exp\left(\frac{1}{\varepsilon}\int_s^t \mu_1(x)dx\right) - z_1(s)\exp\left(\int_s^t \lambda(x)dx\right)\right) + O(\varepsilon)\right],$$

$$K_3(t,s,\varepsilon) = \frac{\varepsilon^2}{\mu_1(s)\mu_2(s)(\mu_2(s) - \mu_1(s))z_1(s)z_2(s)}$$

$$\cdot \left[\mu_1(s)z_1(s)\left(z_2(t)\exp\left(\frac{1}{\varepsilon}\int_s^t \mu_2(x)dx\right) - z_2(s)\exp\left(\int_s^t \lambda(x)dx\right)\right) \right.$$

$$\left. + \mu_2(s)z_2(s)\left(z_1(s)\exp\left(\int_s^t \lambda(x)dx\right) - z_1(t)\exp\left(\frac{1}{\varepsilon}\int_s^t \mu_1(x)dx\right)\right) + O(\varepsilon)\right].$$

Analytical Solution Formula. The unique solution on the segment $[0, 1]$ of the problem (1), (2) is expressed by the formula

$$y(t,\varepsilon) = \alpha_0 K_1(t,0,\varepsilon) + \alpha_1 K_2(t,0,\varepsilon) + \alpha_2 K_3(t,0,\varepsilon)$$

$$+ \frac{1}{\varepsilon^2}\int_0^t K_3(t,s,\varepsilon)F_\varepsilon(s)ds \int_0^1 R_\varepsilon(s,x)F_\varepsilon(x)dx. \qquad (8)$$

Asymptotic Estimates of the Solution. The solution of the problem (1), (2) on the segment $[0, 1]$ has asymptotic estimates in the form

$$|y(t,\varepsilon)| \le C\left[(|\alpha_0| + \varepsilon|\alpha_1| + \varepsilon^2|\alpha_2|)(1 + \|L_0\| + \|L_1\| + \|F\|)\right],$$

$$|y'(t,\varepsilon)| \le C[|\alpha_0|(1 + \|L_0\| + \|L_1\| + \|F\|)$$

$$+ (|\alpha_1| + \varepsilon|\alpha_2|)\left(\varepsilon(1 + \|L_0\| + \|L_1\|) + \exp\left(-\gamma\frac{t}{\varepsilon}\right)\right) + \|F\|],$$

$$|y''(t,\varepsilon)| \le C\left[|\alpha_0|\left(1 + \|L_0\| + \|L_1\| + \frac{1}{\varepsilon}\exp\left(-\gamma\frac{t}{\varepsilon}\right)\right)\right.$$

$$+ |\alpha_1|\left(\varepsilon(1 + \|L_0\| + \|L_1\|) + \frac{1}{\varepsilon}\exp\left(-\gamma\frac{t}{\varepsilon}\right)\right) + |\alpha_2|$$

$$\left. \cdot \left(\varepsilon^2(1 + \|L_0\| + \|L_1\|) + \exp\left(-\gamma\frac{t}{\varepsilon}\right)\right) + \|F\|\left(1 + \frac{1}{\varepsilon}\exp\left(-\gamma\frac{t}{\varepsilon}\right)\right)\right].$$

The unperturbed problem

$$L_0\bar{y} \equiv B(t)\bar{y}' + C(t)\bar{y} = F(t) + \int_0^1 [L_0(t,x)\bar{y}(x) + L_1(t,x)\bar{y}'(x)]dx \qquad (9)$$

$$\bar{y}(0) = \alpha_0. \qquad (10)$$

Asymptotic Estimates of the Difference Between the Solutions of a Perturbed and Unperturbed Problem. Asymptotic estimates of the difference between the solutions of problems (1), (2) and (9), (10) on the segment [0, 1] have the form

$$|y(t,\varepsilon) - \bar{y}(t)| \le C\varepsilon, \quad |y'(t,\varepsilon) - \bar{y}'(t)| \le C\left[\varepsilon + \exp\left(-\gamma\frac{t}{\varepsilon}\right)\right],$$

$$|y''(t,\varepsilon) - \bar{y}''(t)| \le C\left[\varepsilon + \frac{1}{\varepsilon}\exp\left(-\gamma\frac{t}{\varepsilon}\right)\right]. \tag{11}$$

From (11) we immediately obtain the following limit equalities:

$$\lim_{\varepsilon \to 0} y(t,\varepsilon) = \bar{y}(t), \quad 0 \le t \le 1, \quad \lim_{\varepsilon \to 0} y'(t,\varepsilon) = \bar{y}'(t), \quad 0 < t \le 1,$$

$$\lim_{\varepsilon \to 0} y''(t,\varepsilon) = \bar{y}''(t), \quad 0 < t \le 1. \tag{12}$$

Thus, the solution of the singularly perturbed problem (1), (2) tends uniformly over t on the segment [0,1] to solution of the unperturbed problem (9), (10), and its derivatives of the first and second $y'(t,\varepsilon), y''(t,\varepsilon)$ order tend in outside a sufficiently small neighborhood of the point $t = 0$ to $y'(t), y''(t)$ to. Note that the constituent elements and the evidence of all the above formulas were described in more detail in [17].

Numerical Results. We apply the considered method to a singularly perturbed problem

$$L_\varepsilon y \equiv \varepsilon^2 y''' + 3\varepsilon y'' + 2y' = 1 + \int_0^1 y(x,\varepsilon)dx, \tag{13}$$

$$y(0,\varepsilon) = 0, \quad y'(0,\varepsilon) = 1, \quad y''(0,\varepsilon) = 2. \tag{14}$$

Corresponding homogeneous equation to Eq. (13)

$$L_\varepsilon y \equiv \varepsilon^2 y''' + 3\varepsilon y'' + 2y' = 0 \tag{15}$$

has a characteristic equation

$$\varepsilon^2 \lambda^3 + 3\varepsilon \lambda^2 + 2\lambda = 0 \tag{16}$$

Roots of the Eq. (16)

$$\lambda_1 = -\frac{1}{\varepsilon}, \; \lambda_2 = -\frac{2}{\varepsilon}, \; \lambda_3 = 0 \tag{17}$$

Fundamental solution system of the Eq. (15)

$$y_1(t, \varepsilon) = \exp\left(-\frac{t}{\varepsilon}\right), \quad y_2(t, \varepsilon) = \exp\left(-2\frac{t}{\varepsilon}\right), \quad y_3(t, \varepsilon) = 1. \tag{18}$$

Wronskian has the form [17]

$$W(t, \varepsilon) = -\frac{2}{\varepsilon^3} \exp\left(-3\frac{t}{\varepsilon}\right) \neq 0. \tag{19}$$

Determinants $W_i(i = t, s, \varepsilon), i = 1, 2, 3$ have the following representations:

$$\begin{aligned}
W_1(t, s, \varepsilon) &= -\frac{2}{\varepsilon^3} \exp\left(-3\frac{s}{\varepsilon}\right), \\
W_2(t, s, \varepsilon) &= \frac{1}{\varepsilon^2}\left[-3\exp\left(-3\frac{s}{\varepsilon}\right) + 4\exp\left(-\frac{t+2s}{\varepsilon}\right) - \exp\left(-\frac{2t+s}{\varepsilon}\right)\right], \\
W_3(t, s, \varepsilon) &= \frac{1}{\varepsilon}\left[-\exp\left(-3\frac{s}{\varepsilon}\right) + 4\exp\left(-\frac{2t+s}{\varepsilon}\right) - \exp\left(-\frac{t+2s}{\varepsilon}\right)\right].
\end{aligned} \tag{20}$$

The Cauchy functions

$$\begin{aligned}
K_1(t, s, \varepsilon) &= 1, K_2(t, s, \varepsilon) = \frac{\varepsilon}{2}\left[3 - 4\exp\left(-\frac{t-s}{\varepsilon}\right) + \exp\left(-2\frac{t-s}{\varepsilon}\right)\right], \\
K_3(t, s, \varepsilon) &= \frac{\varepsilon^2}{2}\left[1 + \exp\left(-2\frac{t-s}{\varepsilon}\right) - 2\exp\left(-2\frac{t-s}{\varepsilon}\right)\right].
\end{aligned} \tag{21}$$

By formula (8)

$$y(t, \varepsilon) = K_2(t, 0, \varepsilon) + 2K_3(t, 0, \varepsilon) + \frac{1}{\varepsilon^2}\int_0^t K_3(t, s, \varepsilon)f_\varepsilon(s)ds. \tag{22}$$

Substituting (22) in the right side of the equation and writing in the form, we get

$$\begin{aligned}
f_\varepsilon(t) &= 1 + \int_0^1 \left[K_2(t, 0, \varepsilon) + 2K_3(t, 0, \varepsilon) + \frac{1}{\varepsilon^2}\int_0^t K_3(t, s, \varepsilon)f_\varepsilon(s)ds\right]dt \\
&= F_\varepsilon(t) + \int_0^1 \left[\frac{1}{\varepsilon^2}\int_0^t K_3(t, s, \varepsilon)f_\varepsilon(s)ds\right]dt,
\end{aligned}$$

$$F_\varepsilon(t) = 1 + \int_0^1 [K_2(t, 0, \varepsilon) + 2K_3(t, 0, \varepsilon)]dt.$$

$$f_\varepsilon(t) = F_\varepsilon(t) + \int\limits_0^1 K_\varepsilon(t,s)f_\varepsilon(s)ds, K_\varepsilon(t,s) = \frac{1}{\varepsilon^2}\int\limits_s^1 K_3(t,s,\varepsilon)dt.$$

By (21)

$$K_\varepsilon(t,s) = \frac{1-s}{2} - 3\frac{\varepsilon}{4} + \varepsilon\, \exp\left(-\frac{1-s}{\varepsilon}\right) - \frac{\varepsilon}{4}\exp\left(-2\frac{1-s}{\varepsilon}\right) \qquad (23)$$

$$K_\varepsilon(t,s) = \frac{1-s}{2} + O(\varepsilon). \qquad (24)$$

$$f_\varepsilon(t) = F_\varepsilon(t) + \int\limits_0^1 R_\varepsilon(t,s)F_\varepsilon(s)ds.$$

$$F_\varepsilon(t) = 1 + \frac{3}{2}\varepsilon + \varepsilon^2\left[2\mu - \frac{1}{4}\mu^2 - \frac{3}{4}\right] + \varepsilon^3\left[-\frac{3}{2} + 2\mu - \frac{1}{2}\mu^2\right], \mu = \exp\left(-\frac{1}{\varepsilon}\right).$$

To determine $R_\varepsilon(t,s)$ apply the following formula:

$$K_\varepsilon(t,s) = K_1(t,s,\varepsilon),\ldots, K_n(t,s,\varepsilon) = \int\limits_0^1 K_\varepsilon(t,x)K_{n-1}(x,s,\varepsilon)dx, \quad n \geq 2. \qquad (25)$$

By the formula (23),

$$K_1(t,s,\varepsilon) = \frac{1-s}{2} - \frac{3}{4}\varepsilon + \varepsilon\, \exp\left(-\frac{1-s}{\varepsilon}\right) - \frac{1}{4}\varepsilon\, \exp\left(-2\frac{1-s}{\varepsilon}\right).$$

$$K_1(t,s,\varepsilon) = I_0,$$

$$K_2(t,s,\varepsilon) = I_0 \cdot \int\limits_0^1\left[\frac{1-x}{2} - \frac{3}{4}\varepsilon + \varepsilon\, \exp\left(-\frac{1-x}{\varepsilon}\right) - \frac{\varepsilon}{4}\exp\left(-2\frac{1-x}{\varepsilon}\right)\right]dx = I_0 I_1,$$

$$I_1 = \frac{1}{4} - \frac{3}{4}\varepsilon + \varepsilon^2\left(\frac{7}{8}\mu + \frac{1}{8}\mu^2\right), \mu = \exp\left(-\frac{1}{\varepsilon}\right).$$

$$K_3(t,s,\varepsilon) = I_0 I_1 \int\limits_0^1 K_\varepsilon(t,x)dx = I_0 I_1^2,\ldots, K_n(t,s,\varepsilon) = I_0 I_1^{n-1}.$$

We search resolvent in the form of a series

$$R_\varepsilon(t,s) = K_1(t,s,\varepsilon) + K_2(t,s,\varepsilon) + \ldots = I_0 + I_0 I_1 + I_0 I_1^2 + \ldots$$
$$= I_0\left(1 + I_1 + I_1^2 + \ldots\right) = I_0\left(1 + \frac{1}{4} + \frac{1}{4^2} + \ldots + O(\varepsilon)\right), \tag{26}$$

$$R_\varepsilon(t,s) = 2/3(1-s) + O(\varepsilon).$$

$$F_\varepsilon(t) \to 1,\ R_\varepsilon(t,s) \to 2/3(1-s), f_\varepsilon(t) \to 4/3,\ over\ \varepsilon \to 0.$$

Substituting the values of $R_\varepsilon(t,s), f_\varepsilon(t)$ into (22), we obtain the solution in the form

$$y(t,\varepsilon) = \frac{\varepsilon}{2}\left[3 - 4\exp\left(-\frac{t}{\varepsilon}\right) + \exp\left(-2\frac{t}{\varepsilon}\right)\right] + \varepsilon^2\left[1 + \exp\left(-2\frac{t}{\varepsilon}\right) - 2\exp\left(-\frac{t}{\varepsilon}\right)\right]$$
$$+ \frac{2}{3}\left[1 + \frac{3\varepsilon}{2} + \varepsilon^2\left(-\frac{3}{4} + 2\mu - \frac{1}{4}\mu^2\right) + \varepsilon^2\left(-\frac{3}{2} + 2\mu - \frac{\mu^2}{2}\right)\right]$$
$$\cdot\left[t + \varepsilon\left(-\frac{3}{2} - \frac{1}{2}\exp\left(-2\frac{t}{\varepsilon}\right) + 2\exp\left(-\frac{t}{\varepsilon}\right)\right)\right].$$

In this example, we can verify that the solution of the perturbed problem (13), (14) tends to solution of the corresponding unperturbed problem as the small parameter tends to zero. Based on the obtained limit equalities (12), it was concluded that the difference between the solutions of the considering singularly perturbed and unperturbed problems tends to zero when a small parameter tends to zero. Based on the main results of this part, approximate concepts of the conditions and parameters of problems for modeling physical processes by mathematical methods, as well as techniques of neural networks, can be formed.

4 Conclusions

In this paper, the basic principles and general approaches to the development of a predictive model of hydrodynamic processes using neural networks based on mathematical models are theoretically investigated. Since this work is of a general character, further research will be conducted to identify specific problems of hydrodynamics and their mathematical modeling based on singularly perturbed differential equations, as well as practical results of prediction using neural networks model.

Acknowledgements. This research was supported by the MSIT, Korea, under the ITRC support program (IITP-2019-2017-0-01630) supervised by the IITP and in part by the NRF-2018R1D1A 1A09084151.

References

1. Landau, L.D., Lifshits, E.M.: Hydrodynamics. Theoretical Physics: Volume 6, 3rd edn. Nauka, Moscow (1986)
2. Galkin, V.A., Urmantseva, N.R.: Mathematical modeling of hydrodynamic processes in the blood of the brain. Vestnik kibernetiki **4**(16), 35–42 (2014)
3. Markku, V.: Mathematical modelling of flow and transport as link to impacts in multidiscipline environments. Oulu University Press, Oulu (2009)
4. Hydrodynamics. https://ru.wikipedia.org. Accessed 12 Apr 2019
5. Wassermann, F.: Neurocomputer Techniques: Theory and Practice. Mir, Moscow (1992)
6. Barsky, A.B.: Neural networks: recognition, management, decision-making: finance and statistics, Moscow (2004)
7. Hagras, M.A.: Prediction of hydrodynamic coefficients of permeable paneled breakwater using artificial neural networks. IJEST **5**(8), 1616–1627 (2013)
8. Elsafi, S.H.: Artificial neural networks (ANNs) for flood forecasting at Dongola Station in the River Nile. Sudan. Alexandria Eng. J. **53**, 655–662 (2014)
9. Andronov, Yu.V., Strekalov, A.V.: Application of neural networks for predicting the efficiency of formation hydraulic fracturing. Dev. Oil Gas Fields **12**(2), 64–68 (2014)
10. Yasinsky, I.F., Yasinsky, F.N.: Simulation of a hydrodynamic problem using the combined neural network and dynamic models. Vestnik ISEU **1**, 77–79 (2013)
11. Valyuhov, S., Kretinin, A., Burakov, A.: Neural network modeling of hydrodynamics processes. In: Harry, E.S., André, L.A.S., Raquel, J.L. (eds.) Hydrodynamics-Optimizing Methods and Tools, pp. 201–222. InTech, Croatia (2011)
12. Vasilyeva, A.B., Butuzov, V.F.: Asymptotic Methods in the Theory of Singular Perturbations. Visshaya shkola, Moscow (1990)
13. Nayfe, A.Kh.: Perturbation Methods. Mir, Moscow (1976)
14. Kasymov, K.A.: Singularly perturbed boundary value problems with initial jumps. Sanat, Almaty (1997)
15. Vishik, M.I., Lyusternik, L.A.: On the initial jump for nonlinear differential equations containing a small parameter. Dokl. Akad. Nauk SSSR **132**(6), 1242–1245 (1960)
16. Imanaliev, M.I.: Asymptotic methods in the theory of singularly perturbed integro-differential systems. Ilim, Frunze (1972)
17. Kasymov, K.A., Zhumanazarova, A.M.: On the Cauchy problem for linear singularly perturbed integro-differential equations of Fredholm type. Izv. Minist. Nauki Vyssh. Obraz. Nats. Akad. Nauk Resp. Kaz. **1**, 45–54 (1999)
18. Vasilyeva, A.B.: Asymptotic methods in the theory of ordinary differential equations with small parameters at the higher derivatives. Vychl. mat. and mat. phys. **3**(4), 611–642 (1963)
19. Lomov, S.A.: Perturbation method for singular problems. Izvestiya Akad. Nauk SSSR **36**(3), 635–651 (1972)

Modelling and Optimization

Multi-criteria Decision Making Problem for Doing Business: Comparison Between Approaches of Individual and Group Decision Making

Daniela Borissova[1,2]($\boxtimes$) ⓘ, Dilian Korsemov[1] ⓘ, and Ivan Mustakerov[1] ⓘ

[1] Institute of Information and Communication Technology at Bulgarian Academy of Sciences, 1113 Sofia, Bulgaria
{dborissova,mustakerov}@iit.bas.bg,
dilian_korsemov@abv.bg
[2] University of Library Studies and Information Technologies, 1784 Sofia, Bulgaria

Abstract. The selection of location for doing business can be realized by using of several aspects of business regulations as reported by the World Bank. For the goal, a multi-criteria decision making problem is formulated to determine the most preferable city to invest. This decision making problem is solved by two optimization models – by individual decision making preferences expressed in weighted sum method and group decision making considering the proposed modified simple additive weighting. In group decision making, the experts usually are with different background and field of competency. The proposed modification takes into account the difference in experts' experience by considering all experts' opinions with different importance in the aggregated final group decision. It is shown that new utility function based on simple additive weighting method more accurately reflect the existing differences in background and field of competency of each expert. Due the multidimensional nature of the problem for doing business, the group decision making approach seems to be more precisely in determination of the best selection to invest.

Keywords: MCDM · Weighted sum method · Group decision making · Modified simple additive weighting · Economies ranking

1 Introduction

Doing of business recognized as investment decision making, is influenced by different factors including country business atmosphere, macroeconomic stability, economic policy environment, etc. Many of investment decisions rely on the index of ease of doing business where different indicators are considered (Pinheiro-Alves and Zambujal-Oliveira 2012). Due the globalization, the growing business is faced with the problem of competitiveness and choice of most appropriate location for investments. A large part of doing business is related with making the decisions. These decisions are

K. Saeed et al. (Eds.): CISIM 2019, LNCS 11703, pp. 385–396, 2019.
https://doi.org/10.1007/978-3-030-28957-7_32

usually related with different measurable indicators. Usage of performance indicators allows to measure the degree of realization of the defined goals and to point the key factors responsible to improve or deterioration of business results (Jaksic et al. 2018; Ruiz et al. 2018).

In most cases the investment decisions require selection of particular geographical location where to make the investments (Ruiz et al. 2018). There exist a number of factors influencing on this decision, but the doing business project of the World Bank provides objective measures of business regulations across 190 economies (Doing Business, http://www.doingbusiness.org/). In such way, different economies can be compared or ranked accordingly different objective criteria. It is possible even to make comparison between some given cities from particular country or comparison between given cities from different countries. This comparison is important, because the business regulations and their implementation could vary considerably both among different countries even in different cities in same country.

The aim of the paper is to compare the approaches of individual and group decision making to sustainable location assessment and selection for doing business. In addition, a new modified utility function is proposed to cope with different level of knowledge and experience of group members when aggregating the final group decision.

Due the multidimensional nature of the problem for doing business, the group decision making approach seems to be more precisely in determination of the best selection to invest. This is a result of variety of business regulations required different and specific competences. Making the decisions is relatively easy in case when only one person is involved or affected by this decision. In case of group decision making, authorized group with experts collectively have to make a choice from the alternatives. That is why the current paper aims to compare these two approaches (individual and group) for selection of the city for doing business.

The rest of the paper is structured as follows: Sect. 2 provide a literature review of some methods for selection in multi-attribute decision problems; Sect. 3 describes the problem and provide the input data; Sect. 4 contains mathematical models for selection a city for doing business – individual and group decision making approaches; Sect. 5 presents the result from numerical testing of formulated mathematical models and provide analysis and discussion, while Sect. 6 contains the conclusions.

2 Literature Review

The goal of doing business is to tracks the business regulations that affect small and medium-size domestic companies. The business regulations involve different criteria related to the most essential aspects to establish a business. This means that different kind of specialists is needed to assess these business regulations. To rank the economy, an algorithm based on multi-criteria optimization could be used (Mustakerov and Borissova 2013). This algorithm sequentially solves a series of multi-criteria optimization tasks and reduces the number of alternatives on each subsequent iteration. Other authors propose an approach for ranking of alternatives by pairwise comparisons matrix and priority vector (Ramik 2017). Gokmenoglu and Alaghemand (2015) suggest methodology that combines AHP, TOPSIS and multi-period multi-attribute decision making technique. In some cases it makes sense to combine some stochastic local search and genetic algorithms to optimize the model parameters to achieve the desired solution (Skraba et al. 2016).

The strategy identification is considered as the most important component in strategic management and sometimes is even more important than it implementation. This is why the proper mathematical models or simulations are needed (Angarita-Zapata et al. 2016). Due the multidimensional of the strategy, the multi-criteria decision making models seems to be suitable. Considering the fuzzy environment and multi-criteria decision making models, the hybrid fuzzy AHP and TOPSIS are developed to perform the proper selection (Wang et al. 2018). They applied fuzzy AHP for determination of alternative weights while the TOPSIS is used for ranking of all potential alternatives. In the modern society, identifying the best suited alternative is of high importance. To indentify such alternative, the authors propose AHP-GTMA (analytic hierarchy process and graph theory and matrix approach) and AHP-TOPSIS for determination of selection decision (Zhuang et al. 2018). It should be noted that key indicators identifying in grouped factors in the field of financial performance is a crucial issue for all individuals and organizations (Hornungova and Milichovsky 2019). The usage of mathematical multi-criteria methods based on analytical hierarchical process and data envelopment analysis contribute to rank different project activities evaluated by several indexes (Hadad et al. 2016). In the field of efficiency evaluation the different variants of DEA is possible to utilize as it is demonstrated in the case of transport sector (Markovits-Somogyi 2011). The business decision for supplier selection could involve evaluation toward some environmental (green) factors. It is shown that usage of DEA with common weights analysis the decision maker can influence a decision with the choice of weight system (Vorosmarty and Dobos 2019).

Besides the existence of variety of multi-criteria decision making models, the age and qualification of managers and experts who forming the group for decision making are to be considered. This is due the fact, that the empirical study results show that the younger age of managers is more competent in the company's management capabilities (Fujianti 2018). It is expedient to consider the preferences about criteria and evaluations with different importance in case of group decision making (Korsemov et al. 2018; Borissova 2018). Because of differences in field of competence, backgrounds, and experience of decision makers, the difference in opinions is observed (Shih et al. 2007). This should be taken into account in determination of final preferred selection of group decision making (Borissova 2018; Chen et al. 2015). The growing complexity in financial investment due the specific nature of alternatives' representations requires new algorithms to overcome such difficulties or using of fuzzy networks with feedback rule bases to improve the transparency in decision making (Gegov et al. 2017). In this regard, Brester et al. propose multi-objective optimization algorithms with the island metaheuristic for effective problem solving (Brester et al. 2017). The decision making problem of doing business is related with different aspects of financial investment and using of proper business model is of highly importance, especially in the fast changing business environment (Marolt et al. 2016).

All these aspects of different business activity and models can be used for evaluation and selection of the most suitable location for doing business considering some business regulations considered as evaluation criteria toward some possible locations within East Europe.

3   Problem Descriptions

The rapidly changing environment required to take responsible action to be able to reflect the different changes. There exists a difference in the objective criteria within the same country. For this reason, some major cities from Bulgaria, Romania and Hungary are used as possible locations for doing business. These economies are evaluated toward five business regulations in accordance to the most recent report of the World Bank for 2017. The used regulations that are considered as evaluation criteria are as follows: (1) starting a business; (2) deal with construction permit; (3) getting electricity; (4) registering property and (5) enforcing contracts (see Table 1).

Table 1. Normalized scores for the business regulations

#	Alternatives (cities)	Criteria				
		Starting a business, (C_1)	Deal with construction permit, (C_2)	Getting electricity (C_3)	Registering property, (C_4)	Enforcing contracts, (C_5)
		Score	Score	Score	Score	Score
1	Burgas (Bg)	90.05	69.23	65.49	70.67	72.68
2	Pleven (Bg)	90.50	71.92	54.66	70.44	73.63
3	Plovdiv (Bg)	90.05	68.30	65.06	69.59	72.36
4	Ruse (Bg)	88.33	71.34	54.71	71.53	75.38
5	Sofia (Bg)	86.82	72.75	54.64	69.23	67.04
6	Varna (Bg)	90.56	70.53	59.05	70.19	74.23
7	Budapest (Hu)	87.28	67.89	63.25	80.08	73.75
8	Debrecen (Hu)	87.61	72.71	63.36	81.16	81.72
9	Gyor (Hu)	87.32	73.35	63.25	80.80	74.20
10	Miskolc (Hu)	87.61	73.47	61.76	80.92	79.53
11	Pecs (Hu)	87.61	75.58	65.21	79.96	77.07
12	Szeged (Hu)	87.57	74.38	67.46	80.80	75.98
13	Szekesfeharvar (Hu)	87.32	73.70	65.53	80.92	79.12
14	Brasov (Ro)	88.78	56.28	49.56	74.65	64.24
15	Bucharest (Ro)	89.53	58.09	53.23	74.65	72.25
16	Cluj-Napoca (Ro)	88.78	54.32	50.41	73.81	73.34
17	Constanta (Ro)	87.52	49.26	49.06	74.65	75.04
18	Craiova (Ro)	86.27	61.31	53.01	74.65	73.37

(continued)

Table 1. (*continued*)

#	Alternatives (cities)	Criteria				
		Starting a business, (C_1)	Deal with construction permit, (C_2)	Getting electricity (C_3)	Registering property, (C_4)	Enforcing contracts, (C_5)
		Score	Score	Score	Score	Score
19	Iasi (Ro)	88.28	56.01	57.76	74.65	72.64
20	Oradea (Ro)	89.53	57.84	50.80	75.48	72.01
21	Ploiesti (Ro)	89.53	54.40	47.22	74.64	65.86
22	Timisoara (Ro)	89.53	48.92	43.56	74.65	76.13

Source: http://www.doingbusiness.org/~/media/WBG/DoingBusiness/Documents/Special-Reports/DB17-EU-Report-ENG.PDF

The score about the business regulations in Table 1 are normalized within the range from 0 to 100, where 100 represent the best practices, i.e. the higher the score is the better. The report of the World Bank rang the cities toward only one of the business regulations criteria and do not have information how the particular city is situated in rang accordingly these 5 evaluation criteria (starting a business, deal with construction permit, getting electricity, registering property and enforcing contracts).

To determine the most appropriate city to invest considering simultaneously all five criteria representing the five business regulations, a group of three experts with different area of competency is defined to perform the selection. The expertise of the group members covers the areas of finance, project management and legislation.

Depending on different investment interests, the priority of these business regulations could be in different interest of importance. In this respect, the current article deals with comparison between individual and group decision making.

4   Mathematical Models for Selection a City for Doing Business

4.1   Individual Decision Making Model

Due the multiple business regulations that are to be considered as evaluation criteria, the problem of selection can be considered as multi-criteria decision making problem. To realize the most appropriate selection, the decision maker should express preferences about the importance for each criterion. In this context the individual preferences will define Pareto-optimal alternative in accordance to the given preferences. For the goal, the following combinatorial mathematical model is formulated:

$$\min \; (c_1, c_2, \ldots, \; c_{j-s})$$
$$\max \; (c_{j-(s+1)}, \ldots, c_{j-1}, \; c_j) \tag{1}$$

subject to

$$\forall j = 1, 2, \ldots, J : c_j = \sum_{i=1}^{N} c_j^i x_i, \ldots i = 1, 2, \ldots, N \tag{2}$$

$$\sum_{i=1}^{N} x_i = 1, \; x_i \in \{0, 1\} \tag{3}$$

where $j = 1, \ldots, J$ is the number of evaluation criteria and some of them $(j - s)$ achieve the best value if they are minimized and rest of them achieve the best value if they are maximized $(j - (s + 1))$; $i = 1, 2, \ldots, N$ is the number of alternatives (cities); and x_i are decision variables of type binary integers.

Widely used approach for solving multi-criteria optimization problems is done by transformation into single scalar optimization problem (Marler and Arora 2004). This approach requires selecting a proper transformation method. In this article, the weighted sum method is used to solve the formulated problem (1)–(3). To perform the weighted sum method, the normalization scheme is to be applied for all criteria. The weighted sum method transforms the original multi-criteria problem into scalar problem by aggregated maximization function of normalized criteria and weighting coefficient assigned by the decision maker (DM). The obtained transformation is expressed as follows:

$$\max(w_1(c_1)^* + w_2(c_2)^* + w_3(c_3)^* + w_4(c_4)^* + w_5(c_5)^*) \tag{4}$$

subject to

$$\forall j = 1, 2, \ldots, 5 : c_j = \sum_{i=1}^{22} c_j^i x_i \tag{5}$$

$$\sum_{i=1}^{22} x_i = 1, \; x_i \in \{0, 1\} \tag{6}$$

$$\sum_{j=1}^{5} w_j = 1 \tag{7}$$

where $w_1, \ldots, w_5$ are non-negative weighted coefficients for relative importance between criteria and $(c_j)^*$ are normalized criteria. The weighted coefficients w_j express the subjective point of view of DM toward importance of evaluation criteria. The normalization is needed if the criteria evaluations are with different dimensions.

4.2 Group Decision Making Model

To express the different investment interests toward the business regulations for doing of business, some experts are involved. Each expert determines his own weighted coefficients in regard to the importance of evaluation criteria concerning business regulations. The maximum of overall score for business regulations criteria should determine the most preferable place to make the investments. It should be noted that these experts probably will have different knowledge and experience and the final selection have to be able to consider this difference.

The goal of the article is to use only evaluation scores from Table 1 as objective measure and to consider weighed coefficients for relative importance of business regulations in accordance to different expert' point of view. This requires formulation a new mathematical model to involve: (1) normalized scores for business regulations (Table 1); (2) weighted coefficients for criteria importance given from each expert; (3) differences in experts' expertise. To cope with presence of differences in evaluations of group members', a modification of classical simple additive weighting (MSAW) model is proposed for alternatives evaluation:

$$\max E_i = \sum_{k=1}^{K} \lambda^k \sum_{j=1}^{N} w_j^k a_{ij}, \text{ for } i = \{1, 2, \ldots, \text{M}\} \tag{8}$$

$$\sum_{j=1}^{N} w_j^k = 1 \tag{9}$$

$$\sum_{k=1}^{K} \lambda^k = 1 \tag{10}$$

where $i = 1, \ldots, \text{M}$ is the number of alternatives; $j = 1, \ldots, \text{N}$ is the number of evaluation criteria; a_{ij} express the normalized scores of i-th alternative toward j-th criterion accordingly the World Bank report; w_j^k is the coefficient for relative importance of j-th criterion from the k-th expert point of view; and coefficients λ^k express the importance of expertise for the k-th expert within the group.

In contrast to the classical simple additive weighting model, where each expert evaluate alternatives toward performance criteria, in (8) the same evaluation scores of alternatives performance are used. So, the normalized scores a_{ij} contains the same as determined by the report of the World Bank (Table 1). The essence in proposed formulation (8)–(10) is the usage of weighted coefficients λ^k to express the differences between group members' expertise (10) and considering also the coefficients w_j^k for relative importance of j-th criterion from the k-th expert point of view (9). The overall performance of particular alternative (city) will obtain by summing the multiplication of evaluations scores, weighted coefficients for criteria importance from the experts' perspective and weighted coefficients for group members' expertise. The best city (alternative) to invest will be the city with maximum performance score.

The formulation (8)–(10) allows to determine the preferable alternative of the group, taking into account not only alternatives' evaluations (a_{ij}) in accordance to the criteria and relative importance of these criteria (w_j), but also considers the weighted coefficients for expertise of each group members (λ^k).

When different locations in the same city are to be considered, some new business regulations should be added in Table 1. The weights about the additional regulations (criteria) will stay remain subjective to the point of view of particular DM in both cases of individual and group decision making.

5   Result Analysis and Discussion

5.1   Results from Individual Decision Making Implementation

Using of formulated optimization problem (4)–(7) together with input data from Table 1 determine the following selection as shown in Table 2.

Table 2. Selected alternative by individual decision making implementation

Cases	Coefficients for criteria importance					Objective function value	Selected alternative
	C_1	C_2	C_3	C_4	C_5		
Case-1	0.20	0.20	0.20	0.20	0.20	77.318	A-13 (Szekesfeharvar-Hu)
Case-2	0.40	0.25	0.10	0.15	0.10	80.161	A-11 (Pecs-Hu)

Two different cases are investigated to illustrate how the weighted coefficients influence on the final optimal decision. The Case-1 considers all 5 business regulations with equal importance. The solution in this situation determines the alternative A-13 (Szekesfeharvar-Hu) as optimal selection for doing business. In Case-2, the coefficients for criteria importance about considered business regulations emphasize on C1, followed by C2, C4 and C5. The optimal solution in this case determines alternative A-11 (Pecs-Hu) as the optimal selection.

Disadvantage of this classical approach is the fact, that it takes into account the preferences only of one decision maker. By usage of different weighted coefficients for relative importance between criteria, it is possible to generate different Pareto-optimal selections, but without any relation between them. So, to make more detailed and realistic selection, the group decision making approach should be applied, where the different points of view can be aggregated by using of suitable utility function as shown in the formulation (8)–(10).

5.2   Results from Group Decision Making Implementation

The input data from Table 1 and proposed formulation (8)–(10) together with the same weighted coefficients for relative importance of between criteria for three experts are considered. The proposed group decision making formulation (8)–(10) takes into account simultaneously the different points of view of the experts toward criteria importance. Using the normalized scores about the business regulations (Table 1) and equal importance for the knowledge and experience of group members, the task solution determine as the best selection city Debrecen (Hu) for doing business, as shown in Table 3.

Table 3. Results of proposed group decision making model using

Group members	Coefficients for criteria importance					Expertise weights	MSAW	
	C1	C2	C3	C4	C5		Objective function value	Selected alternative
E-1	0.20	0.20	0.20	0.20	0.20	0.34	77.938	A-8 (Debrecen-Hu)
E-2	0.12	0.21	0.17	0.23	0.27	0.33		
E-3	0.40	0.25	0.10	0.15	0.10	0.33		

All alternatives performance toward 5 business regulations for: starting a business; deal with construction permit; getting electricity; registering property and enforcing contracts, considering the opinion of group members with equal importance are illustrated in Fig. 1. As it could be seen, there are several alternatives with good performance observed at A-8, A-11, A-12 and A-13 (see Fig. 1).

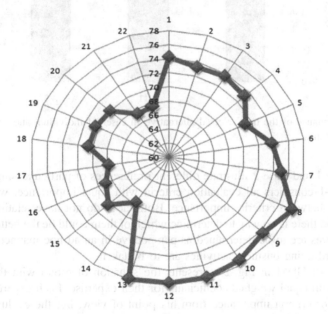

Fig. 1. Performance of the alternatives using the proposed group decision making model

The described in Sect. 4.1 different cases for three different preferences of DM are considers as the same preferences of experts from the group (Table 3). The expertise of these group members are taken into account by corresponding weighted coefficients to express their experience and knowledge relevant to investigated problem. The solution of this group decision making problem determines alternative A-8 (Debrecen-Hu) as optimal selection for doing business.

In such way different points of view of the group members together with level of knowledge and experience about each expert can be aggregated to get a single optimal solution.

5.3   Comparison Between Individual and Group Decision Making Implementation

The objective function values of the selected best alternative in both cases – individual and group decision making approaches are illustrated in Fig. 2.

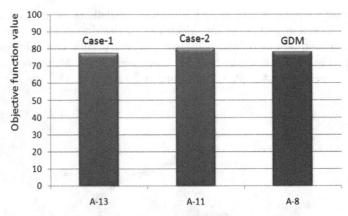

Fig. 2. Performance of the best selected alternative in cases of individual and group decision making approaches

The Case-1 and Case-2 illustrate different preferences of particular single decision maker. Case-1 considers all evaluation criteria with equal importance, while Case-2 distinguishes between criteria' importance. Both cases do not have relations between each other and there is no way to determine which of them could be the better selection. One these cases are to be determined as perspective in an ad-hoc manner and proper actions toward doing business activities are to be taken.

The case of GDM in Fig. 2 represents the situation of group with three experts considered with equal weighed coefficients for their expertise. Each expert determines coefficients for criteria importance from his point of view, but the evaluations score about the business regulations are the same as shown in Table 1. In GDM case, the equal weighted coefficients for experts' expertise are used, to simulate more closely the Case-1 of multi-criteria decision making. The obtained result for Case-1 determined as optimal alternative A-13 (Szekesfeharvar-Hu) as the objective function achieves the maximum value equal to 77.318. In case of GDM, the optimal alternative is A-8 (Debrecen (Hu)) as this alternative has the maximum value (77.938). Although both approaches cannot be compared, it should be noted that reasonable selection for location for doing business should reflect more than one point of view, so the group decision making model can be seen as the more promising approach.

In case of evaluation the possible locations for doing business in the same city it is needed to involve additional sub-criteria to distinguish the advantages and disadvantages for particular specific business activities. For example, the additional sub-criteria in case of hotel business will differ from the sub-criteria for shopping business. This is because the shopping business needs a popular or urban location to be successful, while the successful hotel business will benefit from quiet and rural location.

6 Conclusions

The paper deals with problems of optimal selection of location for doing business. Five indicators (business regulations) are considered as evaluation criteria and are taken into account in accordance to the recent report of the World Bank for 2017. The used input data from this report represents normalized scores within the range between 0 and 100 for different business regulations. Some major cities from Bulgaria, Romania and Hungary are used for numerical testing of the proposed approaches.

Two approaches with ability to cope with different points of view toward the importance of business regulation are proposed – individual and group decision making. The first classical approach considers the selection problem as multi-objective optimization problem, while the second approach considers selection as group decision making by proposed modified simple additive weighting. The proposed group decision making model considers not only different point of view of group' members toward criteria importance, but also take into account the differences between experts. In such way the importance of level in knowledge and experience for each expert is taken into account to get a single and optimal solution. The proposed group decision making approach benefits by using a single aggregate function considering not only alternatives performance, but also the importance of point of view for group members. Furthermore, the optimal alternative is determined by a single run of optimization task.

The proposed group decision making approach could be applied for other indicators and different size on group to consider different requirements. The proposed group decision making approach could be implemented in a software tool for GDM. As future investigation other modifications of aggregation function could be examined to consider different requirements.

References

Angarita-Zapata, J.S., Parra-Valencia, J.A., Andrade-Sosa, H.H.: Understanding the structural complexity of induced travel demand in decision-making: a system dynamics approach. Organizacija 49(3), 129–144 (2016)

Borissova, D.: A group decision making model considering experts competency: an application in personnel selections. Compt. rendus de l'Acad. bulgare des Sci. 71(11), 1520–1527 (2018)

Brester, C., Ryzhikov, I., Semenkin, E.: Multi-objective optimization algorithms with the island metaheuristic for effective project management problem solving. Organizacija 50(4), 364–373 (2017)

Chen, M., Wan, Z., Chen, X.: New min-max approach to optimal choice of the weights in multi-criteria group decision-making problems. Appl. Sci. 5, 998–1015 (2015)

Doing Business. http://www.doingbusiness.org/. Accessed 27 July 2018

Fujianti, L.: Top management characteristics and company performance: an empirical analysis on public companies listed in the Indonesian stock exchange. Eur. Res. Stud. J. **XXI**(2), 62–76 (2018)

Gegov, A., Arabikhan, F., Sanders, D., Vatchova, B., Vasileva, T.: Fuzzy networks with feedback rule bases for complex systems modelling. Int. J. Knowl.-Based Intell. Eng. Syst. **21**(4), 211–225 (2017)

Gokmenoglu, K.K., Alaghemand, Sh.: A multi-criteria decision-making model for evaluating priorities for foreign direct investment. Croat. Oper. Res. Rev., **6**, 489–510 (2015)

Hadad, Y., Keren, B., Laslo, Z.: Multi-criteria methods for ranking project activities. Yugosl. J. Oper. Res. **26**(2), 201–219 (2016)

Hornungova, J., Milichovsky, F.: Evaluations of financial performance indicators based on factor analysis in automotive. Period. Polytech. Soc. Manage. Sci. **27**(1), 26–36 (2019)

Jaksic, M., Mimovic, P., Lekovic, M.: A multi-criteria decision-making approach to performance evaluation of mutual funds: a case study in Serbia. Yugosl. J. Oper. Res. **28**(3), 385–414 (2018)

Korsemov, D., Borissova, D., Mustakerov, I.: Combinatorial optimization model for group decision-making. Cybern. Inform. Technol. **18**(2), 65–73 (2018)

Markovits-Somogyi, R.: Data envelopment analysis and its key variants utilized in the transport sector. Period. Polytech. Transp. Eng. **39**(2), 63–68 (2011)

Marler, R., Arora, J.: Survey of multi-objective optimization methods for engineering. Struct. Multidisc. Optim. **26**(6), 369–395 (2004)

Marolt, M., Lenart, G., Maletic, D., Borštnar, M.K., Pucihar, A.: Business model innovation: insights from a multiple case study of slovenian SMEs. Organizacija **49**(3), 161–171 (2016)

Mustakerov, I., Borissova, D.: Investments attractiveness via combinatorial optimization ranking. Int. J. Econ. Manage. Eng. **7**(10), 2674–2679 (2013)

Pinheiro-Alves, R., Zambujal-Oliveira, J.: The ease of doing business index as a tool for investment location decisions. Econ. Lett. **117**(1), 66–70 (2012)

Ramik, J.: Ranking alternatives by pairwise comparisons matrix and priority vector. Sci. Ann. Econ. Bus. **64**(SI), 85–95 (2017)

Ruiz, F., Cabello, J.M., Perez-Gladish, B.: Building ease-of-doing-business synthetic indicators using a double reference point approach. Technol. Forecast. Soc. Chang. **131**, 130–140 (2018)

Shih, H.-S., Shyur, H.-J., Lee, E.S.: An extension of TOPSIS for group decision making. Math. Comput. Model. **45**, 801–813 (2007)

Skraba, A., Stanovov, V., Semenkin, E., Kofjac, D.: Hybridization of stochastic local search and genetic algorithm for human resource planning management. Organizacija **49**(1), 42–54 (2016)

Vorosmarty, G., Dobos, I.: Supplier evaluation with environmental aspects and common DEA weights. Period. Polytech. Soc. Manage. Sci. **27**(1), 17–25 (2019)

Wang, C.-N., Huang, Y.-F., Chai, Y.-C., Nguyen, V.T.: A multi-criteria decision making (MCDM) for renewable energy plants location selection in Vietnam under a fuzzy environment. Appl. Sci. **8**, 2069 (2018). https://doi.org/10.3390/app8112069

Zhuang, Z.-Y., Lin, C.-Ch., Chen, Ch.-Y., Su, C.-R.: Rank-based comparative research flow benchmarking the effectiveness of AHP-GTMA on aiding decisions of shredder selection by reference to AHP–TOPSIS. Appl. Sci. **8**, 1974 (2018). https://doi.org/10.3390/app8101974

The Modeling of a Programming Language Syntax Based on Positional Entropy

Marcin Cholewa[✉]

Institute of Computer Science, University of Silesia,
Będzińska 39, 41-205 Sosnowiec, Poland
marcin.cholewa@us.edu.pl

Abstract. This paper presents the method of modeling the syntax of a programming language that can be used to design a new language. The purpose of this method is to create a syntax adapted to faster implementation and to embrace a larger class of algorithms. The method can also improve the readability of the source code by programmer. The article also presents the new interpretation of the concept of entropy and complexity, which is applicable in computer science. In experiments many examples of source codes were used, for which the complexity was examined, and then the syntax was optimized according to preset syntactic features (e.g. number of tokens or lines, characteristic tokens, length of tokens etc.). The source code comes down to a structure for which the complexity of its subpart can be explored. Some subparts are modified by reducing or increasing complexity. At the stage of modifying the code the syntactic features determine the change in complexity. The optimization was multi-stage and partly performed by human, to check at each stage whether the modified code obtained the expected syntactic structure. The proposed method is universal and suitable for modeling a new syntax based on existing and modern imperative languages. During syntax modeling, only the syntactical structure of the algorithm changes, not what the algorithm has to do. With an appropriate choice of syntactic features, a completely new language can be designed.

1 Introduction

The coding of the algorithm by means of formal syntactic rules of a programming language is a tedious process and it is highly probable that errors will be made during editing. Particularly troublesome are errors that will appear only during the program execution. Such errors arise as a result of confusion between the marks, too complex instructions, unexpected separators the separating individual tokens etc. Nowadays used languages with their syntax do not make it easy to code complex algorithms, and even obscure its implementations, making it difficult to read and understand the subsequent algorithm by man. The form of the instruction is made by man and intended for man. Therefore, a number of specialized programming languages adapted to implement certain types of algorithms. These languages are of very narrow specialization. It contributed to the improvement of the implementation process, but in a narrow scope. For each class, the class of algorithms needs another language. The solution could be a

© Springer Nature Switzerland AG 2019
K. Saeed et al. (Eds.): CISIM 2019, LNCS 11703, pp. 397–409, 2019.
https://doi.org/10.1007/978-3-030-28957-7_33

language with variable syntax. The programmer could imagine a language that would modify its syntactic rules depending on the type of algorithm implemented. This would help to reduce errors made by programmers, because the same algorithm could be viewed in the chosen syntax, which would highlight the most important features of the code. A variable syntax would semantically preserve an algorithm. The concept of entropy comes with the help of modifying the syntax of the programming language and is derived from physics [1]. It has many interpretations and has found a wide application in information theory and information technology [2–5]. The most important interpretation is a measure of the disorder of the system [6]. The source code of a programming language is composed of discrete components – tokens. The arrangement of tokens in the code interpreted as disorder can be described by entropy. The motivation to write this article is the curiosity to explore the source code in terms of the complexity of the syntactic structure and the possibilities of its simplification in order to develop a better syntax - a more friendly to a programmer. Syntax modification can apply to existing languages as well as creating a new language from scratch.

2 Positional Entropy

The author introduced the positional entropy [7] for the purposes of the article. The positional entropy of the discrete and finite system is a measure of ordering resulting from the mutual arrangement of the components of this system. The ordering as well as the chaos is the state of the system, which is subject to interpretation and assumptions needed for further analysis of the system. The position of the elements acts a significant measurable role, because any change in the elements of the system generates changes in the value of positional entropy. Although there are many definitions of complexity in literature [8–10], the author decided that the best interpretation of the positional entropy is the complexity of the system. Only the static system comes into consideration. The complexity is defined as the number of differences between neighboring elements. The more differences, the more complex the system is (Fig. 1). To define formal the positional entropy, there is need to be defined an auxiliary comparison function.

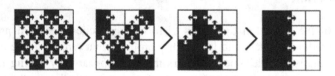

Fig. 1. The black and white fields show the degree of complexity according to positional entropy. The black and white arrows show differences between adjacent fields. The number of arrows shows the degree of complexity. Each square has the same number of black and white fields and they are arranged in descending order of complexity

Definition 1. The comparison function $Eq:\Omega \rightarrow N$ for two elements $x \in \Omega$ and $y \in \Omega$ is determined as follow $Eq(x, y) = |f(x) - f(y)|$, where $f:\Omega \rightarrow N$ is simple function that returns a numeric value for its argument. What the Ω contains can be any, for example

$\Omega = \{|, \|, \|\|\}$ and then $f(|) = 1$, $f(\|) = 6$, $f(\|\|) = 2$ etc. without established order $f(|) < f(\|) < f(\|\|)$.

Definition 2. The positional entropy $EnpC:X\rightarrow[0,1]$ (only for adjacent pairs) of sequence symbols $\langle a_0 a_1 a_2 a_3 \ldots a_{n-1}\rangle \in X$ is a measure of the degree of symbols diversity and is defined as:

$$EnpC(\langle a_0 a_1 a_2 \ldots a_{n-1}\rangle) = \frac{\sum_P \gamma(\{a_i, a_j\})}{Card(P)}$$

where $P = \{\{a_0, a_1\}, \{a_1, a_2\}, \{a_2, a_3\}, \ldots, \{a_{n-2}, a_{n-1}\}\}$ and γ is function for 2-level adjacent differences determined as:

$$\gamma(\{a_i, a_j\}) = \begin{cases} 1, & Eq(a_i, a_j) \neq 0 \\ 0, & Eq(a_i, a_j) = 0 \end{cases} \quad \text{for } i,j = 0, 1, \ldots, n-1 \wedge i = j+1$$

The sequence of symbols can also be represented in the form of a rectangular matrix, so that another definition of positional entropy can be derived.

Definition 3. The positional entropy (*M*-type) $EnpM:X\rightarrow[0,1]$ (only for orthogonally adjacent pairs) is a measure of the degree of symbols diversity in 2-dimension matrix:

$$A_{m\times n} = \begin{bmatrix} a_{0,0} & a_{0,1} & \cdots & a_{0,n} \\ a_{1,0} & a_{1,1} & \cdots & a_{1,n} \\ \vdots & \vdots & \ddots & \vdots \\ a_{m,0} & a_{m,1} & \cdots & a_{m,n} \end{bmatrix}$$

and is defined as:

$$EnpM(A) = \frac{\sum_P \gamma(\{a_{i_1 j_1}, a_{i_2 j_2}\})}{Card(P)}$$

where $P = \left\{ \{a_{i_1 j_1}, a_{i_2 j_2}\} : \begin{cases} i_1 = i_2 \in [0, m] \wedge j_1, j_2 \in [0, n-1] \wedge j_1 = j_2 + 1 \\ j_1 = j_2 \in [0, n] \wedge i_1, i_2 \in [0, m-1] \wedge i_1 = i_2 + 1 \end{cases} \right\}$ and γ is function for 2-level adjacent differences defined as:

$$\gamma(\{a_{i_1 j_1}, a_{i_2 j_2}\}) = \begin{cases} 1, & a_{i_1 j_1} \neq a_{i_2 j_2} \\ 0, & a_{i_1 j_1} = a_{i_2 j_2} \end{cases} \quad \text{for } i,j = 0, 1, \ldots, n-1 \wedge i = j+1$$

The function γ can be defined in a different way (for 3-level adjacent differences), such that:

$$\gamma(\{a_i, a_j\}) = \begin{cases} 1, & Eq(a_i, a_j) \in [h_1, h_2) \\ \frac{1}{2}, & Eq(a_i, a_j) \in [h_2, h_3) \\ 0, & Eq(a_i, a_j) \in [h_3, h_4] \end{cases}$$

where $i, j = 0, 1, \ldots, n - 1 \wedge i = j + 1 \wedge h_1, h_2, h_3 \in [0, 1] \wedge h_1 < h_2 < h_3$. The function γ can be defined more general way (for d-level adjacent differences), such that:

$$\gamma(\{a_i, a_j\}) = \begin{cases} 1, & Eq(a_i, a_j) \in [h_1, h_2) \\ \sum_{i=1}^{d-1} \frac{1}{d-1}, & Eq(a_i, a_j) \in [h_2, h_3) \\ \sum_{i=1}^{d-2} \frac{1}{d-1}, & Eq(a_i, a_j) \in [h_3, h_4) \\ \vdots & \vdots \\ 0, & Eq(a_i, a_j) \in [h_{d-1}, h_d] \end{cases}$$

where $i, j = 0, 1, \ldots, n - 1 \wedge i = j + 1 \wedge h_1, h_2, \ldots, h_d \in [0, 1] \wedge h_1 < h_2 < \ldots < h_d$. To reveal how this function working, the following example shows the calculation of positional entropy for the image (Fig. 2), which afterward can be presented in the matrix $A_{4 \times 4}$.

$$\begin{bmatrix} 1 & 0 & 1/2 & 0 \\ 1 & 0 & 1/2 & 0 \\ 0 & 0 & 1 & 4/5 \\ 1/3 & 1 & 0 & 0 \end{bmatrix} = A_{4 \times 4}$$

Fig. 2. The example of matrix for calculates the positional entropy (*M*-type and 3-level adjacent differences). The black color determines the degree of filling rectangle

Then the positional entropy will be equal to:

$$EnpM(A_{4 \times 4}) = \frac{\sum_{j=0}^{j=4} \sum_{i=0}^{i=3} \gamma(\{a_{j,i}, a_{j,i+1}\}) + \sum_{j=0}^{j=4} \sum_{i=0}^{i=3} \gamma(\{a_{i,j}, a_{i+1,j}\})}{24} =$$

$$\frac{\left(1 + \frac{1}{2} + \frac{1}{2} + 1 + \frac{1}{2} + \frac{1}{2} + 1 + \frac{1}{2} + \frac{1}{2} + 1\right)}{24} + \frac{\left(1 + \frac{1}{2} + 1 + \frac{1}{2} + 1 + \frac{1}{2} + \frac{1}{2}\right)}{24} = \frac{12}{24} = \frac{1}{2}$$

Theorem 1. If matrix $A_{m \times n}$ can be divided into equal sub-matrixes $B_{0,0}, B_{0,1}, \ldots, B_{M,N}$ such that each sub-matrix is self-similar to the whole matrix $A_{m \times n}$, then:

$$EnpM\left(\begin{bmatrix} a_{0,0} & a_{0,1} & \cdots & a_{0,n} \\ a_{1,0} & a_{1,1} & \cdots & a_{1,n} \\ \vdots & \vdots & \ddots & \vdots \\ a_{m,0} & a_{m,1} & \cdots & a_{m,n} \end{bmatrix}\right) = EnpM\left(\begin{bmatrix} EnpM(B_{0,0}) & EnpM(B_{0,1}) & \cdots & EnpM(B_{0,N}) \\ EnpM(B_{1,0}) & EnpM(B_{1,1}) & \cdots & EnpM(B_{1,N}) \\ \vdots & \vdots & \ddots & \vdots \\ EnpM(B_{M,0}) & EnpM(B_{M,1}) & \cdots & EnpM(B_{M,N}) \end{bmatrix}\right) = EnpM(B_0)$$

Theorem 2. If B is any sub-matrix of A, and when *EnpM*(B) is increased, then *EnpM* (A) will also increase. Analogously, when *EnpM*(B) is decreased, then *EnpM*(A) will also decrease.

The article does not provide proofs of the above theorems, because it is not a theoretical work and there is a limit to the number of pages in the article. Theorem 2 is important from the point of view of the analysis, because it talks about how to modify matrix values to decrease or increase its positional entropy. The positional entropy has a useful feature that is applicable to comparing the syntactic complexity of two algorithms - the length of the samples is not significant, so the length of codes is not valid.

3   Method

In order to be able to do an entropy analysis of the source code, it is necessary to determine the structure on which any source code written in any programming language can be represented. The most important feature of the described structure is its universality. The structure resembles a cellular automaton [11].

Definition 4. Any source code of any programming language can be presented as a 2-dimensional grid, each field representing one of the three basic components of the source code: token, character or shape of the character.

Listing 1. The construction of the conditional statement *if* written in languages: C, C++, C#, Java. All white characters have been replaced with visible special symbols. The *space* is shown as · and the *tab* as →.

```
if·(cond) {
→nop
}else·if·(cond) {
→nop
}else {
→nop
}
```

For the exemplary construction of the *if* statement from Listing 1, there is a 2-dimensional token grid according to Definition 4:

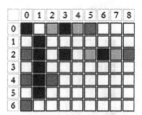

Fig. 3. The 2-dimensional grid shows only tokens for the code from Listing 1. The black fields indicate literals or keywords, gray means brackets, and white marks mean white or blank tokens

To make a more thorough analysis, the source code should be divided into single characters and present it using the characters grid:

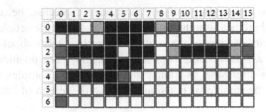

Fig. 4. The 2-dimensional grid shows only characters for the code from Listing 1. The black fields indicate literal or keyword characters, gray fields mean parentheses and the rest of white represent white or blanks characters

It is also possible to present the source code using a character shape grid, in which each glyph of the character is represented as a black and white bitmap [7]. This technique allows examining the similarity between adjacent characters and by changing the similarity it can improve the readability between neighboring characters. It leads to reduce the number of errors when reading the source code and in addition to more effective reading. Often, to draw a feature code, it must be submitted using the simplified grid tokens. Listing 2 shows the program code, and in Fig. 5 is a simplified tokens grid for this code. The simplification consists in the isolation of only keywords and literals.

Listing 2. The complex source code containing conditional statements *if* written in languages: C, C++, C#, Java. All white characters have been replaced with visible special symbols. The *space* is shown as · and the *tab* as →.

```
if·(x==object.methodA(y+1)){
→ object.methodB(y+1·)=1;
}else·if·(x== object.methodA(y+1)-n){
→ object.methodB(object.methodB(y-1)=x+1);
}else·{
→ object.methodB(0)·=·1;
→if·(·object.methodB(1)·>·n)·{object={0}};
}
```

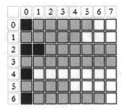

Fig. 5. The 2-dimensional grid shows only keywords and literals code from the Listing 2. Black fields are literals or keywords, gray are parentheses, and white are whitespaces or empty tokens

In the further part of the article, the character grid is used because it allows for a more detailed analysis of keywords or literals. It also fully reflects the source code built from characters, because a constant character width font (*monospaced*) is used to edit the code [12]. After constructing the grid from syntactic elements of the code, syntactic features should be determined and their values should be estimated. Below is a list of syntactic features that will be used to analyze the source code. The syntactic features are divided into two groups. The first group defines the most basic and indivisible features. The second group defines features consisting of the features of the first group and specific elements of the source code. Each syntactic feature has an abbreviation to facilitate identification in the equations. Below are basic syntactic features:

- *Number of syntactic elements* (Nx) - The basic measure that indicates the number of all is the type of item in the source code.
- *Mean elements* (Mx) - If the source code is divided into subparts, with each subpart it can get the number of items of a certain type, and then calculate the average of the number of items of that type code of all the subparts.
- *The ratio of the number of A group elements to the number of B group elements* (Rx2y) - This feature gives the percentage value of number of A group elements in proportion to the number of B group elements.
- *Diversity of elements* (Dx) - The arrangement of syntactic elements of different types can be measured as a degree of their grouping in terms of value [13]. In addition to the element's value, its location can also be taken into account.
- *Arrangement of elements* (Ax) - The syntactic structures of the program code are built according to grammatical rules. In the entropy analysis, these rules are expressed as the shape of the elements' arrangement. Unlike other features, this feature takes into account the position of the syntactic elements in the code. This feature allows studying the structure of the code by estimating the distance between tokens.

The concretion of the type elements from source code and their grouping generates more complex features such as: Number of lines (NL), Number of tokens (NT), Number of characters (NC), Number of conditional statements (NCInstr), Number of tokens and lines in conditional statement (NTLCInstr), Length of token (NLT), Mean of line length (MLL), Mean of tokens length (MTL), Diversity of token types (DTT), Positional diversity of token types (PDTT), Diversity of tokens in line (DTL), Number of nested blocks (NNB) and Characteristic token (CT).

Some features may relate to the entire source code, and some locally to a subpart code. For example, Diversity feature (Dx) can apply to all source code or to a subpart that is a block of conditional statements – Diversity of conditional statement (DCInstr).

On the basis of the already existing features built new and more complex features. For example, the Diversity of token (DT) and Number of lines (NL) features combine to create the Diversity of Line token (DTL) feature. These features are used to rebuild the program code. For example, to modify existing source code to make it shorter, the following features are used: Number of lines (NL) and Number of tokens (NT). If the code is to be more resistant to programmer errors generated by distinguishing tokens, the combination of features is used: Diversity of type tokens (DTT) and Diversity of the token (DT). In a situation where the designed language needs to emphasize conditional instructions, the following features are combined: Diversity of characters in the token (DCT), Length of tokens associated with the conditional instruction (NLTCInstr) and the Number of tokens associated with the conditional instruction (NTCInstr).

The use of syntactic features involves the transformation of the source code. The main type of transformation is the exchange subpart of source code (tokens, characters) according to Theorem 2, to adapt to the complexity of the set parameters. An example of such a change might be to change the constructions of the binary operator *mod(a, b)* to *a mod b* or *a%b*. Nested block statements can be problematic in the syntax modeling process. However, according to Theorem 1, nested instructions in the source code can be considered as single such instruction without losing the positional entropy value.

The optimization equations are constructed from the syntactic features. The purpose of these equations will determine the direction of changes in syntactic complexity. The *i*-th optimization p-equation for *q*-th syntactic feature *r* is defined as:

$$p_i = (\max \mid \min \mid bound)\left(\sum_{q=1}^{Q} r_q\right)$$

In the given formula, the *max*, *min* and *bound* functions are used only once. These functions determine the direction of change in value for the *i*-th p-equation. The *max* function means the maximum value that can be gained, and the *min* function is the opposite of *max*. The *bound* function means the value of the change from the interval. An example of an equation is the lowest sum of the Number of lines (NL) and Number of tokens (NT) related to the whole code. It can be presented as:

$$p_1 = \min(r_{NL} + r_{NT})$$

After each application of the p-equation, the complexity in the source code changes. The optimization equations are built hierarchically, because some equations depend on others. It follows that there are equations that are essential to the subparts of the code, and some even fundamental to the whole code.

4 Analysis

The course of the analysis is multi-stage and begins with the preparation of the source code sample in the selected language. The prepared sample is inputted into the optimization program. Subsequently, based on the guidelines inputted by the programmer - syntactic features, the program generates optimization equations that will be used to search for the optimal syntax. Only small code samples are analyzed. The solutions found are used to generate code samples, which the programmer finally assesses. There may be many output samples, therefore these samples must be assessed by man. In the last stage of the analysis, the grammar for the new language can be generated based on the generated code. Many samples can be obtained to create a new language. Generating grammar is an activity that is completely done by human (Fig. 6).

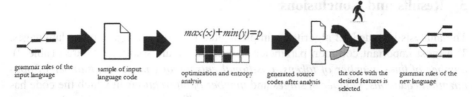

grammar rules of the   sample of input   optimization and entropy   generated source   the code with the   grammar rules of the
input language   language code   analysis   codes after analysis   desired features is   new language
selected

Fig. 6. The course of the optimization analysis that is used to design or modify the programming language

The most important stage - optimization and entropy analysis - is a multi-stage process. This stage is performed partly by humans due to the need to evaluate subsequent stages of optimization. Completely automatic analysis (without the use of artificial intelligence methods) could lead to the creation of useless language constructions. Human supervision is necessary at every stage in which the appropriate optimization p-equation is chosen. After applying the equation in a single stage, it is unknown how the code will change, therefore the change is accepted manually, and then it will go to the next stage. With each stage, a p-equation is related, and the selection of these equations is important in the whole process. The choice of the order of equations is a heuristic process and the proper order of choosing the equations leads to finding the code with the optimal syntactic features. There may be a situation in which several optimal solutions will be obtained. Then the human must decide which code he accepts. The worst is the situation in which the optimal code cannot be found. In this situation, optimization equations must be changed. The sample size affects the code search time. The smaller is the sample, the faster the code search time is and the easier is the evaluation of the partial answers of the analyzer (Fig. 7).

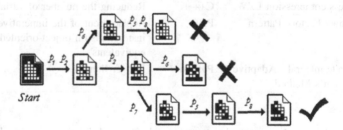

Fig. 7. A gradual process that modifies the source code based on optimization equations: p_1, p_2, p_3, ..., p_8. The order of the equations that led to finding the optimal code: $\{p_1, p_2\}, p_2, p_7, p_5, p_8$

From the result of the analysis, semantically any algorithm implemented in the input language must remain the same algorithm in the newly created language. The new language created (grammar) acquires features that are useful for a human programmer. The new syntax may involve an increase in the number of tokens, but it can have a positive and purposeful effect.

5   Results and Conclusions

The analysis included 12 algorithms implemented in various programming languages. The most important common parameters measured by the source code are (Table 2): *number of lines, number of tokens, positional entropy of characters, number of optimization equations, number of stages* and *number of bifurcations* in which the code has been modified until the expected syntactic effect. The last parameter is the cost of obtaining optimization. The choice of algorithms was dictated by the willingness to test the method, because each algorithm presents a different programming solution (Table 1).

Table 1. The table shows the algorithms and optimization goals

No.	Algorithm	Language	Purpose description
1	Greatest Common Divisor (GCD)	C++	As fewer tokens and lines as possible
2	Fast Fourier Transformata (FFT)	C	Maximum getting rid of the implementation details
3	Sieve of Eratosthenes	Python	Many instructions in one line
4	Quick-Sort	Java	Increased code redundancy
5	Min-Max	Java	Increased readability
6	Toom-Cook multiplication	C	Each instruction is on a separate line
7	Luhn's Number Validation	C#	Increasing the number of instructions along with keywords
8	RSA key generation	JavaScript	The shortest length of the keywords in the control flow instructions
9	Finding the shortest path in graph – Dijikstra's Method	Visual Basic 6.0	Reduction of conditional instructions to a minimum
10	Losless compression LZW	C++	Reducing the number of variables
11	Abstract Factory Pattern	PHP	Replacement of the imperative *if, for* instructions on object-oriented equivalents
12	Definite integral - Adaptive Simpson's Method	Python	Longer literals

Some implementation remarks must be clarified. All source codes have been implemented by the author based on the constructional remarks provided by their creators. The *QuickSort* algorithm was implemented based on the algorithm given by Hoare [14]. This implementation includes its function of splitting the data array [14]. The artificial intelligence field uses *Min-Max* algorithms [15]. These algorithms were used to implement the algorithm of a two-player game strategy based on a binary tree, because it contains recursive calls, which can be better written in the code after analysis. The *RSA* [16] algorithm consists of three main parts that can operate separately and in appropriate situations - key generation, encryption and decryption. The key generation algorithm was chosen for the analysis, because it is composed of too many keywords. The object paradigm affects the building of complex business applications, therefore a design pattern - the abstract generator has been implemented [17]. Other algorithms have been implemented based on the following literature: Dijikstra's algorithm [18], calculation of definite integrals by the Simpson's method [19], algorithm for multiplying large numbers (Toom-Cook multiplication) [20], lossless compression algorithm LZW [21] and Fast Fourier Transform [22].

Table 2. The results of the optimization analysis performed on the source codes

No.	Before optimization			After optimization			p-eqs	Cost/stages	Bifs
	Lines	Tokens	Pos. entrop.	Lines	Tokens	Pos. entrop.			
1	9	82	0.529	6	69	0.610	4	10	3
2	48	945	0.381	48	798	0.417	8	15	5
3	17	310	0.518	9	270	0.498	4	6	1
4	55	556	0.410	60	643	0.425	9	17	8
5	31	444	0.377	57	721	0.431	8	15	7
6	184	2648	0.446	235	2854	0.489	3	4	2
7	20	268	0.351	20	294	0.387	6	11	3
8	107	1241	0.396	107	1241	0.421	2	4	0
9	134	2854	0.282	132	2820	0.306	2	5	6
10	315	5247	0.360	305	5129	0.289	4	31	14
11	80	837	0.456	104	1023	0.564	9	3	0
12	21	493	0.369	21	493	0.467	2	4	0

In Table 2, the p-eqs field is the number of p-equations, the cost/stages field is the cost of optimization as the number of analysis steps, and *bifs* is the number of bifurcations during optimization. Changes in the code are best illustrated by two parameters: the *number of tokens* and *lines*, for that reason is why they were shown before and after optimization. These are initial studies in this field using specified methods and continue the exploration area for further research. The conclusions after analysis are as follows. For each code, the expected modifications have been obtained, although their cost varies considerably.

Not every modification reduces the number of tokens, therefore a situation may arise in which readability increases their number. After the results obtained, a method for designing new programming languages and modifying the existing syntax is acceptable. In any case, there was no disruption in the structure of the algorithm (in modified code), which could lead to potential syntactic errors and errors of execution time. This is a stable method, because the positional entropy changes for the two examined algorithms (*RSA* and *Definite Integral*). For these cases the smallest number of p-equations, analysis stages were used and no bifurcations occurred. These changes were very simple and that influenced the readability of the code. In subsequent cases, there has been a significant change in the number of syntactic elements, as the changes were more detailed. The longest code tested (*LZW*) has been optimized to reduce the number of variables. It was the most difficult case, because it involved interference in the algorithm, but apparently. Some variables were excessive, because they mediated in data operations and their removal did not affect the structure of the algorithm in any way. In turn in the *QuickSort* algorithm, the situation is opposite to *LZW*, because there are changes that are aimed at increasing code redundancy. The redundancy means increasing the variety of tokens and characters, increasing instruction tokens, and generally increasing the visibility of instructions. The number of tokens and the number of lines has actually increased. This effect was obtained at a fairly high cost, as 17 stages and 8 bifurcations were needed.

An experiment was also conducted in which the imperative code containing (*Abstract Factory Pattern*) conditional statements and loops was converted into objects that perform the same functions. In this way, full objectivity was achieved. The conversion of an imperative style into an object-oriented one does not generate a large cost, although it requires a large number of p-equations in comparison with others. A desirable syntactic feature when implementing algorithms is to reduce implementation details. This was checked on the *FFT* algorithm and introduced p-equations, which reduce the number of implementation details such as hiding counter variables, reducing the number of tokens in instructions, shortening instructions and reducing diversity. Optimization significantly reduced the number of tokens, which obviously shows the code itself with fewer implementation details. The cost of this change is above average of all costs.

For each programming paradigm, a set of p equations can be found that modify the syntax to obtain the desired changes. As can be seen in Table 2, the costs of changes can be sometimes significant (number of stages and bifurcations) and this is already for short codes, but the optimization algorithms created by the author worked very quickly. The right selection of optimization equations (p-equations) has an impact on the optimization time and is more important than their quantity, which was also done by the author. Hence, an important conclusion is that optimization algorithms can be successfully used to present the same algorithm in different syntaxes when editing it.

The positional entropy *EnpM* for 3-level adjacent differences (γ-function) was calculated for a 2-dimensional character grid. No clear relationship was found between language and positional entropy. Although the lowest value was obtained for Visual Basic 6.0 and for values in the range of [0.350, 0.550] for all C-style languages, this is not significant in any way. If used higher gamma functions and tokens grid, then it would probably be a relationship.

6   Further Work

The presented method of analysis was carried out partly with human participation. The next step in the development of this technique will be the complete automation of this process. The described positional entropy can also be used to create an overall classification of programming languages in terms of the complexity of their syntax. Moreover, the entropy optimization method is suitable for integration with programs used to design and generate compilers and interpreters.

References

1. Clausius, R., Hirst, T.A.: The Mechanical Theory of Heat: With Its Applications to the Steam-engine and to the Physical Properties of Bodies. John Van Voorst, London (1867)
2. Shannon, C.E.: A mathematical theory of communication. Bell Syst. Techn. J. **27**, 379–423, 623–653 (1948)
3. Bernstein, E., Vazirani, U.: Quantum complexity theory. SIAM J. Comput. **26**(5), 1411–1473 (1997)
4. MacKay, D.: Heapsort, Quicksort, and Entropy (2005)
5. Jost, L.: Entropy and diversity. Oikos **113**, 363–375 (2006)
6. Michaelides, E.E.: Entropy, order and disorder. Open Thermodyn. J. **2**, 7–11 (2008)
7. Cholewa, M.: The readability model for natural and artificial languages. J. Med. Inf. Technol. **27**, 21–28 (2018)
8. Adami, C.: What is complexity? BioEssays **24**(12), 1085–1094 (2002)
9. Adami, C., Cerf, N.J.: Physical complexity of symbolic sequences. Physica D **137**(1–2), 62–69 (2000)
10. Chaitin, G.J.: Algorithmic information theory. IBM J. Res. Dev. **21**(4), 350–359 (1977)
11. Von Neumann, J., Burks, A.W. (eds.): Theory of Self-Reproducing Automata. University of Illinois Press, Champaign (1966)
12. Spolsky, J.: User Interface Design for Programmers. Apress, Berkeley (2006)
13. Simpson, E.H.: Measurement of diversity. Nature **163**, 688 (1949)
14. Hoare, C.A.R.: Quicksort. Comput. J. **5**(1), 10–15 (1962)
15. Von Neumann, J.: Zur Theorie der Gesellschaftsspiele. Math. Ann. **100**(1), 295–320 (1928)
16. Rivest, R., Shamir, A., Adleman, L.: A method for obtaining digital signatures and public-key cryptosystems. Commun. ACM **21**(2), 120–126 (1978)
17. Gamma, E., Helm, R., Johnson, R., Vlissides, J.: Design Patterns: Elements of Reusable Object-Oriented Software, p. 99. Addison-Wesley, Boston (1994)
18. Dijkstra, E.W.: A note on two problems in connexion with graphs. Numer. Math. **1**(1), 269–271 (1959)
19. Kuncir, G.F.: Algorithm 103: Simpson's rule integrator. Commun. ACM **5**(6), 347 (1962)
20. Bodrato, M.: Towards optimal toom-cook multiplication for univariate and multivariate polynomials in characteristic 2 and 0. In: Carlet, C., Sunar, B. (eds.) WAIFI 2007. LNCS, vol. 4547, pp. 116–133. Springer, Heidelberg (2007). https://doi.org/10.1007/978-3-540-73074-3_10
21. Welch, T.A.: A technique for high-performance data compression. Computer **17**(6), 8–19 (1984)
22. Press, W.H., Teukolsky, S.A., Vetterling, W.T., Flannery, B.P.: Numerical Recipes in C++, p. 513. Cambridge University Press, Cambridge (1992)

Two FPGA Devices in the Problem
of Finding Minimal Reducts

Mateusz Choromański[✉][iD], Tomasz Grześ[iD], and Piotr Hońko[iD]

Faculty of Computer Science, Białystok University of Technology,
Wiejska 45A, 15-351 Białystok, Poland
{m.choromanski,t.grzes,p.honko}@pb.edu.pl

Abstract. Speeding up attribute reduction process is an important issue in data mining. The goal of this paper is to compare two hardware implementations of minimal reducts computation, i.e. the previously introduced implementation on Intel Arria V SoC and a newly proposed solution on Xilinx Zynq Ultrascale+ MPSoC. Two versions of an attribute reduction algorithm, i.e. blind and frequency based breadth search strategies, were implemented on the two frameworks. Experimental research showed that finding minimal reducts can be accelerated several times when using the new device.

Keywords: Attribute reduction · Minimal reducts ·
Breadth search strategy · Hardware implementation ·
Field programmable gate arrays

1 Introduction

In the Big Data era the problem of data size reduction, especially attribute reduction, becomes more and more significant. Attribute reduction has extensively been investigated from a theoretical and practical viewpoint (e.g. [1,3,7,9,11–13,17]) in rough set theory [6] that is viewed as a mathematical tool to deal with inconsistent data. One of the ways of speeding up the computations is to use a field programmable gate arrays framework (FPGA).

Hardware support of rough set-based data processing, especially attribute reduction, has a long history and is strictly connected with the rough set theory beginnings.

In [10] an FPGA-based implementation of rough set methods for technology research in fault diagnosis is presented. The FPGA-based hardware is used among others for data reduction and rule extraction.

Hardware implementation of the reduct generation problem is described in [14]. Authors designed and implemented a reduct calculation block that uses the binary discernibility matrix and put it into the rough set processor used for the robotics application.

Real applications of the FPGA-based rough set data processing systems are described in [15,16]. In [15] the rough set coprocessor is introduced. Authors used

This work was supported by the grant S/WI/1/2018 of the Polish Ministry of Science and Higher Education.

K. Saeed et al. (Eds.): CISIM 2019, LNCS 11703, pp. 410–420, 2019.
https://doi.org/10.1007/978-3-030-28957-7_34

the dual port RAM as well as pipelining to increase the efficiency thus making the solution suitable for the real-time applications. For the reduct generation, the discernibility matrix is used.

A previous work of one of the authors on the hardware implementations of the rough sets methods was introduced in [4], where the system for calculating the core and the superreduct is described. The core and reduct are calculated from the discernibility matrix obtained from the decision table stored in FPGA. Another superreduct generating device was described in [5]. None of the described previously solutions allows calculating all the reducts.

The first hardware approach for computing minimal reducts was proposed in [2]. Two strategies, namely blind and frequency based search, were implemented in C and VHDL languages to investigate the run-time differences between software and hardware approaches.

The goal of this paper is to verify how big speedup can be achieved on a relatively new device, i.e. Xilinx Zynq Ultrascale+ MPSoC compared with Intel Arria V SoC. To this end, the solution previously developed and implemented on Intel Arria V SoC (5ASTFD5K3F40I3) was transferred to Xilinx Zynq Ultrascale+ MPSoC (XCZU9EG-2FFVB1156). The solution is provided in two versions. The first one relies on finding minimal reducts using blind search strategy, whereas the second one uses frequency based search strategy. To compare both strategies implemented on both devices, the same database that concerns diabetic patients was tested.

The rest of the paper is organized as follows. Section 2 introduces the basic notions regarding minimal reducts as well as describes breadth search strategies to be implemented. Section 3 proposes a hardware implementation of the strategies for finding minimal reducts. The concluding remarks are given in Sect. 4.

2   Breadth Search Strategies for Finding Minimal Reducts

This section restates the attribute reduction problem and introduces approaches for finding minimal reducts using blind and frequency based breath search strategies.

Firstly, the basic notions that regard attribute reduction will be introduced.

To store the data to be processed, a decision table is used.

Definition 1. *([6]) A decision table is a pair $DT = (U, A \cup \{d\})$, where U is a nonempty finite set of objects, called the universe, A is a non-empty finite set of condition attributes, and $d \notin A$ is the decision attribute.*
Each attribute $a \in A \cup \{d\}$ is treated as a function $a : U \rightarrow V_a$, where V_a is the value set of a.

To compute reducts the discernibility matrix of the decision table can be used.

Definition 2. *([7]) The discernibility matrix $(c_{x,y}^d)$ of a decision table $DT = (U, A \cup \{d\})$ is defined by $c_{x,y}^d = \{a \in A : a(x) \neq a(y), d(x) \neq d(y)\}$ for any $x, y \in U$.*

A reduct is defined as follows.

Definition 3. *A subset $B \subseteq A$ is a reduct of in a decision table $DT = (U, A \cup \{d\})$ if and only if*

1. $\quad \forall_{x,y \in U, d(x) \neq d(y)} \exists_{a \in B} a \in c_{x,y},$

2. $\forall_{C \subset B} \exists_{x,y \in U, d(x) \neq d(y)} \forall_{a \in C} a \notin c_{x,y}.$

A reduct with the minimal cardinality is a minimal one.

The below describes the algorithms used for finding minimal reducts.

The blind version of breadth search based strategy starts with computing the discernibility matrix and attribute core. Next, all combinations of the smallest cardinality (i.e. each combination consists of the core attributes and one extra attribute) are checked for being a reduct. The searching is interrupted after finding the required number of reducts or after checking all combinations and finding at least one reduct. If no reduct is find, all combinations with the cardinality greater by one (i.e. each combination is constructed based on a combination from the previous cardinality level by adding another attribute) are checked in the same way. Combinations are constructed according to alphanumeric order, thanks to this each new combination is not a repetition of any previously generated.

The frequent version of breadth search based strategy starts with the same computations as the blind one, i.e. the discernibility matrix and attribute core. Next, for each attribute that is not included in the core its occurrence frequency in the discernibility matrix is computed. Combinations with the smallest cardinality (i.e. the core attributes plus one attribute) are constructed starting with the most frequent attribute and finishing after using all attributes or the l most frequent attributes (l defined by a user). The combinations are verified for being a reduct in the same way as by the blind version. Combinations of a higher cardinality level are constructed based on those from the previous level by adding one attribute chosen according the occurrence frequency order. One should stress that this way of attribute combination construction does not guarantee that only unique combinations are generated. Hence, each new combination is first compared to other combinations of the same cardinality level that have been generated so far.

3   Hardware Approach

The below subsections describe the dataset, the implemented blocks for finding minimal reducts, and the used FPGA integrated circuit with its resources' utilization.

3.1   Used Data and Its Structure

For this project, the authors used data about children with insulin-dependent diabetes mellitus (type 1) [8]. The data consists of 107 cases. Each case has 12 attributes and is represented as a 16-bit word: sex (1b), age of disease diagnosis (2b), disease duration (2b), appearance diabetes in the family (1b), insulin therapy type (1b), respiratory system infections (1b), remission (1b), HbAlc (2b), hypertension (1b), body mass (2b), hypercholesterolemia (1b), hypertriglyceridemia (1b) and microalbuminuria (decision attribute, 1b). Data is divided into two separate sets:

- **Positive** – with 56 cases having Microalbuminuria (decision attribute value is '1'),
- **Negative** – with 51 cases not having Microalbuminuria (decision attribute is to '0').

3.2 Implemented Hardware Blocks

The architecture of the proposed solution is presented in Fig. 1 (cf. [2]).

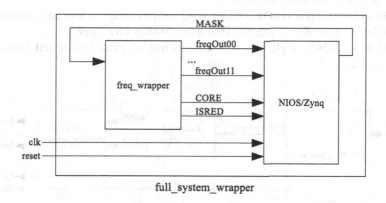

Fig. 1. Solution architecture

Full_system_wrapper is the top level file which contains the connected *freq_wrapper* and *nios/Zynq* components (depends on the used device). This block can be treated as the whole system and has two input ports:

- **clk** – 50 MHz (100 MHz for *Zynq*) clock input for *nios* processor;
- **reset** – reset signal for resetting all the components.

This block has no output ports.

The whole system is composed of the following components:

●**nios/Zynq** - Nios II/f (fast)(in Arria device) or Zynq (in Zynq US+ device) processor instance used for controlling the execution of the algorithm. The main aim of this block is to launch the controlling application written in C. It uses data from the remaining hardware blocks of the system while executing the program: receives the attribute core calculated in *freq_wrapper* and according to it sends reduct candidates until ISRED signal changes the value to '0'. This block has four input ports:
   - **clk** – clock input: 50 MHz for Arria,100 MHz for Zynq US+;
   - **reset** – signal for resetting the processor;
   - **freqOut00...freqOut11** – 16-bit word with frequency of each attribute;
   - **CORE** – provides the attribute core from *freq_wrapper* component;
   - **ISRED** – signal for indicating that the signal sent from MASK output is a reduct.

This block has one output port:

- **MASK** – sends to *freq_wrapper* a reduct candidate based on calculated *CORE* given on input. This signal is also used in other components.

●**freq_wrapper** - component in which attributes frequencies are calculated and sorted (from most to least frequent) using the bitonic sort algorithm. Each result is represented by a 16-bit vector, where the first 4 bits contain the attribute number and the remaining 12 bits are the number of occurrences. *freq_wrapper* contains *DMBlock-Wrapper* component that is responsible for calculating the core and minimal reducts. This block has one input port:

- **MASK** – reduct candidate provided from *nios* component.

This block has fourteen output ports:

- **freqOut00…freqOut11** – 16-bit word with the frequency of each attribute;
- **CORE** – calculated core provided from *DMBlockWrapper*;
- **ISRED** – sends single bit which informs that the candidate passed from *nios* is a reduct.

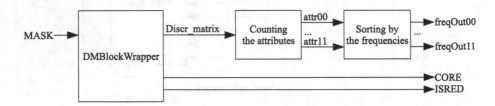

Fig. 2. Freq_wrapper block architecture

The architecture of *freq_wrapper* block is shown in Fig. 2. As mentioned before, this component consists of one block *DMBlockWrapper*, which is described below:

●**DMBlockWrapper** - wrapper for components that are used to calculate the core and reducts. It consists of *DM_block*, *Core_block* and *isZero* (which is generated 2856 times, for every item from discernibility matrix) components. When a reduct is found, then it sends 1-bit signal '0' to *freq_wrapper*. *DMBlockWrapper* component contains also positive and negative datasets described in Sect. 3.1 which is passed to *DM_block* module in *DT_pos* and *DT_neg* signals. This block has one input port:

- **MASK** – reduct candidate provided from *nios* component.

This block has three output ports:

- **Disc_matrix** - the array that contains the calculated discernibility matrix;
- **CORE** – sends the calculated core to *freq_wrapper* where it is passed to *nios* component;
- **ISRED** – sends 1-bit signal, which indicates that vector given on MASK input is a reduct or not to *freq_wrapper* where it is passed to *nios* component.

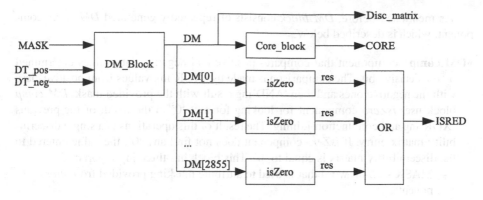

Fig. 3. DMBlockWrapper schema

The connections of components inside the wrapper is shown in Fig. 3. The blocks that create *DMBlockWrapper* component are described below:

- **DM_block** - component that creates the discernibility matrix using the data given from generated 2856 *DM_comp* modules. This block has three input ports:
    - **MASK** – reduct candidate provided from *nios* component;
    - **DT_pos** – provides a 56-element array of 16-bit word positive class data set from *DMBlockWrapper* component;
    - **DT_neg** – provides a 51-element array of 16-bit word negative class data set from *DMBlockWrapper* component.
  This block has one output port:
    - **DM** – sends an array of 2856 12-bit words (which contains the whole discernibility matrix) to *DMBlockWrapper*.
- **Core_block** - component where the core is calculated. This block has one input port:
    - **DM** – 2856-element array of 12-bit words which contains the whole discernibility matrix provided from *DMBlockWrapper*.
  This block has one output port:
    - **CORE** – sends to *DMBlockWrapper* the core calculated from provided the discernibility matrix.
- **isZero** - component that looks for '0' in given 12-bit word by performing OR operation on every single bit from the provided vector. The result is passed to *DM_sing*, where it is used to determine whether the new discernibility matrix entry should be equal to '0' or not. This block has one input port:
    - **inval** - 12-bit word that is the result of comparison of two values from positive and negative data sets.
  This block has one output ports:
    - **res** - single bit which is '0' only if the signal given on input equals to '0'.

As mentioned before, *DM_block* consists of repeatedly generated *DM_comp* component, which is described below:

- **DM_comp** - component that compares positive and negative data values determined by the decisive bit. The comparison is made by 'XOR'ing values from positive class with the negative ones and then 'AND'ing result with the provided mask. *DM_comp* block uses *isZero* component for looking for any '0' in the result of the previous 'XOR'ing and conjunction-joining. The result of this operations is a single discernibility matrix entry. If *isZero* component does not find any '0', the value entered to the discernibility matrix is equal to '0'. This block has three input ports:
    - **MASK** - 12-bit word that is used to attribute masking provided from *nios* component;
    - **DT_pos** – decision table entry from the positive class data set (16-bit word) from *DMBlockWrapper* component;
    - **DT_neg** – decision table entry from the negative class data set (16-bit word) from *DMBlockWrapper* component.
  This block has one output port:
    - **DM_entry** – sends the calculated entry for the discernibility matrix (12-bit word) to *DM_block*.

3.3   Used Hardware and the Resources' Utilization

The project was implemented on two different devices. First was Intel Arria V SoC (5ASTFD5K3F40I3) further referred to as "Arria", which is 28 nm FPGA with 462K logic elements and integrated with ARM Cortex-A9 dual-core processor clocked at 1.05 GHz. In our solution the embedded processor was not used, the Nios II softcore processor was utilized instead. The choice was made because of easier debugging on registry and ALU levels. Nios II was clocked at 50 MHz, which gave a better chance to observe the differences between the solutions. Software used for VHDL compilation, synthesis and generate configuration files for Arria was Quartus Prime 17.1.0 Build 590 10/25/2017 SJ Standard Edition. The C code was compiled with Eclipse Mars.2 Release (4.5.2) Build 20160218-0600 with GCC compiler version 4.8.3.

The project was built using the Quartus Prime by Altera. The compilation reports show the described below utilization of the FPGA resources:

- **Logic utilization (in ALMs):** 15,492/176,160 (9%)
- **Total registers:** 2763
- **Total pins:** 1/876 ($< 1\%$)
- **Total block memory bits:** 8,452,928/23,367,680 (36%)
- **Total DSP Blocks:** 3/1,090 ($< 1\%$)

The utilization of FPGA resources is low. Namely, the project needed less than 10% of the adaptive logic modules (ALMs). It should be noted that the project uses the softcore processor, which needs some resources (about 3500 of ALM was used to implement the Nios II processor). Therefore the total utilization can be even decreased after switching to the embedded processor.

The second device was Xilinx Zynq Ultrascale+ MPSoC (XCZU9EG-2FFVB1156) further referred to as "Zynq US+", which is 16 nm FPGA with 600K logic elements and integrated with quad-core ARM Cortex-A53 (clocked at 1.5 GHz), dual-core Cortex-R5 real-time processors (clocked at 600 MHz), and a Mali-400 MP2 graphics processing unit (clocked at 667 MHz). Software used for Zynq US+ was Vivado Design Edition 2018.3 (64-bit) SW Build 2405991, IP Build: 2404404. The C code was compiled with Xilinx SDK, which is based on Eclipse Version: 4.6.1.v20160907-1200, Build id: M20160907-1200 with GCC compiler version 7.3.1.

The project was built using the Vivado by Xilinx. The compilation reports show the described below utilization of the FPGA resources:

- **LUT utilization:** 26,930/274,080 (9.83%)
- **LUTRAM:** 70/144,000 (0.05%)
- **Total registers:** 3,161/548,160 (0.58%)
- **Total global buffers (BUFG):** 1/404 (0.25%)

The utilization of FPGA resources is very low. The project prepared for Zynq US+ needed less than 10% of Look-Up Tables (LUTs) and less than 1% of available registers.

3.4 Implementation

All hardware components for calculating the discernibility matrix and the core and for checking candidates whether they are reducts or not were written in VHDL language.

Hardware implementation is supported by the application written in C language, which on the basis of data provided by the hardware creates combinations of attributes and sends it back to the hardware.

The discernibility matrix is calculated in DM_Block which consists of many comparators, which compares values of two objects from the decision tables. The decision table is passed from DMBlockWrapper component, where both negative and positive classes were declared. Calculation results are passed back to DMBlockWrapper, where it is used to calculate the core for given data.

The core is calculated in Core_Block which consists of a cascade of singleton checkers. Core_Block is a combinational circuit and does not need clock signal, so calculation time depends only on the propagation time of FPGAs logic blocks.

The calculated core is also used as a first mask, which zeroizes already used attributes in the discernibility matrix. After zeroizing, freq_wrapper calculates for each attribute how many times it is used, and then sorts this data from the most to least frequent ones. Sorted data is sent with the calculated core and ISRED flag (which informs whether the current mask is reduct or not) to Nios/Zynq processor instance.

In Nios/Zynq, C application on the basis of frequency data, picks the most likely candidate for reduct and send it back to freq_wrapper component as a mask. The provided mask is then checked for being a reduct by FPGA.

New frequencies with ISRED flag are sent back to Nios/Zynq processor which types the next candidate. The process is repeated until all minimal reducts are found.

4   Experiments

This section describes experimental research that concerns finding minimal reducts using hardware implementation of the chosen breadth search based algorithms on both devices.

Every calculation of the minimal reducts was performed 10, 100, 1000 and 10000 times in order to obtain the most precise time result. All experiments were performed on the dataset described in Sect. 3.1.

The goal of the first experiment is to check how much time is taken when using the BBFS on Arria. Table 1 shows run-time for finding all minimal reducts for the given dataset.

Table 1. Runtime (in ms) of calculating reducts on Arria

Times calculated	BBFS	FBFS
10	6	5
100	59	48
1000	590	482
10000	5898	4817

The second experiment checks the time needed for the calculations when using the FBFS on Arria. Results presented in Table 1 compared to the previous test shows that no matter what kind of the algorithm was used, since the obtained run-times are almost the same.

After determining the reference times from Arria, the same hardware configuration was launched on Zynq US+. Next experiments were performed in the same way as the previous ones.

In the third experiment, the BBFS was used (Table 2). Comparing the result with the times obtained from Arria, it can be concluded that the execution time is much lower (about 15.5 times).

Table 2. Runtime (in ms) of calculating reducts on Zynq US+

Times calculated	BBFS	FBFS
10	0.38	0.67
100	3.80	6.69
1000	38.13	66.94
10000	380.10	665.80

The goal of the last experiment is to check how much time is taken to calculate the core and the reducts when using FBFS. The results presented in Table 2 shows that this strategy gives almost 1.75 times higher values than the BBFS and about 7.2 times better results than Arria.

The results presented in Tables 1 and 2 show that using the same hardware design on two different devices can lead to an improvement of the performance. The described experiments proved that it is possible to achieve 15.5 times better times (in the case of BBFS) and 7.2 times better (in the case of FBFS). It should be noticed that the clock used for Zynq is 2 times faster than the clock used for Nios, so if we take that difference, the speed factor is about 7.75 for BBFS and 3.6 for FBFS.

For test purposes, the clock used for AXI bus, which is used to transfer data between *Zynq* component and *freq_wrapper*, was raised from 100 MHz first to 250 MHz and finally to 300 MHz. For all clock speeds, the core and reducts were calculated 10000 times.

Table 3. Runtime (in ms) of calculating reducts on Zynq US+ with different AXI clocks

AXI clock in [MHz]	BBFS	FBFS
100	380.10	665.80
250	283.73	462.02
300	272.97	439.53

As can be seen in Table 3, the results are much better when AXI bus clock is faster, but the speedup is not proportional (increasing clock frequency by 2 times does not give 2 times better results). For the used dataset increasing clock by 3 times gives about 40% better results for BBFS and about 50% better results for FBFS.

5 Conclusion

This paper has investigated the problem of speeding up the process of finding minimal reducts by supporting with two FPGA devices: Intel Arria V SoC (5ASTFD5K3F40I3) and Xilinx Zynq Ultrascale+ MPSoC (XCZU9EG-2FFVB1156). Based on the experimental research reported in this paper we can formulate the following conclusions.

1. An essential acceleration in finding minimal reducts can be achieved by replacing the Arria device with the Zynq US+ one.
2. Increasing the clock frequency on the data bus can clearly speed up the system performance thanks to the reduction of the number of processor cycles needed to complete the task.

This study should be treated as preliminary research on minimal reducts computation using the Zynq US+ device. The future work is to make the hardware implementation more flexible so that it can be used for datasets with arbitrary number of attributes and objects.

References

1. Chen, D., Zhao, S., Zhang, L., Yang, Y., Zhang, X.: Sample pair selection for attribute reduction with rough set. IEEE Trans. Knowl. Data Eng. **24**(11), 2080–2093 (2012)
2. Choromański, M., Grześ, T., Hońko, P.: Breadth search strategies for finding minimal reducts - towards hardware implementation. Neural Comput. Appl. (2019, under review)
3. Degang, C., Changzhong, W., Qinghua, H.: A new approach to attribute reduction of consistent and inconsistent covering decision systems with covering rough sets. Inf. Sci. **177**(17), 3500–3518 (2007)
4. Grześ, T., Kopczyński, M., Stepaniuk, J.: FPGA in rough set based core and reduct computation. In: Lingras, P., Wolski, M., Cornelis, C., Mitra, S., Wasilewski, P. (eds.) RSKT 2013. LNCS (LNAI), vol. 8171, pp. 263–270. Springer, Heidelberg (2013). https://doi.org/10.1007/978-3-642-41299-8_25
5. Kopczyński, M., Grześ, T., Stepaniuk, J.: FPGA in rough-granular computing: reduct generation. In: Proceedings of the 2014 IEEE/WIC/ACM International Joint Conferences on Web Intelligence (WI) and Intelligent Agent Technologies (IAT) - Volume 02, WI-IAT 2014, pp. 364–370. IEEE Computer Society, Washington (2014)
6. Pawlak, Z.: Rough Sets. Theoretical Aspects of Reasoning about Data. Kluwer Academic, Dordrecht (1991)
7. Skowron, A., Rauszer, C.: The discernibility matrices and functions in information systems. In: Słowiński, R. (ed.) Intelligent Decision Support. Theory and Decision Library (Series D: System Theory, Knowledge Engineering and Problem Solving), vol. 11, pp. 331–362. Springer, Dordrecht (1992). https://doi.org/10.1007/978-94-015-7975-9_21
8. Stepaniuk, J.: Rough set data mining of diabetes data. In: Raś, Z.W., Skowron, A. (eds.) ISMIS 1999. LNCS, vol. 1609, pp. 457–465. Springer, Heidelberg (1999). https://doi.org/10.1007/BFb0095133
9. Stepaniuk, J.: Rough-Granular Computing in Knowledge Discovery and Data Mining. Studies in Computational Intelligence, vol. 152. Springer-Verlag, Heidelberg (2008). https://doi.org/10.1007/978-3-540-70801-8
10. Sun, G., Qi, X., Zhang, Y.: A FPGA-based implementation of rough set theory. In: 2011 Chinese Control and Decision Conference (CCDC), pp. 2561–2564 (2011)
11. Swiniarski, R.: Rough sets methods in feature reduction and classification. Int. J. Appl. Math. Comput. Sci. **11**(3), 565–582 (2001)
12. Swiniarski, R.W., Skowron, A.: Rough set methods in feature selection and recognition. Pattern Recogn. Lett. **24**(6), 833–849 (2003)
13. Thi, V.D., Giang, N.L.: A method for extracting knowledge from decision tables in terms of functional dependencies. Cybern. Inf. Technol. **13**(1), 73–82 (2013)
14. Tiwari, K.S., Kothari, A.G.: Architecture and implementation of attribute reduction algorithm using binary discernibility matrix. In: 2011 International Conference on Computational Intelligence and Communication Networks, pp. 212–216 (2011)
15. Tiwari, K., Kothari, A.: Design and implementation of rough set co-processor on FPGA. Int. J. Innovative Comput. Inf. Control **11**(2), 641–656 (2015)
16. Tiwari, K., Kothari, A.: Design of intelligent system for medical applications using rough set theory. Int. J. Data Min. Model. Manag. **8**(3), 279–301 (2016)
17. Zhang, X., Mei, C., Chen, D., Li, J.: Multi-confidence rule acquisition oriented attribute reduction of covering decision systems via combinatorial optimization. Knowl.-Based Syst. **50**, 187–197 (2013)

An Event-Based Parameterized Active Scheduler for Classical Job Shop Problem

Luis Carlos dos Santos Júnior[1] (ID), Aparecida de Fátima Castello Rosa[1] (ID),
and Fabio Henrique Pereira[1,2] (✉) (ID)

[1] Universidade Nove de Julho - Informatics and Knowledge Management Graduate
Program - PPGI/UNINOVE, Vergueiro Street 235, São Paulo, Brazil
luissantos@uni9.edu.br, afc.rosa@uninove.edu.br, fabiohp@uni9.pro.br
[2] Universidade Nove de Julho - Industrial Engineering Graduate
Program - PPGEP/UNINOVE, Vergueiro Street 235, São Paulo, Brazil
http://www.uninove.br

Abstract. In this work, an event-based genetic procedure for creating
parameterized active schedules is proposed to solve the classical job shop
scheduling, modelled as a continuous optimization problem. Instead of
work with priorities values, the genetic algorithm defines values of delay
times while the priorities are determined on the basis of the Last In First
Out rule. The hypothesis is that any delay must end when the priority
task arrives the machine. The scheduler is applied in a hybrid approach
to solve the scheduling, which is a well-known NP-hard combinatorial
optimization problem. After an initial schedule is created, it is refined by
a local search and used as a seed in a final phase of optimization, in which
a binary genetic indirect coding to induce permutations and generate new
solutions is used. Preliminary results on a set of standard instances from
literature validate the effectiveness of the proposed approach.

Keywords: Parameterized active scheduler · Genetic algorithms ·
Combinatorial optimization · Job shop

1 Introduction

The job shop scheduling is a well-known NP-hard combinatorial optimization
problem, which deals with the task of finding an optimal schedule from a finite,
but very large, set of all possible schedules. It has a set jobs to be processed in
a strictly order in a set of machines, in which each operation has a processing
time associated to. Moreover, no machine can process more than one operation
at a time, and preemption is not allowed. The most common single objective
in job shop problems (JSPs) are the minimization of the makespan, which are
associated to the overall completion time of all jobs [32].

Comprehensive studies related to the approaches to solve the JSP demonstrate that it has been moved towards the use of hybrid metaheuristics techniques
[1,6,11,12,15]. However, although the multitude of techniques and their success

© Springer Nature Switzerland AG 2019
K. Saeed et al. (Eds.): CISIM 2019, LNCS 11703, pp. 421–432, 2019.
https://doi.org/10.1007/978-3-030-28957-7_35

in the outcome of many classical benchmark problems, no one seems to be robust enough to solve optimally all of them, within a reasonable amount of time.

In fact, performance comparable to the state-of-the-art seems to depend on an efficient exploration of the solution space features. In this sense, the space of feasible solutions can be divided into three subsets: semi-active, active and non-delayed solutions. A solution is semi-active if the anticipation of the start of an operation implies a change in the sequence of operations. If the anticipation of an operation causes delays in another operation or violates some precedence constraint, then the schedule is classified as active. Finally, if no machine is kept idle when it can start processing an operation so we have a non-delayed solution.

It is known that the active solution space is dominant over the semi-active, since it is smaller and contains at least one optimal solution of the problem. On the other hand, despite being the subspace that represents the smallest set, the non-delayed space does not always contain the optimal solution. Thus, typical algorithms for this problem search the active space to ensure that the optimum is considered. These algorithms, in general, are based on the Giffler and Thompson method [8] that consists of an active schedule builder.

However, although the active space always contains an optimal solution, this subset is still very large and contains many low-quality schedules in terms of the makespan [9,25]. In order to overcome this limitation, the authors in [29] proposed the generation of an intermediate subspace of *parametrized active schedules*, between the spaces of active and non-delayed solutions. The basic idea for generating this subset is to control the maximum delay times allowed for each operation, so that the search space contains the optimal solution without the need to explore the whole set of active solutions [9].

Since it was created, the concept of parameterized active schedule has been successfully explored in numerous researches [9,20,21,23–27]. Generally, these approaches are based on metaheuristics and represent solutions in different ways, from priorities list for all operations to binary or real representations, based on random keys. In addition, these methods either use fixed values of *acceptable idle-time limit* or require an additional procedure to optimize this parameter for creating parameterized active schedules. The authors in [9], for example, defined a genetic algorithm in which each chromosome has the size $2n$, where n is the number of operations of the problem, in which the first half of the chromosome represents priority values and the second half defines idle times for each operation. Despite the good results obtained by those authors that approach increases the search space and possibly the computational time. Many approaches are based on similar ideas [20,27].

More recently, a two-level metaheuristic algorithm has been proposed in [25], in which an upper-level population-based metaheuristic algorithm is only designated to adjust the parameters, among them, the *acceptable idle-time limit*.

In this paper, we propose a new procedure to construct parameterized active schedules, which works from the non-delayed to the active space. Instead of work with priorities values, the genetic algorithm defines n values of delays while the priorities are determined on the basis of the Last In First Out (LIFO) rule.

The hypothesis is that any delay must end when the priority operation reaches the machine. So, it is not necessary to define idle-time values explicitly.

After an initial schedule is created a local search method is applied to refine the solution, which is used as a seed in a final stage of optimization, in which a binary genetic indirect coding is used to induce permutations and generate other solutions.

This paper is organized as follows. First, Sect. 2 presents some definitions about the types of schedules: active, non-delay and parameterized active. Section 3 describes the proposed optimization approach detailing the procedure to generate parameterizes active schedules based on values of delay times defined by genetic algorithm (GA), the local search method using the neighborhood of van Laarhoven [16], and the final phase of optimization using the binary indirect dynamic seed genetic algorithm. Section 4 then lays out the design of the experiments and Sect. 5 discusses the experimental results. Finally, Sect. 6 concludes this paper and draws some perspectives.

2   Types of Schedules

Schedules are classified into three types: semi-active schedule, active schedule, and non-delay schedule, according [22].

- Semi-active schedule: a feasible schedule is called semi-active if no operation can be completed earlier without changing the order of processing on any one of the machines;
- active schedule: a feasible schedule is called active if it is not possible to construct another schedule, through changes in the order of processing on the machines, with at least one operation finishing earlier and no operation finishing later; and
- non-delay schedule: no machine is kept idle while an operation is waiting for processing.

It is important notice that the subset of active schedules constitutes a subset of semi-actives schedules and thus the active schedule contains optimal schedule [9]. According Smutnicki and Bożejko, another interesting relation found is that, although the semi-actives schedules are located relatively close to best known solutions, they offer makespans of very poor quality [28].

Generally the set of active schedules is very large and contains many schedules with large delay. In order to reduce the search space the concept of parametrized active schedules has been developed [9].

2.1   Parametrized Active Schedules

The basic idea for parametrized active schedule is to control the maximum delay time allowed, one can reduce or increase the solution space [9]. In this approach, a maximum delay time of zero is equivalent to restricting solution space to non-delay times, and a maximum delay time equal to infinity is equivalent to allowing active scheduling.

3   Proposed Optimization Approach

The proposed approach is divided into three stages: a procedure to create parameterized active schedules, a local search method, and a binary genetic indirect coding to induce permutations and generate new solutions.

First the GA defines values of delay to create an initial parameterized active schedule. The chromosome representation is based on real numbers to solve a continuous optimization problem. As hypothesis of this approach any delay time must end when the priority task reaches the machine, so the priorities are defined based on LIFO rule.

After an initial schedule is created, it is refined by the van Laaehoven neighborhood local search and used as a seed in a final stage of optimization, in which a binary genetic indirect coding is used to induce permutations and generate new solutions.

3.1   Procedure to Create Parameterized Active Schedules

The procedure is based on concepts of discrete-event simulation using a modified time advanced algorithm with a combination of event scheduling and activity scanning. An event is an instantaneous occurrence that changes some variable necessary to describe the system while an activity represents a processing time of an operation [13].

In the original time advanced algorithm two kind of events exist: the beginning of processing an operation and the end of processing an operation. So, at the beginning of an operation the end of processing is calculated and the corresponding events are chronologically ordered in a future event list. In a modified time advanced algorithm used here a new kind of event is defined as the end of the delay time stipulated by the GA. Additionally, each machine can assume three different status: busy, idle and delayed. The algorithm has three phases as illustrated in Algorithm 1.

3.2   Local Search Method

In order to reach better results for solving JSPs and to avoid local optimal solutions, local search has been used. The main idea of local search is to improve a schedule since there is no guarantee of its optimality with respect to the local neighborhood [15].

The local search procedure begins by identifying the critical path in the current solution and then apply elementary perturbations of the machines critical operations based on the neighborhood of van Laarhoven [16]. If the permutation improves the solution then it is accepted, a new critical path is calculated and the process continues. If there is no improvement the local search ends [9].

Algorithm 1. Schedule generator procedure

Input: chromosome with values of delay times
Output: parameterized active schedule and its makespan
Initialization:
    Move jobs to corresponding queues
    Create the future event list: end-delay events
Phase A: advance clock to next event time
Phase B: execute the end-processing events
    Move jobs to next queue
    Update future event list: end-delay events
    Update status of machine(s)
Phase C: execute the beginning-processing events
    Remove Last In job(s) from queue
    Scheduling job(s) on machine(s)
    Update future event list: end-processing events
    Update status of machine(s)
    Update makespan with time of the last end-processing event

---

3.3 Binary Indirect Dynamic Seed Genetic Algorithm

The Dynamic Seed Genetic Algorithm (DSGA) utilizes the classical Genetic Algorithm (GA) as the central optimization technique. In this phase the chromosome representation of the problem is based on an indirect binary 2D matrix.

After a parameterized active schedule is created by the local search approach it is used as a seed for other solutions and permuted according a binary 2D chromosome of dimension $m \times (n - 1)$, where m is the number of the machines and n is the number of jobs.

The matrix is scanned from left-to-right, top-to-down fashion and, whenever an allele 1 is present in a locus, a permutation must occurs between the current job and its successor in the seed, for each machine, and no permutation is taken place otherwise.

The resulting permuted matrix is evaluated as a possible solution and ranked based upon its makespan value. This process is parametrically repeated based upon the convergence analysis of the GA. Figure 1 depicts the matrix-related representation mechanism considering a specific instance of JSP, known as LA01, available at the OR-Library [4], while a more detailed explanation of the whole process can be found in [10].

The binary matrix has the advantages to be easy to implement and allow simpler crossover and mutation types to be applies to.

The optimization process of this third phase is iteratively applied until the stop criteria is reached. After a few GA generations the best solution found is used to update the seed dynamically by a number of external iterations defined as *outIter*.

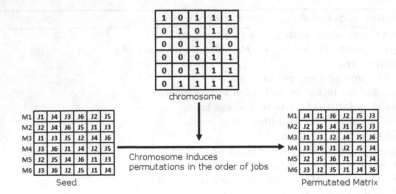

Fig. 1. The indirect binary representation mechanism. The chromosome induces permutations in the order of jobs in the seed setting processing priorities.

4   Experimental Design

In the first phase the GA is applied within the schedule generator procedure to define a parameterized active schedule and its makespan, according Algorithm 1. The chromosome representation is based on real numbers using `GARealGenome` genome from GAlib [30].

For defining lower bound and upper bound for delay times of operations we create a genome whose elements may assume any value in the interval $[0.0, 60.0]$ discretized on the interval 10.0 (5.0 for the instance LA04).

Additionally, we apply a steady state GA with parameters defined according Table 1. The parameters of the proposed approach were experimentally defined by trial-and-error.

Table 1. Parameters of the continuous genetic optimization.

Parameter	Value
Crossover operator	Two-point crossover
Mutator	Swap mutator
Replacement rate	90%
Mutation rate	5%
Crossover rate	90%
Population size	2000
Number of generations	200
Fitness	Minimize makespan

As there is no guarantee of optimality of the schedule returned by the Algorithm 1, it is refined in a local search phase based on neighborhood of van

Laarhoven [16], as depicted in Subsect. 3.2. We start this phase finding the critical path of the solution and then permuting critical operations on the block of those operations on the same machine [9].

This local operation is performed until permutations of critical operations in the same block do not promote any improvement of the solution.

The critical path can be defined as set of the operations with no difference between the late start schedule and the early start schedule, called slack [14]. In an early start schedule the earliest finish of the predecessor becomes the start of an operation processing and, similarly, the late start schedule is one in which the late start is the difference between the late finish and the processing time. This concept is illustrated in Fig. 2 for a job shop problem with 3 jobs and 3 machines.

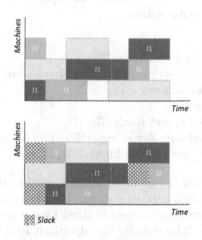

Fig. 2. Illustration of slack and critical operations (no slack) from an early start schedule (upper) and a late start schedule.

Finally, the parameters of the last phase of optimization using the binary indirect dynamic seed genetic algorithm are presented in Table 2. The parameters in this table were also experimentally defined by trial-and-error.

5   Experimental Results

This section presents some results on a set of standard instances from literature to illustrate the effectiveness of the proposed approach.

We have considered the instances LA01 to LA20 from Lawrence [17].

In order to evaluate the performance of the proposed genetic algorithm, results are compared with the following algorithms:

- GRASP by Binato et al. [5];
- GLS1 and GLS2 by van Laarhoven, Aarts, and Lenstra [16];

Table 2. Parameters of the binary 2D genetic algorithm.

Parameter	Value
Crossover operator	Uniform crossover
Mutator	Swap mutator
Replacement rate	90%
Mutation rate	1%
Crossover rate	90%
Population size	10
Number of generations	$3mn$ generations without convergence
outIter^a	20
Fitness	Minimize makespan

^{a}Number of external iterations.

– PaGA by Asadzadeh and Zamanifar [3];
– Parameterized Active (HGA) by Gonçalves, Mendes, and Resende [9];
– LSGA by Ombuki and Ventresca [19];
– aLSGA by Asadzadeh [2];
– Adaptive (Adp) by Gabel and Riedmiller [7];
– Hybrid Genetic and Simulate Annealing (HGSA) by Wang and Zheng [31];
– Tabu Search (TS) by Nowicki and Smutnicki [18].

Table 3 shows a summary of experimental results. It lists problem name (Prob), problem size (number of jobs × number of machines), the best known solution (BKS), the average solutions obtained by our genetic continuous optimization approach (GAC) by running the algorithm 10 times, and the solutions as reported by each of the other algorithms.

From the results, the proposed method (GAC) did not find the optimal for instances LA03, LA16, LA17, LA19 and LA20, like what happens with many other approaches especially for 10×10 problems that are admittedly more complex. However, when comparing the gap for these problems (Table 4), we observed that our approach equals or exceeds more than 60% of the other methods, reaching 70% for LA03 and 90% for LA20, being overcome only by TS in the latter case.

Overall, the GAC presents a general average gap (GAG) smaller than 6 of the 10 methods tested, and it presented at least an improvement with respect to almost all others algorithms, except the HGA and TS, which proves the robustness of the proposed methodology while keeping a simple implementation through binary representation scheme. The authors believe that a simple representation (and thus, the possibility to choose also simple genetic operators rather than specialized ones) are an important aspect to be considered, which allows the use of wider range of implementations and evolutionary algorithm libraries by the research community.

Table 3. Experimental results. The highlight means that the result is not the BKS.

Prob	size	BKS	GAC	GRASP	GLS1	GLS2	Adp	HGA	HGSA	TS	aLSGA	LSGA	PaGA
LA01	10 × 5	666	666	666	666	666	666	666	666	666	666	666	666
LA02	10 × 5	655	655	655	**668**	**659**	**687**	655		655	655	655	655
LA03	10 × 5	597	**599**	**604**	**613**	**609**	**648**	597		597	**606**	597	**617**
LA04	10 × 5	590	590	590	599	594	611	590		590	593	590	607
LA05	10 × 5	593	593	593	593	593	593	593		593	593	593	593
LA06	15 × 5	926	926	926	926	926	926	926	926	926	926	926	926
LA07	15 × 5	890	890	890	890	890	890	890		890	890	890	890
LA08	15 × 5	863	863	863	863	863	863	863		863	863	863	863
LA09	15 × 5	951	951	951	951	951	951	951		951	951	951	951
LA10	15 × 5	958	958	958	958	958	958	958		958	958	958	958
LA11	20 × 5	1222	1222	1222	1222	1222	1222	1222	1222	1222	1222	1222	1223
LA12	20 × 5	1039	1039	1039	1039	1039	1039	1039		1039	1039	1039	1039
LA13	20 × 5	1150	1150	1150	1150	1150	1150	1150		1150	1150	1150	1150
LA14	20 × 5	1292	1292	1292	1292	1292	1292	1292		1292	1292	1292	1292
LA15	20 × 5	1207	1207	1207	1207	1207	1207	1207		1207	1207	1207	1273
LA16	10 × 10	945	**980**	**946**	**977**	**977**	**996**	945		945	**946**	**959**	**994**
LA17	10 × 10	784	**787**	784	**791**	**791**	**793**	784		784	784	**792**	**793**
LA18	10 × 10	848	848	848	**856**	**858**	**890**	848		848	848	**857**	**860**
LA19	10 × 10	842	**858**	842	**863**	**859**	**875**	842		842	**852**	**860**	**873**
LA20	10 × 10	902	**907**	**907**	**913**	**916**	**941**	907		902	**907**	**907**	**912**

It worth to mention that the authors did not present a comparison regarding the computational efficiency due the fact that not all of the studies presented in the beginning of this section reported the computational resources on which the experiments were conducted. Also, comparison related to computational efficiency of an algorithm is highly dependant on the hardware specs and the programming expertise of the researcher, as both can affect the efficiency of the algorithm as perceived by the researchers.

Table 4. Gap from solution found (SF) in relation to BKS ($Gap = |SF - BKS|/BKS$).

Prob	GAC	GRASP	GLS1	GLS2	Adp	HGA	HGSA	TS	aLSGA	LSGA	PaGA
LA03	0.003	0.012	0.027	0.020	0.085	0.000	-	0.000	0.015	0.000	0.033
LA16	0.037	0.001	0.034	0.034	0.054	0.000	-	0.000	0.001	0.015	0.052
LA17	0.004	0.000	0.009	0.009	0.012	0.000	-	0.000	0.000	0.010	0.012
LA19	0.019	0.000	0.025	0.020	0.039	0.000	-	0.000	0.012	0.021	0.037
LA20	0.006	0.006	0.012	0.016	0.043	0.006	-	0.000	0.006	0.006	0.011
GAG	**0.003**	**0.001**	**0.008**	**0.006**	**0.018**	**0.000**	**0.850**	**0.000**	**0.002**	**0.003**	**0.012**

6   Conclusion

This work presents a genetic approach to solve the job shop scheduling problem. The JSP is modelled as a continuous optimization problem to find an initial parameterized active schedule. Instead of work with priorities values, the genetic algorithm defines values of delay times while the priorities are defined based on Last In First Out rule.

The proposed approach seems to be very promising since it found optimal or near-optimal solutions for all instances. More specifically, the GAC produced similar results to the original parameterized active approach (HGA) indicating that the hypothesis of that any delay must end when the priority task reaches the machine seems to be valid. To reinforce this hypothesis, eleven of the twenty tested problems were solved optimally only with steps 1 and 2 of the approach.

Regarding to the computational time, the proposed method presented an average of 5 min to find the optimal solution. However, there is opportunity to improve this aspect, for example, by applying a more efficient local search such as the neighborhood of Nowicki and Smutnicki [18]. The implementation of a more efficient local search and the application of the method in larger problems are being focused on new research.

Acknowledgement(s). This work was partially supported by grant #2018/08326−6, São Paulo Research Foundation (FAPESP). Additionally, the authors would like to thank Universidade Nove de Julho for the support and the scholarship granted to the first two of them.

References

1. Akay, B., Yao, X.: Recent advances in evolutionary algorithms for job shop scheduling. In: Uyar, A., Ozcan, E., Urquhart, N. (eds.) Automated Scheduling and Planning. Studies in Computational Intelligence, vol. 505, pp. 191–224. Springer, Heidelberg (2013). https://doi.org/10.1007/978-3-642-39304-4_8
2. Asadzadeh, L.: A local search genetic algorithm for the job shop scheduling problem with intelligent agents. Comput. Ind. Eng. **85**, 376–383 (2015). https://doi.org/10.1016/j.cie.2015.04.006
3. Asadzadeh, L., Zamanifar, K.: An agent-based parallel approach for the job shop scheduling problem with genetic algorithms. Math. Comput. Model. (2010). https://doi.org/10.1016/j.mcm.2010.04.019
4. Beasley, J.: OR-Library (1990). http://people.brunel.ac.uk/~mastjjb/jeb/orlib/files%0A/jobshop1.txt
5. Binato, S., Hery, W.J., Loewenstern, D.M., Resende, M.G.C.: A grasp for job shop scheduling. In: Ribeiro, C.C., Hansen, P. (eds.) Essays and Surveys in Metaheuristics Operations. Research/Computer Science Interfaces Series, vol. 15, pp. 59–79. Springer, Boston (2002). https://doi.org/10.1007/978-1-4615-1507-4_3
6. Chaudhry, I.A., Khan, A.A.: A research survey: review of flexible job shop scheduling techniques. Int. Trans. Oper. Res. **23**(3), 551–591 (2016)
7. Gabel, T., Riedmiller, M.: Scaling adaptive agent-based reactive job-shop scheduling to large-scale problems. In: 2007 IEEE Symposium on Computational Intelligence in Scheduling, pp. 259–266, April 2007. https://doi.org/10.1109/SCIS.2007.367699

8. Giffler, B., Thompson, G.L.: Algorithms for solving production-scheduling problems. Oper. Res. **8**(4), 487–503 (1960)
9. Goncalves, J.F., Mendes, J.J.M., Resende, M.G.C.: A hybrid genetic algorithm for the job shop scheduling problem. Eur. J. Oper. Res. **167**(1), 77–95 (2005). https://doi.org/10.1016/j.ejor.2004.03.012
10. Grassi, F., Schimit, P.H.T., Pereira, F.H.: Dynamic seed genetic algorithm to solve job shop scheduling problems. In: Nääs, I., et al. (eds.) APMS 2016. IAICT, vol. 488, pp. 170–177. Springer, Cham (2016). https://doi.org/10.1007/978-3-319-51133-7_21
11. Jain, A., Meeran, S.: Deterministic job-shop scheduling: past, present and future. Eur. J. Oper. Res. **113**(2), 390–434 (1999)
12. Jones, A., Rabelo, L.C., Sharawi, A.T.: Survey of Job Shop Scheduling Techniques. Wiley Encyclopedia of Electrical and Electronics Engineering. Wiley, London (2001)
13. Kelton, D.W.: Simulation with Arena. McGraw Hill, Boston (1998)
14. Kerzner, H.: Project Management: A Systems Approach to Planning, Scheduling, and Controlling, 10th edn. Wiley, Hoboken (2009)
15. Kotthoff, L.: Algorithm selection for combinatorial search problems: a survey. In: Bessiere, C., De Raedt, L., Kotthoff, L., Nijssen, S., O'Sullivan, B., Pedreschi, D. (eds.) Data Mining and Constraint Programming. LNCS (LNAI), vol. 10101, pp. 149–190. Springer, Cham (2016). https://doi.org/10.1007/978-3-319-50137-6_7
16. van Laarhoven, P.J.M., Aarts, E.H.L., Lenstra, J.K.: Job shop scheduling by simulated annealing. Oper. Res. **40**(1), 113–125 (1992). https://doi.org/10.1287/opre.40.1.113
17. Lawrence, S.: Resource constrained project scheduling: an experimental investigation of heuristic scheduling techniques (Supplement). Ph.D. thesis, Graduate School of Industrial Administration, Carnegie-Mellon University (1984)
18. Nowicki, E., Smutnicki, C.: A fast taboo search algorithm for the job shop problem. Manag. Sci. **42**(6), 797–813 (1996). https://doi.org/10.2307/2634595
19. Ombuki, B.M., Ventresca, M.: Local search genetic algorithms for the job shop scheduling problem. Appl. Intell. **21**(1), 99–109 (2004). https://doi.org/10.1023/B:APIN.0000027769.48098.91
20. Palacios, J.J., González-Rodríguez, I., Vela, C.R., Puente, J.: Robust swarm optimisation for fuzzy open shop scheduling. Nat. Comput. **13**(2), 145–156 (2014)
21. Petrovic, D., Castro, E., Petrovic, S., Kapamara, T.: Radiotherapy scheduling. In: Uyar, A., Ozcan, E., Urquhart, N. (eds.) Automated Scheduling and Planning. Studies in Computational Intelligence, vol. 505, pp. 155–189. Springer, Heidelberg (2013). https://doi.org/10.1007/978-3-642-39304-4_7
22. Pinedo, M.L.: Scheduling: Theory, Algorithms, and Systems, 4th edn. Springer, Boston (2012). https://doi.org/10.1007/978-1-4614-2361-4
23. Pongchairerks, P.: A self-tuning PSO for job-shop scheduling problems. Int. J. Oper. Res. **19**(1), 96–113 (2014)
24. Pongchairerks, P.: Efficient local search algorithms for job-shop scheduling problems. Int. J. Math. Oper. Res. **9**(2), 258–277 (2016)
25. Pongchairerks, P.: A two-level metaheuristic algorithm for the job-shop scheduling problem. Complexity **2019**, 1–11 (2019)
26. Pongchairerks, P., Kachitvichyanukul, V., et al.: A two-level particle swarm optimisation algorithm on job-shop scheduling problems. Int. J. Oper. Res. **4**(4), 390–411 (2009)
27. Sha, D., Hsu, C.Y.: A new particle swarm optimization for the open shop scheduling problem. Comput. Oper. Res. **35**(10), 3243–3261 (2008)

28. Smutnicki, C., Bożejko, W.: Tabu search and solution space analyses. The job shop case. In: Moreno-Díaz, R., Pichler, F., Quesada-Arencibia, A. (eds.) EUROCAST 2017. LNCS, vol. 10671, pp. 383–391. Springer, Cham (2018). https://doi.org/10.1007/978-3-319-74718-7_46

29. Storer, R.H., Wu, S.D., Vaccari, R.: New search spaces for sequencing problems with application to job shop scheduling. Manag. Sci. **38**(10), 1495–1509 (1992)

30. Wall, M.: GAlib: a C++ library of genetic algorithm components. Mechanical Engineering Department, Massachusetts Institute of Technology (1996). https://doi.org/citeulike-articleid:4305029. http://lancet.mit.edu/ga/dist/

31. Wang, L., Zheng, D.Z.: An effective hybrid optimization strategy for job-shop scheduling problems. Comput. Oper. Res. **28**(6), 585–596 (2001). https://doi.org/10.1016/S0305-0548(99)00137-9

32. Yamada, T.: Studies on metaheuristics for jobshop and flowshop scheduling problems. Ph.D. thesis, Kyoto University, Kyoto, Japan (2008)

Lossless and Lossy Audio Codecs for Low-Performance Microcontrollers for Use in IoT

Tomasz Grzes[✉] [ID]

Faculty of Computer Science, Bialystok University of Technology, Bialystok, Poland
t.grzes@pb.edu.pl
http://www.wi.pb.edu.pl

Abstract. Internet of Things (IoT) is a very fast developing branch of IT. IoT needs low-power systems, that are often also low-performance. For such devices, there is a problem to use one of the popular audio codecs because of very high-performance demand, for example floating point operations. In this paper, two codecs: lossless and lossy are proposed.

Lossless codec makes use of the simple bit operations for reducing the number of bits needed to store one sample and therefore lead to reduce the size of the whole audio file. All needed arithmetic operations are executed very fast and thus don't need a high performance of the microcontroller. Lossy codec additionally utilizes some principles borrowed from the decision systems, among them from rough-set theory. In this case, the resulting audio is lossy, but the difference is very small and thus could not be heard.

Experiments show that either lossless, as well as lossy codec, reduces the size of the audio file, and are very fast (don't need high-performance microcontrollers), so can be used in IoT systems.

Keywords: Lossy audio codec · Lossless audio codec ·
Low-performance microcontroller · Internet of Things

1 Introduction

There are many audio codecs used in contemporary multimedia systems. The most popular and widely used codecs are generally connected with MPEG (Moving Picture Experts Group), among them mp3 (MPEG-1, layer 3), which is widely used in mobile systems [2,3]. Mp3, originally developed in Fraunhofer Institute [12], is a lossy codec, i.e. the audio after coding and decoding is different from the original.

Mp3 is not the only lossy audio codec. Except for mp3, there are also many proprietary and free, open source codecs. One of the open-source codecs is Vorbis [13]. Because of the properties of lossy codecs, they are not suitable in some applications, especially when interesting parts of the signal are destroyed during the processing. In the opposite to the lossy audio codecs, there are lossless audio codecs. One of them is FLAC [11].

Audio codecs development is in field of interest of contemporary scientific researches. In [6] the Block Truncation Coding (BTC) is used. BTC is a digital

© Springer Nature Switzerland AG 2019
K. Saeed et al. (Eds.): CISIM 2019, LNCS 11703, pp. 433–444, 2019.
https://doi.org/10.1007/978-3-030-28957-7_36

image compression algorithm, but in [6] was used for encoding audio data. In [7] for audio compression was used the multi-frame coding method. The proposed method was based on Principal Component Analysis (PCA). In [8] to compress the audio the separating amplitude and phase components are used. After separation, the individual components encoding into a suitable pattern is done.

All these algorithms need big computational power of the device for code and decode the audio signal. Therefore are not suitable for very low-performance devices. Presented in this paper codecs are a try to fill the gap in the development of the low demand codecs suitable to use in IoT.

The paper is organized as follows. In Sect. 2 the information about proposed codecs is provided. There are both algorithms described in detail with pseudocode of operation, and signal transformations used. In Sect. 3 there are results of experimental research of both algorithms. Finally in Sect. 4 all the paper is summarized with conclusions and proposed future work.

2   Audio Compression Algorithms

Below one can find proposed algorithms for audio compression. First, the lossless compression algorithm is described. The algorithm makes use of the assumption, that there is no need for using all the bits assigned to every sample.

Second, the lossy algorithm is described. The lossy algorithm uses one of the rough sets theory operation: discretization [4]. Mentioned operation is generally used to prepare the decision table's values for its easier processing, but here were adopted to use with the audio streams.

Both algorithms need at the input the audio stream S. Let $S = \{s_1, s_2, ..., s_N\}$ is the audio stream consisting of the samples s_i, where $i \in \langle 1, N \rangle$. Every sample is coded as M-bits long integer binary.

2.1   Signal Transformations Used in Algorithms

Visualization of a sample audio stream encoded on 16 bits is shown in Fig. 1. Every neighboring sample is connected to each other, making the plot of signal changes. It can be noticed from the plot in Fig. 1 that the amplitude of the signal is equal to about 18,000 and thus all the 16 bits are needed to encode every sample.

The signal can be encoded using the differences between samples, instead of the samples' values themselves. It this case the codes can be smaller, giving the possibility to use a smaller number of bits to encode. Figure 2 shows the proportion between the values (gray) and the differences between the values of samples (black).

Another transformation that can be used is the rectifying of the signal. The rectifier is the circuit, which converts the bipolar signal to unipolar. In terms of the sample value, rectifying is the process of changing the negative values to the positive, while leaving the positive values unchanged.

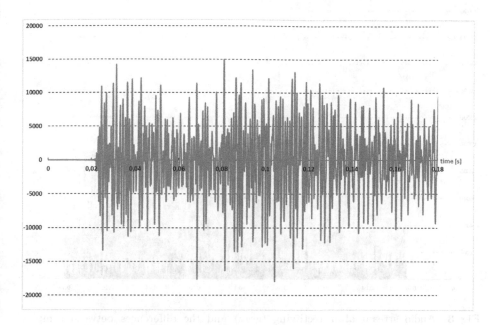

Fig. 1. A sample audio stream visualization. Visible silence at the beginning.

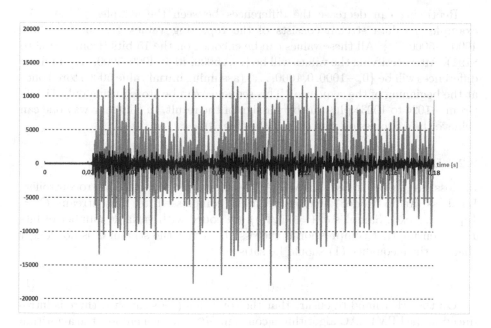

Fig. 2. Values of the differences between samples (black) of the audio stream used in Fig. 1.

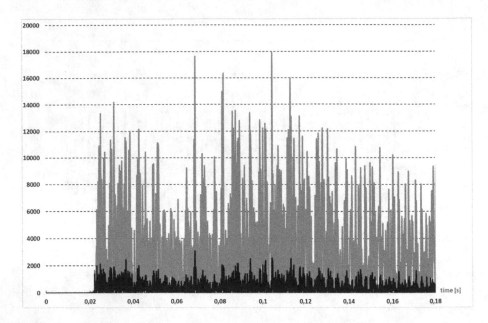

Fig. 3. Audio stream after rectifying (gray) and the differences between samples (black).

Rectifying can decrease the differences between the samples' values. For example the data stream consists of the repeating values $\{\ldots, 5000, -4000, 4000, -5000, \ldots\}$. All these values can be encoded on the 15 bits (from -8192 to 8191). After rectifying the values will be $\{\ldots, 5000, 4000, 4000, 5000, \ldots\}$, and the differences will be $\{0, -1000, 0, 1000, \ldots\}$ (assuming initial value 5000 stored once at the beginning of the sequence). This sequence can be stored using only 11 bits (from -1024 to 1023) plus one bit for sign of the result. In this easy way one can achieve the compression rate of $\frac{12}{15} = 0.8$ (Fig. 3).

2.2   Lossless Compression Algorithm

In lossless audio codec (LPMLLAC – Low Performance Microcontrollers LossLess Audio Codec) audio stream is compressed to new stream $C = \{c_1, c_2, \ldots, c_N\}$. Samples c_i $(i \in \langle 1, N \rangle)$ are coded with variable number of bits L_i. To ensure that compression is successful, so that the stream C is not longer than S, the inequality (1) should be satisfied:

$$\forall_{i \in \langle 1, N \rangle} L_i \leq M \tag{1}$$

On the other hand to ensure that the condition (1) is satisfied there is introduced in the LPMLLAC algorithm a constant $bits_{th}$, which enforce the algorithm to start a new block after crossing the threshold $bits_{th}$.

Because the audio signals are variable ones with the DC signal component equal to or near 0V, one can use e.g. U2 encoding to preserve the sign of the signal. Additionally, the difference between neighboring values is limited. All mentioned observations lead to the proposition of calculating the value of x_i, which depends on the sample values s_i and s_{i-1}:

$$x_i = \begin{cases} ||s_i| - |s_{i-1}||, & \text{if } i > 1 \\ |s_i|, & \text{otherwise} \end{cases} \qquad (2)$$

where $|a|$ is an absolute value of a.

Below is the pseudocode of the algorithm LPMLLAC.

Algorithm LPMLLAC of lossless audio compression.

INPUT: Audio stream S of samples s_i
INPUT: $bits_{th}$ – threshold for starting a new block
OUTPUT: Compressed stream C

```
 1: x_min ← ∞, x_max ← 0
 2: C ← {∅}
 3: T ← {∅} – temporary buffer for samples
 4: i ← 1
 5: while i ≤ N do
 6:    Calculate x_i from formula (2)
 7:    if x_i > x_max then
 8:       x_max ← x_i
 9:    end if
10:    if x_i < x_min then
11:       x_min ← x_i
12:    end if
13:    bits_i ← ⌈log₂(x_max − x_min)⌉
14:    if bits_i − bits_{i−1} > bits_th OR bits_i ≥ M then
15:       Encode elements from T with bits_i bits
16:       C ← C ∪ T
17:       T ← {x_i}
18:       x_min ← ∞, x_max ← 0
19:    else
20:       bits_{i−1} ← bits_i
21:       T ← T ∪ {x_i}
22:    end if
23:    i ← i + 1
24: end while
25: Encode elements from T with bits_i bits
26: C ← C ∪ T
```

In the beginning, the initialization is performed (lines 1–4). Then loop (lines 5–24) processes every sample s_i. Value x_i is calculated using the formula (2) in line 6, subsequently the x_{max} and x_{min} are updated according to the conditions in lines 7–9 and 10–12 respectively. After calculating the number of bits needed to encode the values of current block T, the condition for starting a new block is tested in line 14. A new block should be started after reaching the maximum number of bits ($bits_i \geq M$) or the increase of this number is greater than the

$bits_{th}$. If the block should be started, then the current block T is encoded using $bits_{i-1}$ bits, added to result in C, and finally cleared (lines 15–17). Otherwise value x_i is joined with the block T (line 21). After reaching the end of stream S all remaining values in block T are copied to result in C (line 26).

Although the algorithm looks quite complicated, it doesn't use the time-consuming operations, such as multiplying or dividing. The only problematic operation is logarithm, but it can be easily replaced by the series of bit-shift operations.

2.3   Lossy Compression Algorithm

In lossy audio codec (LPMLAC – Low-Performance Microcontrollers Lossy Audio Codec), the samples from the audio stream are first reduced in terms of bits used by every sample. This process can be compared to the data discretization in rough sets. Example algorithm can be found in [1], and its implementation in FPGA [5]. This algorithm was used for the sample discretization.

Discretization of every full sample is a very time-consuming process and thus is not suitable to use on low-performance microcontrollers. Therefore the discretization is performed on the lowest Q bits. Also, the lowest bits have the least influence on the sample value (have the least weight). After discretization the $CUTS$ cuts (subranges of values) are created, such that $2^Q > CUTS$. $CUTS$ should be the power of 2.

After discretization of the lowest bits, the audio stream is then processed by the LPMLLAC algorithm.

Below is the pseudocode of the algorithm LPMLAC. Operation $LB^Q(x)$ means "extract Q lowest bits from value x".

Algorithm LPMLAC of lossy audio compression.
INPUT: Audio stream S of samples s_i
INPUT: $bits_{th}$ – threshold for starting a new block
INPUT: Q, $CUTS$
OUTPUT: Compressed stream C
 1: **for** $i \in \langle 1, \ldots, 2^Q \rangle$ **do**
 2:     $F_i \leftarrow 0$
 3: **end for**
 4: **for** $i \in \langle 1, \ldots, N \rangle$ **do**
 5:     $B \leftarrow LB^Q(s_i)$
 6:     $F_B \leftarrow F_B + 1$
 7: **end for**
 8: **for** $i \in \langle 1, \ldots, CUTS \rangle$ **do**
 9:     Find cut c_i – median of set F
10:     Divide F according to cut c_i
11: **end for**
12: Assign codes to cuts
13: **for** $i \in \langle 1, \ldots, N \rangle$ **do**
14:     $LB^Q(s_i) = Code(LB^Q(s_i))$
15: **end for**
16: Pass S to LPMLLAC and generate C

Lines 1–3 clears the frequency table of every value $LB^Q(s_i)$. In the next lines 4–7, the frequency table is updated. After this process, the frequency table is ready to discretization. Lines 8–11 find $CUTS$ cuts of the frequency table. In every step, the median is calculated, and the frequency table is divided. Then in the next step, the median is calculated on two divided tables. In line 12 there is a code assigned to every cut. Finally, in every sample (lines 13–15) lowest bits are exchanged with codes obtained in line 12. After processing all samples resulting stream is passed to LPMLLAC algorithm (line 16).

3   Experimental Results

Both algorithms (LPMLLAC and LPMLAC) were implemented in C language and compiled using gcc version 5.1.0 (tdm-1) included to Code::Blocks integrated development environment version 17.12 for Windows. Compiled console application was run on PC equipped with Intel i7-8550U processor (base clock frequency 1.8 GHz, maximum turbo frequency 4.0 GHz), 8 GB DDR4 RAM and 256 GB M.2 SSD hard drive.

Tests were performed on real audio files with various genres of music, downloaded from the website Free Music Archive (http://freemusicarchive.org/). Selected files include:

- Dee_Yan-Key_-_02_-_Somni_soror.mp3 by Dee Yan-Key,
- Don_Aman_-_09_-_Douglas.mp3 by Don Aman,
- Koresma_-_04_-_Big_Sky.mp3 by Koresma,
- Night_Birds_-_17_-_Left_In_The_Middle.mp3 by Night Birds,
- Traveling_Horse_ID_1207.mp3 by Lobo Loco,
- TRG_Banks_-_08_-_A_Christmas_adventure_Part_1.mp3 by TRG Banks.

All files were converted using Audacity version 2.1.0 for Windows [10] to wave audio file format at 44.1 kHz sample rate, 16-bits per channel stereo. Table 1 shows summary information of the audio files used for tests. Files have different sizes from about 24 MB to over 190 MB and represent different music genres.

Experimental results of compression using LPMLLAC are presented in Table 2. For experiments the value $bits_{th} = 8$ was selected. Following columns inform about file ID, original file size in [B], compressed file size in [B], and the compression rate as fraction $\frac{C}{O}$, where C – compressed file size, O – original file size.

Results presented in Table 2 show that the compression rate is in the range from 54% to over 80%. Mean compression rate is equal to about 68%. All files were compressed successfully, with the ratio not related to the original size of the file. Smallest file (*TRG Banks*) has compression rate bigger that largest file (*Don Aman*). But the best compression rate has a second smallest file (*Lobo Loco*).

Table 1. Summary information about the audio files used in experiments.

ID	File name	Size in [B]
Dee Yan-Key	Dee_Yan-Key_-_02_-_Somni_soror.mp3	57.176.064
Don Aman	Don_Aman_-_09_-_Douglas.mp3	192.503.808
Koresma	Koresma_-_04_-_Big_Sky.mp3	40.237.056
Night Birds	Night_Birds_-_17_-_Left_In_The_Middle.mp3	34.647.552
Lobo Loco	Traveling_Horse_ID_1207.mp3	28.071.936
TRG Banks	TRG_Banks_-_08_-_A_Christmas_adventure_Part_1.mp3	24.809.472

Table 2. Experimental results of the LPMLLAC compression rate of audio files.

ID	Original size in [B]	Compressed size in [B]	Compression rate in [%]
Dee Yan-Key	57.176.064	39.765.169	69.5
Don Aman	192.503.808	117.284.025	60.9
Koresma	40.237.056	27.903.077	69.3
Night Birds	34.647.552	27.924.929	80.6
Lobo Loco	28.071.936	15.177.841	54.1
TRG Banks	24.809.472	18.308.022	73.8

Table 3 shows the relation between the compression rate and the compressing time. Results show that the compression rate is not related to the time needed to compress the audio stream. This can be also noticed after analyzing Fig. 4, where bars represent compression rate, and the line represents compression time.

Table 3. Experimental results of the LPMLLAC: compression rate vs. compression time of audio files.

ID	Compression rate in [%]	Compressing time in [s]
Dee Yan-Key	69.5	2.07
Don Aman	60.9	6.39
Koresma	69.3	1.47
Night Birds	80.6	1.34
Lobo Loco	54.1	0.86
TRG Banks	73.8	0.91

Results in Tables 2 and 3 show that the compressing time mostly depend on the file size.

Compression rate and compression time for other algorithms compared to algorithm LPMLLAC are presented in Table 4. To comparison the FLAC [11] and

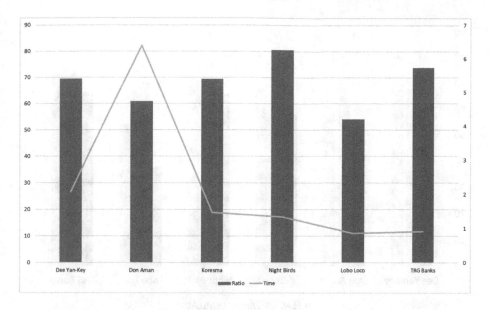

Fig. 4. Relation between compression rate and compressing time.

7zip [9] codecs were selected. First is a popular lossless audio codec, and second is the compression utility. Column "FLAC rate" shows the compression ratio, and the column "FLAC time" shows the compressing time for FLAC codec. Column "7zip rate" shows the compression ratio, and the column "7zip time" shows the compressing time for 7zip compression utility. Last two columns: "LPMLLAC rate" and "LPMLLAC time" show the ratio and the time of compression for LPMLLAC algorithm respectively.

Table 4. Compression rate and compression time for other algorithms compared to algorithm LPMLLAC.

ID	FLAC rate [%]	FLAC time [s]	7zip rate [%]	7zip time [s]	LPMLLAC rate [%]	LPMLLAC time [s]
Dee Yan-Key	54.3	5.17	72.4	9.12	69.5	2.07
Don Aman	48.8	15.82	64.3	30.39	60.9	6.39
Koresma	58.0	3.37	72.5	6.20	69.3	1.47
Night Birds	65.6	2.96	82.3	4.84	80.6	1.34
Lobo Loco	37.9	2.17	52.6	10.19	54.1	0.86
TRG Banks	66.4	2.01	75.8	3.63	73.8	0.91

Results shown in Table 4 were additionally presented in charts Fig. 5 (compression ratio) and Fig. 6 (compressing time). The best results in terms of compression ratio had FLAC codec. The most compressed file was *Lobo loco* with

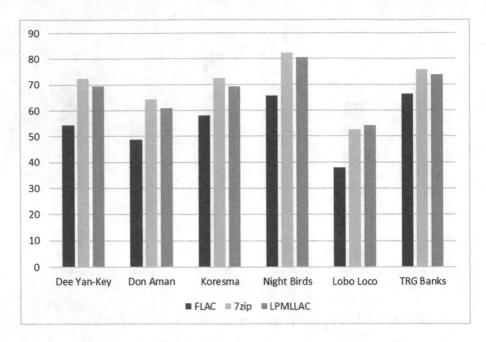

Fig. 5. Compression ratio for FLAC, 7zip and LPMLLAC.

Table 5. Experimental results of the LPMLAC compression rate of audio files.

ID	Original size [B]	Compressed size [B]	Compression rate [%]	Compressing time [s]	LPMLLAC rate [%]
Dee Yan-Key	57.176.064	29.101.037	50.90	8.96	69.5
Don Aman	192.503.808	85.025.862	44.17	11.6	60.9
Koresma	40.237.056	20.520.906	51.00	2.92	69.3
Night Birds	34.647.552	21.444.438	61.89	2.58	80.6
Lobo Loco	28.071.936	11.240.741	40.04	1.56	54.1
TRG Banks	24.809.472	13.644.459	55.00	1.94	73.8

37.9% compression ratio. All compression ratios for FLAC codec was below 67%. In terms of speed, the best results were for LPMLLAC codec. Compression time was mostly less than half of the time for FLAC codec, and at least 4 times shorter than the times for 7zip compression utility.

Experimental results of compression using LPMLAC are presented in Table 5. Following columns inform about file ID, original file size in [B], compressed file size in [B], and the compression rate as fraction $\frac{C}{O}$, where C – compressed file size, O – original file size.

Results presented in Table 2 show that the compression rate is in the range from 40% to over 60%, and all compression ratios are lower than for

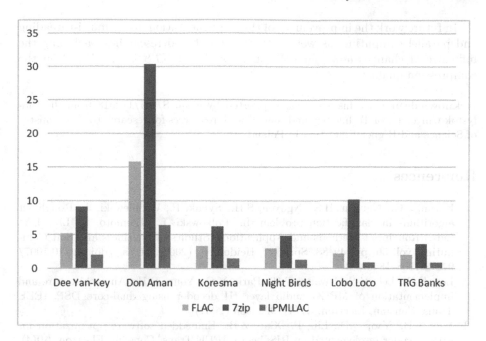

Fig. 6. Compressing time for FLAC, 7zip and LPMLLAC.

LPMLLAC codec. Mean compression rate is equal to about 50%. Smallest file (*TRG Banks*) has compression rate bigger that largest file (*Don Aman*). But the best compression rate has a second smallest file (*Lobo Loco*). The results are similar to LPMLLAC. Additionally, the resulting file is smaller by a similar factor comparing LPMLLAC and LPMLAC. This can be explained by the identical part of the algorithms.

4   Conclusions and Future Work

Presented algorithms LPMLLAC and LPMLAC are an interesting alternative for existing audio codecs to use in very low-performance microcontrollers. Especially lossless LPMLLAC proved its very good performance: the time was at least 2–3 times shorter than other codecs. Very important is a fact, that proposed algorithm was implemented as one-thread application. Other implementations use multithreading and therefore are more optimized and faster.

Lossy LPMLAC didn't give as good results in terms of the compression ratio, as is could be expected, compared to e.g. mp3. The decrease in the compression rate was about 15% of the value between LPMLAC and LPMLLAC. Additionally, the time was 2–3 times bigger, which shows that the LPMLAC is not a good alternative to other lossy codecs.

In future work the improvement of the implementation, using multi-threading and parallel computing, as well as the more detailed researches, including the influence of changes $bits_{th}$ in LPMLLAC and $Q, CUTS$ in LPMLAC on the compression quality.

Acknowledgment. This work was supported by grant S/WI/1/2018 from the Bialystok University of Technology and funded with resources for research by the Ministry of Science and Higher Education in Poland.

References

1. Bazan, J.G., Nguyen, H.S., Nguyen, S.H., Synak, P., Wróblewski, J.: Rough set algorithms in classification problem. In: Polkowski, L., Tsumoto, S., Lin, T.Y. (eds.) Rough Set Methods and Applications. Studies in Fuzziness and Soft Computing, vol. 56, pp. 49–88. Springer, Heidelberg (2000). https://doi.org/10.1007/978-3-7908-1840-6_3
2. Lee, K.H., Lee, K.S., Hwang, T.H., Park, Y.C., Youn, D.H.: An architecture and implementation of MPEG audio layer III decoder using dual-core DSP. IEEE Trans. Consum. Electron. **47**(4), 928–933 (2001)
3. Yao, Y.B., Yao, Q.D., Liu, P., Xiao, Z.B.: Embedded software optimization for MP3 decoder implemented on RISC core. IEEE Trans. Consum. Electron. **50**(4), 1244–1249 (2004)
4. Stepaniuk, J.: Rough-Granular Computing in Knowledge Discovery and Data Mining. Studies in Computational Intelligence, vol. 152. Springer, Heidelberg (2008). https://doi.org/10.1007/978-3-540-70801-8
5. Kopczynski, M., Grzes, T., Stepaniuk, J.: Maximal Discernibility Discretization of Attributes—A FPGA Approach. In: Ryżko, D., Gawrysiak, P., Kryszkiewicz, M., Rybiński, H. (eds.) Machine Intelligence and Big Data in Industry. SBD, vol. 19, pp. 171–180. Springer, Cham (2016). https://doi.org/10.1007/978-3-319-30315-4_15
6. Dacles, M.D.I.: Block truncation coding-based audio compression technique. In: Proceedings of 2nd International Conference on Digital Signal Processing (ICDSP 2018), pp. 137–141 (2018)
7. Wang, J., Zhao, X.H., Xie, X., Kuang, J.M.: A multi-frame PCA-based stereo audio coding method. Appl. Sci-Basel **8**(6), 967 (2018)
8. Mondal, U.K.: Achieving lossless compression of audio by encoding its constituted components (LCAEC). Innovation. Syst. Softw. Eng. **15**(1), 75–85 (2019)
9. 7zip homepage. https://www.7-zip.org/. Accessed 1 Apr 2019
10. Audacity homepage. https://sourceforge.net/projects/audacity/. Accessed 1 Apr 2019
11. Xiph.org web page on FLAC codec. https://xiph.org/flac/. Accessed 1 Apr 2019
12. Fraunhofer Institute for Integrated Circuits IIS: the mp3 history. https://www.mp3-history.com/. Accessed 1 Apr 2019
13. Xiph.org web page on Vorbis codec. https://xiph.org/vorbis/. Accessed 1 Apr 2019

Performance and Resilience to Failures of an Cloud-Based Application: Monolithic and Microservices-Based Architectures Compared

Michał Jagiełło[iD], Marian Rusek[✉][iD], and Waldemar Karwowski[iD]

Faculty of Applied Informatics and Mathematics, Warsaw University
of Life Sciences — SGGW, ul. Nowoursynowska 159, 02-776 Warsaw, Poland
{marian_rusek,waldemar_karwowski}@sggw.pl

Abstract. Traditional cloud applications were based on monolithic processes started inside virtual machines. The development of virtualization containers and automated orchestration systems made a new microservices-based architecture of applications possible. The advantages and disadvantages of both application architectures have been already discussed in the literature. However there still a shortage of direct performance comparisons for both application versions. In this paper we present such an experimental study of response times and transaction rates for the same application implemented in monolithic and microservices-based architectures. The ability to survive database failures is also analyzed.

Keywords: Microservice architecture · Virtualization containers

1 Introduction

Development of internet-based applications and mobile devices connecting to them creates new opportunities and raises new needs. Their users are increasingly demanding and have new requirements for minimal response time and better failure tolerance. In most cases performance problems in such distributed systems are caused by limited capacity of servers or network. They can be solved by scaling the distributed system up, that is by deploying more machines or multiplying instances of application components. The concept of a cloud as a utility computing model comes to help solve these problems. Cloud computing can be characterized by an easily usable and accessible pool of virtualized resources. Which and how resources are used can be configured dynamically, providing the basis for scalability: if more work needs to be done, a customer can simply acquire more resources.

There is no single definition for what a computer cloud is. There are four major characteristics that distinguish today's cloud infrastructures from previous generations of distributed computing systems. They are massive scale, on-demand access, data-intensive nature, and new cloud programming paradigms.

© Springer Nature Switzerland AG 2019
K. Saeed et al. (Eds.): CISIM 2019, LNCS 11703, pp. 445–456, 2019.
https://doi.org/10.1007/978-3-030-28957-7_37

The classification of the cloud services is often based on the nature of the services themselves. It is called an "as a Service" (aaS) classification. Hardware as a Service (HaaS) means that the cloud user gets access to the bare bones hardware machines and he can do whatever he wants with them. But exposing hardware as a service to other users, especially those that the owner of the cloud doesn't trust, may not be a good idea because of the security risks involved. Infrastructure as a Service (IaaS) allows the user to get access to machines and install his own operating systems inside virtual machines instances without having the security risks of the hardware as a service cloud [21].

Recently the cloud industry is moving beyond self-contained, isolated, and monolithic virtual machine images in favor of container-type virtualization [16]. Containers keep applications and their runtime components together by combining lightweight application isolation with an image-based deployment method. Containers introduce autonomy for applications by packaging apps with the libraries and other binaries on which they depend. This avoids conflicts between apps that otherwise rely on key components of the underlying host operating system. Containers do not contain a operating system kernel, which makes them faster and more agile than virtual machines. They provide an ideal way for practical implementation of microservices [13].

In the paper we compare two implementations of the same cloud-based application: monolithic and microservices-based. Each version of the application is packaged inside Docker virtualization containers and studied experimentally in the same environment. We compare their performance, scaling abilities and resilience to failures. This study allows to answer whether the microservices architecture is always a good architectural solution for modern cloud-based applications. In the literature only some case studies can be found [1,10,15], but not a direct comparison of two approaches outside of [19,20] where performance is analyzed in context of infrastructure costs. This paper is organized as follows: in Sect. 2 the main issues connected with microservices are presented. In Sect. 3 the architecture of example application in microservices and monolithic version is described. In Sect. 4 some experimental results for three server analysis tools are presented. We finish with summary and brief conclusions in Sect. 5.

2   Microservice Architecture

Computer applications and their architectures have evolved over time together with the technological development. Microservices are the next step in the development process of software and system architecture [2]. They have its roots in SOA (Service Oriented Architecture), at the beginning were called fine grained SOA and cloud-based systems had impact on their development. Two main trends in the evolution of cloud application architectures are identified [8]. The first, cloud computing and its related application architecture evolution can be seen as a steady process to optimize resource utilization in cloud computing; the second, these resource utilization improvements resulted over time in an architectural evolution of how cloud applications are being built and deployed.

The microservice architectural style is an approach to develop a single application as a suite of small services, each running in its own process and communicating with lightweight mechanisms, often an HTTP resource API [4]. [2] defines microservice as cohesive, independent processes interacting via messages, and microservice architecture as a distributed application where all its modules are microservices. In [6] empirical survey to assess the current state of practice and collect challenges in microservices architecture is presented. The lack of notations, methods, and frameworks to architect microservices were considered as important points. Moreover it was concluded that optimization in security, response time, and performance have higher priorities than resilience, reliability, fault tolerance, and memory usage. In [14] authors identified, classified and systematically compared 21 selected studies of microservices and their applications in the cloud. They concluded that microservices emerge as an architectural style, but one that extends from the design-stage architecture into deployment and operations as a continuous development style.

Still most of enterprise applications are often built in three tiers: a user interface (usually WWW page), a data storage (usually relational database management system), and a server-side application. The server-side application executes business logic, handles all user requests, stores, retrieves and updates data from the database, and sends responses to the browser. This solution has light user interface and a monolithic server-side application. Any changes to the system do not require user interface changes except the browser update but involve building and deploying a new version of the server-side application. Such application is called monolith [4], similar definition is given in [2]: a monolith is a software application whose modules cannot be executed independently. In practice even if a change is made to a small part of the application it implies the rebuilding and deploying entire monolith. Scaling requires scaling of the entire application rather than parts of it that require more resources. Comprehensive list of issues that affect monoliths is presented in [2].

Today many companies decompose their monolithic applications into collection of containerized microservices. There are different refactoring approaches to transform existing enterprise-scale applications to microservices [5]. Comparing scalability of applications written in microservices vs. monolithic architectures is discussed in [3]. It is concluded that microservices have better scalability as confirmed by implemented systems one of such example is Netflix. In [17] the issue of microservice granularity and its effect upon application latency was examined. In this paper two approaches to microservice deployment were simulated; the first with microservices in a single container, and the second with microservices partitioned across separate containers. It was observed a negligible increase in service latency for the multiple container deployment over a single container. Container technologies like Docker shall provide horizontally scalable, easily deployable systems and a high-performance alternative to virtual machine hypervisors [7]. The ping-pong system relied on a REST-like and HTTP-based protocol to exchange data was analyzed. Especially network performance impact of container, software defined virtual networks and encryption layers on the performance impact of distributed cloud based systems using HTTP-based REST-based protocols was discussed. The study shows that container impact on network performance is not negligible. Performance impact for containers is about 10% to 20%. The analyzed software defined virtual networks solution showed a performance impact of about 30% to 70%.

Horizontally scaling of a microservice and relationship between the number of replicas and the performance is presented in [9]. Experiments showed that there was no improvement of the performance when the stateful microservice is scaled out above the determined limit. Another issue is comparing monolithic with analogous microservices application in terms of performance. A case study where an enterprise application was developed and deployed in the cloud using a monolithic approach and a microservice architecture using the Play web framework is presented in [19]. Each of the two versions of the application consisted of two services. The first service implemented CPU intensive algorithms to generate payment plan, and the second service was responsible for returning an existing payment plan and its corresponding set of payments. For the first service average response time was shorter for monolith than microservice about 13.8%, for the second service average response time was shorter for microservices about 35.8%.

Research was continued and reported in [20]. This time additional microservice application operated by AWS Lambda was prepared. The results were calculated by increasing the number of requests until the application began to generate errors or the response time was not met. Such maximum performance was better for microservices than for monolith. Average response time during peak periods was best for AWS Lambda microservices, however solution with Play microservices was three times slower than monolith.

3   Example Application

To make a performance comparison between monolithic and microservices-based application, a sample application in the microservices architecture and the corresponding monolithic application were prepared. As a starting version, we chose the Docker example-voting-app[1] application. It is an application that allows to vote for a favorite house pet, the choice is between dogs and cats. Each user can vote only for one candidate. Application consists of three microservices, two data bases and one data volume. The microservices are described below:

Voting-app – service written in Python using the Flask library. It provides a Web page with two available options. Moreover, it generates voters ID placed in the cookie to prevent user to give two valid votes. The service uses the JINJA2 engine to generate the code for the HTML from the template file that is sent in response to the voter's browser. The voting ID and its selection are saved in the JSON format and stored in the Redis database.

We changed the voting-app in such a way that user can vote many times because every time new ID is generated and user is treated as a different person.

---

[1] https://github.com/docker/example-voting-app.

This modification makes easier to generate load during performance tests. Also an additional HAProxy container has been added to allow scaling the voting service. This is necessary, because in the Docker environment only one container can have an open port exposed to the external network.

Worker – this service uses the Command Query Responsibility Separation (CQRS) design pattern[2]. CQRS separates the logic of recording and the logic of reading data from each other. Worker is written in the C# language, it reads the data stored by the voting-app service in the Redis database and saves processed data in a PostgreSQL relational database in a format that is readable for the result-app service. Moreover, worker verifies if the user with the specified identification number has already given a vote. Very important advantage of worker is that if there is no connection to any database it does not stop its action, but periodically checks whether the connection can be created again. Therefore, if the connection to the PostgreSQL database is lost, the votes stored in the Redis database are not lost. After reconnection to the database the votes may be recorded.

Result-app – the last element of the example-voting-app application is a service that displays the results of voting in a website. The service is written in the JavaScript language, and is running inside the Node.js environment. When started, it connects to the PostgreSQL database in which the worker service has recorded results. The service periodically retrieves results from PostgreSQL using polling. Results are displayed in the user's browser both in text and graphic form. Thanks to pooling and the Node.js environment, the service updates the customer's website automatically. The time window is 1000 ms, thus exactly every one second it executes the query to the database to check the latest voting results. Naturally, if the connection will be lost, service displays the results that were available to it before the crash and tries to connect again on the next call.

To compare the microservices architecture with a monolithic layered architecture, we created a monolithic version of the example-voting-app with the entire data flow carried out in a single process. The resulting application combines the three services outlined above. There was no need for a Redis database, but to make application more flexible Object-Relational Mapping was added, we used Flask-SQLAlchemy library. The polling is also used to retrieve information about the votes. However, monolithic solution has one significant drawback when a PostgreSQL database crashes the user can neither vote nor download votes already cast. For monolithic application, only two containers must be running: one for the application and second for the PostgreSQL database.

4   Experimental Results

It is a common believe, that size scalability problems for centralized services can be formally analyzed using queuing theory [18]. Several simplifying assumptions can be made. Let us consider a situation in which there are no restrictions on the number of requests that can be accepted for processing. Thus a centralized

---

[2] https://martinfowler.com/bliki/CQRS.html

service is modeled as a queuing system with infinite capacity. Assuming that the arrival of requests is a Poisson process with arrival rate λ, and that the processing times of a service have an exponential distribution with rate parameter μ (M/M/1 queue) one can compute the ratio of the response time R to the service time S as a function of server utilization U [11]:

$$\frac{R}{S} = \frac{1}{1-U} \tag{1}$$

Substituting $U = \lambda/\mu$ and $S = 1/\mu$ Eq. 1 can be rewritten as:

$$\frac{1}{R} = \mu - \lambda \tag{2}$$

Thus the dependence of an inverse response time $1/R$ on request arrival rate λ should be linear. Measuring the experimental points and fitting a straight line would provide the service rate μ characterizing the performance of a cloud application.

4.1   Python Requests and Asyncio

To check this prediction we performed the following experiment. We launched a single instance of the microservices-based example-voting-app described in Sect. 3. The time of the experiment was divided in equal intervals of 5 s each. In the next time window the request arrival rate was doubled. This gives a series of 11 values of λ: 1, 2, 4, 8, 16, 32, 64, 128, 256, 512, 1024. In each interval GET and POST requests were sent to the application with some constant rate λ and its response time R was measured. It was calculated as the difference of times before the GET request (displaying the voting page) and after the POST request (sending a random vote to the server). To perform this experiment a dedicated Python app was written utilizing requests and asyncio libraries.

In Fig. 1 we have the experimental points plotted as purple crosses. They indeed form a straight line but only when plotted on log-log scale. To prove this a fit $y = \beta_2 x + \beta_1$ obtained using linear least squares method is shown as a green line. This means that Eq. 2 should be replaced by:

$$\frac{1}{R} \simeq \beta_1 \lambda^{\beta_2} \tag{3}$$

Such a power-law behavior with low exponent (of the order of $-4/3$ in Fig. 1) of inverse service time plot could be a hint for self-similar behavior of network traffic, that is, a process which is bursty over a wide range of time-scales. It is now an accepted fact that the standard Poisson queue model does not adequately model arrival and service processes in web servers since it does not take into account its inherently bursty nature of the underlying network traffic. This increases the complexity of simulation and modeling tools that can be used for such an analysis. Heavy-tailed distributions of arrival process or a heavy-tailed service-time

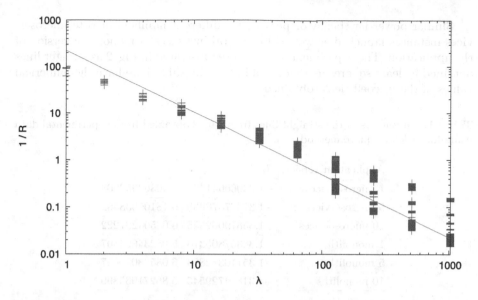

Fig. 1. Inverse response times $1/R$ versus incoming requests rate λ for different numbers of instances of the two application versions. (Color figure online)

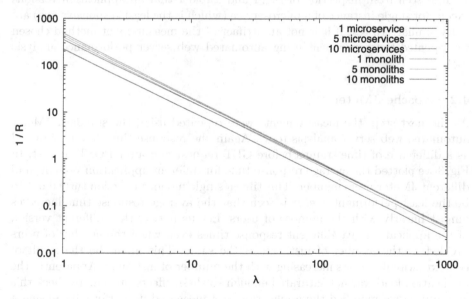

Fig. 2. Straight lines fitted to experimental results similar to these from Fig. 1.

distribution that have tails that follow a power-law with low exponent, in contrast to traditional distributions (e.g., Gaussian, Exponential, Poisson) whose tails decline exponentially (or faster) should be used. This lead to stochastic models of web servers [12].

Similar power-law behavior persists for different numbers of vote microservices instances launched as well as for several instances of monolithic version of the application. The experimental results are illustrated in Fig. 2 as straight lines obtained by least squares method. In addition, in Table 1 we have the numerical values of the β_i coefficients obtained:

Table 1. Parameters of the straight lines from Fig. 2 obtained from experimental data using linear least square method.

Application version	β_2	β_1
1 microservice	−1.33060641421	5.40368952908
5 microservices	−1.37377578935	6.18106638562
10 microservices	−1.35879062555	6.08504297222
1 monolith	−1.36357805378	5.98234694807
5 monoliths	−1.35110382873	6.08568070057
10 monoliths	−1.31844729545	5.86271065899

It is seen from inspection of Fig. 1 and Table 1 that all application versions except for single instance of a microservice (which is the least responsive one) are fairly similar. To test if it is not an artifact of the measurement method chosen we repeated the experiment using automated web server performance analysis tools.

4.2   Apache JMeter

As the next step, the measurements were repeated using the standard JMeter automated web server analysis tool[3]. Again the response time R was obtained as a difference of time stamps before GET request and after POST request. In Fig. 3 we plotted the average response time for different application versions and different JMeter users number. This time a single monolith version turned out to be the least performant one. It is seen that the average response time increases almost linearly with the number of users. Let us notice, that different version of the application give different response times even when the number of users divided by the number of instances is the same. This might be the result of context switching costs increasing with the number of instances. Apparently the application load was not saturated enough so these effects prevail. To check this assumption we modified the application and measured its performance using a yet another tool.

4.3   Siege

To further investigate cloud application performance its code has been rewritten again. We eliminated the necessity for POST request and added another GET

---

[3] https://jmeter.apache.org

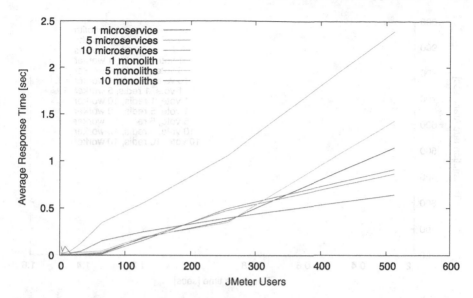

Fig. 3. Average response time for different application versions and different JMeter users number.

endpoint to submit votes. This allowed automated testing using the popular Siege tool[4]. In Fig. 4 we present response time and transaction rate obtained for 255 concurrent users, and 100 repetitions (25 500 total hits in each case). The colored symbols of different shape represent different application versions. The most responsive and with the highest throughput is the version with 10 instances of vote microservice, and 1 instance of Redis and worker (blue circle i the top left corner). On the opposite side is single instance of monolith (purple cross in the bottom right corner). The surprising result of this experiment is that the increase of the number of Redis instances does not yield neither increase of throughput nor better responsiveness of the application studied (c.f., open and filled triangles with sharp edge top corresponding to 1 vote, 10 workers, and 1 or 5 Redis in memory data stores). This might be because all the Redis instances have the same name, and the build Docker DNS resolver working in an application specific network assigns them randomly after each attempt to write or read data. This yields in another context switching and network overhead. A possibility of such an overhead was suggested in [7]. Thus the microservice version of a cloud application can be indeed as fast or faster as the monolithic one but one needs carefully chose the microservices to scale.

---

[4] https://github.com/JoeDog/siege

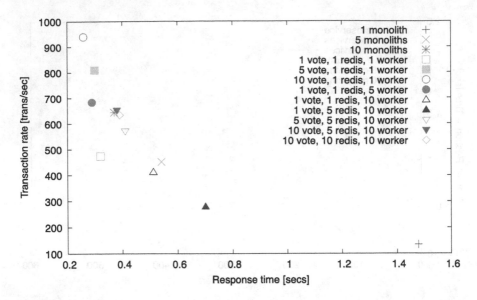

Fig. 4. Response time and transaction rate obtained using the Siege tool for different application versions. (Color figure online)

4.4 Docker Example-Voting-App

The microservices-based version of the Docker example-voting-app uses a CQRS pattern and thus should be resilient to databases failures. To test this behavior a following experiment was performed:

- the application is launched in the background using

```
docker-compose up -d
```

- votes are submitted from a web browser connected to port 5000 (e.g., 2 for a cat)
- results are checked from a web browser connected to port 5001
- database container is killed

```
docker-compose kill db
```

- additional votes are submitted (e.g., 1 for a dog)
- all the remaining containers are stopped

```
docker-compose stop
```

- and relaunched

```
docker-compose up -d
```

- on the results page there are 2 votes for a cat a 1 for a dog.

This works, because the votes are stored in the Redis in memory key value store container. Stoping it causes it to write them to the container disk image. When the application is relaunched worker container reads them and writes to the database. The votes submitted before database kill are also preserved because this container uses a separate data image. It is interesting to note, that relaunching the database only is not sufficient:

```
docker-compose up db
```

By doing so all the votes would be lost. So indeed, an microservices-based version of the application is resilient to failures, but to gracefully recover from them an exceptional knowledge of the cloud administrator is required.

5   Conclusions

In this paper performance of two versions of an simple cloud-based voting application was compared. Both the monolithic and microservices-based versions were placed inside Docker virtualization containers. The monolithic version consisted of one container whereas the microservice version used four containers and utilized a CQRS design pattern. In order to run both versions were supplemented with a SQL database container storing the vote results and a proxy container distributing the incoming load. It was shown that both versions scored similar results when sufficient numbers of its instances were provided to survive the incoming requests. In addition the microservice version was resilient to database failures. The votes submitted when the database was down were not lost.

It was shown that it is difficult to describe performance of such internet-based cloud applications using analytic models from queuing theory. Thus automated load generating tools were used instead. The somewhat surprising result of our studies is that only needs to carefully chose the microservices to scale. When increasing the number of the wrong ones the performance gains are lost due to increasing communication between microservices and context switching overhead of the launched virtualization containers. Otherwise the monolithic version starts to perform better. In future work it would be interesting to study these effects for an application launched in a cluster, e.g., Docker Swarm.

References

1. Balalaie, A., Heydarnoori, A., Jamshidi, P.: Migrating to cloud-native architectures using microservices: an experience report. In: Celesti, A., Leitner, P. (eds.) ESOCC Workshops 2015. CCIS, vol. 567, pp. 201–215. Springer, Cham (2016). https://doi.org/10.1007/978-3-319-33313-7_15
2. Dragoni, N., et al.: Microservices: yesterday, today, and tomorrow. In: Mazzara, M., Meyer, B. (eds.) Present and Ulterior Software Engineering, pp. 195–216. Springer, Cham (2017). https://doi.org/10.1007/978-3-319-67425-4_12

3. Dragoni, N., Lanese, I., Larsen, S.T., Mazzara, M., Mustafin, R., Safina, L.: Microservices: how to make your application scale. In: Petrenko, A.K., Voronkov, A. (eds.) PSI 2017. LNCS, vol. 10742, pp. 95–104. Springer, Cham (2018). https://doi.org/10.1007/978-3-319-74313-4_8

4. Fowler, M., Lewis, J.: Microservices a definition of this new architectural term (2014). http://martinfowler.com/articles/microservices.html

5. Fritzsch, J., Bogner, J., Zimmermann, A., Wagner, S.: From monolith to microservices: a classification of refactoring approaches. In: Bruel, J.-M., Mazzara, M., Meyer, B. (eds.) DEVOPS 2018. LNCS, vol. 11350, pp. 128–141. Springer, Cham (2019). https://doi.org/10.1007/978-3-030-06019-0_10

6. Ghofrani, J., Lübke, D.: Challenges of microservices architecture: a survey on the state of the practice. In: ZEUS (2018)

7. Kratzke, N.: About microservices, containers and their underestimated impact on network performance. arXiv preprint arXiv:1710.04049 (2017)

8. Kratzke, N.: A brief history of cloud application architectures. Appl. Sci. 8(8), 1368 (2018)

9. López, M.R., Spillner, J.: Towards quantifiable boundaries for elastic horizontal scaling of microservices. In: Companion Proceedings of the 10th International Conference on Utility and Cloud Computing, pp. 35–40. ACM (2017)

10. Malavalli, D., Sathappan, S.: Scalable microservice based architecture for enabling DMTF profiles. In: 11th International Conference on Network and Service Management (CNSM), pp. 428–432. IEEE (2015)

11. Menasce, D.A., Almeida, V.A.: Capacity Planning for Web Services: Metrics, Models, and Methods, vol. 2. Prentice Hall PTR, Upper Saddle River (2002)

12. Nossenson, R.: Stochastic models for web servers. Ph.D. thesis, Technion – Israel Institute of Technology (2005)

13. Pahl, C.: Containerisation and the paas cloud. IEEE Cloud Comput. 2(3), 24–31 (2015)

14. Pahl, C., Jamshidi, P.: Microservices: a systematic mapping study. In: CLOSER (2016)

15. Savchenko, D., Radchenko, G., Taipale, O.: Microservices validation: Mjolnirr platform case study. In: 38th International Convention on Information and Communication Technology, Electronics and Microelectronics (MIPRO), pp. 235–240. IEEE (2015)

16. Scheepers, M.J.: Virtualization and containerization of application infrastructure: a comparison. In: 21st Twente Student Conference on IT, pp. 1–7 (2014)

17. Shadija, D., Rezai, M., Hill, R.: Microservices: granularity vs. performance. In: UCC (2017)

18. Van Steen, M., Tanenbaum, A.S.: Distributed Systems. CreateSpace Independent Publishing Platform, Scotts Valley (2017)

19. Villamizar, M., et al.: Evaluating the monolithic and the microservice architecture pattern to deploy web applications in the cloud. In: 10th Computing Colombian Conference (10CCC), pp. 583–590 (2015)

20. Villamizar, M., et al.: Cost comparison of running web applications in the cloud using monolithic, microservice, and AWS lambda architectures. Serv. Oriented Comput. Appl. 11, 233–247 (2017)

21. Zhang, Q., Cheng, L., Boutaba, R.: Cloud computing: state-of-the-art and research challenges. J. Internet Serv. Appl. 1(1), 7–18 (2010)

Design of a State Estimation Considering Model Predictive Control Strategy for a Nonlinear Water Tanks Process

Wiktor Jakowluk(✉) ⓘ

Faculty of Computer Science, Bialystok University of Technology,
Wiejska 45a, 15-351 Bialystok, Poland
w.jakowluk@pb.edu.pl

Abstract. The Model predictive control (MPC) is a generally accepted control method which has been widely employed in the industry processes. This control strategy is based on an established model of the true system. The selection of the appropriate model is often costly. For this reason the state-space model parameters should be estimated with maximum accuracy. To ameliorate the system tracking and reduce the experimental costs, the Kalman filter (KF) was introduced. In this paper a novel technique of the plant parameter estimation for MPC purposes was verified on the multivariable nonlinear water tanks system. The linearized and discretized water tanks model has been employed in the control design. The fundamental objective of the identification experiment was to estimate the plant model parameters subject to additive white noise affecting the output of the model. The introduced scheme was verified using a numerical examples, and the results of the control performance and the state estimates were discussed.

Keywords: Optimal control · Kalman filtering · Model predictive control · Parameter identification

1 Introduction

The model predictive control (MPC) is the modern technique which has an important impact for advanced process control in many industrial applications, especially in the petrochemical processes. In fact, most petrochemical plants have employed the MPC in practice [1]. In conjunction with the speed of modern microprocessors, MPC has the application in many areas (e.g. heating control and ventilation systems) [2–4]. The main advantage of MPC method is the possibility to control multivariable nonlinear processes and its ability to handle constraints on inputs, states and output signals [5–7]. This method uses a model of the system and the collected data to predict a plant's future output signal with respect to a future input signal [8, 9]. The performance index is based on the predicted input and output signals and it is optimized subject to the future input signal sequence.

The control performance assessment has a great impact on the economic condition of the real-life processes [10]. An identification experiment is usually performed by

© Springer Nature Switzerland AG 2019
K. Saeed et al. (Eds.): CISIM 2019, LNCS 11703, pp. 457–468, 2019.
https://doi.org/10.1007/978-3-030-28957-7_38

exciting the system using an input signal and by applying the resulting data to extract expected values of the model parameters [11, 12]. It has been reported that the model construction absorbs over 75% of the cost related to industrial control loops design [13]. Consequently, some authors proposed an idea of the efficiency degradation minimization in exchange for the variance minimization of the parameters to be estimated. The robust control identification examines the uncertainty of the approximated model using the designed closed-loop system implementation [14]. The least-costly identification method for control purposes, with the aim to design an experiment guaranteeing a small uncertainty region but still providing a sufficient efficiency of control, was presented in [15, 16]. The plant-friendly system identification is assigned as the application-oriented technique. The objective of the plant-friendly identification is to find a trade-off between the minimal disruption to the nominal operation conditions, and the most exact system identification [17, 18]. One of the main trends in connection with application-oriented input design is to employ the model predictive control methodology [19, 20].

The main contribution of this paper is to introduce a novel data-driven and model based technique oriented to the construction of the robust controller to improve liquid flow prediction for the nonlinear tanks interacting system. The control scheme consists of the linearized discrete time actual model with unknown parameters, the MPC optimizer with the reference plant of the two water tanks system, and the Kalman filter as the prediction model. The implementation of the proposed state error compensation strategy has been performed in the Matlab-Simulink environment. The issues of the input design for integer and fractional-order reference systems perturbation have been considered in earlier works of the author [21–24].

2 The Liquid Double-Tank Process

The second-order nonlinear water tanks system is presented in Fig. 1. The cylindrical water tank model is specified by the relation of the volumetric flow $Q_{in}(t)$ into the first tank to the outflow of water $Q_{out}(t)$ through the valve at the second tank. One can express a balance of water flow in each tank with the following expression:

$$A\frac{dh(t)}{dt} = Q_{in}(t) - Q_{out}(t) , \tag{1}$$

where: A is the cross-sectional surface of the tank, and $h(t)$ is the height of the fluid level in the tank.

Given the cross sectional area a of the outlet hole of the tank and assuming an ideal sharp edged orifice, the outflow of water of each tank can be found using Torricelli's principle, expressed as:

$$Q_{out}(t) = a \cdot \sqrt{2gh(t)} . \tag{2}$$

The cross sectional area a of the orifice is sometimes multiplied by the constant C_d (called the discharge coefficient of the valve), which represents fluid characteristics, losses and irregularities in the system and g is the gravitational constant (9.8 m/s^2).

Substituting Eq. (2) to (1) and assuming that the output of the first tank is connected to the input to the second one, we obtain the following system of nonlinear deferential equations:

$$\begin{cases} A_1 \frac{dh_1(t)}{dt} = -a_1 \cdot \sqrt{2gh_1(t)} + Q_{in}(t) & h_1(0) = h_{10}, \\ A_2 \frac{dh_2(t)}{dt} = a_1 \cdot \sqrt{2gh_1(t)} - a_2 \cdot \sqrt{2gh_2(t)} & h_2(0) = h_{20}. \end{cases} \quad (3)$$

The index $n = 1, 2$ signifies one of the system's two tanks. The nonlinear differential equations (3) describe the mathematical model of the double tank liquid system illustrated in Fig. 1.

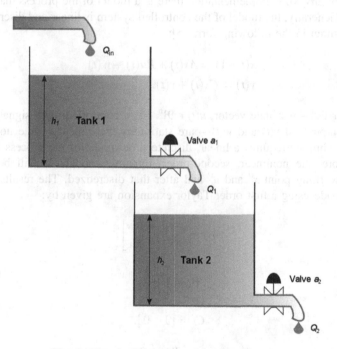

Fig. 1. The double tank water system diagram

The following substitutions were made to obtain the standard form of the state-space equations: $Q_{in}(t) = u(t)$, $x_1(t) = h_1(t)$, $x_2(t) = h_2(t)$, $y(t) = h_1(t)$. The parameters to be identified are the cross sectional areas of the orifices: a_1, a_2. From the nonlinear model, described earlier by Eq. (3), it is possible to obtain the mathematical expressions for a state equation in the form:

$$\begin{cases} \dot{x}_1 = -\frac{a_1}{A_1} \cdot \sqrt{2gx_1} + \frac{1}{A_1}u & x_1(0) = h_{10}, \\ \dot{x}_2 = \frac{a_1}{A_2} \cdot \sqrt{2gx_1} - \frac{a_2}{A_2} \cdot \sqrt{2gx_2} & x_2(0) = h_{20}. \end{cases} \quad (4)$$

where: $x_1 = x_1(t, a_1)$, $x_2 = x_2(t, a_1, a_2)$. The water levels in the tanks have the real working constraints:

$$h_{i, max} \geq x_i(t) \geq 0 \qquad i = 1, 2. \tag{5}$$

For the purposes of the model parameters estimation the linearized and discrete time state-space equations should be utilized.

3   Model Linearization and Discretization

In the case of any MPC implementation there is a model of the process that should be controlled. Generally, the model of the controlled system is linear and discrete in time. It can be written in the following form [5]:

$$\begin{aligned} x(t+1) &= Ax(t) + Bu(t) + w(t), \\ y(t) &= Cx(t) + v(t). \end{aligned} \tag{6}$$

where: $x(t) \in \mathfrak{R}^n$ – is a state vector, $u(t) \in \mathfrak{R}^n$ – is a controlled input signal, $y(t)$ – is a measured output and $v(t)$ and $w(t)$ – are stationary, zero-mean, white noise signals. The MPC technique requires a linear, discrete time model of the process in the form (6). Therefore, the nonlinear, second-order, dynamic model (4) will be linearized around its working point x^0 and u^0 and after that discretized. The results of the linearization made using a first order Taylor expansion are given by:

$$A_l = \begin{bmatrix} -\tau_1 & 0 \\ \tau_3 & -\tau_4 \end{bmatrix}, \tag{7}$$

$$B_l = \begin{bmatrix} \frac{1}{A_1} \\ 0 \end{bmatrix}, \tag{8}$$

$$C_l = [1 \quad 0], \tag{9}$$

$$\tau_n = \frac{a_i}{A_i} \sqrt{\frac{g}{2x_i^0}}. \tag{10}$$

For the discretization purposes, zero-order hold with a rate period of $T_s = 1$ [s] was used. The following matrices were used by the MPC to predict system output [25].

$$A_d = e^{A_l}, \quad B_d = \int_0^1 e^{A_l(1-t)} B_l dt, \quad C_d = C_l. \tag{11}$$

The MPC optimizer was applied to control a liquid level of the upper tank (Fig. 1). The MPC controller utilizes the linearized model of the plant around its working point $(x^0; u^0)$, according to (6), to estimate the future output of the system which is given by:

$$\hat{y}(t+k|t) = CA^k x(t) + \sum_{i=0}^{k-1} A^{k-i-1} Bu(t+i).$$ (12)

The above formula requires the complete knowledge of the state variable $x(t)$. When the measurement of the state variable is impossible, a state variable estimator could be used instead. The Kalman filter method will be then used for the purpose of the estimation of the unknown state.

4 Model Predictive Control Problem Formulation

In this section the model predictive control block diagram containing the Kalman filter (KF) for the nonlinear double tank interacting system was introduced. Model predictive control is a special kind of controller which makes use of a reference plant to predict the behavior of the controlled system, starting at the current time, over a future prediction horizon. The MPC makes use of a model of the system and the measured data from the reference plant to anticipate the system's future output, as a function of future input signals. The predicted inputs and outputs are then utilized by a performance function which is minimized with respect to the future input sequence. The Kalman filter is used to estimate states of a linear dynamic system in the state space form. The KF algorithm is composed of two steps: prediction and update. The control scheme (Fig. 2) consists of the discrete time actual plant model with unknown parameters, the MPC optimizer with the linearized discrete reference plant of the system, and the KF as a prediction model [26]. The MPC acts as a nominal controller for the reference plant and produces input u for actual plant model and Kalman filter. The reference plant is given by:

$$\begin{cases} \dot{x}_r = A_d x_r + B_d u_r \\ y_r = C_d x_r \end{cases},$$ (13)

where u_r is the reference plant input signal. The system under diagnosis with respect to Eq. (6) has a following form:

$$\begin{cases} \dot{x}_d = A_d x_d + B_d u + w \\ y_d = C_d x_d + v \end{cases}.$$ (14)

The main objective of the MPC design is to balance the faulty system by the MPC, in such a way that the actual plant has an output signal very similar to the reference plant output. The performance degradation problem can be obtained by the objective function minimization subject to the control input u, as shown below:

$$J = \int_t^{t+N_c \Delta t} \left(\|x_d - x_r\|_Q^2 + \|\hat{u}\|_R^2 \right) d\tau.$$ (15)

The state-state equation (14), containing matrices A_d, B_d and C_d, represents a discrete, linearized dynamic system. The output measurement signals, marked as y_d, x_d, represent the state of the faulty model, x_r is the state variable of the reference model and y_r denotes the reference model output. The vectors w and v signify the process noise and the measurement noise, respectively. The Kalman filter assumes that w and v are zero-mean, independent random variables with known variances. In the objective function (15) t is the current time, Δt is the control interval, and N_c is the length of the control horizon. The prediction horizon, denoted as N_c, defines the number of samples of the input and output signals that are used in the optimization procedure. Matrices Q and R are the covariances of the process noise and observation noise, respectively. The Kalman filter is utilized to estimate the state vector x_f and the output flow y_f of the faulty water tanks system, according to the following equations:

$$\begin{cases} \dot{x}_f = A_d x_f + B_d u + K_f \left(y_d - C_d x_f \right) \\ y_f = C_d x_f \end{cases}, \tag{16}$$

where K_f is the KF gain.

The structure diagram of the fault degradation MPC is illustrated in the figure below. The reference plant has been perturbed using reference input signal $u_r = x_r$, shown in Fig. 3.

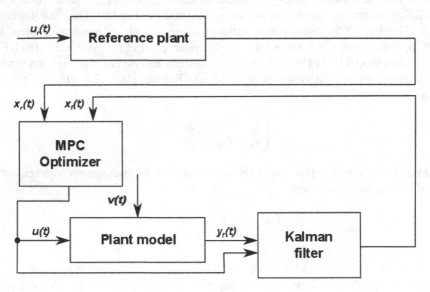

Fig. 2. The block diagram of the fault compensated MPC

The model predictive control structure includes the reference model (13), the filtered system (16) and the MPC optimizer was used to solve the problem of finding control input u that minimizes the performance criterion:

$$J = \int_{t}^{t+N_c\Delta t} \left[(x_f - x_r)^T Q (x_f - x_r) + \dot{u}^T R \dot{u} \right] d\tau, \tag{17}$$

where x_f and x_r are the states of the filtered and the reference models. In order to predict the future output signals with respect to the future input signals, the MPC requires the data from the model of the system to be obtained. The objective function utilizes the estimated inputs and outputs to penalize undesirable changes. It is minimized with respect to the forthcoming input sequence. Once an optimal input signal has been designed, then the first element of the input sequence is adopted by the system. This algorithm is subsequently recurred at the next time interval [26].

5   MPC - Experimental Results

For the numerical solution of the above MPC problem the Matlab-Simulink package was employed. Simulink is a block diagram environment for model-based design. It supports simulation, automatic code generation, and continuous testing of embedded systems. All computations were made utilizing low-cost PC (Intel®, 2.40 GHz, 4 GB RAM) running Windows 10 and Matlab 9.3 (R2017b).

For the simulation purposes the second-order nonlinear dynamic system was used, (Fig. 1). The cylindrical water tanks model was specified by the relation of the volumetric flow $Q_{in}(t)$ into the first tank to the outflow of water $Q_{out}(t)$ through the valve at the second tank. The physical constraints and the plant model parameters of the liquid tanks process are summarized in Table 1.

Table 1. The physical constraints and the model parameters.

Parameter	Value	Unit	Description
$h_{1,max}$	4.00	[m]	Maximum water level of tank 1
$h_{1,min}$	0.00	[m]	Minimum water level of tank 1
$h_{2,max}$	2.00	[m]	Maximum water level of tank 2
$h_{2,min}$	0.00	[m]	Minimum water level of tank 2
h_{10}	0.61	[m]	Initial condition of water level of tank 1
h_{20}	0.50	[m]	Initial condition of water level of tank 2
$a_1 = a_2$	0.05	[m]	Cross sectional area of water outlet holes
A_1	1.50	[m^2]	Cross sectional area of the first tank
A_2	0.75	[m^2]	Cross sectional area of the second tank
u_0	0.05	[m^3/s]	Initial water inflow to the first tank

According to Sect. 3, the matrices A_d, B_d and C_d in the models (13) and (16) were obtained considering a linearization of the nonlinear water tanks process described by the matrices (18). The selected unknown plant model parameters (19) are to be estimated by the MPC optimizer shown in Fig. 2.

$$A_d = \begin{bmatrix} -0.085 & 0 \\ 0.171 & -0.209 \end{bmatrix}, \ B_d = \begin{bmatrix} 0.667 \\ 0 \end{bmatrix}, \ C_d = [1 \quad 0]. \tag{18}$$

$$A_d = \begin{bmatrix} -\theta_1 & 0 \\ 0.171 & -0.209 \end{bmatrix}, \ B_d = \begin{bmatrix} \theta_2 \\ 0 \end{bmatrix}, \ C_d = [1 \quad 0]. \tag{19}$$

The Kalman filter is a recursive algorithm where additional measurements are used to update states x and an uncertainty specification as a covariance matrix P. The KF gain in (16) and the steady-state error covariance matrix P were obtained accordingly, e.g. by solving the related dual algebraic Riccati problem:

$$K_f = \begin{bmatrix} 0.1301 \\ 0.0151 \end{bmatrix}, \ P = \begin{bmatrix} 0.0015 & 0.0002 \\ 0.0002 & 0.0001 \end{bmatrix}. \tag{20}$$

The Kalman filter (16) was designed taking into consideration the covariance matrices of the normally distributed process with white noise and observation noise, respectively, using $Q=$ diag[0.005] and $R =$ diag[0.001]. The nominal response signals were obtained for fixed values of parameters: $a = 0.05$, $b = 0.05$ and for the chosen time interval of t = [0, 20] [s], utilizing the sequential quadratic programming (SQP) algorithm. The dynamic model is expected to be at the initial conditions: $x_1(0) = 0.61$, $x_2(0) = 0.5$. The initial value of the input signal is established as $u(0) = 0.05$. The response signals were obtained utilizing the fixed-step, 4th order Runge-Kutta method with a grid period of 0.1 [s]. To avoid the risk of the reaching a local minimum by the minimisation algorithm implemented in the Simulink package, we repeated the simulations several times using alternative initial conditions.

The plant model shown in Fig. 2 was affected by the white noise signal of variance from the interval $1e-5 \le v(t) \le 1e-1$. As it could be noticed in Fig. 3, the MPC responses are considerably different, while the value of the noise variance increases. The plot shown on the bottom right-hand side of Fig. 3 contains the comparison of the state variables $x_r(t)$ and a $x_f(t)$ according to the noise variance value of $1e-1$. It could be noticed that the filtered state variable exhibits sharp edges while the estimated plant model parameter error compared to the initial parameter values of the reference model is equal to about 7% and 5%, respectively. The nominal parameter values of the reference plant and the estimated parameters of the plant model were compared in Table 2.

Table 2. Initial and estimated parameters for different variance values.

Parameters	Variance values v(t)					
	Initial	1e−5	1e−4	1e−3	1e−2	1e−1
θ_1	0.0851	0.0865	0.0868	0.0876	0.0877	0.0913
θ_2	0.6667	0.6749	0.6718	0.6700	0.6584	0.6375

As it has been mentioned before, an increasing value of the noise variance makes the plant model parameters to be estimated less precise. The conducted experimental research confirms that the inaccuracy of the estimated parameters do not exceed seven 7% of the initial values.

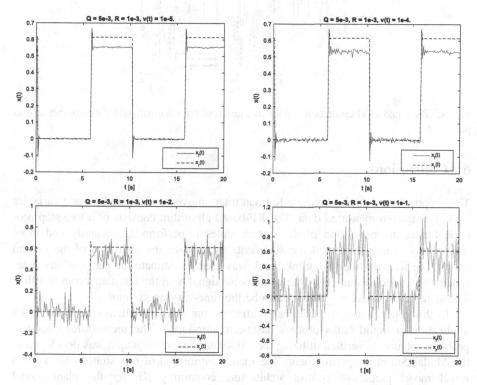

Fig. 3. The filtered state of the linear model controlled with the MPC compared to the state of the reference model

Figure 4 shows the curves of the upper tank water level measurement and the estimation error normalized by the number of data points. The Kalman filter estimates have about 20% less error than the raw measurements.

As it has been shown in Fig. 4, the green (solid line) curve represents the water level measurements. The measurement error was obtained as a difference between the measurements and the true states. The black (dashed line) curve illustrates the Kalman filter water level. The KF level error was calculated as a difference between estimated states and the real states of the system.

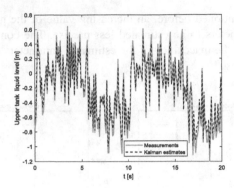

Fig. 4. The liquid level estimation and the measurement error normalized by the number of data points

6 Conclusions

The proposed method, involving a Kalman filter, allows to estimate the state variables of a system from measured data. The KF-based algorithm consists of a two-step process. Firstly the prediction of the system states is performed. Secondly and more importantly, it uses disturbed measurements to improve the estimates of the system states. The Kalman filter Simulink block was used to estimate the states of the state-space plant model disturbed by the white noise signal with the constant variance value. The state-space model was assumed to be the time-varying system.

In this paper, a novel model-based strategy for model predictive controller with application to liquid tanks process has been introduced. The methodology for this problem solution is verified utilizing the exploratory example which was developed in the Matlab-Simulink environment. The main contribution of this strategy is to use a novel model predictive control architecture containing KF for the plant model parameter estimation. The control approach is composed of the linearized discrete time actual model with unknown parameters, MPC optimizer with the reference plant, and the Kalman filter as a prediction model.

The numerical experiments confirm that the increasing value of the noise signal variance makes the estimated plant model parameters imprecise. However, it has been confirmed that the inaccuracy of the identified parameters do not exceed 7% of the magnitude of the initial values. It was also shown that the performance of the Kalman filter estimates is about 20% better than the raw measurements. It is worth noting that the implementation of this model-based strategy for system identification guarantees a slight confidence region of the estimated parameters. However, the proposed methodology require further investigations of the stability properties especially in the transient conditions.

Acknowledgement. I am deeply indebted to Prof. M. Świercz, Faculty of Electrical Engineering, Bialystok University of Technology, for his guidance during model design. The present study was supported by a grant S/WI/3/18 from the Bialystok University of Technology and funded from the resources for research by the Ministry of Science and Higher Education.

References

1. Zhu, Y.: System identification for process control: recent experience and outlook. Int. J. Model. Ident. Control **6**, 89–103 (2009)
2. Aste, N., Manfren, M., Marenzi, G.: Building automation and control systems and performance optimization: a framework for analysis. Renew. Sustain. Energy Rev. **75**, 313–330 (2017)
3. Perez, K., Baldea, M., Edgar, T.: Integrated HVAC management and optimal scheduling of smart appliances for community peak load reduction. Energy Build. **123**, 34–40 (2016)
4. Afram, A., Janabi-sharifi, F., Fung, A., Raahemifar, K.: Artificial neural network (ANN) based model predictive control (MPC) and optimization of HVAC systems: a state of the art review and case study of a residential HVAC system. Energy Build. **141**, 96–113 (2017)
5. Camacho, E.F., Bordons Alba, C.: Model Predictive Control. Advanced Textbooks in Control and Signal Processing, 2nd edn. Springer, London (2007). https://doi.org/10.1007/978-0-85729-398-5
6. Tran, T., Ling, K., Maciejowski, J.M.: Economic model predictive control - a review. In: Proceedings of the 31st International Symposium Automation Robotics in Construction and Mining (ISARC), Sydney, Australia, pp. 1–8 (2014)
7. Maciejowski, J.: Modelling and predictive control: enabling technologies for reconfiguration. Annu. Rev. Control **23**, 13–23 (1999)
8. Rawlings, J.B., Mayne, D.Q.: Model Predictive Control: Theory and Design, 5th edn. Nob Hill Pub., Madison (2012)
9. Bernardini, D., Bemporad, A.: Stabilizing model predictive control of stochastic constrained linear systems. IEEE Trans. Autom. Control **57**, 1468–1480 (2012)
10. Hugo, A.J.: Process controller performance monitoring and assessment. Control Arts Inc. (2001). http://www.controlarts.com/. Accessed 8 May 2018
11. Kalaba, R., Spingarn, K.: Control, Identification, and Input Optimization, pp. 225–299. Plenum Press, New York (1982)
12. Ljung, L.: System Identification: Theory for the User, pp. 358–406. Prentice-Hall, Englewood Cliffs (1999)
13. Hussain, M.: Review of the applications of neural networks in chemical process control-simulation and online implementation. Artif. Intell. Eng. **13**, 55–68 (1999)
14. Gevers, M., Ljung, L.: Optimal experiment designs with respect to the intended model application. Automatica **22**(5), 543–554 (1986)
15. Bombois, X., Scorletti, G., Gevers, M., Van den Hof, P.M.J., Hildebrand, R.: Least costly identification experiment for control. Automatica **42**(10), 1651–1662 (2006)
16. Bombois, X., Hjalmarsson, H., Scorletti, G.: Identification for robust deconvolution filtering. Automatica **46**(3), 577–584 (2010)
17. Narasimhan, S., Rengaswamy, R.: Plant friendly input design: convex relaxation and quality. IEEE Trans. Automat. Control **56**, 1467–1472 (2011)
18. Steenis, R., Rivera, D.: Plant-friendly signal generation for system identification using a modified simultaneous perturbation stochastic approximation (SPSA) methodology. IEEE Trans. Control Syst. Technol. **19**, 1604–1612 (2011)
19. Larsson, C.A., Rojas, C.R., Bombois, X., Hjalmarsson, H.: Experiment evaluation of model predictive control with excitation (MPC-X) on an industrial depropanizer. J. Process Control **31**, 1–16 (2015)

20. Annergren, M., Larson, C.A., Hjalmarsson, H., Bombois, X., Wahlberg, B.: Application-oriented input design in system identification: optimal input design for control. IEEE Control Syst. Mag. **37**, 31–56 (2017)
21. Jakowluk, W.: Plant friendly input design for parameter estimation in an inertial system with respect to D-efficiency constraints. Entropy **16**(11), 5822–5837 (2014)
22. Jakowluk, W.: Free final time input design problem for robust entropy-like system parameter estimation. Entropy **20**(7), 528 (2018)
23. Jakowluk, W.: Design of an optimal actuation signal for identification of a torsional spring system. Przegląd Elektrotechniczny **87**(6), 154–160 (2011)
24. Jakowluk, W.: Optimal input signal design for fractional-order system identification. Bull. Pol. Acad. Sci. Tech. Sci. **67**(1), 37–44 (2019)
25. Maciejowski, J.M.: Predictive Control: with Constraints. Prentice-Hall, Upper Saddle River (2002)
26. Simani, S., Alvisi, S., Venturini, M.: Fault tolerant model predictive control applied to a simulated hydroelectric system. In: Proceedings of the 3rd Conference on Control and Fault-Tolerant Systems, Barcelona, Spain, pp. 245–250 (2016)

Balanced Power, Speed and Area Minimization of Finite State Machines for FPGA Devices

Adam Klimowicz[✉] [iD]

Bialystok University of Technology, Bialystok, Poland
a.klimowicz@pb.edu.pl

Abstract. A balanced method for the minimization of incompletely specified finite state machines (FSMs) implemented on Field Programmable Logic Devices (FPGA) is proposed. In this method, such optimization criteria as the power consumption, speed of operation and device area are taken into account already at the stage of minimizing internal states. The method also takes into consideration the technological features of programmable logic and the state encoding method. The method is based on sequential merging of two internal states. For this purpose, the set of all pairs of states that can be merged is found, and the pair of states that has the highest rank is chosen for merging. The rank is calculated on the base of estimations of power, speed and area parameters and the user is able to choose the direction of minimization by setting weights for each criteria. In addition, the proposed method allows to minimize the number of transitions and redundant input variables of the FSM. Algorithms for the estimation of optimization criteria values are described and experimental results are also discussed.

Keywords: Finite state machines · Logic synthesis · Speed optimization · Power optimization · Area optimization · FPGA

1 Introduction

A widespread of digital and embedded systems in all spheres of human activity imposes more severe restrictions on the parameters of the designed equipment. These parameters are the cost of implementation (area), speed and power consumption. Depending on the specific conditions a single parameter or all of them can be used as optimization criteria.

The finite state machine (FSM) is a mathematical model that is widely used in the design process of various computational structures, such as the sequential circuits, control devices, microprocessor controllers, digital telecommunications systems, networks, and others. So the problem of optimization of finite state machines is actual according to parameters such as cost, speed and power consumption.

The traditional approach to the synthesis of finite state machine consists of the following steps which are performed sequentially: minimization of internal states, state assignment and synthesis of combinational part of a finite state machine. The combinational part of the finite state machine is usually presented in the form of set of Boolean functions, the synthesis of which is allocated to a separate task and, as a rule,

© Springer Nature Switzerland AG 2019
K. Saeed et al. (Eds.): CISIM 2019, LNCS 11703, pp. 469–480, 2019.
https://doi.org/10.1007/978-3-030-28957-7_39

not considered at synthesis of finite state machines. Thus, in traditional approach optimization in finite state machine involves minimizing internal states and optimizing state assignment.

However, such an approach often contradicts to the objectives of optimization of state machine logic synthesis phase, because both the minimization of internal states, and their encoding does not take into account the particular requirements of technological base and the tasks of logic synthesis, in particular, restrictions on the parameters of the designed device in terms of cost, speed and power consumption.

2 State of the Art

The first attempts to combine the two design procedures for minimization and encoding of the internal states of finite state machines, were made in [1, 2]. In work [1], the problem of minimization and state assignment was considered for asynchronous FSMs. The method proposed in [2] is applicable only to FSMs with the number of states not exceeding 10.

The power consumption of an FSM can be directly reduced by special encoding of internal states [3]. In [4], the implementation cost is minimized simultaneously with the minimization of the power consumption at the stage of state assignment. In the majority of these works, genetic algorithms are used. In [5], the minimization of power consumption and delay is considered for asynchronous FSMs. The concept of a low power semi-synchronous FSM operating on a high frequency is proposed that can be implemented and tested as an ordinary synchronous FSM. In [6], the conventional approach to the synthesis of FSMs is considered, under which the number of internal states is first minimized, then the internal states are encoded; next, the program ESPRESSO is used to build disjunctive normal forms (DNFs) of the functions to be realized and, finally, the cost, power consumption, and speed of operation are estimated. A set of algorithms is proposed to select the best state assignment so as to minimize the parameters mentioned above.

The problem of the simultaneous minimization of area and signal delay on the critical path is considered in works [7–9]. In [7], a structural model of the FSM called MAR model is proposed, which consists of an FSM and a combinational circuit with flip-flops in the feedback loops. In [8], codes with two unities (two-hot) and three unities (three-hot) are used. In [9], a two-level structural model is proposed to minimize the power consumption, area and delay. The first level of this model consists of sequential units, while the second level consists of combinational units of limited size. The paper [10] proposes to use the evolutionary methodology to yield optimal evolvable hardware that implements the state machine control component. The evolved hardware requires a minimal hardware area and introduces a minimal propagation delay of the machine output signals.

In following works the chip area (implementation cost) is minimized simultaneously with the minimization of the power consumption at the stage of state assignment. In the majority of works [11] genetic algorithms are used. In [12], an internal state splitting procedure is used; in this case, no minimization of the number of internal states of the FSM is required. The parametric methods of the minimization of finite state machines are proposed in [13, 14]. In these methods, such optimization criteria as the power consumption [13], critical delay path [14] and also possibility of merging other states are taken into account already at the early stage of minimization of internal FSM states.

The analysis of available studies showed that the number of internal states and other parameters such as power, area and speed of FSM are not simultaneously minimized in one procedure. The methods that claim to simultaneously take into account several optimization criteria actually are often related to the conventional approach where a few different algorithms are proposed for each stage. In the present paper, we propose a heuristic method for the minimization of FSMs that makes it possible to optimize an used area (a number of logic elements of FPGA) already at the stage of minimization of the number of internal states. The proposed approach suits well for the implementation of FSMs on FPGA devices.

3 Idea of the Approach

The proposed approach is based on the method for the minimization of the number of internal states of FSMs proposed in [15] for Mealy machines and in [16] for Moore machines. A FSM behavior can be described by the *transition list*. This is a table which consists of four columns: a_m, a_s, $X(a_m, a_s)$, and $Y(a_m, a_s)$. Each row in the table corresponds to one FSM transition. The column a_m contains the present, the column a_s contains the next state, the column $X(a_m, a_s)$ contains the set of values of the input variables that initiates this transition (*a transition condition* or *an input vector*), and the column $Y(a_m, a_s)$ contains the set of values of the output variables that is generated by FSM at this transition (*an output vector*).

The idea of the method [15] is to consecutively merge two states. For this purpose, the set G of all pairs of internal states of the FSM which satisfies the merging conditions must be found at each step. Then, for every pair in set G, a trial merging is done. Next, the pair (a_i, a_j) that leaves the maximum possibilities for merging other pairs in set G is chosen for final merging.

In distinction from [15], in this paper we chose for merging at each step the pair (a_i, a_j) that best satisfies the optimization criteria in terms of power consumption, speed and area occupation, and leaves the maximum possibilities for merging other pairs in G. This procedure is repeated while at least one pair of states can be merged.

Let (a_s, a_t) be a pair of states in G. The parameter Q_{st} is the estimate of FSM quality in terms of power, speed and area, M_{st} is the estimate of the possibility to merge other states. Then, with regard to the above considerations, the main FSM minimization algorithm can be described as on Fig. 1.

Algorithm of minimization of the number of transitions is based on some observations. Suppose, that one transition from a state a_1 under condition x_1 leads to a state a_2 and the second transition from a_1 under condition $\bar{x}_1$ leads to another state a_3 and on each of these transitions non-orthogonal output vectors are formed. After possible merging a_2 and a_3, a new state a_{23} is formed. Now two transitions lead from a_1 to a_{23}, one under condition x_1 and the second under condition $\bar{x}_1$. It means that the transition from a_1 to a_{23} is unconditional and two transitions can be replaced by one unconditional transition.

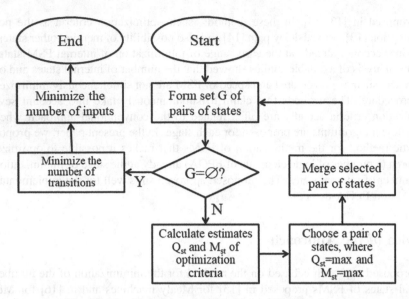

Fig. 1. Algorithm 1 (general algorithm of FSM synthesis)

At minimization of the number of FSM inputs can appear in a situation when some input variables have no impact on the transition conditions. Suppose, that one transition from a state a_1 under condition x_1 leads to a state a_2 and another transition from a_1 under condition $\bar{x}_1$ leads to a state a_3 and the variable x_1 does not meet anywhere else in transition conditions of the FSM. Suppose that after merging states a_2 and a_3, the transition from the state a_1 to the state a_{23} becomes unconditional, i.e. it does not depend on values of input variables. The latter means that the variable x_1 has no impact on any FSM transition and therefore it is redundant.

4   Estimation of Balanced Optimization Criteria

To estimate the optimization criteria, all pairs of states in G are considered one after another. For each pair of states (a_s, a_t) in G, a trial merging is performed. After merging the internal states are encoded using one of three state assignment methods (binary, one-hot and sequential [17]) and the system of Boolean functions corresponding to the combinational part of the FSM is built. Next, for the pair (a_s, a_t), power consumption P_{st}, maximum critical delay path (speed) S_{st}, cost of implementation (area) C_{st}, and the possibility of minimizing other states M_{st} are estimated. After selecting an optimal pair of states for merging, the final merging can be done.

In order to jointly use all three criteria to assess the quality of the pairing of states, one of the classic solutions for discrete multicriteria optimization was used – a weighted sum [18]. The weighted sum method is probably the most widespread approach due to its simplicity. A scalar cost function is defined as an aggregation of costs using weights as defined below.

Let $C = (C_1 \ldots, C_d)$ be a d-dimensional function and let $\lambda = (\lambda_1, \ldots, \lambda_d)$ be a vector such that:

$$\forall j \in [1 \ldots d], \lambda_j > 0 \tag{1}$$

$$\sum_{j=1}^{d} \lambda_j = 1 \tag{2}$$

The λ-aggregation of C is the function:

$$C^{\lambda} = \sum_{j=1}^{d} \lambda_j C_j \tag{3}$$

Intuitively, the components of λ represent the relative importance (weight) one associates with each objective. In this case, we have three criteria: power P_{st}, cost C_{st} and speed S_{st}, for which the weights can be specified by the user, accordingly w_P (power), w_C (cost) and w_S (speed). Regarding to above consideration the merging quality (aggregation) function Q_{st} for each pair of states (a_s, a_t) can be specified as follows:

$$Q_{st} = w_P \hat{P}_{st} + w_C \hat{C}_{st} + w_S \hat{S}_{st} \tag{4}$$

where $\hat{P}_{st}$, $\hat{C}_{st}$ and $\hat{S}_{st}$ are normalized criteria parameters P_{st}, C_{st} and S_{st}, for all pairs of states in set G.

The optimization criteria for each pair of states (a_s, a_t) in G are estimated using the algorithm presented on Fig. 2.

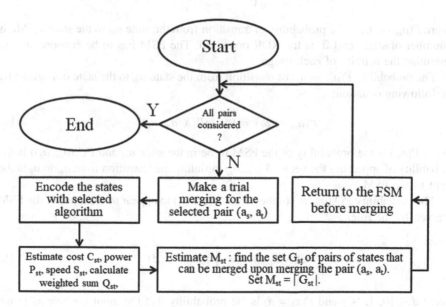

Fig. 2. Algorithm 2 (estimation of optimization criteria).

The estimate M_{st} is determined by the number of pairs of the FSM that can be merged after merging the pair (a_s, a_t). To provide the best possibilities for merging other states, M_{st} should be maximized. Using the method described in [15], the set G_{st} of pairs of states that can be merged upon merging the pair (a_s, a_t) must me find. After that, the parameter M_{st} can be calculated as the cardinality of the set G_{st} ($M_{st} = |G_{st}|$).

5   Estimation of Optimization Criteria

5.1   Estimation of Power Dissipation

According to [19], the power consumption of the FSM is determined by the rule:

$$P = \sum_{r=1}^{R} P_r = \frac{1}{2} V_{DD}^2 fC \sum_{r=1}^{R} N_r \tag{5}$$

where P_r is the power consumed by the trigger r, V_{DD} is the supply voltage, f is the frequency at which the FSM operates, C is the capacity of trigger output, and N_r is the activity of the trigger r.

Let k_i be a binary code of a state a_i. Denote by k_r^i the value of the bit r in the code k_i of the state a_i. Then, the activity N_r of switching the memory element r of the FSM satisfies the following equation

$$N_r = \sum_{m=1}^{M} \sum_{s=1}^{M} P(a_m \rightarrow a_s)(k_m^r \oplus k_s^r) \tag{6}$$

where $P(a_m \rightarrow a_s)$ is the probability of transition from the state a_m to the state a_s, Ma is a number of states and $\oplus$ is the XOR operation. The FSM has to be encoded first to determine the activity of each trigger.

The probability $P(a_m \rightarrow a_s)$ of transition from the state a_m to the state a_s is given by the following equation:

$$P(a_m \rightarrow a_s) = P(a_m)P(X(a_m, a_s)) \tag{7}$$

where $P(a_m)$ is the probability of the FSM to be in the state a_m and $P(X(a_m, a_s))$ is the probability of appearing the vector $X(a_m, a_s)$ initiating the transition from a_m to a_s at the input of the FSM.

The probability $P(X(a_m, a_s))$ of the vector $X(a_m, a_s)$ to appear at the input of the FSM is given by the rule:

$$P(X(a_m, a_s)) = \prod_{b=1}^{L} P(x_b = d) \tag{8}$$

where $d \in \{0, 1, '-'\}$ and $P(x_b = d)$ is the probability that the input variable x_b in the input vector $X(a_m, a_s)$ takes the value d.

5.2   Estimation of Implementation Cost

When the cost of implementation of the FPGA based FSM is estimated, the implementation of the FSM memory is ignored and the cost is determined only by the cost of the combinational part of the FSM. The point is that the logic elements of the FPGA admit configurations with the combinational or register output. For that reason, in order to introduce a memory registers in the FSM circuit, it suffices to configure the logic element output on which the activation function of the corresponding memory element is realized as a register output. No additional resources of FPGA are needed; therefore, the cost of the FSM memory implementation does not increase.

Note that, before calculating the implementation cost, the system of Boolean functions corresponding to the combinational part of the FSM can be minimized using the method that will be used for synthesis.

In the general case, the architecture of modern FPGAs can be represented as a set of logic elements based on functional LUT generators. A feature of LUT functional generators is that they can realize any Boolean function but with a small number of arguments (typically, 4–6 and more often 4). In the case when the number of arguments of functions to be realized exceeds the number of LUT inputs n, the Boolean function must be decomposed with respect to the number of arguments [20]. When the cost of implementation of a function w_i ($w_i \in W$) is calculated, only the restriction on the number of LUT inputs is taken in account. Among the great number of decomposition methods for Boolean functions with respect to the number of arguments, linear decomposition methods are most popular.

With regard to the above considerations, the implementation cost $C(w_i)$ for each function $w_i \in W$ is calculated as

$$C(w_i) = 1 +](|Z(w_i)| - n)/(n - 1)[, \tag{9}$$

where $Z(w_i)$ is the set of arguments of the function w_i, $|Z(w_i)|$ is the cardinality of the set $Z(w_i)$ and operator $]A[$ is the minimum integer greater than or equal to A.

The implementation cost of the whole FSM is a sum of implementation costs of all functions $w_i \in W$:

$$C_{st} = \sum_{w_i \in W} C(w_i) \tag{10}$$

5.3   Estimation of Speed

The speed of operation of an FSM is determined by the length of the critical path of its combinational part, which is equal to the FPGA logic elements involved in the critical path. First, we determine the maximum number L_{max} of arguments of the functions realized by the combinational part of the FSM.

$$L_{\max} = \max_{w_i \in W} |L(w_i)|, \tag{11}$$

where $L(w_i)$ is a set of arguments of the function w_i.

The next step is to calculate the length of the critical path in the combinational part of the FSM. If the FSM is implemented on the basis of FPGA, the length of the critical path is determined only based on the maximum number of arguments:

$$S_{st} = 1 +](L_{max} - n)/(n - 1)[. \tag{12}$$

6   Experimental Results

The method of minimization of finite state machines was implemented in a program called ZUBR. To preliminary examine the efficiency of the offered method we used MCNC FSM benchmarks [21]. The experiments were performed using IntelFPGA Quartus Prime version 17.1 EDA tool.

Three parameters were taken from report files for further analysis: Total Logic Elements (C), Core Dynamic Power (P) in mW and Maximum Clock Frequency - Fmax (F) in MHz. For an implementation author has chosen the EP4CE115F29I8L device – a popular low cost FPGA from the Cyclone IV E family. For estimation of power, cost, speed and further implementation three state assignment methods have been chosen: binary encoding, one-hot encoding and sequential encoding [17]. The two sets of balance weights were used:

- $w_P = 0.8$, $w_C = 0.1$, $w_S = 0.1$ - for power direction optimization (PDO),
- $w_P = 0.1$, $w_C = 0.1$, $w_S = 0.8$ - for speed direction optimization (SDO).

All benchmarks in all three cases (without minimization, minimized with PDO and SDO styles) were implemented using identical design flow optimization parameters.

The experimental results for binary encoding are presented in Table 1, where M_{0B}, C_{0B} F_{0B} and P_{0B} are, respectively, the number of internal states, the number of used logic elements, maximum working frequency and dissipated dynamic power of the initial FSM (without minimization); M_{1B}, C_{1B}, F_{1B} and P_{1B} are, respectively, the number of internal states, number of logic elements, maximum frequency and dissipated power after minimization using power direction optimized (PDO) method. Finally, parameters M_{2B}, C_{2B}, F_{2B} and P_{2B} are, respectively, the number of internal states, number of logic elements, maximum frequency and power after synthesis using speed direction optimized (SDO) method. *Mean* row contains the average values.

The analysis of Table 1 shows that application of the proposed method allows to reduce the number of internal states of the initial FSM in 6 cases. The average power reduction for PDO method makes 1.13 times and for SDO method – also 1.13 times. The average speed increase for PDO method makes 1.33 times and for SDO method – 1.44 times. For binary encoding the speed optimized method was better in terms of speed than power optimized method 1.08 times. Results in terms of power dissipation were identical for both methods. Additionally, an application of both variants SDO and PDO causes significant implementation cost reduction (on average 1.21 times).

Table 1. The experimental results for binary encoding

Name	M_{OB}	C_{OB}	F_{OB}	P_{OB}	M_{1B}	C_{1B}	F_{1B}	P_{1B}	M_{2B}	C_{2B}	F_{2B}	P_{2B}
BBSSE	16	70	239,69	0,22	13	57	293,34	0,21	13	57	293,34	0,21
BEECOUNT	7	19	497,76	0,20	5	13	500,75	0,20	5	13	500,75	0,20
EX1	20	297	108,86	0,43	18	198	126,81	0,28	18	198	126,81	0,28
EX2	19	58	254,26	0,22	19	58	265,75	0,22	19	58	265,75	0,22
EX7	10	27	344,12	0,21	10	8	504,03	0,20	10	8	504,03	0,20
LION9	9	15	429,55	0,20	4	3	894,45	0,20	4	3	900,90	0,20
S1488	48	491	98,38	0,87	48	468	100,84	0,79	48	468	100,84	0,79
S208	18	145	124,05	0,24	18	122	134,55	0,23	18	122	134,55	0,23
S820	25	247	100,00	0,34	25	216	121,94	0,30	25	216	121,94	0,30
SAND	32	328	100,83	0,47	32	266	129,08	0,33	32	266	129,08	0,33
SSE	16	70	239,69	0,22	13	57	293,34	0,21	13	57	293,34	0,21
TRAIN11	11	19	416,67	0,20	6	9	564,65	0,20	4	3	895,26	0,20
Mean	**19,25**	**148,83**	**246,16**	**0,32**	**17,58**	**122,92**	**327,46**	**0,28**	**17,42**	**122,42**	**355,55**	**0,28**

The experimental results for one-hot encoding are presented in Table 2, where M_{OO}, C_{OO}, F_{OO} and P_{OO} are, respectively, the number of internal states, the number of used logic elements, maximum working frequency and dynamic power of the initial FSM (without minimization); M_{1O}, C_{1O}, F_{1O} and P_{1O} are, respectively, the number of states, number of logic elements, maximum frequency and dissipated power after minimization using PDO method. Finally, parameters M_{2O}, C_{2O}, F_{2O} and P_{2O} are, respectively, the number of internal states, number of logic elements, maximum frequency and power after synthesis using SDO method. *Mean* row contains the average values.

Table 2. The experimental results for one-hot encoding

Name	M_{OO}	C_{OO}	F_{OO}	P_{OO}	M_{1O}	C_{1O}	F_{1O}	P_{1O}	M_{2O}	C_{2O}	F_{2O}	P_{2O}
BBSSE	16	37	333.33	0.22	13	40	356.38	0.22	13	40	356.38	0.22
BEECOUNT	7	29	400.32	0.21	5	22	486.62	0.20	5	22	486.62	0.20
EX1	20	216	166.17	0.30	18	158	181.49	0.27	18	158	181.49	0.27
EX2	19	32	504.03	0.21	19	31	508.39	0.21	19	31	508.39	0.21
EX7	10	11	525.76	0.20	10	11	525.76	0.20	10	11	525.76	0.20
LION9	9	20	486.85	0.21	5	11	504.80	0.20	4	8	512.30	0.20
S1488	48	364	169.89	0.47	48	335	175.44	0.46	48	335	175.44	0.46
S208	18	150	178.16	0.27	18	115	185.70	0.25	18	115	185.70	0.25
S820	25	227	151.79	0.35	25	209	160.08	0.43	25	209	160.08	0.43
SAND	32	221	164.10	0.34	32	189	192.46	0.31	32	189	192.46	0.31
SSE	16	37	333.33	0.22	13	40	356.38	0.22	13	40	356.38	0.22
TRAIN11	11	19	515.46	0.21	4	7	577.03	0.20	4	7	577.03	0.20
Mean	**19.25**	**113.58**	**327.43**	**0.27**	**17.50**	**97.33**	**350.88**	**0.26**	**17.42**	**97.08**	**351.50**	**0.26**

The analysis of Table 2 shows that application of the proposed method allows to reduce the number of internal states of the initial FSM in 6 cases. The average power reduction for PDO and SDO methods makes 1.01 times The average speed increase for

PDO method makes 1.07 times and for SDO method – also 1.07 times. For one-hot encoding the results in terms of power dissipation and speed were almost identical for both methods. Additionally, an application of both variants SDO and PDO causes significant implementation cost reduction (on average 1.17 times).

The experimental results for power optimized sequential encoding are presented in Table 3, where M_{0S}, C_{0S}, F_{0S} and P_{0S} are, respectively, the number of internal states, the number of used logic elements, maximum working frequency and dissipated dynamic power of the initial FSM (without minimization); M_{1S}, C_{1S}, F_{1S} and P_{1S} are, respectively, the number of internal states, number of logic elements, maximum frequency and dissipated power after minimization using PDO method. Finally, parameters M_{2S}, C_{2S}, F_{2S} and P_{2S} are, respectively, the number of internal states, number of logic elements, maximum frequency and power after synthesis using SDO method. *Mean* row contains the average values.

Table 3. The experimental results for sequential encoding

Name	M_{0S}	C_{0S}	F_{0S}	P_{0S}	M_{1S}	C_{1S}	F_{1S}	P_{1S}	M_{2S}	C_{2S}	F_{2S}	P_{2S}
BBSSE	16	57	289.27	0.22	13	53	308.83	0.22	13	53	308.83	0.22
BEECOUNT	7	20	480.31	0.20	6	14	465.98	0.20	5	14	507.36	0.27
EX1	20	282	116.77	0.43	18	205	145.16	0.27	18	205	145.16	0.27
EX2	19	74	224.32	0.22	19	76	235.24	0.22	19	76	235.24	0.22
EX7	10	20	371.89	0.20	10	10	426.80	0.20	10	10	426.80	0.20
LION9	9	15	421.41	0.20	5	9	582.75	0.20	4	3	893.66	0.21
S1488	48	474	104.30	1.00	48	459	101.73	0.81	48	459	101.73	0.81
S208	18	181	121.43	0.29	18	138	130.74	0.24	18	138	130.74	0.24
S820	25	282	107.63	0.39	25	242	115.51	0.33	25	242	115.51	0.33
SAND	32	321	106.59	0.41	32	270	129.22	0.36	32	270	129.22	0.36
SSE	16	57	289.27	0.22	13	53	308.83	0.22	13	53	308.83	0.22
TRAIN11	11	17	423.73	0.20	10	18	411.18	0.20	4	3	894.45	0.23
Mean	**19.25**	**150.00**	**254.74**	**0.33**	**18.08**	**128.92**	**280.16**	**0.29**	**17.42**	**127.17**	**349.79**	**0.30**

The analysis of Table 3 shows that application of the proposed method allows to reduce the number of internal states of the initial FSM in 6 cases. The average power reduction for PDO method makes 1.15 times and for SDO method – 1.11 times. The average speed increase for PDO method makes 1.1 times and for SDO method – 1.37 times. For sequential encoding the speed optimized method was better in terms of speed than power optimized method 1.25 times. The PDO variant was better in terms of power dissipation than SDO variant 1.03 times. Additionally, an application of both variants SDO and PDO causes significant implementation cost reduction (on average 1.16 times).

The comparison of average results for all state assignment methods is presented in Table 4. The analysis shows that the average results obtained using presented approach are better than results obtained using initial FSM in all styles of encoding used. The one-hot encoding style was the least area and power consumable and for all minimization styles used, but in terms of speed the best result were obtained using binary encoding and SDO variant of minimization method.

In lot of cases the cost or speed obtained from proposed method was lower than obtained from initial FSM, although the number of the states was identical. It is related to the fact that the proposed method allows to minimize not only the number of FSM states, but also the number of FSM transitions and input variables what has an impact on the cost of synthesized circuits.

Table 4. The comparison of average results for all state assignment methods

Encoding	No minimization			PDO variant			SDO variant		
	Cost	Speed	Power	Cost	Speed	Power	Cost	Speed	Power
Binary	148,83	246,16	0,32	122,92	327,46	0,28	122,42	355,55	0,28
One-hot	113,58	327,43	0,27	97,33	350,88	0,26	97,08	351,50	0,26
Sequential	150,00	254,74	0,33	128,92	280,16	0,29	127,17	349,79	0,30

7 Conclusion

In this paper a balanced method for FSM minimization was presented. Using the proposed method there are always obtained machines with less cost of implementation, less power dissipation and higher speed as the initial machines. The proposed method allows, at the first stage, to take into account the parameters of the target programmable system in order to optimize the parameters of the machine. The direction of minimization depends on user defined weights in terms of power, speed and cost of implementation.

Presented method is the part of future work on the complex minimization method, where not only criteria weights will be used. It is planned to use automatic selection of weights in such a way as to obtain a machine that is optimal in terms of the three criteria considered above. In the offered method of FSM minimization only two states merging is considered. The given algorithm can be modified to merge a group of states containing more than two states.

Acknowledgements. The research was done in the framework of the grant S/WI/3/2018 and financed from the funds for science by MNiSW.

References

1. Hallbauer, G.: Procedures of state reduction and assignment in one step in synthesis of asynchronous sequential circuits. In: Proceedings of the International IFAC Symposium on Discrete Systems, Riga, Pergamons, pp. 272–282 (1974)
2. Lee, E.B., Perkowski, M.: Concurrent minimization and state assignment of finite state machines. In: Proceedings of the IEEE International Conference on Systems, Man and Cybernetics, Minneapolis. IEEE Computer Society (1984)
3. Benini, L., De Micheli, G.: State assignment for low power dissipation. IEEE J. Solid State Circuits **30**(3), 259–268 (1995)

4. Aiman, M., Sadiq, S.M., Nawaz, K.F.: Finite state machine state assignment for area and power minimization. In: Proceedings of the IEEE International Symposium on Circuits and Systems (ISCAS), pp. 5303–5306. IEEE Computer Society (2006)
5. Lindholm, C.: High frequency and low power semi-synchronous PFM state machine. In: Proceedings of the IEEE International Symposium on Digital Object Identifier, pp. 1868–1871. IEEE Computer Society (2011)
6. Shiue, W.-T.: Novel state minimization and state assignment in finite state machine design for low-power portable devices. Integration, VLSI J. **38**, 549–570 (2005)
7. Rama Mohan, C., Chakrabarti, P.: A new approach to synthesis of PLA-based FSM's. In: 1994 Proceedings of the 7th International Conference on VLSI Design, Calcutta, India, pp. 373–378. IEEE Computer Society (1994)
8. Gupta, B.N.V.M., Narayanan, H., Desai, M.P.: A state assignment scheme targeting performance and area. In: 1999 Proceedings of the Twelfth International Conference on VLSI Design, Goa, India, pp. 378–383. IEEE Computer Society (1999)
9. Liu, Z., Arslan, T., Erdogan, A.T.: An embedded low power reconfigurable fabric for finite state machine operations. In: 2006 Proceedings of the International Symposium on Circuits and Systems (ISCAS), Island of Kos, Greece, pp. 4374–4377. IEEE Computer Society (2006)
10. Nedjah, N., Mourelle, L.: Evolutionary synthesis of synchronous finite state machines. In: Proceedings of the International Conference on Computer Engineering and Systems, Cairo, Egypt, pp. 19–24, 5–7 November 2006
11. Chaudhury, S., KrishnaTejaSistla, K.T., Chattopadhyay, S.: Genetic algorithm based FSM synthesis with area-power trade-offs. Integration, VLSI J. **42**, 376–384 (2009)
12. Yuan, L., Qu, G., Villa, T., Sangiovanni-Vincentelli, A.: An FSM reengineering approach to sequential circuit synthesis by state splitting. IEEE Trans. CAD **27**, 1159–1164 (2008)
13. Klimowicz, A., Solov'ev, V., Grzes, T.: Minimization method of finite state machines for low power design. In: Proceedings of Euromicro Conference on Digital System Design, Funchal, 2015, pp. 259–262 (2015)
14. Klimowicz, A.: Performance targeted minimization of incompletely specified finite state machines for implementation in FPGA devices. In: 2017 Proceedings of Euromicro Conference on Digital System Design, Vienna, pp. 145–150 (2017)
15. Klimovich, A., Solov'ev, V.V.: Minimization of mealy finite-state machines by internal states gluing. J. Comput. Syst. Sci. Int. **51**(2), 244–255 (2012)
16. Klimovich, A., Solov'ev, V.V.: A method for minimizing moore finite-state machines by merging two states. J. Comput. Syst. Sci. Int. **50**(6), 907–920 (2011)
17. Grzes, T.N., Solov'ev, V.V.: Sequential algorithm for low-power encoding internal states of finite state machines. J. Comput. Syst. Sci. Int. **53**(1), 92–99 (2014)
18. Zadeh, L.A.: Optimality and non-scalar-valued performance criteria. IEEE Trans. Automat. Contr. AC **8**, 59–60 (1963)
19. Tsui, C.-Y., Monteiro, J., Devadas, S., Despain, A.M., Lin, B.: Power estimation methods for sequential logic circuits. IEEE Trans. VLSI Syst. **3**, 404–416 (1995)
20. Zakrevskij, A.D.: Logic Synthesis of Cascade Circuits. Nauka, Moscow (1981). (in Russian)
21. Yang, S.: Logic synthesis and optimization benchmarks user guide, Version 3.0. Technical report. Microelectronics center of North Carolina, North Carolina (1991)

An Addressing Scheme for Massive Sensor Networks

Rakesh Kumar Mishra[1]([✉]) , Nabendu Chaki[2] ,
and Sankhayan Choudhury[2]

[1] Feroze Gandhi Institute of Engineering and Technology, Rae Bareli, India
rakesh.mishra.rbl@gmail.com
[2] Department of Computer Science and Engineering, University of Calcutta,
Kolkata, India
nchaki@gmail.com, sankhayan@gmail.com

Abstract. Generally, sensors do not come with on-board address except
for specialized protocols like RFID, 6LowPAN and some typical location aware sensing applications. Identity establishment with id-less sensor devices is often a centralized activity. Manual assignment of the
addresses will be a costly alternative, also would result in long setup
time for a large network. Effectiveness of provisioning additional hardware, like GPS, will be subject to weather conditions, nature of deployment, etc. The performance of conventional addressing schemes relies
on prior knowledge of network topology. This assumption fails for typical applications, especially in the era of Internet of Things (IoT), that
demands massive deployment of sensor nodes with a nearly unstructured
topology. IPv6 could be an alternative, having ability to support large
address spaces. However, inherent assumption of IPv6 is the presence of
identity and reliability at link layer hence, its adaptation is doubtful for
sensor networks with massive deployment and unknown topology. Moreover, applications having inherent security concern, require to identify
the malicious node rather than zone from where the node belongs. This
paper presents dynamic address allocation scheme for applications like
Smart-Cities having massive sensor node deployment with an indefinite
topology. Algorithm works over a flat network and can even build a clusters among the nodes in the process. Proposed algorithm is simulated
over Omnet++ for large sensor network having upto 5000 nodes. The
simulated algorithm has given approx 99.7% resolved address irrespective of number of nodes in the network. Proposed distributed address
allocation approach reduces the task load of base stations with a small
number of packet exchanges hence conserves energy dissipation within
the network.

Keywords: Wireless sensor network · Addressing scheme ·
Energy efficiency · Flat topology · Clustering

© Springer Nature Switzerland AG 2019
K. Saeed et al. (Eds.): CISIM 2019, LNCS 11703, pp. 481–492, 2019.
https://doi.org/10.1007/978-3-030-28957-7_40

1   Introduction

A wireless sensor network have typical features like frequent node failure resulting in inconsistent topology, broadcasting nature of communication, limited power and lack of global network wide identity [1,2]. In contrary, Self-identification and quick deployment could be useful for the smooth functioning of the network in a typical scenario. Its indeed a fact that many applications involving deployment of large sensors, work well with techniques like data-centric routing. In such cases, it may not be important to identify each sensor node; rather the data from a region of the deployment area drive the operations.

However, there exist typical application(s) where unique identification of each node is a desirable and even mandatory requirement. Let us take an example, in this era of Internet of Things (IoT) realization, situations demand massive deployment of nodes for a sensing based application [3]. The need to scale an application and volume of nodes deployed for sensing often do not guarantee for structured topology hence ultimately could become simple flat topology with huge number of sensor nodes. In most of the application(s), from a functional perspective, it is sufficient to know the direction or area from where the data is coming, rather than the exact identification of the sensing node from where the data is sensed. However, say, a hoax message is introduced in the network by an intruder. This message, leads to wrong interpretation and false positive threat perception. Thus, to safeguard from such events, the identity of compromised node that sources hoax messages needs to be tracked. Hence, the prerequisite for taking any action is the identification of each node independently rather than just identifying the region of data generation. Tracking wild life in a reserve forest may be another application with similar concern. The network is not structured, deployment becomes huge and each animal needs to be tracked for analyzing their respective behavioral/migration pattern.

An address helps to identify a sensor node regardless of the context in which the name is used i.e., MAC address or network address, [4]. Moreover, the reliability of communication emphasizes over the exposure of identity that demands a network-wide unique addressing scheme. Random assignment of addresses across the network possesses the problem of implosion. Implosion, is the inability of designated nodes to detect the duplicates. Its a peculiar problem of a sensor network having thousands of nodes. As a result of implosion, overlapping happens because two data streams are generated by two or more sensing devices and those streams cannot be segregated on the basis of origin [5]. The other reasons behind the requirement for the addressing of each sensor node, as refer in [6] include System Development, Bug fixes, Reconfiguration and Dynamic Application Deployment etc.

The massive deployment of sensors, with unrestricted scalability and change in topology, across a geographical area requires a very large address space to uniquely identify each of sensing nodes. This specific requirement needs self-identification of sensor devices and it still remains an open challenge, [4,7]. In this context, it may be considered that the IPv6 protocol provides a vast address space and dynamic identity allocation. However, the adaptability of IPv6 for sensor networks is doubtful because IPv6 presumes reliable link layer addressing and highly reliable medium. These assumptions cannot prevail for the above said applications. Thus a localized dynamic addressing scheme is necessary for the applications demanding huge deployment with irregular topology.

The desirable feature of an addressing scheme discussed in [8] as follows:

1. **Efficiency:** The node address naming scheme would be efficient if it requires less power. It can be achieved through reducing the size of header. The lesser transmit power will be required if header bits are less. Similarly, in a drive to obtain address if number of message exchanges become independent of the topology and neighborhood the required power can be further minimized.
2. **Accuracy:** The addressing scheme should guarantee absence of address collisions at allocation time and also maintains the collision free state of the network.
3. **Distributed:** The nomenclature algorithm should not be centralized as it adds additional load to arbitrator and increases set up time. In case of decentralized algorithm, load can be shared by other participatory nodes but count of such nodes must remain within predefined limits. This will reduce noise level during address allocation and resolution stage.
4. **Scalability:** The addressing scheme should scale well with increase in network size. Any periodic broadcast is not desirable for a large system.

Rest of the paper is organized as: in Sect. 2, state of the art review is done with necessary comparative study. It concludes with the scope of the work that presents a precise objective statement towards proposing the new addressing scheme. Section 3 describes our proposed solution, Simulation of solution and discusses the result obtained there from and Sect. 4 concludes highlighting the merits of the algorithm in comparison to the comparable existing addressing schemes.

2 State of the Art Review on Addressing Schemes for WSN

Conventional address allocation scheme is not applicable in sensor network because the nodes are energy constrained and underlying layer two address missing, except for specific cases. In Smart-City like deployment scenario topology based addressing scheme cannot scale up [7]. In this section the overall review regarding the present state of art is classified into five categories decided on the basis of how the addresses are structured and provisioned.

2.1 Multi-label Addressing

Under this approach address is segmented into two or more parts. Each part of the address is associated with specific meaning as per deployment scenario. The addressing mechanism demands a definite topology perceived beforehand say, a *tree topology*. This is a routing enabled form of addressing where by merely processing the address a node takes the decision for dropping or forwarding a packet. This is a scalable and accurate approach as addition of node at any level will affect the only local parent node.

The algorithm in [9] divides IPv6 address is into 3 segments representing a hierarchy within the sensor network. A similar, hierarchical addressing algorithm is given in [10]. Algorithms [11] and [12] define addressing with respect to the role of node in the network. Dynamic address allocation mechanism in [12] (DAAM) and [11] causes the address exhaustion problem due to the skip range. The presence of network controller and flooding are two overheads in this scheme. In [10], address are provided by blending the clustering and role based approach.

[13] proposed address allocation scheme that uses a short address within the network and a global IPv6 for inter-network messaging. Scheme is simple but it contradicts the fact that sensor does not have unique ids [7]. All the above mentioned techniques are typically centralized and implemented as post network setup activity.

2.2 Location Aware Addressing

Sensors in most of the application areas are essentially known by either their role or location of the subject under monitoring using a sensing platform that could be GPS or any other device. It is efficient as header overhead is consistent and addresses are undisputed. But the approach is power consuming and costly due to additional unit like GPS. [14], uses location information, equal-distance/equal size partitioning and scan-line scheme to ensure that each node will be assigned a unique IP address as well as spatial relation between nodes is maintained. These are location aware centralized addressing scheme and mainly dependent upon distribution of the sensor over the area.

2.3 Randomized Address Allocation

One of the best approaches to start with addressing is to let nodes to acquire address on their own using a unique property of interest. The probability of having unique id is very high if the nodes do not have same value for the property. IPv6 is the best example of random address assignment by the node to itself and is distributed also. IPv6 is a well-known stateless address auto-configure scheme [7]. Here each node selects an address randomly and floods for the verification by the other nodes in a network. Though the scheme is simple and easy to implement, but flooding induces high packet overhead. Moreover, IPv6 assumes the presence of unique layer-2 ids for node which is a contradiction. In [7] class based IPv6 approach is suggested for IoT in cloud infrastructure. This [15] is a probabilistic spatially reusable and locally unique identifier, chosen out of binary digits from the packet randomly, to each initiated stream. However, assuring the uniqueness of bit stream is a tedious task and is a serious bottleneck of the scheme.

2.4 State-full Approach

State is represented by a set of attributes pertaining to either network or node itself. In State-full approach, the identity of a node is given through certain properties including deployment strategy or role assigned to the nodes. This is a distributed approach where all the nodes proceed for address assignment independently and concurrently. Accuracy depends totally upon which properties of the network/node is used for the definition of address and that needs to be known to all other nodes of the network.

[4] uses the link characteristics, [16] scheme uses battery to define the state, and [17] uses battery level to derive address from the property. The papers [11,12], attempt to overcome the local address exhaustion while having network controller and flooding as overheads. [18], suggested a distributed address allocation scheme using function that produces an integer sequence. [19] proposed unique addressing scheme based on the factorization theorem of positive numbers.

2.5 Address Space Partitioning

This is most commonly used and conventional approach also. In this approach local or global controller is allocated with a pool of addresses. The address pool is successively partitioned in tree like fashion and allocated to joining child nodes. The main problem here is address leakage and exhaustion. In first case address remain available but cannot be used while in latter case there is no address left for node to be assigned for its child/new entrants. [20] and [21], assumes primary node has the pool of IP available for allocation which is equally divided among the new entrant in hierarchy. The management of pool and effect on pool status in the case of quick failures is a concern with the approach.

A comparative study on the above classes of addressing scheme in terms of the desirable features is illustrated in Table 1.

It can be observed from the Table 1, that Location Aware Addressing requires additional hardware. Address Space Partitioning Scheme, which is IPv6 based, have the deficiency in multiple features. Multi-label is more accurate and scalable but the performance in terms of efficiency depends on the topology awareness. However, it is not distributed, and efficient only if label size and count remain within certain limits. Randomized and State-full approaches are distributed and energy efficient as prior topology assessment is not a mandatory requirement. None of the approach in their pure form has the capability to generate address space for randomly spilled large number of sensors. Solution to the problem of address assignment for massive deployments may lie with a hybrid approach that amalgamates the best practice of the individual approaches.

3   Proposed Solution

In this paper a *randomized, state-full* and *multi-label* addressing scheme is proposed that starts with random address, appends the role to node and finally puts

Table 1. Comparing addressing classes' as per [8]

	Multi Label	Location aware	Randomized	State-full approach	Addressing space partitioning
Efficiency	Size of address is defined by span of tree	Depends upon GPS coordinates	Defined by number of bits used in address	Depends on the network topology	128 bit address as IP-v6 is used
Accuracy	Yes	Yes	Difficult to assure[a]	Depends on reliability of attributes used	Yes
Distributed	No	No	Yes	Yes	No
Scalability	Limited	If sensor are GPS enabled	Difficult to assure[a]	Depends on reliability of attributes used	Limited due to partitioning of address space
Topology dependency	Yes	No	No	No	Implementation specific
Addl H/w	No	Yes	No	No	No

[a]Consistency in establishing the desired property is doubtful with larger number of nodes.

suitable labels to make it globally unique. The proposed solution is supposed to be effective for the target application as stated in Sect. 1 An attempt has been made to achieve the primary objective of node identity while maintaining the other desirable features like scalability, energy efficiency etc.

The assumptions for the proposed algorithm are:

- Nodes are distributed randomly and evenly across the space.
- Nodes have consistent transmission range and static neighborhood during address allocation.
- Nodes are identical with respect to computation and memory.
- Restrict the length of address to 36 bits.
- Node maintains a local clock.

Network comprises of two classes of node: Initiators and common nodes (non-initiators). Initiators are the arbitrator nodes and are entrusted with resolving addressing anomalies at local level. Proposed algorithm works in multiple stages to acquire and resolve the address. Algorithm is stated through following steps:

1. Each node assigns itself an address using pseudo number generator with local clock as seed.
2. A set of nodes establishes themselves as initiator and rest become non-initiators.

3. Initiator and non-initiator exchange their interim addresses for address allocation and collision resolution.
4. Finally, multi-label address is formed in form of $A_1 \ldots A_{n-1}A_n$ where each component is either obtained locally (A_n) or from initiator (A_1, A_{n-1}). In the proposed solution $n = 3$.

3.1 Simulation of Algorithm with Omnet++ Using MiXim Framework

Proposed algorithm is simulated using Omnet++ for establishing the proof-of-concept for the algorithm in massive sensor deployment scenario. The network comprises of two classes of node; Initiators and common nodes (non-initiators). Initiators are the arbitrator nodes entrusted with resolving addressing anomalies at local level.

- addNode - 32 bit Address composed from {subnet, atbit, addr}
  - addr - 8 bit field for initial local address.
  - arbit - 8 bit field used for resolving the address collision at initiator level.
  - subnet - 16 bit field for arbitrator.

The simulation environment that has been chosen for implementation is given in Table 2. The SensorAppLayer module in the MiXim Framework is modified to implement the algorithm. The MAC layer is implemented through BMAC module (Berkeley Mac) for sensor nodes. No changes are made to MAC layer module except for out-of-turn node awakening.

Table 2. Simulation setup parameter for OMNET

[General]	
cmdenv-express-mode	True
network	ksenmote.KSenMote
experiment-label	${configname}
record-eventlog	False
Repeat	50
sim-time-limit	100 s
tkenv-image-path	../../images;
**.playgroundSizeX	6200 m
**.playgroundSizeY	6200 m
**.playgroundSizeZ	100 m
**.numNodes	5000
**.minDist	65 m
**.connectionManager-.sendDirect	False

3.2   Experimental Findings

Experiment is executed for 100 to 5000 nodes without using any constraint. Nodes are randomly distributed over the play ground and simulation is repeated for 50 times over each configuration. The results are averaged over the runs.

Address Collision. Address collision percentage is the percentage of nodes failed to obtain the unique address during the address assignment. The address collision percentage of the algorithm is well contained with the limit of 0.28% to 0.35% (Fig. 1). This is a very narrow window of 3 to 40 nodes for a network of 100 to 5000 nodes respectively. It is expected that these small number of nodes, suffering collision, can be mitigated by the base station when it starts the topology assessment. This establishes accuracy of the algorithm to allocate the unique address. The address size in proposed algorithm is 36 bit long. Hence energy requirement will be much less as number of lesser bits are to be transmitted. Moreover, in IPv4/IPv6, the address is assigned in two layers and are 32/128 bit long. Hence effective address size in proposed algorithm is much smaller than what is used conventionally. Scalability is exhibited as the algorithm performs well over any topology and span of network.

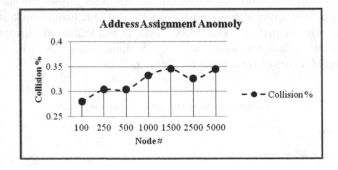

Fig. 1. Address assignment with 32 bit address space

Initiator Counts. Number of initiators is also remained well below 25% of the total number of sensors as depicted in Fig. 2. A limited number of nodes act as initiator and control the address allocation. If all nodes participate as initiator, then the network-wide energy dissipation will be considerably high. The addressing scheme obtains the address from the three different components namely, address of local initiator, arbitration address from the initiator and locally generated address. Algorithm allocate addresses with a small number of initiators hence there is less energy dissipation in the process. The initiator count, far below the node count, indirectly indicates towards formation of clustering. Thus by virtue of its design it may exhibit some sort of clustering that may not be even throughout. Finally, the formation of possible clusters exhibits the distributed nature of algorithm.

Message Exchanged. The Fig. 3 shows that the message exchanged by each node is approximately 3 irrespective of the size of the network. The overall messaging overhead for the proposed algorithm is:

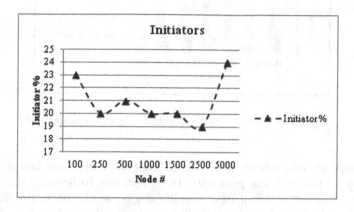

Fig. 2. Number of initiators in OMNET simulation

- The 2 broadcast messages from $N/4$ initiators $= 2N/4$ network wide messages.
- The address production messages from $3N/4$ non-initiators $= 3N/4$ network wide messages.
- The arbitration message from $N/4 = N/4$ network wide messages.

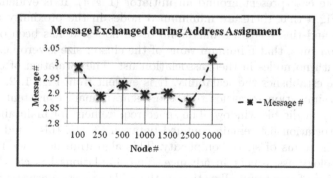

Fig. 3. Average number of message exchanged

Total messaging overhead imposed by the proposed algorithm is $2N$ irrespective of the underlying topology and degree of node. In actual simulation environment, the message exchange count reaches to $3N$ across the network. The count escalates due to provisions for re-association even when a node has skipped the

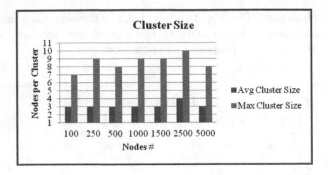

Fig. 4. Cluster formation within algorithm design

initial broadcasts and retries (from the initiator) to make their broadcast to be listened by all the nodes in proximity. In comparison to flooding that requires messaging overhead of $2Nrd$ (d = Average degree of the node, r = Number of retries required to resolve address collision), hence the performance is better. The performance is even better than the Prophet scheme as reported in [18] where the messaging overhead is dN. The exchange of a small number of messages ensures the energy efficiency as with increase in size of network message exchange remains constrained within a limit $< 3N$. This is also resemblance of distributed nature of algorithm as assignment is accomplished through message exchanges.

Inherent Clustering. The simulation is rerun for the possibility of existence of cluster is also discovered. This property also defines the number of nodes in an average case present around an initiator (Fig. 4). It is evident from the results in Fig. 4 that there are minimum 3 nodes in the proximity of any initiator node and this reaches a maximum of 10 nodes. It has been observed in all simulation runs, that minimum value of the cluster size is zero i.e., there are initiators with no nodes in their association list. The formation of cluster and its existence establishes the scalability. It is evident from Figs. 1, 2, 3 and 4 in all possible simulation scenarios that the results remain consistent and varies within a very negligible window. The space requirement for maintaining neighborhood association list remain confined between (3–11). this could be treated as efficient in terms of space complexity. This algorithm does not require any kind of topology assessment in advance. The simulations has clearly revealed that for 99.7% of successful allocation of the address, entire process is executed with mere 3 message exchanges. Besides, there is fair level of clustering exhibited by the initiators all together. This is good for scalability of algorithm. Thus the proposed algorithm appears to satisfy the property of being Accurate, Scalable, Distributed and Energy Efficient.

Compressing the address by few bits saves a considerable amount of energy in transmission/forwarding of data. The proposed scheme has three logical components namely, subnet_addr, atbit, and node_addr. The subnet_addr field is the longest of the all fields (16 bit) and can be dropped for the communication with 1-hop neighborhood of an initiator. This inherent capability of the algorithm of omission of the longest segment of the address for local communication, makes it even more energy efficient.

4   Conclusion

The overall challenge of the work is to offer an address allocation methodology for applications with massive deployment of sensors and require unique identification of nodes. The existing works are not readily usable for applications with unknown topologies hence implosion can degrade the situation more. The proposed solution performs well for the application requiring massive deployment of sensors and same has been substantiated by the simulation results. Our result shows 99.7% fully resolved address allocation for the nodes with only 3 messages exchanged per node.

Another, very important characteristic of the proposed solution is that it is a decentralized algorithm and its independent of the underneath topology or routing protocol. Unlike IPv6 protocol, the address usability and availability are not any concern in the proposed solution. There is no need for network wide authentication or approval from any centralized entity in the network. Furthermore, topology knowledge is mandatory for the most of the addressing scheme as stated in [11,16,17] etc. This is not the case with the proposed algorithm. Proposed algorithm satisfies the desired characteristics viz. efficiency, accuracy, distributed, scalability and thus could be an effective solution for our target applications as mentioned in Sect. 1 requiring massive sensor node deployment.

References

1. Al-Karaki, J.N., Kamal, A.E.: Routing techniques in wireless sensor networks: a survey. IEEE Wirel. Commun. **11**, 6–28 (2004). https://doi.org/10.1109/MWC.2004.1368893
2. Akyildiz, I.F., Su, W., Sankarasubramaniam, Y., Cayirci, E.: Wireless sensor networks: a survey. Comput. Netw. **38**, 394–422 (2002). https://doi.org/10.1016/S1389-1286(01)00302-4
3. Lin, J., Yuy, W., Zhangz, N., Yang, X., Zhangx, H., Zhao, W.: A survey on Internet of Things: architecture, enabling technologies, security and privacy, and applications. IEEE Internet Things J. **4**, 1125–1142 (2017). https://doi.org/10.1109/JIOT.2017.2683200
4. Schurgers, C., Kulkarni, G., Srivastava, M.B.: Distributed on-demand address assignment in wireless sensor networks. IEEE Trans. Parallel Distrib. Syst. **13**, 1056–1065 (2002). https://doi.org/10.1109/TPDS.2002.1041881
5. Huang, P., Xiao, L., Soltani, S., Mutka, M.W., Xi, N.: The evolution of MAC protocols in wireless sensor networks: a survey. IEEE Commun. Surv. Tut. **15**, 101–120 (2013). https://doi.org/10.1109/SURV.2012.040412.00105
6. Savolainen, T., Soininen, J., Silerajan, B.: IPv6 addressing strategies for IoT. IEEE Sens. J. **13**, 3511–3519 (2013). https://doi.org/10.1109/JSEN.2013.2259691

7. Ziegler, S., Crettaz, C., Thomas, I.: IPv6 as a global addressing scheme and integrator for the Internet of Things and the cloud. In: 28th International Conference on Advanced Information Networking and Applications Workshops, pp. 797–802. IEEE Press (2014). https://doi.org/10.1109/WAINA.2014.157

8. Ali, M., Uzmi, Z.A.: An energy-efficient node address naming scheme for wireless sensor networks. In: International Networking and Communication Conference (INCC 2004), pp. 1–6 (2004). https://doi.org/10.1109/INCC.2004.1366571

9. Cheng, C., Chuang, C., Chang, R.: Three-dimensional location-based IPv6 addressing for wireless sensor networks in smart grid. In: 26th International Conference on Advanced Information Networking and Applications, pp. 824–831. IEEE Press (2012). https://doi.org/10.1109/AINA.2012.42

10. Pan, M., Fang, H., Liu, Y., Tseng, Y.: ZigBee-based long-thin wireless sensor networks: address assignment and routing schemes. Int. J. Ad Hoc Ubiquitous Comput. **12**, 147–156 (2013). https://doi.org/10.1109/VETECS.2008.48

11. Kim, H., Han, J., Bang, J., Lee, Y.: Distributed scalable network association in wireless sensor networks. In: International Conference on Green Computing and Communications (GreenCom-2012), pp. 179–186. IEEE Press (2012). https://doi.org/10.1109/GreenCom.2012.36

12. ZigBee Specification, Document 053474. http://www.zigbee.org/download/standards-zigbee-specification/

13. Ma, L., Li, D., Zeng, Y., Liu, X., Wang, X.: Address allocation in IPv6 sensor networks for medical monitoring applications. In: International Conference on Internet of Things (iThings-2011) and 4th International Conference on Cyber, Physical and Social Computing(iThings/CPSCom-2011), pp. 768–771. IEEE Press (2011). https://doi.org/10.1109/iThings/CPSCom.2011.47

14. Ray-I Chang, R., Chuang, C.: A new spatial IP assignment method for IP-based wireless sensor networks. Pers. Ubiquit. Comput. **16**, 913–928 (2011). https://doi.org/10.1007/s00779-011-0446-5

15. Elson, J., Estrin, D.: Random, ephemeral transaction identifiers in dynamic sensor networks. In: 21st International Conference on Distributed Computing Systems, pp. 459–468 (2001). https://doi.org/10.1109/ICDSC.2001.918976

16. Saad, L.B., Tourancheau, B.: Address allocation scheme to improve lifetime of IPv6 cluster-based WSNs. In: Proceeding of 5th IEEE International Conference on New Technologies, Mobility and Security (NTMS 2012), pp. 131–135 (2012). https://doi.org/10.1109/NTMS.2012.6208699

17. Kronewitter, F.D.: Dynamic Huffman addressing in wireless sensor networks based on the energy map. In: Military Communications Conference (MILCOM 2008), pp. 1–6 (2008). https://doi.org/10.1109/MILCOM.2008.4753639

18. Zhou, H., Ni, L.M., Mutka, M.W.: Prophet address allocation for large scale MANETs. Ad Hoc Netw. **1**, 423–434 (2003). https://doi.org/10.1109/INFCOM.2003.1208966

19. Yuan-Ying Hsu, Y., Tseng, C.: Prime DHCP: a prime numbering address allocation mechanism for MANETs. IEEE Commun. Lett. **9**, 712–714 (2005). https://doi.org/10.1109/LCOMM.2005.1496591

20. Liu, Y., Zhong, P., Li, J.: Dynamic address allocation protocols for mobile ad hoc networks based on genetic algorithm. In: 5th International Conference on Wireless Communications, Networking and Mobile Computing (WiCom 2009), pp. 1–4 (2009). https://doi.org/10.1109/WICOM.2009.5301704

21. Thoppian, M.R., Prakash, R.: A distributed protocol for dynamic address assignment in mobile ad hoc networks. IEEE Trans. Mob. Comput. **9**, 4–19 (2006). https://doi.org/10.1109/TMC.2006.2

Coding Techniques in Verilog for Finite State Machine Designs in FPGA

Valery Salauyou$^{(\boxtimes)}$ and Łukasz Zabrocki$^{(\boxtimes)}$

Faculty of Computer Science,
Bialystok University of Technology, Bialystok, Poland
valsol@mail.ru, lukasz.zabrocki@gmail.com

Abstract. Coding techniques in Verilog HDL of finite state machines (FSMs) for synthesis in field programmable gate arrays (FPGAs) are researched, and the choice problem the best FSM coding styles in terms of an implementation cost (area) and a performance (speed) are considered. The problem is solved empirically by executing of experimental researches on the FSM benchmarks. Seven coding styles in Verilog are offered for coding of combinational circuits for FSMs from those two styles are selected. On the basis of these two coding styles of combinational circuits six coding styles of FSMs are offered. The efficiency of the coding styles was researched for the synthesis of FSM benchmarks in two classes of programmable devices: CPLD (Complex Programmable Logic Device) and FPGA. The experimental results showed that the choice of coding styles allows to reduce the implementation cost of FSMs by a factor of 3.06 and to increase the speed of FSMs by a factor of 1.6. In conclusion, the prospective directions for coding styles of FSMs are specified.

Keywords: Finite state machine · Field programmable gate array ·
Coding styles · Verilog · CPLD · FPGA · Implementation cost · Speed · CAD

1   Introduction

Hardware Description Languages (HDLs) have a pivotal role in computer aided design (CAD). In CAD, today two HDLs are widely used: Verilog and VHDL. Verilog has been created by developers of CAD tools as an alternative of VHDL and it quickly became popular among digital logic engineers. As of now Verilog has several standards, which are supported by most vendors of CAD. Today, Verilog is supported by CAD tools of such firms as Intel, Xilinx, Synopsys, Cadence, Mentor Graphics, etc.

A finite state machine (FSM) is one of the most important components in the design of a sequential circuit. The efficient Verilog coding styles are necessary to infer synthesizable FSM from a project code. However, the Verilog standards do not give the answer to a question: how to code the FSM in Verilog.

To date, there are few studies that have investigated the coding styles of FSM in Verilog for synthesis in programmable devices. In [1], the encoding styles of the FSMs in Verilog and VHDL which are provided in design tools from Synopsys are considered. The general principles of representation of FSMs in the HDL languages are stated; two structural models are offered: with two and with one combinational circuit;

© Springer Nature Switzerland AG 2019
K. Saeed et al. (Eds.): CISIM 2019, LNCS 11703, pp. 493–505, 2019.
https://doi.org/10.1007/978-3-030-28957-7_41

different ways of state encoding are described: binary, one-hot, and almost one-hot. It also is considered using *case* and *if* statements for the description of the transition functions in different ways of state encoding, the error recovery and illegal states, asynchronous inputs, and unknown inputs.

In [2], the standardized FSM coding style in Verilog that is used in Cisco design tools is considered. In this style, the description of FSM transitions is carried out by *case* statement, the states are declared by local parameters, the FSM transitions are described by means of two variables: *current* and *next*. Using the compiler directives cisco_fsm is presented. The application of the offered standardized style of the FSM allows to analyze accessibility of each state, to find terminal states (from which there are no exits), to carry out a dynamic FSM verification, and to build a state diagram.

The FSM coding styles of [1] are detailed and extended in [3]. In [3], the two FSM coding styles are considered: with one and two processes; for each used style its advantages and shortcomings are noted; the possible ways of state encoding are described; the use of Synopsys FSM Tool for generation binary, Gray, and one-hot coding is discussed. The coding style for synthesis of register outputs of the Mealy FSM is offered.

The FSM coding styles of [3] have been developed in [4]. In [4], it is offered to use register outputs of FSM to eliminate glitch upon transitions between states. Two methods are for this purpose offered. The first method repeats the method [3] for the installation of registers on outputs of the Mealy FSM. In the second method, the output values of the Moore FSM are used for state encoding.

In [5], the five FSM coding styles are offered: style 1 with three processes for Mealy and Moore machines; style 2 and 3 with two processes for Mealy and Moore machines; style 4 with one process for Moore machines, and style 5 with two processes for Moore machines. The question what of FSM coding styles is better is set, but the answer to this question is not provided.

In [6], the FSM coding styles in Verilog and the different ways of state encoding that implemented in design tool ISE from Xilinx are investigated. Experimental researches were conducted for FPGA Spartan-6. Three FSM coding styles are considered: with one, two, and three processes; and also the next ways of state encoding are considered. The experimental researches have been conducted for one simple FSM example, which has one input, one exit, four states and five state transitions. Following parameters were analyzed: the number of used flip-flops, the number of used FPGA logic elements, and the maximum frequency of FSM. In [6], the following conclusions are drawn: for speed optimization prefer *one-hot* and *speed1* option, and for area optimization chose *gray* or *Johnson* or *sequential* encoding scheme.

Overall, these studies indicate that most studies in the field of FSM coding have only focused on coding styles that have been implemented in CAD tools. Such approaches, however, have failed to address all coding styles which are possible in Verilog.

In this paper, we study the coding styles of FSMs in Verilog that can differ from the traditional coding styles. A problem is to choose a best coding style for an optimization of the area and the speed of FSMs. The problem is solved empirically by fulfilment of a great number of experimental researches. The received results give recommendations that allow to reduce considerably the FSM area and to increase the FSM speed without the application of any special synthesis methods.

2 FSMs with Three and Two Processes

Two types of FSMs are most known: Mealy machines and Moore machines. Previous studies showed that there are three main coding styles of FSMs in Verilog: with three processes, with two processes, and with one process, where the process is the *always* block in Verilog.

Coding of the FSM by one process is possible only for Moore machine, and as the Mealy machine is the most general model of the FSMs, in this paper we will study only two coding styles: with three processes and with two processes.

In the FSM coding style with three processes, the first process describes a combinational circuit CL_φ, which implements the state transitions, the second process describes a combinational circuit CL_ψ, which implements the FSM outputs, and the third describes the FSM memory. In the coding style with two processes, the first and the second processes are combined in one process.

Before proceeding to examine coding styles of FSMs, we will study coding styles of combinational circuits for FSMs.

3 Coding Styles of Combinational Circuits for FSMs in Verilog

In general, Verilog does not superimpose any restrictions on the coding styles of FSMs, therefore we can use any Verilog statements and any constructions of these statements. Commonly, to check that the FSM is in a certain state the *case* statement is used, and to check transition conditions from some state both the *if* statement and the *case* statement can be used. We will consider various ways of usage of *if* and *case* statements for check of transition conditions and for forming FSM outputs.

Developers of the Verilog compilers recommend in the description of FSMs to use constructions *else* and *default* in *if* and *case* statements, and besides as the next state specify the present state in the constructions *else* and *default*. For completely specified FSMs [7], the usage of the additional *else* and *default* constructions does not influence in any way behavior of the FSM because this constructions will never be executed. For incompletely specified FSMs [8], the usage of the additional *else* and *default* constructions determines indefinite transitions from each state by the transition to the present state. Actually, the incompletely specified FSM is replaced by the completely specified FSM. Since for incompletely specified FSMs it is guaranteed that on the FSM inputs never there will be the vectors corresponding to the indefinite transition conditions, such additional definitions do not influence behavior of the FSM. Thus, the use of the *else* and *default* constructions do not influence on behavior of the FSM, however it allows to reduce sometimes the implement cost of the combinational circuits CL_φ and CL_ψ.

We will study the possible constructions of the *if* and *case* statements for assignment of the values to the output vector *out* depending on the values of the input vector *in*. In case of determination of the next state, the constructions of the *if* and *case* statements have similar forms.

The following variants of the usage of the *if* statement for coding the FSM combinatorial circuits are possible:

(1) IF_1 – the check of each transition condition by means of the separate *if* statement (it is considered that the given approach leads to of the minimum implementation cost):

```
if (in==2`b00)           out = 2`b11;
if (in==2`b01)           out = 2`b01;
if (in==2`b10)           out = 2`b10;
```

(2) IF_2 – the check of the first transition condition from some state by means of the *if* statement, and the check of each following transition condition by means of the construction *else if* (the traditional approach for coding incompletely specified FSMs):

```
if (in==2`b00)           out = 2`b11;
else if (in==2`b01)      out = 2`b01;
else if (in==2`b10)      out = 2`b10;
```

(3) IF_3 – this variant repeats the previous case except that the last transition condition from some state is implemented by means of the construction *else* (the traditional approach for coding completely specified FSMs):

```
if (in==2`b00)           out = 2`b11;
else if (in==2`b01)      out = 2`b01;
else                     out = 2`b10;
```

(4) IF_4 – this variant repeats the construction IF_2 except that the construction *else* is added, which implements the transition to the present state (in coding transition functions), and the zero or unknown output (in coding outputs):

```
if (in==2`b00)           out = 2`b11;
else if (in==2`b01)      out = 2`b01;
else if (in==2`b10)      out = 2`b10;
else                     out = 2`b00;// or out = 2`bxx;.
```

Similarly, following variants of the usage of the *case* statement for coding the FSM combinatorial circuits are possible:

(5) CASE_1 – the check of each transition condition by means of the separate case item (the traditional approach for coding incompletely specified FSMs):

```
                    case (in)
                        2`b00: out = 2`b11;
                        2`b01: out = 2`b01;
                        2`b10: out = 2`b10;
                    endcase
```

(6) CASE_2 – this variant repeats the previous case except that the last transition condition from some state is implemented by means of the construction *default* (the traditional approach for coding completely specified FSMs):

```
                    case (in)
                        2`b00: out = 2`b11;
                        2`b01: out = 2`b01;
                        default: out = 2`b10;
                    endcase
```

(7) CASE_3 – this variant repeats the CASE_2 construction except that the construction *default* is added, which implements the transition to the present state (in coding transition functions), and the zero or unknown output (in coding outputs):

```
                    case (in)
                        2`b00: out = 2`b11;
                        2`b01: out = 2`b01;
                        2`b10: out = 2`b10;
                        default: out = 2`b00;    // or out = 2`bxx;
                    endcase
```

Note that in coding the transitions in the construction IF_4 after last *else* and in the construction CASE_3 after *default*, it is described the transition to the present state, and also here can it is described the transition to the initial state or to the recovery state. Thus, we have 7 the coding variants in Verilog of the combinative circuits of FSMs.

In Listing 1, the variant IF_1 is used for check of three transitions conditions from some state. The *clk* and *reset* inputs are included in this code to simulate switching between states, and also the code contains a process for the generation of outputs. The examples of usage for other variants the *if* and *case* statements for a check of the transition conditions are built similarly.

Listing 1. Example of the variant IF_1 for three transition conditions

```
module IF_1_3 (input clk, reset, input [5:0] in, output reg [5:0] out);
reg [5:0] out_t;
always@(*) begin        /* IF_1 variant */
        if(in==0)       out_t=2;
        if(in==1)       out_t=1;
        if(in==2)       out_t=0;
end
always@(posedge clk)           /* coding the outputs */
        if (~reset)     out<=out_t;
        else            out<=6'bx;
endmodule
```

To estimate the efficiency of the Verilog constructions that can be used for coding combinational circuits of FSMs we will consider 19 examples. Each example differed from another by the number of the checked conditions. The synthesis of combinational circuits was made for FPGA families Cyclone III by Quartus version 17.1, all options of synthesis were assigned by default.

The experimental research results for the implementation cost (the number of used logic elements of the FPGA) are presented in Table 1, where ex_n is the name of a example; n is the number of the checked conditions, $n \in [3, 21]$; IF_1, ..., IF_4 are the coding variants with the *if* statement; CASE_1, ..., CASE_3 are the coding variants with the *case* statement; C_{max} and C_{min} is the maximum and minimum implementation cost of the example for various coding variants; *mid* is the arithmetic mean value.

Table 1. Experimental research results of the coding styles of combinational circuits of FSMs

The example	IF_1	IF_2	IF_3	IF_4	CASE_1	CASE_2	CASE_3	C_{max}	C_{min}	C_{max}/C_{min}
ex_3	7	7	3	3	7	3	3	7	3	2.33
ex_4	6	7	3	3	3	3	3	7	3	2.33
ex_5	10	10	4	4	10	5	5	10	4	2.50
ex_6	10	10	4	4	10	5	5	10	4	2.50
ex_7	10	10	4	4	11	6	6	11	4	2.75
ex_8	9	9	3	3	4	3	3	9	3	3.00
ex_9	17	17	5	5	13	7	7	17	5	**3.40**
ex_10	15	14	6	6	13	7	7	15	6	2.50
ex_11	18	17	8	8	14	8	8	18	8	2.25
ex_12	13	13	5	5	9	6	6	13	5	2.60
ex_13	15	18	7	7	14	8	8	18	7	2.57
ex_14	15	14	6	6	14	8	8	15	6	2.50
ex_15	16	17	7	7	9	8	8	17	7	2.43

(continued)

Table 1. (*continued*)

The example	IF_1	IF_2	IF_3	IF_4	CASE_1	CASE_2	CASE_3	C_{max}	C_{min}	C_{max}/C_{min}
ex_16	9	12	4	4	5	4	4	12	4	3.00
ex_17	23	21	7	7	11	7	7	23	7	3.29
ex_18	22	17	7	7	10	7	7	22	7	3.14
ex_19	28	23	10	10	11	10	10	28	10	2.80
ex_20	18	18	6	6	8	7	7	18	6	3.00
ex_21	26	22	9	9	11	10	10	26	9	2.89
mid	15.11	14.53	5.68	5.68	9.84	6.42	6.42	15.58	5.68	2.73

Table 1 shows that the coding variants IF_3 and IF_4 with the *if* statement, and also the coding variants CASE_2 and CASE_3 with the *case* statement produce the identical results. The coding variants IF_3 and IF_4 produce the best results at implementation cost, the variants CASE_2 and CASE_3 follow them. One interesting finding is that the worst results are received by means of the IF_1 variant, which was considered earlier as the best at implementation cost.

The results of this investigation show that the coding styles of combinational circuits of FSMs appreciably influence on the implementation cost. This fact is proved by relation C_{max}/C_{min}, which equal to 2.73 on average and 3.4 at maximum.

To create the FSM coding styles, we select the constructions IF_4 and CASE_3 because these constructions provide the low implementation cost and provide additional possibilities for FSM coding.

4 Coding Styles of FSMs

We consider two main coding styles of FSMs in Verilog: with three processes and with two processes. The description of FSMs with three processes contains first process for the description of the combinational circuit CL_φ, which implements the transition functions, the second process for the description of the combinational circuit CL_ψ, which implements the output functions, and the third process, which implements the FSM memory. In the FSM description with two processes, the combinational circuits CL_φ and CL_ψ are represented by means of one process.

Each combinative circuit of the FSM is described or by means of the construction IF_4 with *if* statement, or by means of the construction CASE_3 with *case* statement. In this way, we can build six coding styles M_1, ..., M_6 of FSMs, which are given in Table 2.

Note that the coding style M_1 corresponds to the traditional style of coding of FSMs with three processes, and the coding style M_5 corresponds to the traditional style of coding of FSMs with two processes.

The fragments of FSM coding for IF_4 and CASE_3 constructions are shown in listing 2 and 3 accordingly. Here in construction CASE_3, the *casex* statement is used instead the *case* statement because input vectors of FSMs can contain *don't care* values.

Table 2. Coding styles of FSMs

Coding style	The number of process	Construct for coding CL_Φ	Construct for coding CL_Ψ
M_1	3	IF_4	IF_4
M_2	3	CASE_3	IF_4
M_3	3	IF_4	CASE_3
M_4	3	CASE_3	CASE_3
M_5	2	IF_4	
M_6	2	CASE_3	

Listing 2. Fragment of FSM coding with construction IF_4

```
casex(state)
s0:     if(in==2'b00)            nextstate=s1;
        else if(in==2'b01)       nextstate=s2;
        else if(in==2'b11)       nextstate=s3;
        else                     nextstate=s0;
s1:     if(in==2'b10)            nextstate=s2;
        else if(in==2'b00)       nextstate=s0;
        else if(in==2'b01)       nextstate=s3;
        else                     nextstate=s1;
    ...
endcase
```

Listing 3. Fragment of FSM coding with construction CASE_3

```
casex(state)
s0:    casex(in)
            2'b00:   nextstate=s1;
            2'b01:   nextstate=s2;
            2'b11:   nextstate=s3;
            default: nextstate=s0;
       endcase

s1:    casex(in)
            2'b10:   nextstate=s2;
            2'b00:   nextstate=s0;
            2'b01:   nextstate=s3;
            default: nextstate=s1;
       endcase
    ...
endcase
```

5   Experimental Research Coding Styles of FSMs

To estimate the efficiency of the offered FSM coding styles in Verilog we used MCNC benchmarks of FSMs [9]. The synthesis of FSMs was fulfilled for three FPGA families which are related to three classes of programmable devices: MAX II family is Complex Programmable Logic Devices (CPLD), Cyclone III and Stratix III family is Field Programmable Gate Arrays (FPGA). The synthesis of the FSMs was made by Quartus tool with the parameters of logical synthesis that set by default.

Criteria for selecting the best coding styles were as follows: the FSM implementation cost (the number of used logical elements of the FPGA) and the FSM speed (the maximum frequency of the FPGA). Note that the coding style influences not all benchmarks of FSMs. The coding styles make noticeable impact on the implementation cost or the maximum frequency only in 23 FSM benchmarks from 44. Therefore such examples were researched, for which the implementation cost or the maximum frequency was changed.

The results of the experimental research for the FSM implementation cost and for the FSM speed of family MAX II are presented in Tables 3 and 4 respectively, where C_n is the implementation cost (the number of logic elements of FPGA) and F_n is the speed (in MHz) of the FSM that coded by style M_n, $n \in [1, 6]$; C_{min}, C_{max}, F_{min}, and F_{max} are the maximum cost, the minimum cost, the maximum speed, and the minimum speed of same benchmark for various coding styles; C_{max}/C_{min}, F_{max}/F_{min} are the relation of corresponding parameters.

Table 3. Results of the FSM implementation cost for family MAX II

Benchmarks	C_1	C_2	C_3	C_4	C_5	C_6	C_{min}	C_{max}	C_{max}/C_{min}
BBARA	33	30	29	29	33	29	29	33	1.14
BBSSE	57	57	58	58	57	58	57	58	1.02
BEECOUNT	21	21	14	14	21	14	14	21	1.50
CSE	104	103	101	101	104	98	98	104	1.06
DK14	40	41	39	39	40	39	39	41	1.05
DK15	17	16	16	16	17	16	16	17	1.06
EX1	132	129	121	118	138	118	118	138	1.17
EX3	24	27	22	22	24	22	22	27	1.23
EX5	19	21	20	20	19	20	19	21	1.11
EX6	55	58	56	56	55	56	55	58	1.05
KEYB	83	80	100	87	83	87	80	100	1.25
PLANET	210	224	225	230	216	230	210	230	1.10
S1	160	166	157	156	164	156	156	166	1.06
S1488	211	221	212	212	212	212	211	221	1.05
S1494	209	218	217	219	213	219	209	219	1.05
S208	24	55	41	41	18	41	18	55	**3.06**
S386	59	59	64	64	61	64	59	64	1.08
S420	34	18	19	19	34	19	18	34	1.89
S820	128	138	137	137	128	137	128	138	1.08

(*continued*)

Table 3. (*continued*)

Benchmarks	C_1	C_2	C_3	C_4	C_5	C_6	C_{min}	C_{max}	C_{max}/C_{min}
S832	135	132	132	132	134	132	132	135	1.02
SAND	209	213	199	198	208	198	198	213	1.08
STYR	249	252	216	221	258	225	216	258	1.19
TBK	434	328	422	298	449	282	282	449	1.59
mid	115.09	113.35	113.78	108.13	116.78	107.48	103.65	121.74	1.26

Table 4. Results of the FSM speed for family MAX II

Benchmarks	F_1	F_2	F_3	F_4	F_5	F_6	F_{min}	F_{max}	F_{max}/F_{min}
BBARA	221	203	225	225	221	225	203	225	1.11
BBSSE	155	138	156	156	155	156	138	156	1.13
BEECOUNT	304	304	284	284	304	284	284	304	1.07
CSE	131	123	127	127	131	124	123	131	1.07
DK14	234	192	223	223	234	223	192	234	1.22
DK15	258	413	389	389	258	389	258	413	**1.60**
EX1	111	144	139	137	127	137	111	144	1.30
EX3	256	230	206	206	256	206	206	256	1.24
EX5	266	229	216	216	266	216	216	266	1.23
EX6	211	195	171	171	211	171	171	211	1.23
KEYB	143	136	112	114	143	114	112	143	1.28
PLANET	111	108	100	91	111	91	91	111	1.22
S1	113	119	111	120	120	120	111	120	1.08
S1488	114	112	112	112	108	112	108	114	1.06
S1494	119	121	105	114	121	114	105	121	1.15
S208	265	192	240	240	253	240	192	265	1.38
S386	166	149	176	176	145	176	145	176	1.21
S420	278	306	319	319	278	319	278	319	1.15
S820	97	115	118	124	107	124	97	124	1.28
S832	118	128	117	114	116	114	114	128	1.12
SAND	105	108	110	109	114	109	105	114	1.09
STYR	91	98	110	101	109	118	91	118	1.30
TBK	86	80	97	83	82	93	80	97	1.21
mid	171.87	171.43	172.30	171.78	172.61	172.83	153.52	186.52	1.21

The analysis of Table 3 shows that for FPGA family MAX II the relation between the maximum and minimum implementation cost of the FSMs is equal to 1.26 on average and to 3.06 at maximum (the example S208). Table 4 shows that for FPGA family MAX II the relation between the maximum and minimum speed of the FSMs is equal to 1.21 on average and to 1.60 at maximum (the example DK14). For family MAX II, the coding style M_6 is the best at implementation cost, and the coding style M_2 is the best at speed.

Similar experimental researches also were made for families Cyclone III and Stratix III. Table 5 provides the generalised results of the experimental researches of the FSM benchmarks, where C_{max}/C_{min} is the relation of the maximum and minimum implementation cost of the FSMs for various coding styles; F_{max}/F_{min} is the same, only for FSM speed.

Table 5. Relation of the best and worst results for the various FPGA families

Family	C_{max}/C_{min}	F_{max}/F_{min}
MAX II	3.06	1.60
Cyclone III	2.50	1.46
Stratix III	1.69	1.33

Table 5 shows that by a choice of the FSM coding style, the implementation cost can be reduced by a factor of 3.06 for family MAX II, by a factor of 2.5 for family Cyclone III, and by a factor of 1.69 for family Stratix III. Similarly, the FSM speed can be increased by a factor of 1.6 for family MAX II, by a factor of 1.46 for family Cyclone III, and by a factor of 1.33 for family Stratix III.

The best coding styles at implementation cost and at speed for the FPGA families are presented in Table 6, where M_1 is the FSM coding with three processes when the next-state logic and the output logic is described by means of construction IF_4 (if ... else if ... else); M_2 is the FSM coding with three processes when the next-state logic is described by means of construction CASE_3 (case (...) ... default: ...), and the output logic is described by means of construction IF_4; M_4 is the FSM coding with three processes when the next-state logic and the output logic is described by means of construction CASE_3; M_6 is the FSM coding with two processes when the next-state logic and the output logic is described by means of single construction CASE_3.

Table 6. The best coding styles of the FSMs for the various FPGA families

Family	Cost	Speed
MAX II	M_6	M_2
Cyclone III	M_6	M_2
Stratix III	M_4	M_1

Surprisingly, only one traditional FSM coding style M_1 (from six offered) is in Table 6, which provides the maximum speed for family Stratix III.

The fulfilled researches showed that coding style of FSMs in Verilog makes essential impact as on the FSM implementation cost (for separate examples by a factor of 3.06), and on the FSM speed (for separate examples by a factor of 1.6). Therefore in packet ZUBR [10] the program has been developed, which allows to form automatically the FSM code in Verilog from the FSM representation in language KISS2 [9]. The program allows to generate the FSM codes in Verilog according to offered coding styles M_1, ..., M_6 and to select from them the most suitable description at the FSM cost and the FSM speed.

6 Conclusions

This study has shown that Verilog gives a great variety of the FSM coding styles, which are researched till now not completely. This project is the first comprehensive investigation of the FSM coding styles in Verilog. The traditional coding styles of FSMs not always are the best at the implementation cost and the speed. The results of this investigation show that the offered coding styles of FSMs in Verilog considerably influences on the FSM cost (for our examples by a factor of 2.71 on average) and on the FSM speed. The second major finding was that the FSM coding styles allow to reduce the FSM implementation cost and to increase the FSM speed without using any synthesis methods of FSMs. The findings of this study have a number of important implications for future practice. The present study lays the groundwork for future research into finding the coding styles of FSMs.

A limitation of this study is that all possible the coding styles of FSMs in Verilog are researched not. In particular, such coding styles were not considered as an implicit FSM coding, using *assign* statements, coding the FSM in the form of several separate modules (for example, the combinational circuit and the register), etc.

Traditionally, the check of the FSM present state is made by *case* statement (and also in the given paper), but with the same purpose it is possible to use various constructions of *if* statement. The important problem also is research of coding styles for Moore machines, as the model of the Moore machine of widely is used and it is very popular among developers. The offered technique of creation and choice of effective coding styles of FSMs in Verilog is applied for FPGA from Intel. Similar researches can be made for FPGA from the other vendors. The similar technique can be used also for research of coding styles of FSMs in VHDL. All these problems demand the further careful research.

Acknowledgements. The present study was supported by a grant S/WI/3/2018 from Bialystok University of Technology and founded from the resources for research by Ministry of Science and Higher Education.

References

1. Golson, S.: State machine design techniques for Verilog and VHDL. Synopsys J. High-Level Des. **9**, 1–48 (1994)
2. Wang, T.H., Edsall, T.: Practical FSM analysis for Verilog. In: Verilog HDL Conference and VHDL International Users Forum (IVC/VIUF), Santa Clara, USA, pp. 52–58 (1998)
3. Cummings, C.E.: State machine coding styles for synthesis. In: Synopsys Users Group (SNUG 1998), San Jose, USA, pp. 1–20 (1998)
4. Cummings, C.E.: Coding and scripting techniques for FSM designs with synthesis-optimized, glitch-free outputs. In: Synopsys Users Group (SNUG 2000), Boston, USA, pp. 1–12 (2000)
5. Lee, J.M.: Verilog Quick Start. A Practical Guide to Simulation and Synthesis in Verilog, 3rd edn. Kluwer Academic Publishers, New York (2002)

6. Uma, R., Dhavachelvan, P.: Finite state machine optimization in FPGAs. In: Second International Conference on Computational Science, Engineering and Information Technology (CCSEIT-2012), Coimbatore, India, pp. 205–211 (2012)
7. Klimovich, A.S., Soloviev, V.V.: Minimization of mealy finite-state machines by internal states gluing. J. Comput. Syst. Sci. Int. **2**, 244–255 (2012)
8. Klimovicz, A.S., Solov'ev, V.V.: Minimization of incompletely specified Mealy finite-state machines by merging two internal states. J. Comput. Syst. Sci. Int. **3**, 400–409 (2013)
9. Yang, S.: Logic synthesis and optimization benchmarks user guide. Version 3.0. Technical report. North Carolina. Microelectronics Center of North Carolina (1991)
10. Salauyou, V., Klimowicz, A., Grzes, T., Bulatowa, I., Dimitrowa-Grekow, T.: Synthesis methods of finite state machines implemented in package ZUBR. In: Sixth International Conference Computer-Aided Design of Discrete Devices (CAD DD'7). Minsk, Republic of Belarus, pp. 53–56 (2007)

Various Aspects of Computer Security

CollabChain: Blockchain-Backed Trustless Web-Based Volunteer Computing Platform

K. S. Sagar Bharadwaj$^{(\boxtimes)}$, Samvid Dharanikota$^{(\boxtimes)}$, Adarsh Honawad$^{(\boxtimes)}$, and K. Chandrasekaran$^{(\boxtimes)}$

National Institute of Technology Karnataka, Surathkal, India
sagarbharadwaj50@gmail.com, samvid.dharani@gmail.com, adarsh2397@gmail.com,
kchnitk@ieee.org

Abstract. Volunteer computing is a distributed computing model in which individuals in possession of computing resources volunteer to provide them to a project. Owing to the availability of billions of computing devices all over the world, volunteer computing can help solve problems that are larger in scale even for supercomputers. However, volunteer computing projects are difficult to launch and deploy. These platforms also force volunteers to trust the authenticity of the project owner and to blindly accept credits allotted to their contribution by the project owner. As a result, very few high-profile trusted projects are able to sustain in this system. In this paper, we present an incentivized web-based volunteer computing platform that functions as a market place to buy and sell computing power. Launching a project on the system and contributing to an existing project happens over the browser without the need for a specialized software or hardware. We introduce the application of blockchain to remove the need to trust any other party in the system. We also present a prototype implementation and solve NP-Problems as examples using the proposed prototype.

Keywords: Volunteer computing · CPU cycle · Blockchain · Web · Browser

1 Introduction

Volunteer computing refers to a distributed computing solution where users (called volunteers) contribute their computing power to large-scale projects requiring high throughput and longer computation time. These large-scale projects are usually, but not limited to, research problems in the areas of medicine, meteorology, mathematics and so on. Some examples are Folding@Home [4], that simulates protein folding, computational drug design, and other types of molecular dynamics and Einstein@Home [3] that searches for radiations from neutron stars.

K. S. Sagar Bharadwaj, Samvid Dharanikota and Adarsh Honawad—Contributed equally.

© Springer Nature Switzerland AG 2019
K. Saeed et al. (Eds.): CISIM 2019, LNCS 11703, pp. 509–522, 2019.
https://doi.org/10.1007/978-3-030-28957-7_42

Approximately 10 petaflops of computing power are available from volunteer computing networks [15]. Anderson et al. [9] provide further statistics on the potential of volunteer computing.

In a general volunteer computing model, volunteers pick up tasks (processes) given by a host, perform necessary computation, and submit the output back to the host. Most volunteer computing architectures today are usually supported by unpaid volunteers. They are 'volunteers' in the truest sense. These models can also be based on 'volunteers' 'selling' their resources, and the host 'buying' them. For example, a host that requires high-throughput computation can request a volunteer to run the computation in exchange for payment made to the volunteer. Such an architecture is feasible due to the fact that they do not have to invest in expensive cloud servers or any other computation platform, but can 'buy' computing resources for smaller amounts on a per-process basis. This also allows for systems to accumulate monetary reward during their idle time.

The Blockchain in its basic sense is a distributed ledger that is replicated on all nodes in a distributed system. As the name suggests, it consists of a 'chain' of blocks, that are linked to each other. These blocks contain transaction records and associated data. The hash of the contents of a block is recorded in the following block, and this forms the 'link' between the two blocks. This essentially makes the ledger immutable and append-only, because, tampering of data in a certain block would require re-computation of its hash, and the subsequent modification of this hash in the following block, and this propagates. Generation of these blocks by nodes in the blockchain network is restricted by 'consensus' mechanisms. Hence tampering with the blockchain and creating new blocks is not feasible.

Nodes need only a pair of public and private keys to participate in the blockchain network. This implies that they do not have to use any personal data such as their name, for instance, to create an identity in the network, preserving their privacy.

The blockchain is replicated over all nodes in the P2P network, and its state is made (eventually) consistent over all nodes by exchange of state-update information with its peers. The lack of a central node/server to maintain and enforce the current blockchain state ensures a decentralized environment.

Properties of blockchain such as immutability, privacy and decentralization make it an attractive solution to many development problems that require the same properties. It was initially used as the ledger for the famous Bitcoin [11], where the blockchain stored Bitcoin transaction records. Blockchain has since evolved, and saw applications in many domains not restricted to cryptocurrencies, such as healthcare, Internet of Things (IoT), cloud computing and more.

This paper proposes a novel architecture of browser-based volunteer computing platform that employs blockchain to provide a trusted environment for the volunteers and incentivizes them to devote their computational resources. Without the need of any specialized application, except just the web-browser that is pre-installed on almost all commercially available personal computers, anyone can deploy the platform and use it with ease.

The paper starts with an introduction to volunteer computing and blockchain concepts in general. The following section explores other research works related to volunteer computing. We then define the design goals that our volunteer computing platform must implement in the third section. The fourth section describes the architecture of our volunteer computing platform along with a sample implementation. The fifth section explains the flow of control through whilst using the platform. The final section displays the results of some our tests and drawbacks of our architecture.

2   Related Work

Many researchers and organizations have attempted to create browser-based volunteer computing platforms with varying levels of complexity that cater to general or specific use-cases. The earliest popular volunteer computing project was perhaps SETI@home (Search for Extra Terrestrial Intelligence) proposed by Anderson [8]. The project consisted of a high frequency feed from a radio telescope whose signals could be analysed to determine the presence of extra terrestrial life. Although the project failed to identify extra terrestrial life, it paved the way for *Public-resource computing*. The same group launched a volunteer computing platform called *BOINC* (Berkeley Open Infrastructure for Network Computing) [7]. It was the first platform that allowed participants to volunteer for a number of scientific projects that had massive computation requirements. BOINC projects use a centralised server complex centered around a relational database that stores descriptions of applications, platforms, versions, workunits, results, accounts, teams, and so on. The BOINC project has a large entry barrier for addition of projects. Around 30 projects use BOINC today [6]. Every project must maintain a server complex containing a database server and a web server. BOINC is thus only used to contribute computation power and seldom to request it. The volunteers will also have to spend significant amount of time downloading and setting up the BOINC client. BOINC is also based on a trusted 'credit' system. The volunteers trust the project host and receive credits after completing their share of work. Our design removes the barrier of entry for addition of new tasks, decentralizes the system and also eliminates the need for trust between exchanging parties.

Golem [5] is an incentivized computing market place with based on blockchain. However the tasks that the volunteers on the system can perform are limited to computations such as computer graphics rendering and certain machine learning algorithms. Thus the computations that can be performed are not generic and the platform cannot be used to request computation power for generic tasks.

BOID [1] is another blockchain-backed social computing platform where volunteers get paid in custom BOID cryptocurrency tokens for the resource that they contribute. It is currently in Alpha phase.

Sarmenta and Hirano [13] have proposed a Java based applet, Bayanihan, for a web-based volunteer computing system that consists of worker and watcher clients that connect to a server (via the URL in the browser) that serves 'problems' to the volunteers (clients). Note that Bayanihan is only a framework that can be used to build platforms on top of it with the mentioned underlying architecture. In contrast, our paper is a full-fledged platform.

Ong et al. [12] proposed a volunteer computing platform using a client-broker-host model, based on Java. Clients submit tasks that are distributed to the hosts via the broker, which handles task collection and distribution. Similar to our architecture, the hosts are incetivized by the client based on the amount of data they process/compute on.

Specific to image processing computation, a client-server model is proposed by Zorrilla et al. [16] where the clients are users on a social media service, who run a given algorithm on images from the social media provided by the server. The platform uses JavaScript, similar to our architecture, and spawns threads to perform computation in the browser in the background. It is worth noting that the more recent works on browser-based distributed computation have used JavaScript over Java. One key reason is due to the lack of the need of a separate Java Virtual Machine on JavaScript-based browsers, that needs to be installed on a system to view Java-based web-pages.

Turek et al. [14] also proposed a volunteer computing approach, based on a similar client-server model, for a specific use-case: Web-crawling. Servers first download the content of the web-pages required to be crawled. They then send the content to volunteers and collect the results computed by them. The volunteers initially obtain the algorithm to be run on the web-page content. They then query the server to obtain tasks. On receiving the content, they process it with the given algorithm and return the information to the server.

Although not a volunteer-computing application itself, Merelo-Guervós and García-Sánchez [10] proposed a browser-based distributed computing model for evolutionary computation.

3   Design Goals

Figure 1 shows the architecture of the volunteer computing platform that we have built.

We ensure that the architecture we have proposed adheres to the following design goals:

- *Easy Deployment*: Deployment refers to the steps needed to be taken to make a software system available for use. We aim at building a system which involves minimum effort to deploy. Existing volunteer computing platforms generally have a large deployment overhead, especially for the party seeking computation resources - the task submitter in our case.
- *Decentralization*: Most volunteer computing platforms depend on a central entity to monitor executors, collect results and distribute credits. This means the system is prone to single point of failure problems. We wish to remove centralized entities and make sure there is no single point of failure or a potential bottleneck in the system.

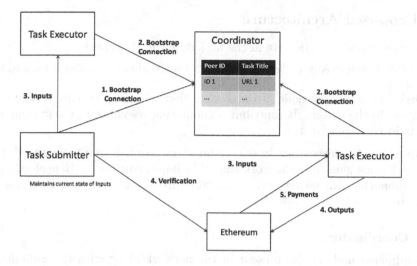

Fig. 1. Architecture

- *Platform independence*: Software systems in the volunteer computing domain are dependent on hardware resources and the underlying platform. Authors have developed clients separately for different platforms. However, we propose a system that is independent of the platform and underlying hardware.
- *Trustlessness*: All volunteer computing systems existent today are reliant on the assumption of presence of trust between participating entities. Submitters rely on executors to not attack the system and executors trust the submitters to distribute unbiased credits proportional to the amount of computation. This trust model is justified as long as nothing of real value is exchanged. However, such an assumption cannot be made when it comes to an incentivized platform. We propose a system where the concept of trustlessness is achieved using blockchain.
- *Privacy*: Privacy refers to a one's choice of withholding private information about oneself from a system. The system developed, although involves incentivization must be capable of payments without the need to discover the individual's personal credentials.
- *Elimination of software and hardware overhead*: Existing volunteer computing platforms mandate the Task submitters to maintain dedicated hardware to sustain the system. We wish to eliminate these software and hardware overheads.
- *Performance*: The system should ideally provide a linear increase in performance with respect to the number of executors.
- *Scalability*: The system should be scalable with respect to the number of nodes as well as the number of tasks it can handle.

The current architecture that our platform uses implements almost all the mentioned design goals to a great extent. However, scalability and decentralization are two design goals that can be improved upon in further works.

4   Proposed Architecture

Two types of nodes participate in the underlying P2P network:

- *Task Submitter*: Any node in the system that wishes to submit a task to the system
- *Task Executor*: Any node in the system that wishes to execute a task submitted to the system. It contributes computing resources to the system and gets incentivized for it.

Note that the 'executors' in our architecture are not true 'volunteers', i.e., they seek some gain from the work that they have contributed. Henceforth, the Task Submitter will be referred to as 'Submitter' and the Task Executor as 'Executor'.

4.1   Coordinator

A coordinator node is also present in the network along with the Submitters and Executors. Nodes initiates their connection to the network by connecting to the coordinator. Every peer to peer system requires a bootstrap connection to a seed node through which it discovers other peers in the system. The coordinator in our system acts like the seed node. The coordinator has two tasks:

- To maintain a database of all the projects utilizing the volunteer computing platform. This enables any Executor node to discover all projects and choose the project of its liking.
- To act as a seed node and let peers discover themselves to initiate connections among themselves. The coordinator acts as a brokering connection initiator.

After the nodes have connected to the coordinator, which only acts like a bootstrapping seed node, they no longer need to communicate with the coordinator, except for heart beats to confirm the node is still alive. The Executor node obtains the 'peer ID' (can also be thought of as a 'task ID') of the Submitter of a particular task through the coordinator's database. Note that the same Submitter node can have different peer IDs for different tasks that they submit to the network, i.e., the peer ID is unique for a task. This ensures brevity in the number of IDs that the coordinator has to store in memory.

Once the Executor has discovered the corresponding Submitter, it does not communicate through the coordinator. Instead, a P2P connection is established between the Submitter and the Executor directly. The Submitter generates a unique URL for its task, and the Executor establishes this connection by accessing the URL in a browser. The task and the its inputs are sent through this connection.

The decoupling of the coordinator from the task of channeling input to executors ensures that the coordinator is no longer the bottleneck. It inadvertently implies that the connection established between the submitter and executor remains intact in spite of failures at the coordinator's end. Such bottlenecks and single point of failure problems, which are prevalent in most existing volunteer computing architectures, are avoided here.

4.2 Task Submitter and Executor

The Submitter creates a task to be distributed along with a set of inputs on which the task/process is to be run, and then submits it to the network. The task comprises of a JavaScript method which conforms to a specified format of input parameters and return values.

Once the connection between the Submitter and Executor is established as stated above, the Submitter provides inputs to the Executors in a batch round robin fashion. It sends a configurable batch of inputs at once to each Executor. The task of dividing an input into independent units is delegated to the user. This decision is made as user of the system is the only actor who can decide the best execution plan for a task.

The Executors complete their tasks independently by executing a procedure defined by the Submitter on their assigned inputs. The output of the Execution, however, is not sent directly to the Submitter. This is to avoid two types of malicious node behaviour:

- Withdrawing payments - The Submitter can choose not to proceed with paying the Executor even after it receives valid outputs.
- Forgoing legitimate computation - The Executor can avoid computing outputs using the given task and instead send garbage output to the Submitter in hopes of getting paid.

The output computed by the Executor is sent to the blockchain to prevent the above behaviour. In addition to sending the task method and set of inputs to the Executor, the Submitter also sends a set of 'pre-computed' outputs to the smart contracts. The following sections explains the role of blockchain and smart contracts in detail.

4.3 Blockchain Incentivization Mechanism

The blockchain ensures the following:

- Payment for the volunteers for successful completion of work
- Honest behaviour of submitters and volunteers

Smart contracts are used to realize the same.

The Submitter, when it creates a task, is mandated to compute the outputs for a randomly chosen subset of the inputs. This subset is very small compared to m, the size of the inputs. These outputs are computed on a per-batch basis, as in, one set of outputs per batch. The batch size determines the degree of legitimate values the Submitter gets. It then invokes the smart contract, providing it with the vector of hashes of the computed outputs as a parameter, along with the price it is ready to pay. The Submitter also makes the payment to the smart contract. These hashes are recorded on the blockchain.

The Executor, on successfully completing the computation, provides the vector of hashes of outputs to a smart contract method. The smart contract then

verifies if the expected outputs (computed values from the Submitter) are present
in the outputs given by the Executor. If so, the smart contract then releases
payments to the executor and the executor then sends over the outputs to the
Submitter directly via its connection.

Since the Executor has no way to know which input of the batch given to
it has its output pre-computed, it has to execute all of it to get paid, thereby
ensuring that the executor will not submit garbage outputs for verification and
falsely be rewarded.

The batch size directly determines the probability of the Submitter receiving
a valid output. If the batch size is small, there the number of inputs per batch
decreases, and the Submitter would have to spend more of its computing power
to pre-compute the outputs at the benefit of receiving more valid outputs. Conversely, if the batch size is large, then the Submitter would have to perform lesser
computation at the risk of receiving wrong outputs from a malicious Executor.

Table 1. Run-times with different browsers

S. No.	Type	Hardware	%age batches	Browser	Time
1	Serial	Intel Core i7-4510U CPU	100%	Mozilla Firefox 64.0	198.64 s
2	Serial	Intel Core i7-4510U CPU	100%	Google Chrome 71.0	88.53 s
3	Distributed	Intel Core i7-4510U CPU	63.63%	Google Chrome 71.0	56.95 s
		Intel Core i5-6200U CPU	36.36%	Google Chrome 71.0	
4	Distributed	Intel Core i7-4510U CPU	54.54%	Google Chrome 71.0	52.06 s
		Intel Core i5-6200U CPU	36.36%	Google Chrome 71.0	
		Qualcomm Snapdragon 650 hexa-core (4 × 1.4 GHz + 4 × 1.8 GHz)	9.09%	Firefox (Android 6.0)	

5   Flow of Control

1. The submitter joins the network by connecting to the coordinator (P2P
   Bootstrap).
2. The submitter writes the task to be executed in the given format and also
   prepares the set of inputs (and also divides them into assignable batches)
   on which this is supposed to be run.
3. The submitter then executes the task on a subset of these batches and
   obtains output.
4. The submitter then decides the reward he is willing to pay, and invokes
   the smart-contract to record the pre-computed outputs (a hash of the pre-
   computed outputs, for practical purposes; one hash is computed for one
   batch) along with the task ID and reward, and a payment is made to the
   contract. The task 'function' is then given to the coordinator.
5. The executor also joins the network by connecting to the coordinator (P2P
   Bootstrap).
6. The executor then picks a task from the list of tasks displayed to it by the
   coordinator.

7. Once the executor picks a task, its connection with the coordinator is terminated. A connection is initiated directly with the corresponding submitter.
8. The submitter then provides the executor with a few batches of inputs corresponding to that task that are still not computed.
9. The executor runs the task function on these inputs and computes the set of outputs.
10. The executor then provides the hashes of the computed batches to the same smart-contract.
11. The smart-contract compares the hashes that have been provided by the submitter (pre-computed outputs) with the hashes given to it by the executor. If all the pre-computed outputs' (in the range of batches given to that executor) hashes are present in the list of hashes given by the executor, the smart-contract then pays the executor with the reward amount as specified by the submitter.
12. If the executor is still connected to the submitter, a new set of batches are given to the executor and the above steps repeat.
13. If the hashes do not match in step 11, then no payment is made as the outputs computed (some or all) by the executor are wrong.

6 Results

To test our system, we executed a simple scenario where the submitter wants to solve the integer factorisation problem. Factorisation does not have a known polynomial solution and is thus an NP-Problem. The problem of finding all factors of n can be distributed among executors by dividing the range of numbers having possible factors (1 to $\sqrt{n}$) into sub ranges. The executors can then launch the factor searching process in their own sub-ranges. For the purpose of demonstrating preliminary results, we make an attempt at factorising a 21 digit (in base 10) number with 67 bits. The submitter function is a simple 8 line JavaScript code which is run in a distributed fashion by all executors in parallel. We have divided our input into sub-ranges as follows:

```
{
  "Input": [
    {
      "start": 1,
      "end": 100000000,
      "num": 123456789123456800000
    },
    {
      "start": 100000001,
      "end": 200000000,
      "num": 123456789123456800000
    }, // and so on
}
```

Our implementation also provides sample scripts to generate input batches in the above format. The following is the code for the 'task' given to the executors:

```
factor = [];
for(var k = input.start; k <= input.end
   && k * k <= input.num; k++) {
    if(obj.num % k == 0) {
        factor.push(k);
        factor.push(obj.num / k);
    }
}
return {Factor: factor};
```

We record several observations in Table 1.

Clearly, distributing the work over several computers reduced the computation time owing to parallel execution. The time required to finish computation decreases inversely with the number of devices. An interesting observation is that the Chrome's V8 engine runs the given JavaScript code faster than the Mozilla's Gecko Engine. We also used a mobile device running the Firefox browser. The Android 6.0 mobile device obviously took more time than a laptop computer, but it was nevertheless able to partake in the voluntary computing platform and yield results. This shows that even mobile devices can participate in the platform.

We also took up the hashing problem to demonstrate our system. The problem is similar to cryptocurrency mining where the executors compute hashes for nonces in the given range. The hash function considered is a Javascript implementation of the String.hashCode() function in Java. The results are shown in Fig. 2. Two Gigahashes were computed in total in total by the system. The nonces required to generate two Gigahashes were divided into 100 subranges. 10 of these subranges were grouped together into a batch. Thus there were a total of 10 batches.

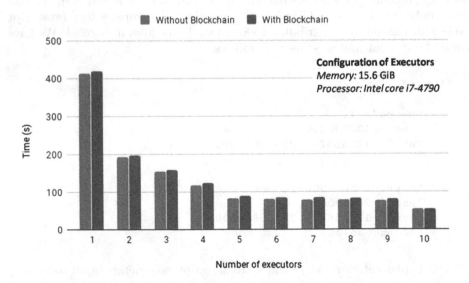

Fig. 2. Running times for the hashing problem

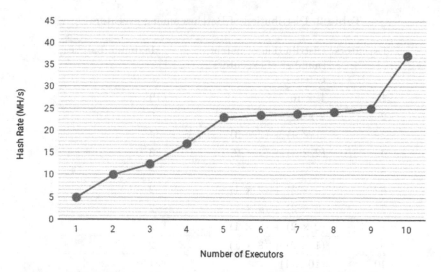

Fig. 3. Increase in hash rate with number of executors

Figure 3 shows how the hash rate of the system varies with respect to the number of executors. As can be seen from the chart, the increase in performance is not always linear with respect to the number of executors. There are regions in the graph where the hash rate remains constant even when the number of executors increases. For instance, the hash rate does not increase when the number of executors increases from 5 to 9. The reason for this behavior is explained by the distribution of the batches given in Table 2. A total of 10 batches is distributed between all the available executors. The runtime of execution is measured as the time elapsed between the first executor joining the system and the last executor finishing the computation. As a result, the hash rate is limited by the last executor to finish. Thus, it is dependent on the the maximum number of batches given to an executor. As shown in Table 2, the maximum number of batches given to an executor remains 2 even when the number of executors increases from 5 to 9. However, there is a slight increase in the hash rate when executors increase from 5 to 9. This is because, only the fastest executors finish fast enough to fetch another batch from the submitter. Thus in case of 5 executors, the fastest 4 executors fetch the next batch. The runtime is limited by the slowest of the fastest four. In case of 9 executors, only the fastest executor fetches the next batch. Thus, it completes faster.

Table 2. Distribution of Batches among executors

Executors	Distribution of batches (number of executors × batches)	Maximum batches
1	1×10	10
2	2×5	5
3	$(1 \times 4) + (2 \times 3)$	4
4	$(2 \times 3) + (2 \times 2)$	3
5	(5×2)	2
6	$(4 \times 2) + (2 \times 1)$	2
7	$(3 \times 2) + (4 \times 1)$	2
8	$(2 \times 2) + (6 \times 1)$	2
9	$(1 \times 2) + (8 \times 1)$	2
10	(10×1)	1

7   Analysis

In this section we explore how the design goals proposed in Sect. 3 were met. Table 3 summarizes the technologies used to meet these design goals.

Table 3. Design goals

Design goal	Technology used
Trustlessness	Blockchain
Easy deployment	Browser
Decentralisation	PeerJS
Platform independence	Browser
Privacy	Ethereum/metamask
Performance	Architecture
Scalability	Architecture

- *Easy Deployment*: The system is easy to deploy. The user will need nothing more than a browser to contribute or request computing power. In order to get incentivized, setting up an Ethereum wallet is required. An Ethereum wallet can be set up in a very short time with the help of tools such as the Metamask wallet browser extension.
- *Decentralisation*: Our design aims at eliminating any form of centralization. The purpose of the volunteer computing system is to impede dependency on a central entity for both computation and incentivization purposes. Our current design uses a coordinator that acts a seed node in the Peer to Peer network, which is inevitable. After establishment of a connection between the

submitter node and executor nodes, the coordinator is no longer involved and a direct P2P connection is established between the nodes.

- *Platform independence*: Our design and implementation is independent of the platform as it runs within the execution environment of a browser. It is only limited by the availability of a web-browser on a device. Any device that can run a browser can contribute computational power including mobile phones, tablets and Desktops.
- *Trustlessness*: Existing Volunteer computing systems are all dependent on trust. They generally do not verify the outputs generated by volunteers. There is little reason for volunteers to submit erroneous values in an un-incentivized system. The volunteers also trust the task owner's authenticity. However, in an incentivized system on the public network, such a trust based model cannot be used. A node may simply submit erroneous values to get the incentive rewards. A simple verification is not sufficient as the task's owner may refuse to compensate the volunteer in spite of receiving valid/correct outputs. In such cases, reliance on a trusted third party who can mediate between the task submitter and the task executor seems necessary. However, our design eliminates the existence of any trusted entity. The execution and incentivization takes place without the need for the involvement of trust using blockchain.
- *Privacy*: The system does not require personal data. Ethereum accounts associated with a person do not have personal data attached to them, which means our system preserves user's privacy.
- *Elimination of software and hardware overhead*: Our implementation does not require additional software or hardware set up. There is no need to set up an Ethereum client or an Ethereum node. A browser and a simple browser based Ethereum wallet would be sufficient to participate in the system.
- *Performance*: The performance of the system increases with the number of executors as shown by the results.
- *Scalability*: The system is scalable with respect to both the number of unique tasks it can handle and the number of nodes. The system has no bottleneck as the connection to the coordinator persists only before a direct connection is established between the task submitter and the task executor.
- *Minimum user prerequisites*: There are no prerequisites for a task executor to contribute computational power. A task submitter can write the task in plain JavaScript. The system does not mandate any special syntax and thus the task submitter need not be familiar with the system to use it. This is generally not the case with most other volunteer computing platforms.

Note that the submitter is required to stay on-line even after delegating the process function and the inputs to the executors in order to obtain computed outputs from the executor. This could be a possible future work direction to remove this constraint.

8   Conclusion

In this paper we have proposed a novel approach of leveraging blockchain technology to build a trustless volunteer computing platform. The platform is completely browser based making it convenient for both the task submitters and executors. This removes the requirement of any additional software or hardware as is necessary in traditional volunteer computing solutions. A proof of concept of the proposal has also been implemented and tested using the open source blockchain, Ethereum. The implementation has been open sourced [2]. The platform also supports incentivization as opposed to traditional solutions because of the trustless and immutable nature of blockchain.

References

1. BOID. https://www.boid.com/
2. CollabChain. https://github.com/SagarB-97/CollabChain
3. Einstein@Home. https://einsteinathome.org/
4. Folding@Home. https://foldingathome.org/
5. The Golem Project, November 2016. https://golem.network/doc/Golemwhite paper.pdf. Accessed 18 Jan 2019
6. BOINC. https://boinc.berkeley.edu/. Accessed 18 Jan 2019
7. Anderson, D.P.: BOINC: a system for public-resource computing and storage. In: Proceedings of the Fifth IEEE/ACM International Workshop on Grid Computing, pp. 4–10. IEEE (2004)
8. Anderson, D.P., Cobb, J., Korpela, E., Lebofsky, M., Werthimer, D.: Seti@ home: an experiment in public-resource computing. Commun. ACM **45**(11), 56–61 (2002)
9. Anderson, D., Fedak, G.: The computational and storage potential of volunteer computing pp. 73–80, June 2006
10. Merelo-Guervós, J.J., García-Sánchez, P.: Designing and modeling a browser-based distributed evolutionary computation system. In: Proceedings of the Companion Publication of the 2015 Annual Conference on Genetic and Evolutionary Computation, pp. 1117–1124. ACM, New York (2015)
11. Nakamoto, S.: Bitcoin: A Peer-to-Peer Electronic Cash System (2008)
12. Ong, T.M., Lim, T.M., Lee, B.S., Yeo, C.K.: Unicorn: voluntary computing over internet. SIGOPS Oper. Syst. Rev. **36**(2), 36–51 (2002)
13. Sarmenta, L.F., Hirano, S.: Bayanihan: building and studying web-based volunteer computing systems using Java. Future Gener. Comput. Syst. **15**(5–6), 675–686 (1999)
14. Turek, W., Nawarecki, E., Dobrowolski, G., Krupa, T., Majewski, P.: Web pages content analysis using browser-based volunteer computing. Comput. Sci. **14**(2), 215–230 (2013)
15. Wikipedia contributors: Volunteer computing – Wikipedia, the free encyclopedia (2018). https://en.wikipedia.org/w/index.php?title=Volunteer_computing&oldid=859975321. Accessed 18 Jan 2019
16. Zorrilla, M., Martin, A., Tamayo, I., Aginako, N., Olaizola, I.G.: Web browser-based social distributed computing platform applied to image analysis. In: 2013 Third International Conference on Cloud and Green Computing (CGC), pp. 389–396. IEEE (2013)

A Fast Method for Security Protocols Verification

Olga Siedlecka-Lamch[1]([⊠])(iD), Sabina Szymoniak[1](iD),
and Miroslaw Kurkowski[1,2](iD)

[1] Institute of Computer and Information Sciences,
Czestochowa University of Technology, Czestochowa, Poland
{olga.siedlecka,sabina.szymoniak}@icis.pcz.pl
[2] Institute of Computer Science, Cardinal St. Wyszyński University, Warsaw, Poland
m.kurkowski@uksw.edu.pl

Abstract. Internet communication is essential for everyone. Algorithms that decide about the correctness of this communication are protocols, and the central part of it that keeps all in safety are security protocols. Because every such program must be implemented and applied, errors are probable. That is why we need verification methods based on mathematical models, and we also need tools checking the new protocols, looking for undiscovered gaps. Existing verification tools and languages describing the protocols are not free of errors or imperfections. Sometimes they neglect some dependencies, and sometimes they are utterly redundant. We present in the article a formal model that we have recently developed. It describes the different behaviours and properties of security protocols. On the base of it, we implemented the tool that verifies many types of protocol, first of all, if they work and then if they meet the security requirements. At the end of the article, we provided a summary of our results with the results obtained from popular tool.

Keywords: Verification of security protocols ·
Security protocols properties · Model checking

1 Introduction

Internet communication affects all areas of our modern life. We use it for virtual conversation, business, shopping, and in our private life. In each of the situations mentioned above, we may wonder if our data is safe, how much potential intruders can learn. Does every Internet user realize what Internet communication is, how many operations hide under it?

The Internet was initially the domain of scientists subsidized by the army. From the very beginning, it was supposed to enable safe communication, even in

The project financed under the program of the Minister of Science and Higher Education under the name "Regional Initiative of Excellence" in 2019–2022 project number 020/RID/2018/19, the amount of financing 12,000,000 PLN.

© Springer Nature Switzerland AG 2019
K. Saeed et al. (Eds.): CISIM 2019, LNCS 11703, pp. 523–534, 2019.
https://doi.org/10.1007/978-3-030-28957-7_43

the event of damage or attack of parts of the network. Many devices, algorithms and software decide about the operation of the modern network. Examples of these algorithms are communication protocols that deal with data exchange. Their most essential parts are security protocols. These are small algorithms consisting of several steps to guarantee correct verification of communicating pages, as well as security of transmitted data.

During these several decades of Internet existence, scientists invented and implemented many protocols, many of them turned out to be defective. Errors and gaps were detected, sometimes only after many years of use [18, 21]. There was and still is a strong need to verify the mechanisms that determine the security of our data.

The verifications were initially carried out experimentally, but of course, there are no better methods than formal verification, allowing the analysis of a much broader spectrum of possible situations. There are several paths for verification. The first approach is deductive verification, the descriptions of which can be found in the works of Burrows, Abbadi and Needham [1, 6]. Basin and Wollf used logic in their work [3]. Another approach was based on inductive methods [20, 22]. Currently, most of the works on verification of security protocols focus on model checking [4, 9, 10, 19].

For each of the developed methods, teams of researchers created dedicated tools, firstly to show their performance and effectiveness, and secondly to provide verification tools to the public. Here is a list of the most popular tools: Scyther [7], ProVerif [5], AVISPA [2], UPPAAL [8], VerICS [13], PathFinder [17].

The question arises whether the topic has not been exhausted with such a long list of methods and tools. We should emphasise that researchers still develop new protocols, adapt them, and existing tools are not free of defects [15]. We also care about the time of the verification, especially since most tools search the redundant space of generated actions and their combination, which not reflects reality.

The article presents our current approach to protocol verification. Our team has been working for years in this field, developed techniques related to automatic machine networks [16], verification using SAT tools [14], probabilistic verification [24], up to the current method. Our methods have also been used in practice to verify the MobInfoSec system, which is a distributed, modular, and configurable cryptographic access control system to sensitive information [23]. In the method described in the article, a tuple represents a step of the protocol. In every tuple, we distinguish elements related to the conditions that the user must meet to send a message, elements related to the message itself, and elements suggesting what knowledge the recipient has gained. This simple structure allows a quick analysis of whether the user can take the next step. If he did not get the right knowledge in previous tuples - he can not. In this way, the model is strictly limited and does not allow for the analysis of paths that do not occur in reality.

The article consists of five sections: introduction, description of an exemplary protocol, description of the formal method, experimental results and a summary.

2   Exemplary Security Protocol

In this part of the article, we show an example of the security protocol used in the MobInfoSec system, which enables encryption and sharing of confidential information to a group of connected users of mobile devices [12,23]. The system includes software and hardware. A team of researchers and programmers developed it for popular mobile devices available on the market. One of the most complex components that met the ORCON rules was a strong mutual authentication scheme between secret protection modules (SP). The system performs communication between multiple users. Each of them on its device has two modules: Module Secret Protection (SP) and Authentication Module (MU) (Fig. 1).

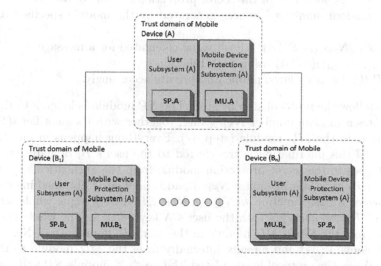

Fig. 1. Trust domains concept for different mobile devices

One of the communication points is taken as the initiator of the protocol (chairman - in the picture described by letter A) and should authenticate with other users (B_i); at the end, it establishes secure communication channels.

The entire communication protocol, which consists of five phases, is described in detail in the article [23], here we describe only the part responsible for authentication, which is a security protocol. For the description, we use the Common Language, which is the most popular form of protocol description appearing in the literature. We assume that before the security protocol, the keys of the $SP.A$ and $SP.B_i$ modules are activated, which is necessary to perform the cryptographic operations; there is also a request from $MU.A$ to $SP.A$ to generate a random number (nonce - a number used once).

$$\alpha_1 \quad SP.A \to MU.A: \{N_{SP.A}, i(SP.A)\}$$
$$\alpha_2 \quad MU.A \to MU.B_i: \{N_{SP.A}, i(SP.A)\}$$
$$\alpha_3 \quad MU.B_i \to SP.B_i: \{N_{SP.A}, i(SP.A)\}$$
$$\alpha_4 \quad SP.B_i \to MU.B_i: \{\{N_{SP.B_i}, -k_{SP.B_i},$$
$$h(N_{SP.B_i}, N_{SP.A}, i(SP.A))\}_{-k_{SP.B_i}}\}_{+k_{SP.A}}$$
$$\alpha_5 \quad MU.B_i \to MU.A: \{\{N_{SP.B_i}, -k_{SP.B_i},$$
$$h(N_{SP.B_i}, N_{SP.A}, i(SP.A))\}_{-k_{SP.B_i}}\}_{+k_{SP.A}}$$
$$\alpha_6 \quad MU.A \to SP.A: \{\{N_{SP.B_i}, -k_{SP.B_i},$$
$$h(N_{SP.B_i}, N_{SP.A}, i(SP.A))\}_{-k_{SP.B_i}}\}_{+k_{SP.A}}$$

where:

- $i(SP.A)$ - the identifier of the secret protection module of user A,
- N_X - random numbers - nonces generated by the module specified in subscript,
- $h(N_{SP.B_i}, N_{SP.A}, i(SP.A))$ - hash value calculated for a message $N_{SP.B_i}, N_{SP.A}, i(SP.A)$ using hash function h.
- $-k_S P.B_i$, $+k_{SP.A}$ - keys, public and private accordingly.

Let's follow the protocol step by step. The SP module belonging to the user A generates a random number $N_{SP.A}$ and, together with its identifier $i(SP.A)$, transmits it to the MU module (step α_1). Everything happens in one trusted domain. All this information is transferred to the user's B_i domain (step α_2), where it goes to the secret protection module from the authentication module (α_3). User B_i generates his nonce $N_{SP.B_i}$, adds previously obtained information and provides a hash function $h(N_{SP.B_i}, N_{SP.A}, i(SP.A))$, signs whole with his key $-kSP.B_i$ and encrypts with the user's A key $+k_{SP.A}$. The whole is sent in sequence from the SP to MU module in the user's B_i domain (α_4). Next to the user's A domain (α_5) and already internally from the MU module to the SP module. When the protocol is completed, the user's A module SP and each SP module of user B_i (for $i = 1, ..., n$) have confidential key materials $N_{SP.A}$ and $N_{SP.B_i}$ ($i = 1, ..., n$). On this basis, each party calculates the new symmetric key for independent, trusted channels.

3   Verification Method

In the paper [16], a mathematical model of a protocol's executions (correct runs) is transformed into a network of finite synchronous automata. Many protocol executions (the runs) were expressed as the computations in this network. The security problems were modelled as a problem of the reachability of desired (unsecured) states in the network. The computations in the network were subsequently encoded as propositional boolean formulas. SAT-solvers answer the question whether a valuation fulfilling the formula exists, and therefore whether an attack on the protocol exists. In the paper [16], several experimental results for untimed protocols were given. In some cases, they were better than those obtained during verification with the AVISPA Tool.

Now, we introduce a new approach. The double translation of the mathematical model of executions proposed in [16] brought along some redundancies, of which the following method is free. The obtained and described experimental results in the last section of the article are promising for the later development of this approach.

In the proposed method, we encode each step of a protocol execution in the form of a tuple (1) containing conditions for executing a given step and actions taking place during its execution. We can analyse many executions that are running in parallel. That is why we mark each step as α_j^i, where i is the number of the execution and j is the number of the protocol step. Each tuple takes the form:

$$\alpha_j^i = (Send, Rec, PreCond(S_j^i), S_j^i, PostKnow(S_j^i)), \tag{1}$$

where $Send$ is the sender, Rec is the receiver, S_j^i is the j-th step of the i-th protocol's execution, $PreCond(S_j^i)$ is the set of conditions that must be met for the step S_j^i to be executed and at the end $PostKnow(S_j^i)$ is the set of knowledge that is gained as a result of the step. As you can see, the order of the elements in the tuple clearly suggests the time sequence of individual actions.

We distinguish two types of $PreCond$, that must be held before a step:

1. G_U^X - represents the generation of new confidential information X (nonces, keys) by the user U (e.g. $G_A^{N_A}$ - the nonce N_A generated by the user A),
2. P_U^X - represents the requirement to have the given knowledge element X necessary for the user U to perform the given step U (e.g. $P_A^{N_B}$ - the user A must have the nonce N_B to perform the step).

In the $PostKnow$ set, you will find the knowledge gained as a result of performing the step, which will be marked as K_U^X - knowledge about the object X gained by the user U.

Example 1. Now we can represent steps of the security protocol part for MobInfoSec system in the form of tuples:

$$\alpha_1 = (SP.A, MU.A, -sender \ \ and \ \ receiver$$

$$\{P_{SP.A}^{I_{SP.A}}, G_{SP.A}^{N_{SP.A}}\}, -PreCond$$

$$\{N_{SP.A}, i(SP.A)\}, -message \tag{2}$$

$$\{K_{MU.A}^{i(SP.A)}, K_{MU.A}^{N_{SP.A}}\}) - PostKnow$$

Since we can consider interleaving of different executions of the same protocol, we enter the designation $alpha_i^j$ where i is the step number, and j is the execution number. For clarity, let's also mark as $hash = h(N_{SP.B_i}, N_{SP.A}, i(SP.A))$ and as $message_{\alpha_4} = \{\{N_{SP.B_i}, -k_{SP.B_i}, h(N_{SP.B_i}, N_{SP.A}, i(SP.A))\}_{-k_{SP.B_i}}\}_{+k_{SP.A}}$. Thus, one arbitrary execution of the entire protocol looks as follows:

$$\alpha_1^1 = (SP.A, MU.A, \{P_{SP.A}^{i(SP.A)}, G_{SP.A}^{N_{SP.A}}\},$$

$$\{N_{SP.A}, i(SP.A)\},$$

$$\{K_{MU.A}^{i(SP.A)}, K_{MU.A}^{N_{SP.A}}\})$$

$$\alpha_2^1 = (MU.A, MU.B_i, \{P_{MU.A}^{i(SP.A)}, P_{MU.A}^{N_{SP.A}}\},$$

$$\{N_{SP.A}, i(SP.A)\},$$

$$\{K_{MU.B_i}^{i(SP.A)}, K_{MU.B_i}^{N_{SP.A}}\})$$

$$\alpha_3^1 = (MU.B_i, SP.B_i \{P_{MU.B_i}^{i(SP.A)}, P_{MU.B_i}^{N_{SP.A}}\},$$

$$\{N_{SP.A}, i(SP.A)\},$$

$$\{K_{SP.B_i}^{i(SP.A)}, K_{SP.B_i}^{N_{SP.A}}\})$$

$$\alpha_4^1 = (SP.B_i, MU.B_i \{P_{SP.B_i}^{i(SP.A)}, P_{SP.B_i}^{N_{SP.A}}, P_{SP.B_i}^{+k_{SP.A}}, G_{SP.B_i}^{N_{SP.B_i}}, G_{SP.B_i}^{hash}\},$$

$$\{message_{\alpha_4}\},$$

$$\{K_{MU.B_i}^{message_{\alpha_4}}\})$$

$$\alpha_5^1 = (MU.B_i, MU.A \{P_{MU.B_i}^{message_{\alpha_4}}\},$$

$$\{message_{\alpha_4}\},$$

$$\{K_{MU.A}^{message_{\alpha_4}}\})$$

$$\alpha_5^1 = (MU.A, SP.A \{P_{MU.A}^{message_{\alpha_4}}\},$$

$$\{message_{\alpha_4}\},$$

$$\{K_{SP.A}^{N_{SP.B_i}}, K_{SP.A}^{hash}\}) \tag{3}$$

Let's explain the above formula on the example of the fourth tuple, which looks the most complex. The module $SP.Bi_i$ sends a message to the module $MU.B_i$. It needs the identifier $i(SP.A)$, the nonce $N_{SP.A}$, the key $+k_{SP.A}$, and must also generate the nonce $N_{SP.B}$, and the hash value. The module $SP.B_i$ sends the entire $message_{\alpha_4}$ to the module $MU.B_i$, but this second one can not do anything with message, $MU.B_i$ can only forward it to the user's A domain. The message reaches the right sender only in the sixth step, and then $SP.A$ can decipher the message and learn the nonce $N_{SP.B_i}$ and the hash value from it.

On this base, we can generate interlaces of many executions from many sessions, for example $\alpha_1^1, \alpha_1^2, \alpha_2^2, \alpha_2^1, ..., \alpha_5^1, \alpha_5^2$. How to check if the generated tuples are real and have the right to exist in actual protocol executions? We must define the so-called correct tuple. Let Π be the base space consisting of the users and their attributes (identifiers, nonces, cryptographic keys, etc.). We have to consider all the executions of the protocol in this space and all tuples for all executions. Under the set of all these tuples, we define a correct tuple represents the real executions of the protocol in the network.

Definition 1. *We call the sequence* $\mathfrak{s} = s_1, s_2, \ldots, s_p$ **a correct tuple** *iff the following conditions hold:*

1. *if* $s_i = S_j^k$ *for some* $j, k \leq p$ *then* $(j = 1 \vee \exists_{t<i}(s_t = S_{j-1}^k))$ *and* $PreCond(S_j^k) \subseteq \{s_1, \ldots, s_{i-1}\} \wedge PostKnow(S_j^k) \subseteq \{s_{i+1}, \ldots, s_p\}$,
2. *if* $s_i = G_U^X$, *then* $\forall_{t \neq i}(s_t \neq G_U^X)$,
3. *if* $s_i = P_U^X$, *then* $\exists_{t<i}(s_t = G_U^X \vee s_t = K_U^X)$.

The first point guarantees a proper dependence on the order of carrying out the individual steps of a given execution. Points second and third, ensure a dependence of the users' knowledge necessary to execute the individual steps. In particular, the second point guarantees that a given knowledge can be generated only once. The third point shows that a given user has some knowledge if he has generated it or obtained it as the result of one of the previous steps.

Thanks to the following theorem, we can reduce verification of considered security protocol for a given set of their executions to the analysis of the corresponding set of tuples that represents executions. Specifically, observe that there is an attack upon the protocol in the considered set of executions if there is an a correct tuple that represents attacking execution. An attacking execution contains an element in which the Intruder I learns secret information (for example $K_I^{N_{SP.A}}$), or can even finish the protocol by impersonating another user without being recognised. For the definition of the correctness of knowledge, see [14].

4   Experimental Results

The tool implemented by us (from now on referred to as an E-Ver from an efficient verifier) enabled modelling and generation of many security protocols, taking into account all the new assumptions described in the previous sections. Then, we compared the time results with the results of the known tool - ProVerif, with which we have not combined our method so far. We obtained all the results presented below on the same computer unit, equipped with an Intel Core i7 processor, 16 GB main memory and Ubuntu Linux operating system.

At the input, the tool accepts the protocol description defined in the ProToc language [11]. This description allows to include information about external and internal actions which are performed during protocol execution.

Table 1. Summary of the MobInfoSec security protocol executions

No.	Execution
1	$SP.A \rightarrow MU.A \rightarrow MU.B_1 \rightarrow SP.B_1$
2	$SP.A \rightarrow MU.A \rightarrow MU.B_2 \rightarrow SP.B_2$
3	$I \rightarrow MU.B_1 \rightarrow SP.B_1$
4	$I \rightarrow MU.B_2 \rightarrow SP.B_2$
5	$I_A \rightarrow MU.B_1 \rightarrow SP.B_1$
6	$I_A \rightarrow MU.B_2 \rightarrow SP.B_2$
7	$SP.A \rightarrow MU.A \rightarrow I$
8	$SP.A \rightarrow MU.A \rightarrow I_{B_1}$
9	$SP.A \rightarrow MU.A \rightarrow I_{B_2}$

Table 1 presents a summary of the MobInfoSec security protocol executions. We can find here all the communication possibilities between users A and B_i. In column 'Executions' is located information about the users according to the order they appear in the protocol. By A and B_i, we mark honest users. By I the Intruder is indicated. Designations I_A and I_{B_i} mean an Intruder impersonate honest users. For every execution in which Intruder take part, there are more possibilities for parameters (nonces, keys). The Intruder can use his own or other users parameters. we show below (example for one chairman and two other users).

Each of the nodes in our executions tree consists of five elements:

- execution's number,
- step's number,
- set of the needs (elements needed to execute a given step - *PreCond*),
- set of generated elements (elements generated in a given step - *PreCond*),
- set of knowledge (elements that increase the set of knowledge after a given step - *PostKnow*).

Elements which are located in mentioned sets are numbers referring to a cryptographic object used by users in protocol's executions. Thanks to such simplification, we can build a tree of nodes and verify a protocol faster than other tools. Also, our structure is smaller than in other tools.

Next, our tool tries to build a tree and find an attack. By following the methodology mentioned earlier, nodes that meet the imposed conditions are added to the tree. If the created path contains an attack, a tool returns information about finding an attack.

Let's show a summary of how our tool works for several popular protocols (Fig. 2.) like The Needham–Schroeder Symmetric Key Protocol ($NSSK$ [21] - It forms the basis for the Kerberos protocol), the Needham–Schroeder Public-Key Protocol corrected by Lowe ($NSPK_{LOWE}$ [21]). Wide-Mouth Frog protocol (WMF [6]) and Woo and Lam Pi protocol [25]. We examined three time parameters:

- node generation time (T_{NG}),
- time of finding attacks (T_{AF}),
- protocol checking time (T_{PC}).

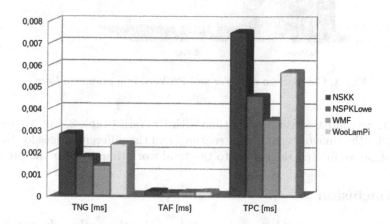

Fig. 2. Summary of protocols verification times in E-Ver in a graphical form

Please note that for all examined protocols an attack was found (normal attack or man-in-the-middle attack). For all protocols and all parameters obtained times were lower than 1 [ms] (Table 2).

Table 2. Summary of protocols verification times in E-Ver

Protocol	T_{NG} [ms]	T_{AF} [ms]	T_{PC} [ms]
NSPK	0.002853	0.000224	0.007503
NSPK$_{Lowe}$	0.001791	0.000145	0.004582
WMF	0.001382	0.000167	0.003488
WooLamPi	0.002378	0.000192	0.005677

Table 3. Comparison of E-Ver and ProVerif

Time [ms]	NSKK	Denning-Sacco
ProVerif	24	9
E-Ver	0.008659	0.005632

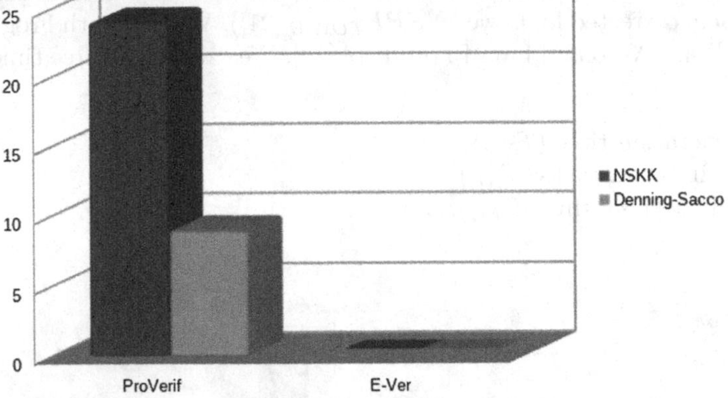

Fig. 3. Comparison of E-Ver and ProVerif in a graphical form

Next, we compared verification time with ProVerif (Table 3, Fig. 3). You can not specify the time of generating structures and the different stages for the tool ProVerif, so we limited the results to the total work time tool for the protocol.

5   Conclusion

The article presents the last work carried out by the authors in the field of verification of security protocols. Previous methods included many redundant operations and steps: building machines, testing with Sat-solver, and so on. The current formal model allows for a broad expression of the parameters of security protocols that are used nowadays. It allows to analyse the conditions needed to perform individual steps, takes into account the knowledge aspect, significantly limiting the searched space. The developed method allows to examine the inter-laces of the same protocols for many sessions, to analyse the difficult-to-study Intruder model, which is Dolev-Yao.

The important thing is that for all of the protocols we examine, the time to detect attacks or search the whole tree in the absence of an attack is surprisingly small. Despite the size of the structure causing the exponential complexity of the algorithm, due to constraints imposed on attachable nodes (considering *PreCond* and *PostKnow*), the tree shrinks to real performances, which allows for quick analysis. Thanks to the structure built on constraints, we are also able to detect a situation in which the algorithm itself is incorrectly constructed, which is not always possible with the use of other tools.

References

1. Abadi, M., Blanchet, B., Fournet, C.: The applied pi calculus: mobile values, new names, and secure communication. J. ACM **65**(1), 1:1–1:41 (2018)
2. Armando, A., et al.: The AVISPA tool for the automated validation of internet security protocols and applications. In: Etessami, K., Rajamani, S.K. (eds.) CAV 2005. LNCS, vol. 3576, pp. 281–285. Springer, Heidelberg (2005). https://doi.org/10.1007/11513988_27
3. Basin, D., Clavel, M., Doser, J., Egea, M.: Automated analysis of security-design models. Inf. Softw. Technol. **51**(5), 815–831 (2009)
4. Basin, D., Cremers, C., Meadows, C.: Model checking security protocols. Handbook of Model Checking, pp. 727–762. Springer, Cham (2018). https://doi.org/10.1007/978-3-319-10575-8_22
5. Blanchet, B.: Modeling and verifying security protocols with the applied pi calculus and ProVerif. Found. Trends Priv. Secur. **1**(1–2), 1–135 (2016)
6. Burrows, M., Abadi, M., Needham, R.: A logic of authentication. ACM Trans. Comput. Syst. **8**(1), 18–36 (1990)
7. Cremers, C., Mauw, S.: Operational Semantics and Verification of Security Protocols. Information Security and Cryptography. Springer, Heidelberg (2012). https://doi.org/10.1007/978-3-540-78636-8
8. David, A., Larsen, K.G., et al.: UPPAAL SMC tutorial. Int. J. Softw. Tools Technol. Transfer (STTT) **17**(4), 397–415 (2015)
9. Dolev, D., Yao, A.: On the security of public key protocols. Technical report, Stanford, CA, USA (1981)
10. Gibson-Robinson, T., Kamil, A., Lowe, G.: Verifying layered security protocols. J. Comput. Secur. **23**(3), 259–307 (2015)
11. Grosser, A., Kurkowski, M., Piątkowski, J., Szymoniak, S.: ProToc—an universal language for security protocols specifications. In: Wiliński, A., El Fray, I., Pejaś, J. (eds.) Soft Computing in Computer and Information Science. AISC, vol. 342, pp. 237–248. Springer, Cham (2015). https://doi.org/10.1007/978-3-319-15147-2_20
12. Hyla, T., Pejas, J., El Fray, I., Mackow, W., Chocianowicz, W., Szulga, M.: Sensitive information protection on mobile devices using general access structures. In: Proceedings of the Ninth International Conference on Systems, ICONS 2014, pp. 192–196. XPS (Xpert Publishing Services) (2014)
13. Kacprzak, M., et al.: Verics 2007 - a model checker for knowledge and real-time. Fundamenta Informaticae **85**(1–4), 313–328 (2008)
14. Kurkowski, M.: Formalne metody weryfikacji własności protokołów zabezpieczajacych w sieciach komputerowych. Informatyka - Akademicka Oficyna Wydawnicza EXIT, Akademicka Oficyna Wydawnicza Exit (2013)
15. Kurkowski, M., Kozakiewicz, A., Siedlecka-Lamch, O.: Some remarks on security protocols verification tools. In: Grzech, A., Świątek, J., Wilimowska, Z., Borzemski, L. (eds.) Information Systems Architecture and Technology: Proceedings of 37th International Conference on Information Systems Architecture and Technology – ISAT 2016 – Part II. AISC, vol. 522, pp. 65–75. Springer, Cham (2017). https://doi.org/10.1007/978-3-319-46586-9_6
16. Kurkowski, M., Penczek, W.: Verifying security protocols modelled by networks of automata. Fundam. Inf. **79**(3–4), 453–471 (2007)
17. Kurkowski, M., Siedlecka-Lamch, O., Dudek, P.: Using backward induction techniques in (timed) security protocols verification. In: Saeed, K., Chaki, R., Cortesi, A., Wierzchoń, S. (eds.) CISIM 2013. LNCS, vol. 8104, pp. 265–276. Springer, Heidelberg (2013). https://doi.org/10.1007/978-3-642-40925-7_25

18. Lowe, G.: An attack on the needham-schroeder public-key authentication protocol. Inf. Process. Lett. **56**(3), 131–133 (1995)
19. Lowe, G.: Breaking and fixing the needham-schroeder public-key protocol using FDR. In: Margaria, T., Steffen, B. (eds.) TACAS 1996. LNCS, vol. 1055, pp. 147–166. Springer, Heidelberg (1996). https://doi.org/10.1007/3-540-61042-1_43
20. Martina, J.E., Paulson, L.C.: Verifying multicast-based security protocols using the inductive method. Int. J. Inf. Secur. **14**(2), 187–204 (2015)
21. Needham, R.M., Schroeder, M.D.: Using encryption for authentication in large networks of computers. Commun. ACM **21**(12), 993–999 (1978)
22. Paulson, L.C.: Inductive analysis of the internet protocol TLS. ACM Trans. Inf. Syst. Secur. **2**(3), 332–351 (1999)
23. Siedlecka-Lamch, O., El Fray, I., Kurkowski, M., Pejaś, J.: Verification of mutual authentication protocol for MobInfoSec system. In: Saeed, K., Homenda, W. (eds.) CISIM 2015. LNCS, vol. 9339, pp. 461–474. Springer, Cham (2015). https://doi.org/10.1007/978-3-319-24369-6_38
24. Siedlecka-Lamch, O., Kurkowski, M., Piatkowski, J.: Probabilistic model checking of security protocols without perfect cryptography assumption. In: Gaj, P., Kwiecień, A., Stera, P. (eds.) CN 2016. CCIS, vol. 608, pp. 107–117. Springer, Cham (2016). https://doi.org/10.1007/978-3-319-39207-3_10
25. Woo, T., Lam, S.: A lesson on authentication protocol design. SIGOPS Oper. Syst. Rev. **28**(3), 24–37 (1994)

Author Index

Printed in the United States
By Bookmasters